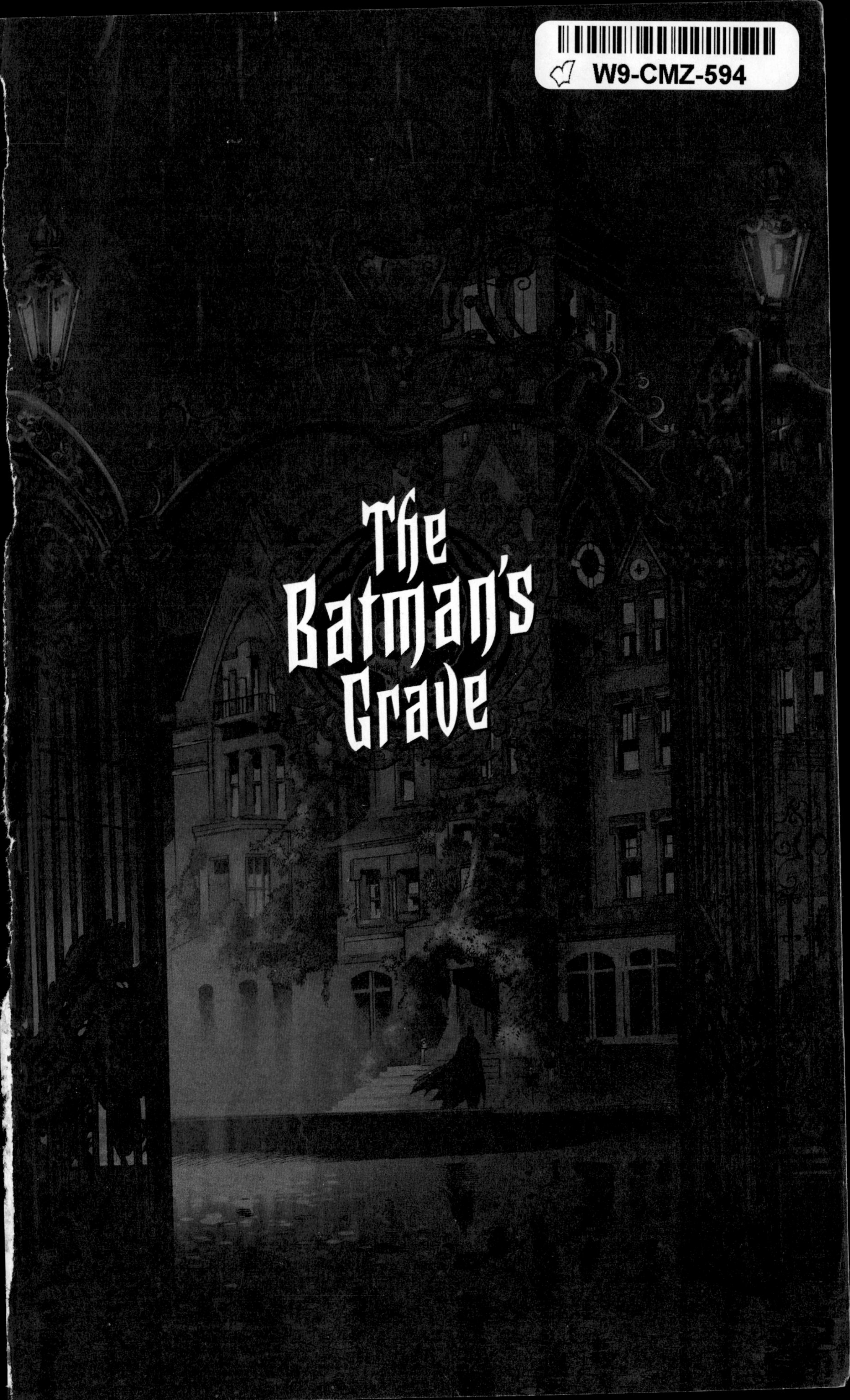
The Batman's Grave

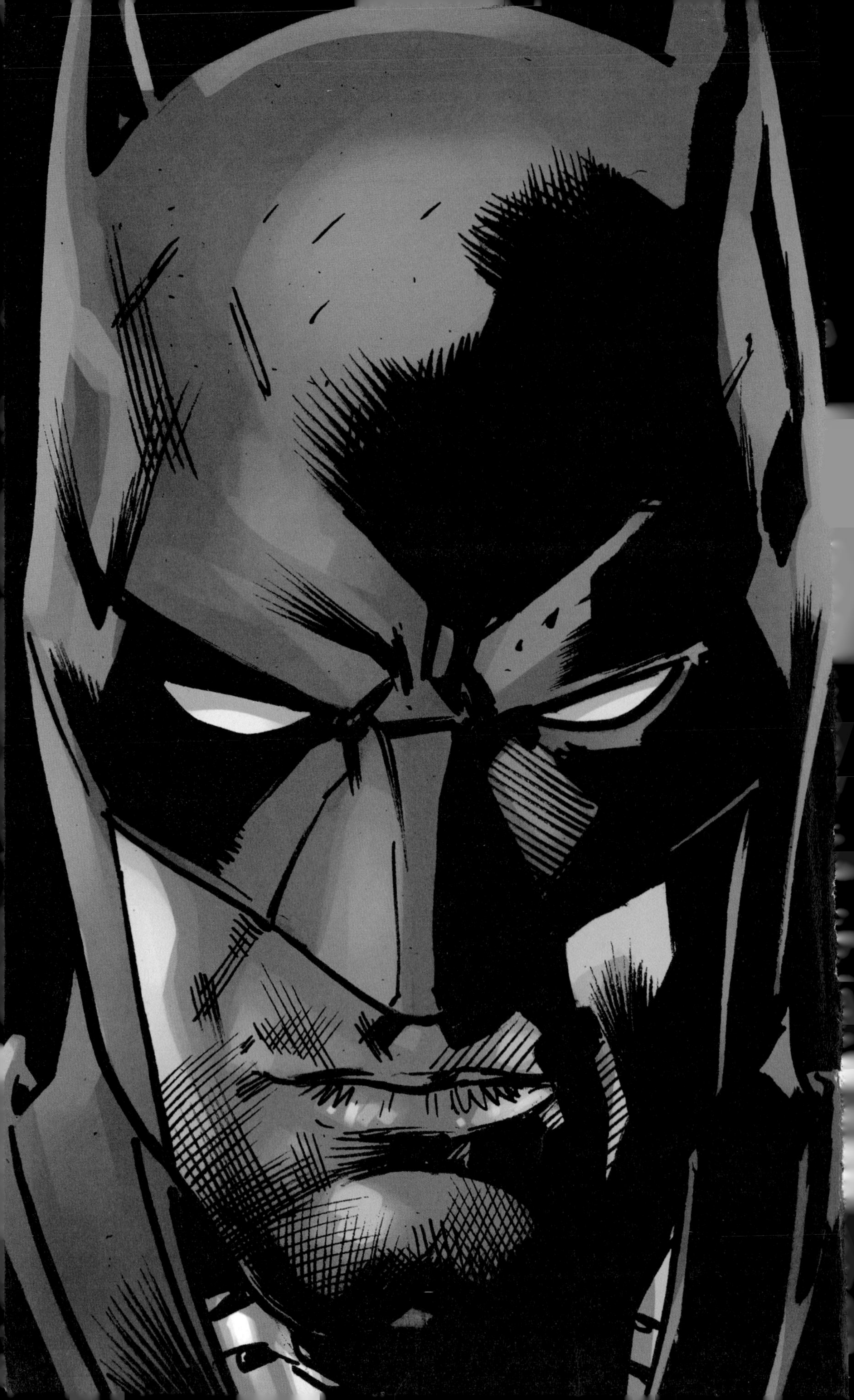

The Batman's Grave

THE COMPLETE COLLECTION

Writer	Penciller
WARREN ELLIS	**BRYAN HITCH**

Inkers
BRYAN HITCH and **KEVIN NOWLAN**

Colors	Letters
ALEX SINCLAIR	**RICHARD STARKINGS**

Collection Cover Artists	BATMAN created by
BRYAN HITCH and **ALEX SINCLAIR**	**BOB KANE** with **BILL FINGER**

MARIE JAVINS	Editor – Original Series
ROB LEVIN	Associate Editor – Original Series
ANDREW MARINO	Associate Editor – Original Series & Editor – Collected Edition
STEVE COOK	Design Director – Books & Publication Design
SUZANNAH ROWNTREE	Publication Production
MARIE JAVINS	Editor-in-Chief, DC Comics
DANIEL CHERRY III	Senior VP – General Manager
JIM LEE	Publisher & Chief Creative Officer
DON FALLETTI	VP – Manufacturing Operations & Workflow Management
LAWRENCE GANEM	VP – Talent Services
ALISON GILL	Senior VP – Manufacturing & Operations
JEFFREY KAUFMAN	VP – Editorial Strategy & Programming
NICK J. NAPOLITANO	VP – Manufacturing Administration & Design
NANCY SPEARS	VP – Revenue

THE BATMAN'S GRAVE: THE COMPLETE COLLECTION

Published by DC Comics. Compilation and all new material Copyright © 2022 DC Comics. All Rights Reserved. Originally published in single magazine form in *The Batman's Grave* 1-12. Copyright © 2019, 2020 DC Comics. All Rights Reserved. All characters, their distinctive likenesses, and related elements featured in this publication are trademarks of DC Comics. The stories, characters, and incidents featured in this publication are entirely fictional. DC Comics does not read or accept unsolicited submissions of ideas, stories, or artwork. DC – a WarnerMedia Company.

DC Comics, 2900 West Alameda Ave., Burbank, CA 91505
Printed by Transcontinental Printing Interweb Montreal,
A division of Transcontinental Printing inc., Boucherville, QC, Canada.
2/4/22. First Printing.
ISBN: 978-1-77951-431-8

Library of Congress Cataloging-in-Publication Data is available.

PEFC Certified

This product is
from sustainably
managed forests and
controlled sources

PEFC/01-31-106   www.pefc.org

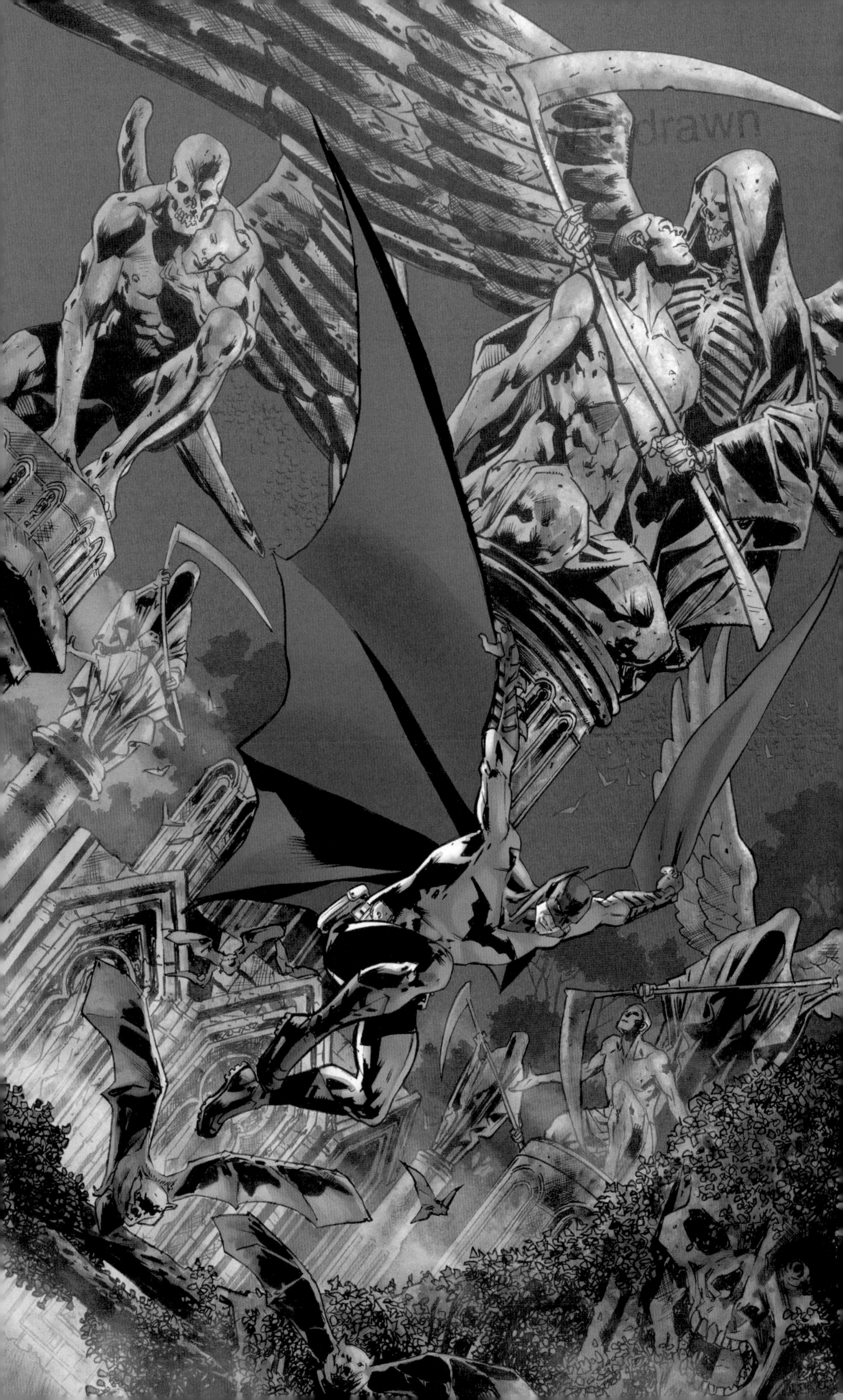

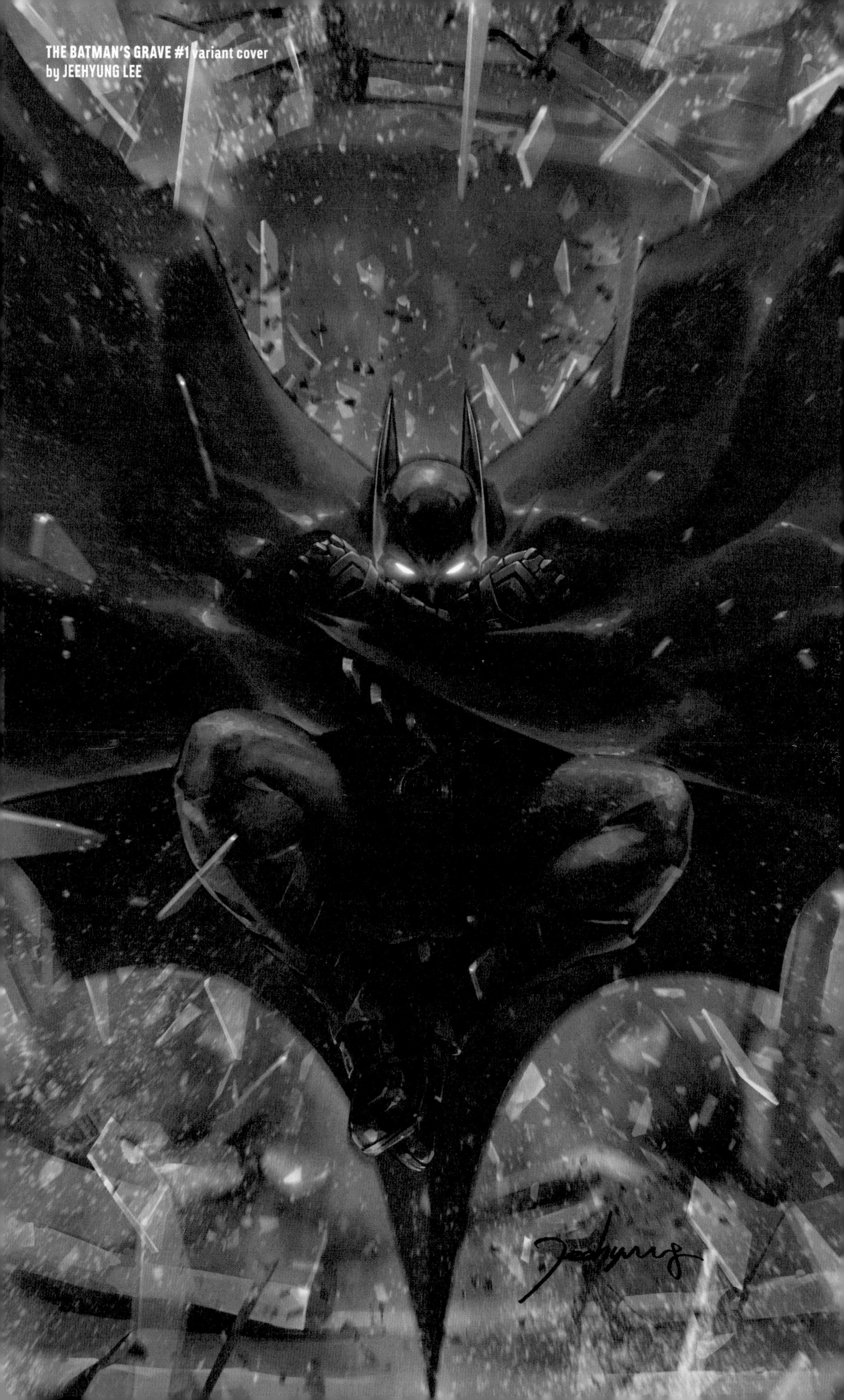

THE BATMAN'S GRAVE #1 variant cover
by JEEHYUNG LEE

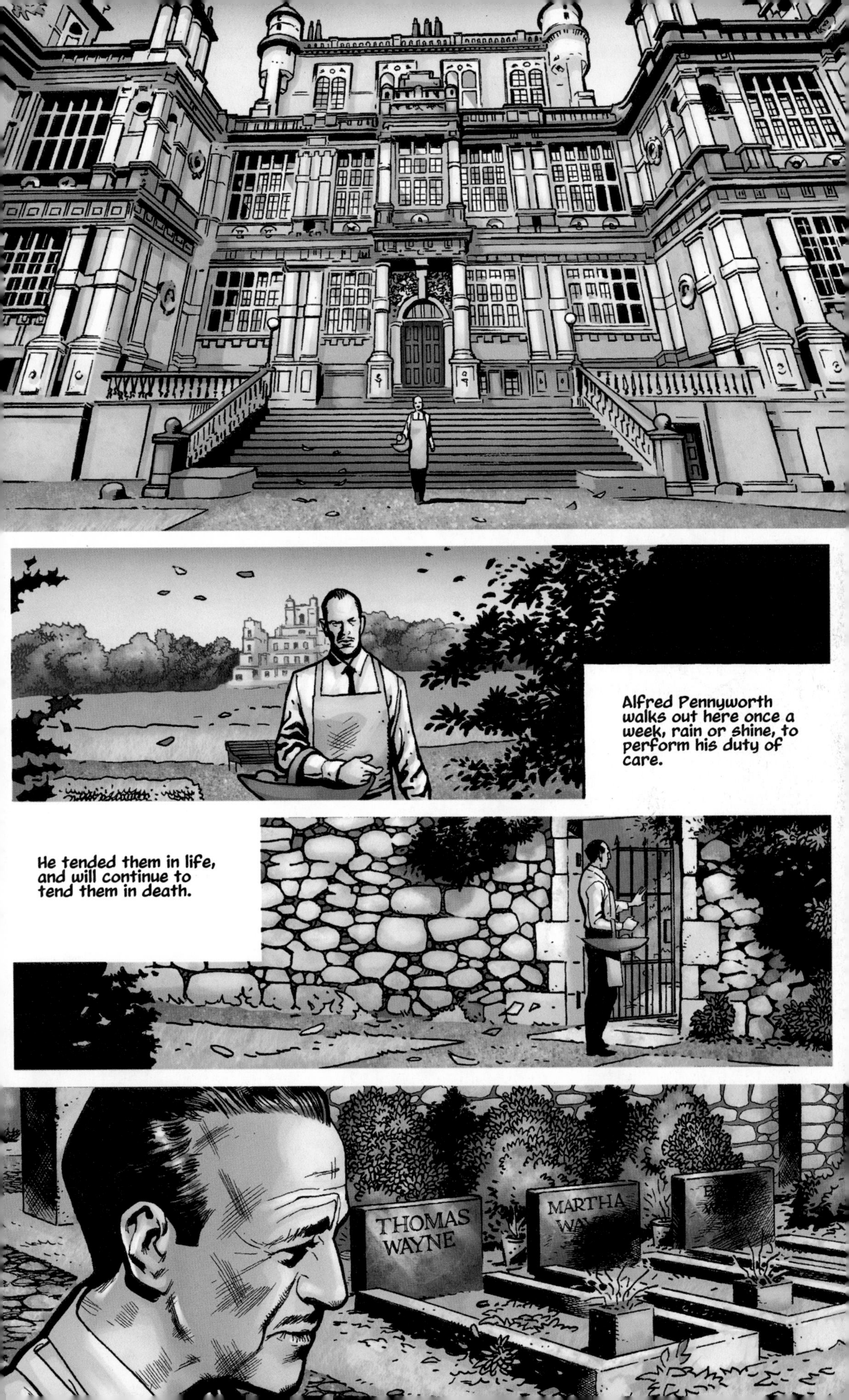
Alfred Pennyworth walks out here once a week, rain or shine, to perform his duty of care.
He tended them in life, and will continue to tend them in death.
THOMAS WAYNE
MARTHA

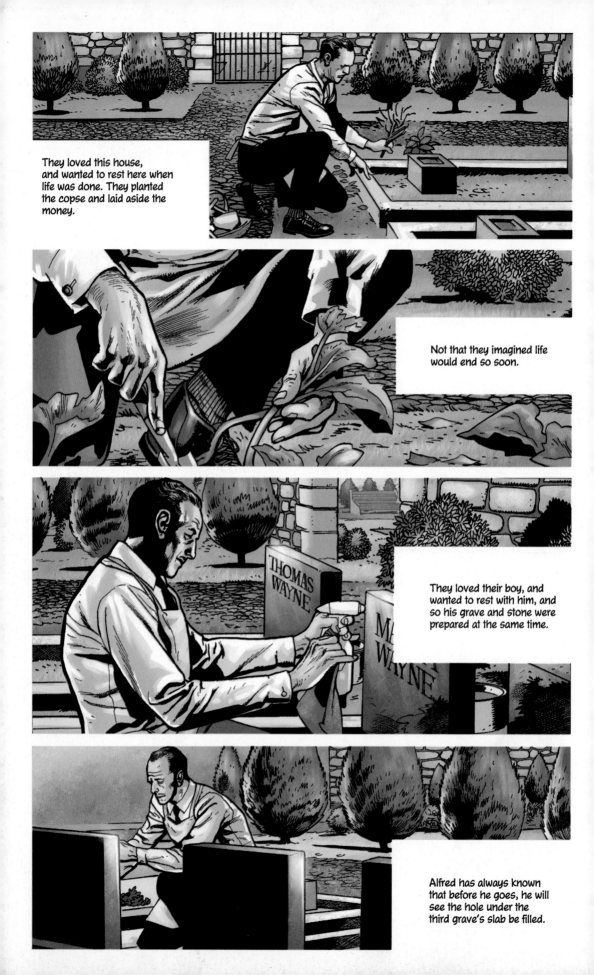

They loved this house, and wanted to rest here when life was done. They planted the copse and laid aside the money.

Not that they imagined life would end so soon.

They loved their boy, and wanted to rest with him, and so his grave and stone were prepared at the same time.

Alfred has always known that before he goes, he will see the hole under the third grave's slab be filled.

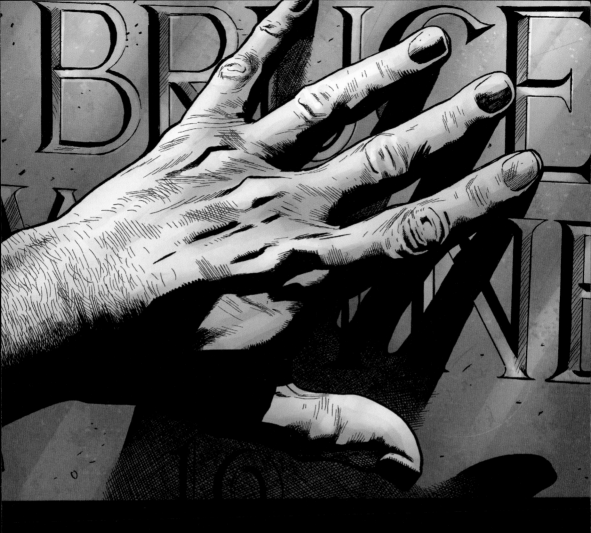

Chapter 1

| Writer | Pencils | Inks |
| WARREN ELLIS | BRYAN HITCH | KEVIN NOWLAN |

| Colors | Letters |
| ALEX SINCLAIR | RICHARD STARKINGS |

| Cover | Variant Cover |
| BRYAN HITCH & ALEX SINCLAIR | JEEHYUNG LEE |

| Associate Editor | Editor |
| ROB LEVIN | MARIE JAVINS |

BATMAN created by BOB KANE with BILL FINGER

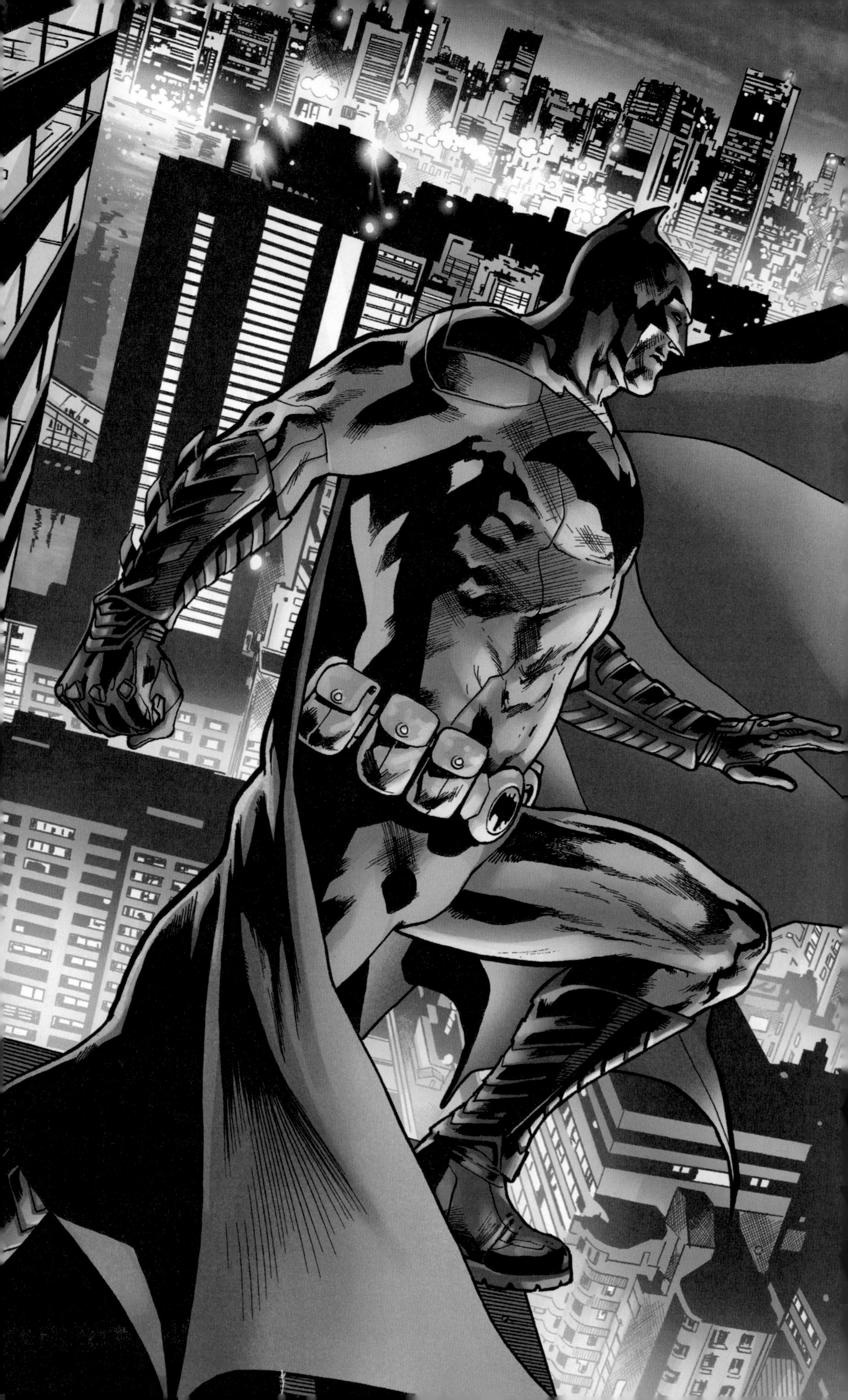

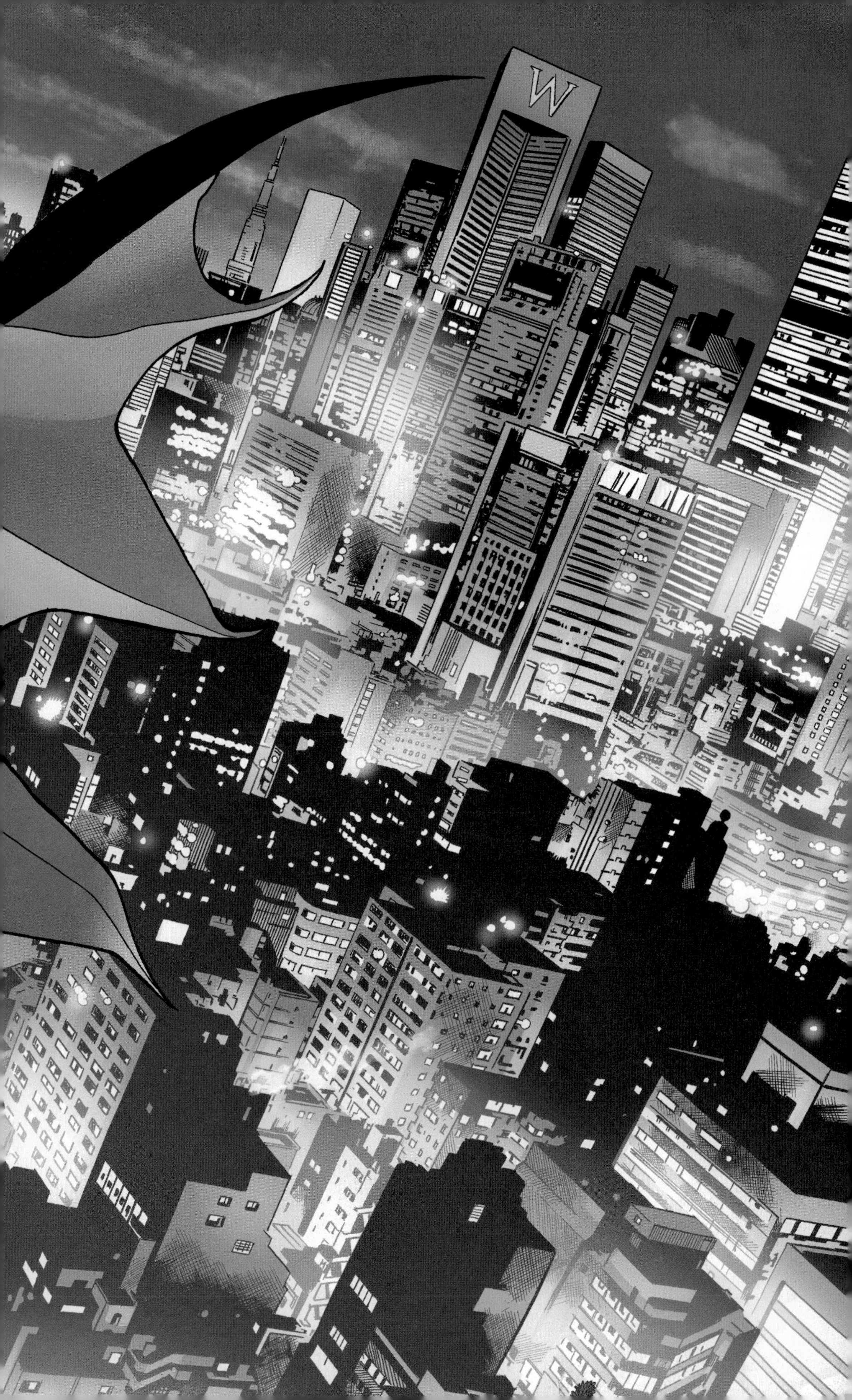
W

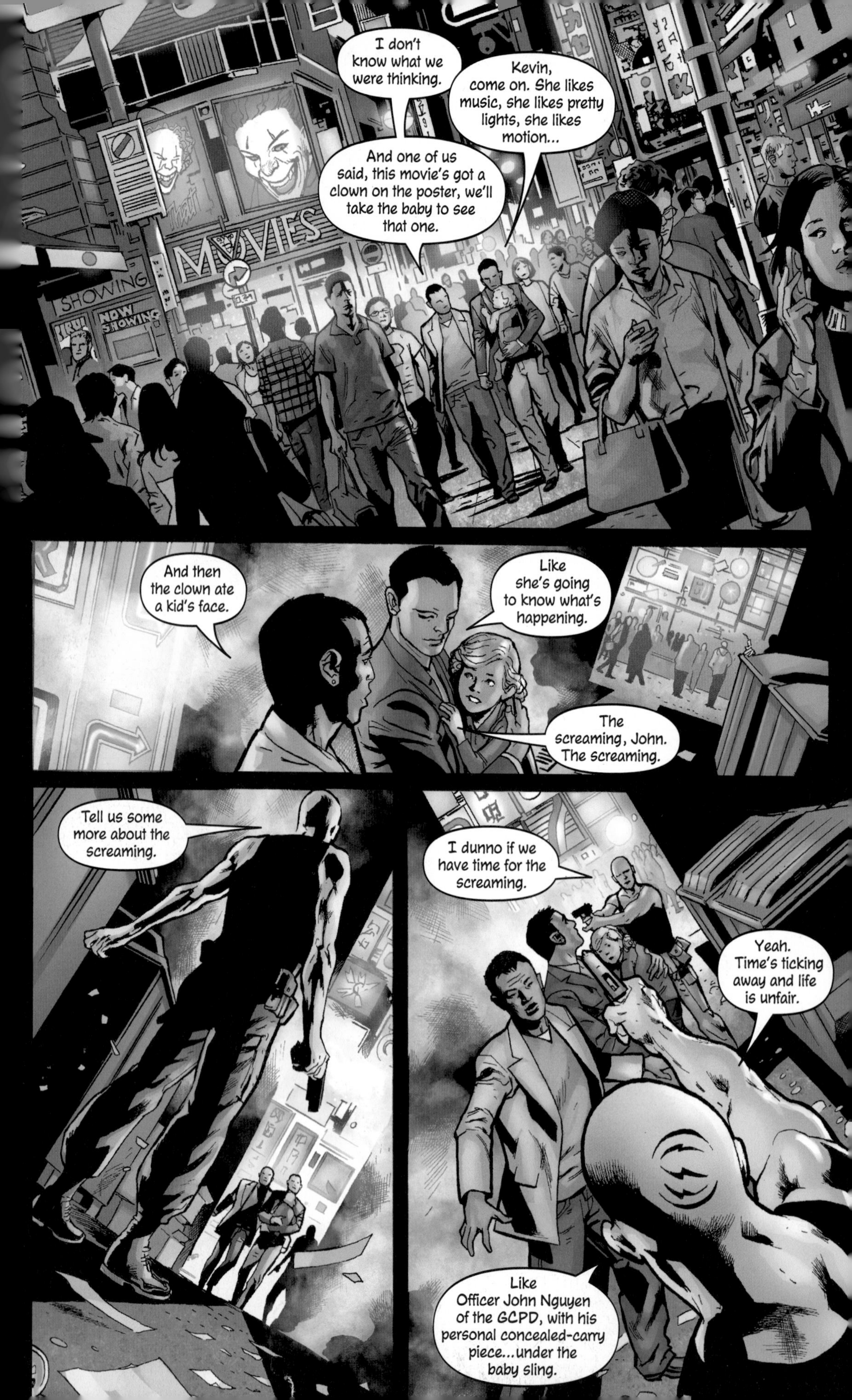

I don't know what we were thinking.
Kevin, come on. She likes music, she likes pretty lights, she likes motion...
And one of us said, this movie's got a clown on the poster, we'll take the baby to see that one.
MOVIES
SHOWING
NOW SHOWING
And then the clown ate a kid's face.
Like she's going to know what's happening.
The screaming, John. The screaming.
Tell us some more about the screaming.
I dunno if we have time for the screaming.
Yeah. Time's ticking away and life is unfair.
Like Officer John Nguyen of the GCPD, with his personal concealed-carry piece...under the baby sling.

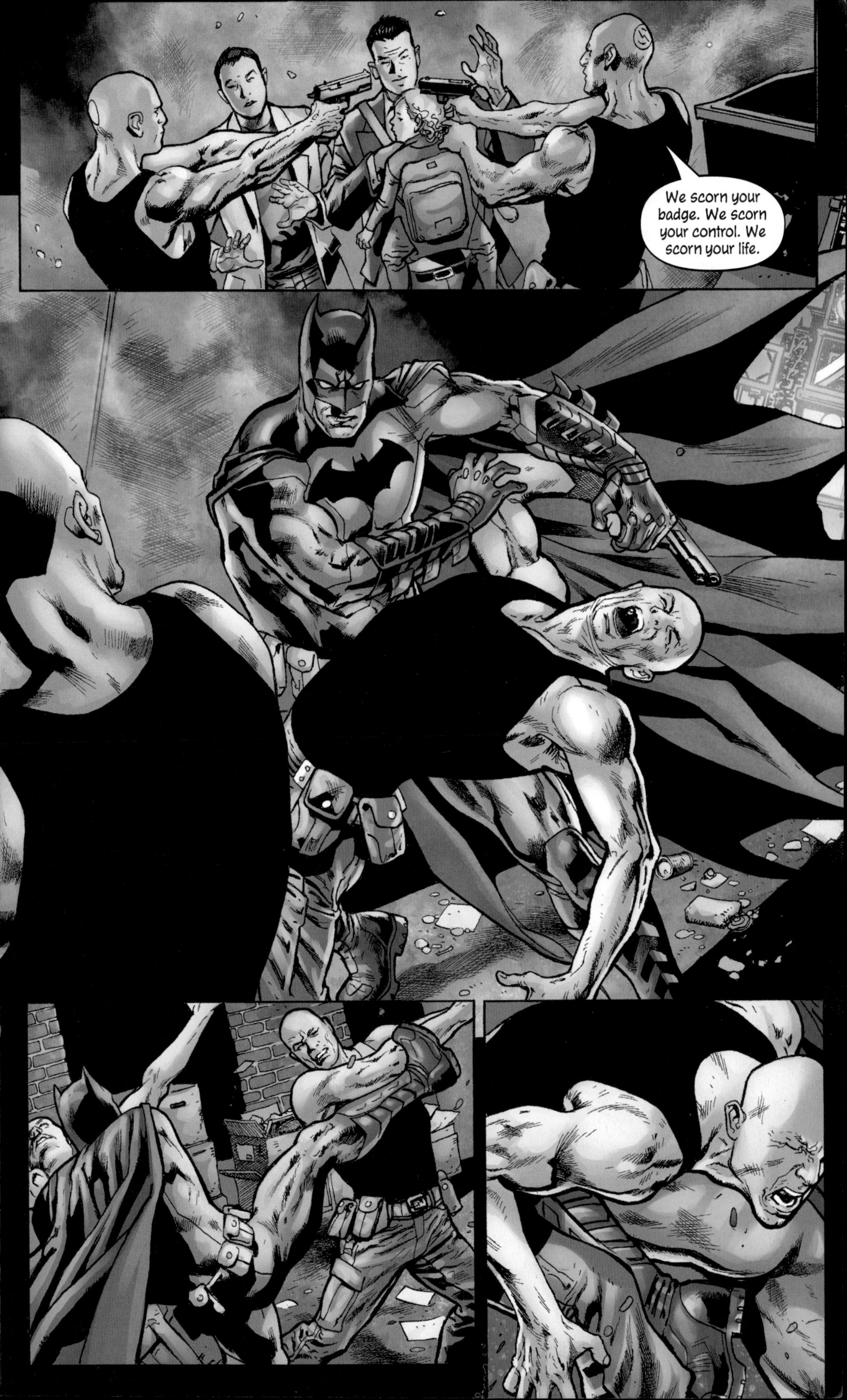
We scorn your badge. We scorn your control. We scorn your life.

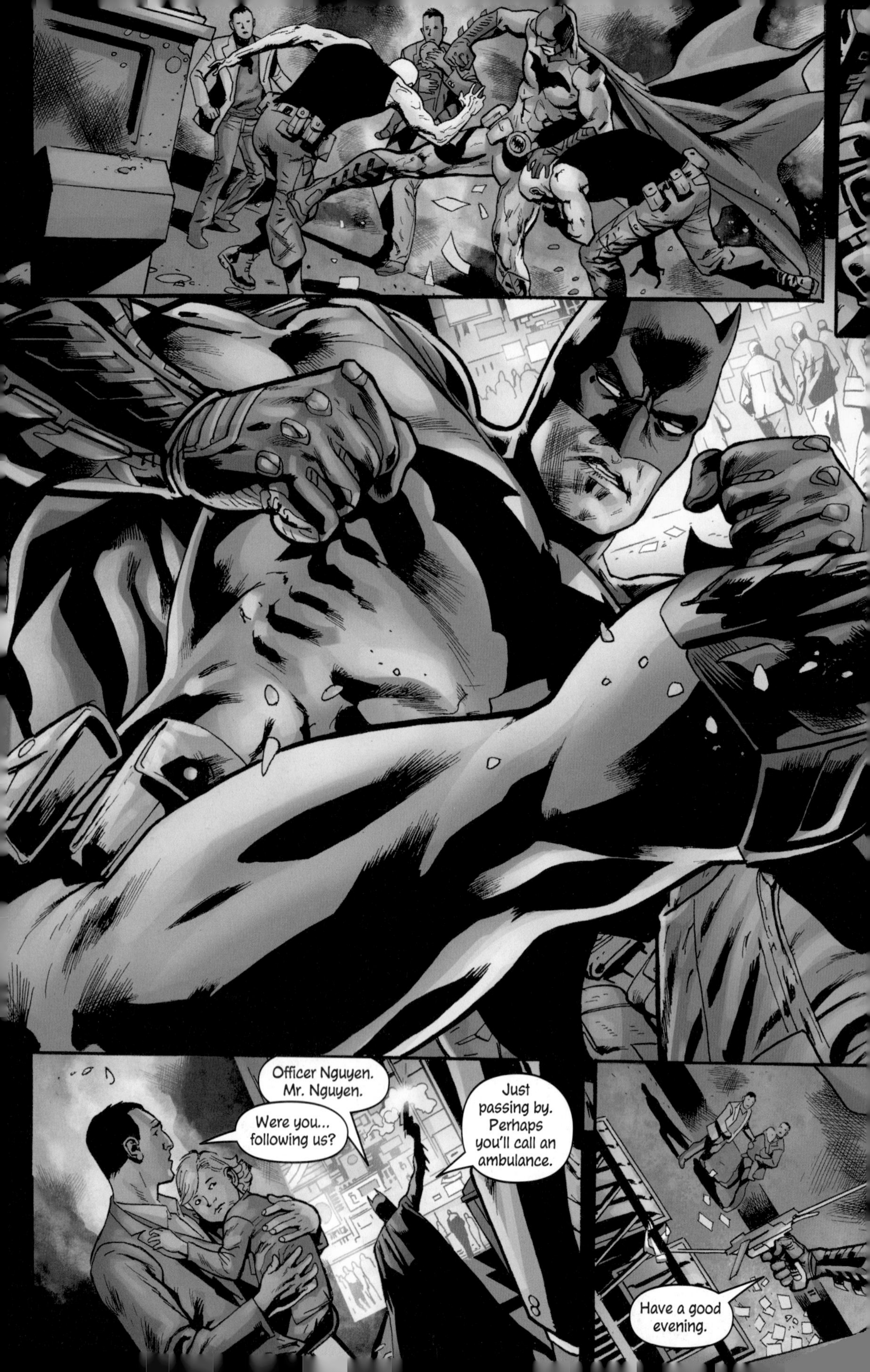
Officer Nguyen. Mr. Nguyen.
Were you... following us?
Just passing by. Perhaps you'll call an ambulance.
Have a good evening.

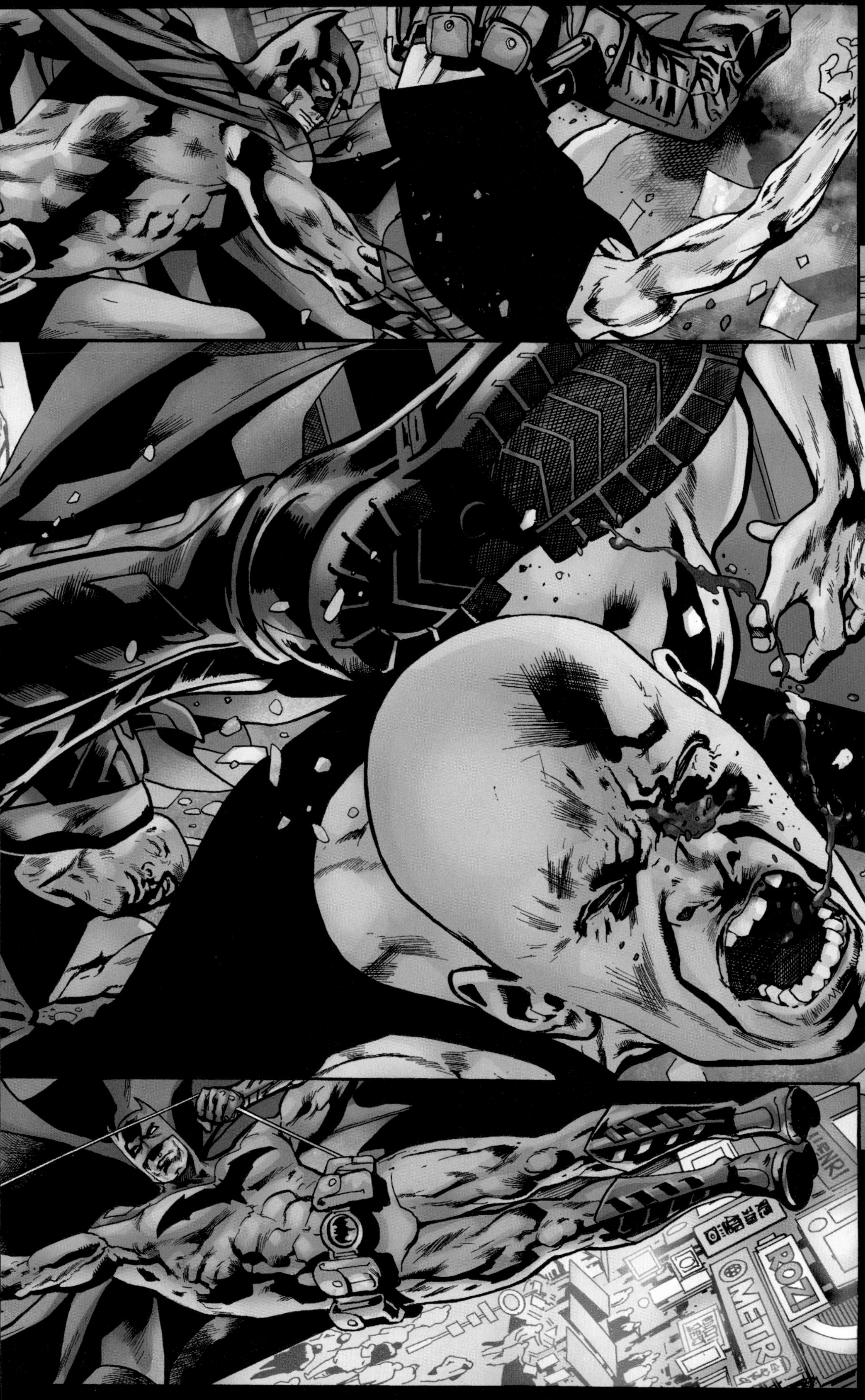

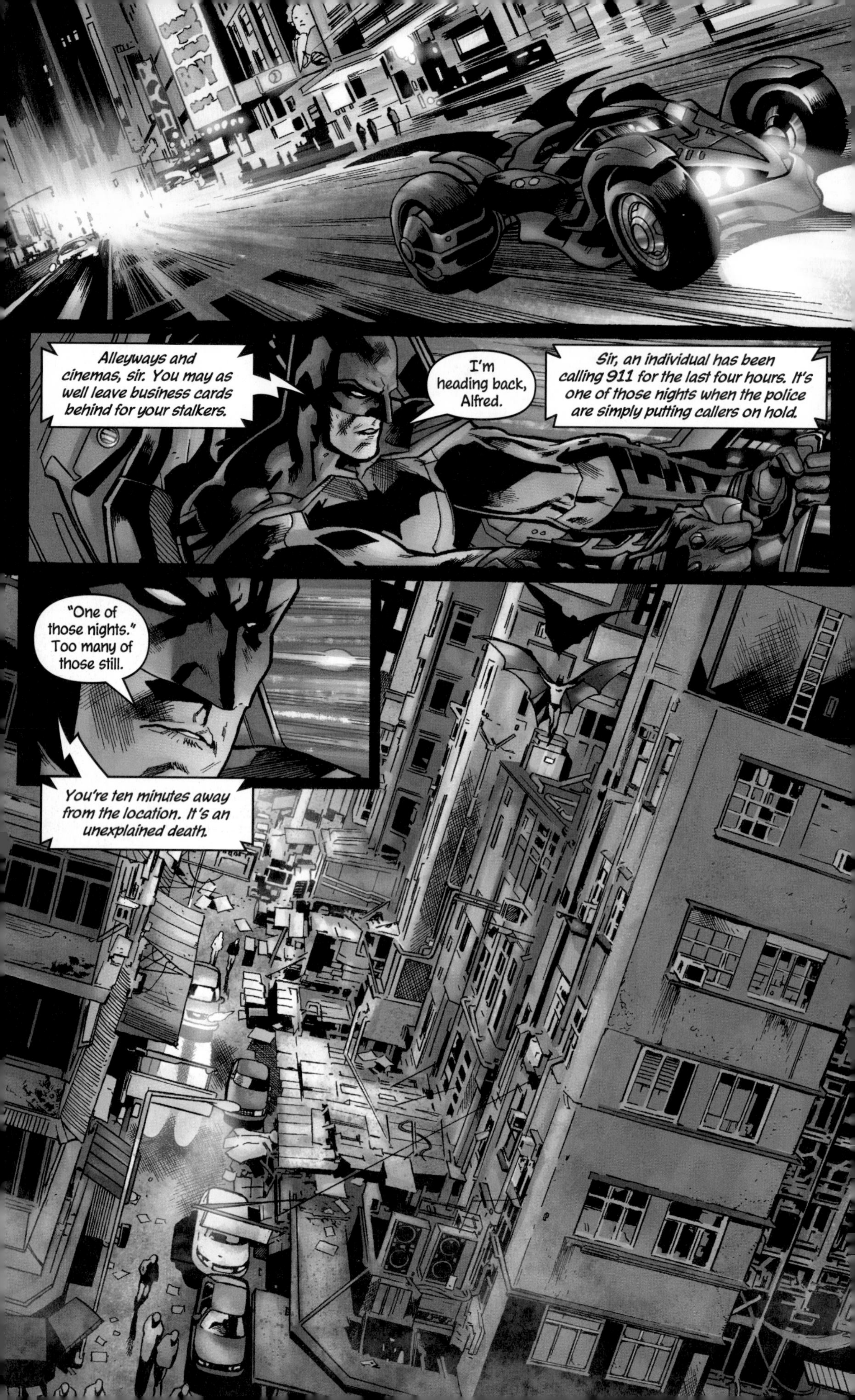
Alleyways and cinemas, sir. You may as well leave business cards behind for your stalkers.
I'm heading back, Alfred.
Sir, an individual has been calling 911 for the last four hours. It's one of those nights when the police are simply putting callers on hold.
"One of those nights." Too many of those still.
You're ten minutes away from the location. It's an unexplained death.

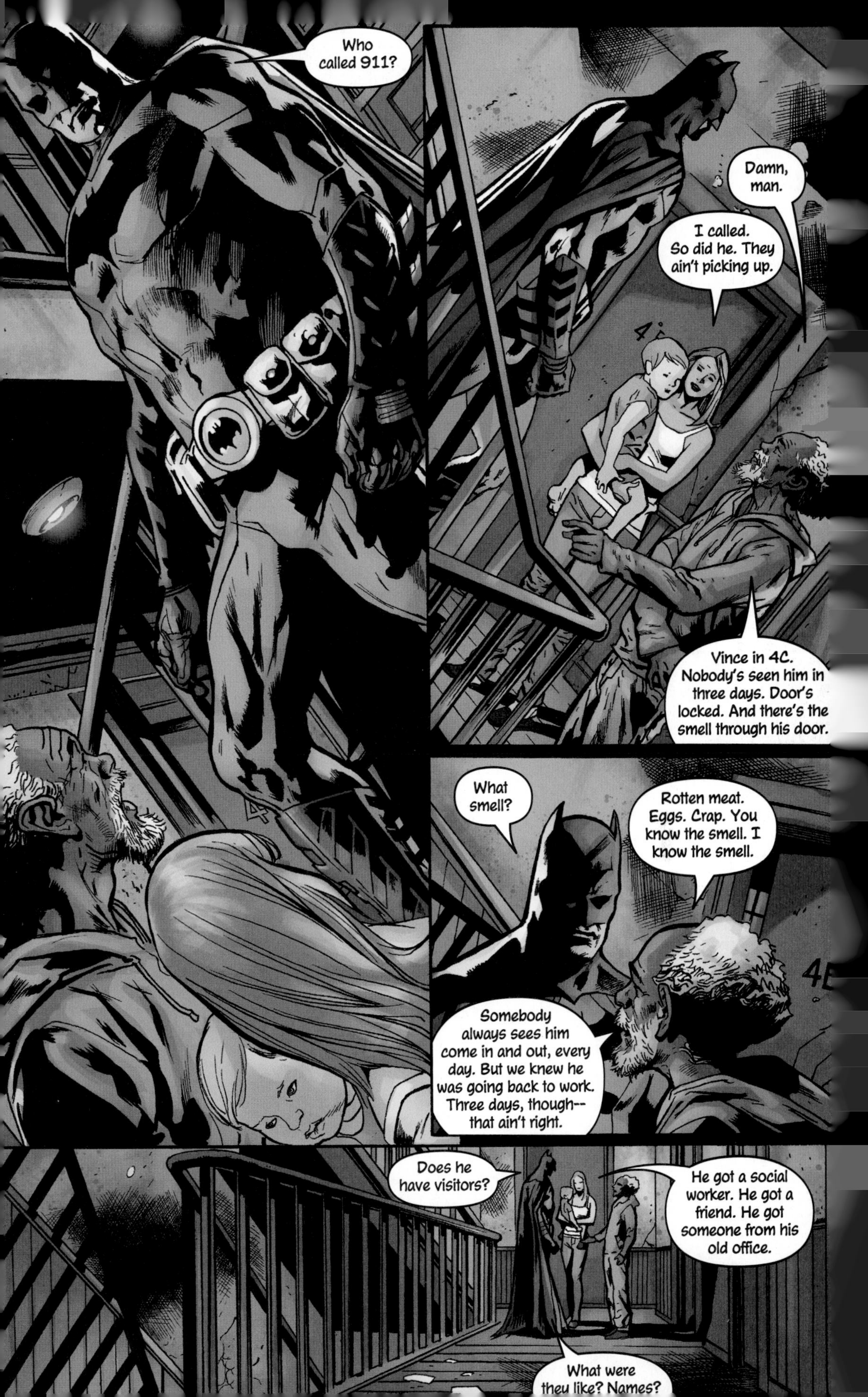
Who called 911?
Damn, man.
I called. So did he. They ain't picking up.
Vince in 4C. Nobody's seen him in three days. Door's locked. And there's the smell through his door.
What smell?
Rotten meat. Eggs. Crap. You know the smell. I know the smell.
Somebody always sees him come in and out, every day. But we knew he was going back to work. Three days, though-- that ain't right.
Does he have visitors?
He got a social worker. He got a friend. He got someone from his old office.
What were they like? Names?

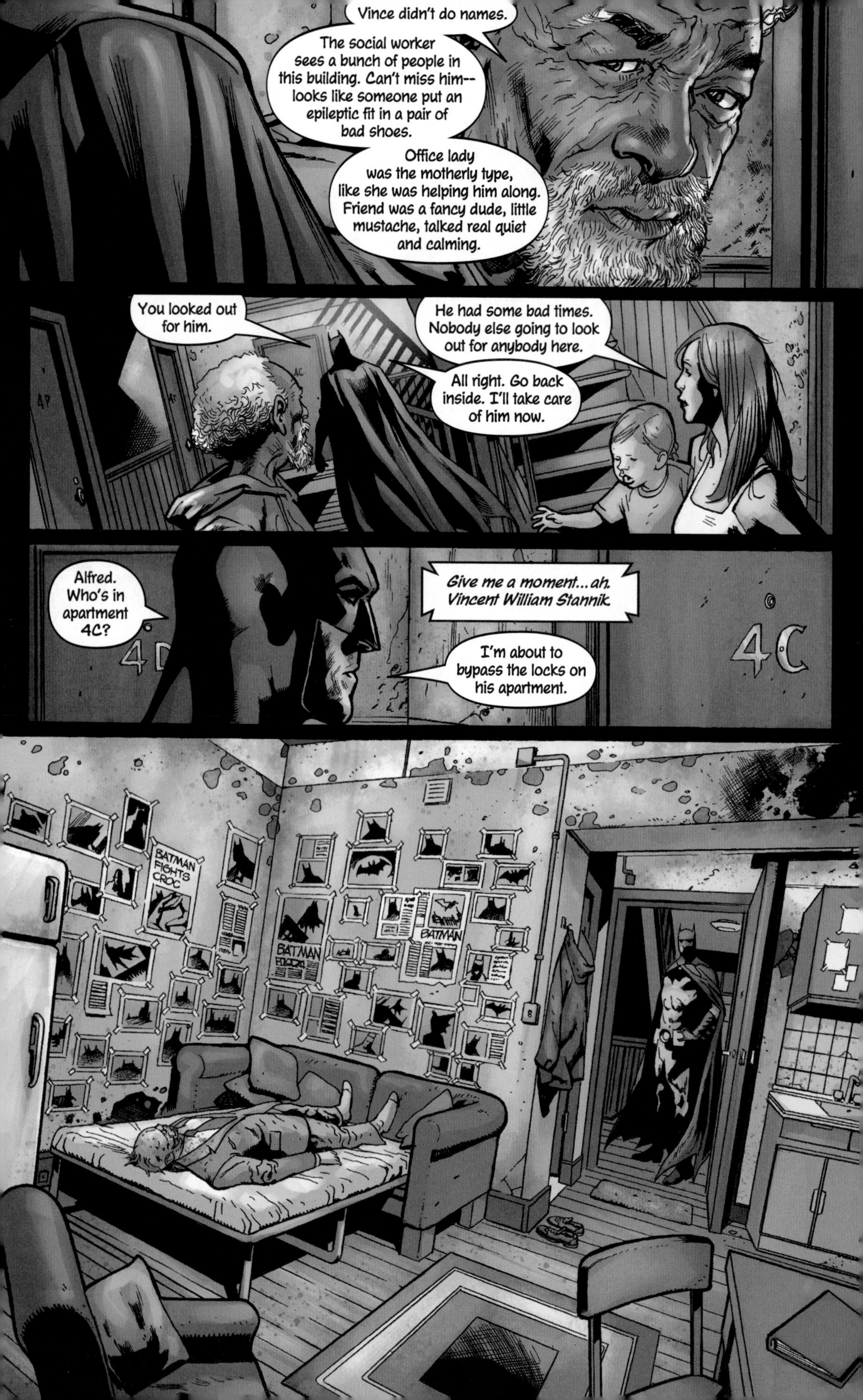
Vince didn't do names.
The social worker sees a bunch of people in this building. Can't miss him-- looks like someone put an epileptic fit in a pair of bad shoes.
Office lady was the motherly type, like she was helping him along. Friend was a fancy dude, little mustache, talked real quiet and calming.
You looked out for him.
He had some bad times. Nobody else going to look out for anybody here.
All right. Go back inside. I'll take care of him now.
Alfred. Who's in apartment 4C?
Give me a moment...ah. Vincent William Stannik.
I'm about to bypass the locks on his apartment.
4C
BATMAN FIGHTS CROC
BATMAN
BATMAN

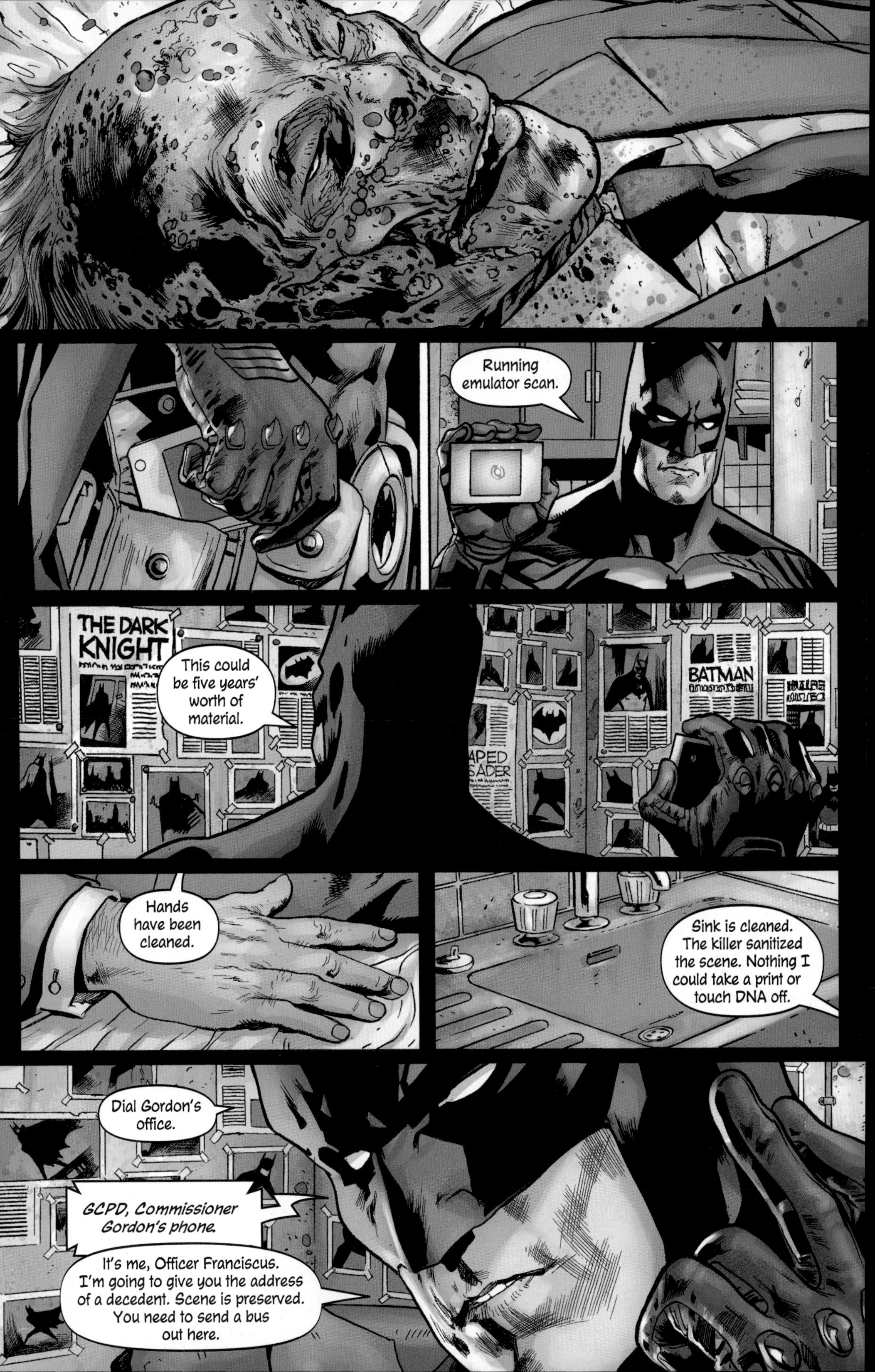
Running emulator scan.
THE DARK KNIGHT
This could be five years' worth of material.
BATMAN
Hands have been cleaned.
Sink is cleaned. The killer sanitized the scene. Nothing I could take a print or touch DNA off.
Dial Gordon's office.
GCPD, Commissioner Gordon's phone.
It's me, Officer Franciscus. I'm going to give you the address of a decedent. Scene is preserved. You need to send a bus out here.

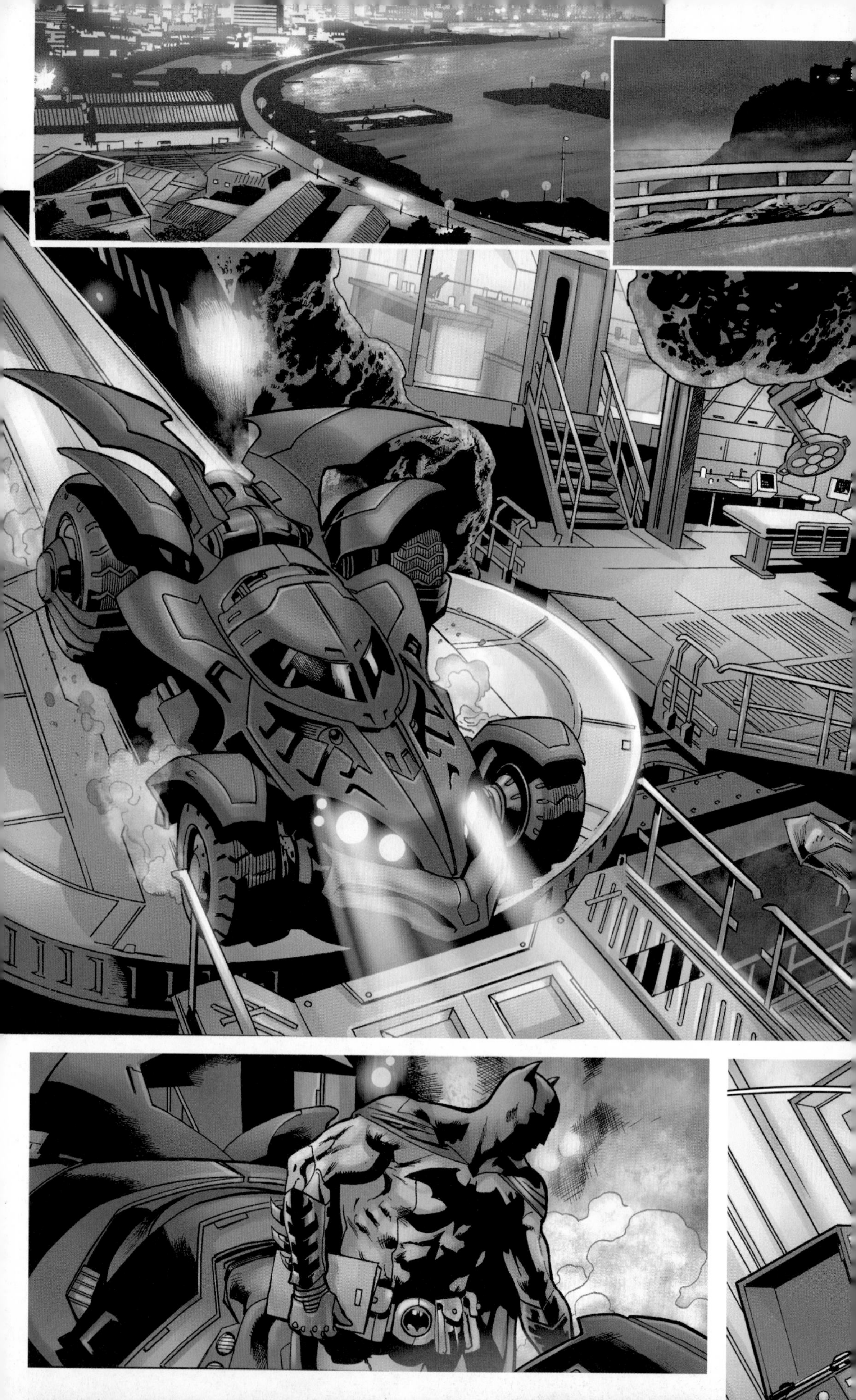

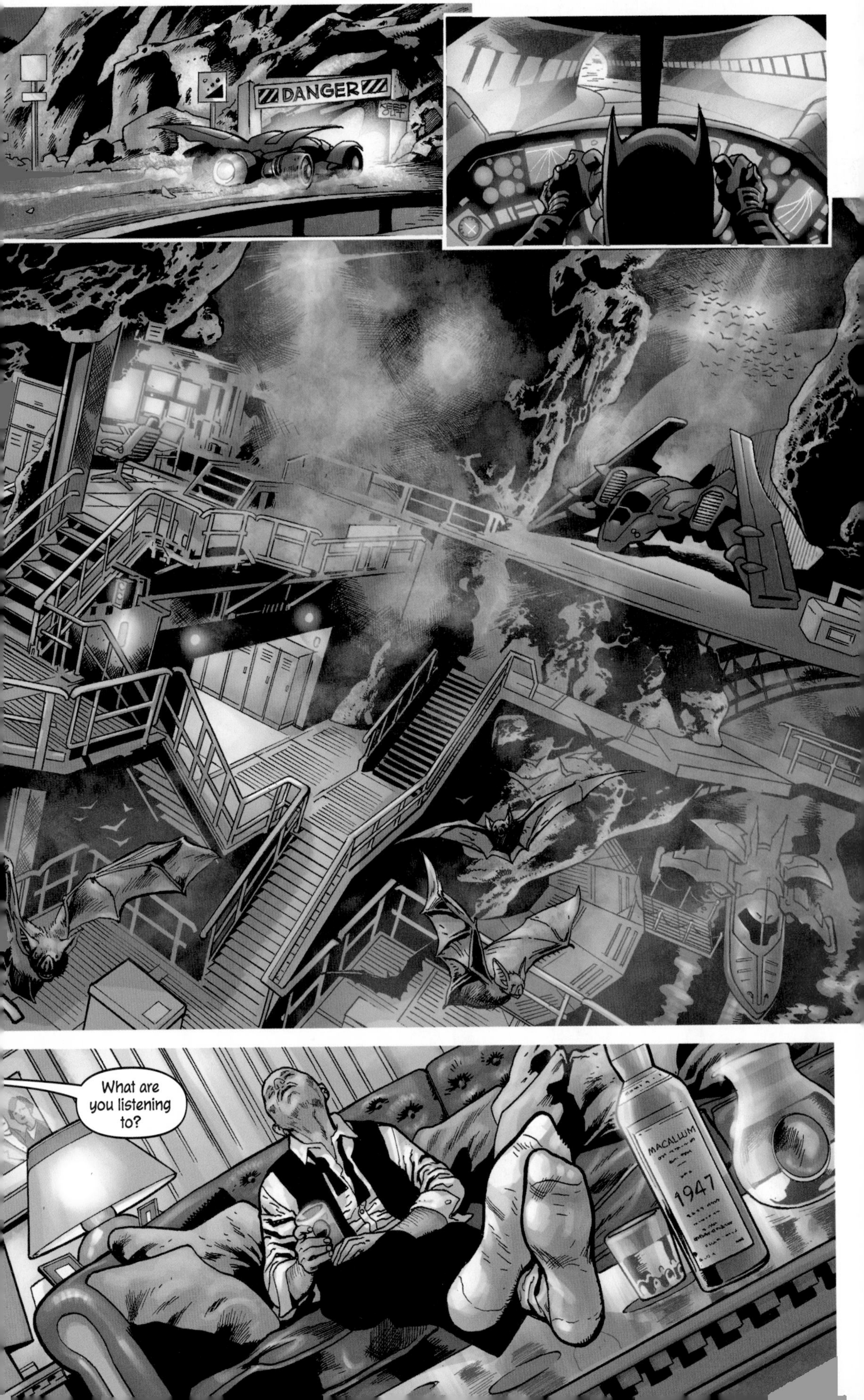
DANGER
KEEP OUT
What are you listening to?
MACALLUM
1947

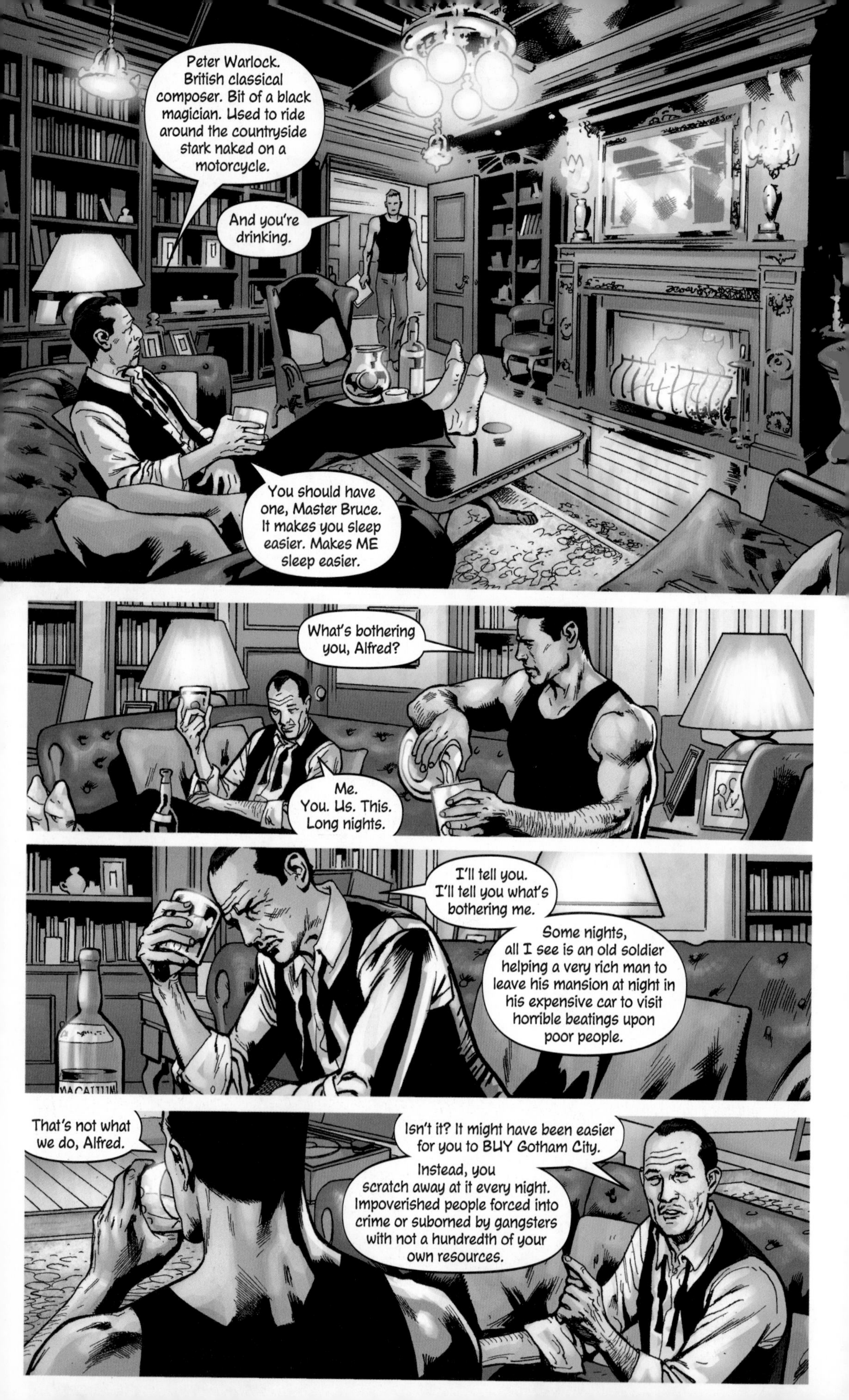
Peter Warlock. British classical composer. Bit of a black magician. Used to ride around the countryside stark naked on a motorcycle.
And you're drinking.
You should have one, Master Bruce. It makes you sleep easier. Makes ME sleep easier.
What's bothering you, Alfred?
Me. You. Us. This. Long nights.
I'll tell you. I'll tell you what's bothering me.
Some nights, all I see is an old soldier helping a very rich man to leave his mansion at night in his expensive car to visit horrible beatings upon poor people.
That's not what we do, Alfred.
Isn't it? It might have been easier for you to BUY Gotham City.
Instead, you scratch away at it every night. Impoverished people forced into crime or suborned by gangsters with not a hundredth of your own resources.

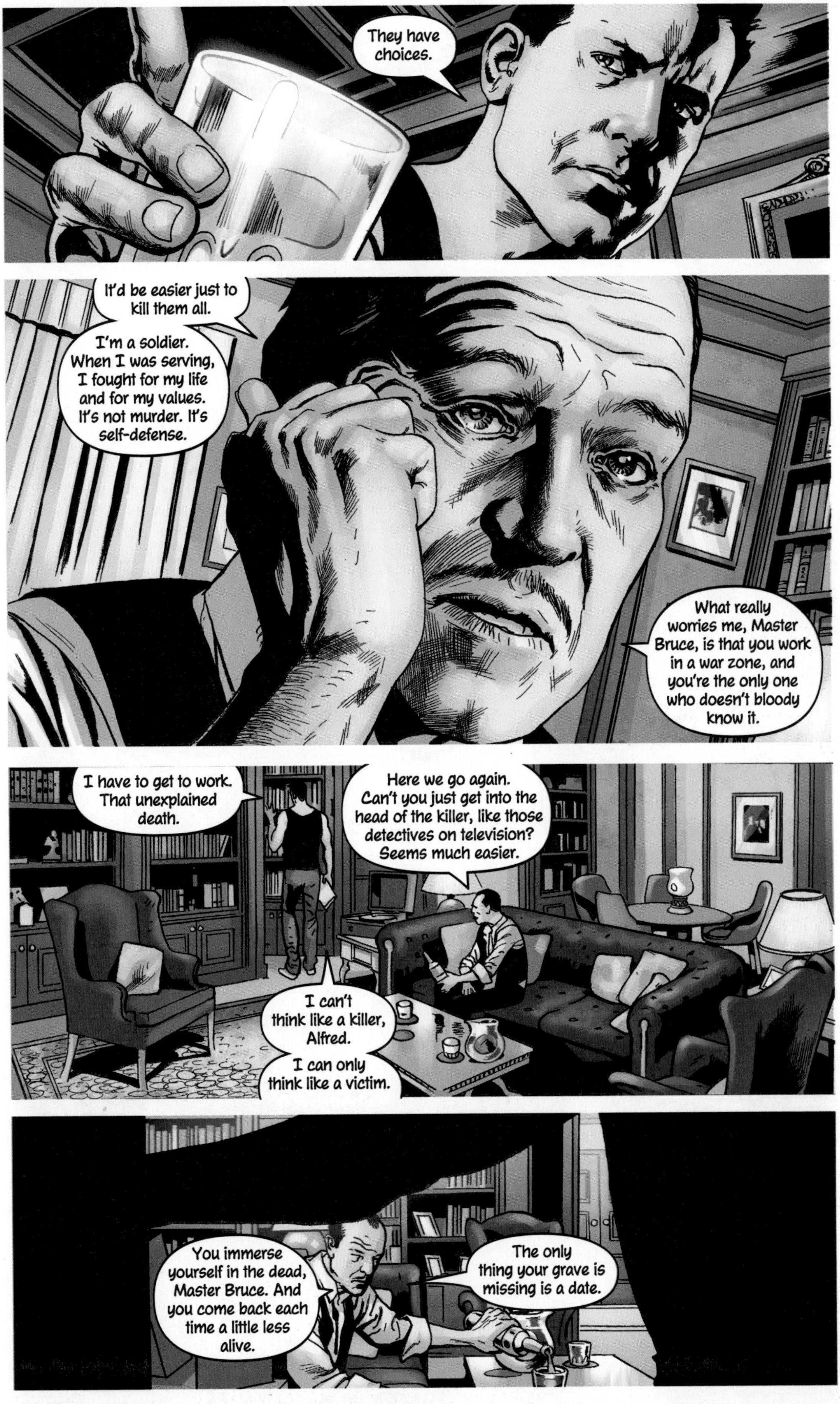

They have choices.
It'd be easier just to kill them all.
I'm a soldier. When I was serving, I fought for my life and for my values. It's not murder. It's self-defense.
What really worries me, Master Bruce, is that you work in a war zone, and you're the only one who doesn't bloody know it.
I have to get to work. That unexplained death.
Here we go again. Can't you just get into the head of the killer, like those detectives on television? Seems much easier.
I can't think like a killer, Alfred.
I can only think like a victim.
You immerse yourself in the dead, Master Bruce. And you come back each time a little less alive.
The only thing your grave is missing is a date.

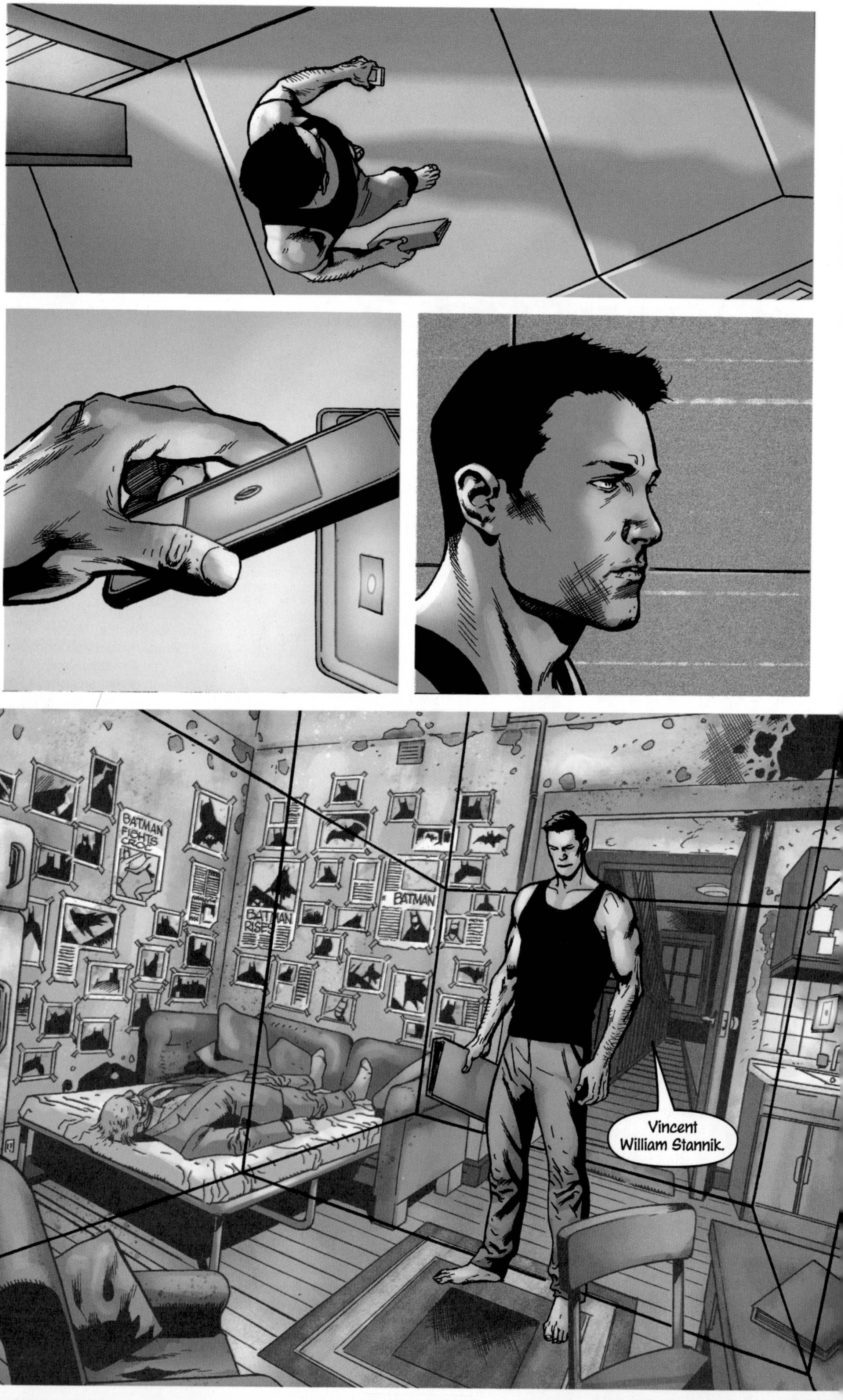
BATMAN FIGHTS CROC
BATMAN RISES
BATMAN
Vincent William Stannik.

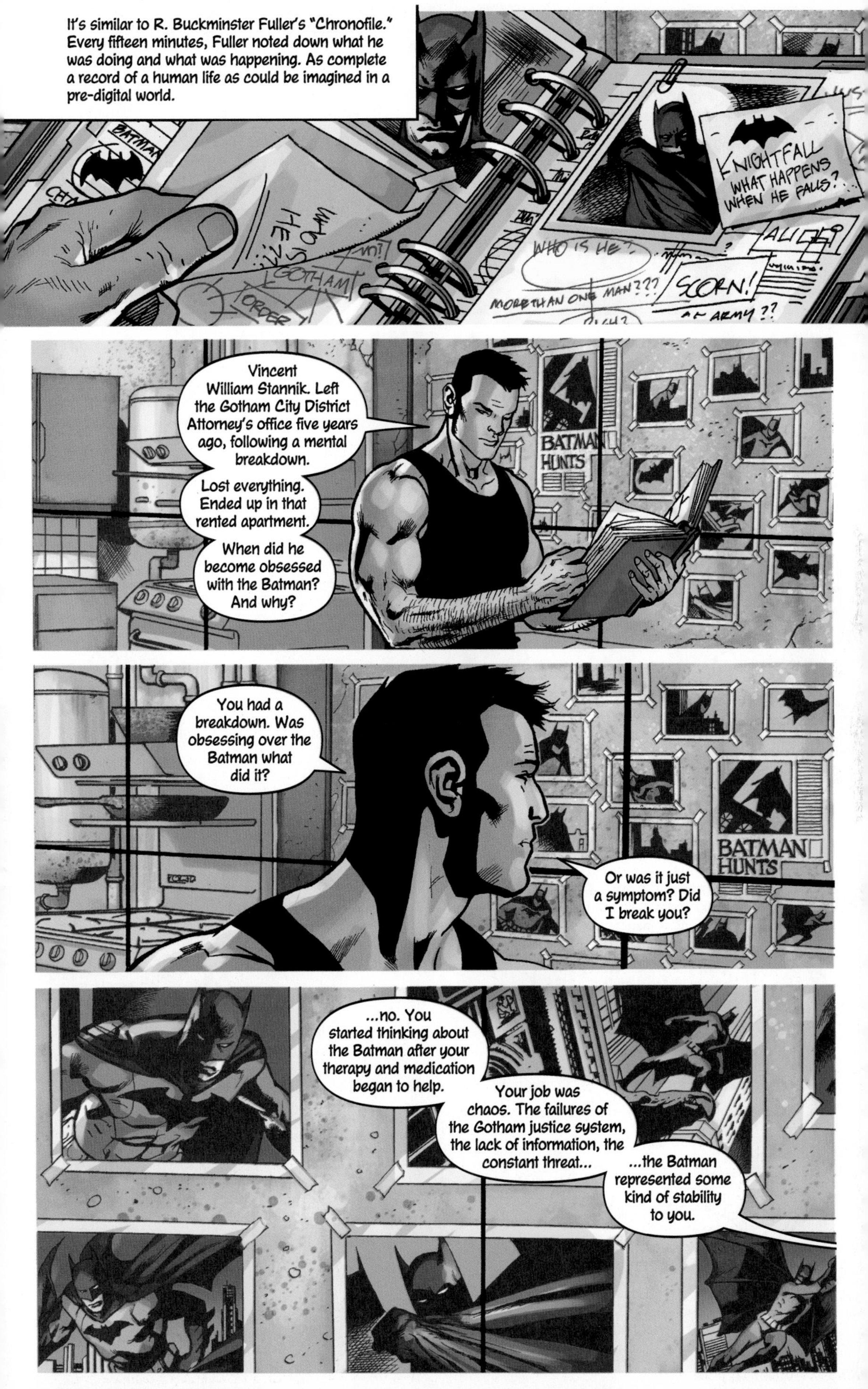
It's similar to R. Buckminster Fuller's "Chronofile." Every fifteen minutes, Fuller noted down what he was doing and what was happening. As complete a record of a human life as could be imagined in a pre-digital world.
BATMAN
KNIGHTFALL WHAT HAPPENS WHEN HE FALLS?
WHO IS HE?
GOTHAM
ORDER
SCORN!
MORE THAN ONE MAN???
Vincent William Stannik. Left the Gotham City District Attorney's office five years ago, following a mental breakdown.
Lost everything. Ended up in that rented apartment.
When did he become obsessed with the Batman? And why?
BATMAN HUNTS
You had a breakdown. Was obsessing over the Batman what did it?
Or was it just a symptom? Did I break you?
BATMAN HUNTS
...no. You started thinking about the Batman after your therapy and medication began to help.
Your job was chaos. The failures of the Gotham justice system, the lack of information, the constant threat...
...the Batman represented some kind of stability to you.

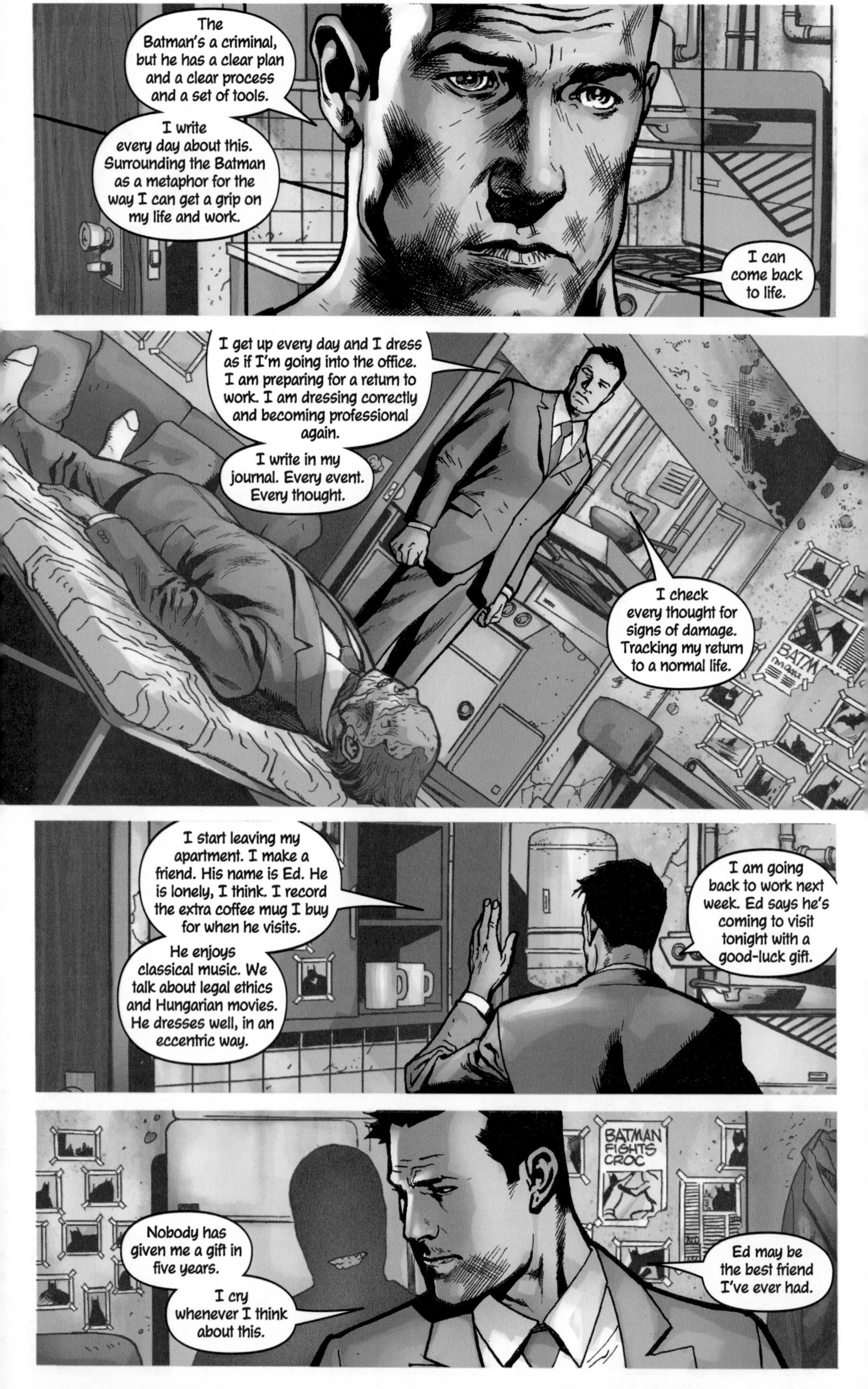

The Batman's a criminal, but he has a clear plan and a clear process and a set of tools.
I write every day about this. Surrounding the Batman as a metaphor for the way I can get a grip on my life and work.
I can come back to life.
I get up every day and I dress as if I'm going into the office. I am preparing for a return to work. I am dressing correctly and becoming professional again.
I write in my journal. Every event. Every thought.
I check every thought for signs of damage. Tracking my return to a normal life.
BATM
I start leaving my apartment. I make a friend. His name is Ed. He is lonely, I think. I record the extra coffee mug I buy for when he visits.
He enjoys classical music. We talk about legal ethics and Hungarian movies. He dresses well, in an eccentric way.
I am going back to work next week. Ed says he's coming to visit tonight with a good-luck gift.
BATMAN FIGHTS CROC
Nobody has given me a gift in five years.
I cry whenever I think about this.
Ed may be the best friend I've ever had.

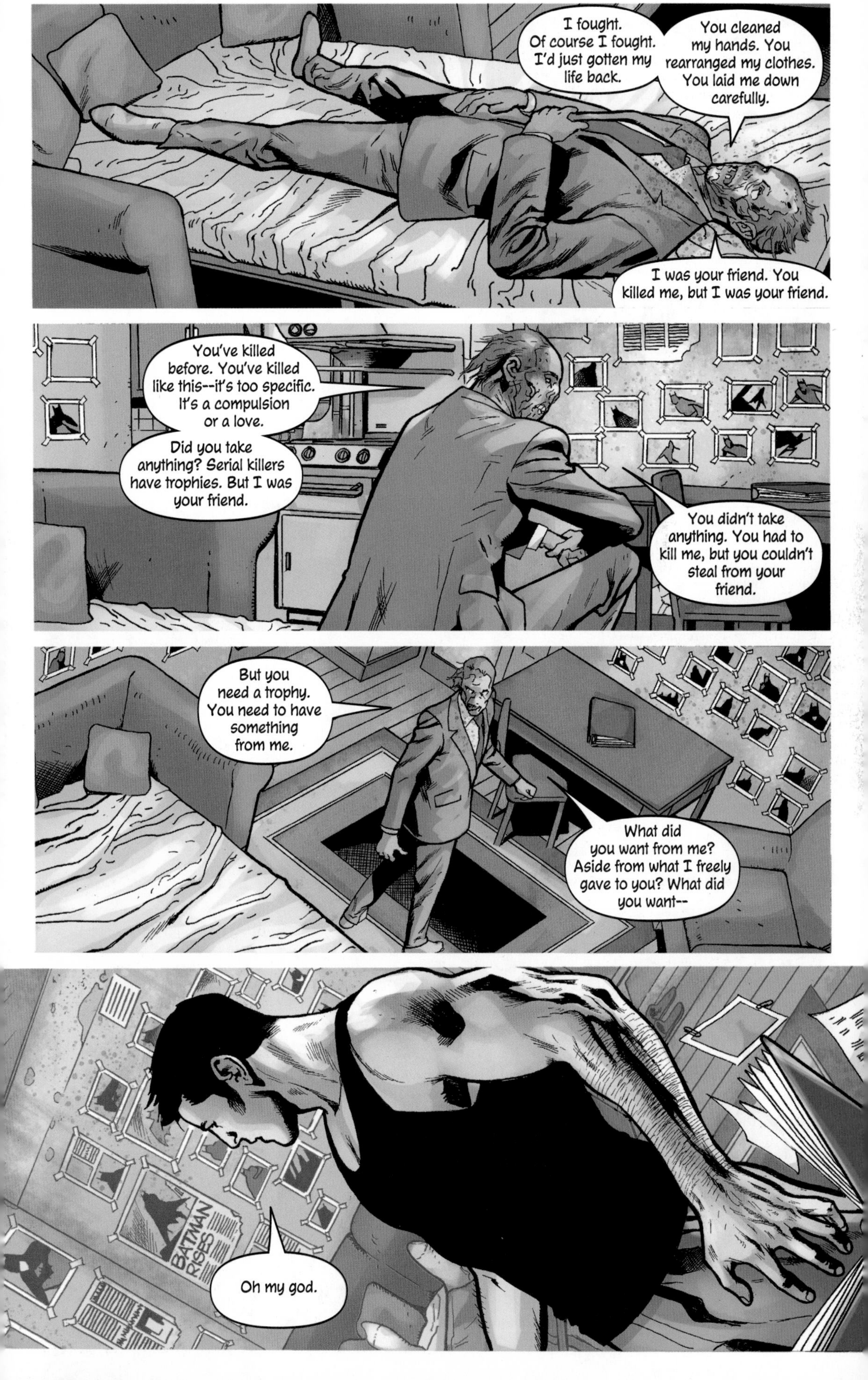
I fought. Of course I fought. I'd just gotten my life back.
You cleaned my hands. You rearranged my clothes. You laid me down carefully.
I was your friend. You killed me, but I was your friend.
You've killed before. You've killed like this--it's too specific. It's a compulsion or a love.
Did you take anything? Serial killers have trophies. But I was your friend.
You didn't take anything. You had to kill me, but you couldn't steal from your friend.
But you need a trophy. You need to have something from me.
What did you want from me? Aside from what I freely gave to you? What did you want--
BATMAN RISES
Oh my god.

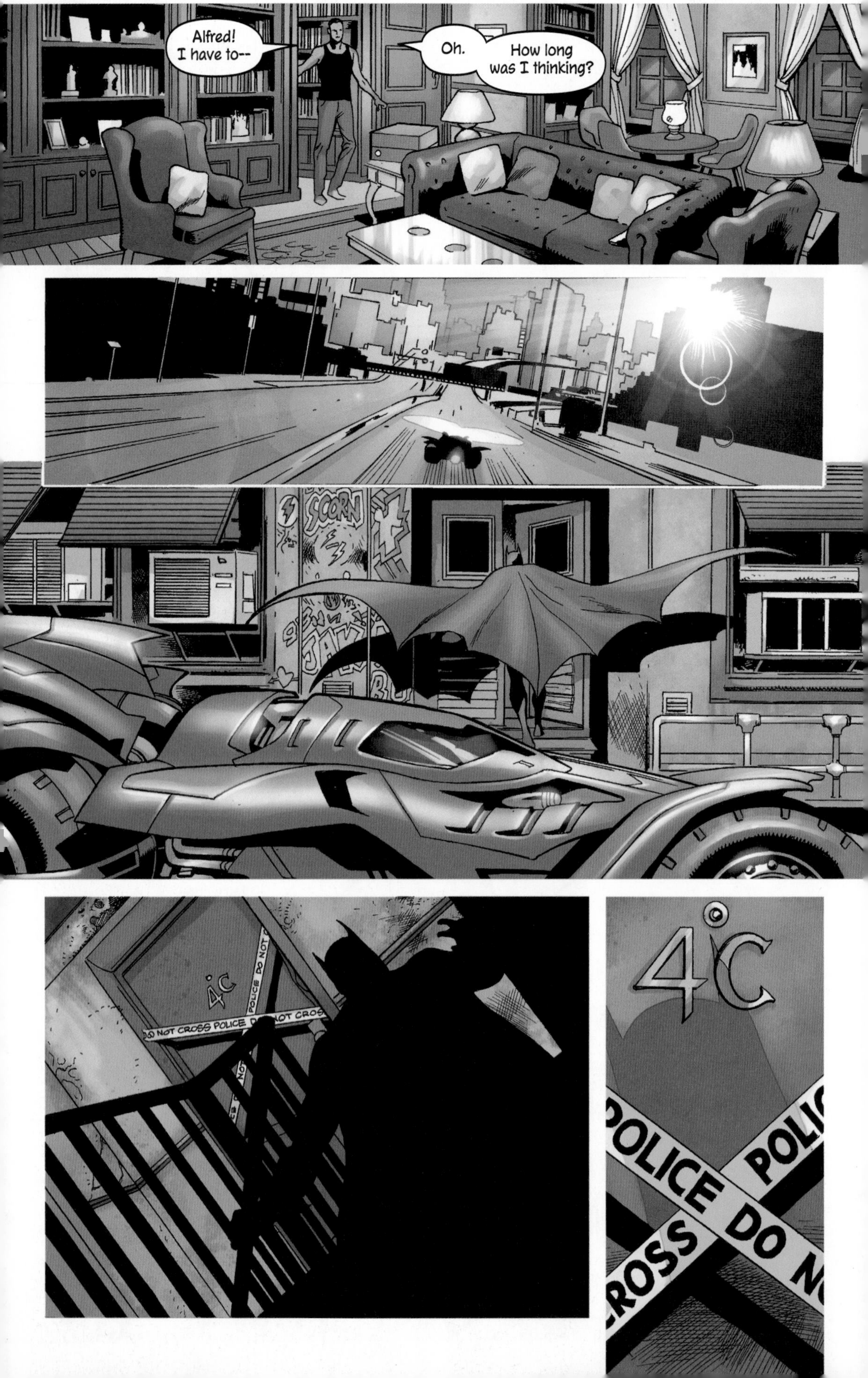
Alfred! I have to--
Oh.
How long was I thinking?
4C
POLICE
CROSS

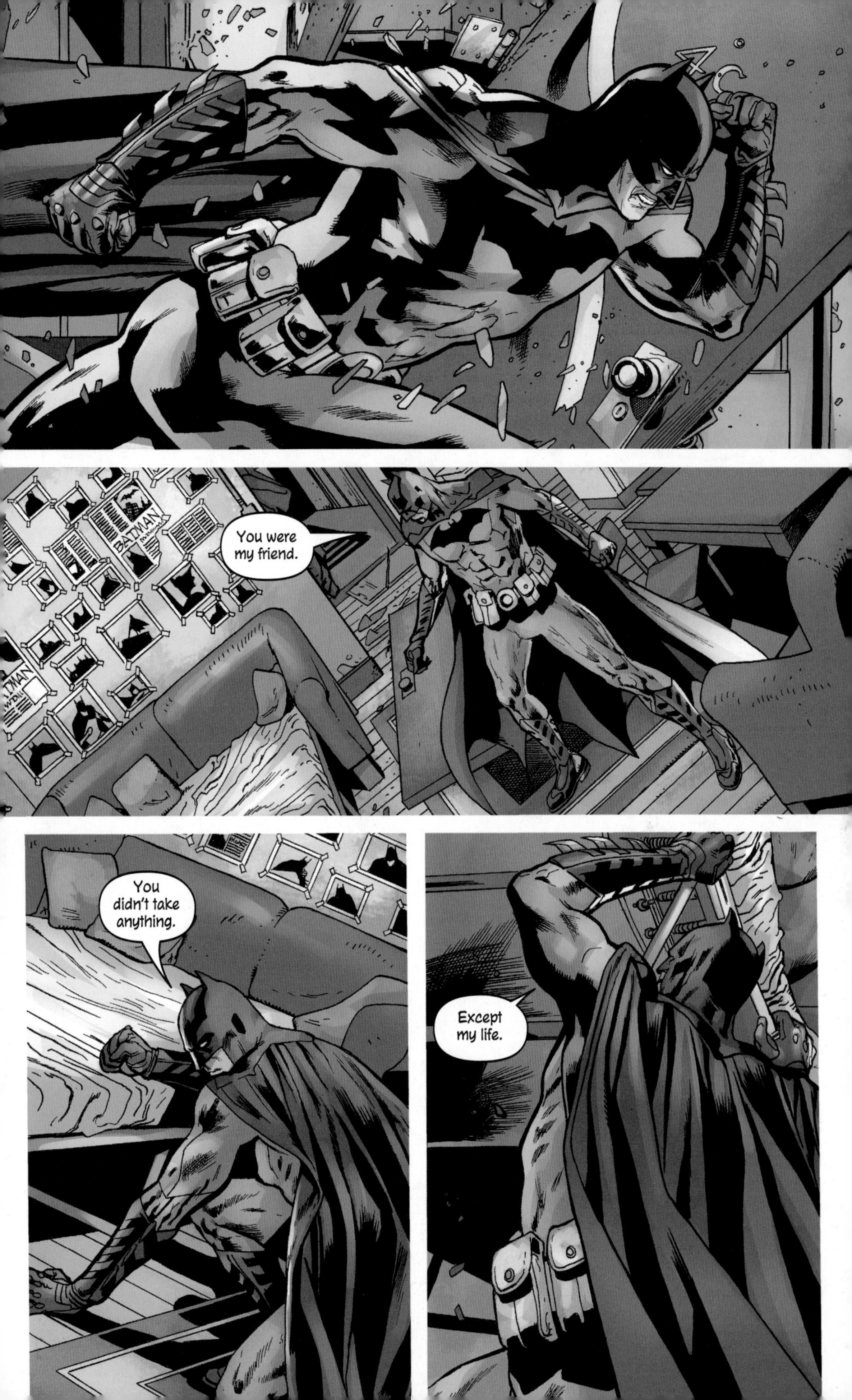
You were my friend.
You didn't take anything.
Except my life.

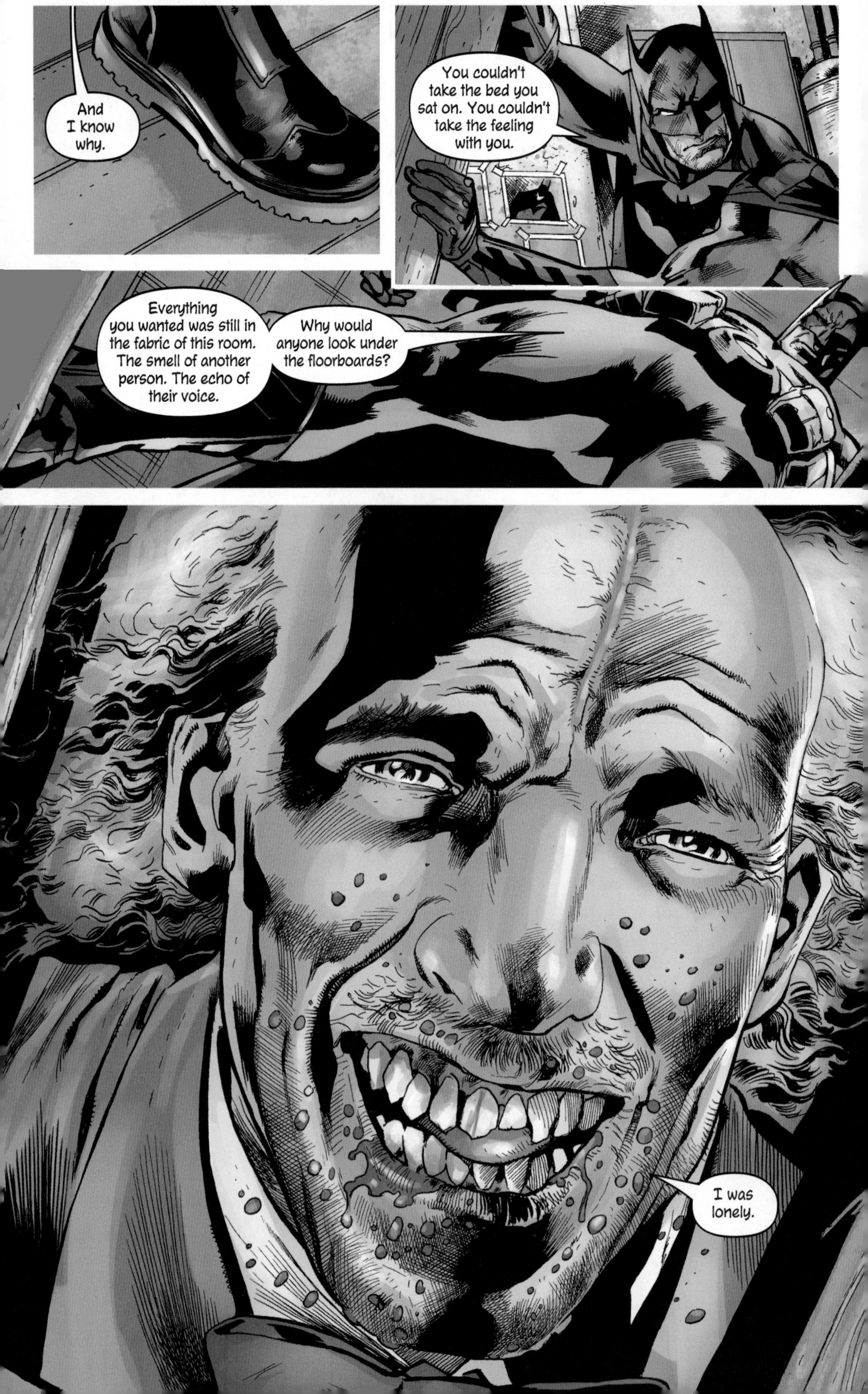
And I know why.
You couldn't take the bed you sat on. You couldn't take the feeling with you.
Everything you wanted was still in the fabric of this room. The smell of another person. The echo of their voice.
Why would anyone look under the floorboards?
I was lonely.

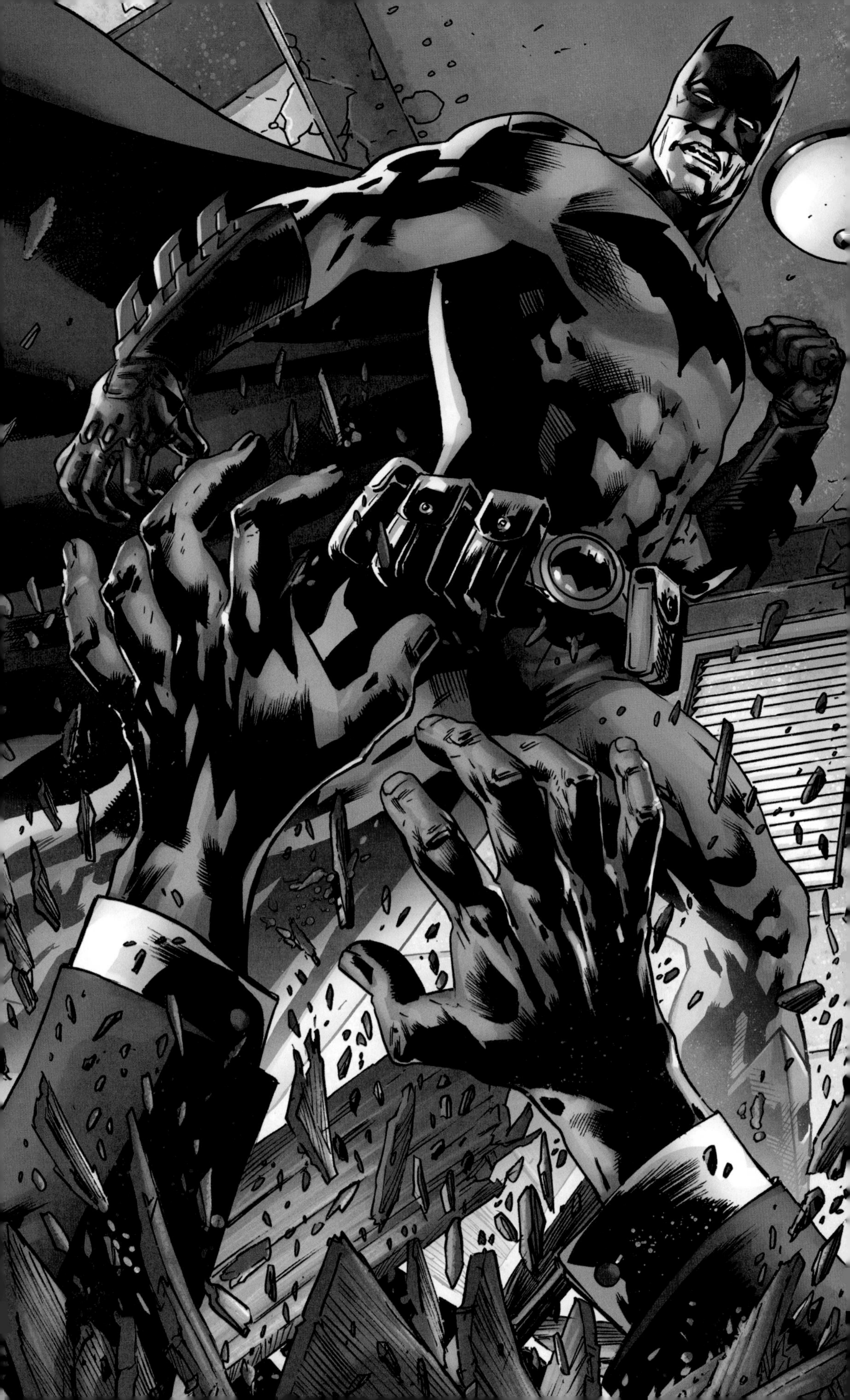

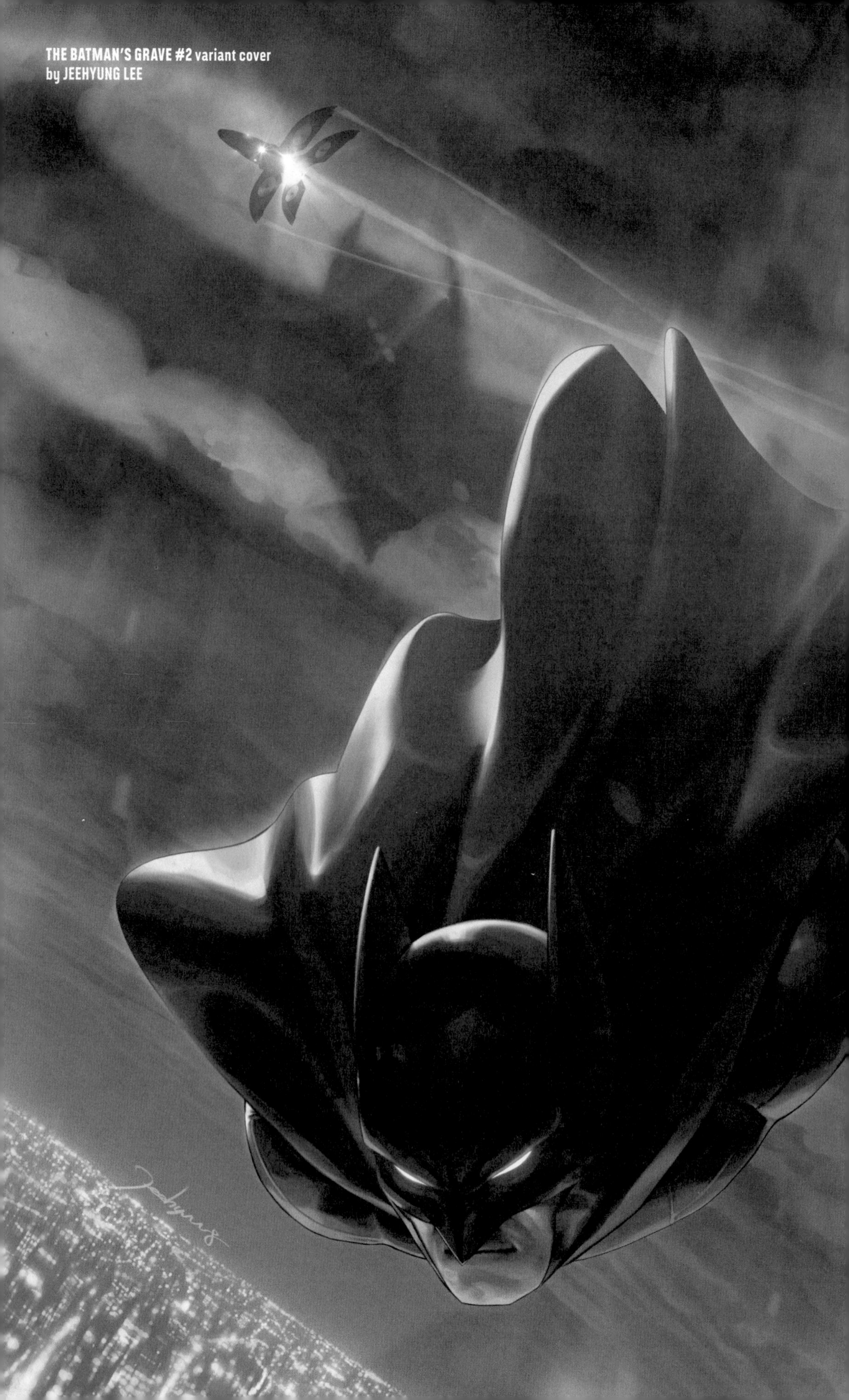

THE BATMAN'S GRAVE #2 variant cover
by **JEEHYUNG LEE**

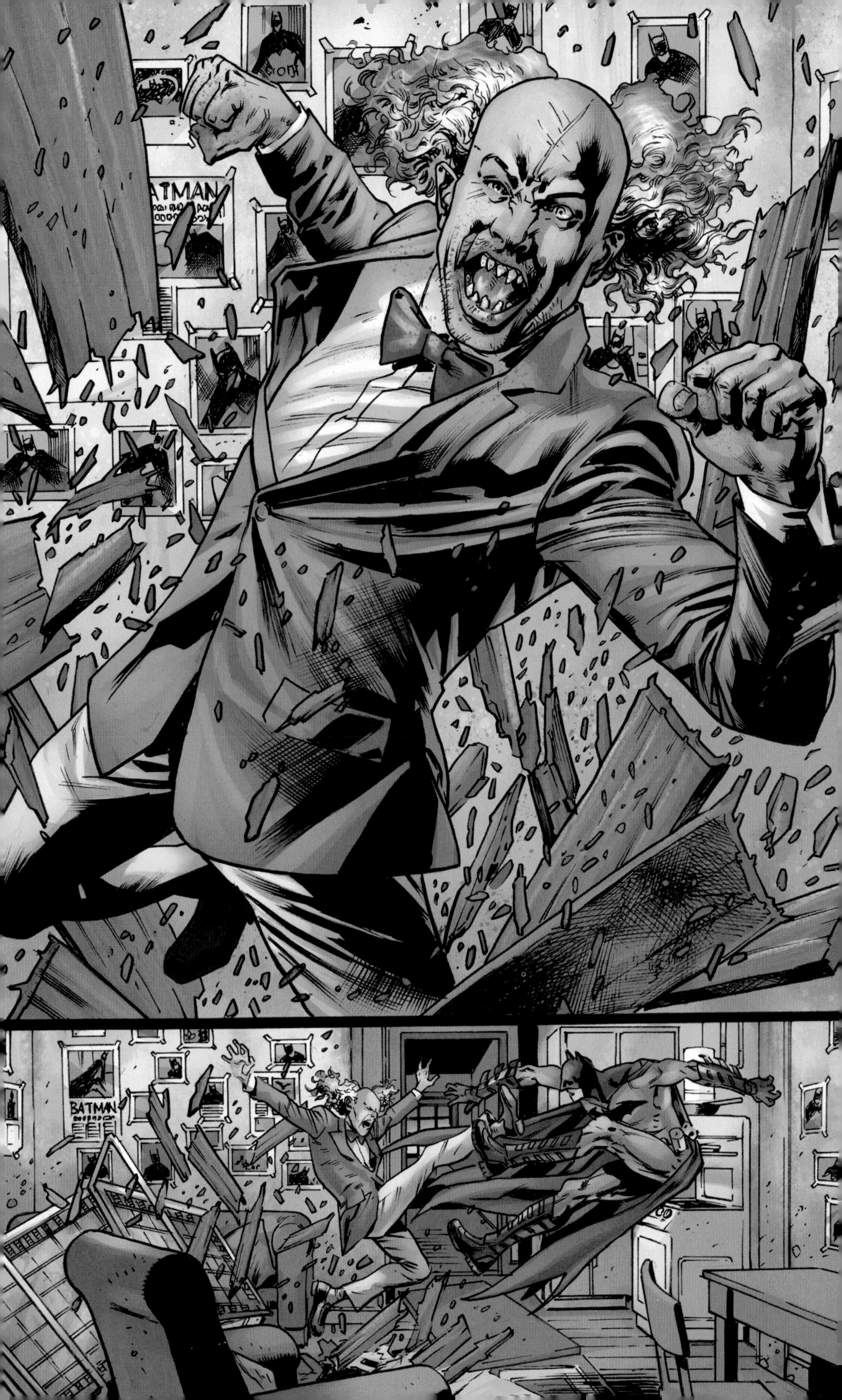
BATMAN

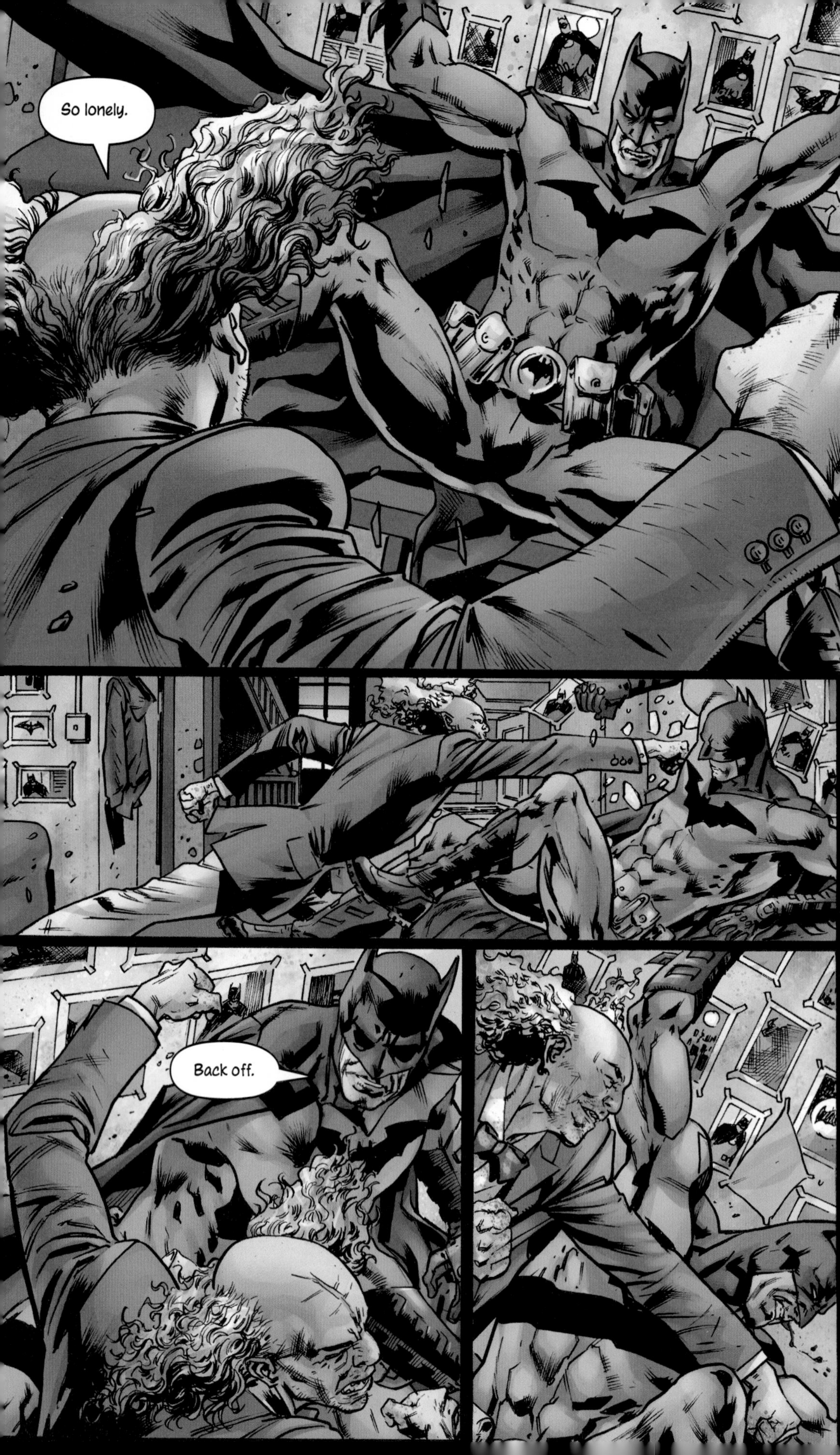
So lonely.
Back off.

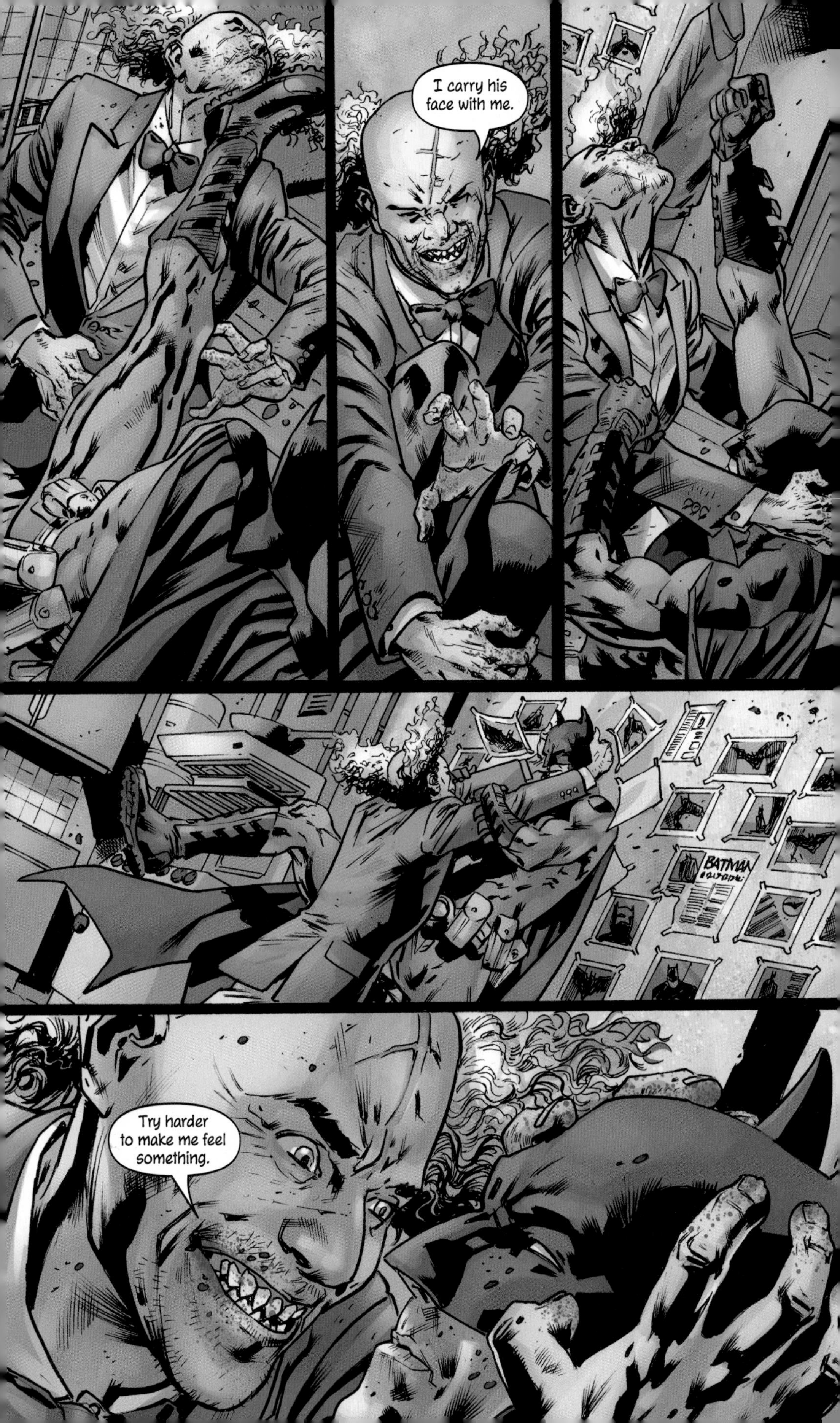
I carry his face with me.
BATMAN
Try harder to make me feel something.

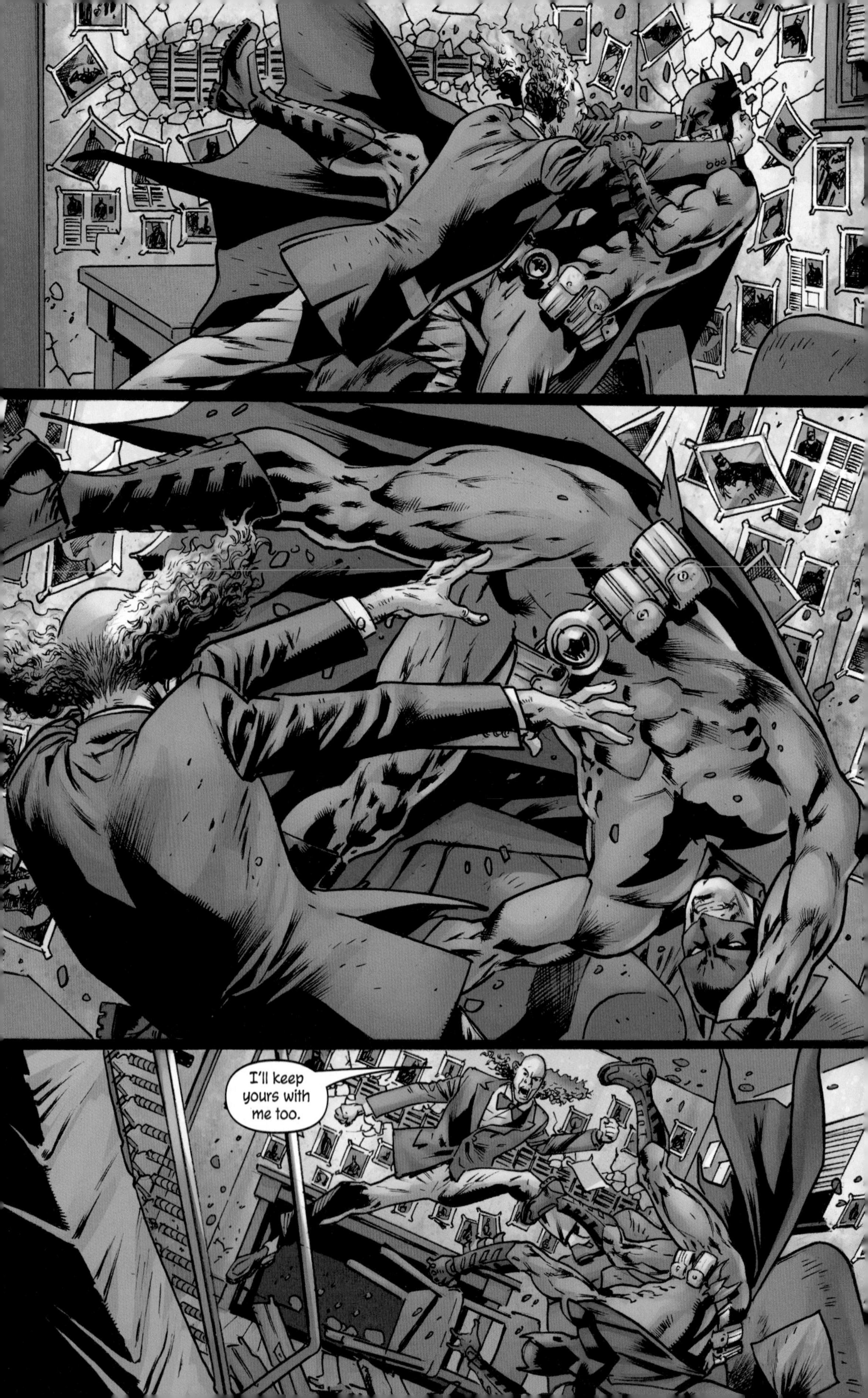
I'll keep yours with me too.

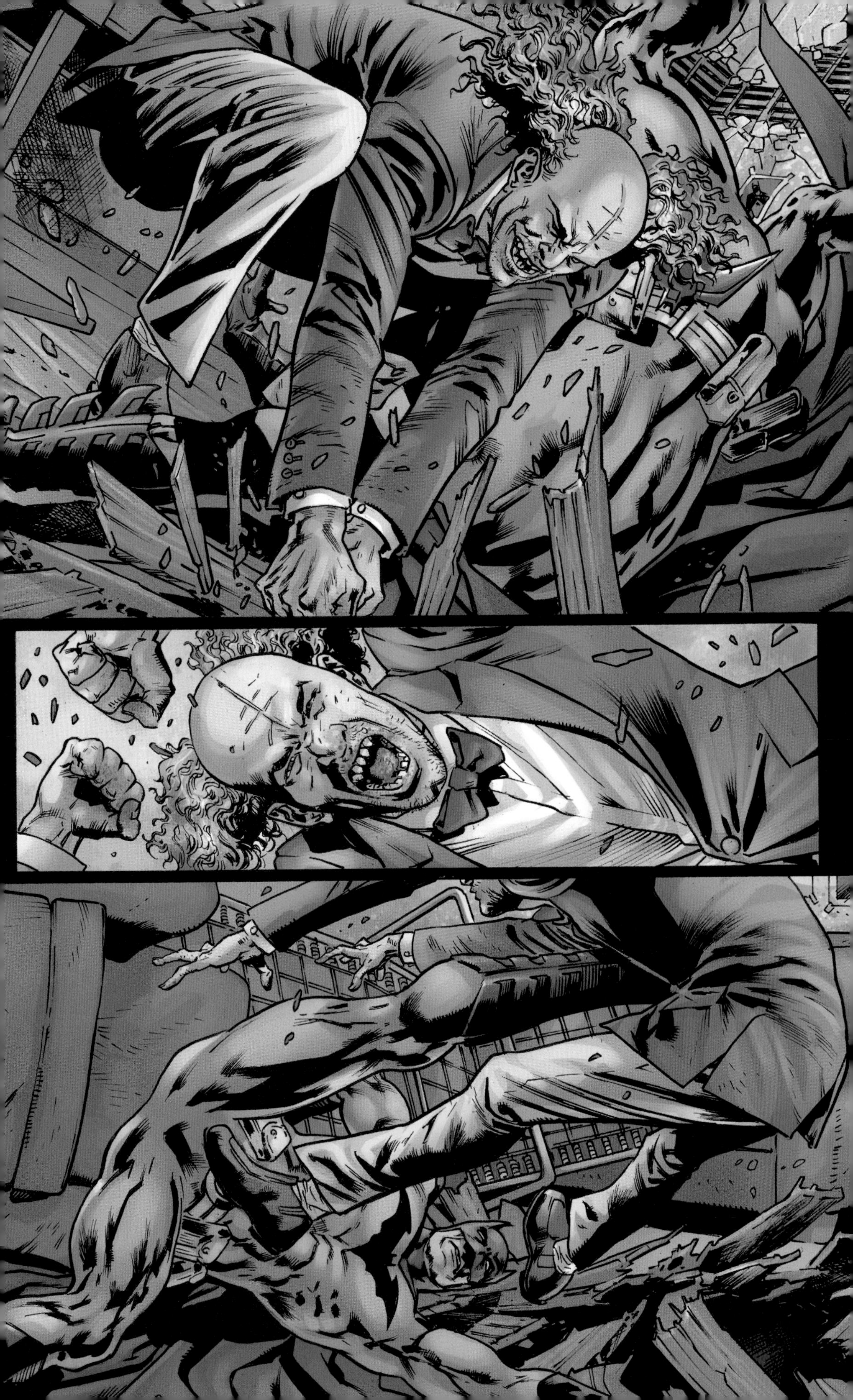

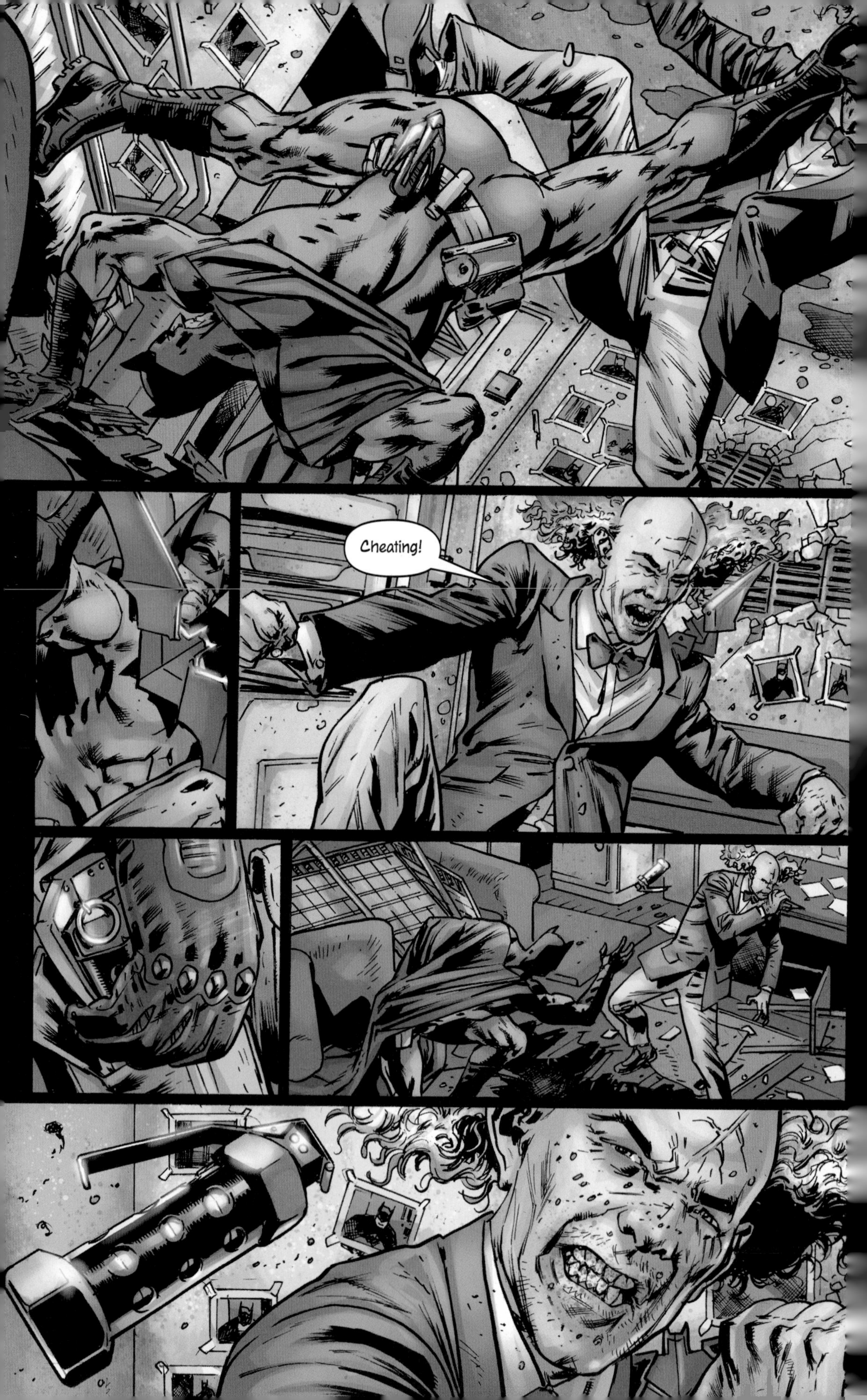
Cheating!

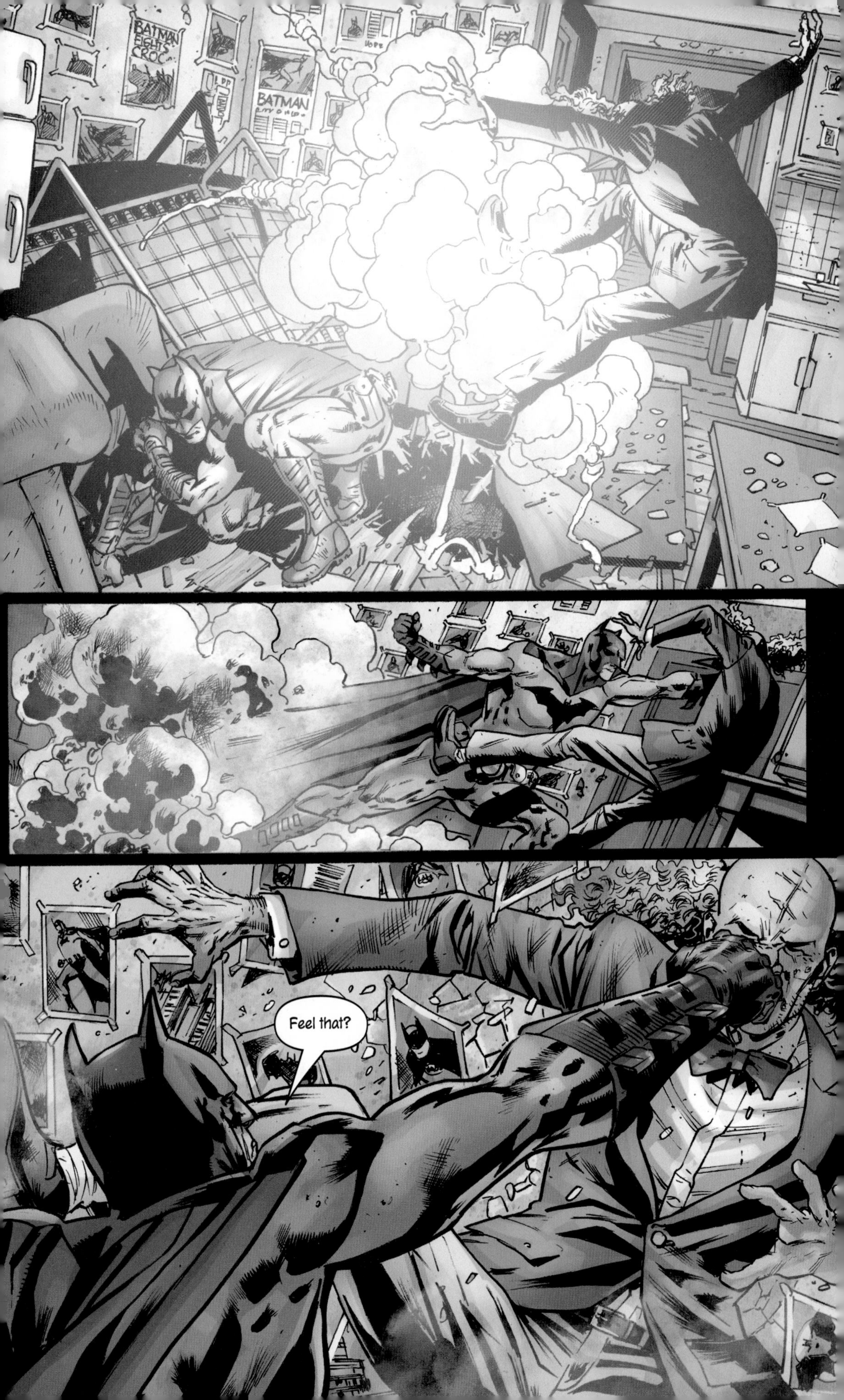
BATMAN FIGHTS CROC
BATMAN
Feel that?

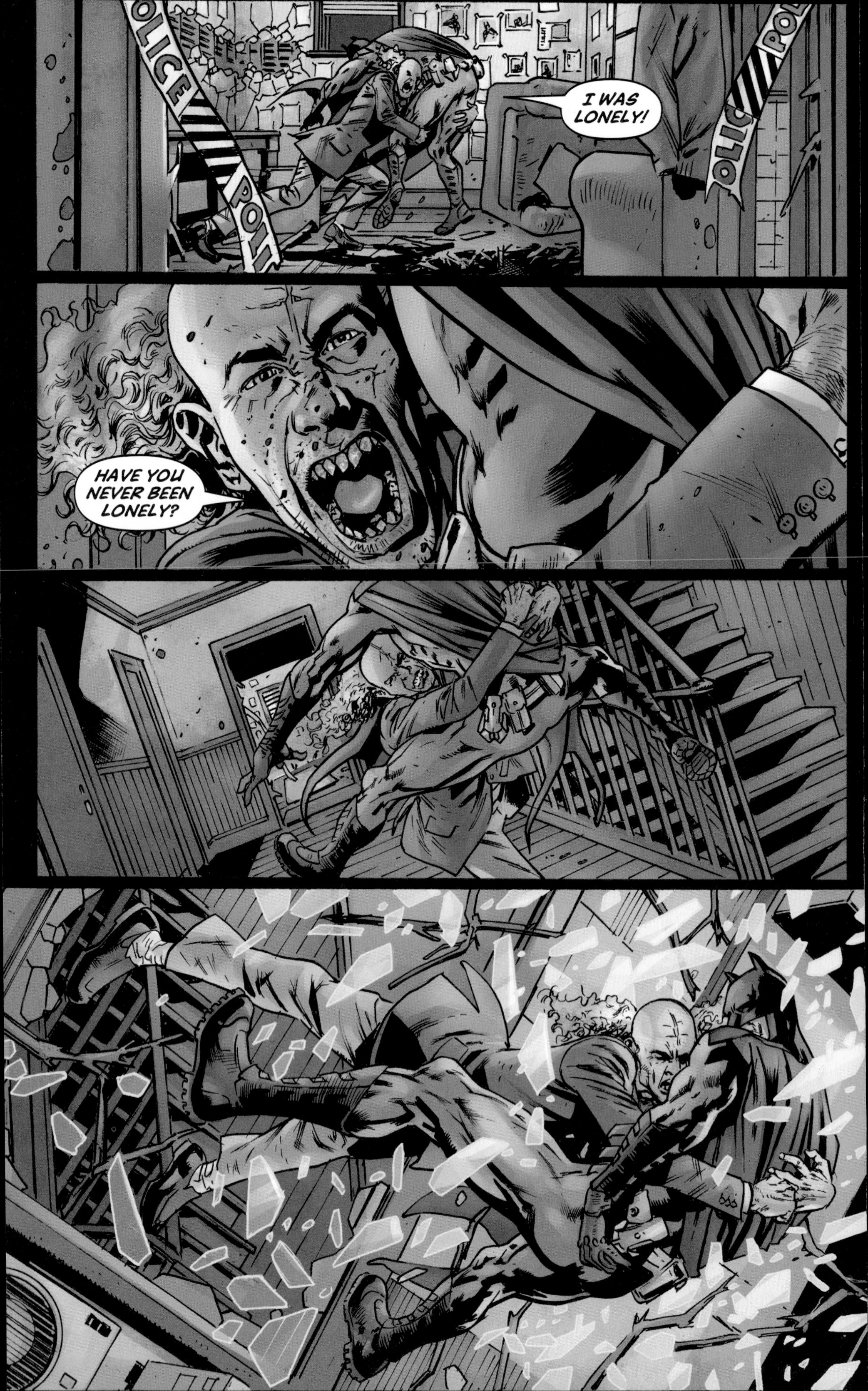

I WAS LONELY!
HAVE YOU NEVER BEEN LONELY?

Chapter 2

Writer	Art
WARREN ELLIS	**BRYAN HITCH**

Colors	Letters
ALEX SINCLAIR	**RICHARD STARKINGS**

Cover	Variant Cover
BRYAN HITCH &	**JEEHYUNG**
ALEX SINCLAIR	**LEE**

Associate Editor	Editor
ANDREW MARINO	**MARIE JAVINS**

BATMAN created by BOB KANE with BILL FINGER

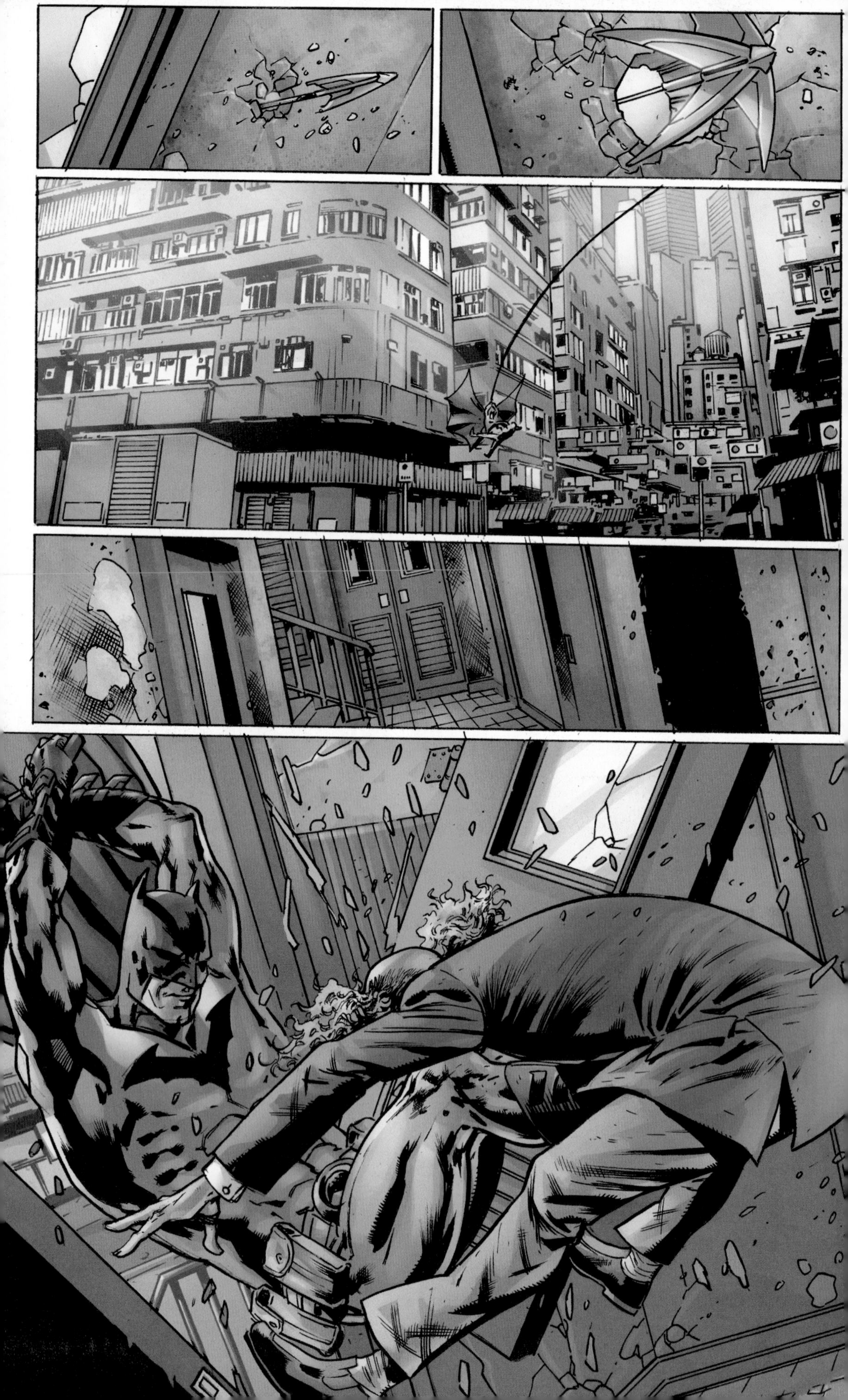

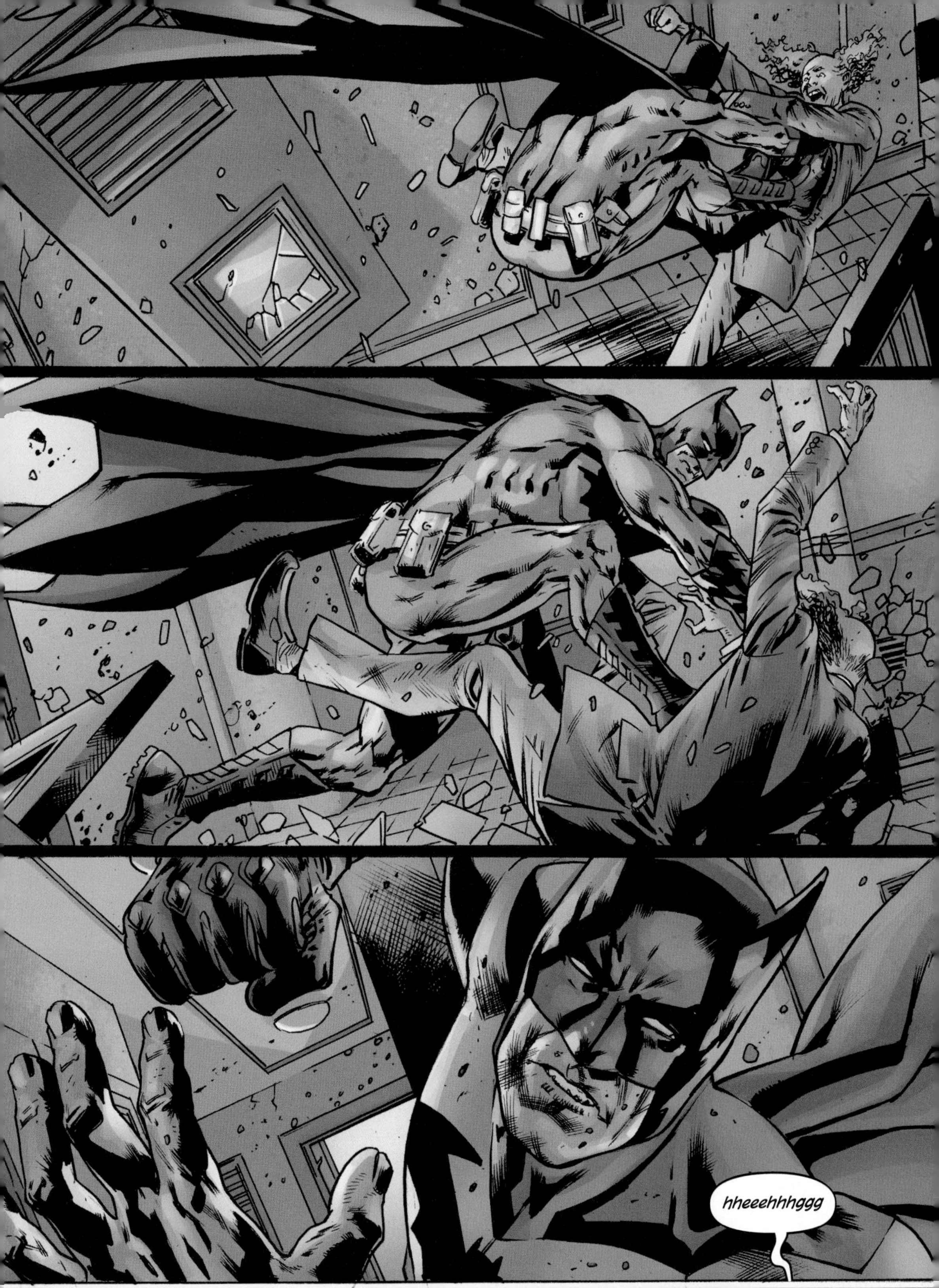
hheeehhhggg

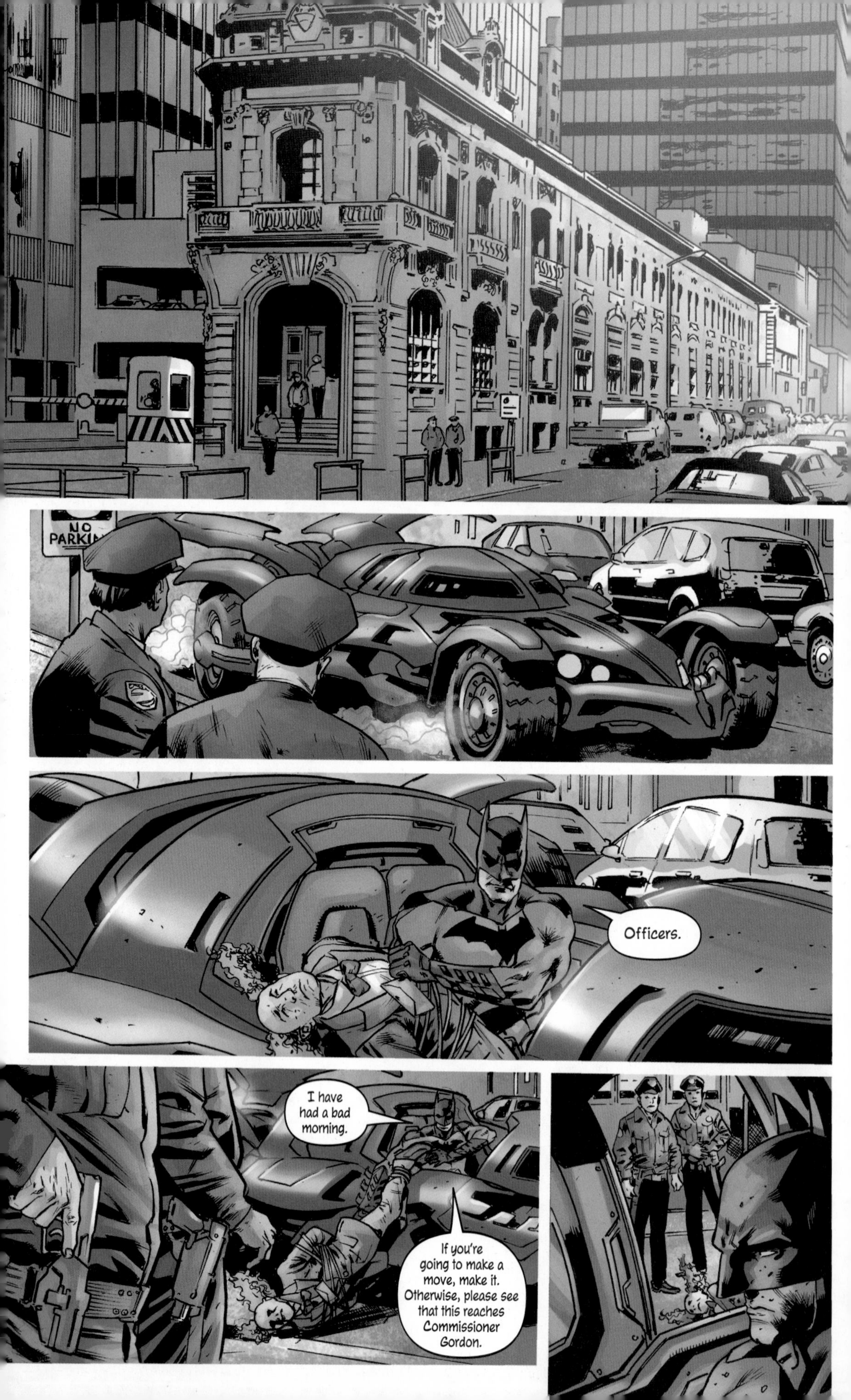
Officers.
I have had a bad morning.
If you're going to make a move, make it. Otherwise, please see that this reaches Commissioner Gordon.

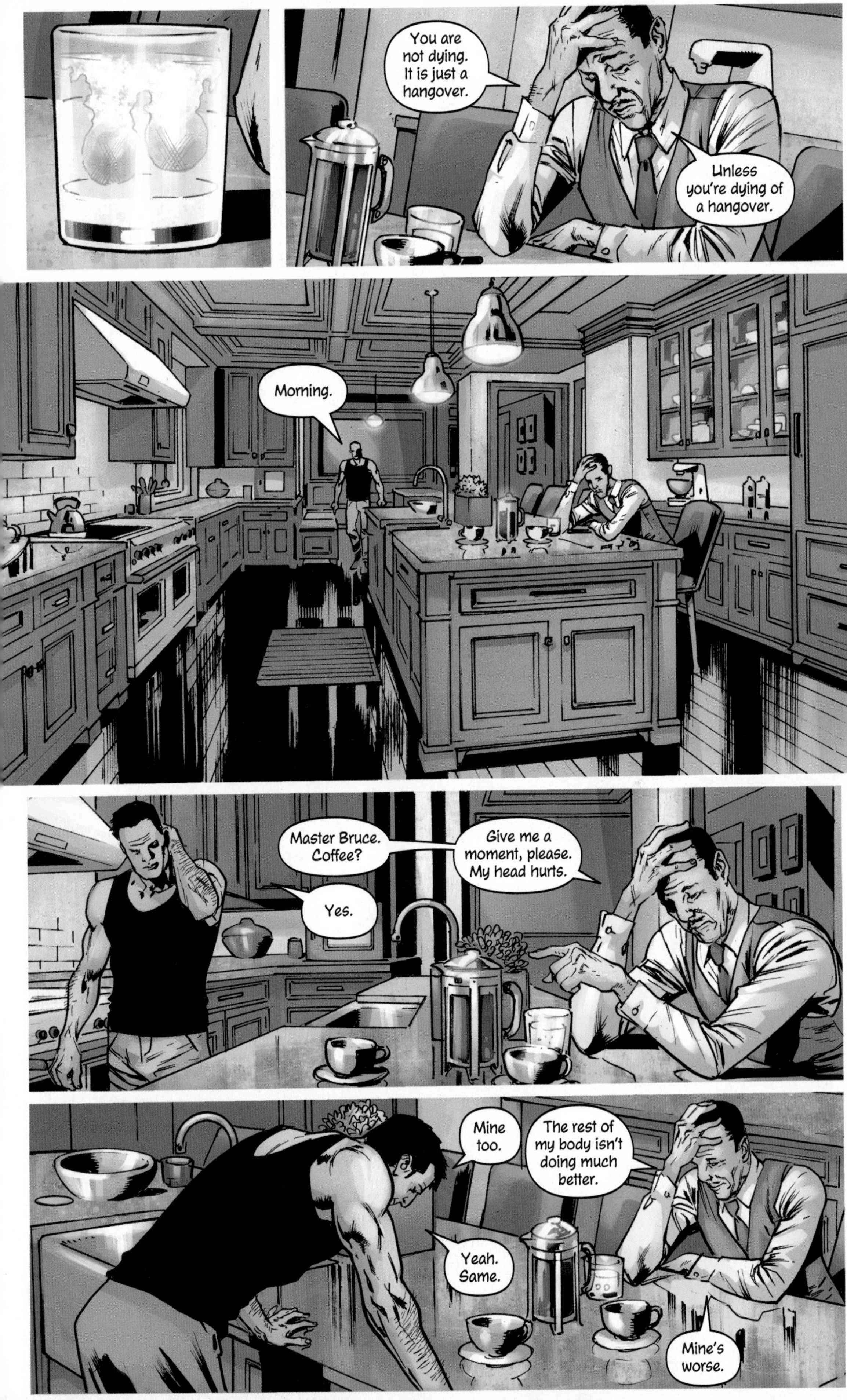
You are not dying. It is just a hangover.
Unless you're dying of a hangover.
Morning.
Master Bruce. Coffee?
Give me a moment, please. My head hurts.
Yes.
Mine too.
The rest of my body isn't doing much better.
Yeah. Same.
Mine's worse.

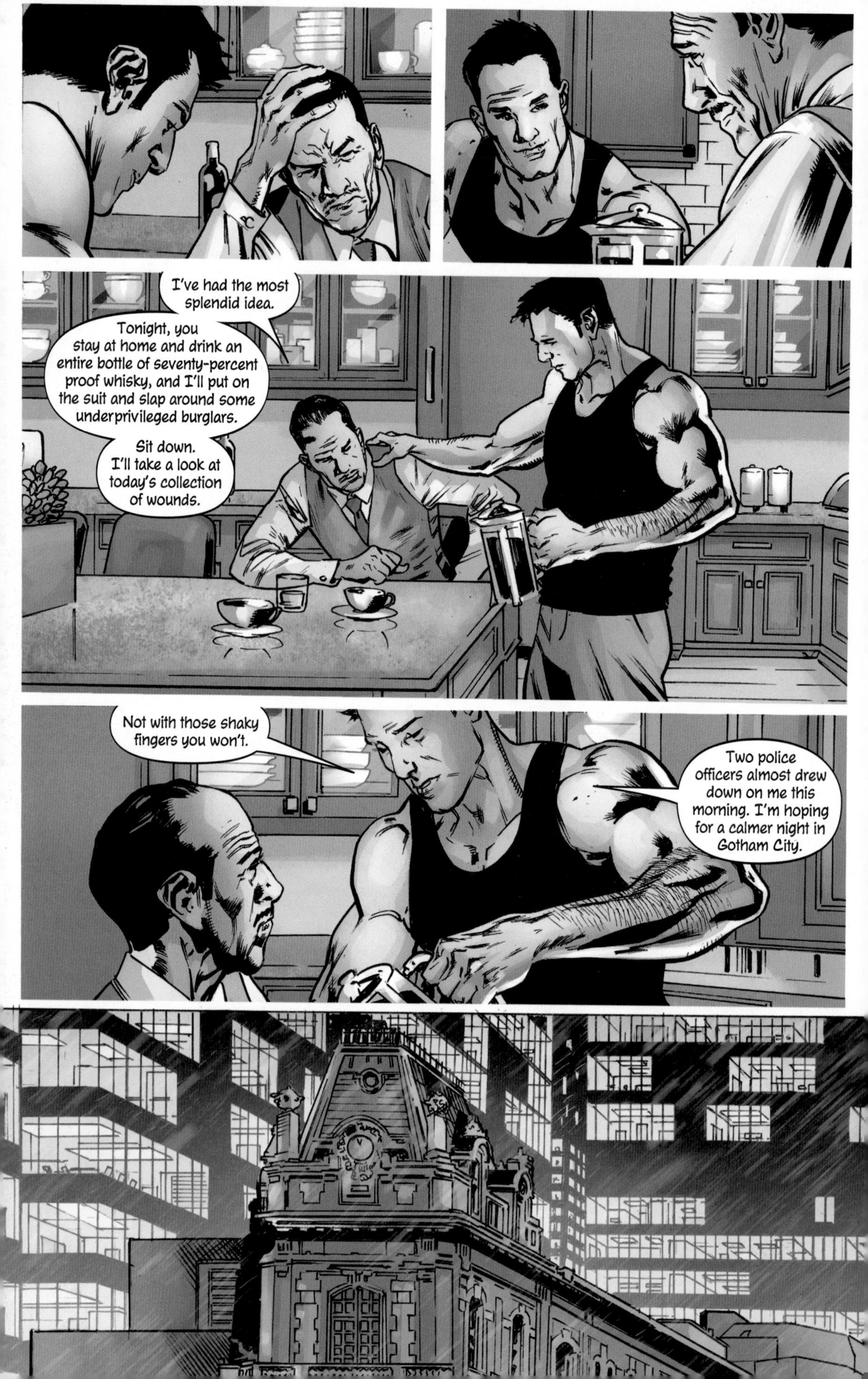
I've had the most splendid idea.
Tonight, you stay at home and drink an entire bottle of seventy-percent proof whisky, and I'll put on the suit and slap around some underprivileged burglars.
Sit down. I'll take a look at today's collection of wounds.
Not with those shaky fingers you won't.
Two police officers almost drew down on me this morning. I'm hoping for a calmer night in Gotham City.

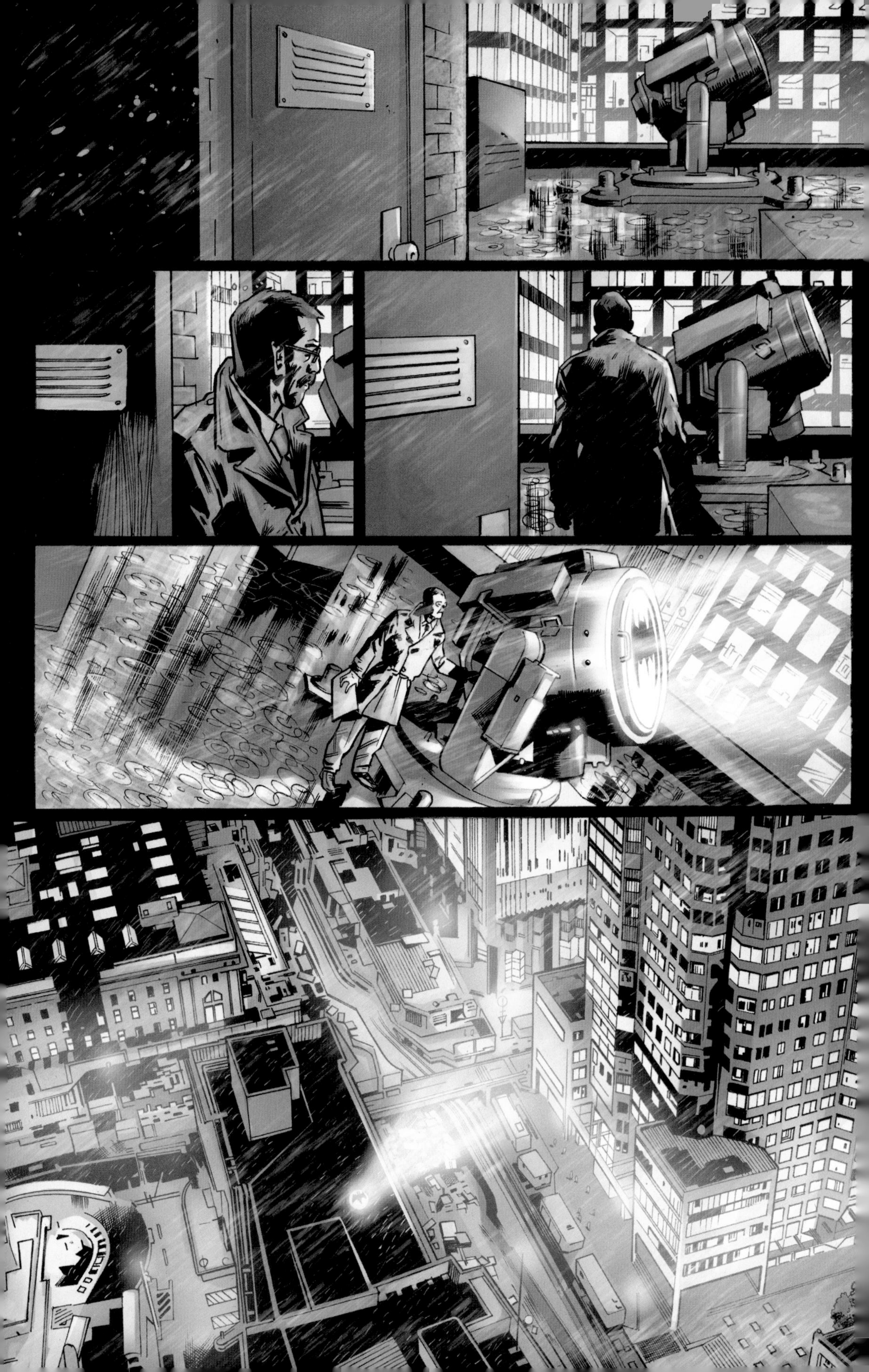

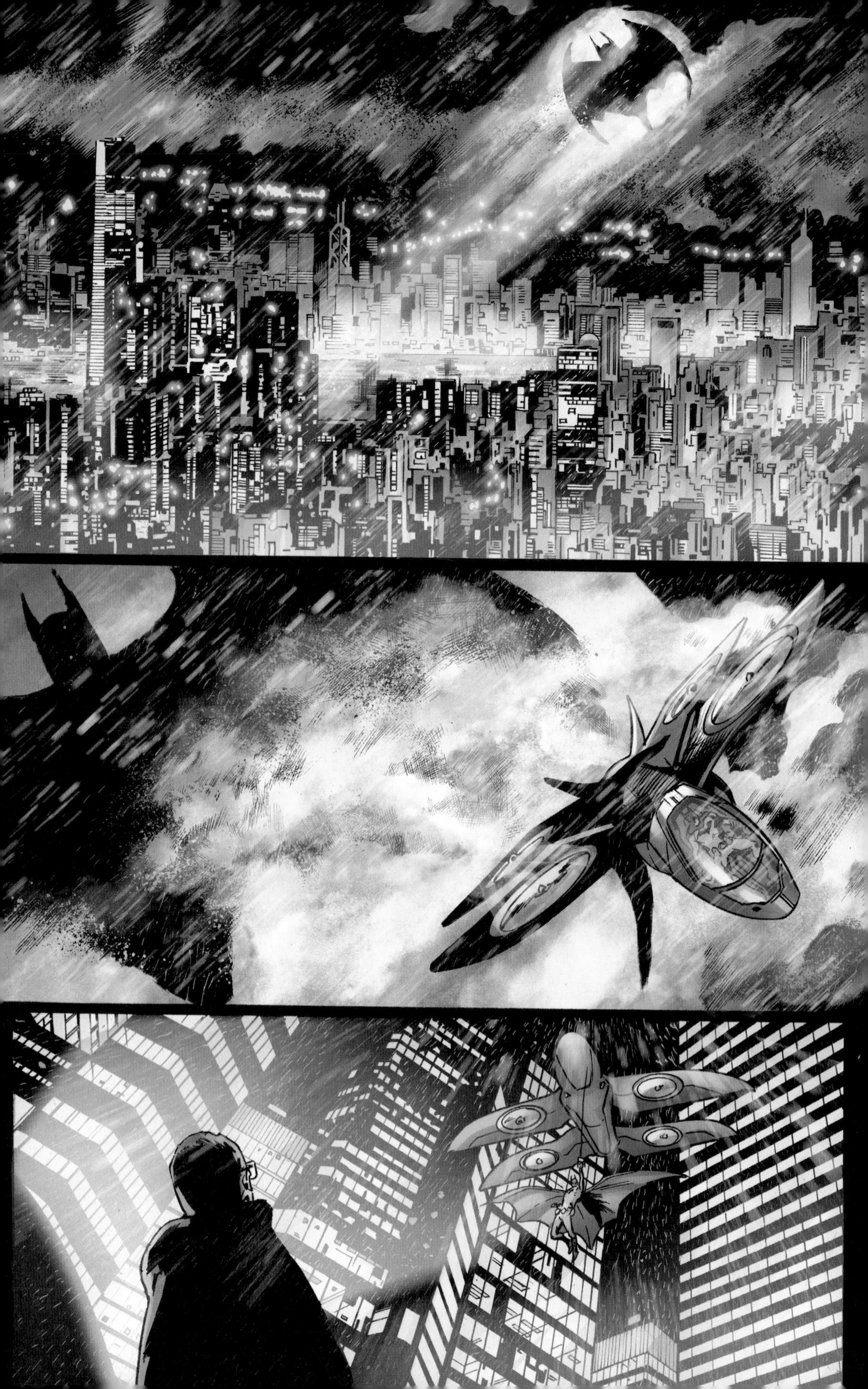

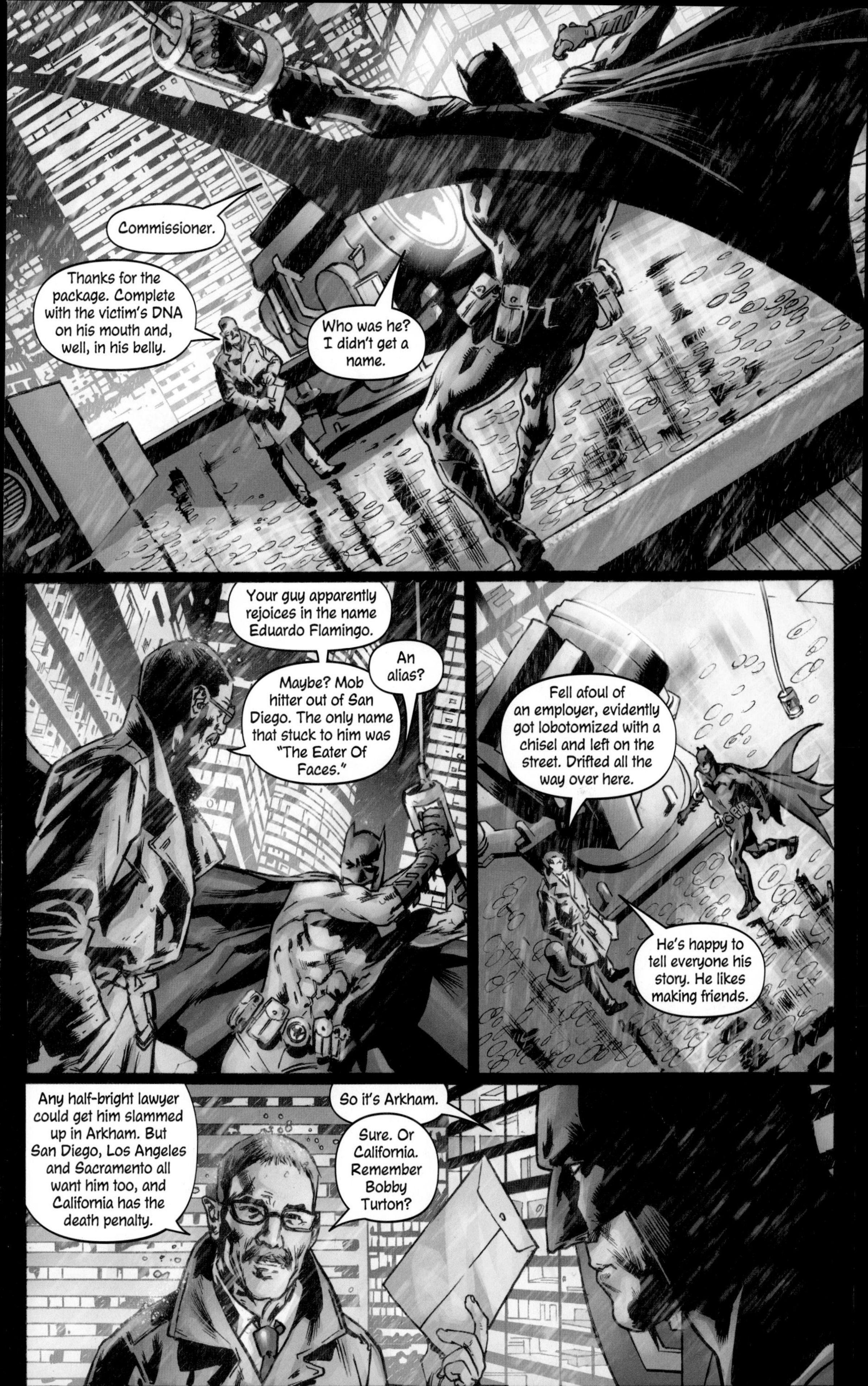
Commissioner.
Thanks for the package. Complete with the victim's DNA on his mouth and, well, in his belly.
Who was he? I didn't get a name.
Your guy apparently rejoices in the name Eduardo Flamingo.
An alias?
Maybe? Mob hitter out of San Diego. The only name that stuck to him was "The Eater Of Faces."
Fell afoul of an employer, evidently got lobotomized with a chisel and left on the street. Drifted all the way over here.
He's happy to tell everyone his story. He likes making friends.
Any half-bright lawyer could get him slammed up in Arkham. But San Diego, Los Angeles and Sacramento all want him too, and California has the death penalty.
So it's Arkham.
Sure. Or California. Remember Bobby Turton?

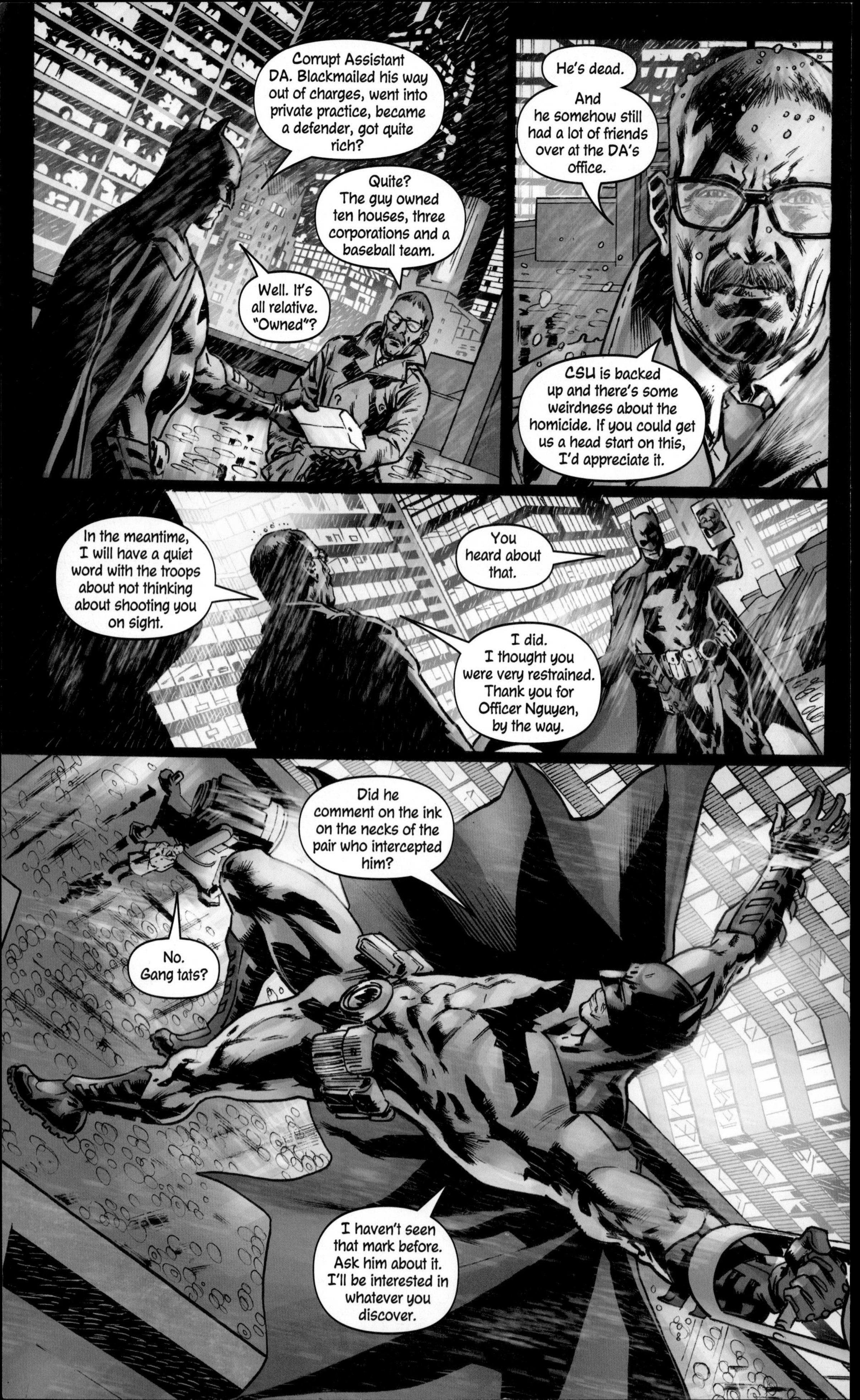

Corrupt Assistant DA. Blackmailed his way out of charges, went into private practice, became a defender, got quite rich?
Quite? The guy owned ten houses, three corporations and a baseball team.
Well. It's all relative. "Owned"?
He's dead.
And he somehow still had a lot of friends over at the DA's office.
CSU is backed up and there's some weirdness about the homicide. If you could get us a head start on this, I'd appreciate it.
In the meantime, I will have a quiet word with the troops about not thinking about shooting you on sight.
You heard about that.
I did. I thought you were very restrained. Thank you for Officer Nguyen, by the way.
Did he comment on the ink on the necks of the pair who intercepted him?
No. Gang tats?
I haven't seen that mark before. Ask him about it. I'll be interested in whatever you discover.

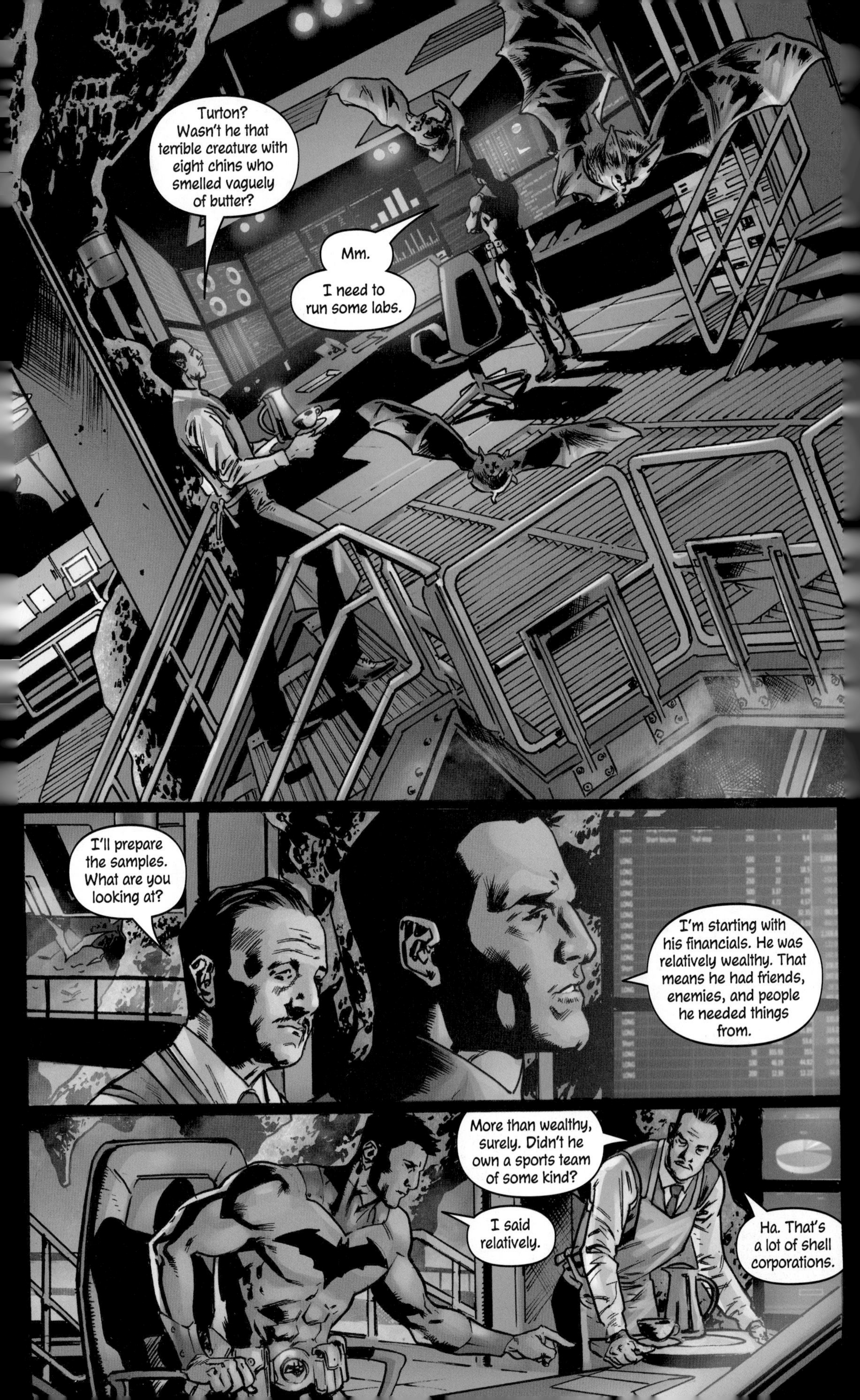
Turton? Wasn't he that terrible creature with eight chins who smelled vaguely of butter?
Mm.
I need to run some labs.
I'll prepare the samples. What are you looking at?
I'm starting with his financials. He was relatively wealthy. That means he had friends, enemies, and people he needed things from.
More than wealthy, surely. Didn't he own a sports team of some kind?
I said relatively.
Ha. That's a lot of shell corporations.

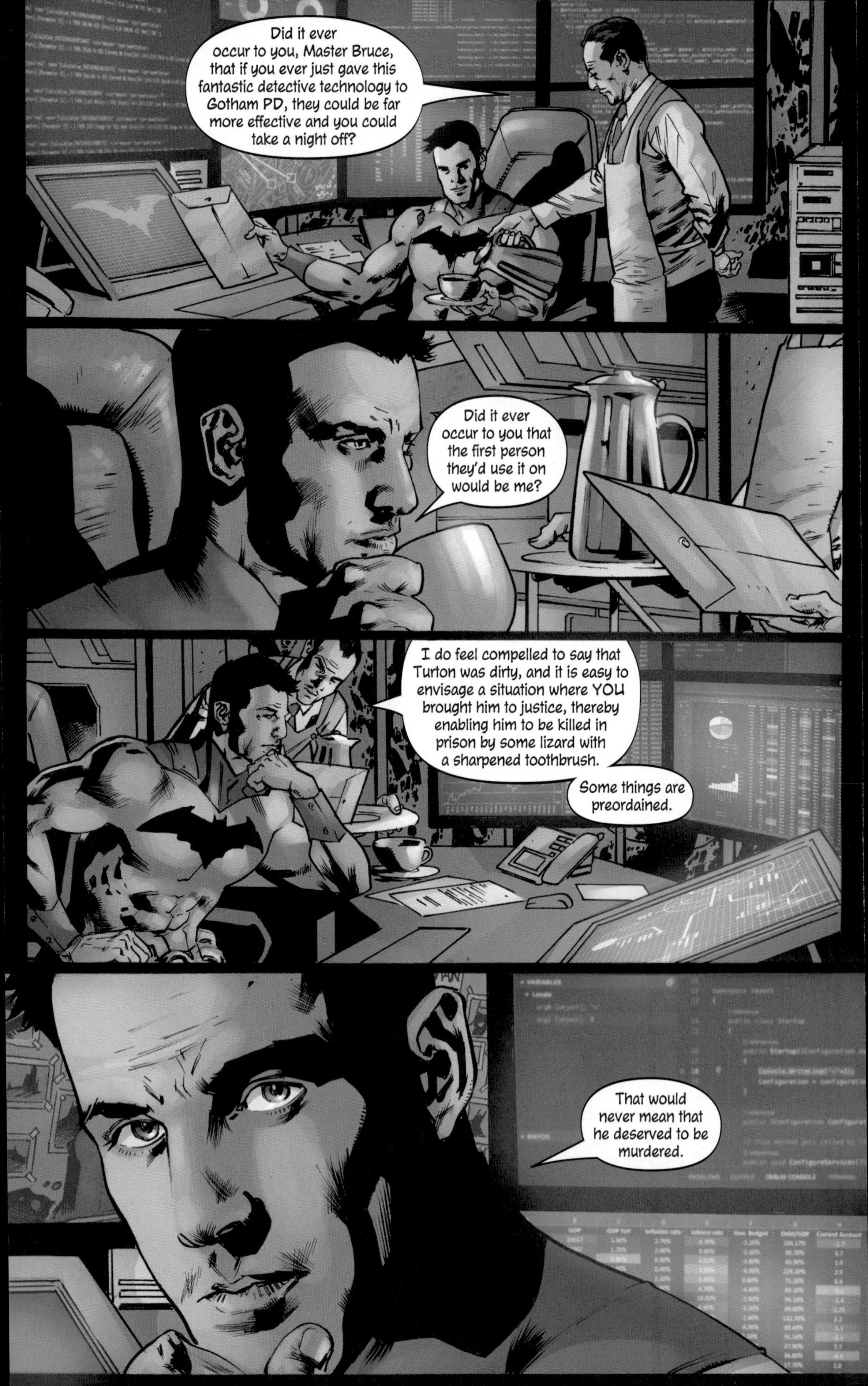
Did it ever occur to you, Master Bruce, that if you ever just gave this fantastic detective technology to Gotham PD, they could be far more effective and you could take a night off?
Did it ever occur to you that the first person they'd use it on would be me?
I do feel compelled to say that Turton was dirty, and it is easy to envisage a situation where YOU brought him to justice, thereby enabling him to be killed in prison by some lizard with a sharpened toothbrush.
Some things are preordained.
That would never mean that he deserved to be murdered.

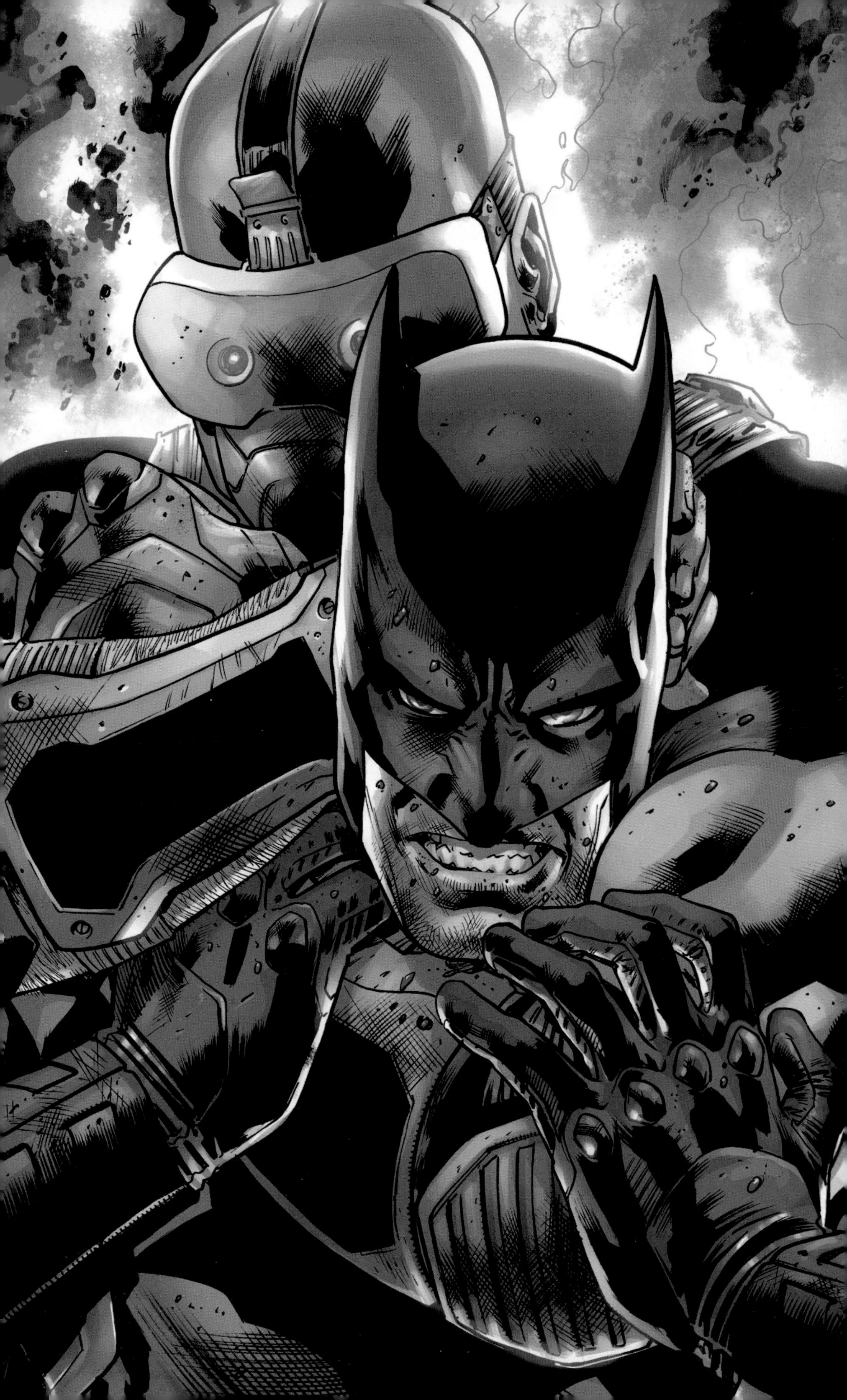

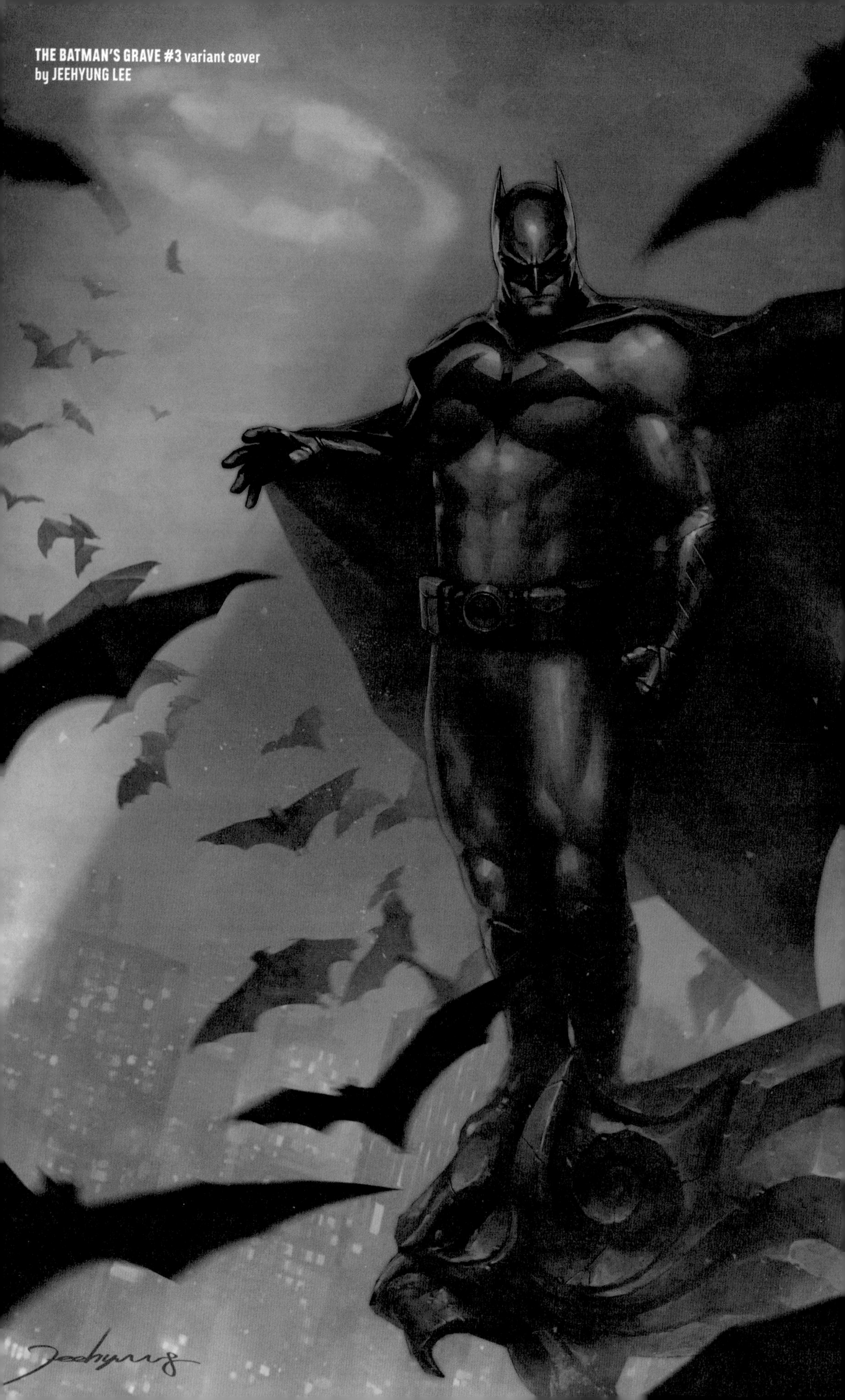

THE BATMAN'S GRAVE #3 variant cover
by **JEEHYUNG LEE**

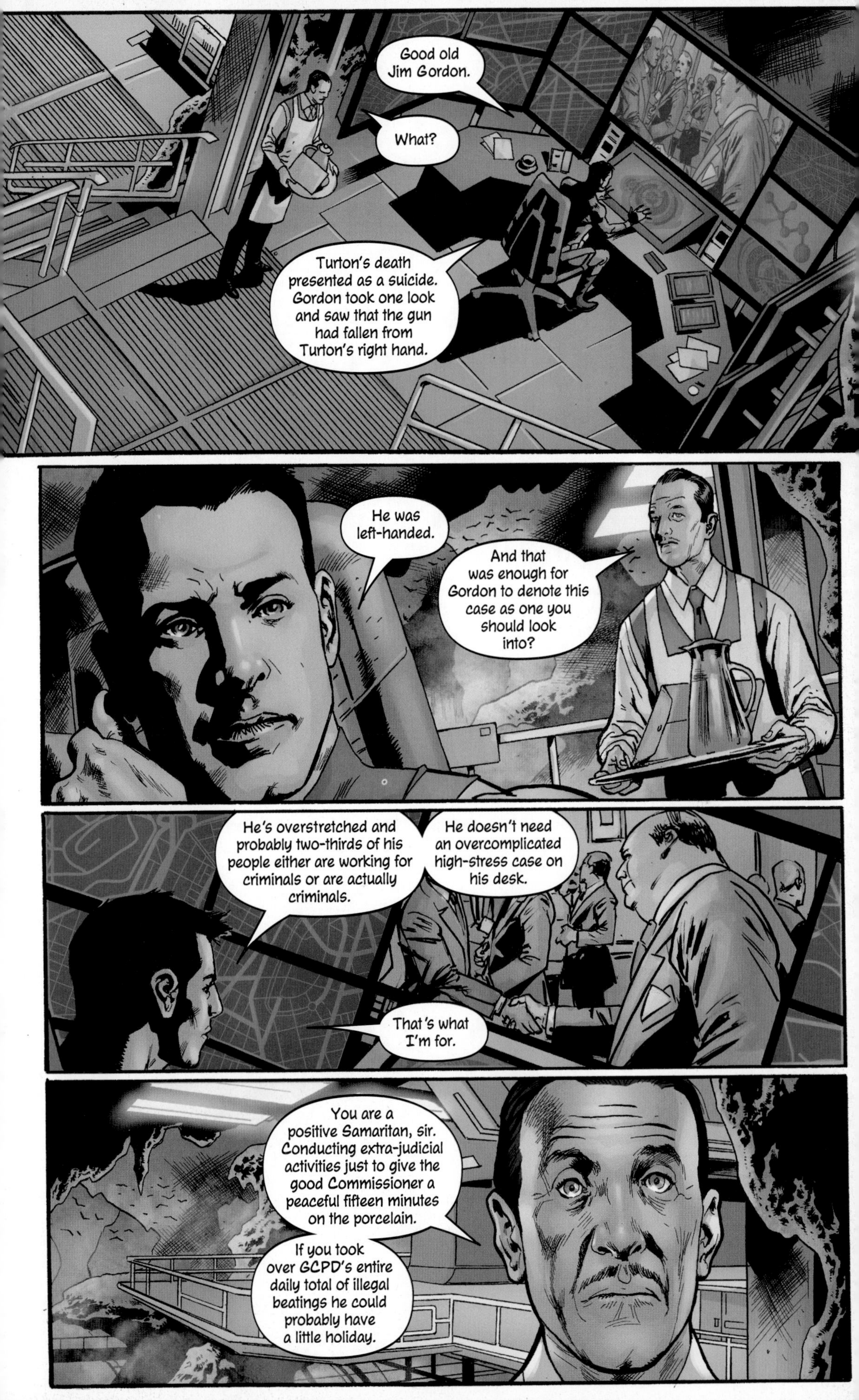
Good old Jim Gordon.
What?
Turton's death presented as a suicide. Gordon took one look and saw that the gun had fallen from Turton's right hand.
He was left-handed.
And that was enough for Gordon to denote this case as one you should look into?
He's overstretched and probably two-thirds of his people either are working for criminals or are actually criminals.
He doesn't need an overcomplicated high-stress case on his desk.
That's what I'm for.
You are a positive Samaritan, sir. Conducting extra-judicial activities just to give the good Commissioner a peaceful fifteen minutes on the porcelain.
If you took over GCPD's entire daily total of illegal beatings he could probably have a little holiday.

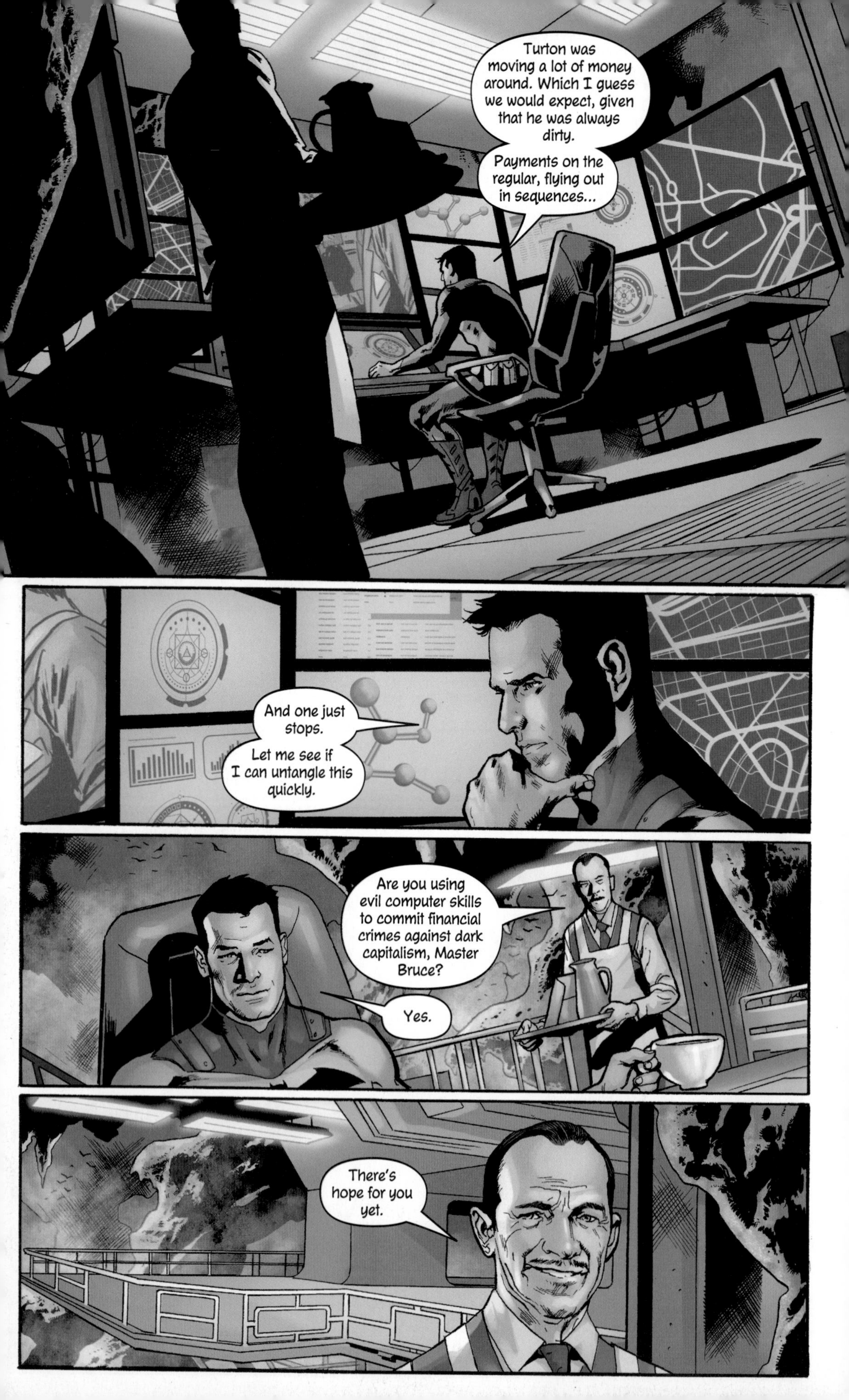
Turton was moving a lot of money around. Which I guess we would expect, given that he was always dirty.
Payments on the regular, flying out in sequences...
And one just stops.
Let me see if I can untangle this quickly.
Are you using evil computer skills to commit financial crimes against dark capitalism, Master Bruce?
Yes.
There's hope for you yet.

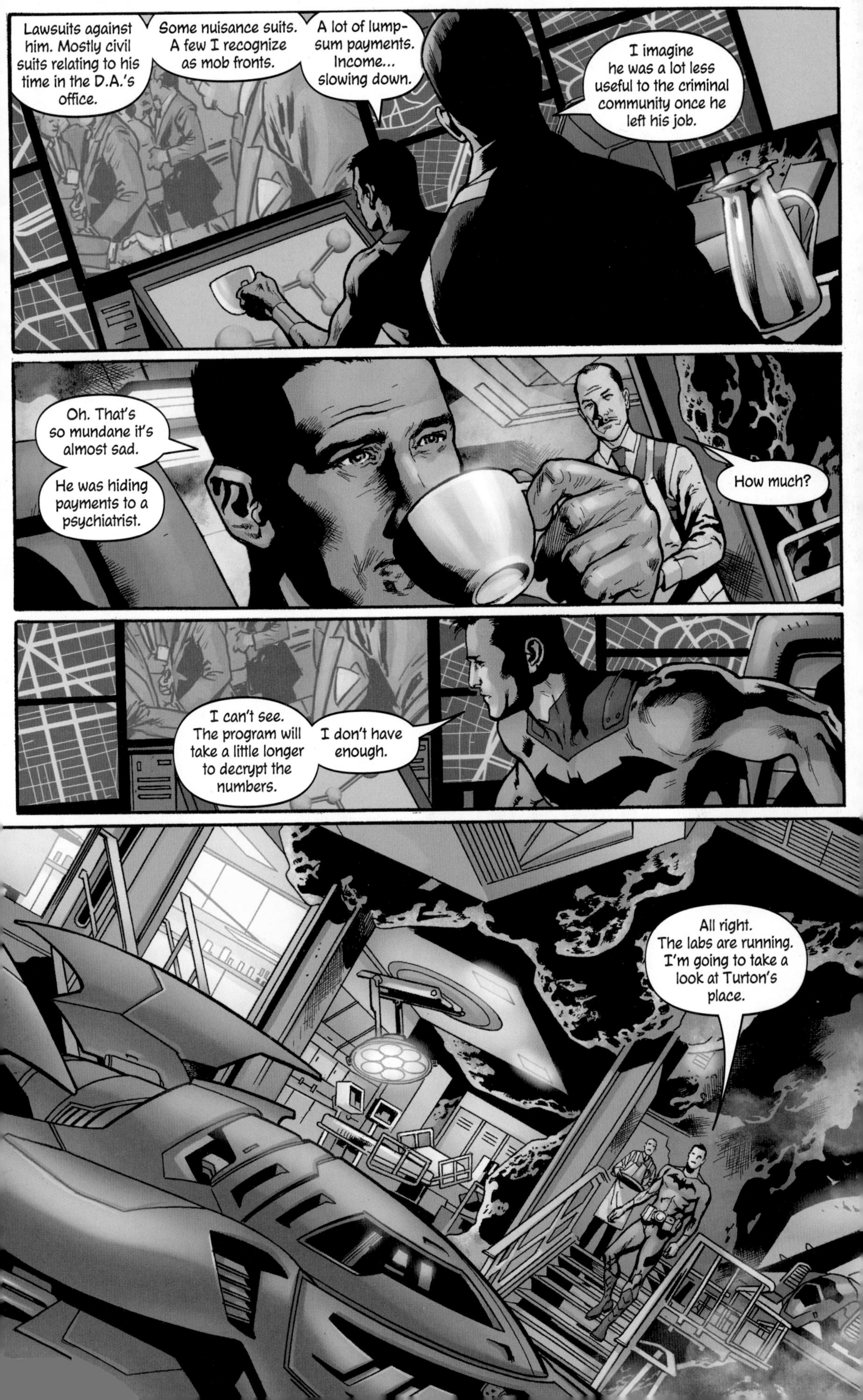
Lawsuits against him. Mostly civil suits relating to his time in the D.A.'s office.
Some nuisance suits. A few I recognize as mob fronts.
A lot of lump-sum payments. Income... slowing down.
I imagine he was a lot less useful to the criminal community once he left his job.
Oh. That's so mundane it's almost sad.
He was hiding payments to a psychiatrist.
How much?
I can't see. The program will take a little longer to decrypt the numbers.
I don't have enough.
All right. The labs are running. I'm going to take a look at Turton's place.

Chapter 3

Writer	Pencils	Inks
WARREN ELLIS	**BRYAN HITCH**	**KEVIN NOWLAN**

Colors	Letters
ALEX SINCLAIR	**RICHARD STARKINGS**

Cover	Variant Cover
BRYAN HITCH &	**JEEHYUNG**
ALEX SINCLAIR	**LEE**

Associate Editor	Editor
ANDREW MARINO	**MARIE JAVINS**

BATMAN created by **BOB KANE** with **BILL FINGER**

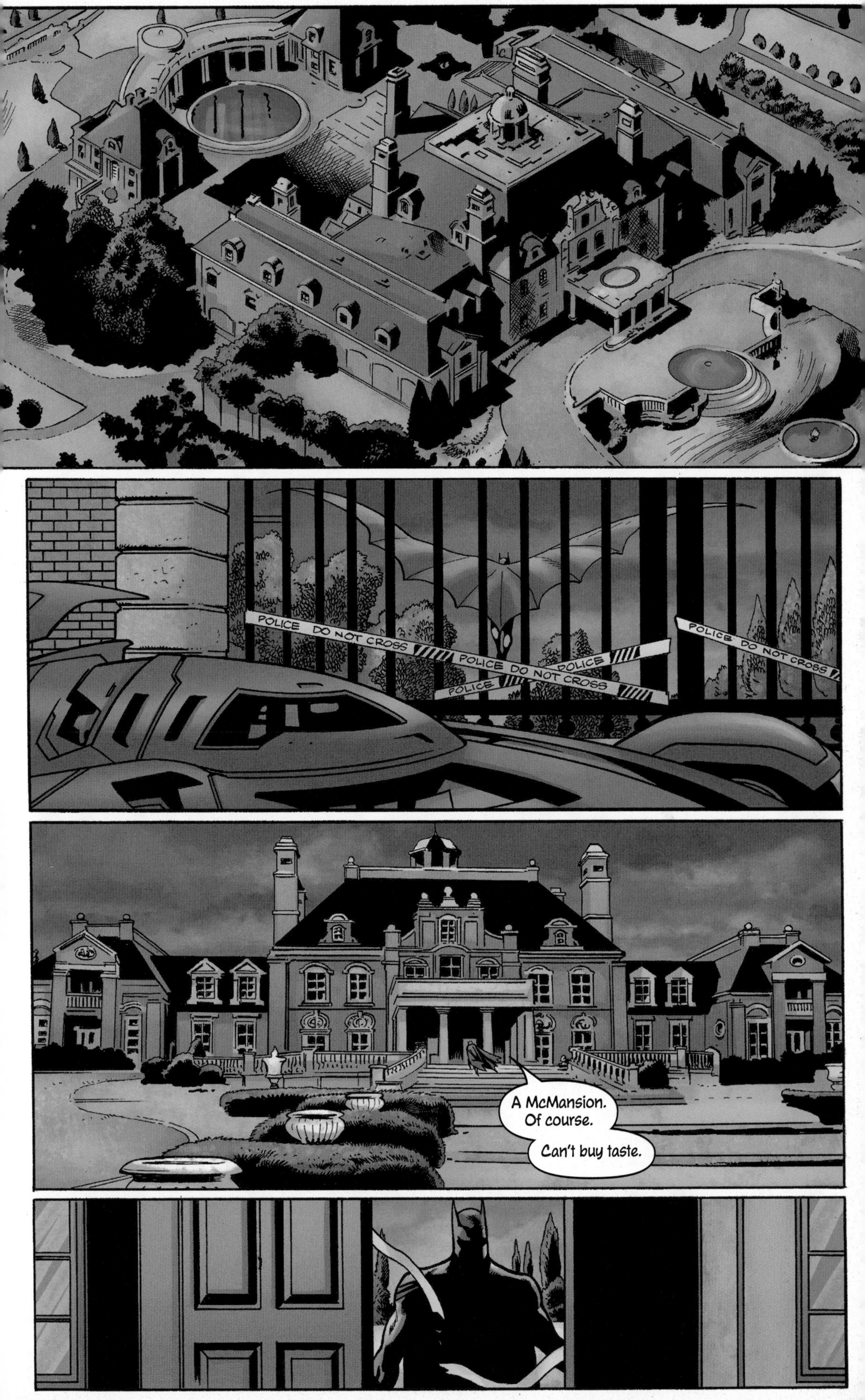
POLICE DO NOT CROSS
POLICE DO NOT CROSS
POLICE DO NOT CROSS
A McMansion. Of course.
Can't buy taste.

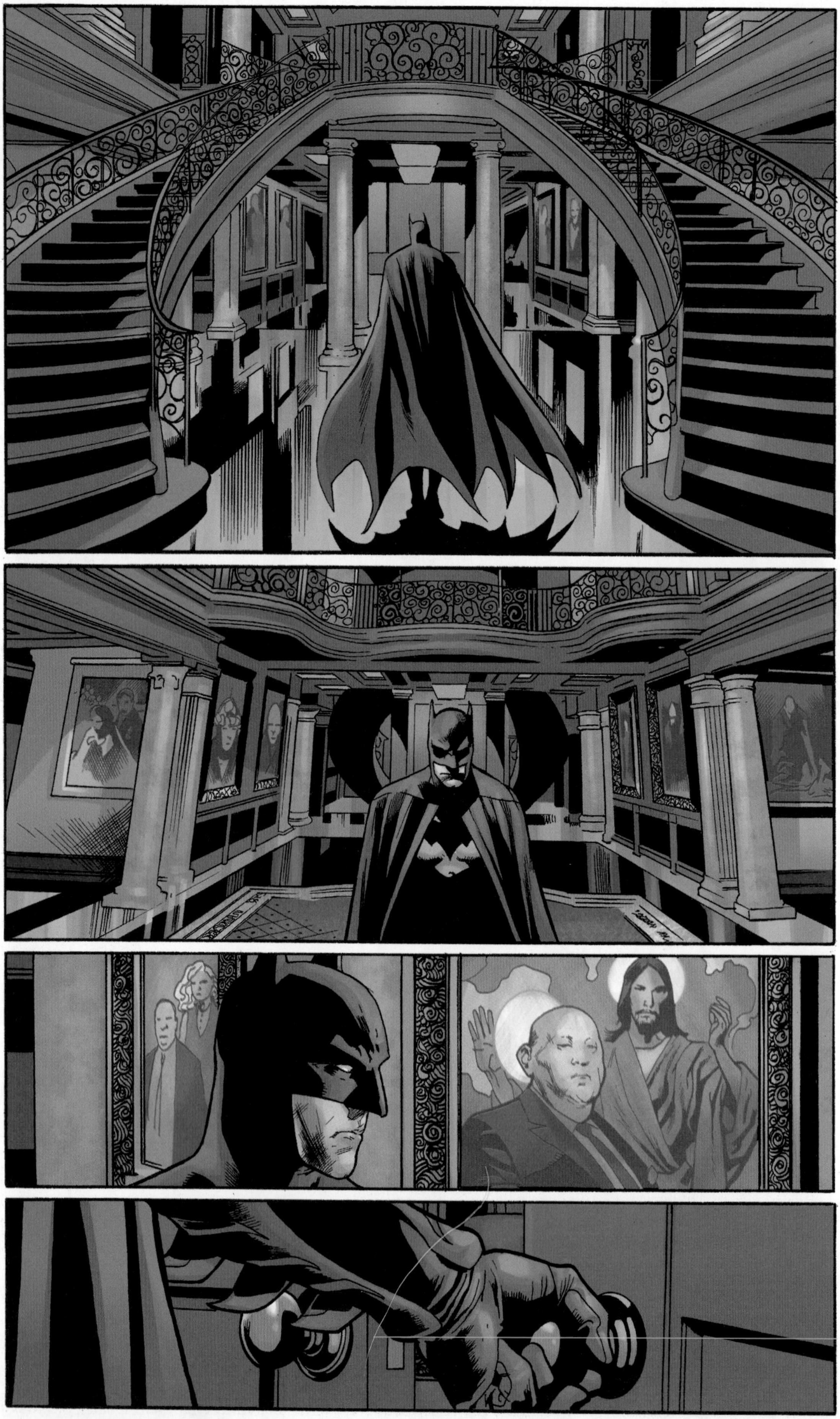

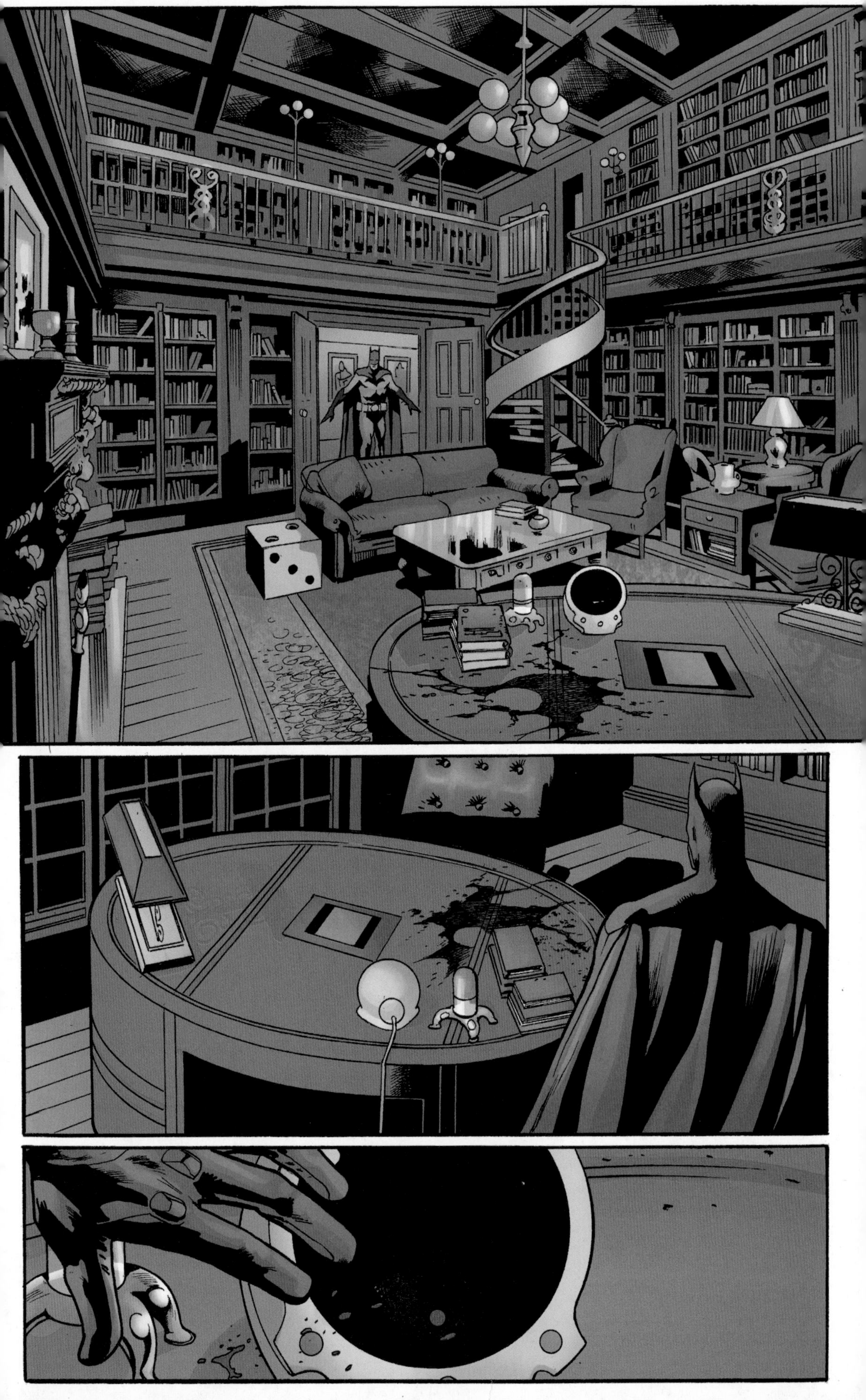

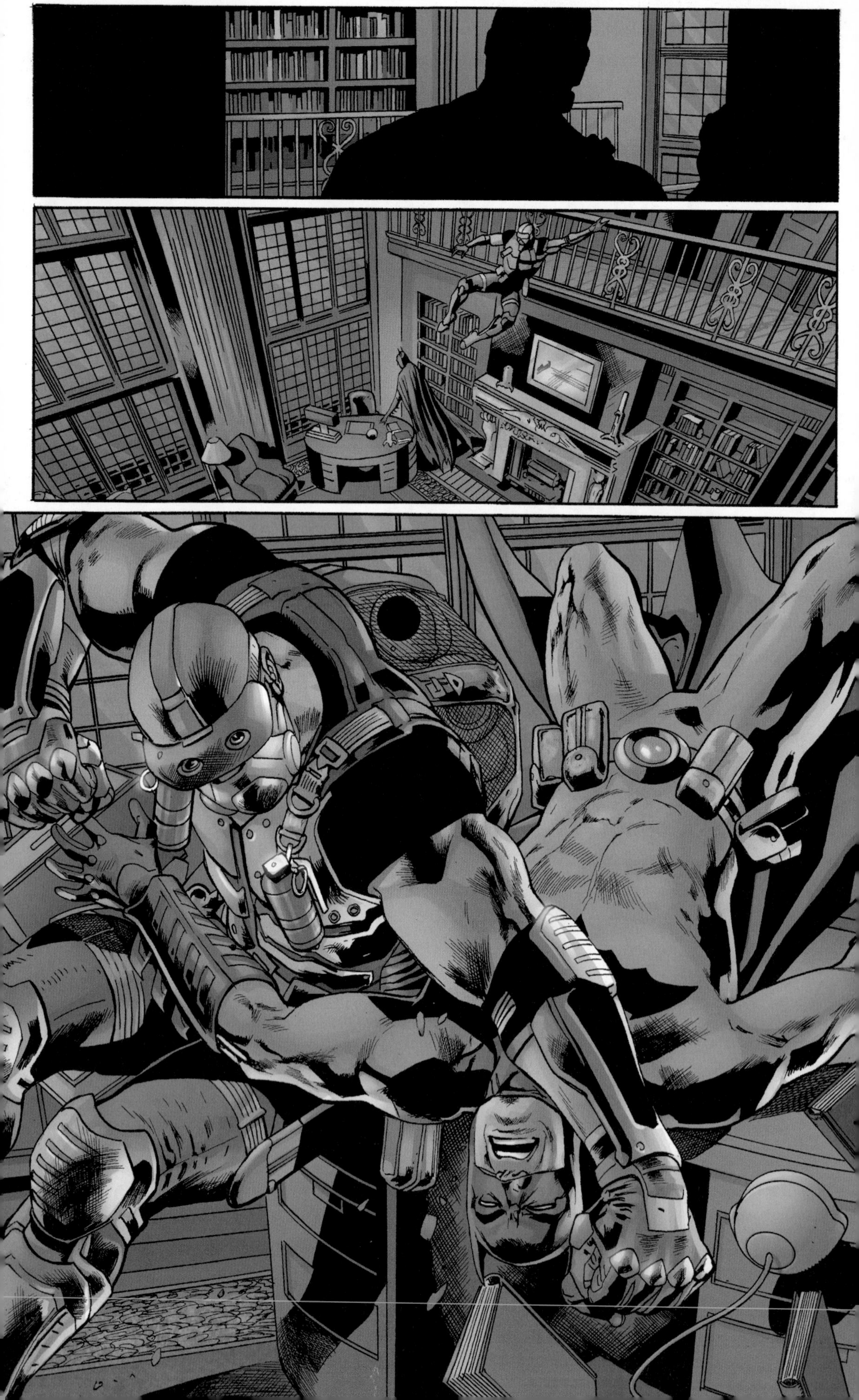

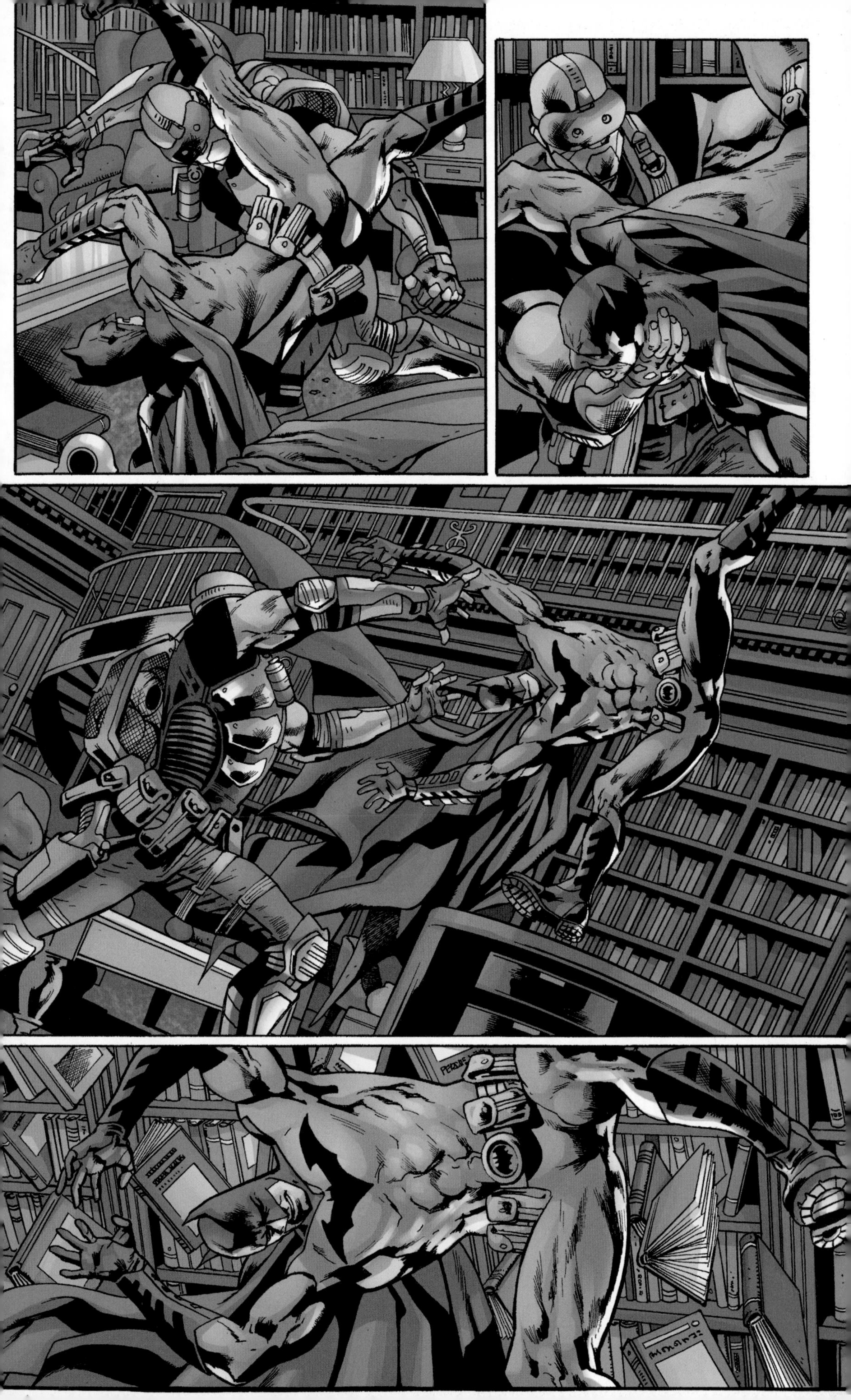

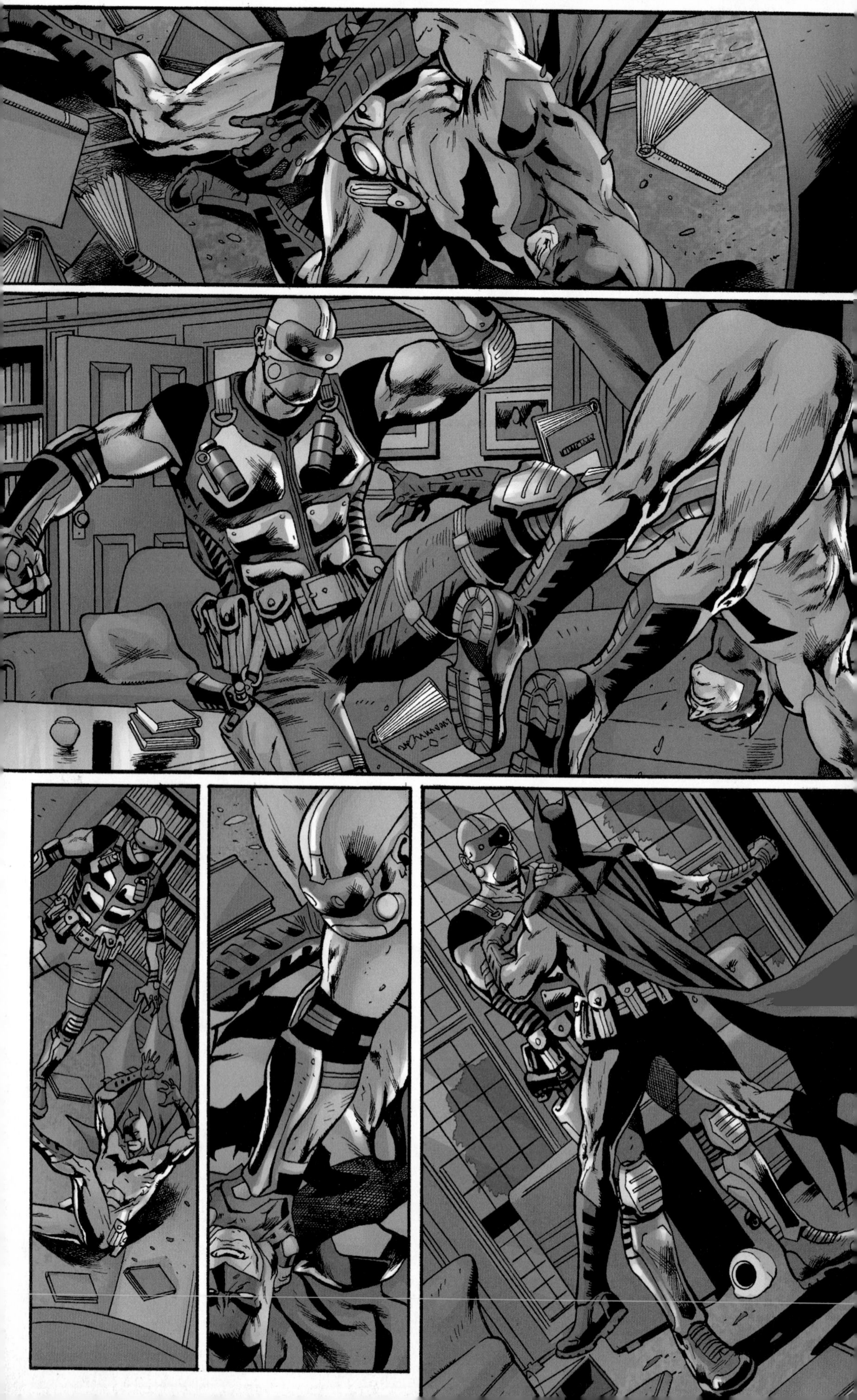

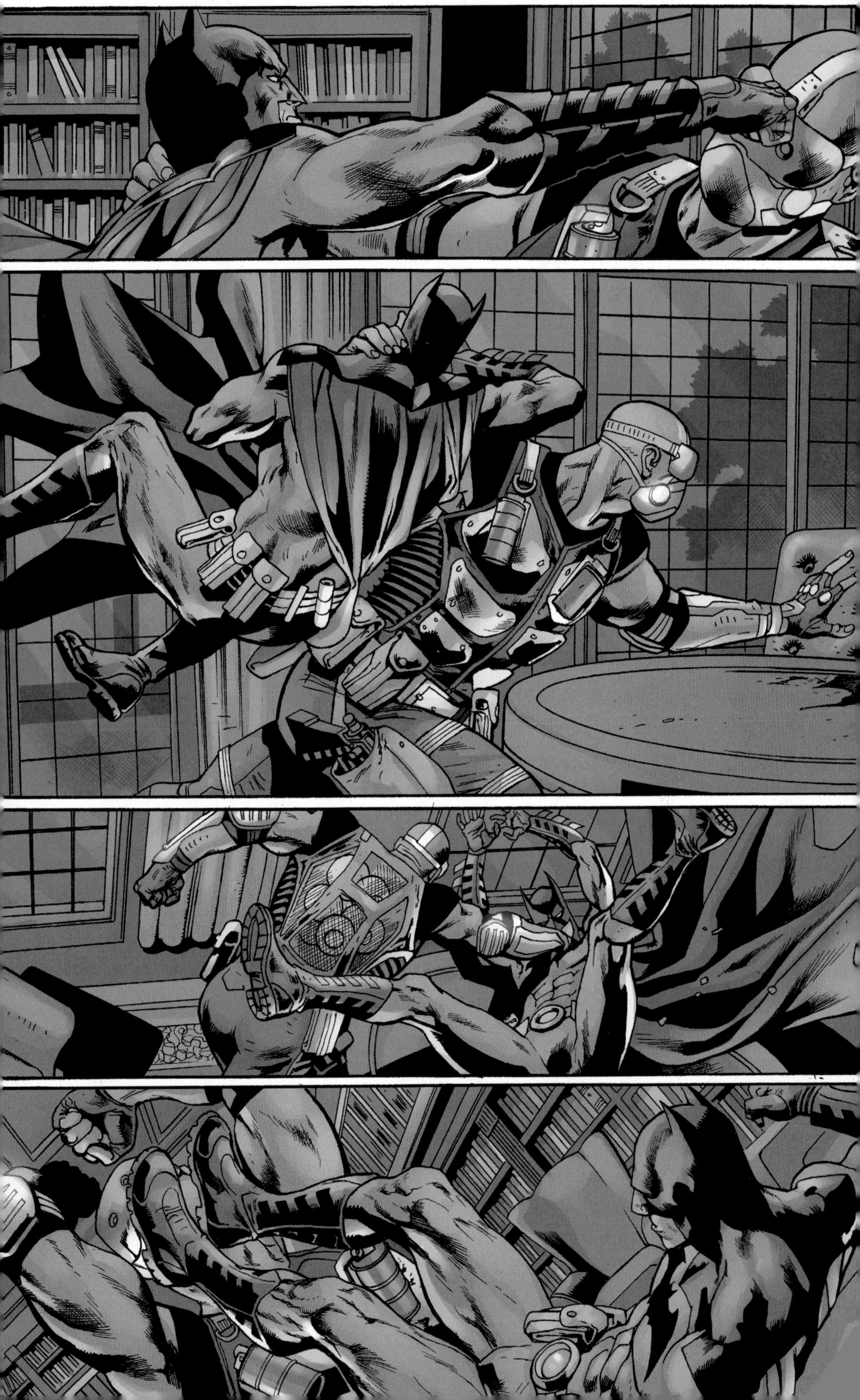

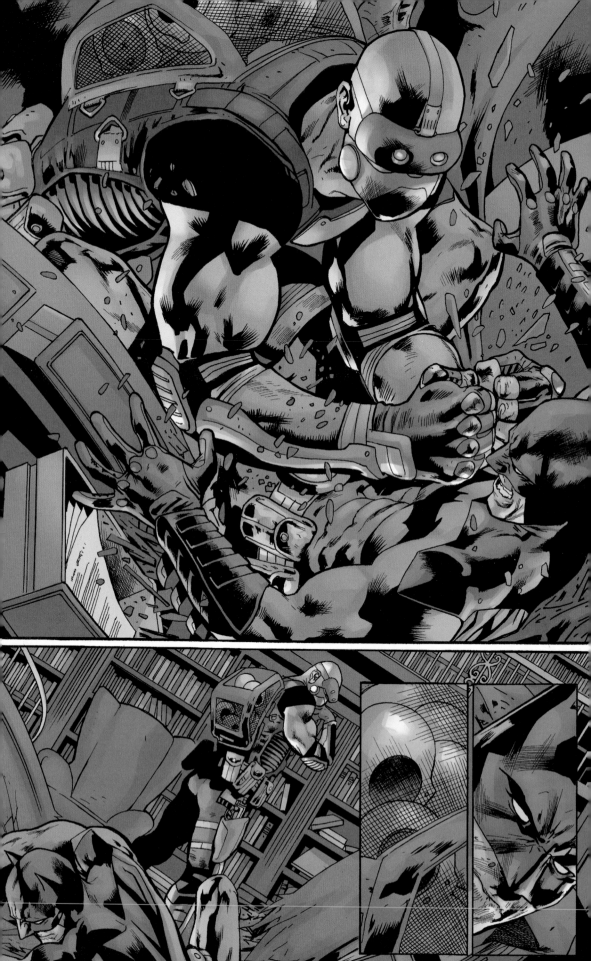

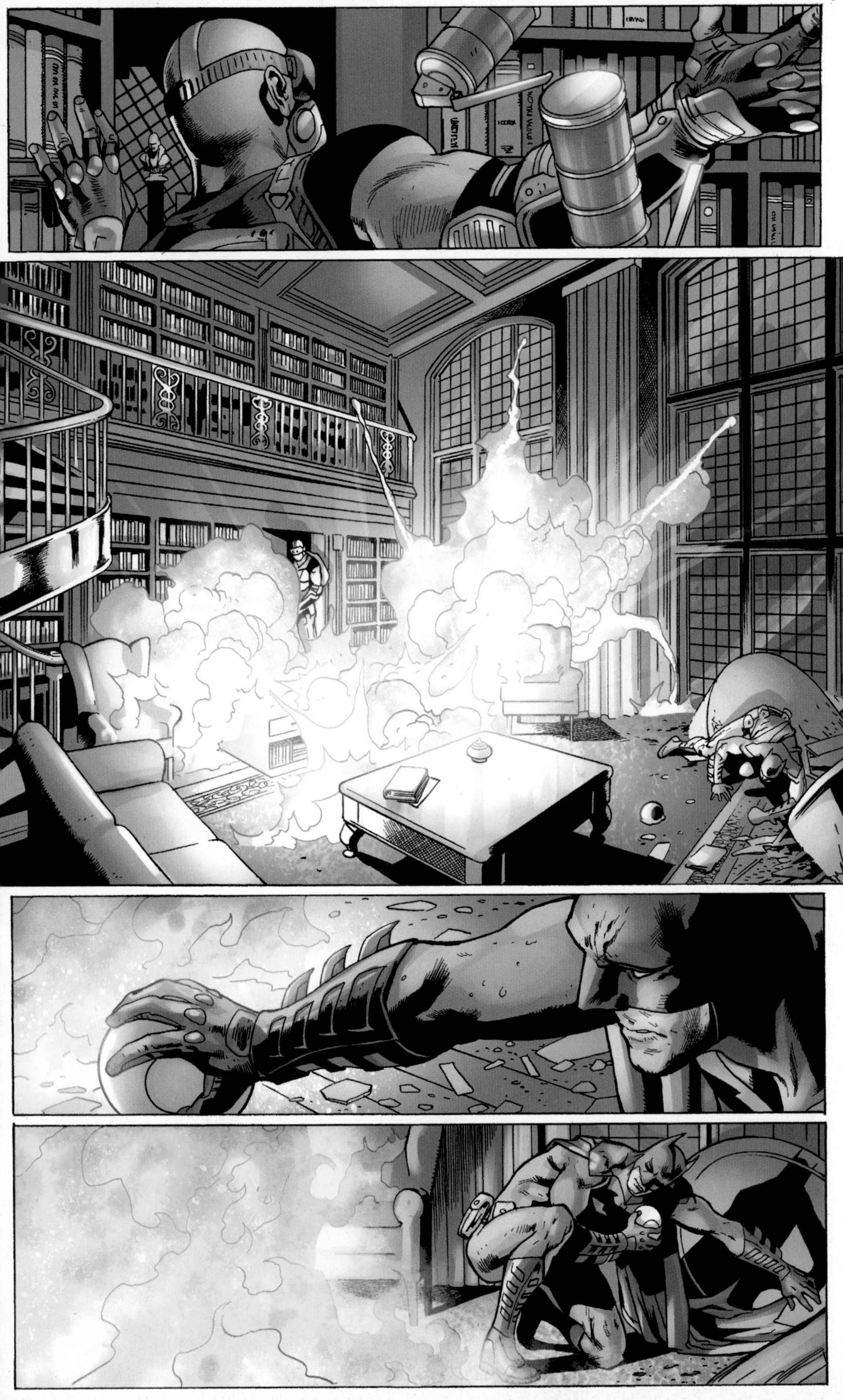

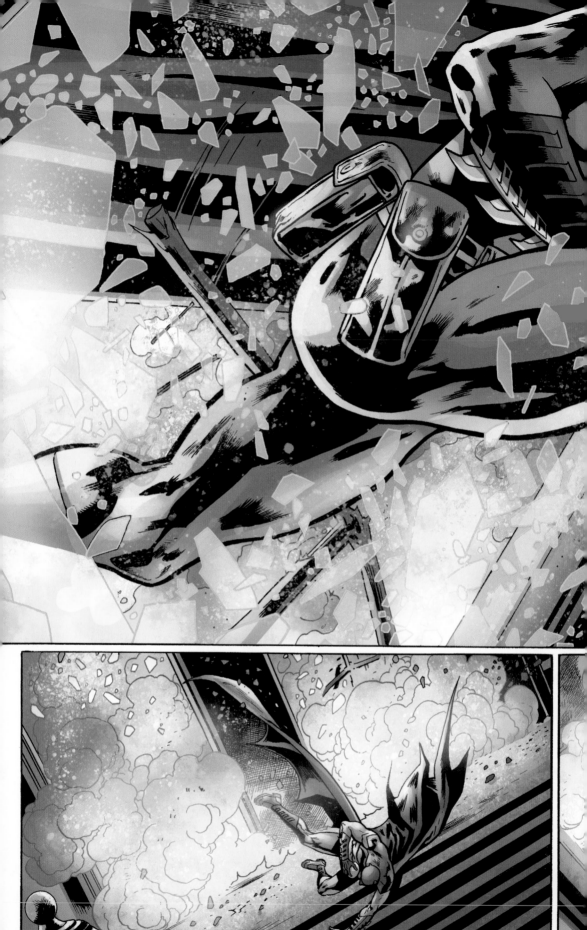

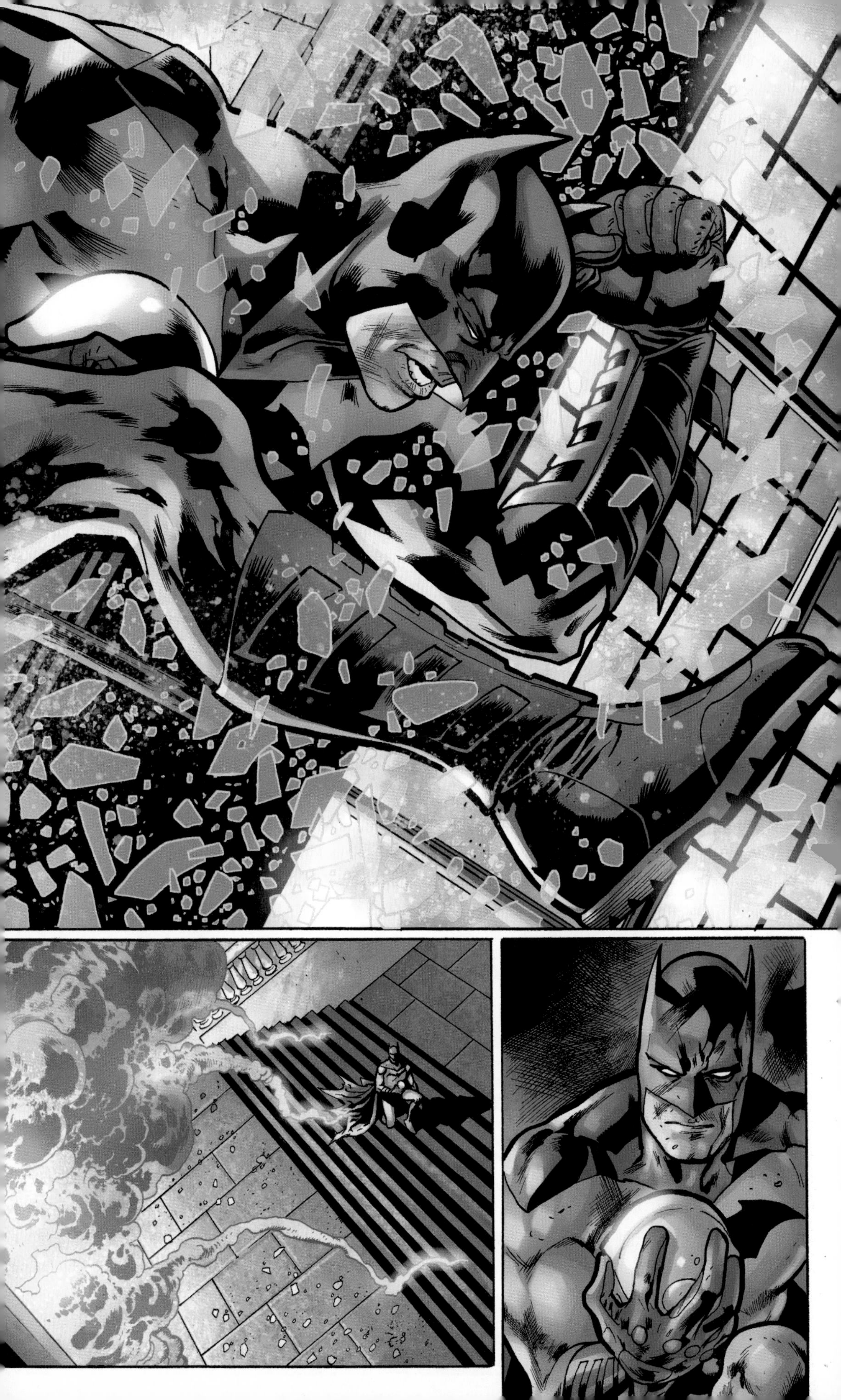

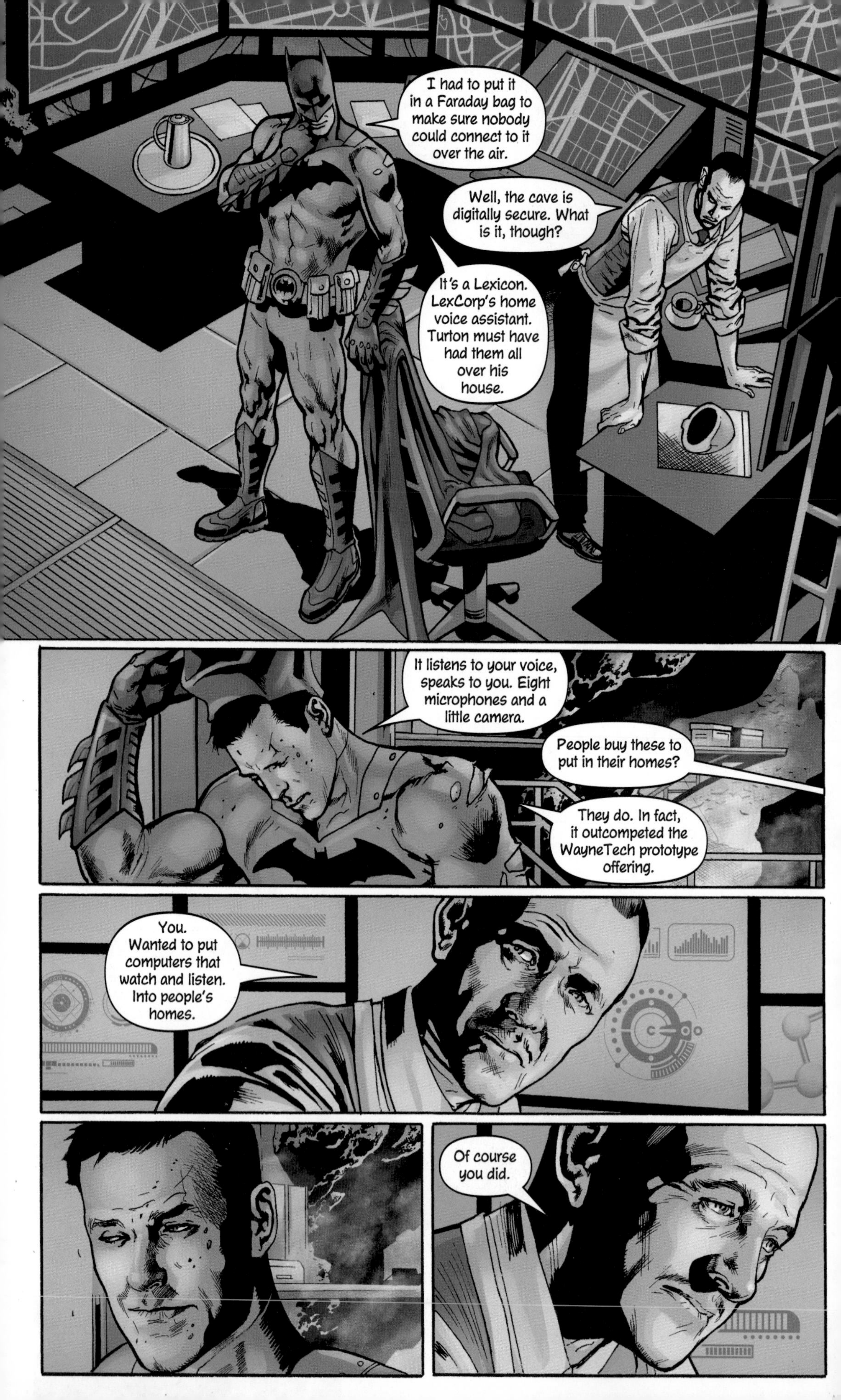
I had to put it in a Faraday bag to make sure nobody could connect to it over the air.
Well, the cave is digitally secure. What is it, though?
It's a Lexicon. LexCorp's home voice assistant. Turton must have had them all over his house.
It listens to your voice, speaks to you. Eight microphones and a little camera.
People buy these to put in their homes?
They do. In fact, it outcompeted the WayneTech prototype offering.
You. Wanted to put computers that watch and listen. Into people's homes.
Of course you did.

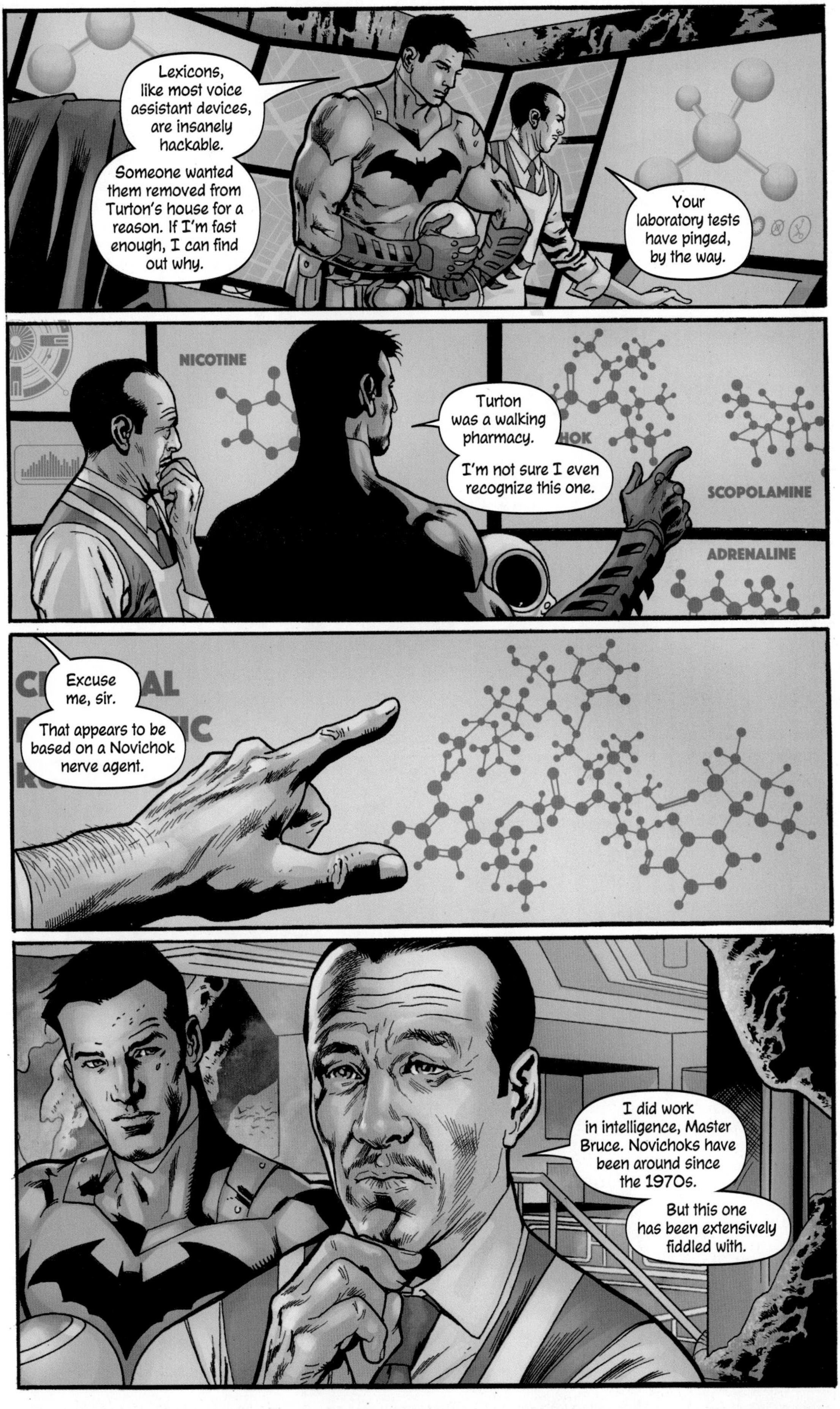
Lexicons, like most voice assistant devices, are insanely hackable.
Someone wanted them removed from Turton's house for a reason. If I'm fast enough, I can find out why.
Your laboratory tests have pinged, by the way.
NICOTINE
Turton was a walking pharmacy.
I'm not sure I even recognize this one.
SCOPOLAMINE
ADRENALINE
Excuse me, sir.
That appears to be based on a Novichok nerve agent.
I did work in intelligence, Master Bruce. Novichoks have been around since the 1970s.
But this one has been extensively fiddled with.

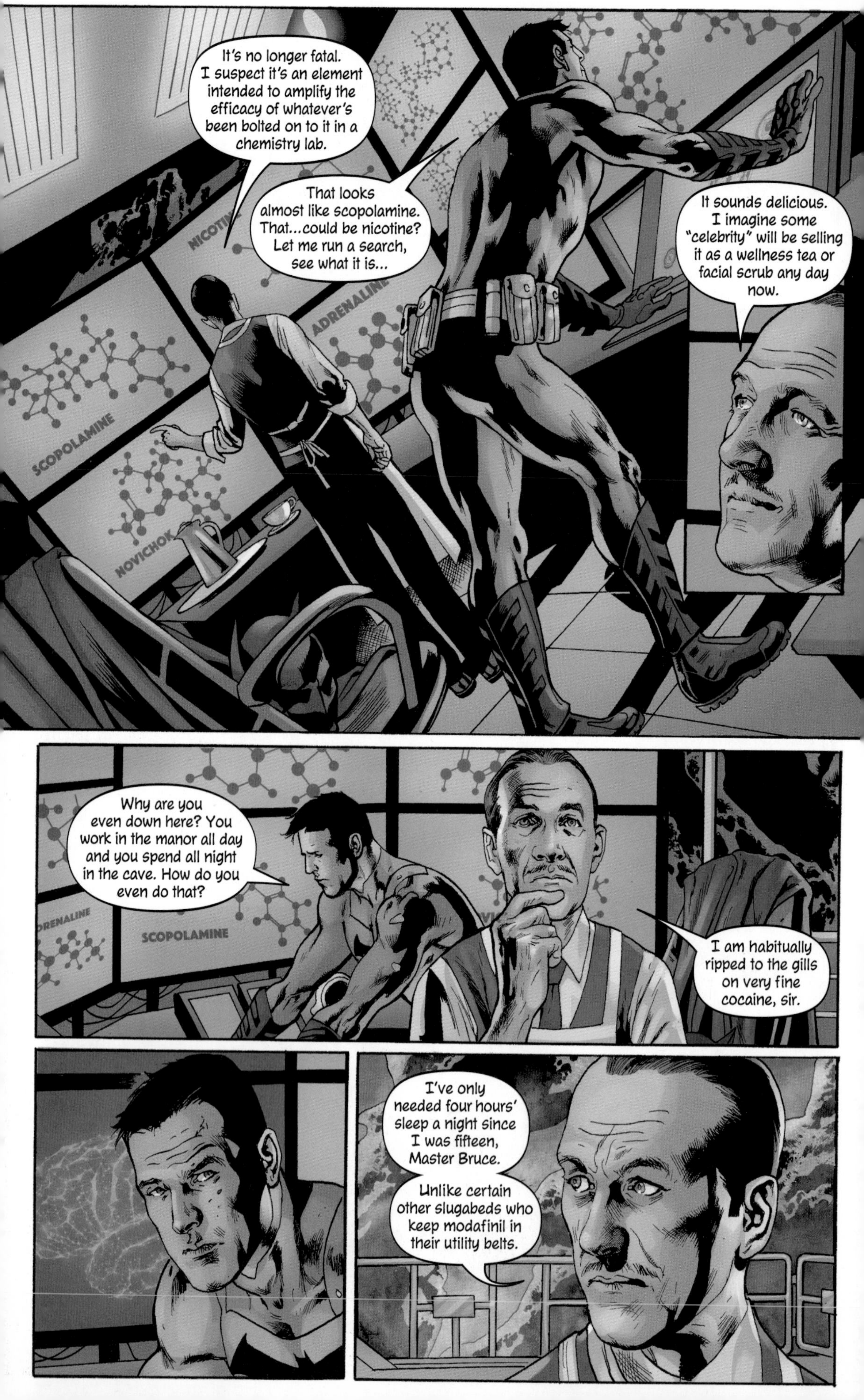

It's no longer fatal. I suspect it's an element intended to amplify the efficacy of whatever's been bolted on to it in a chemistry lab.
That looks almost like scopolamine. That...could be nicotine? Let me run a search, see what it is...
ADRENALINE
SCOPOLAMINE
NOVICHOK
It sounds delicious. I imagine some "celebrity" will be selling it as a wellness tea or facial scrub any day now.
Why are you even down here? You work in the manor all day and you spend all night in the cave. How do you even do that?
SCOPOLAMINE
I am habitually ripped to the gills on very fine cocaine, sir.
I've only needed four hours' sleep a night since I was fifteen, Master Bruce.
Unlike certain other slugabeds who keep modafinil in their utility belts.

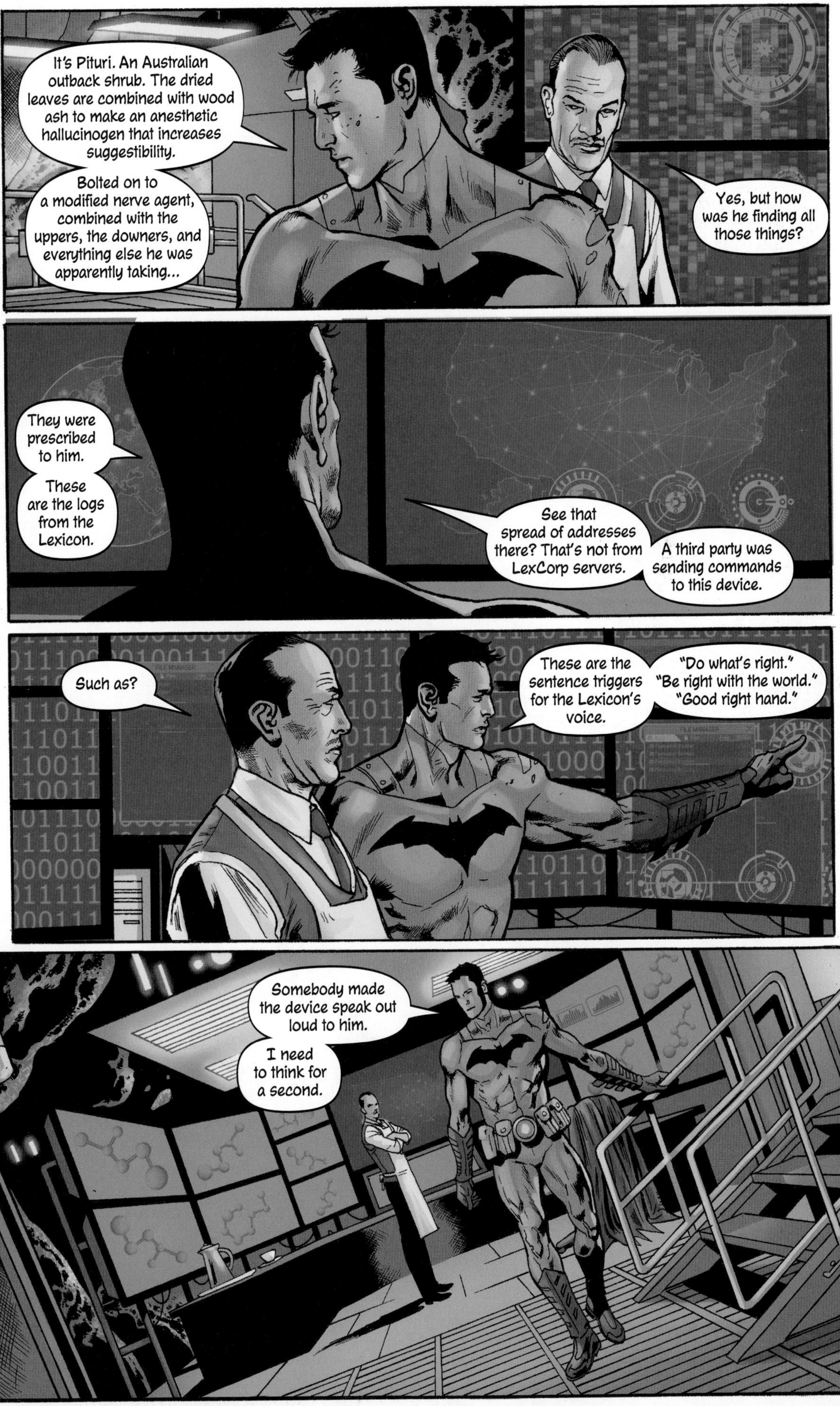
It's Pituri. An Australian outback shrub. The dried leaves are combined with wood ash to make an anesthetic hallucinogen that increases suggestibility.
Bolted on to a modified nerve agent, combined with the uppers, the downers, and everything else he was apparently taking...
Yes, but how was he finding all those things?
They were prescribed to him.
These are the logs from the Lexicon.
See that spread of addresses there? That's not from LexCorp servers.
A third party was sending commands to this device.
Such as?
These are the sentence triggers for the Lexicon's voice.
"Do what's right." "Be right with the world." "Good right hand."
Somebody made the device speak out loud to him.
I need to think for a second.

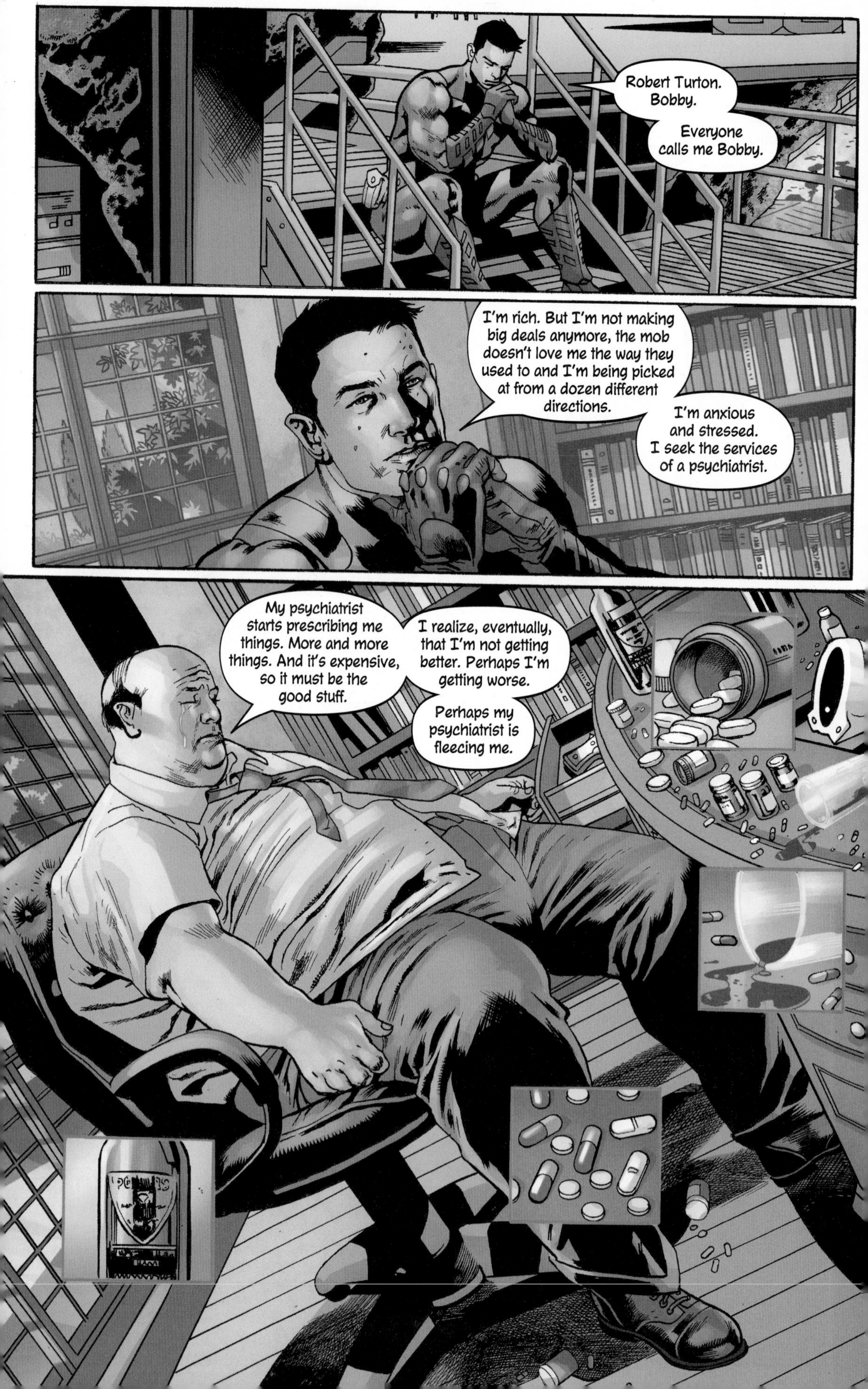
Robert Turton. Bobby.
Everyone calls me Bobby.
I'm rich. But I'm not making big deals anymore, the mob doesn't love me the way they used to and I'm being picked at from a dozen different directions.
I'm anxious and stressed. I seek the services of a psychiatrist.
My psychiatrist starts prescribing me things. More and more things. And it's expensive, so it must be the good stuff.
I realize, eventually, that I'm not getting better. Perhaps I'm getting worse.
Perhaps my psychiatrist is fleecing me.

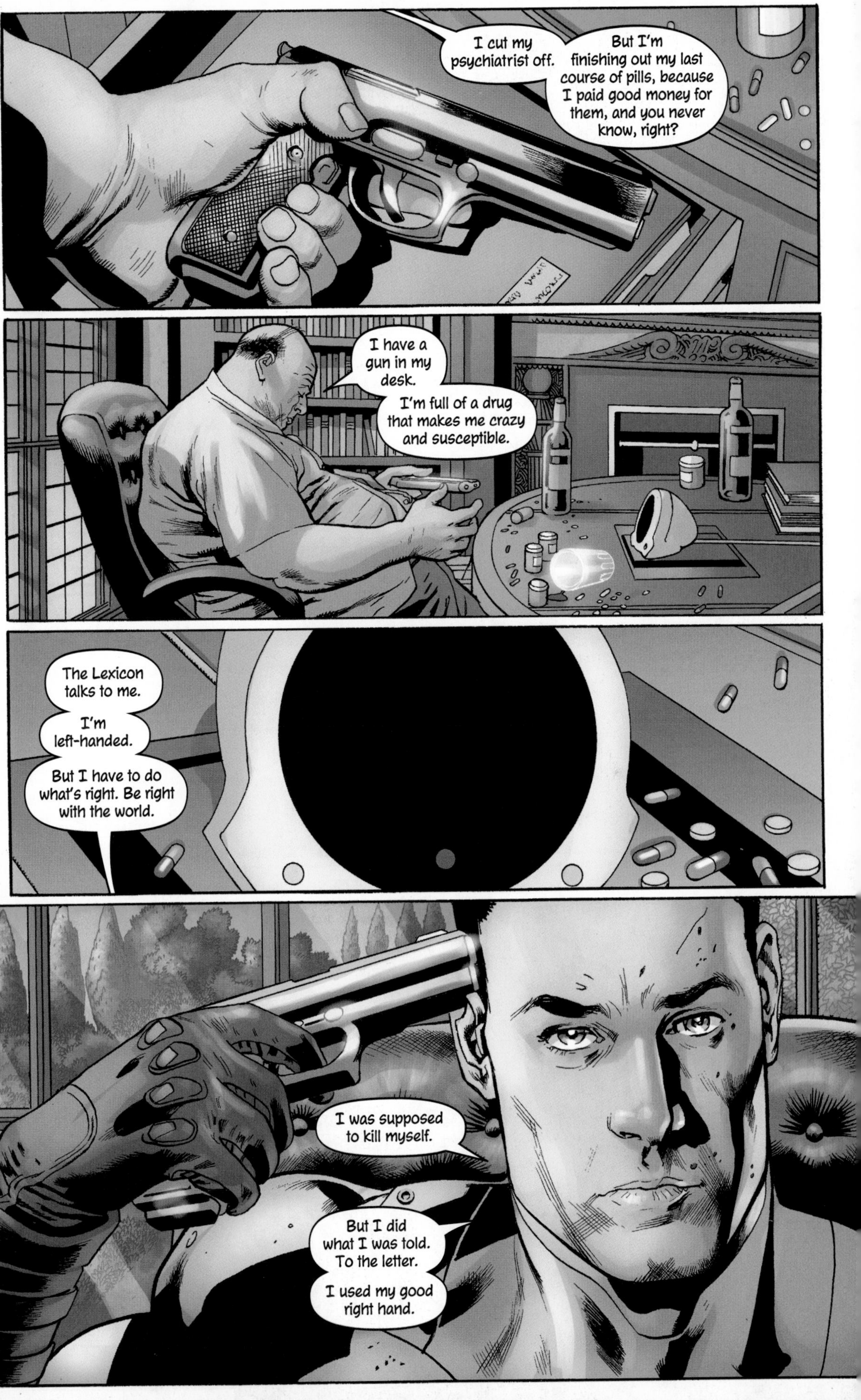
I cut my psychiatrist off.
But I'm finishing out my last course of pills, because I paid good money for them, and you never know, right?
I have a gun in my desk.
I'm full of a drug that makes me crazy and susceptible.
The Lexicon talks to me.
I'm left-handed.
But I have to do what's right. Be right with the world.
I was supposed to kill myself.
But I did what I was told. To the letter.
I used my good right hand.

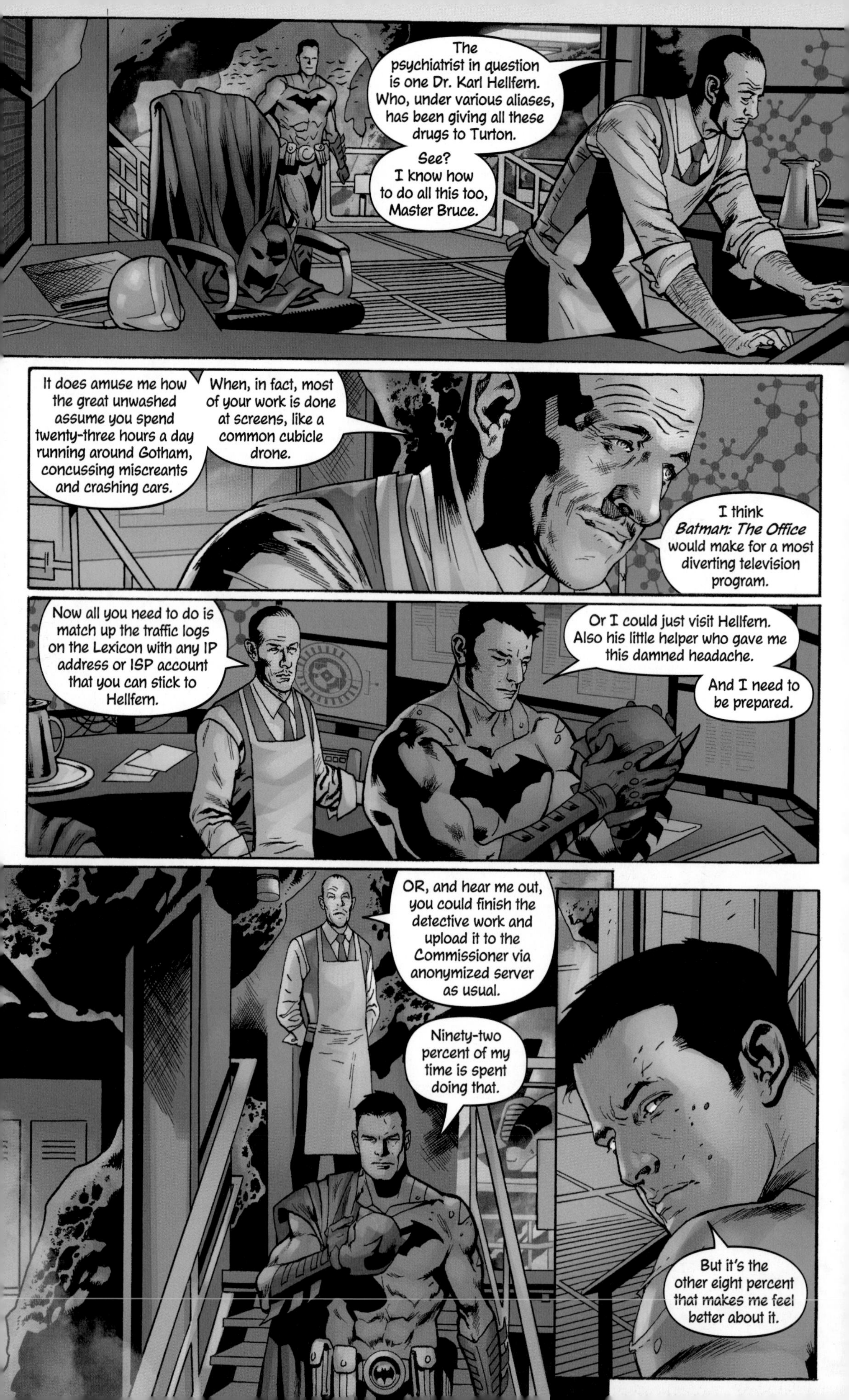
The psychiatrist in question is one Dr. Karl Hellfern. Who, under various aliases, has been giving all these drugs to Turton.
See? I know how to do all this too, Master Bruce.
It does amuse me how the great unwashed assume you spend twenty-three hours a day running around Gotham, concussing miscreants and crashing cars.
When, in fact, most of your work is done at screens, like a common cubicle drone.
I think *Batman: The Office* would make for a most diverting television program.
Now all you need to do is match up the traffic logs on the Lexicon with any IP address or ISP account that you can stick to Hellfern.
Or I could just visit Hellfern. Also his little helper who gave me this damned headache.
And I need to be prepared.
OR, and hear me out, you could finish the detective work and upload it to the Commissioner via anonymized server as usual.
Ninety-two percent of my time is spent doing that.
But it's the other eight percent that makes me feel better about it.

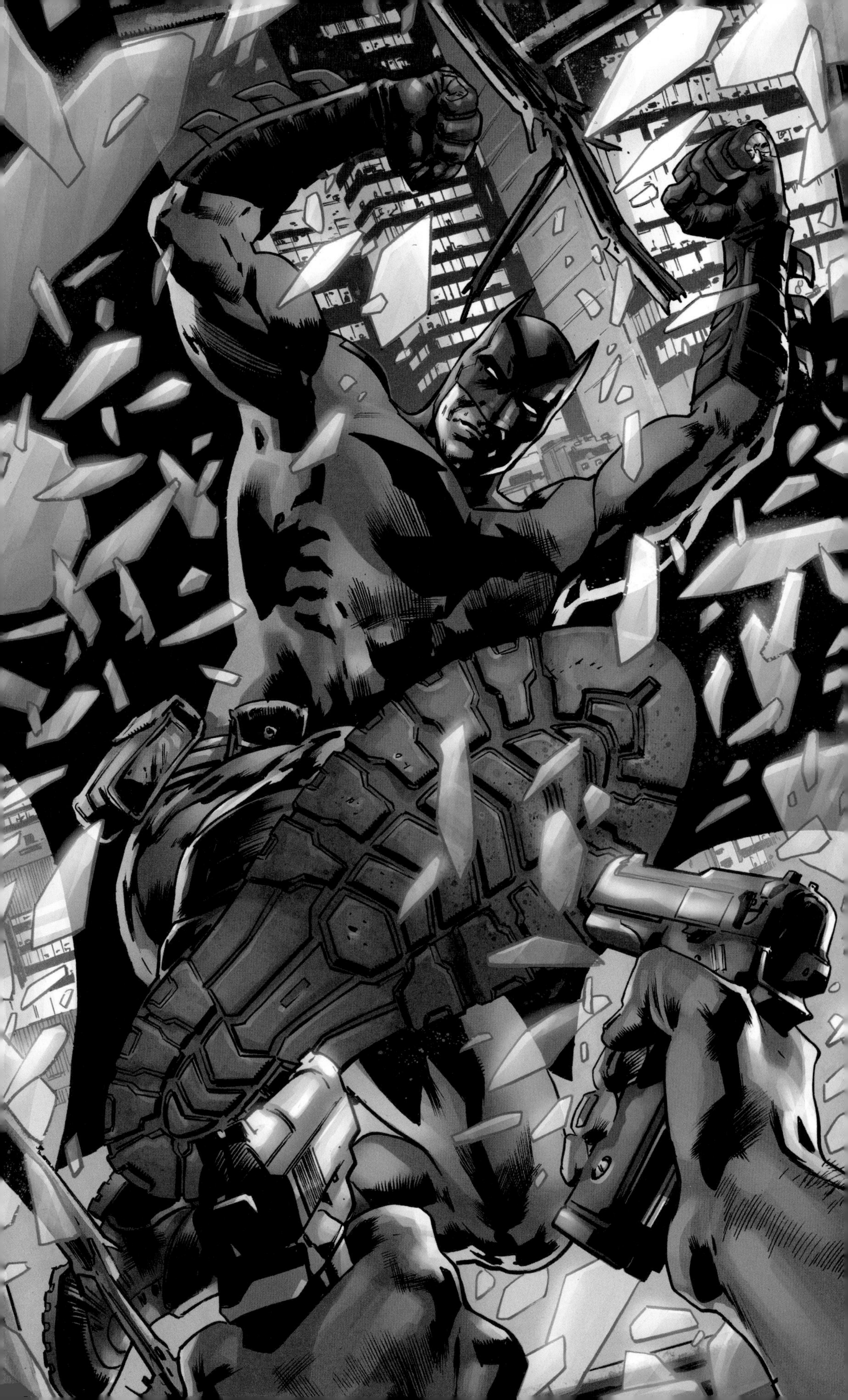

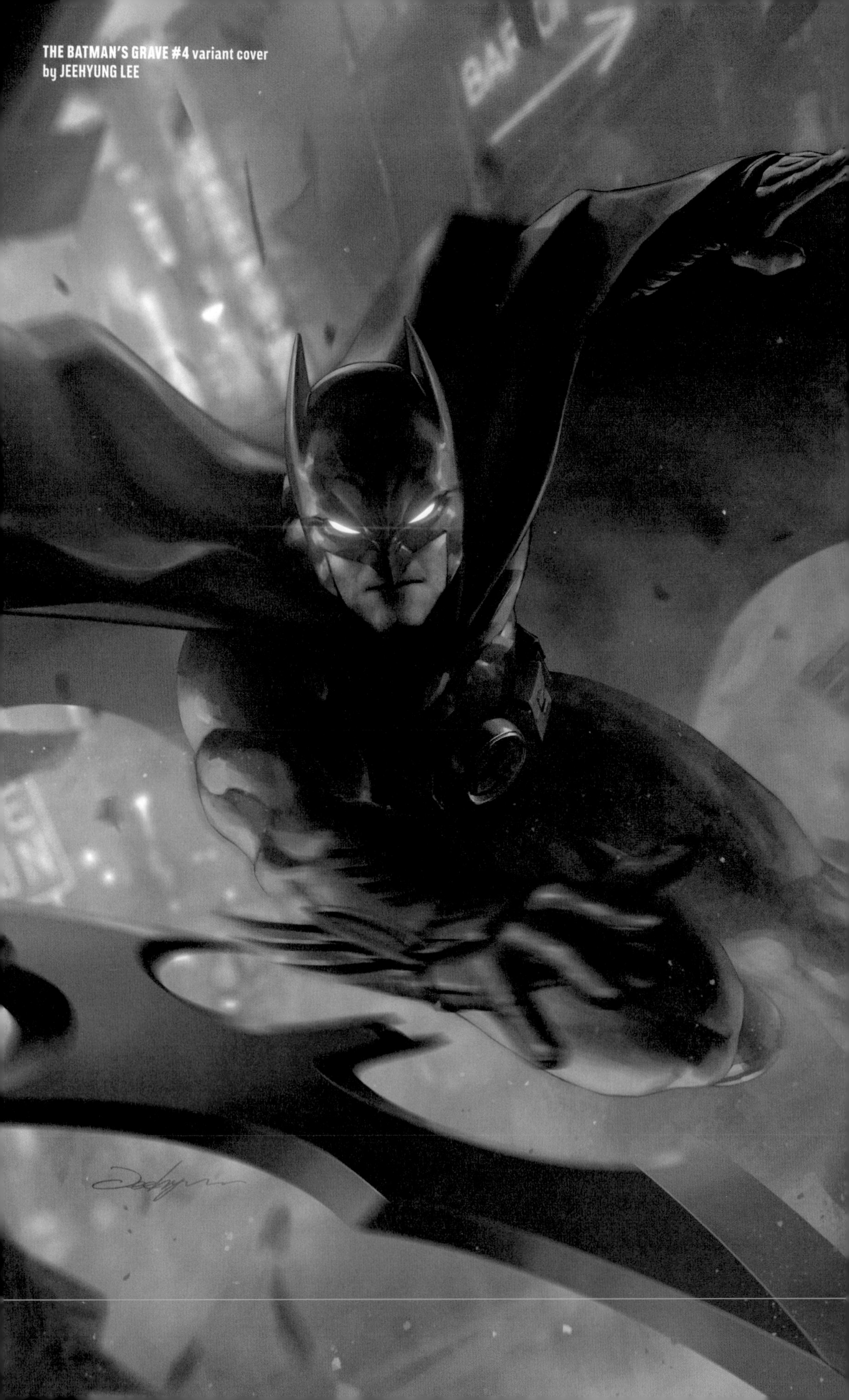

THE BATMAN'S GRAVE #4 variant cover
by **JEEHYUNG LEE**

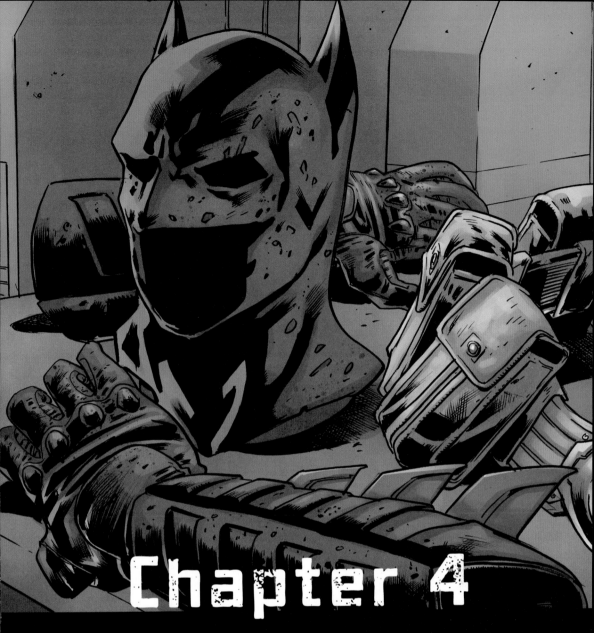

Chapter 4

| Writer | Pencils & Inks |
| WARREN ELLIS | BRYAN HITCH |

| Colors | Letters |
| ALEX SINCLAIR | RICHARD STARKINGS |

Cover	Variant Cover
BRYAN HITCH &	JEEHYUNG
ALEX SINCLAIR	LEE

| Associate Editor | Editor |
| ANDREW MARINO | MARIE JAVINS |

BATMAN created by BOB KANE with BILL FINGER

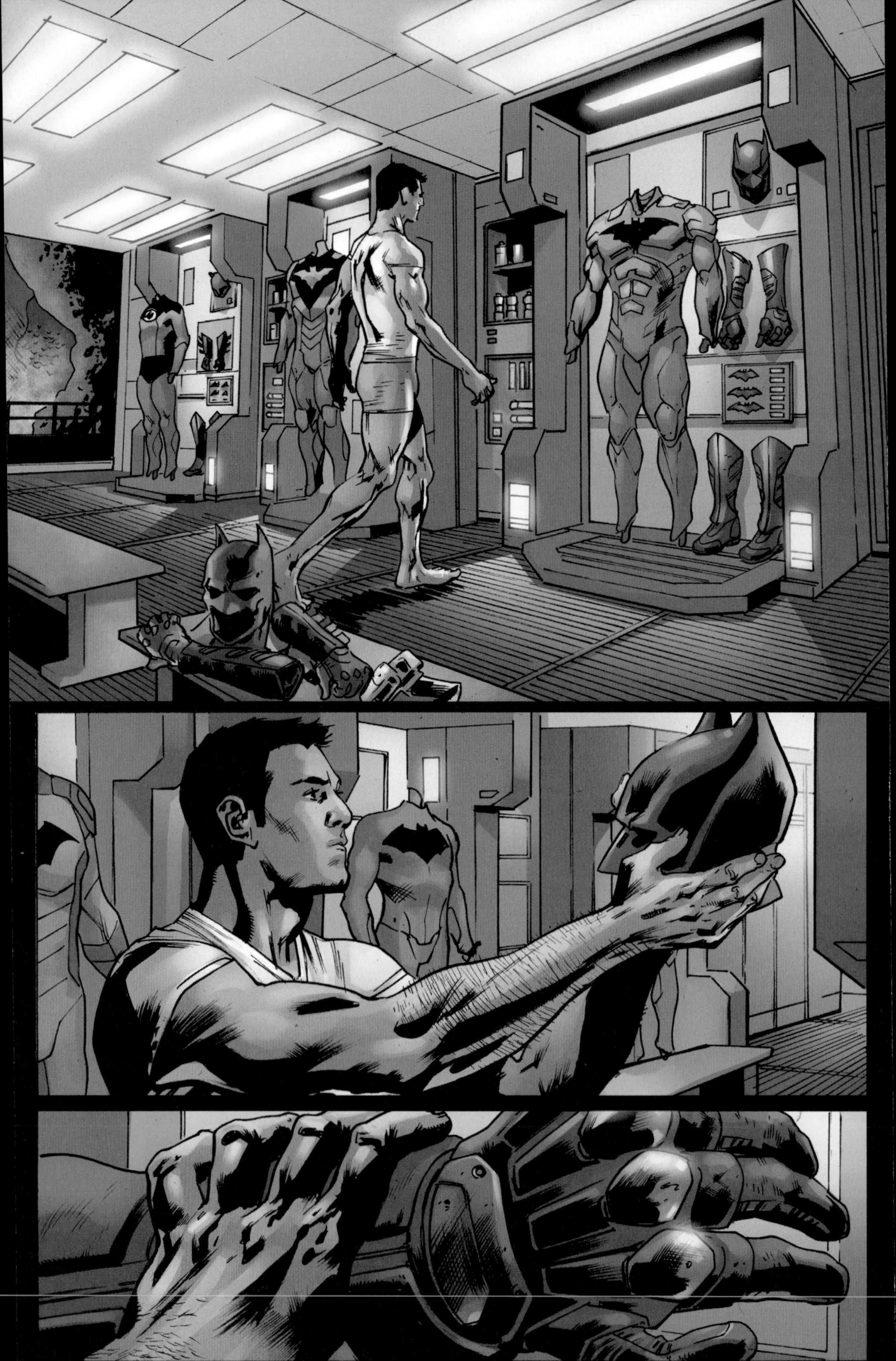

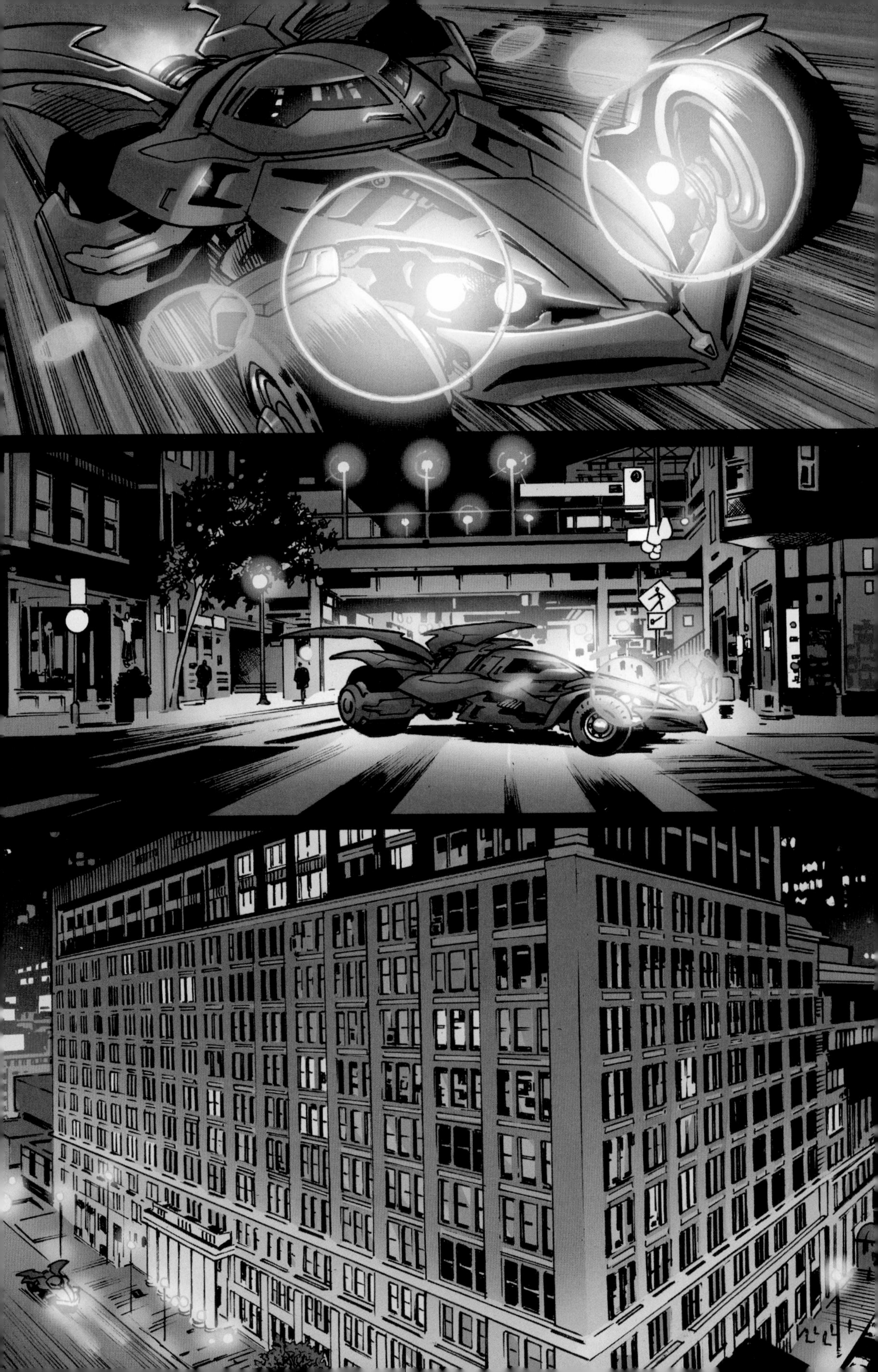

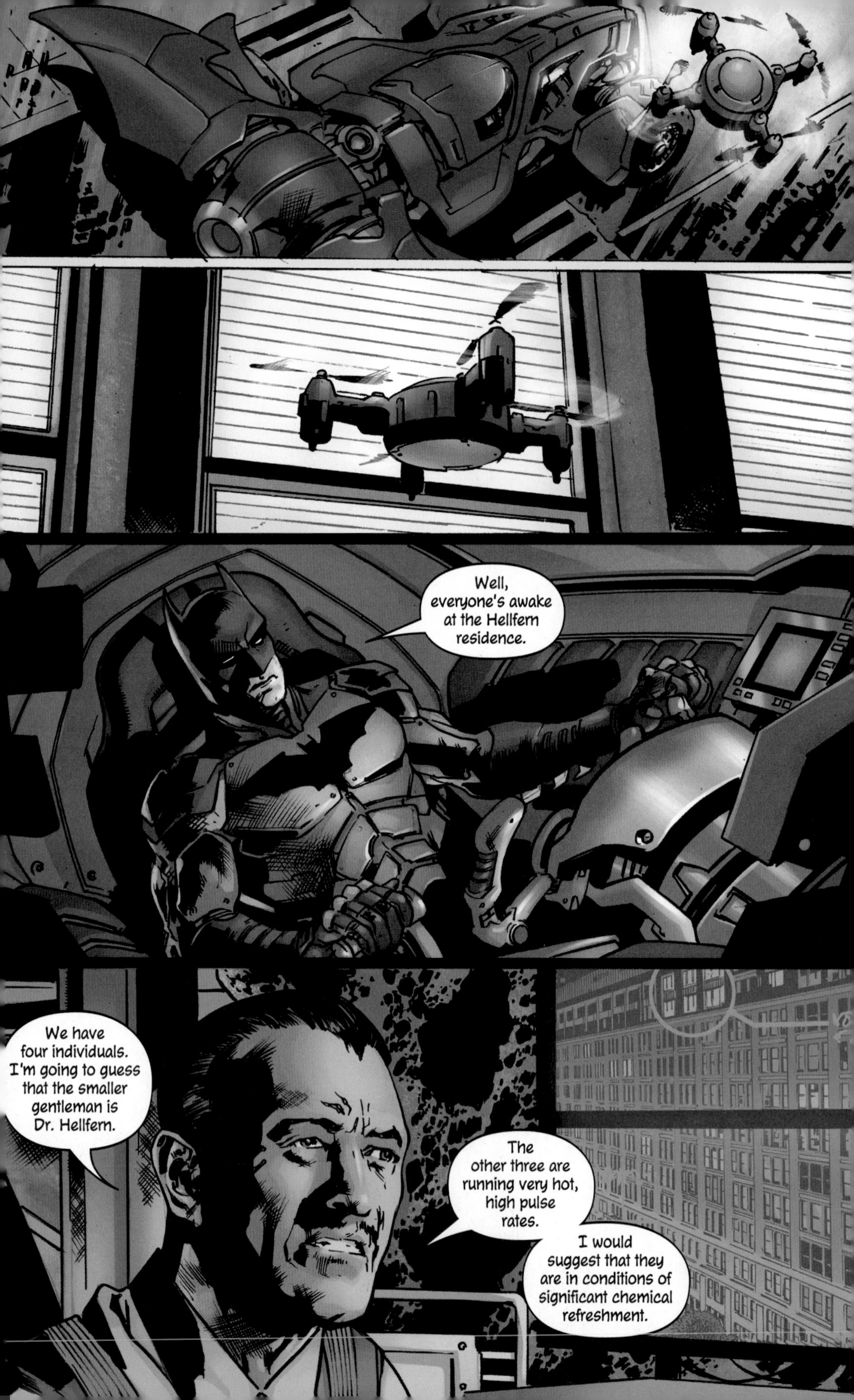
Well, everyone's awake at the Hellfern residence.
We have four individuals. I'm going to guess that the smaller gentleman is Dr. Hellfern.
The other three are running very hot, high pulse rates.
I would suggest that they are in conditions of significant chemical refreshment.

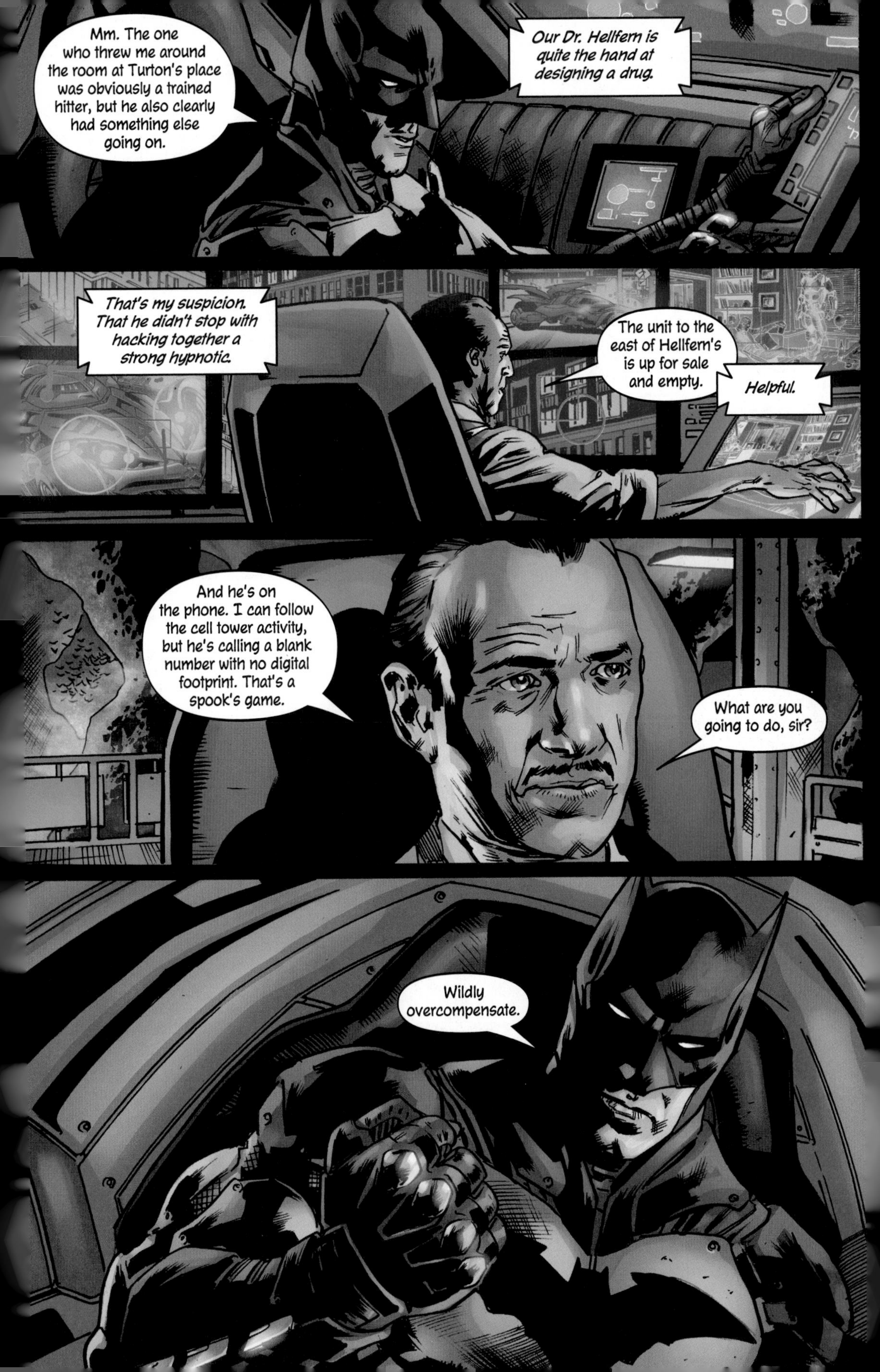
Mm. The one who threw me around the room at Turton's place was obviously a trained hitter, but he also clearly had something else going on.
Our Dr. Hellfern is quite the hand at designing a drug.
That's my suspicion. That he didn't stop with hacking together a strong hypnotic.
The unit to the east of Hellfern's is up for sale and empty.
Helpful.
And he's on the phone. I can follow the cell tower activity, but he's calling a blank number with no digital footprint. That's a spook's game.
What are you going to do, sir?
Wildly overcompensate.

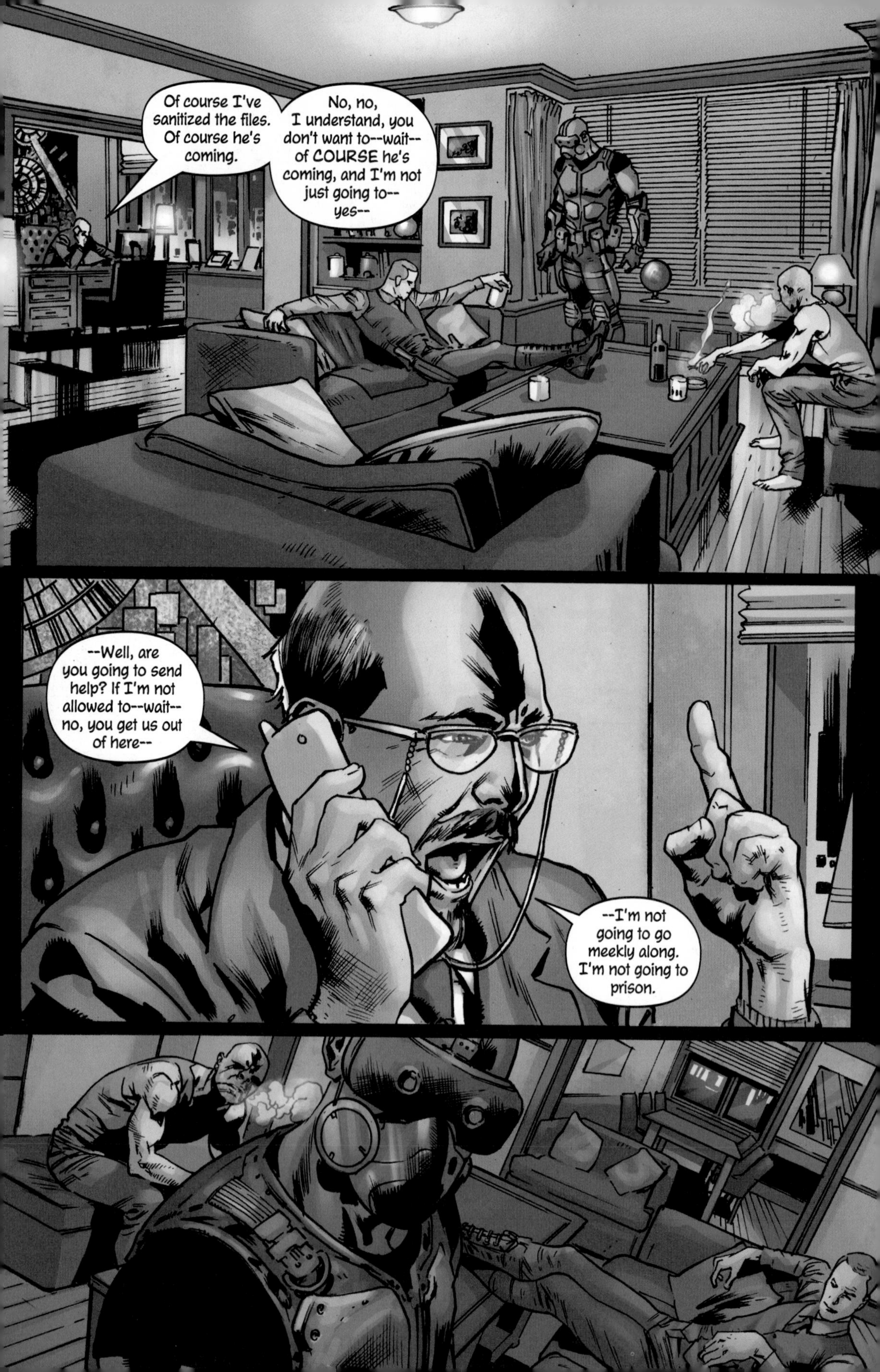
Of course I've sanitized the files. Of course he's coming.
No, no, I understand, you don't want to--wait-- of COURSE he's coming, and I'm not just going to-- yes--
--Well, are you going to send help? If I'm not allowed to--wait-- no, you get us out of here--
--I'm not going to go meekly along. I'm not going to prison.

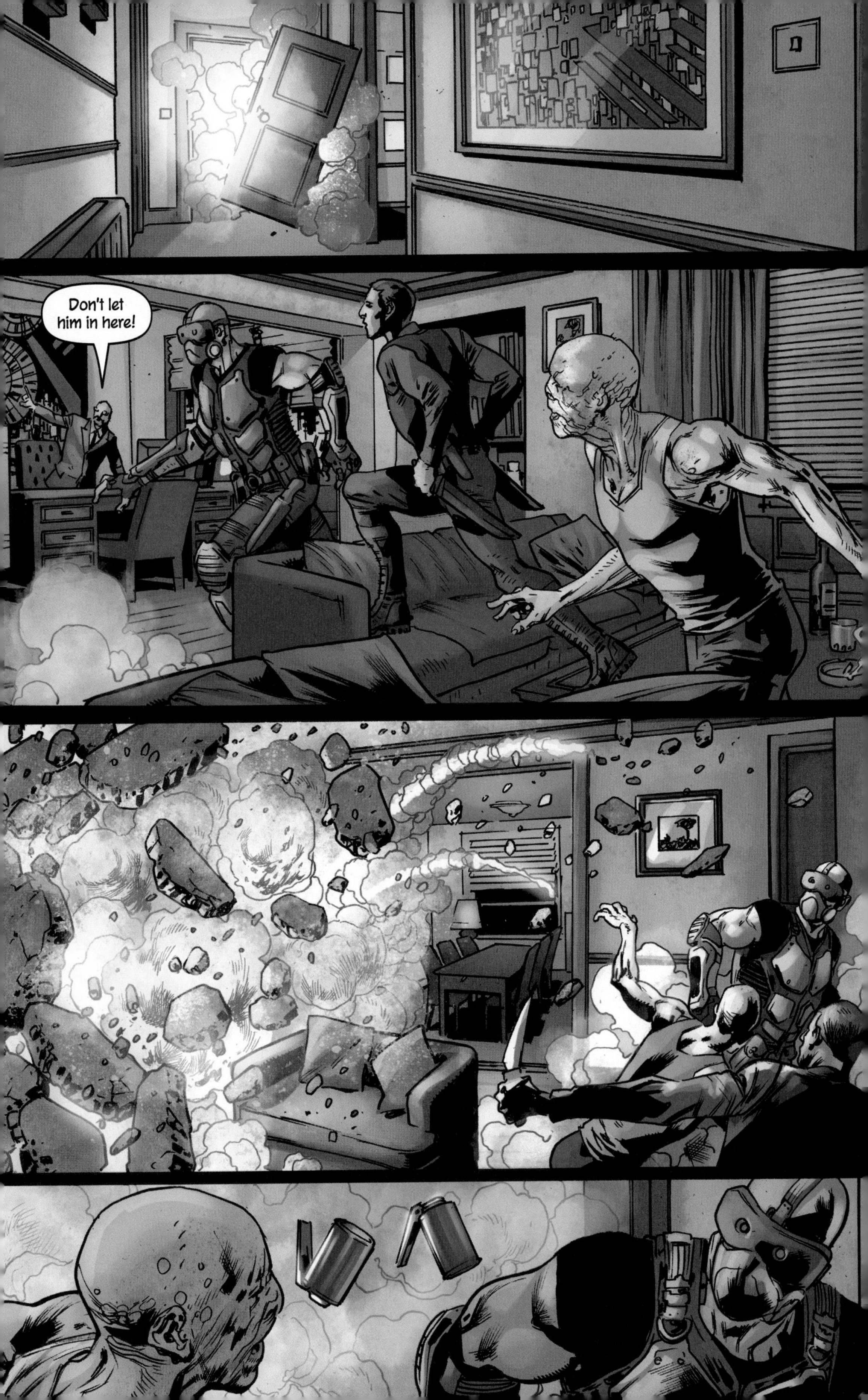
Don't let him in here!

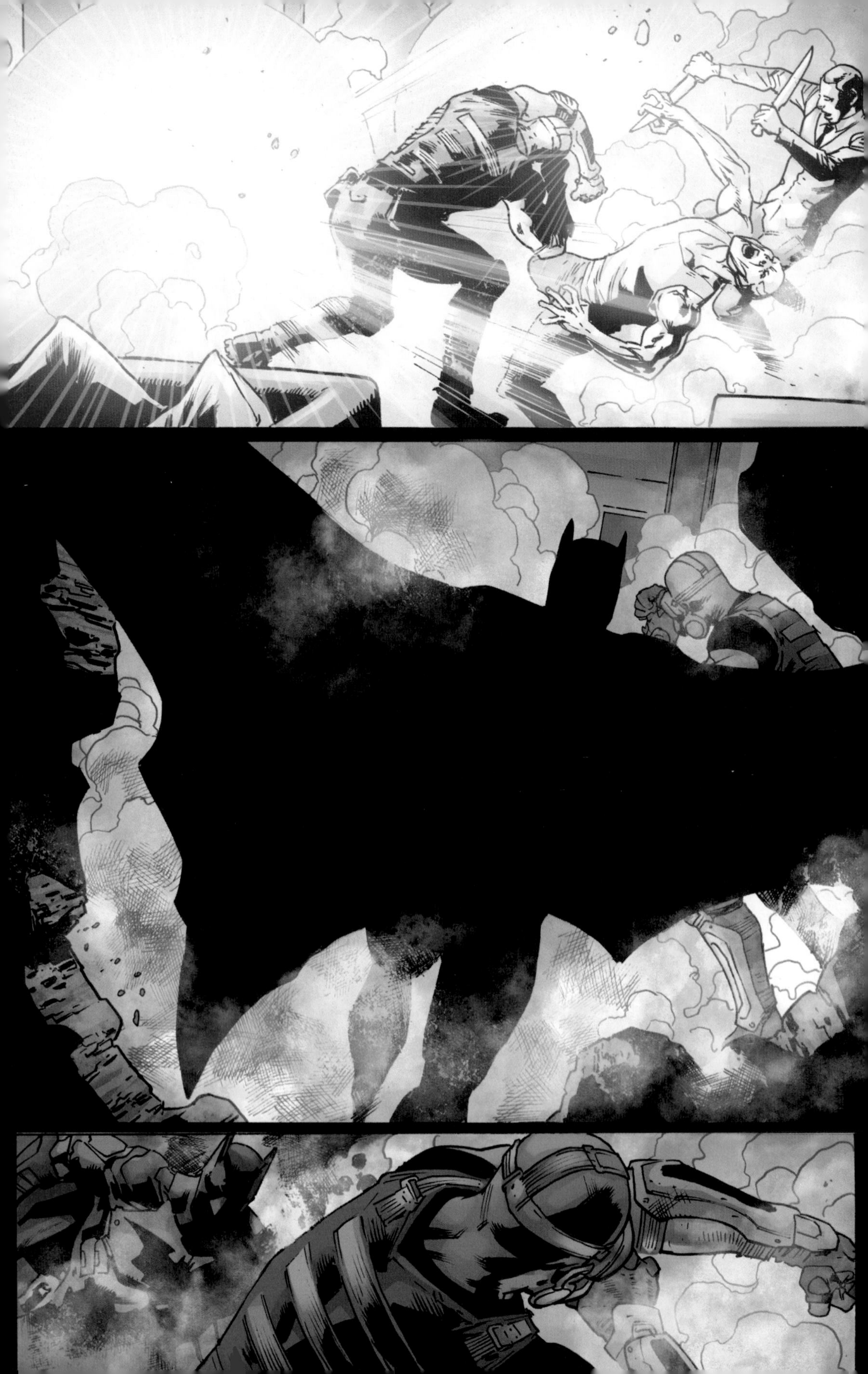

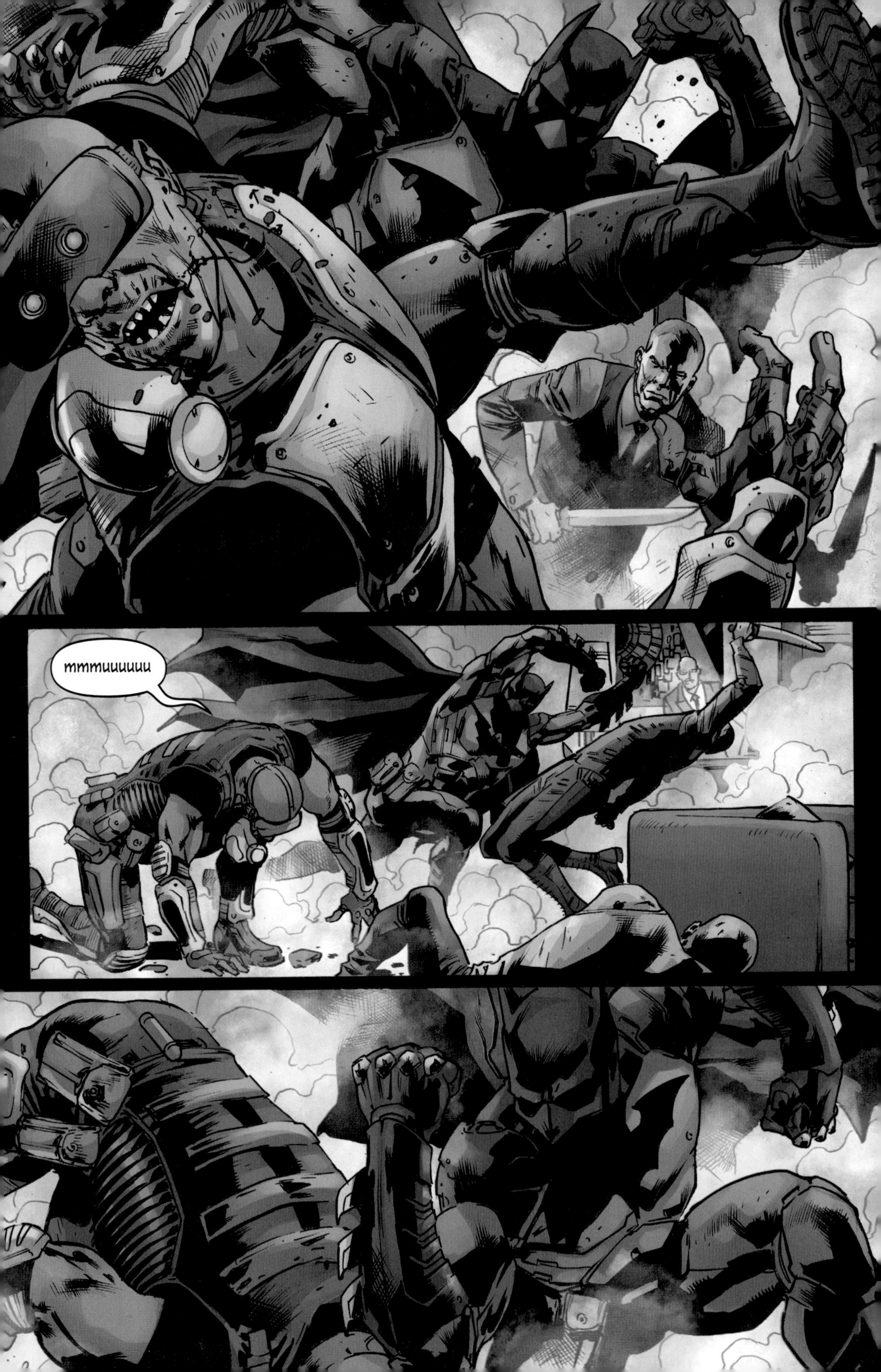
mmmuuuuuu

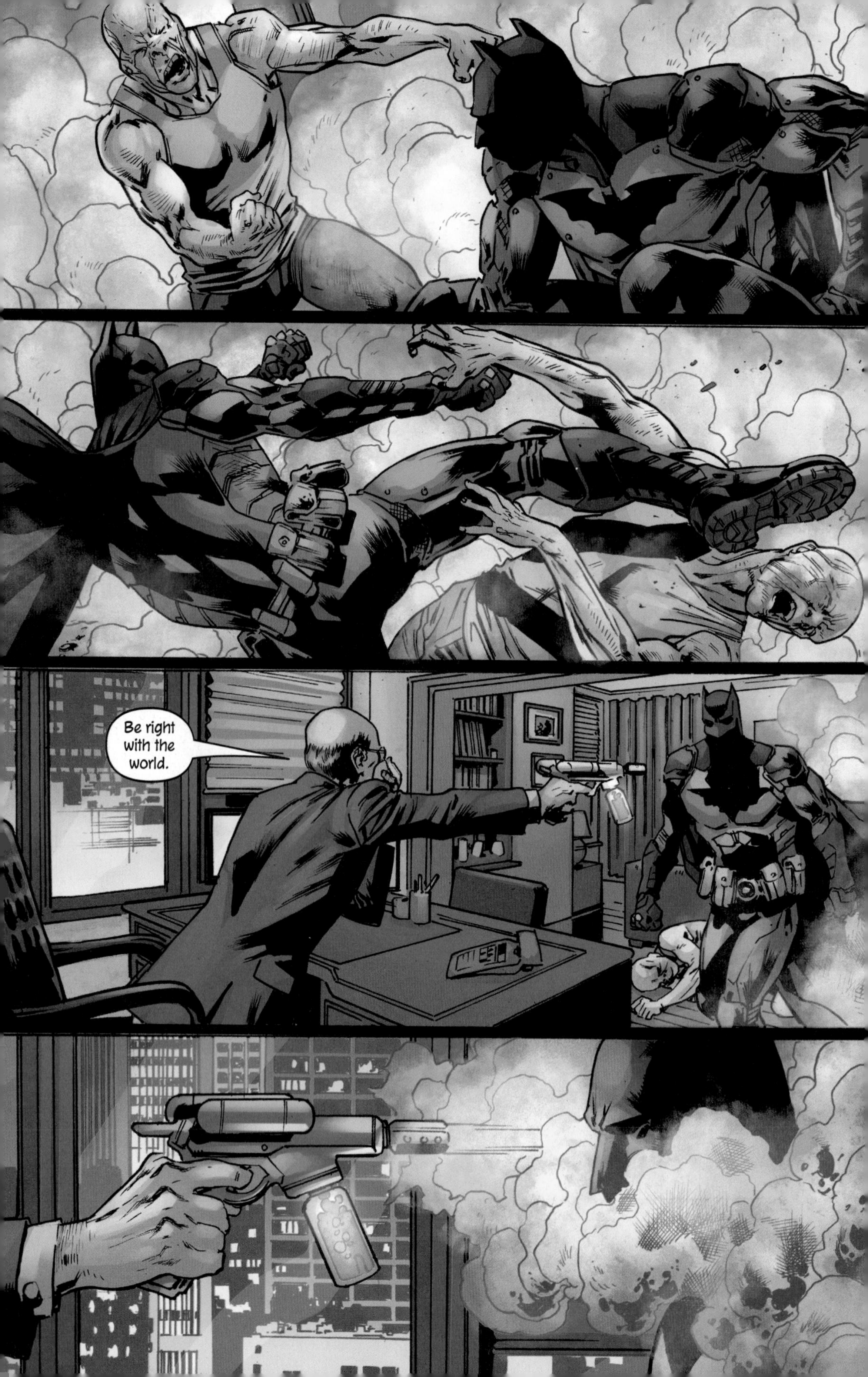

Be right with the world.

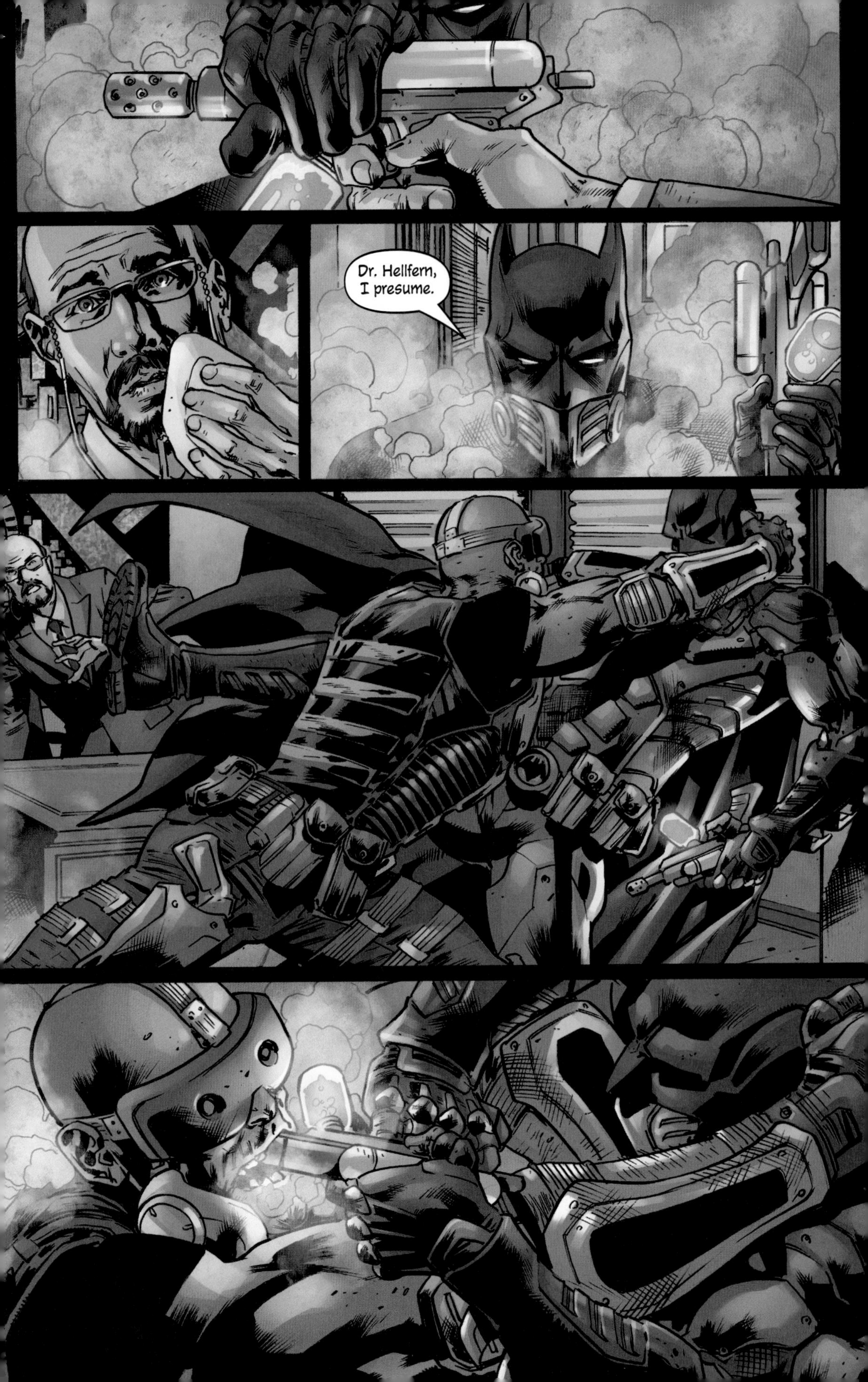
Dr. Hellfern, I presume.

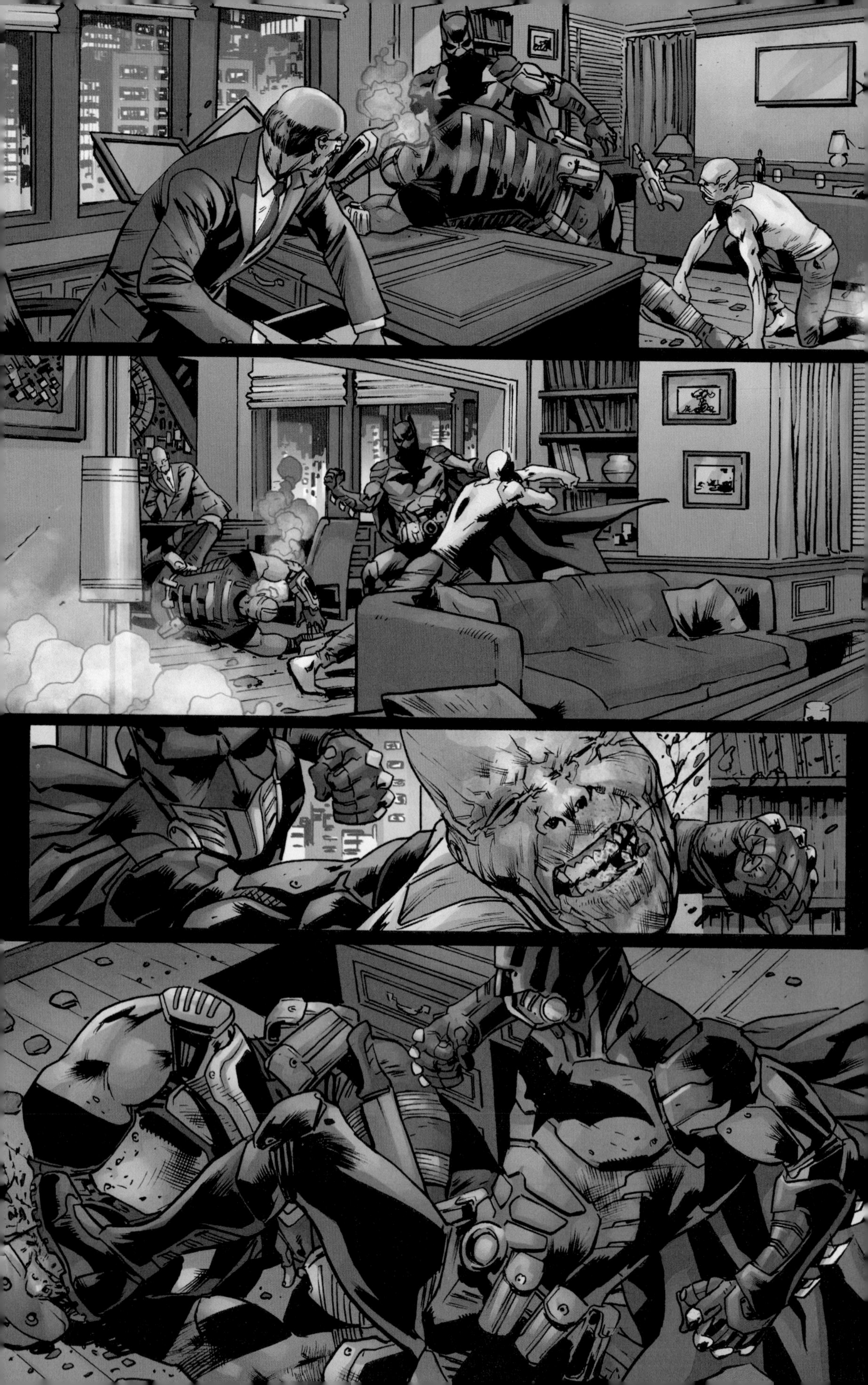

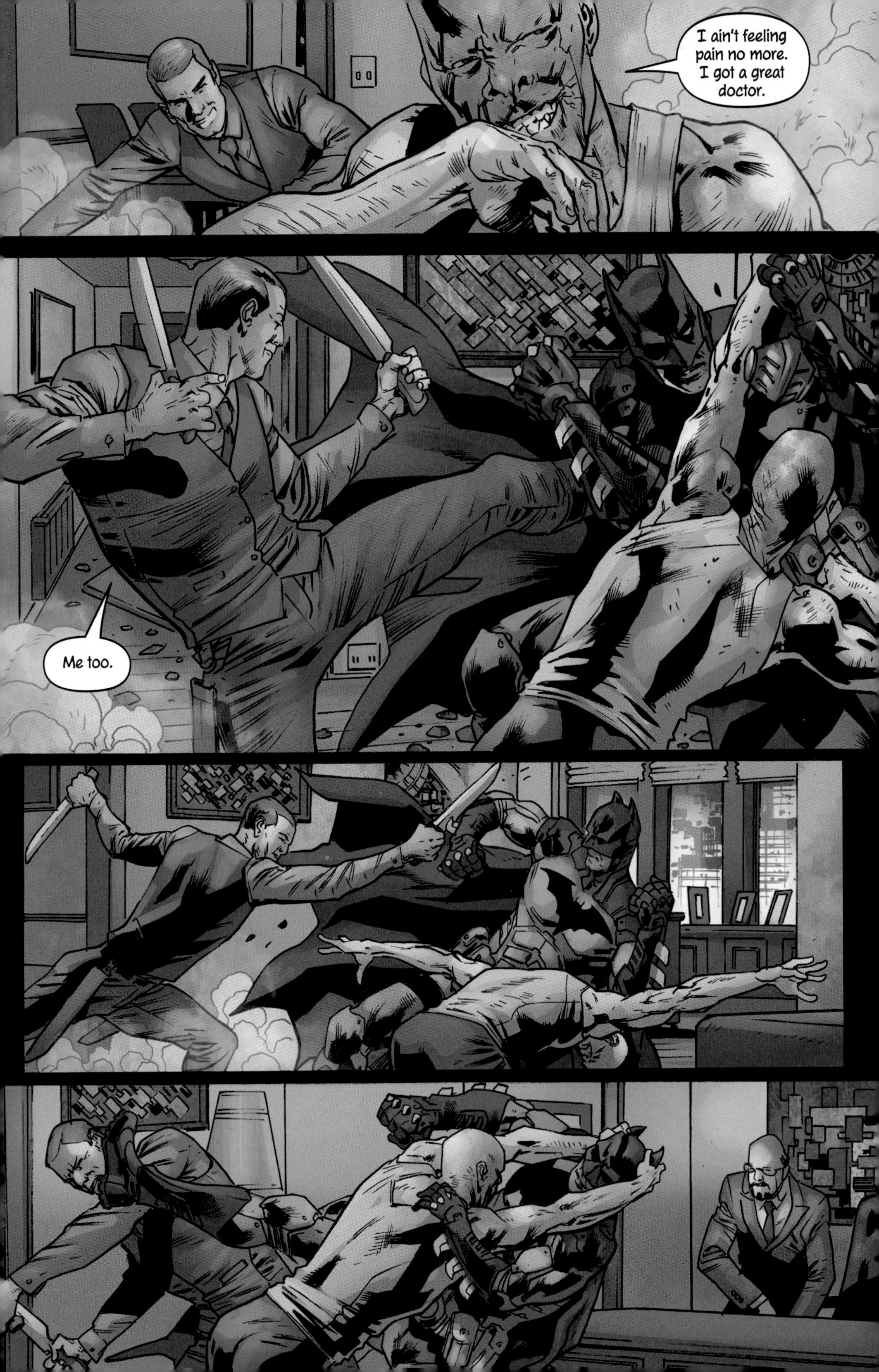
I ain't feeling pain no more. I got a great doctor.
Me too.

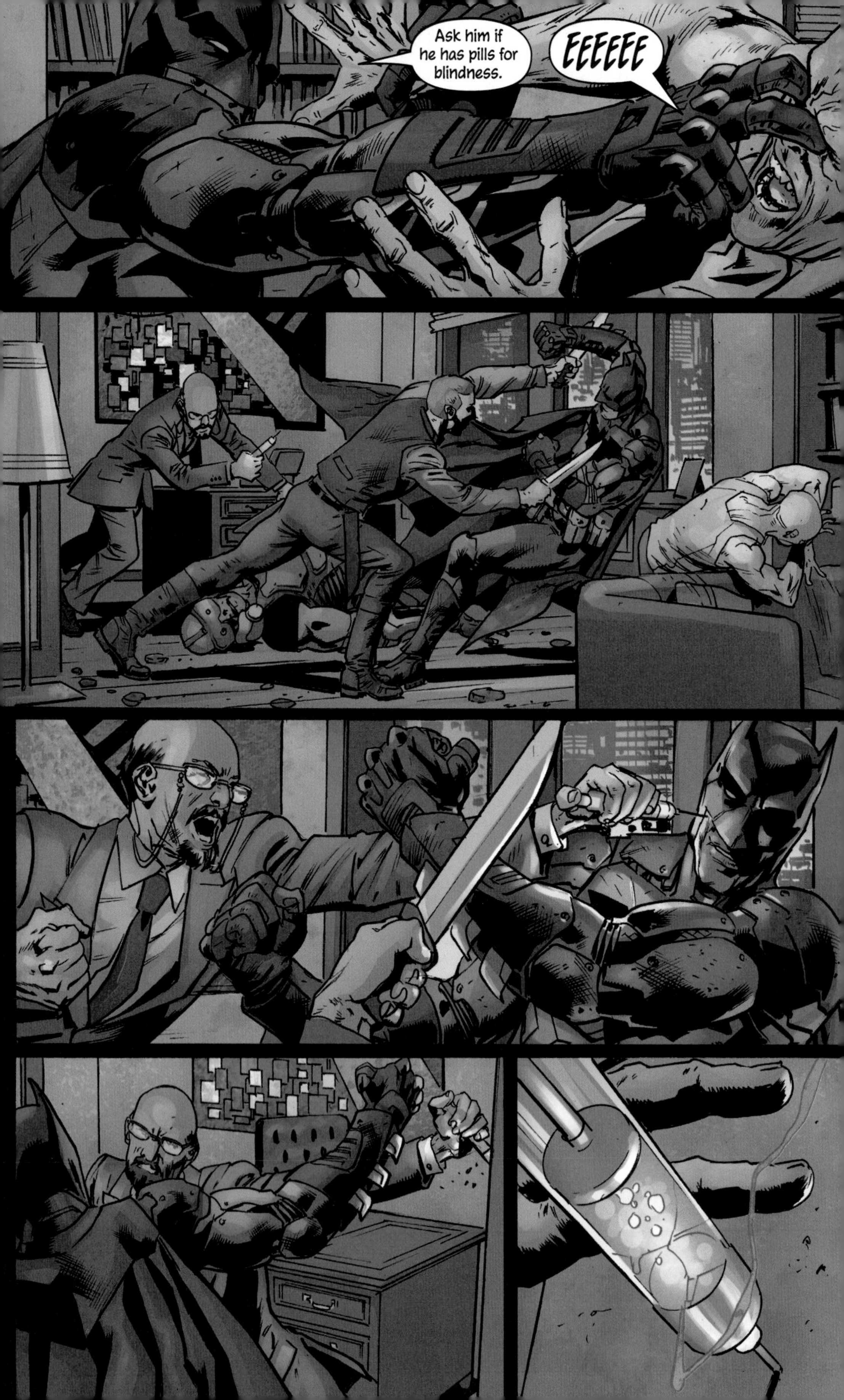
Ask him if he has pills for blindness.
EEEEEE

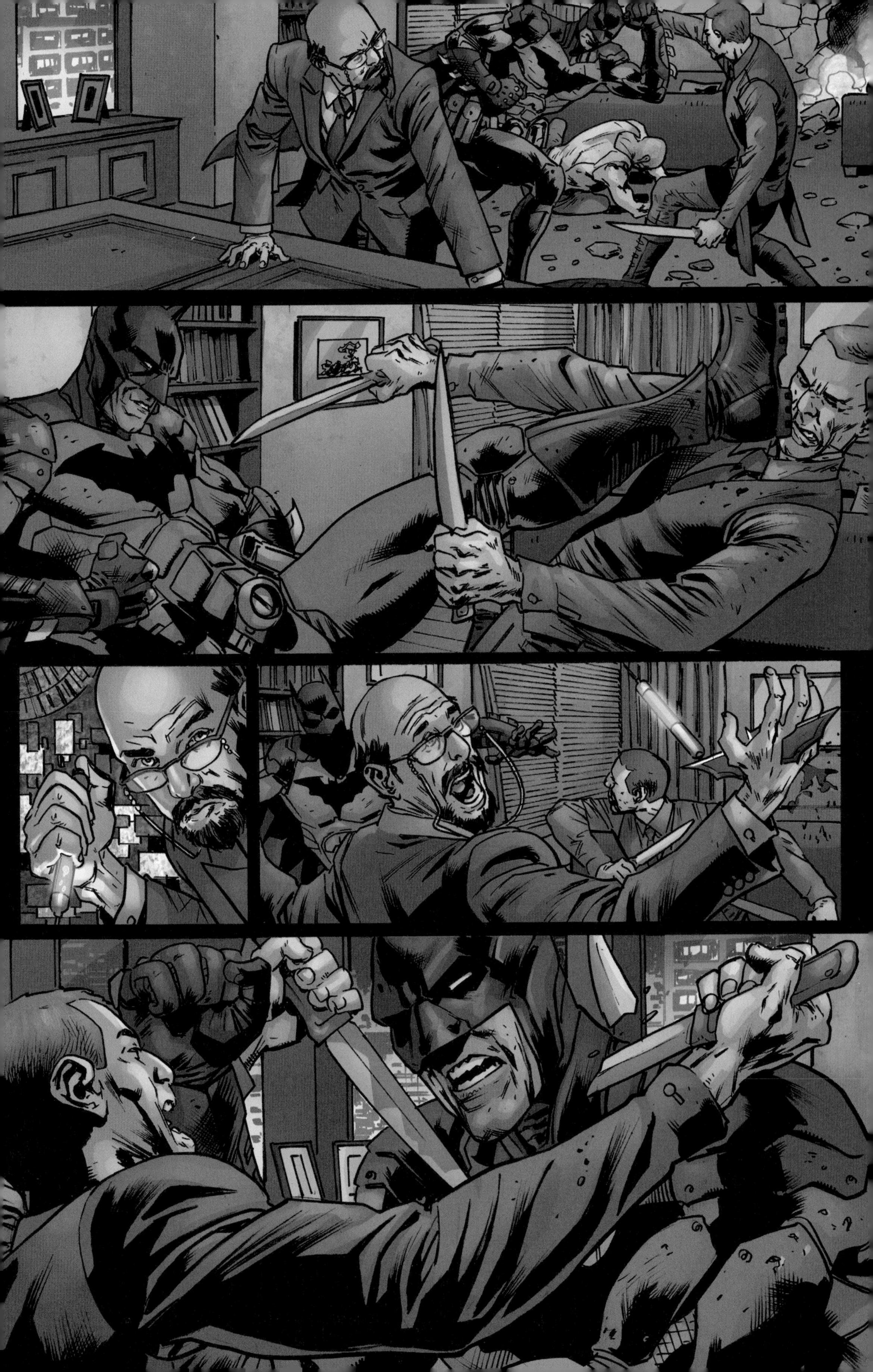

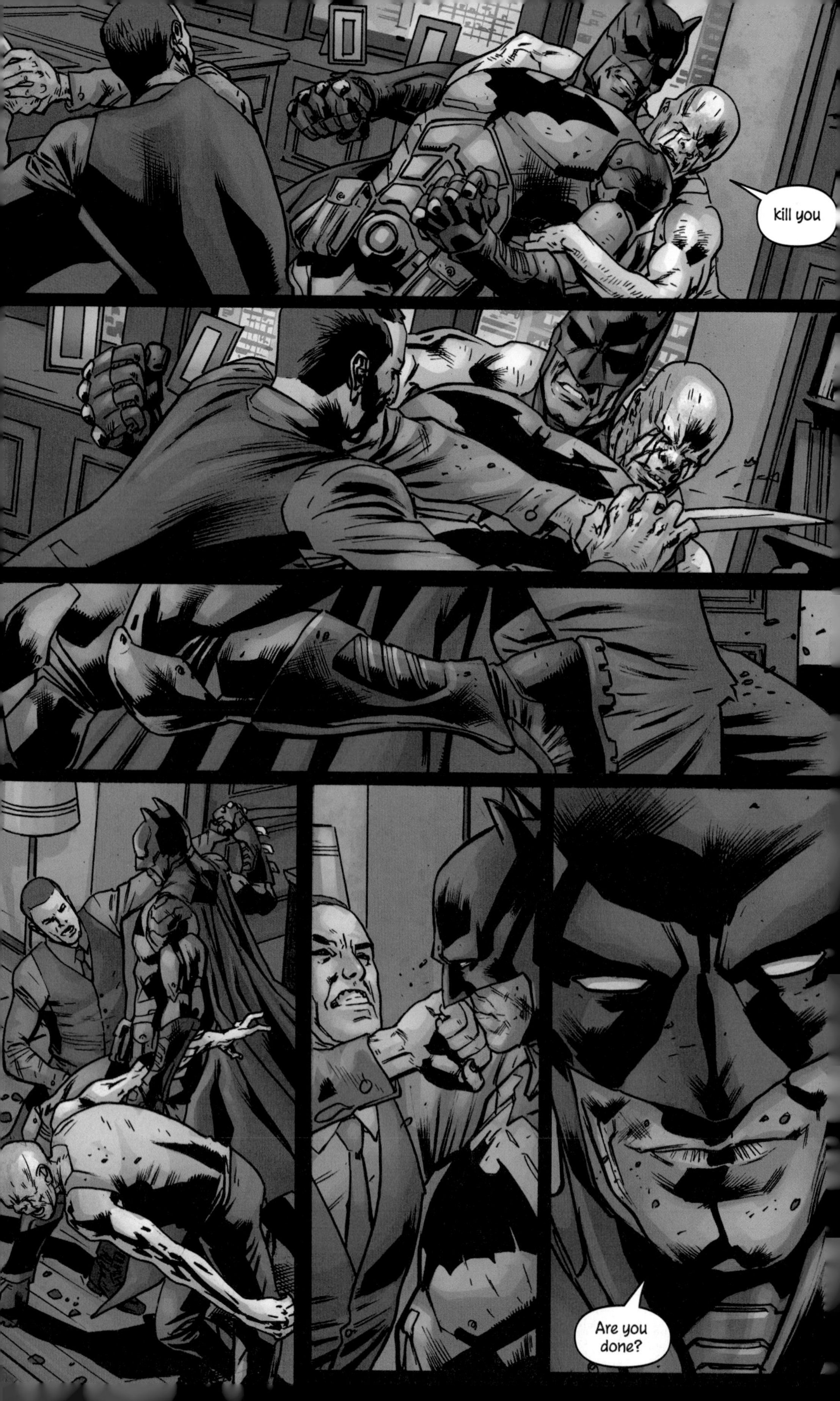
kill you
Are you done?

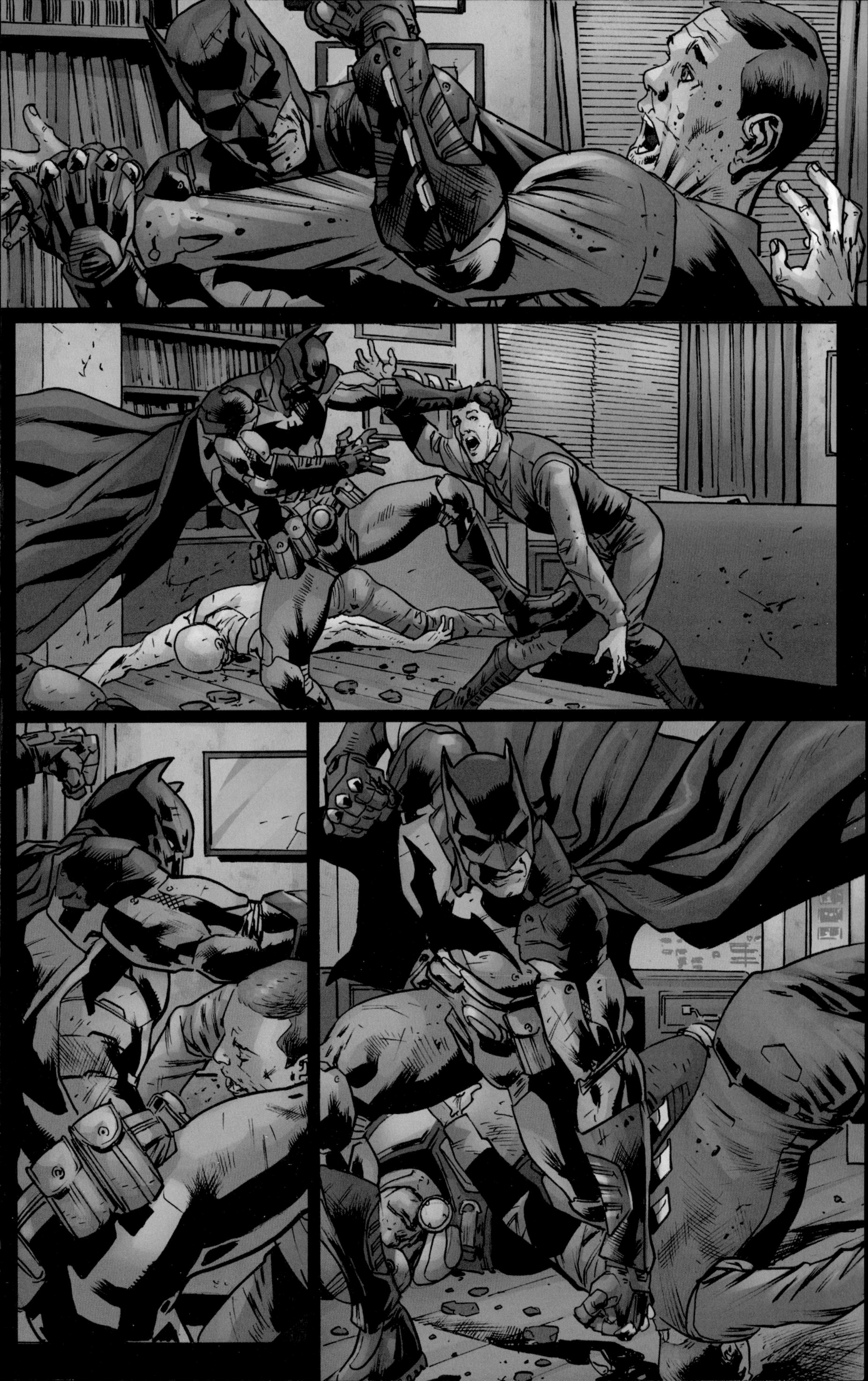

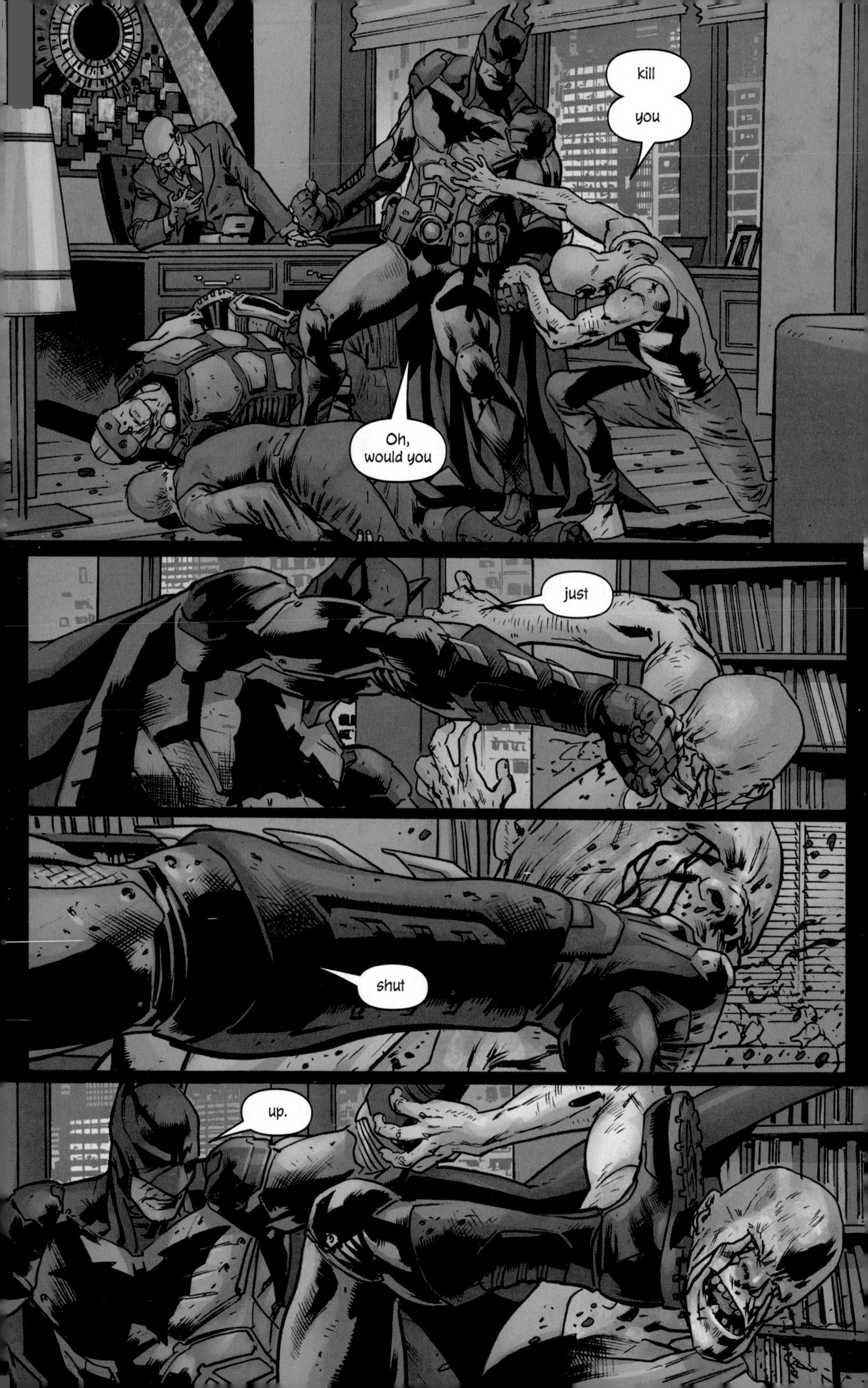
kill
you
Oh, would you
just
shut
up.

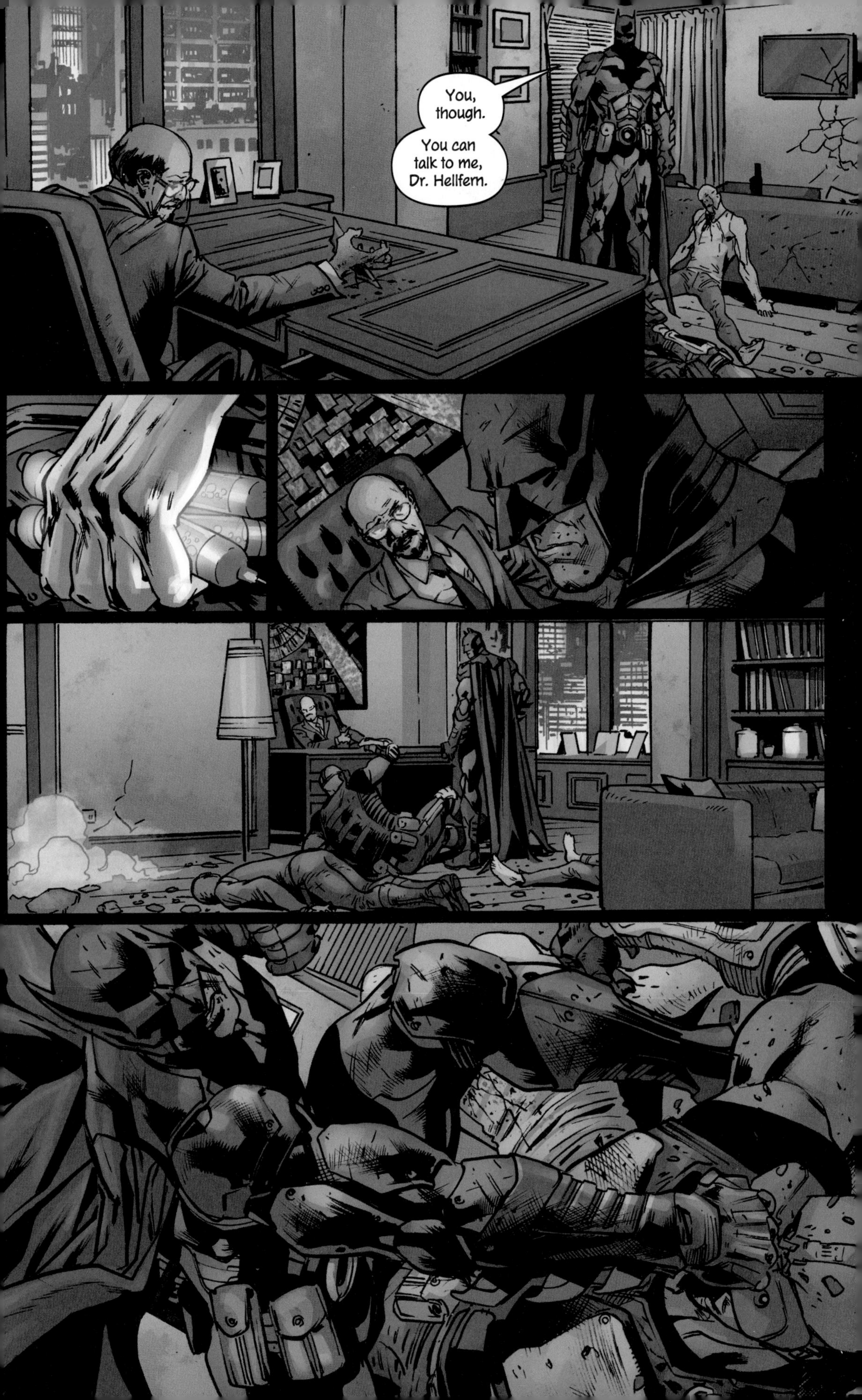
You, though.
You can talk to me, Dr. Hellfern.

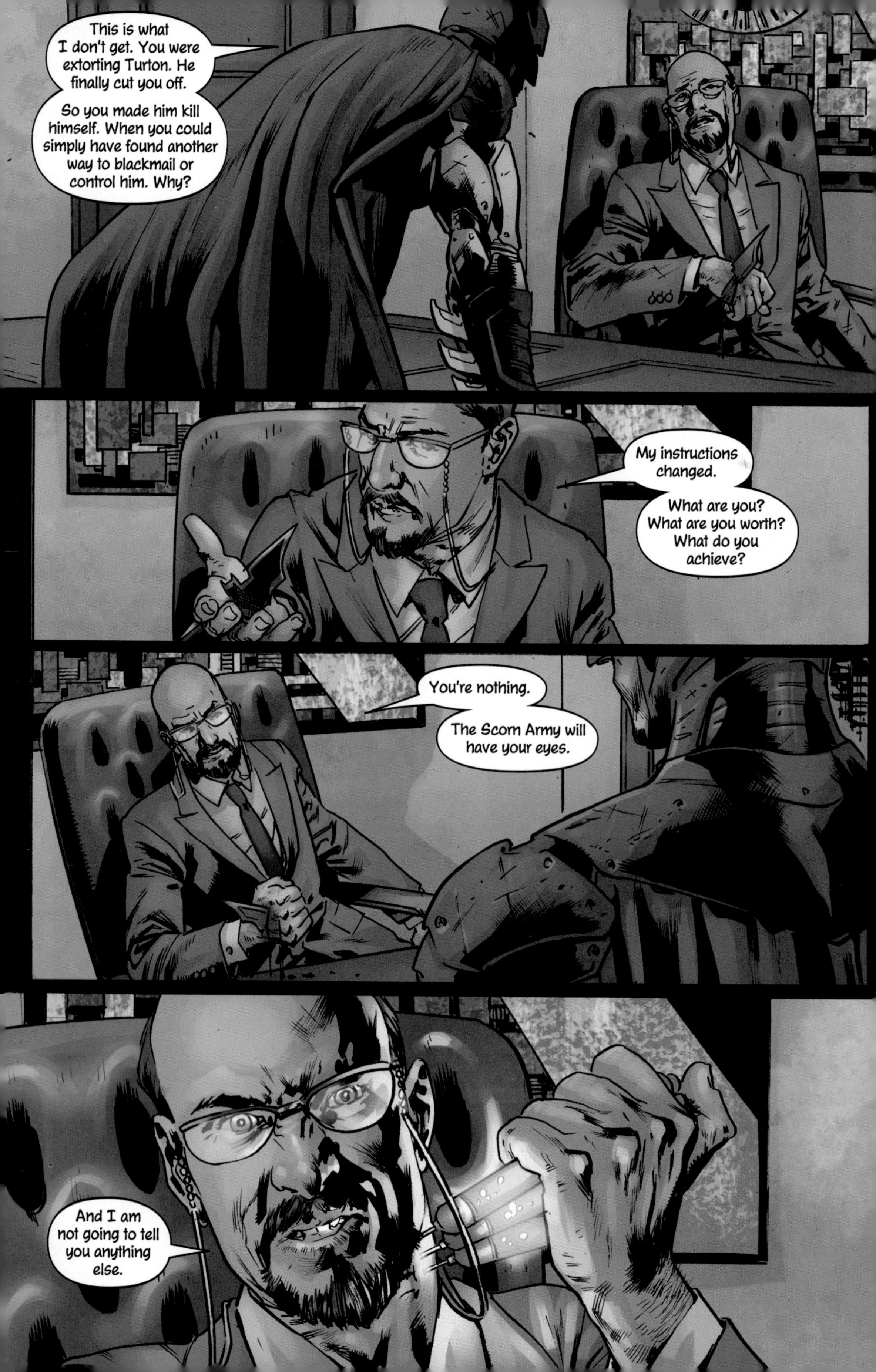
This is what I don't get. You were extorting Turton. He finally cut you off.
So you made him kill himself. When you could simply have found another way to blackmail or control him. Why?
My instructions changed.
What are you? What are you worth? What do you achieve?
You're nothing.
The Scorn Army will have your eyes.
And I am not going to tell you anything else.

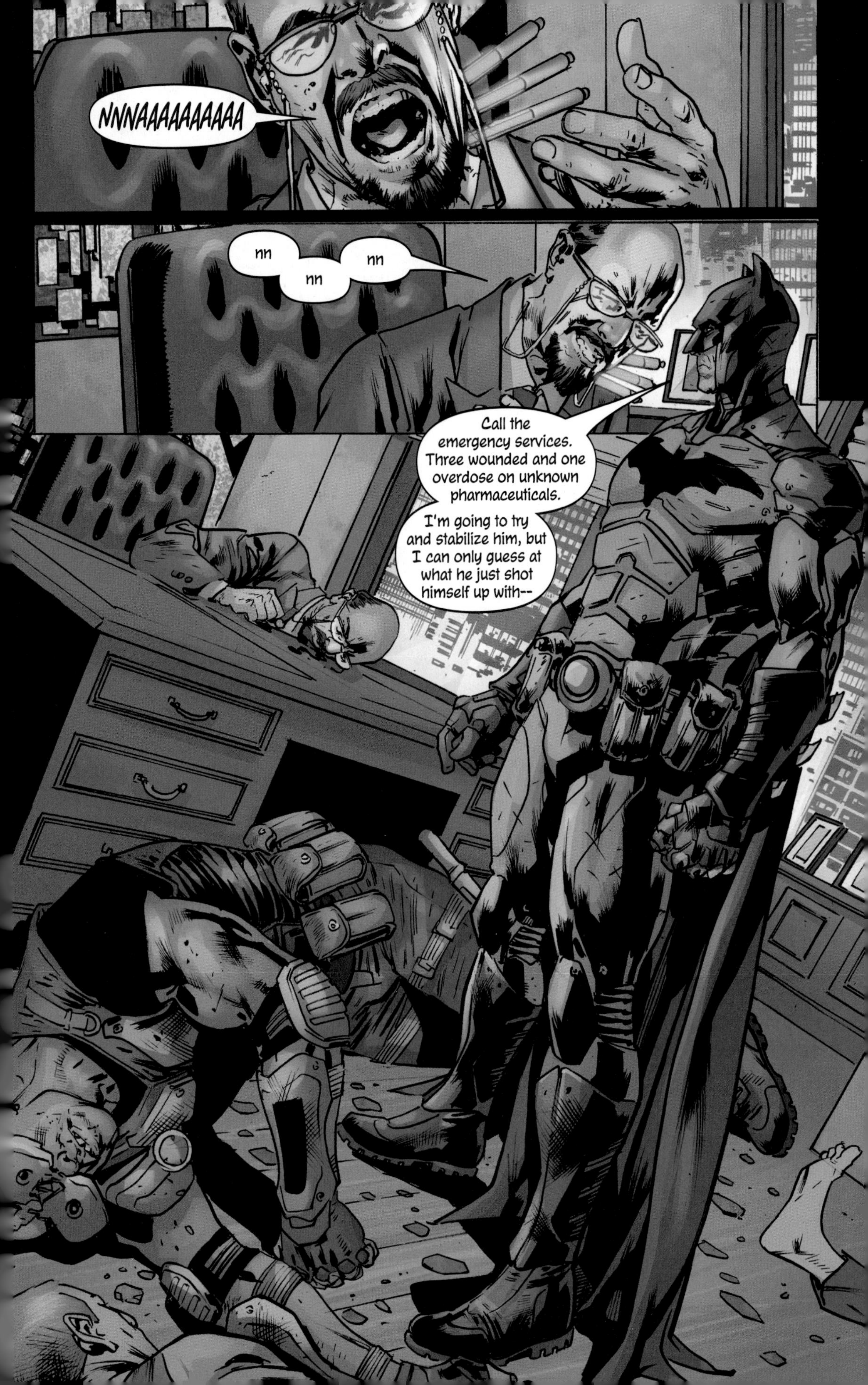
NNNAAAAAAAAAA
nn
nn
nn
Call the emergency services. Three wounded and one overdose on unknown pharmaceuticals.
I'm going to try and stabilize him, but I can only guess at what he just shot himself up with--

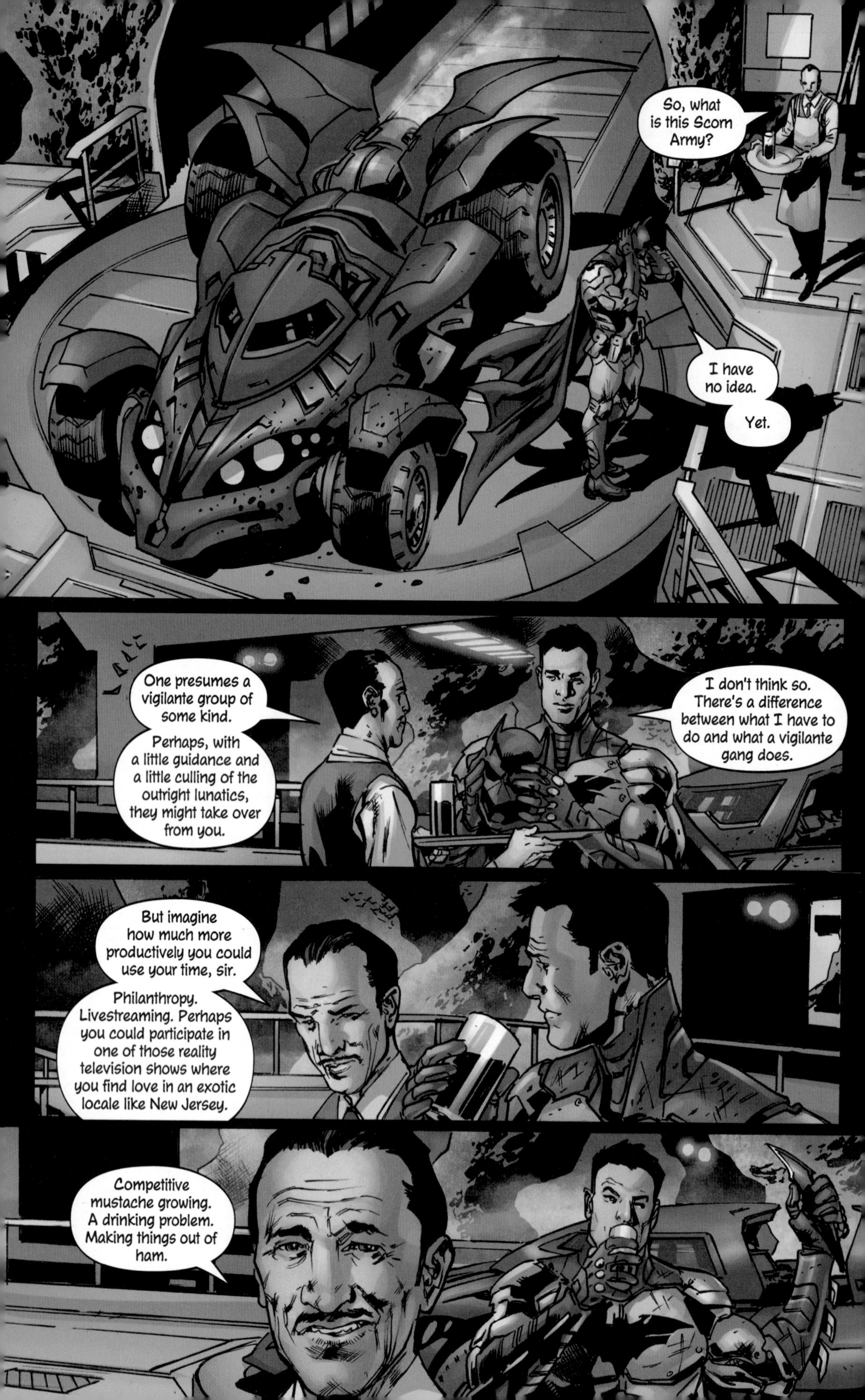
So, what is this Scorn Army?
I have no idea.
Yet.
One presumes a vigilante group of some kind.
Perhaps, with a little guidance and a little culling of the outright lunatics, they might take over from you.
I don't think so. There's a difference between what I have to do and what a vigilante gang does.
But imagine how much more productively you could use your time, sir.
Philanthropy. Livestreaming. Perhaps you could participate in one of those reality television shows where you find love in an exotic locale like New Jersey.
Competitive mustache growing. A drinking problem. Making things out of ham.

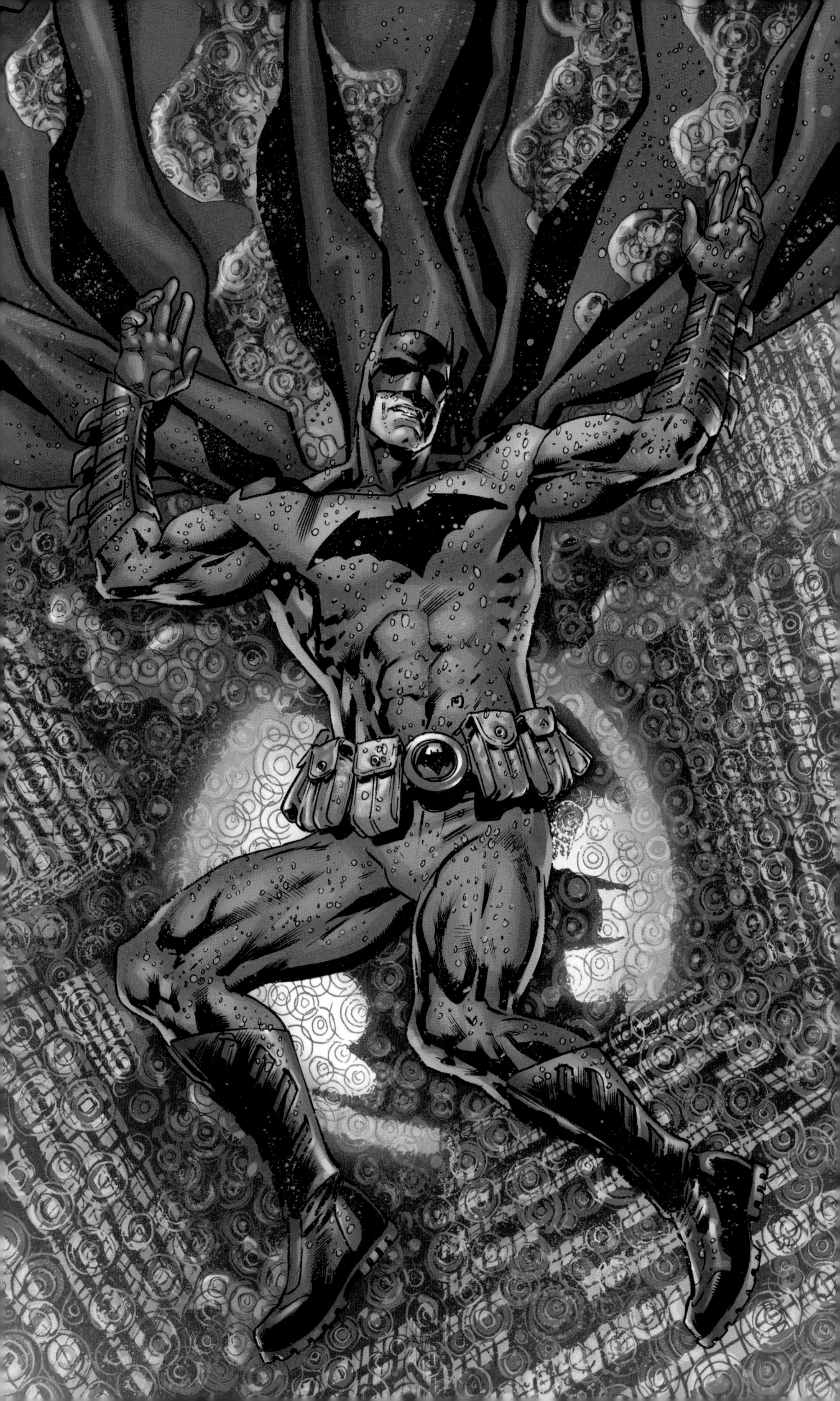

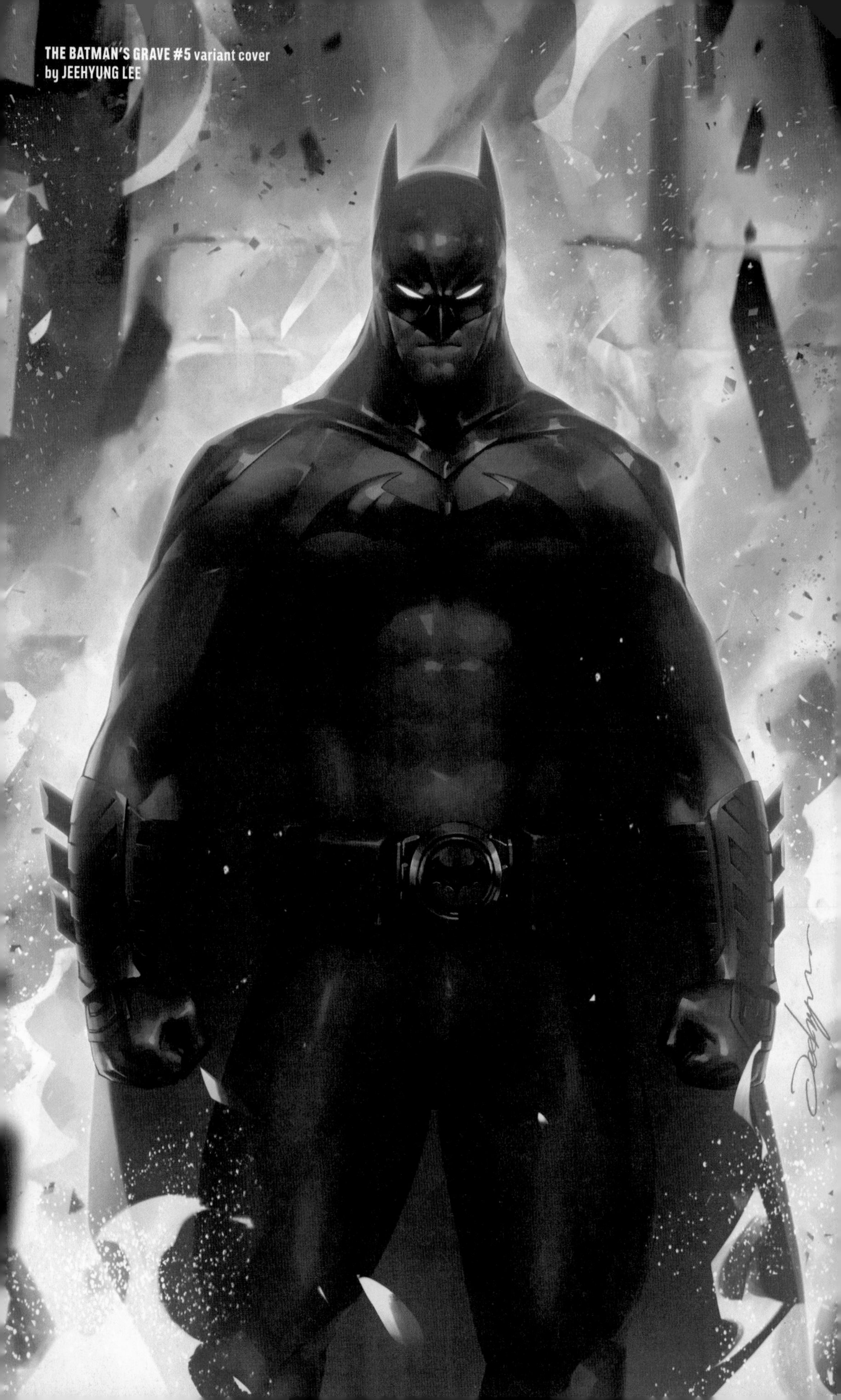

THE BATMAN'S GRAVE #5 variant cover
by JEEHYUNG LEE

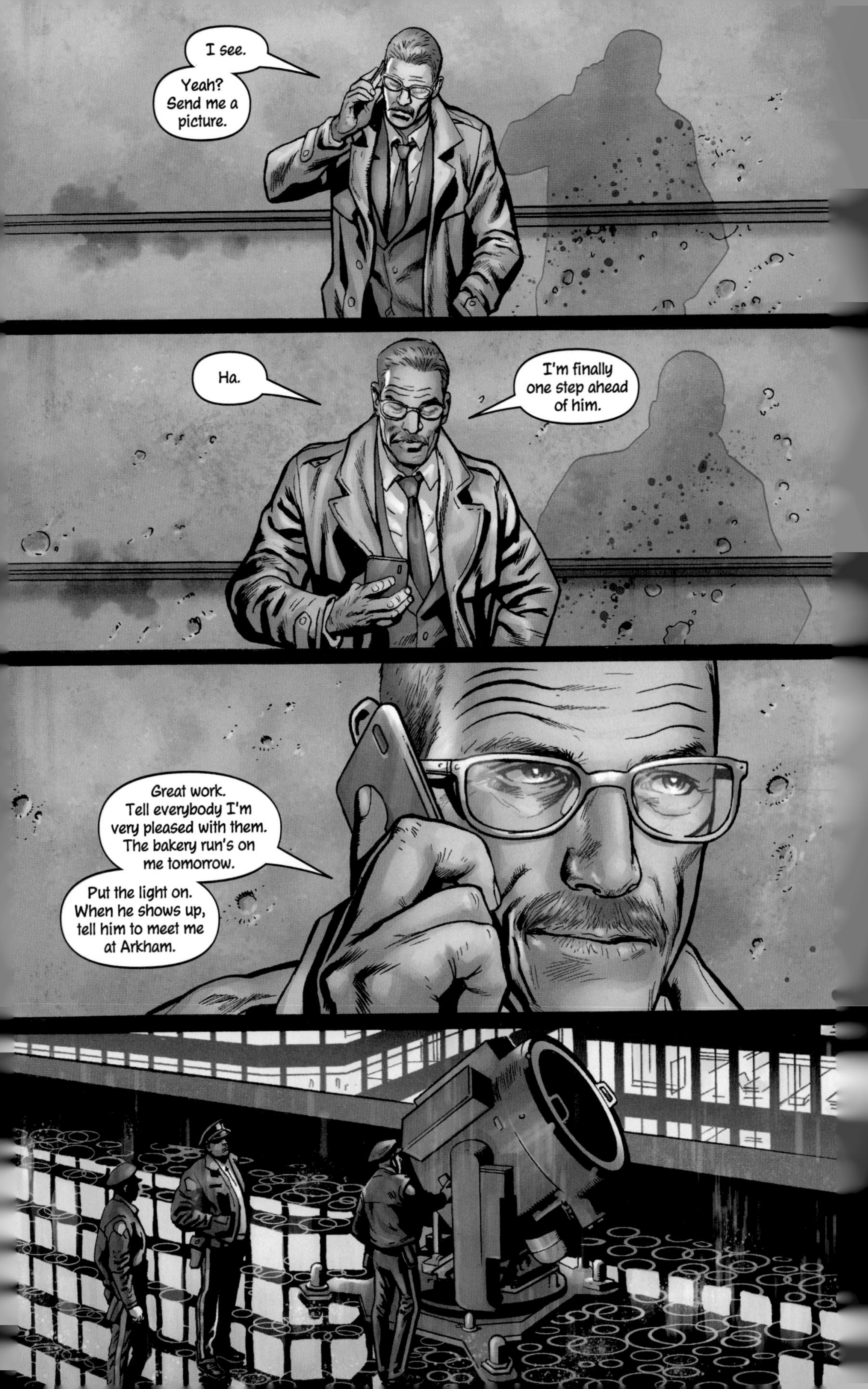
I see.
Yeah? Send me a picture.
Ha.
I'm finally one step ahead of him.
Great work. Tell everybody I'm very pleased with them. The bakery run's on me tomorrow.
Put the light on. When he shows up, tell him to meet me at Arkham.

Chapter 5

Writer	Pencils
WARREN ELLIS	**BRYAN HITCH**

Inks
KEVIN NOWLAN & BRYAN HITCH

Colors	Letters
ALEX SINCLAIR	**RICHARD STARKINGS**

Cover	Variant Cover
BRYAN HITCH &	**JEEHYUNG**
ALEX SINCLAIR	**LEE**

Associate Editor	Editor
ANDREW MARINO	**MARIE JAVINS**

BATMAN created by BOB KANE with BILL FINGER

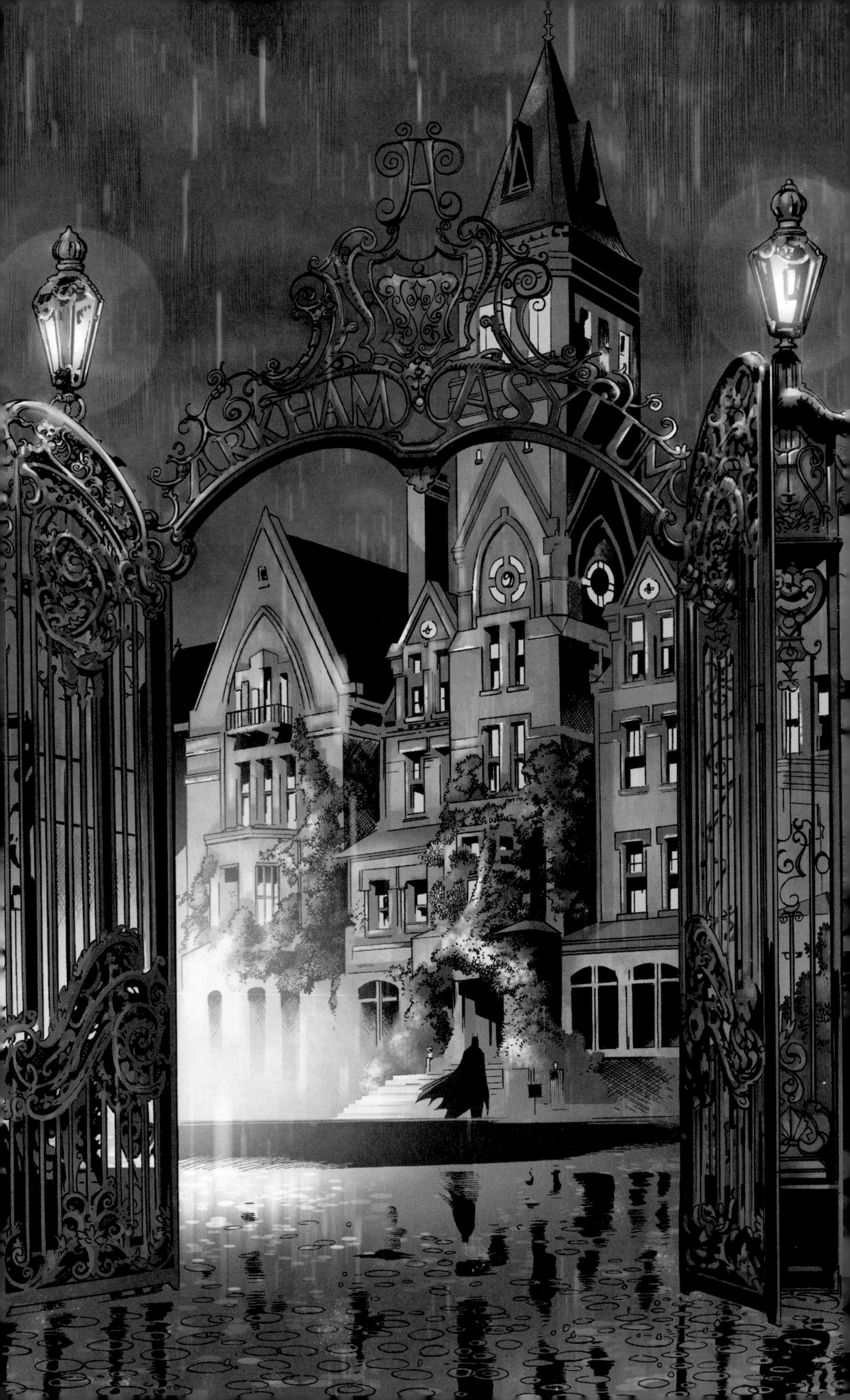
ARKHAM ASYLUM

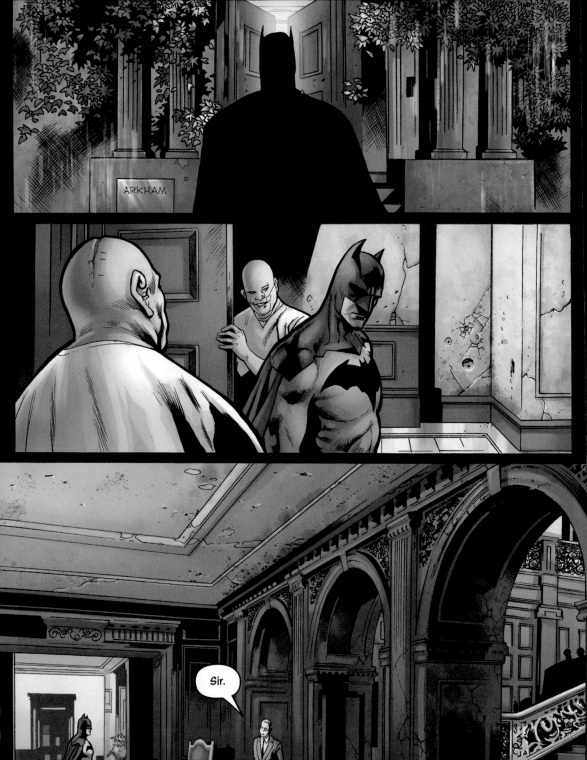

ARKHAM

Sir.

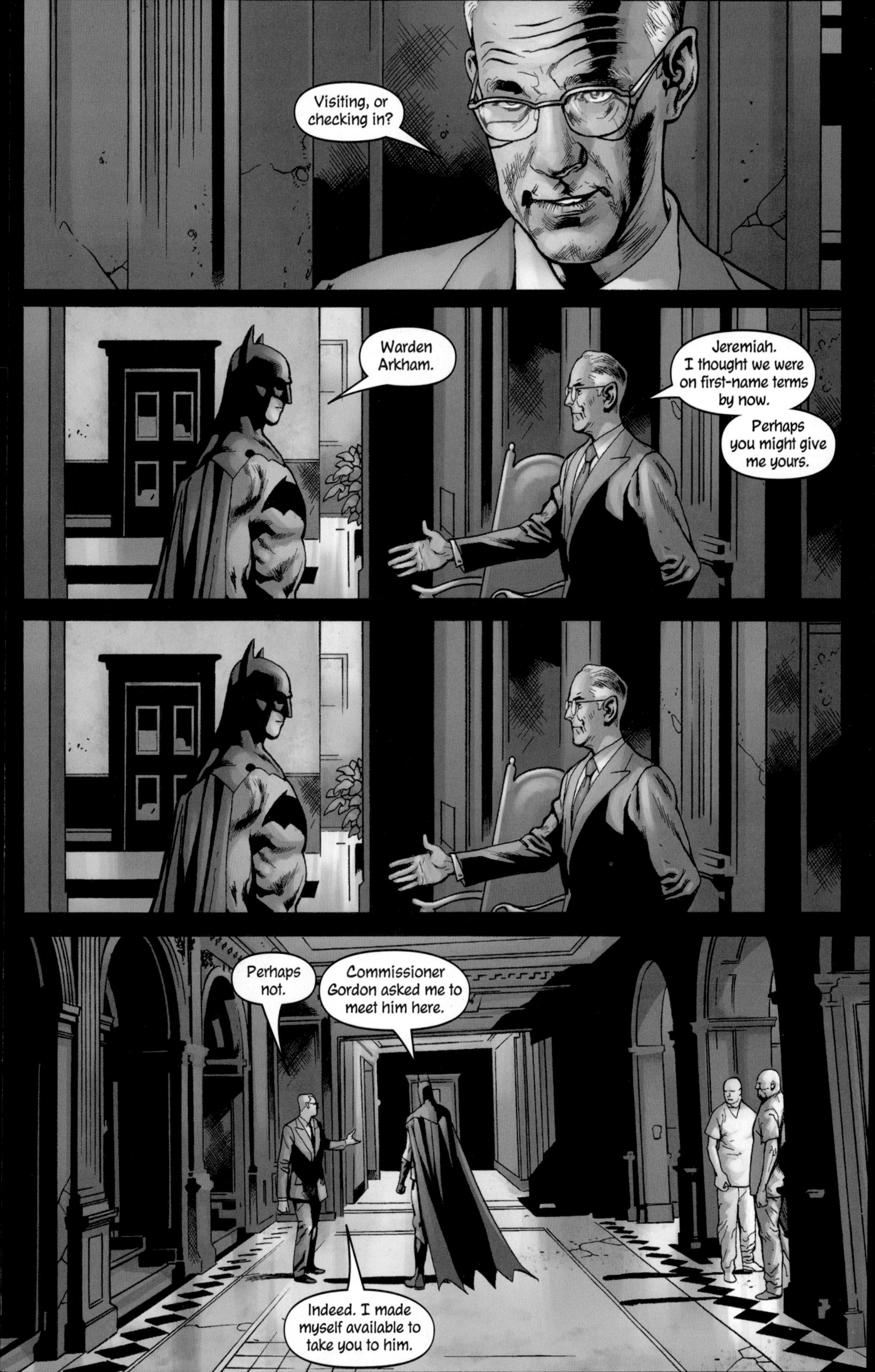
Visiting, or checking in?
Warden Arkham.
Jeremiah. I thought we were on first-name terms by now.
Perhaps you might give me yours.
Perhaps not.
Commissioner Gordon asked me to meet him here.
Indeed. I made myself available to take you to him.

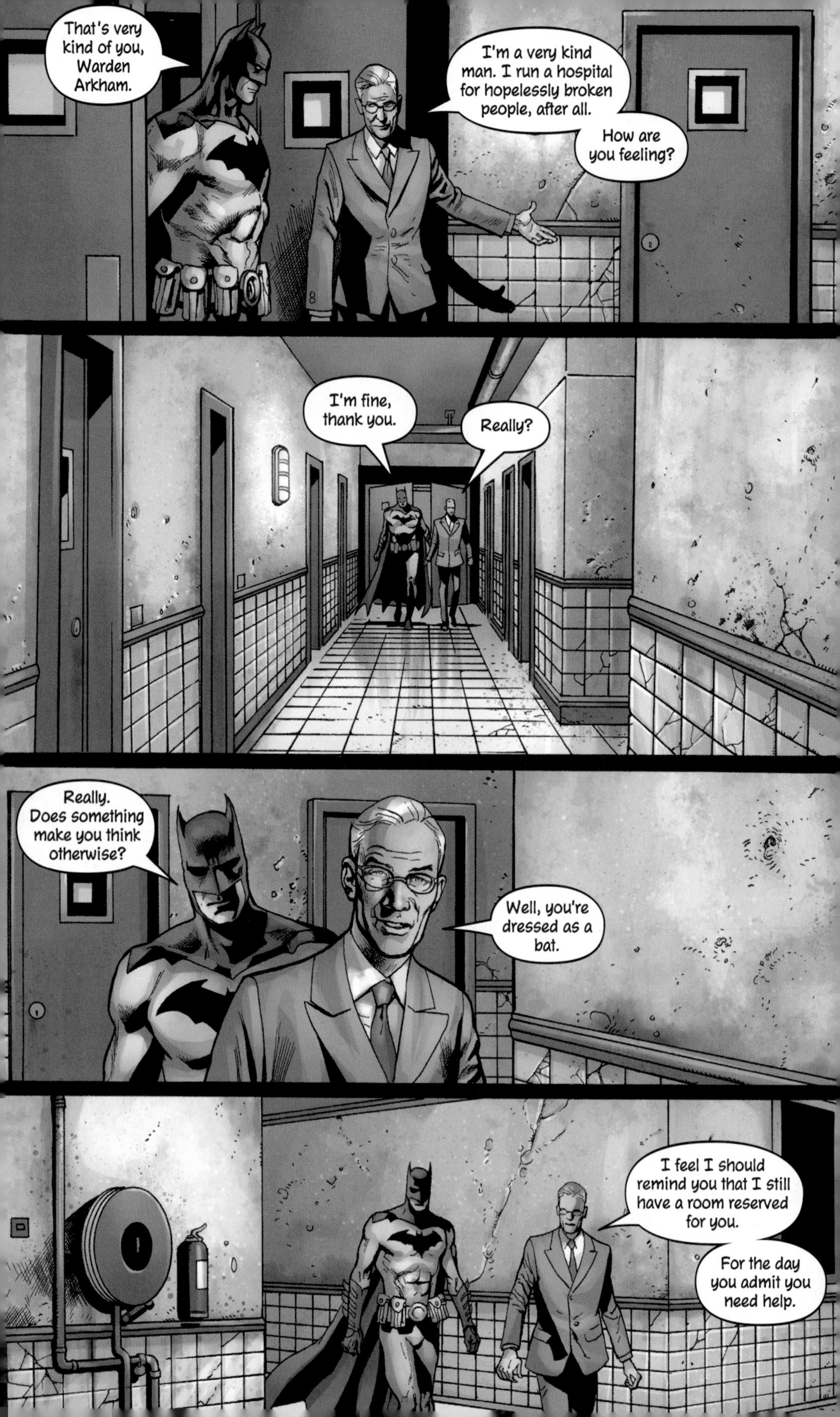
That's very kind of you, Warden Arkham.
I'm a very kind man. I run a hospital for hopelessly broken people, after all.
How are you feeling?
I'm fine, thank you.
Really?
Really. Does something make you think otherwise?
Well, you're dressed as a bat.
I feel I should remind you that I still have a room reserved for you.
For the day you admit you need help.

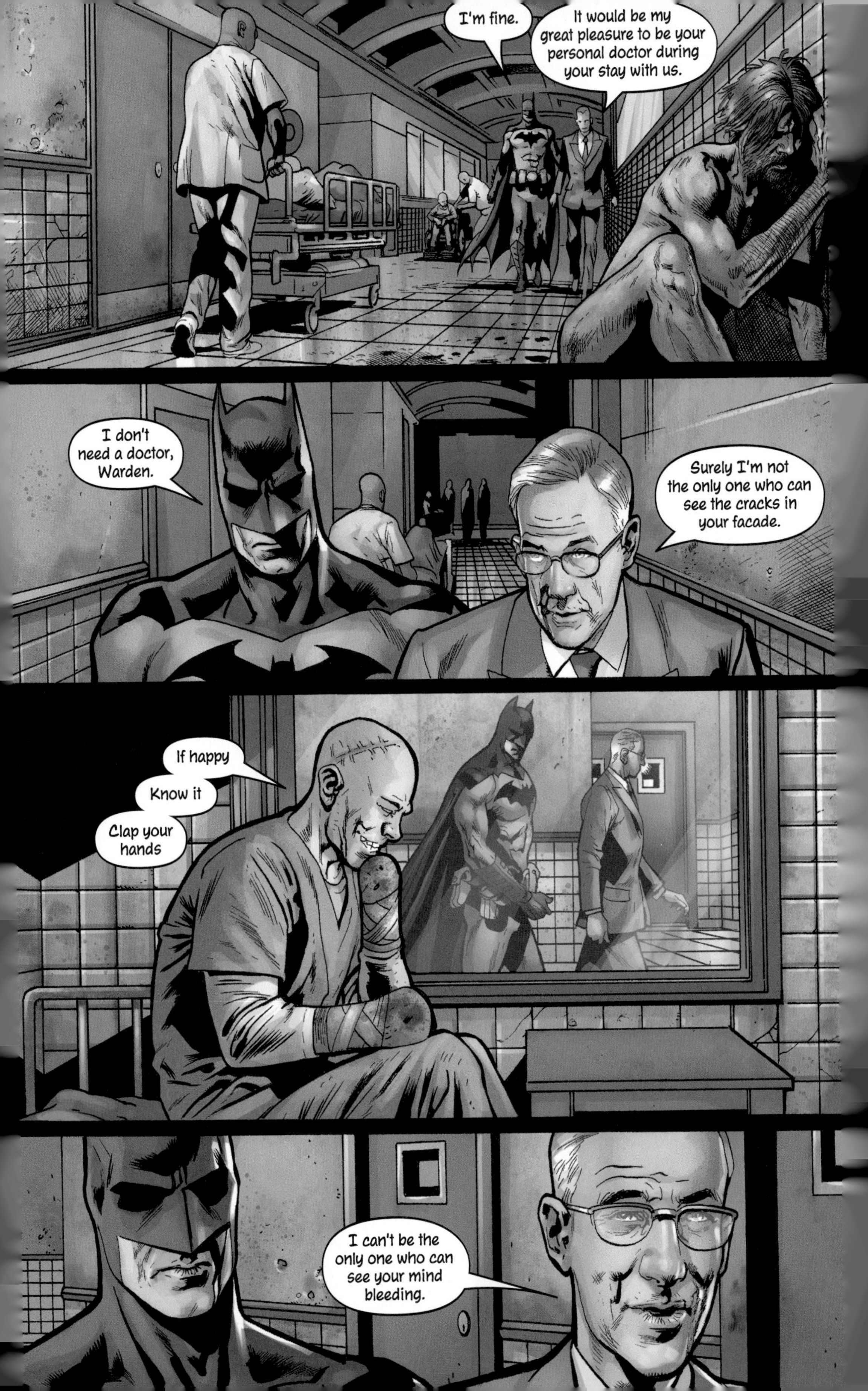
I'm fine.
It would be my great pleasure to be your personal doctor during your stay with us.
I don't need a doctor, Warden.
Surely I'm not the only one who can see the cracks in your facade.
If happy
Know it
Clap your hands
I can't be the only one who can see your mind bleeding.

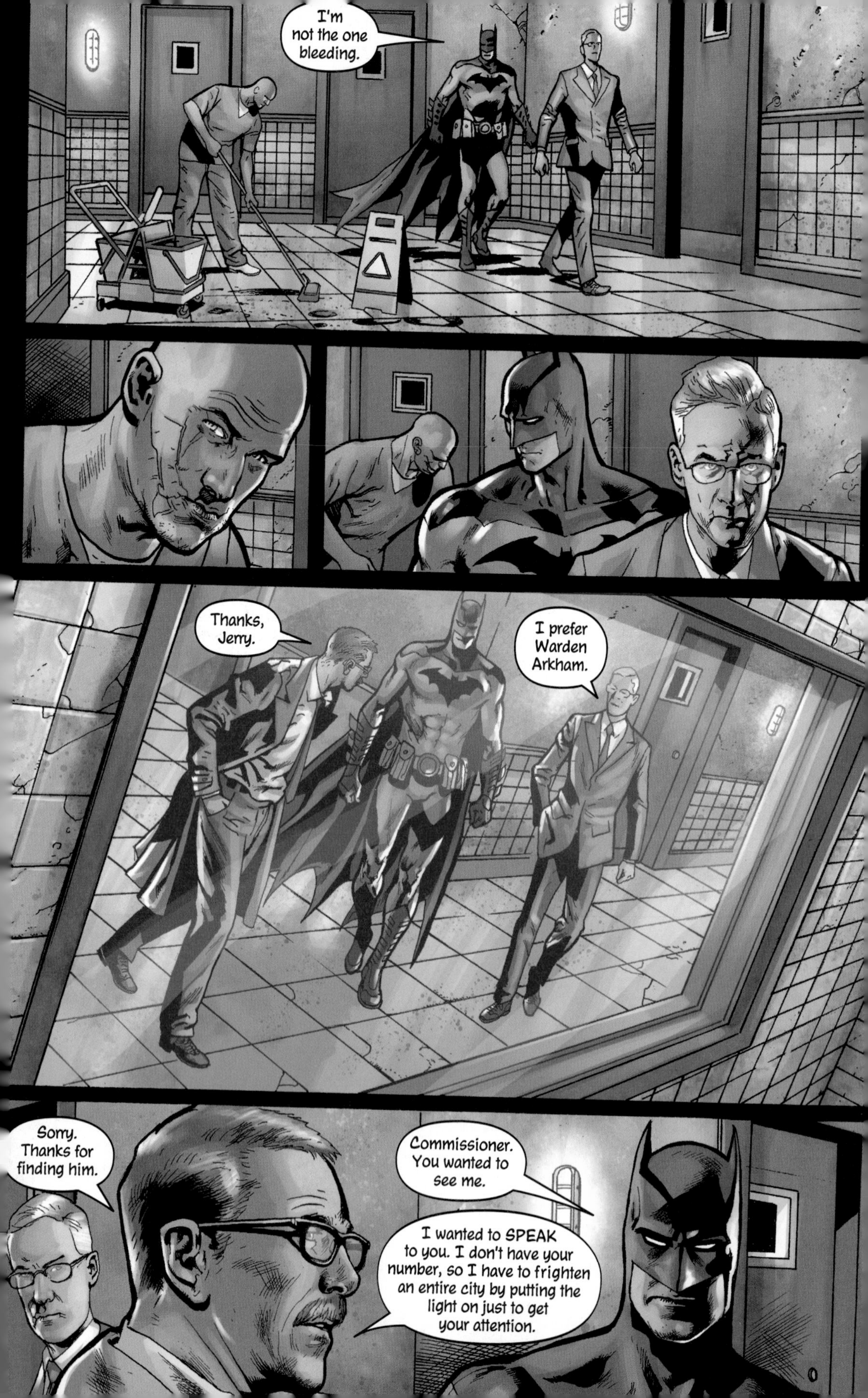
I'm not the one bleeding.
Thanks, Jerry.
I prefer Warden Arkham.
Sorry. Thanks for finding him.
Commissioner. You wanted to see me.
I wanted to SPEAK to you. I don't have your number, so I have to frighten an entire city by putting the light on just to get your attention.

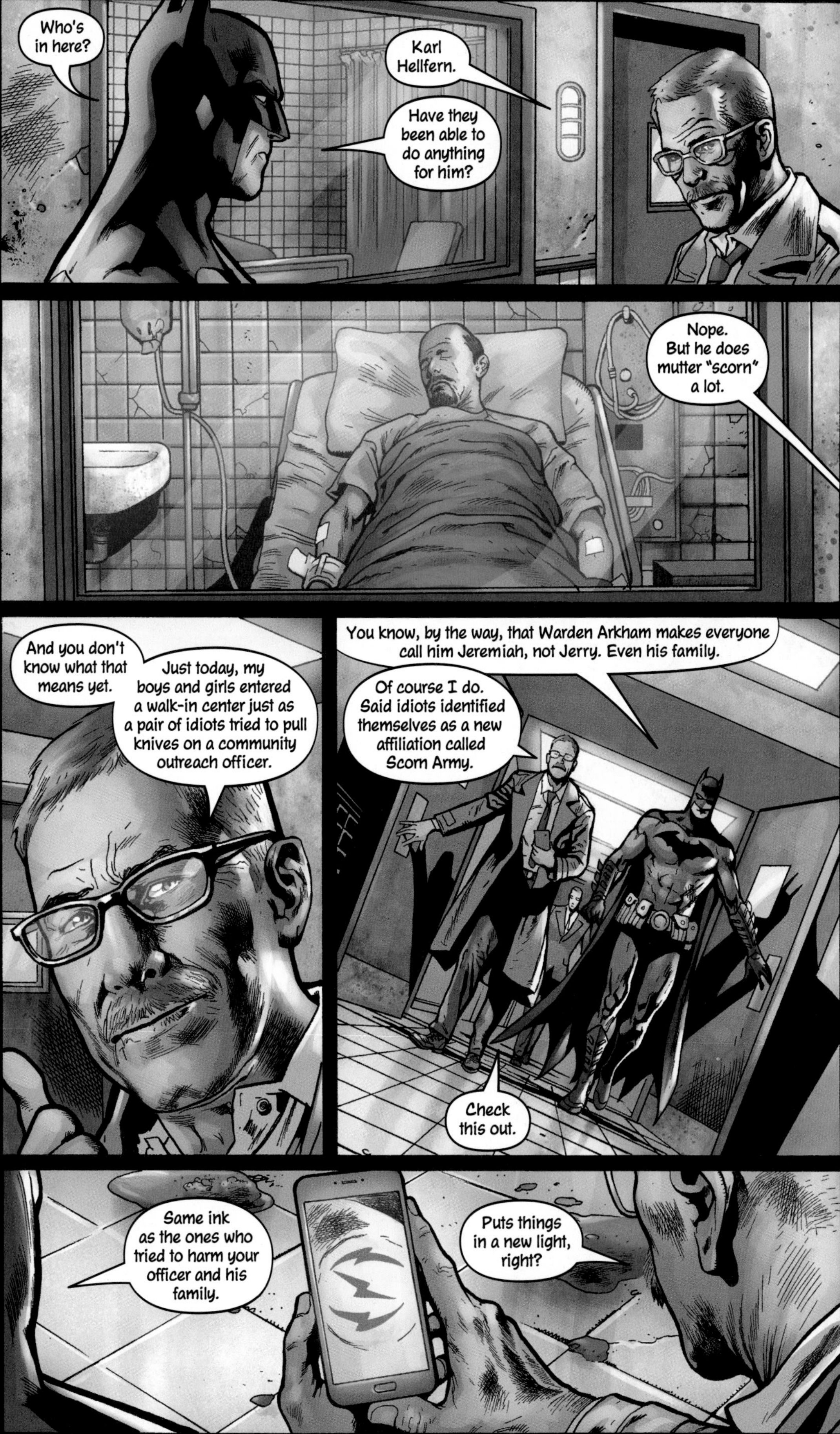
Who's in here?
Karl Hellfern.
Have they been able to do anything for him?
Nope. But he does mutter "scorn" a lot.
And you don't know what that means yet.
Just today, my boys and girls entered a walk-in center just as a pair of idiots tried to pull knives on a community outreach officer.
You know, by the way, that Warden Arkham makes everyone call him Jeremiah, not Jerry. Even his family.
Of course I do. Said idiots identified themselves as a new affiliation called Scorn Army.
Check this out.
Same ink as the ones who tried to harm your officer and his family.
Puts things in a new light, right?

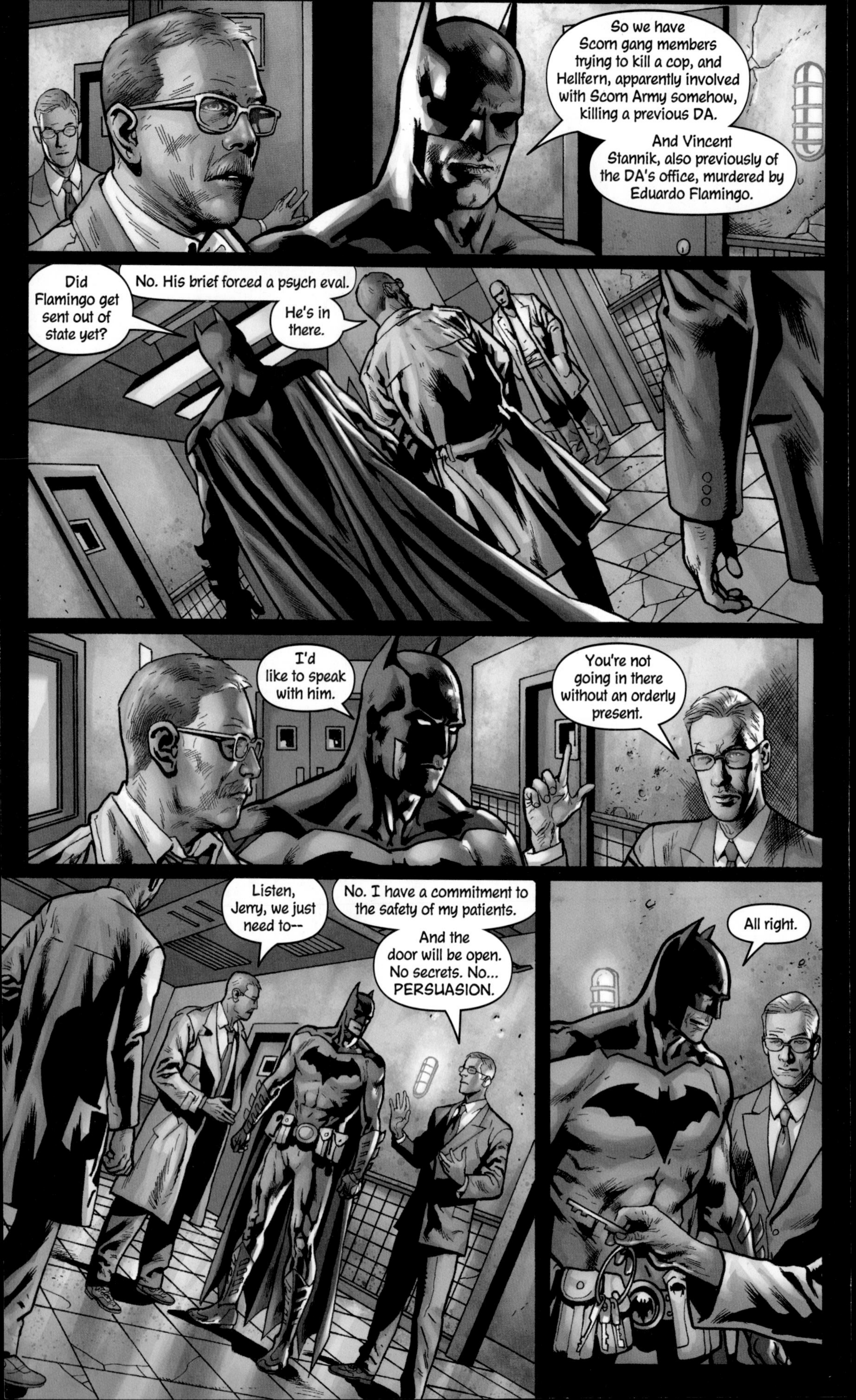
So we have Scorn gang members trying to kill a cop, and Hellfern, apparently involved with Scorn Army somehow, killing a previous DA.
And Vincent Stannik, also previously of the DA's office, murdered by Eduardo Flamingo.
Did Flamingo get sent out of state yet?
No. His brief forced a psych eval.
He's in there.
I'd like to speak with him.
You're not going in there without an orderly present.
Listen, Jerry, we just need to--
No. I have a commitment to the safety of my patients.
And the door will be open. No secrets. No... PERSUASION.
All right.

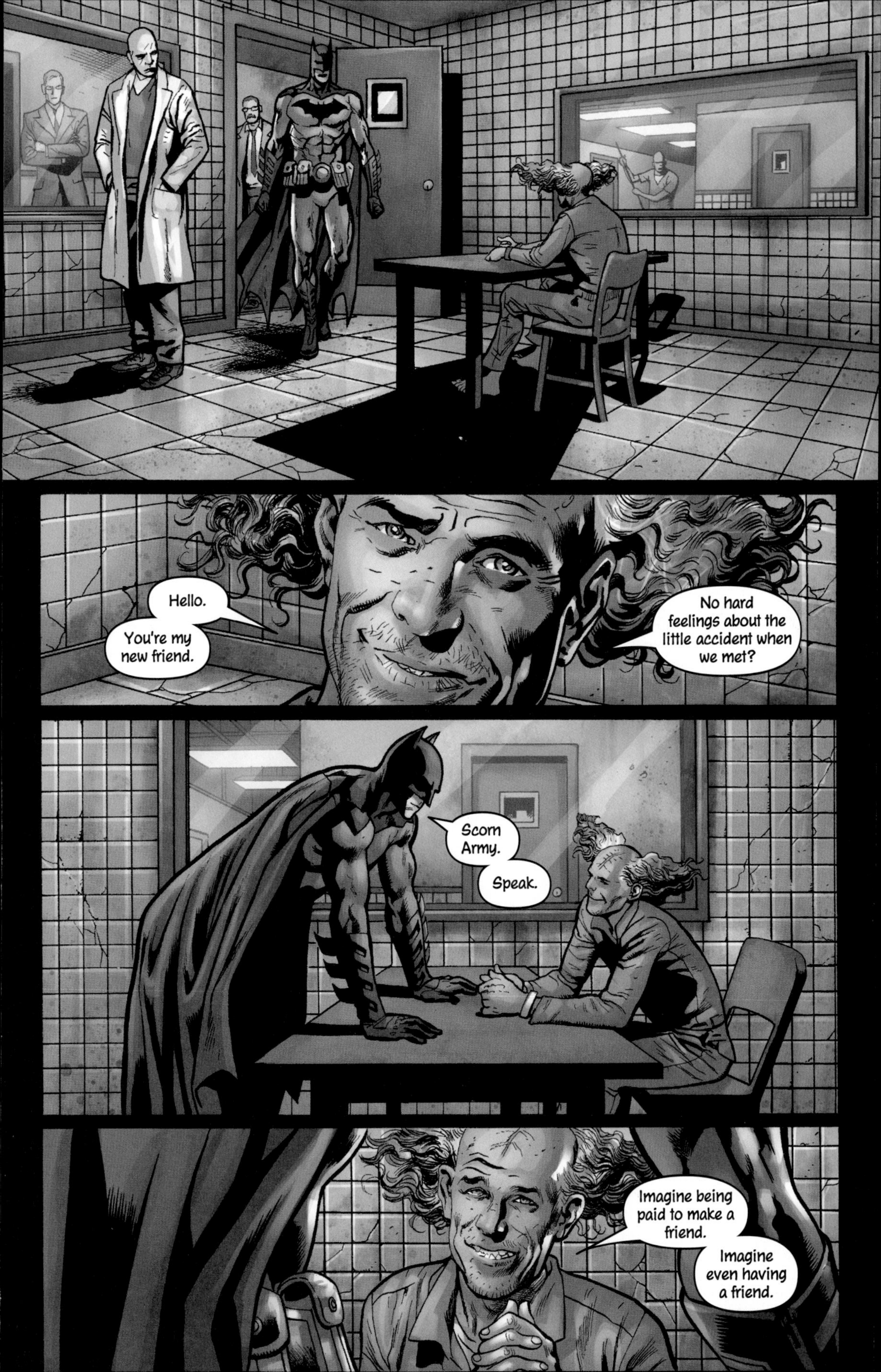
Hello.
You're my new friend.
No hard feelings about the little accident when we met?
Scorn Army.
Speak.
Imagine being paid to make a friend.
Imagine even having a friend.

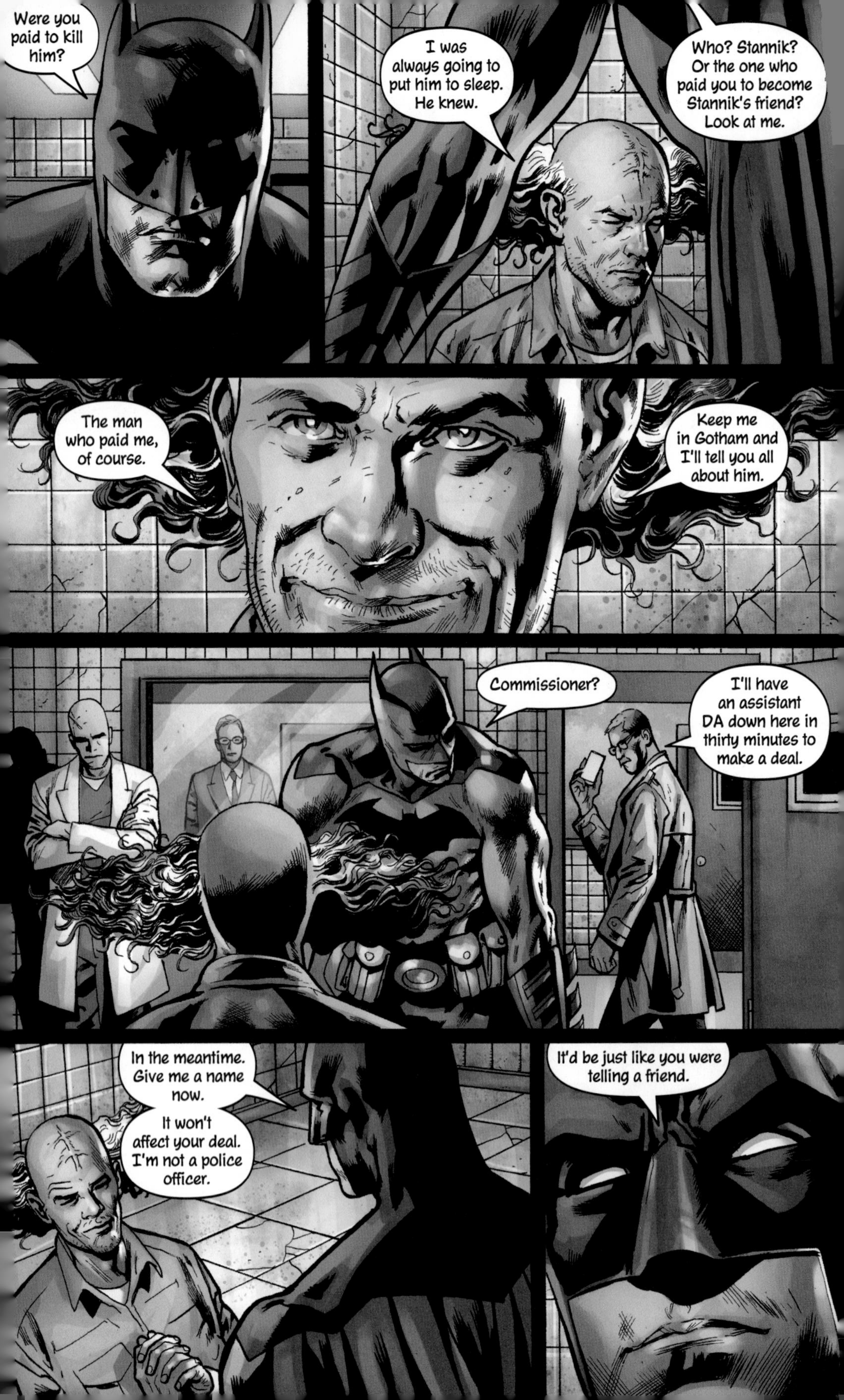
Were you paid to kill him?
I was always going to put him to sleep. He knew.
Who? Stannik? Or the one who paid you to become Stannik's friend? Look at me.
The man who paid me, of course.
Keep me in Gotham and I'll tell you all about him.
Commissioner?
I'll have an assistant DA down here in thirty minutes to make a deal.
In the meantime. Give me a name now.
It won't affect your deal. I'm not a police officer.
It'd be just like you were telling a friend.

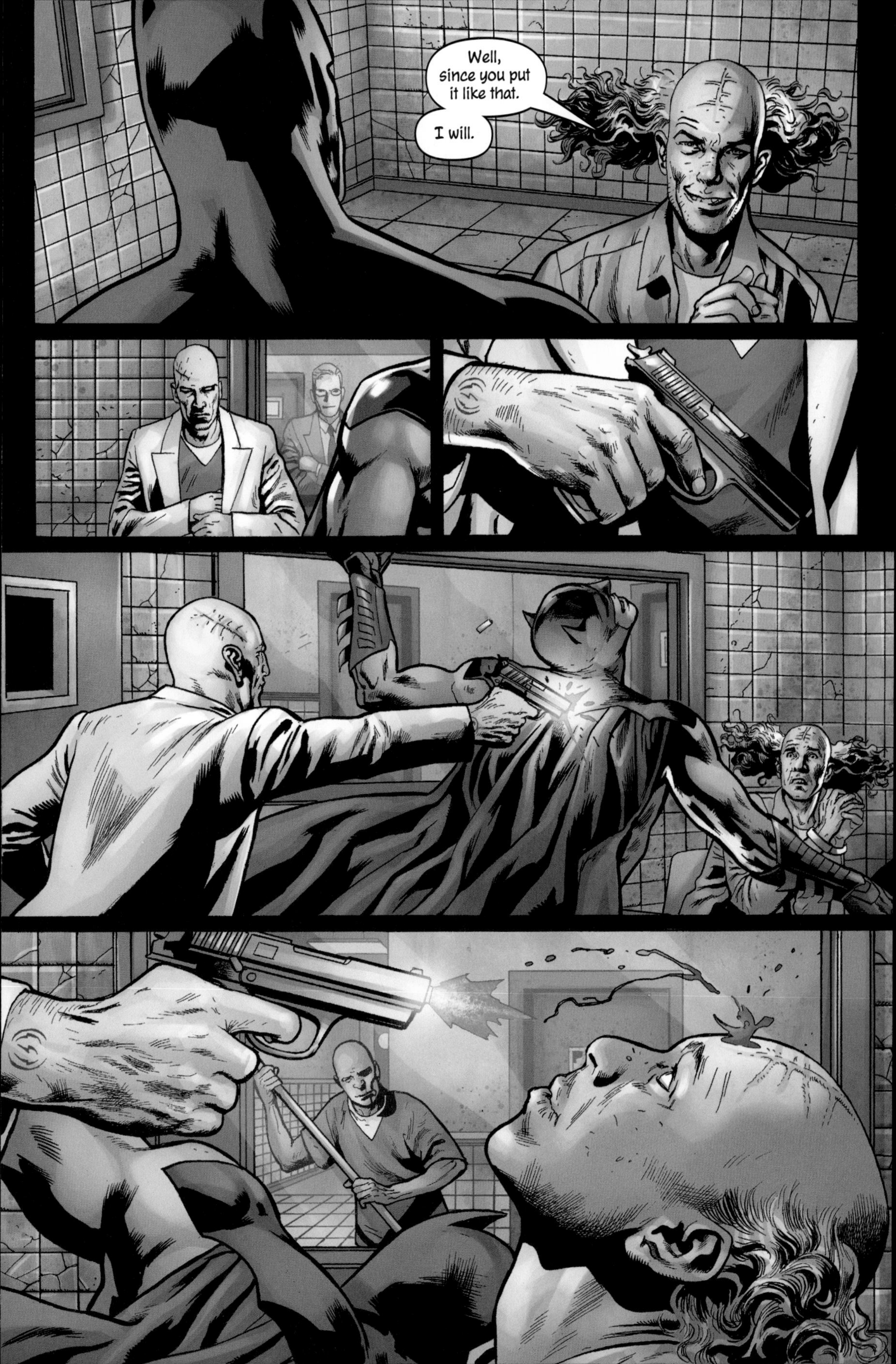
Well, since you put it like that.
I will.

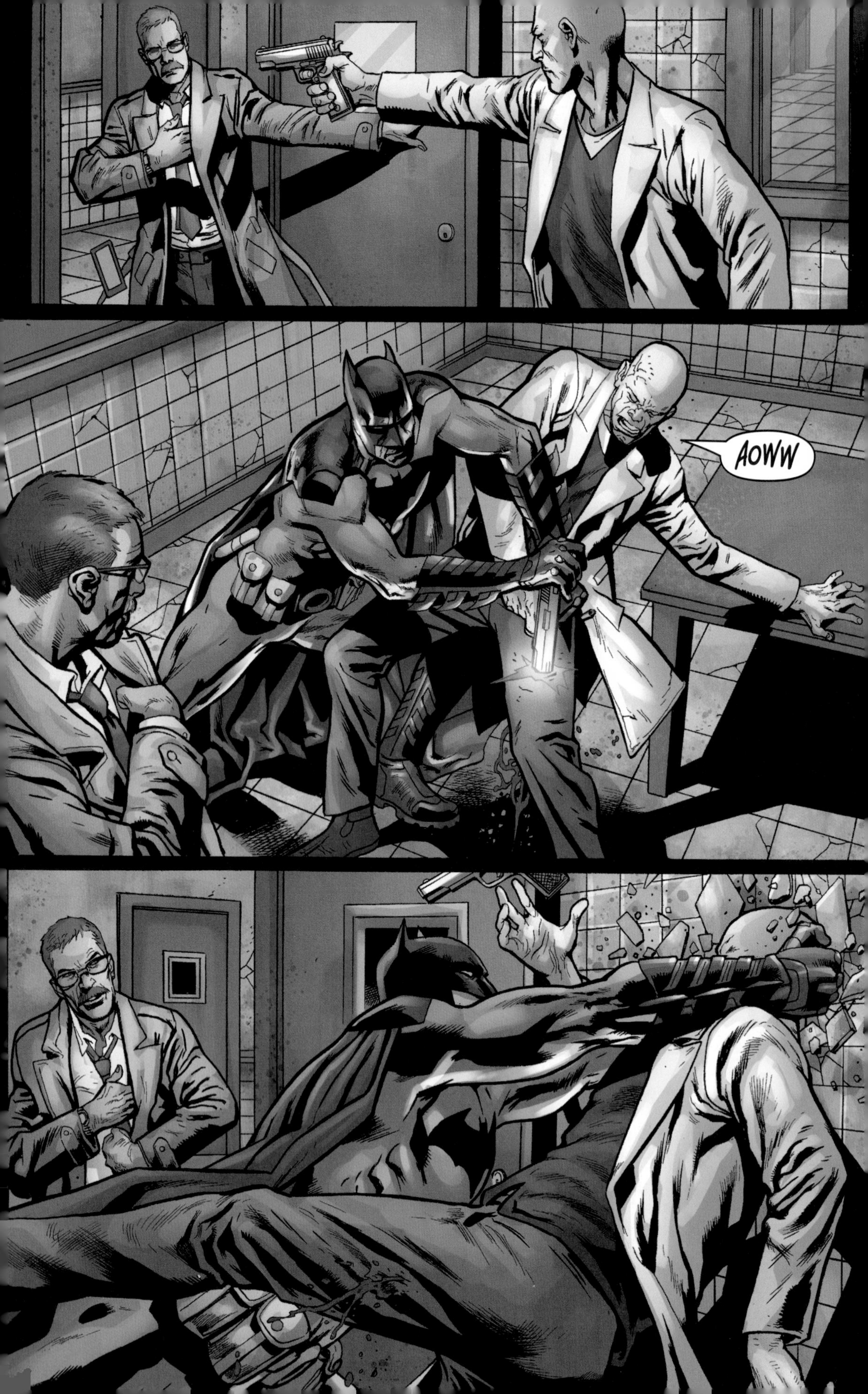
AOWW

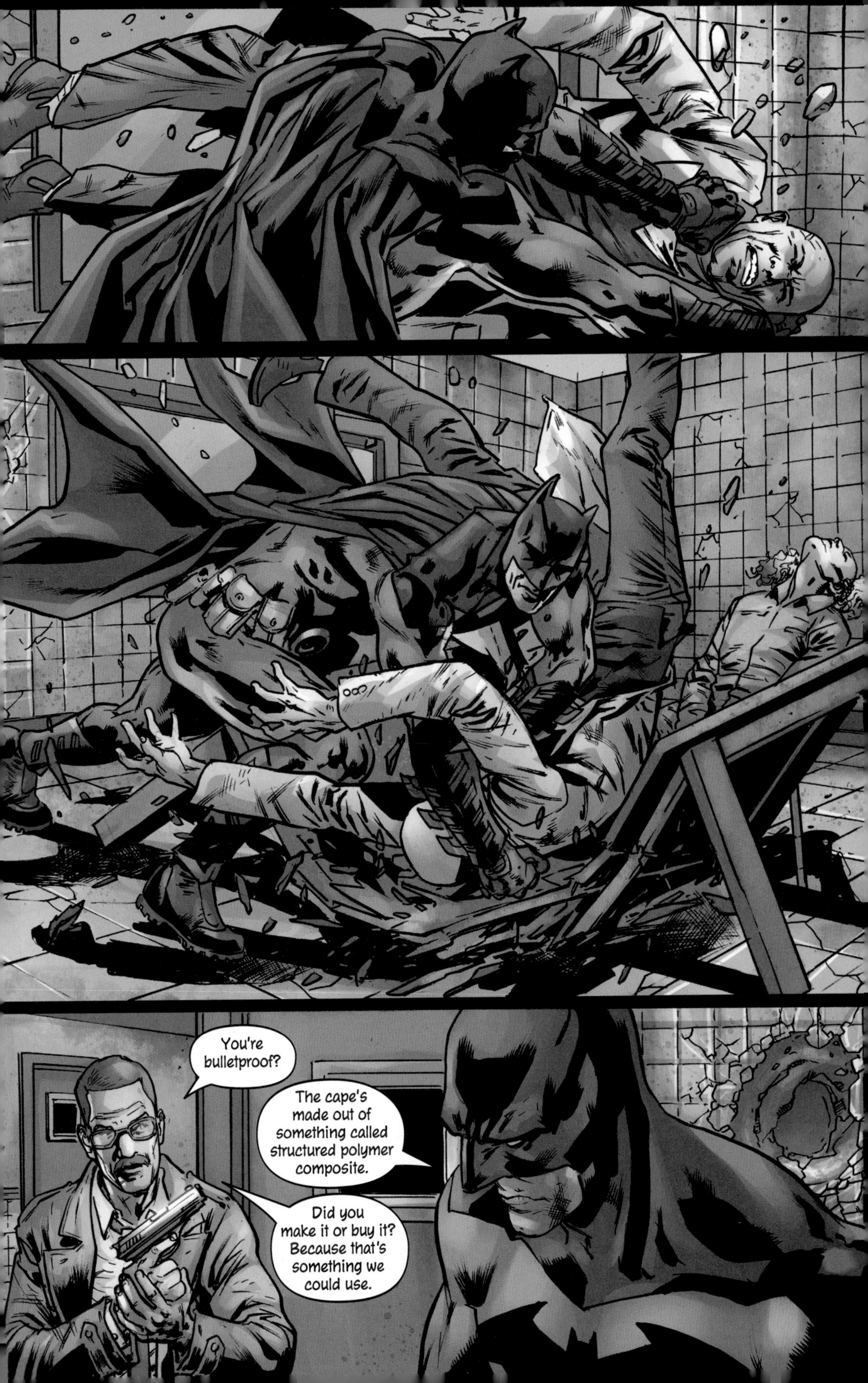
You're bulletproof?
The cape's made out of something called structured polymer composite.
Did you make it or buy it? Because that's something we could use.

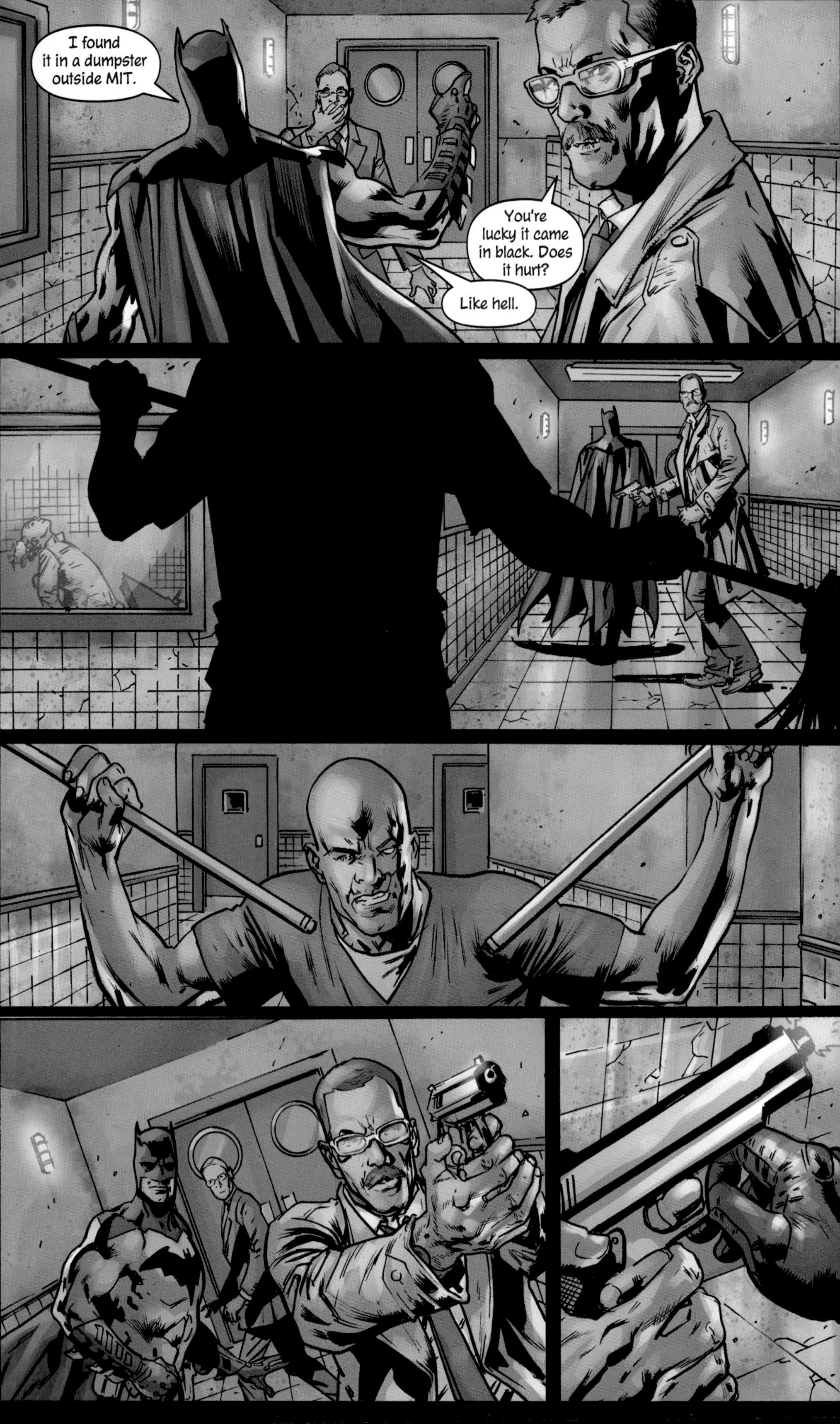
I found it in a dumpster outside MIT.
You're lucky it came in black. Does it hurt?
Like hell.

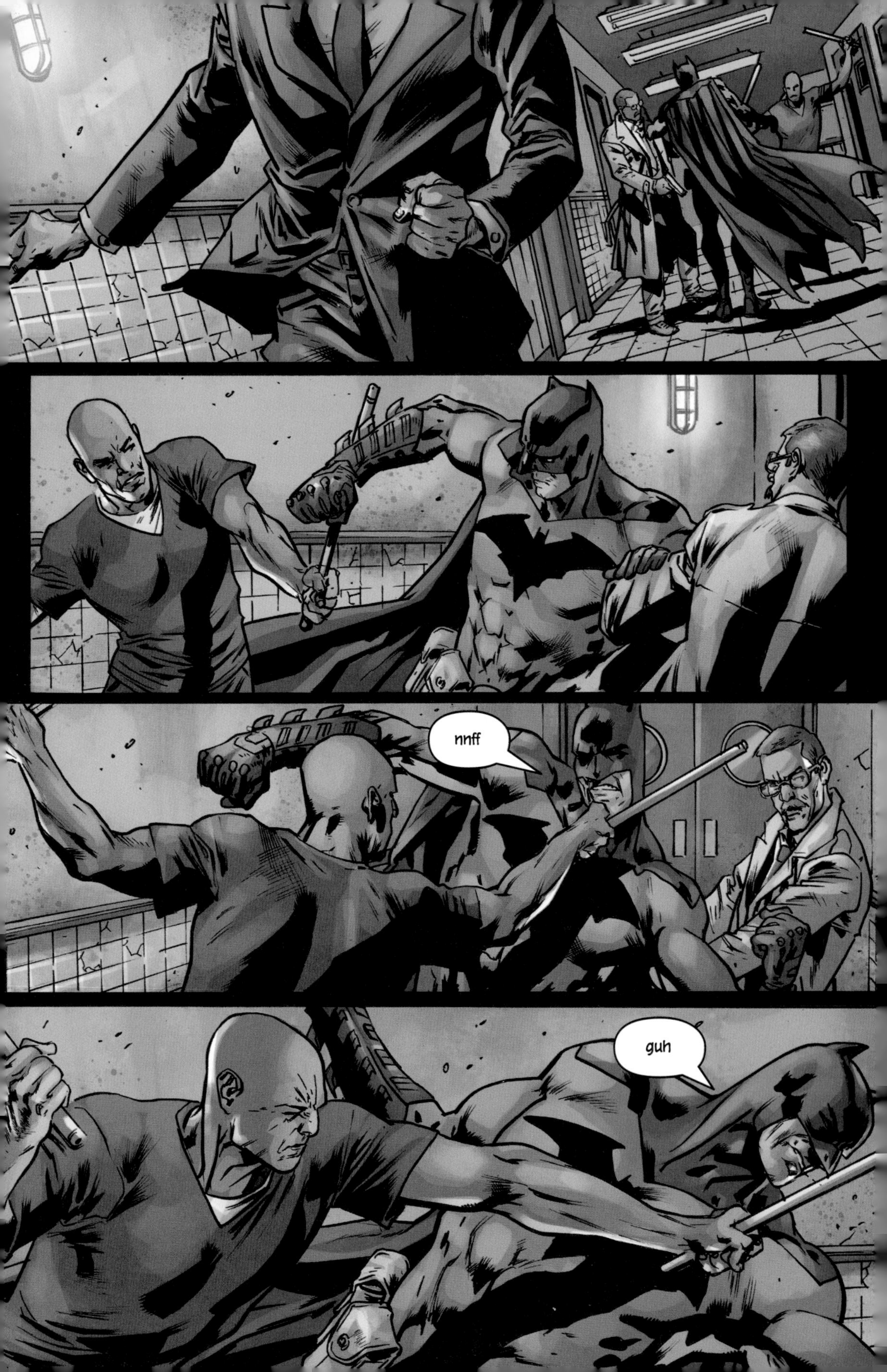
nnff
guh

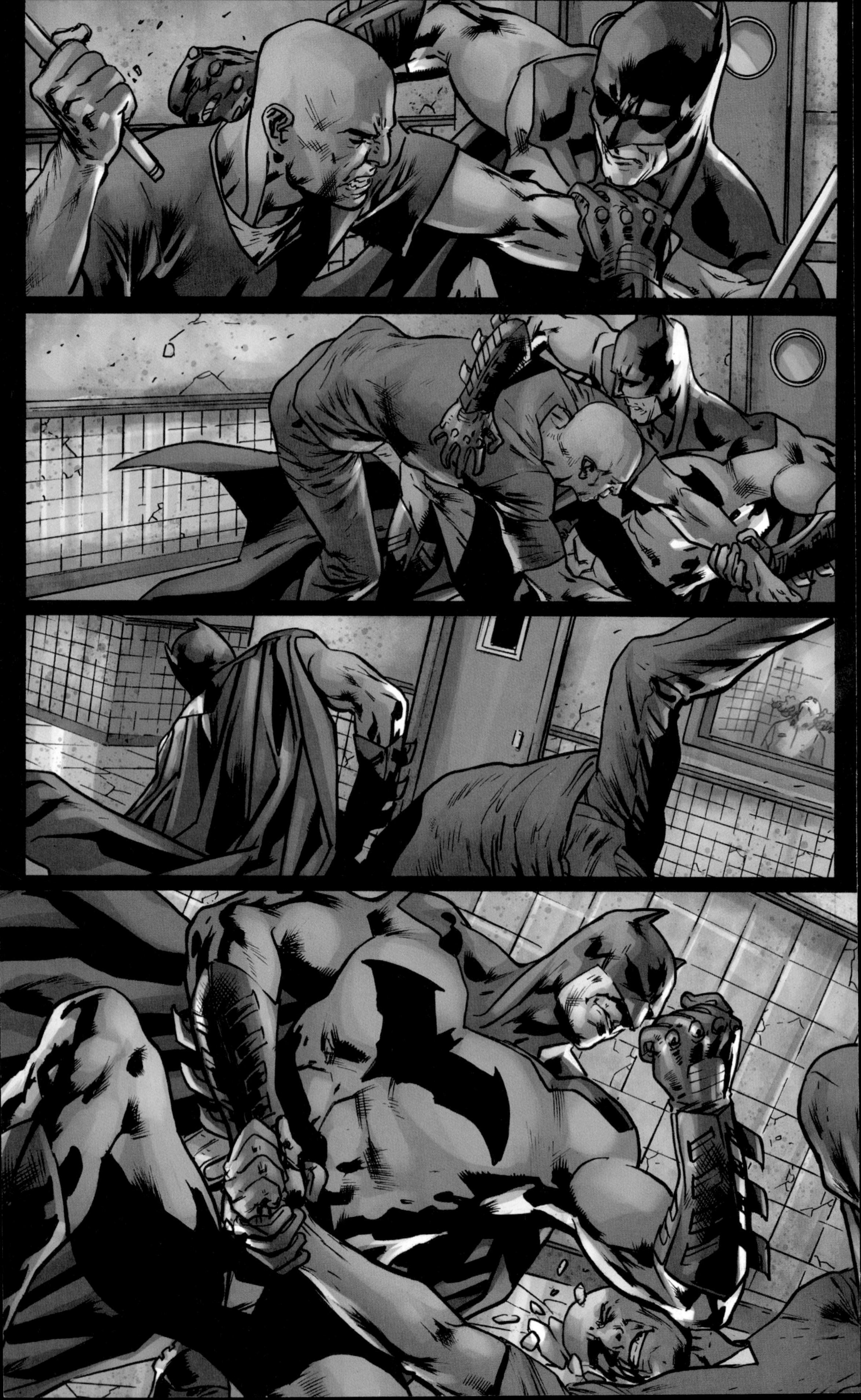

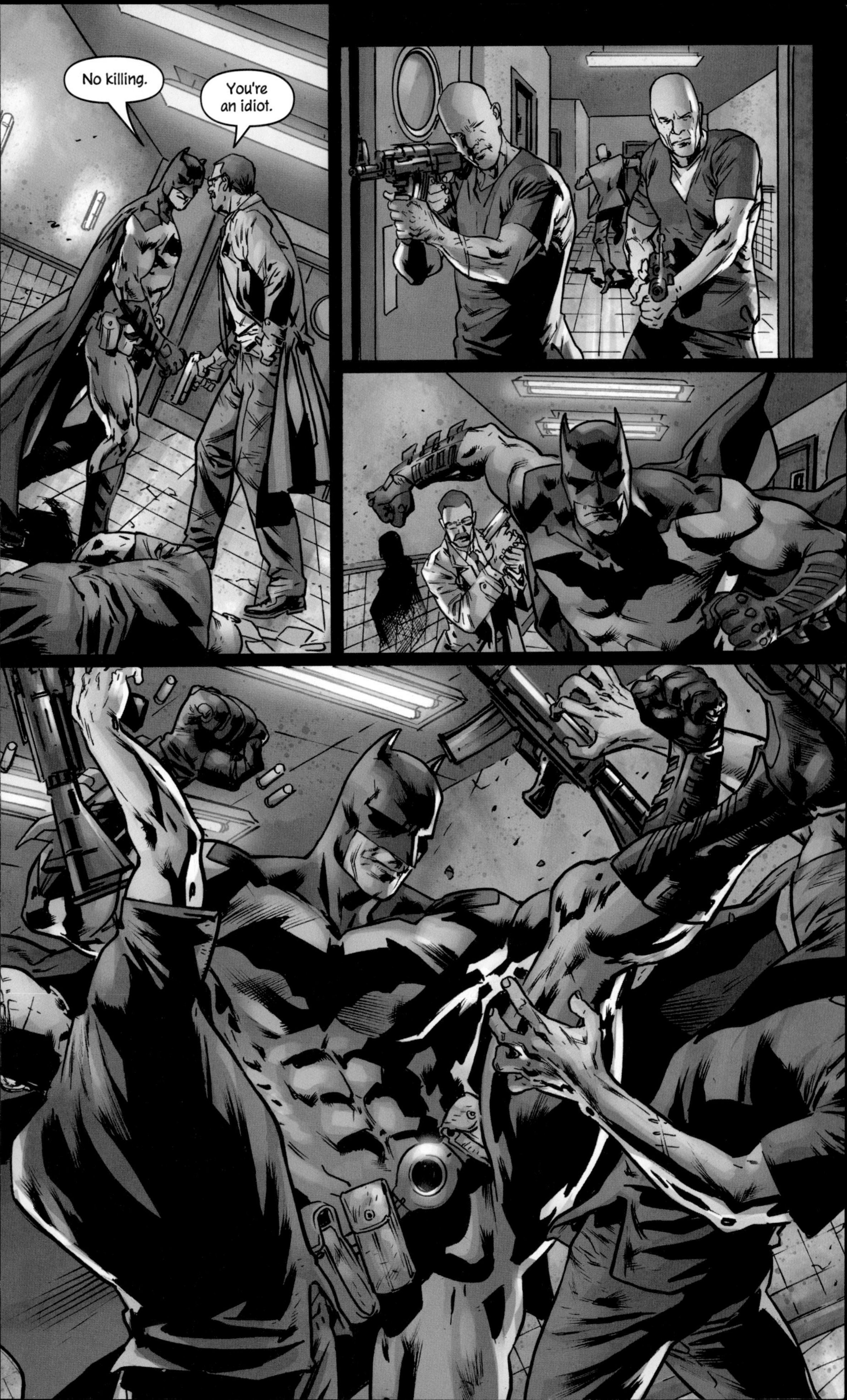
No killing.
You're an idiot.

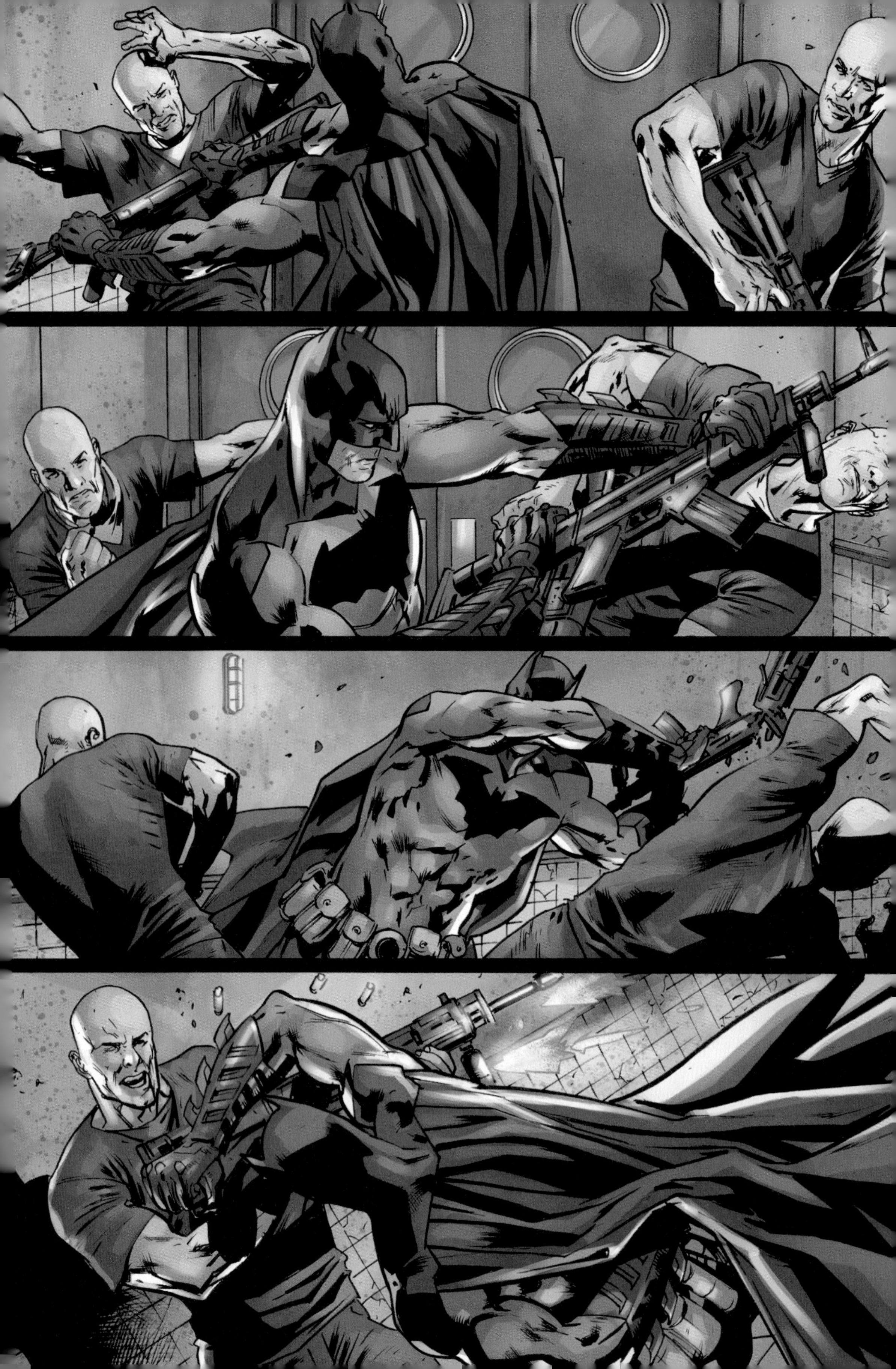

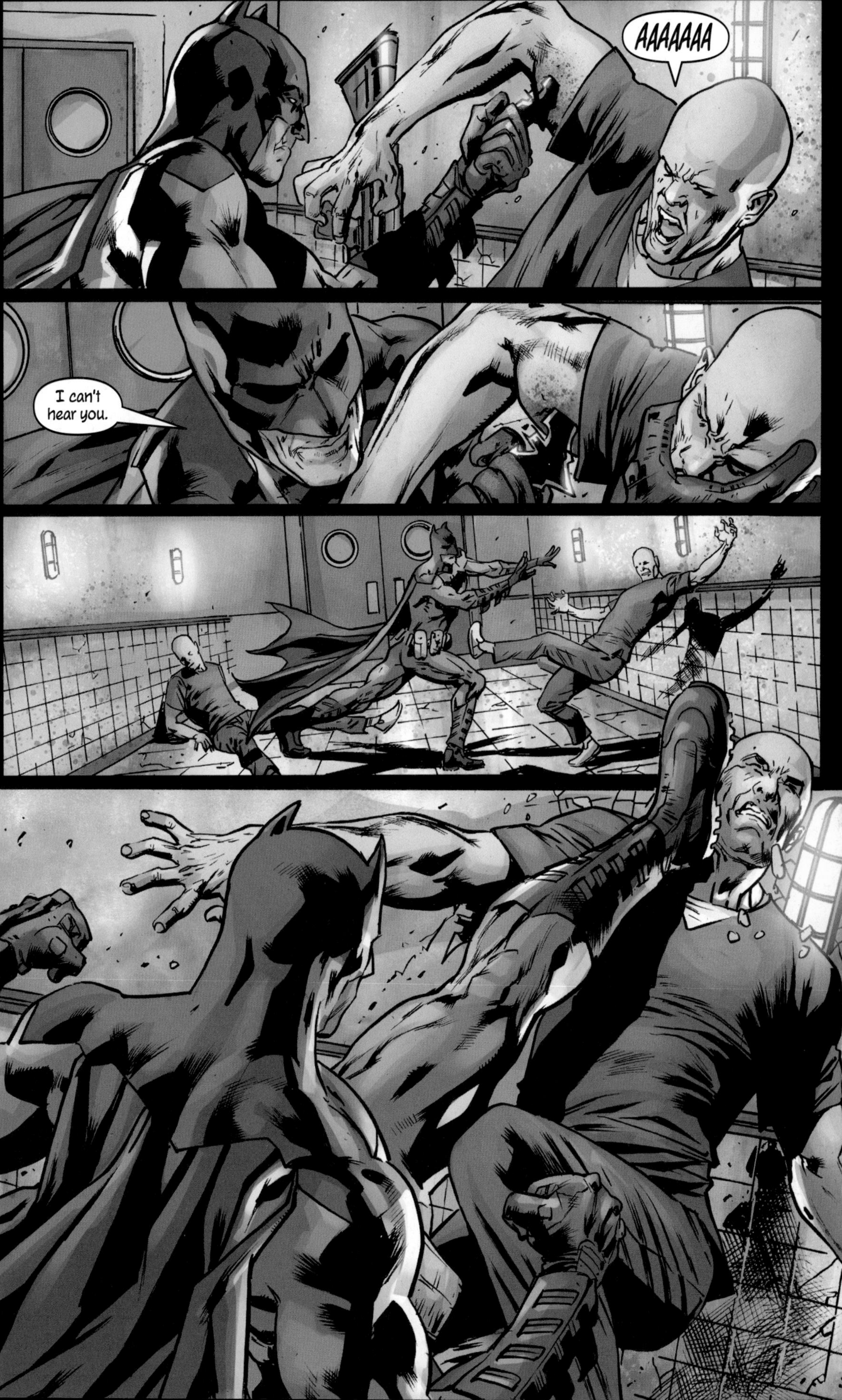
AAAAAAA
I can't hear you.

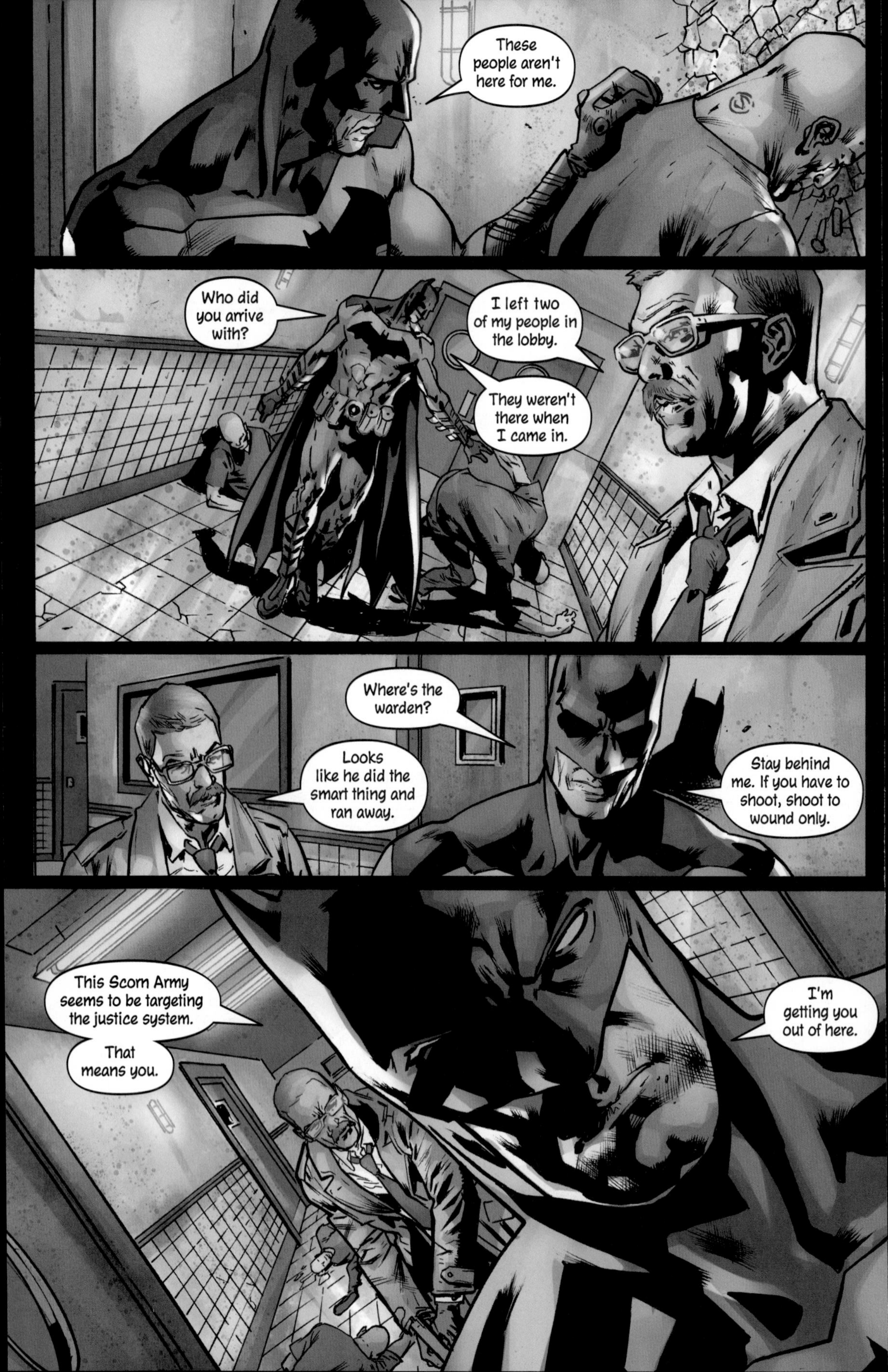
These people aren't here for me.
Who did you arrive with?
I left two of my people in the lobby.
They weren't there when I came in.
Where's the warden?
Looks like he did the smart thing and ran away.
Stay behind me. If you have to shoot, shoot to wound only.
This Scorn Army seems to be targeting the justice system.
That means you.
I'm getting you out of here.

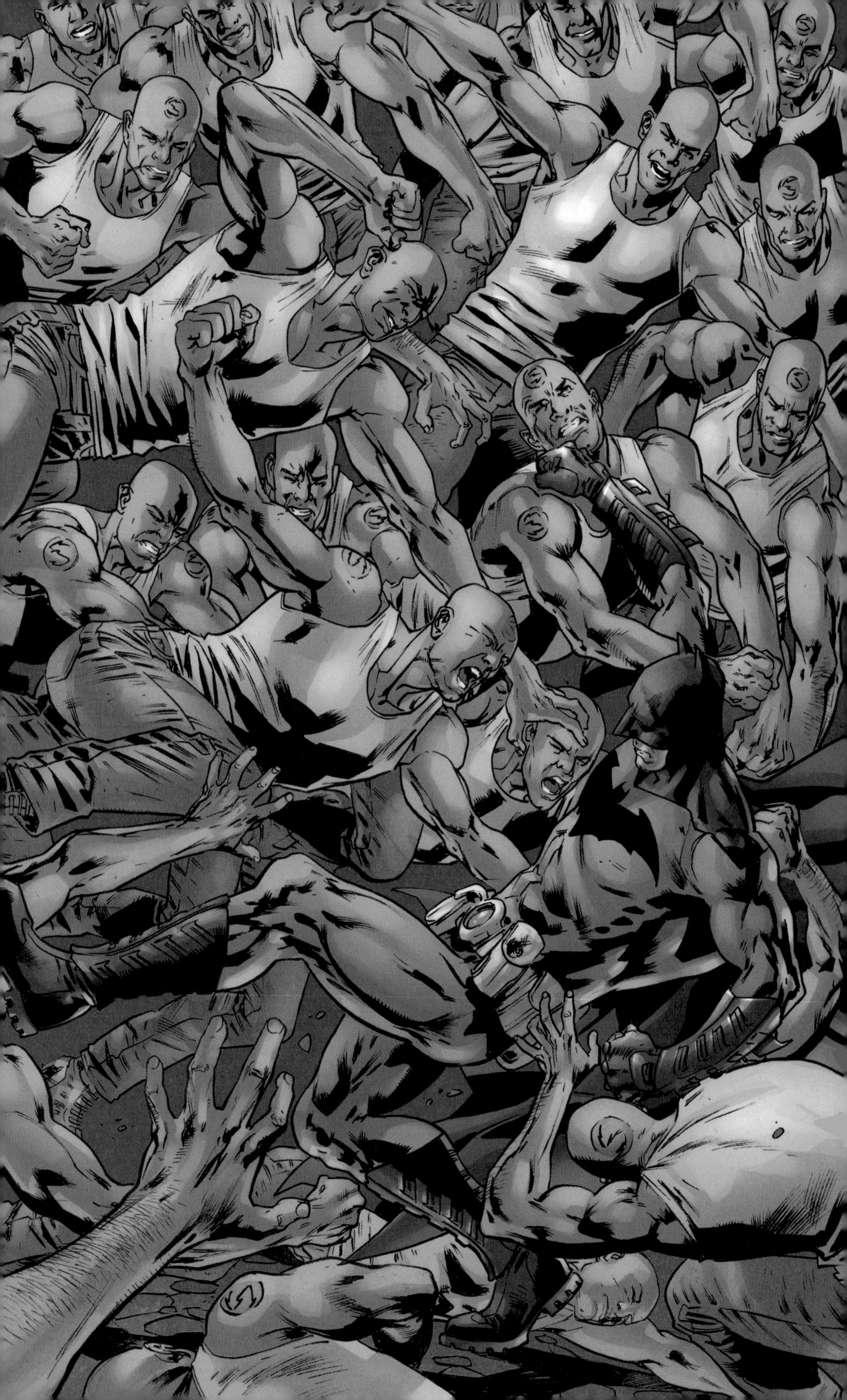

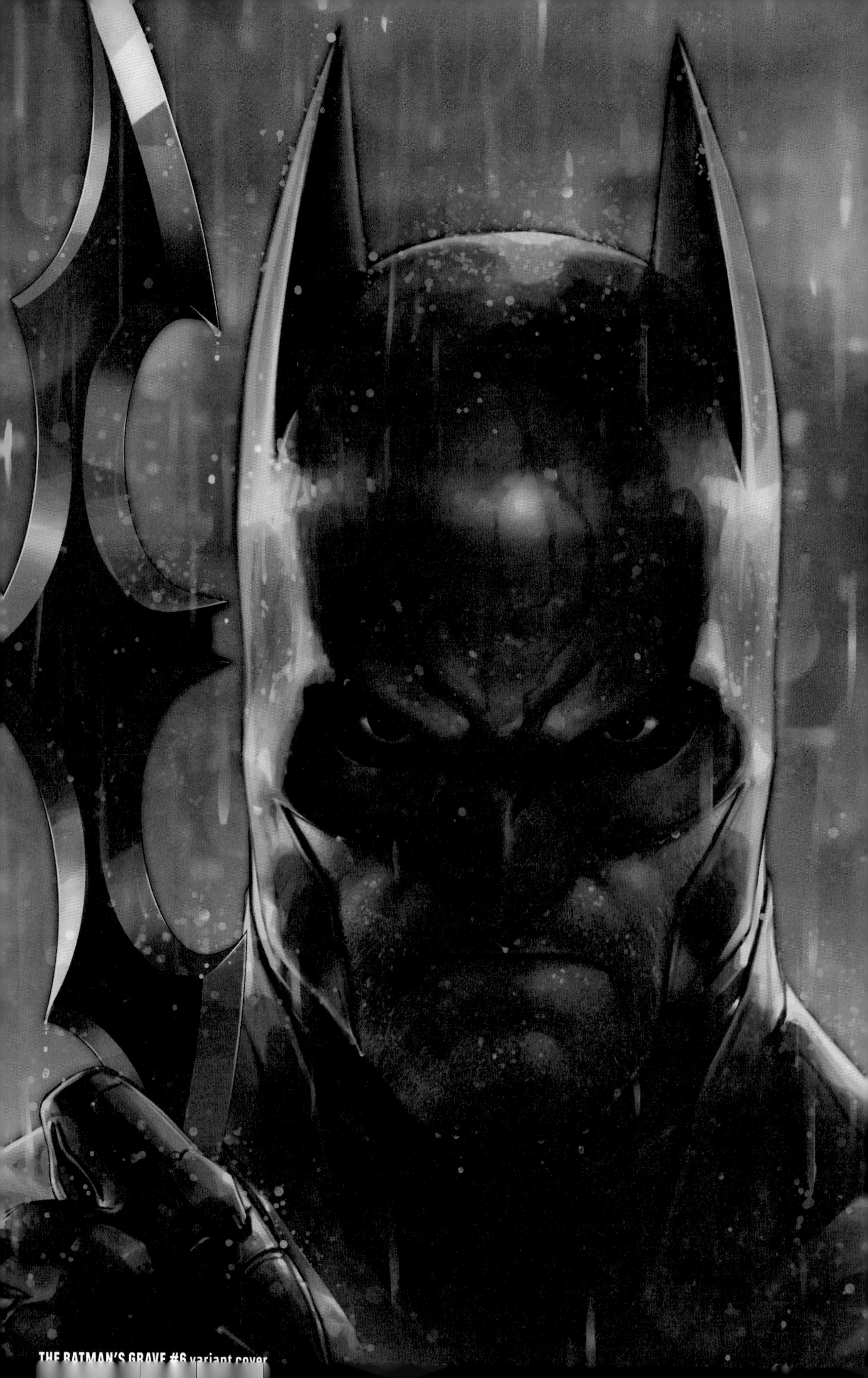

THE BATMAN'S GRAVE #6 variant cover

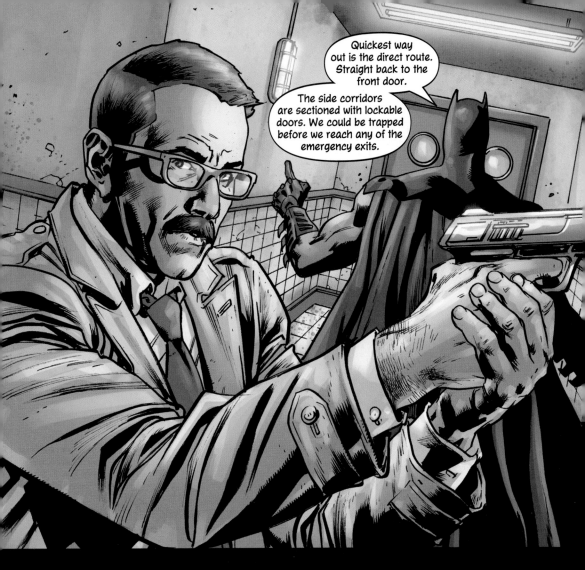

Chapter 6

Writer	Art
WARREN ELLIS	**BRYAN HITCH**

Colors	Letters
ALEX SINCLAIR	**RICHARD STARKINGS**

Cover	Variant Cover
BRYAN HITCH &	**JEEHYUNG**
ALEX SINCLAIR	**LEE**

Associate Editor	Editor
ANDREW MARINO	**MARIE JAVINS**

BATMAN created by BOB KANE with BILL FINGER

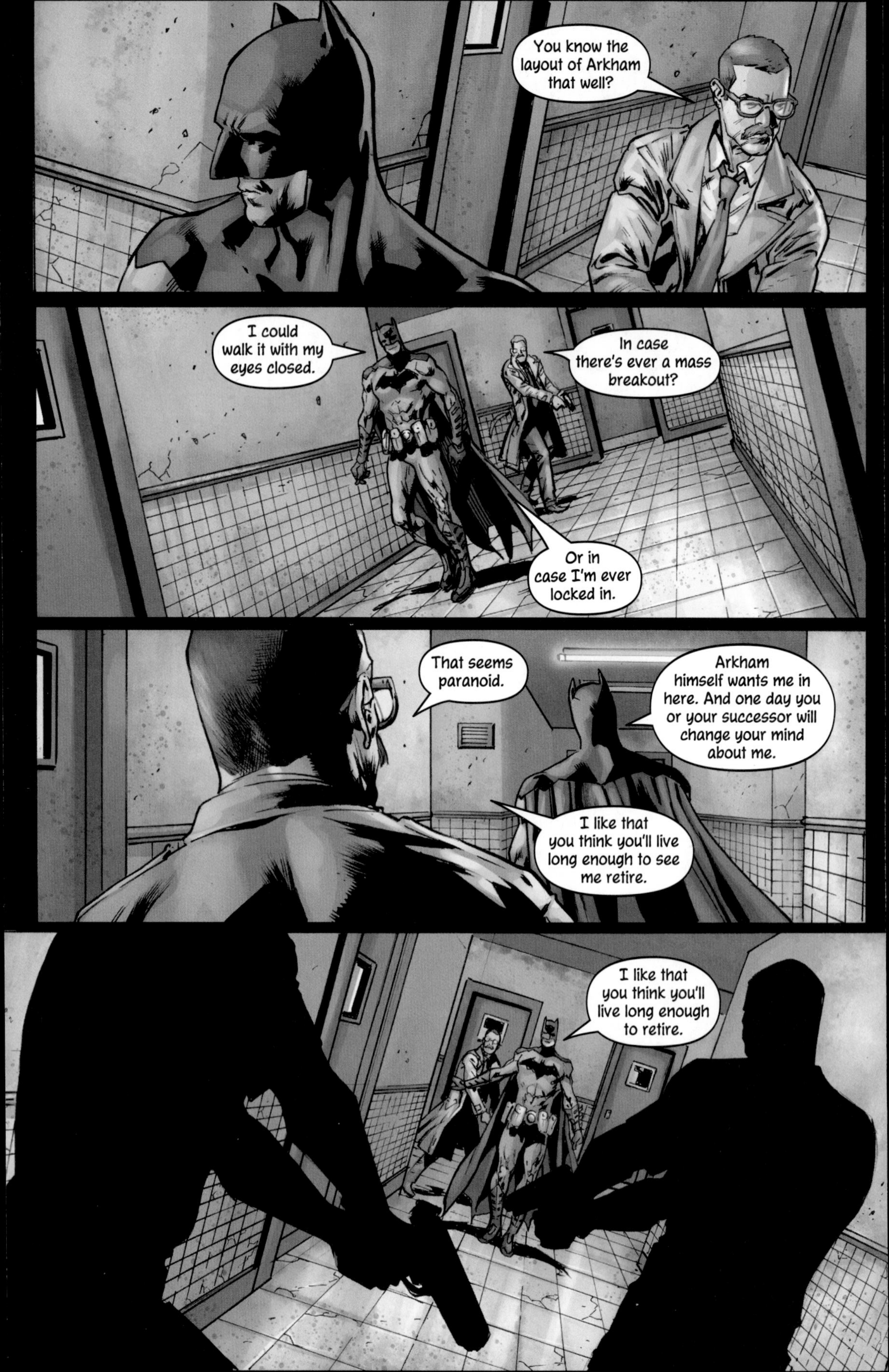
You know the layout of Arkham that well?
I could walk it with my eyes closed.
In case there's ever a mass breakout?
Or in case I'm ever locked in.
That seems paranoid.
Arkham himself wants me in here. And one day you or your successor will change your mind about me.
I like that you think you'll live long enough to see me retire.
I like that you think you'll live long enough to retire.

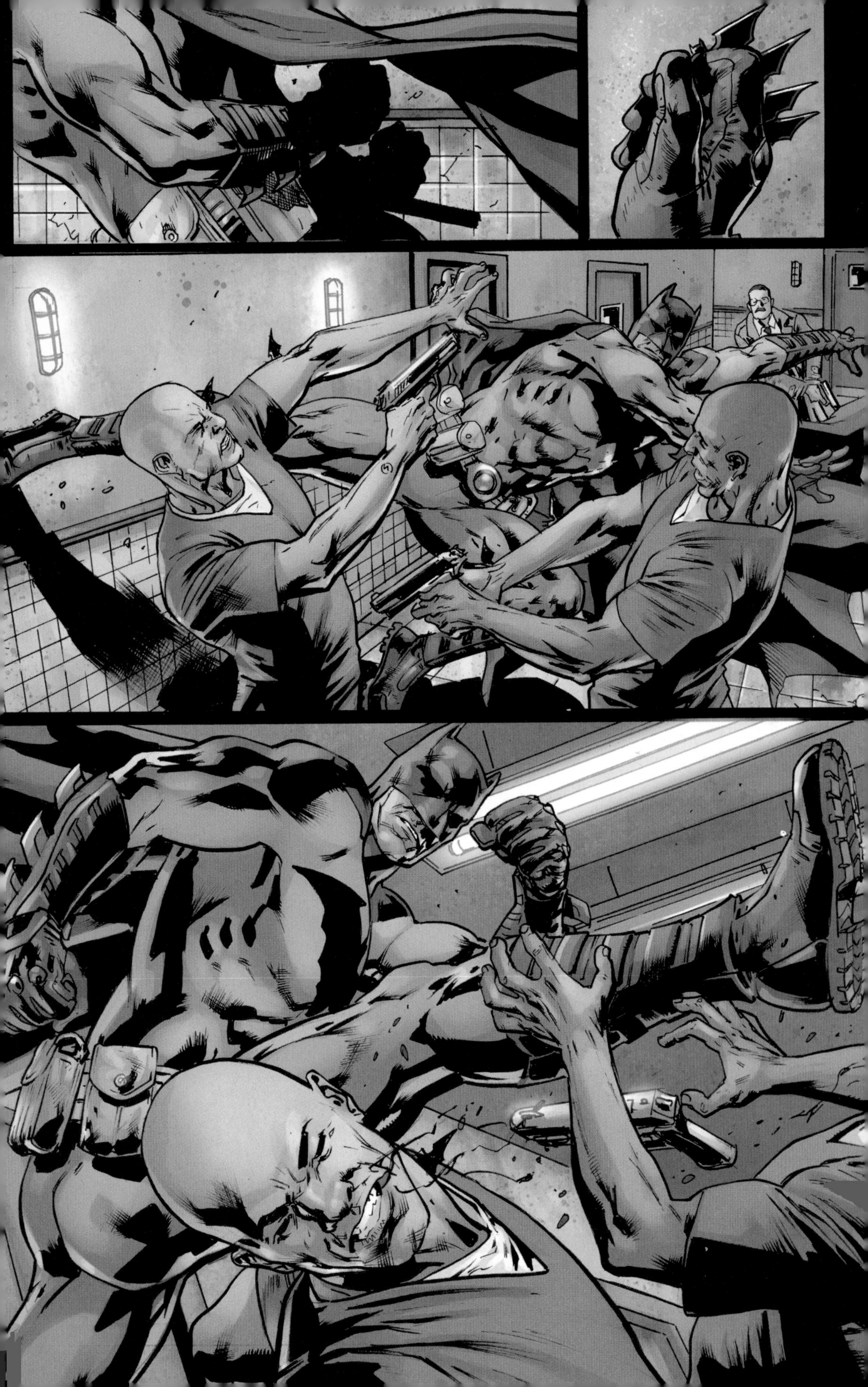

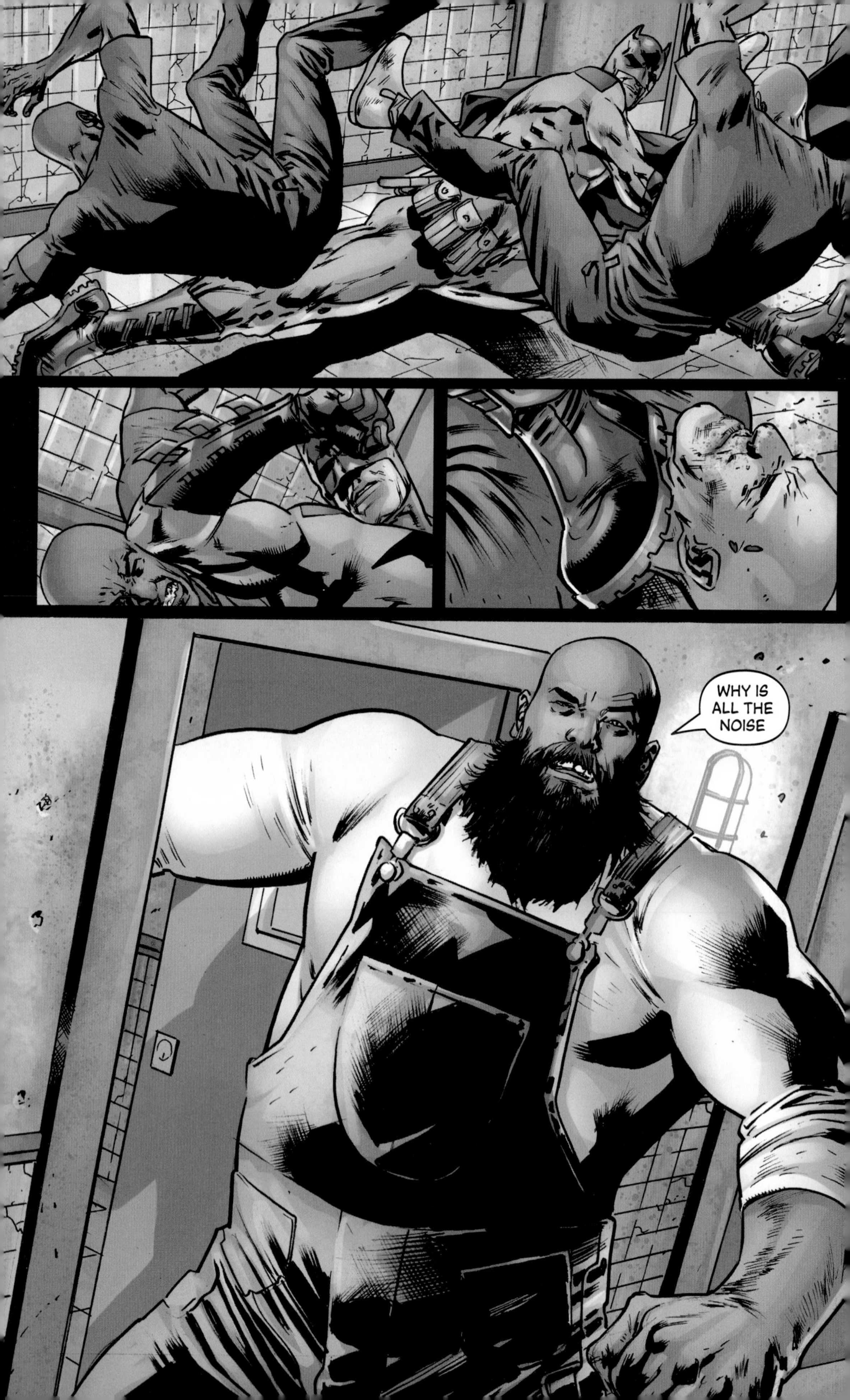
WHY IS ALL THE NOISE

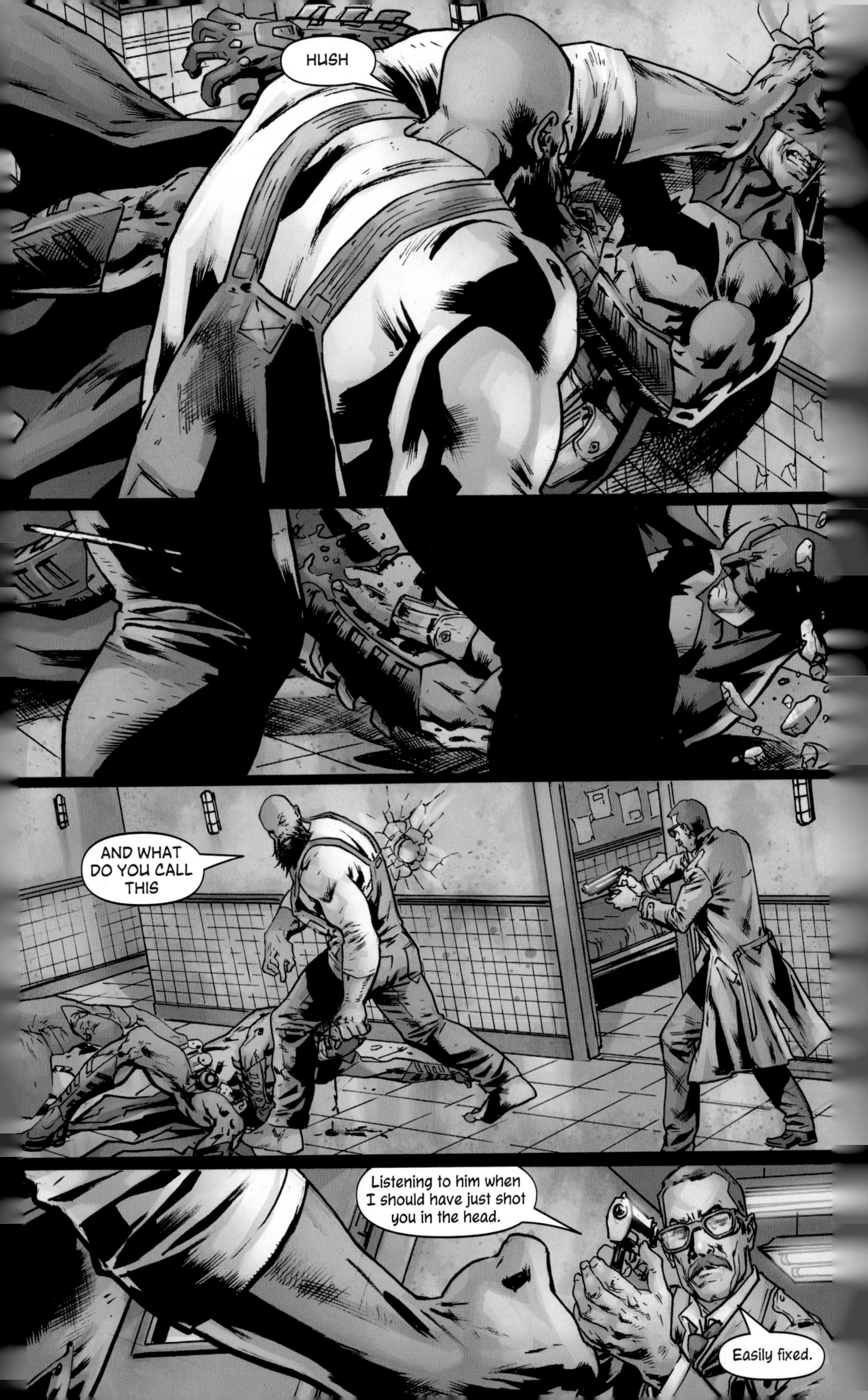
HUSH
AND WHAT DO YOU CALL THIS
Listening to him when I should have just shot you in the head.
Easily fixed.

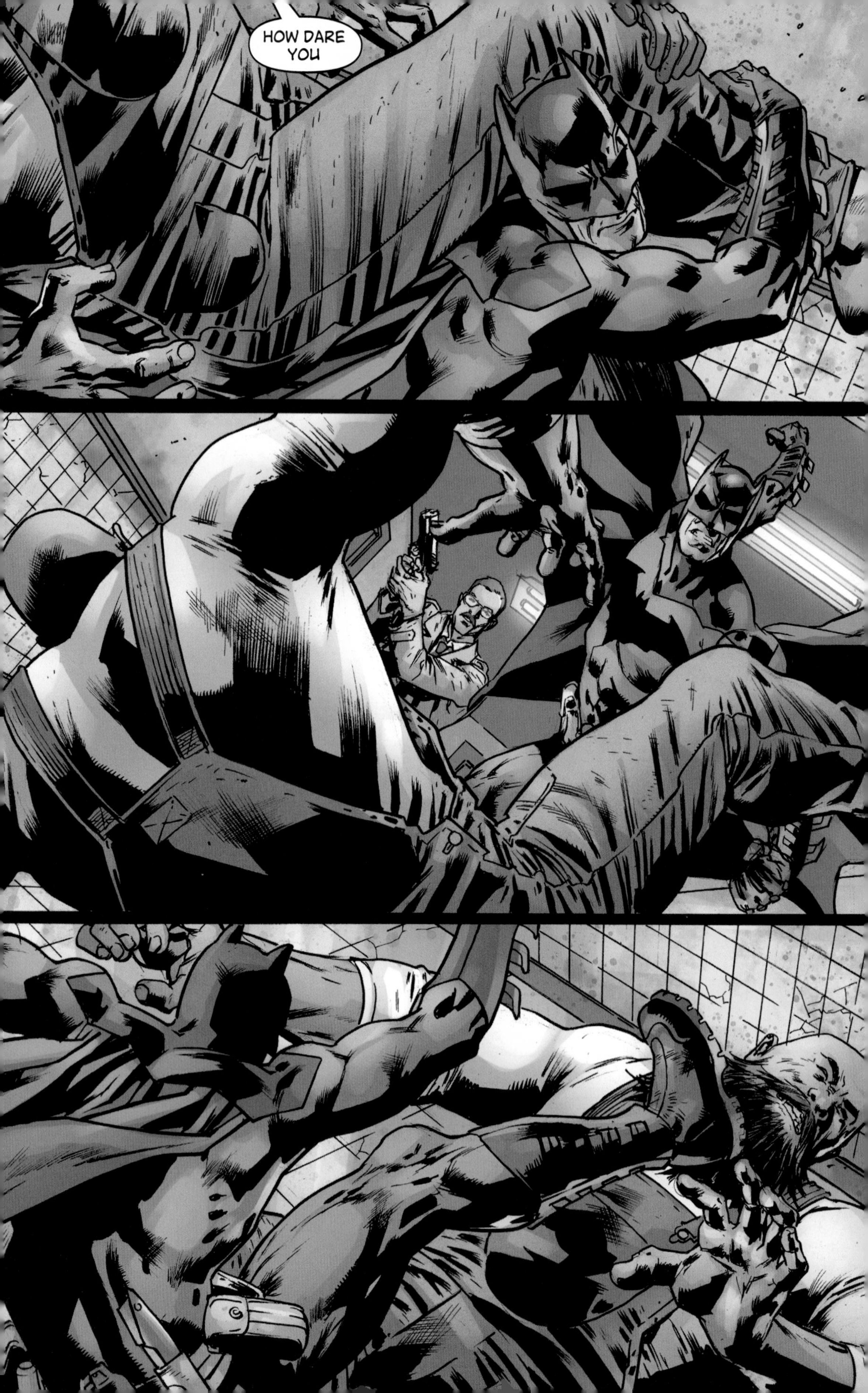
HOW DARE YOU

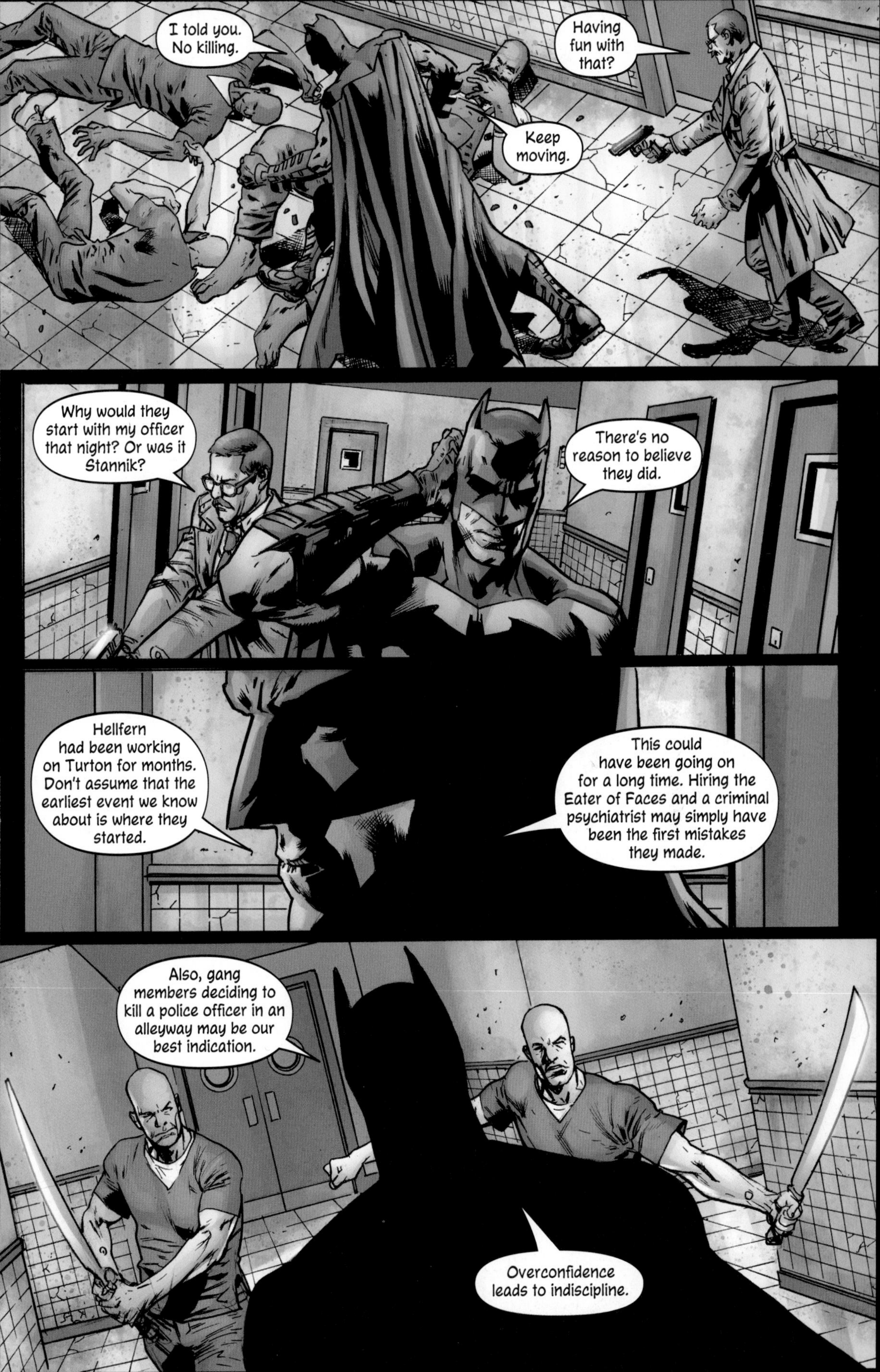
I told you. No killing.
Having fun with that?
Keep moving.
Why would they start with my officer that night? Or was it Stannik?
There's no reason to believe they did.
Hellfern had been working on Turton for months. Don't assume that the earliest event we know about is where they started.
This could have been going on for a long time. Hiring the Eater of Faces and a criminal psychiatrist may simply have been the first mistakes they made.
Also, gang members deciding to kill a police officer in an alleyway may be our best indication.
Overconfidence leads to indiscipline.

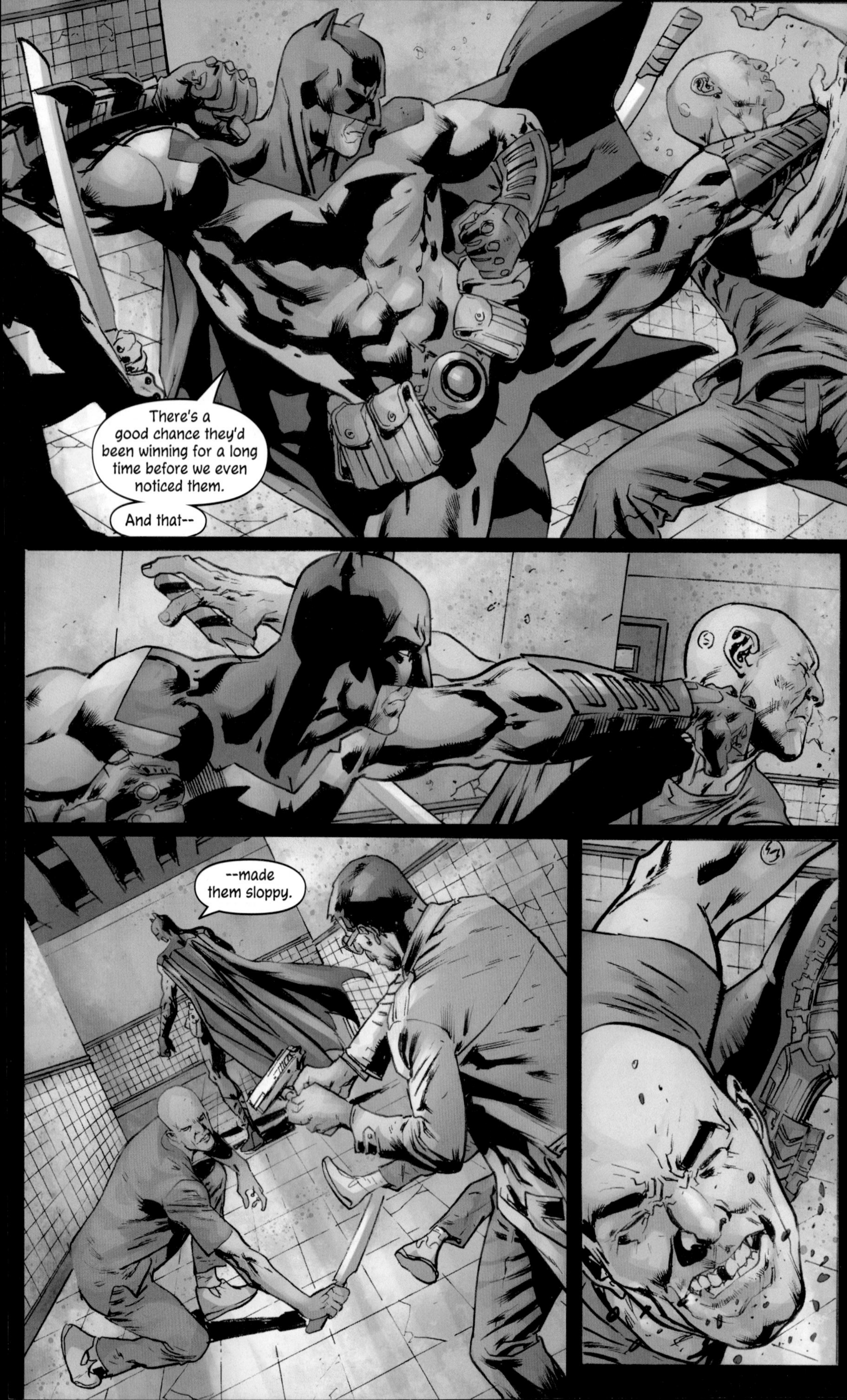
There's a good chance they'd been winning for a long time before we even noticed them.
And that--
--made them sloppy.

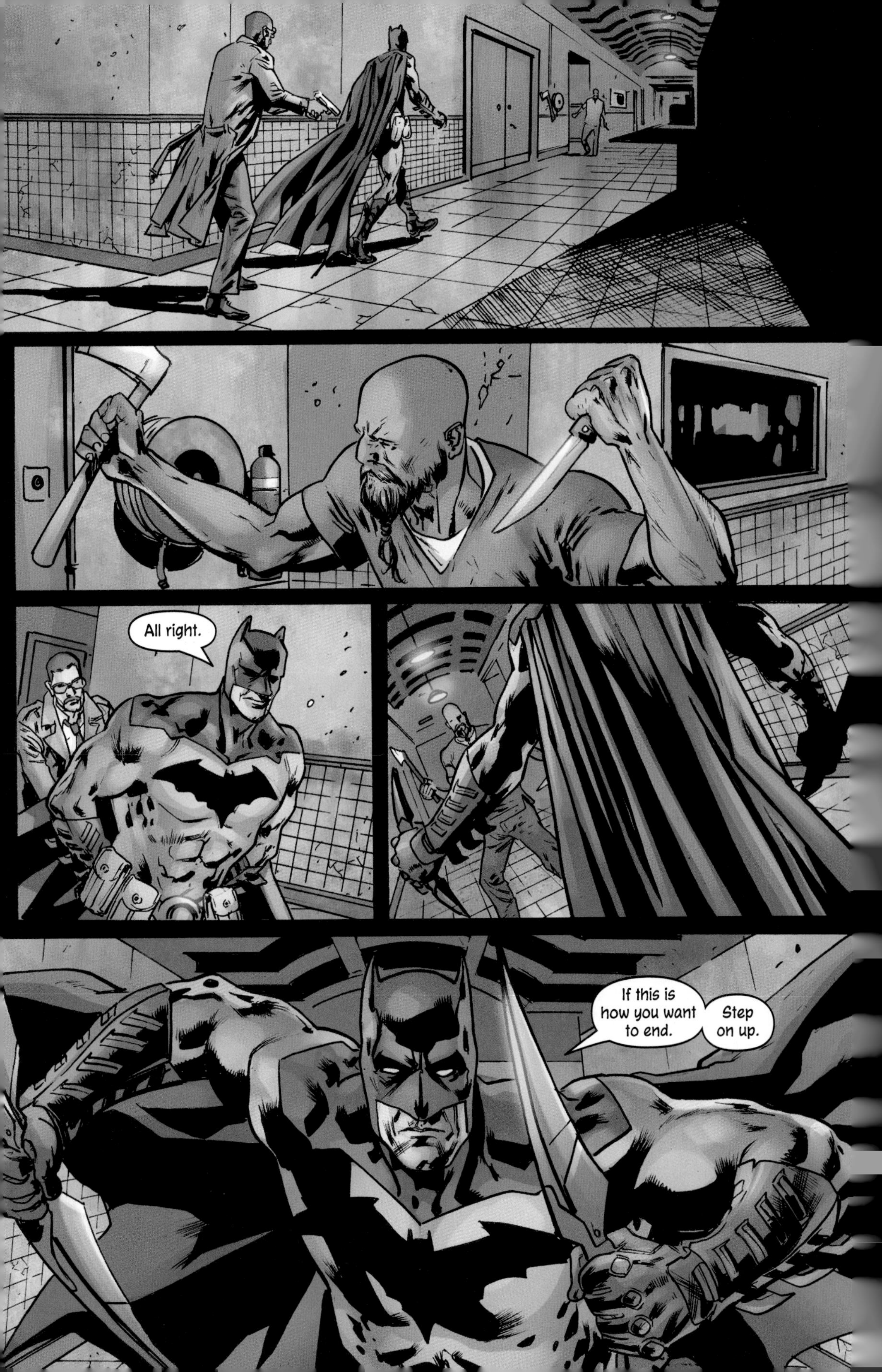
All right.
If this is how you want to end.
Step on up.

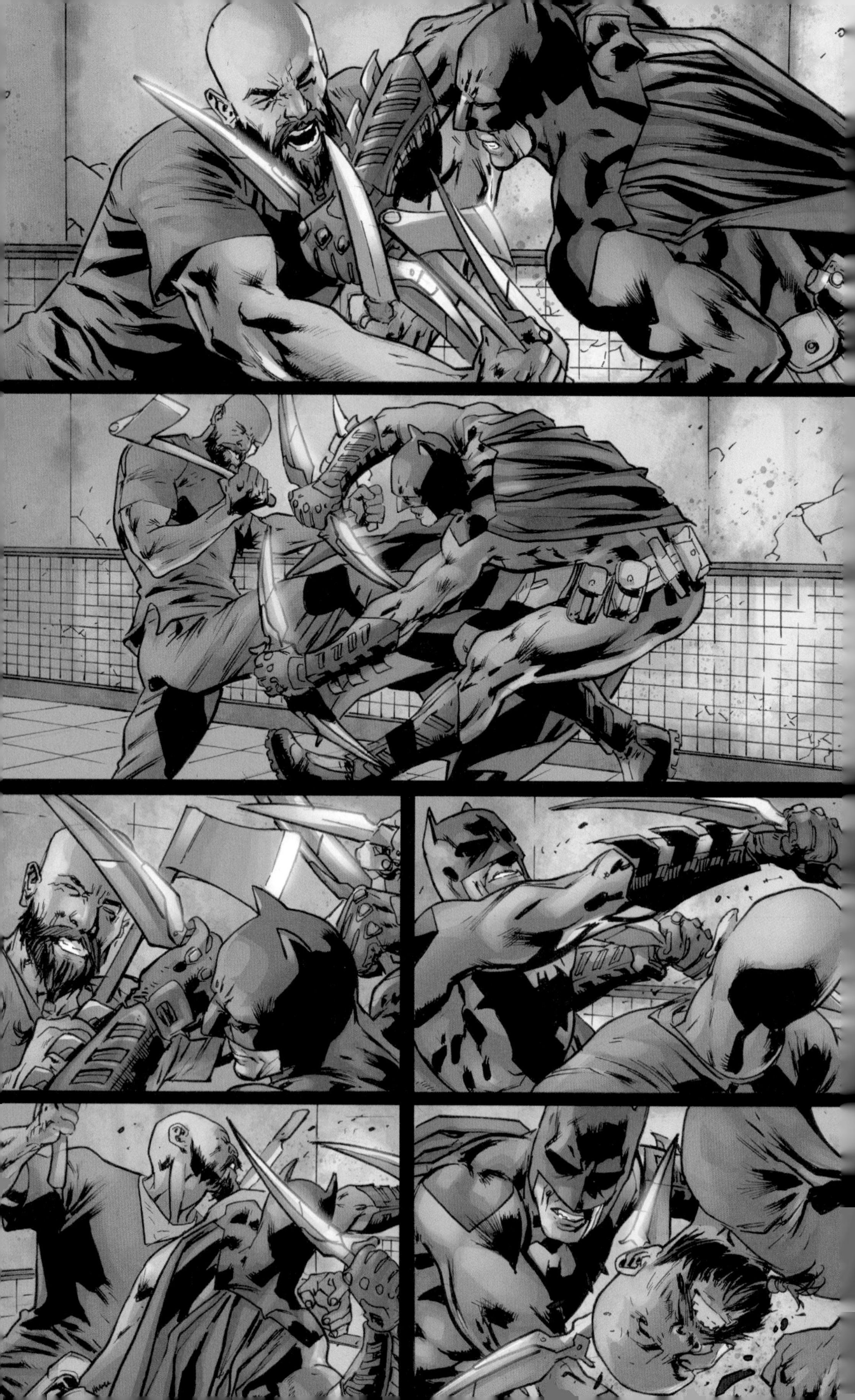

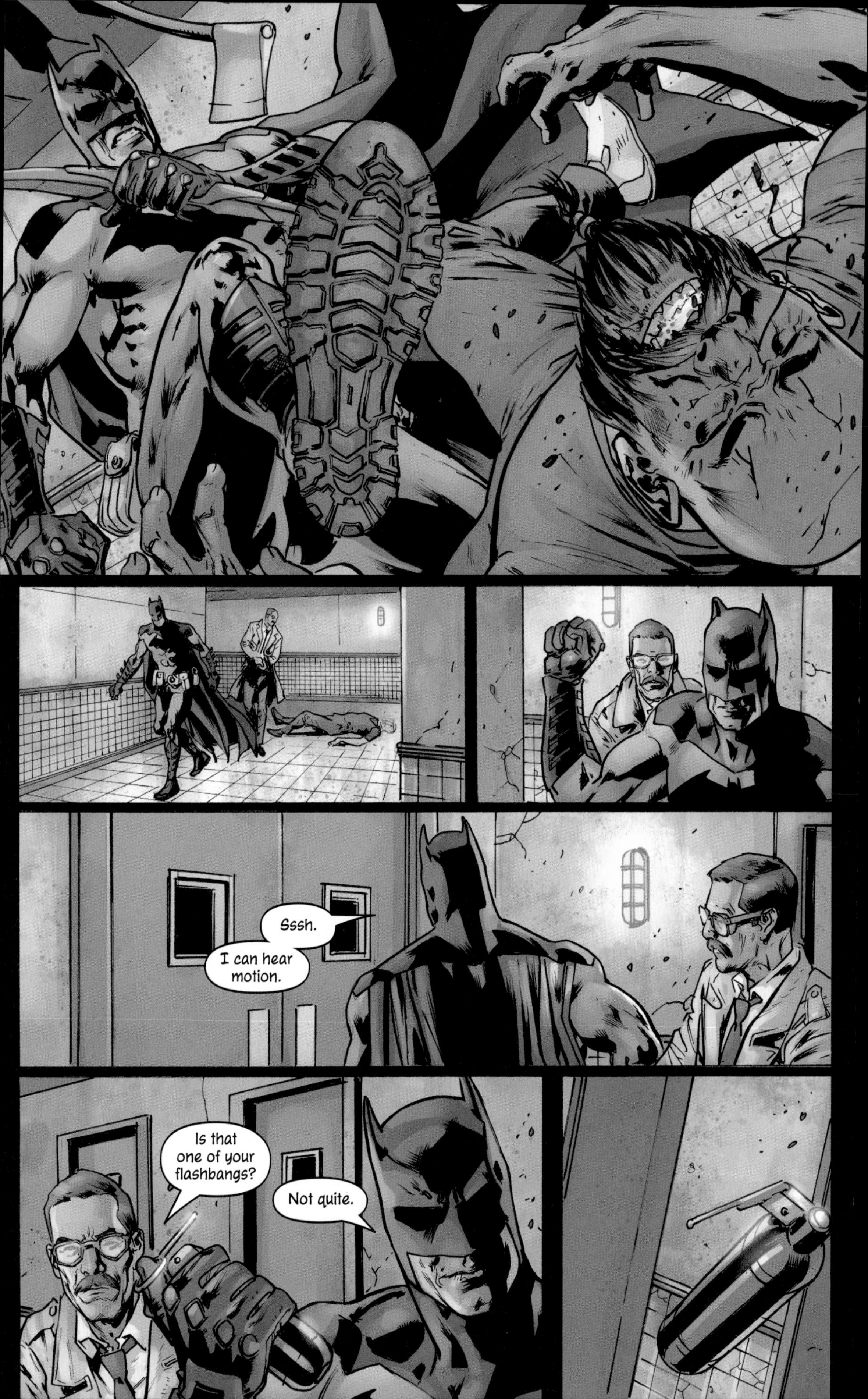
Sssh.
I can hear motion.
Is that one of your flashbangs?
Not quite.

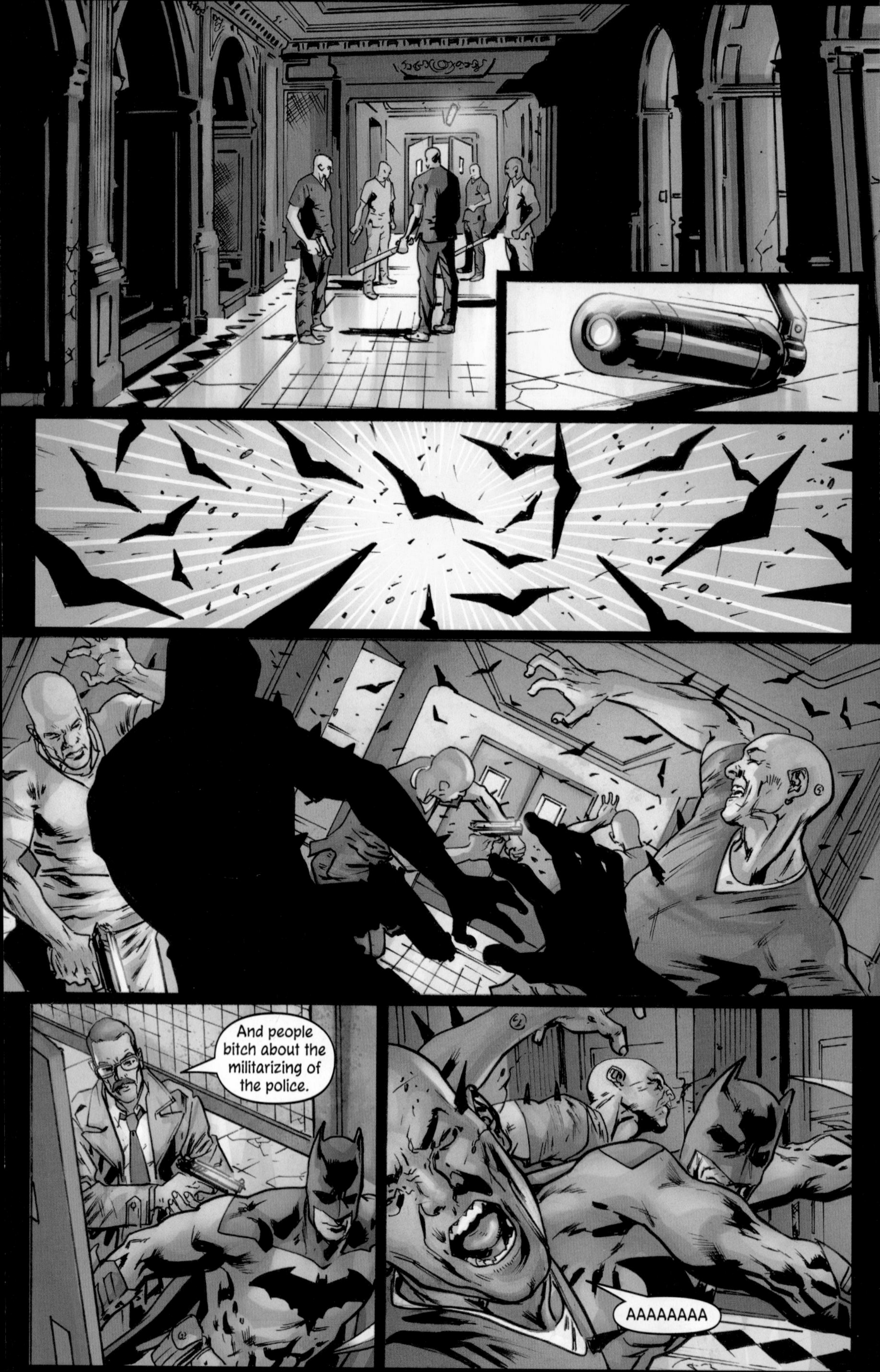
And people bitch about the militarizing of the police.
AAAAAAAA

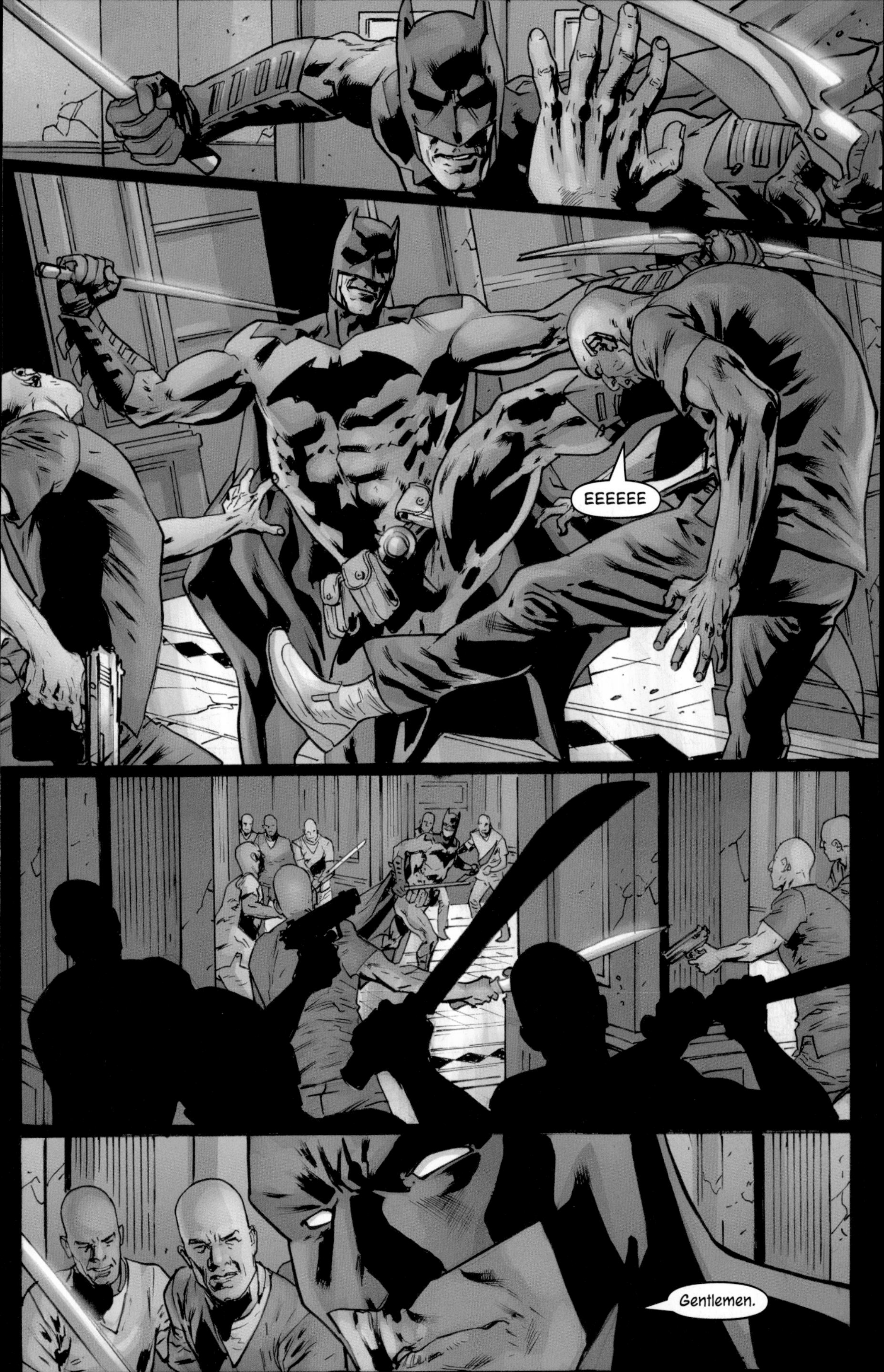
EEEEEE
Gentlemen.

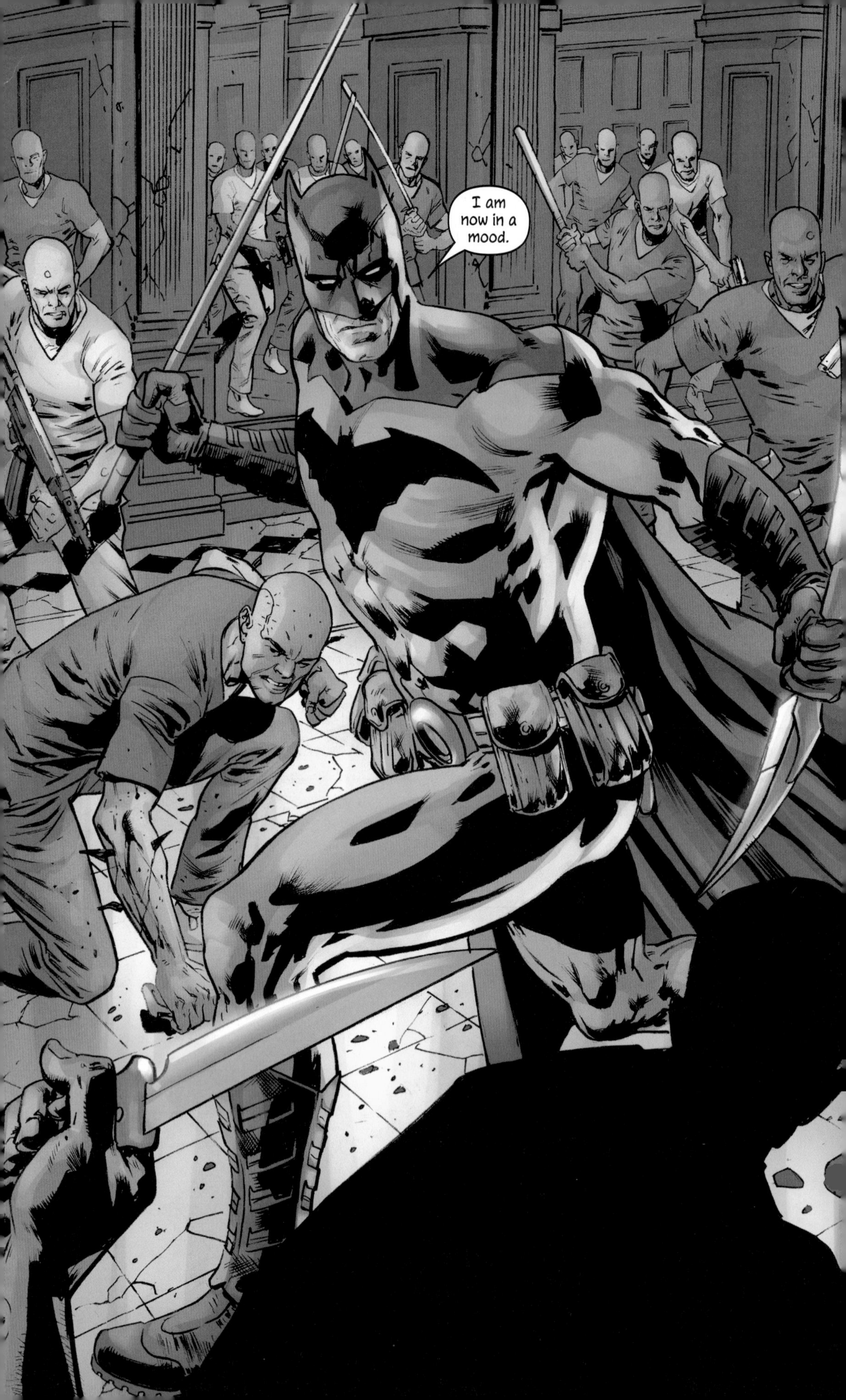
I am now in a mood.

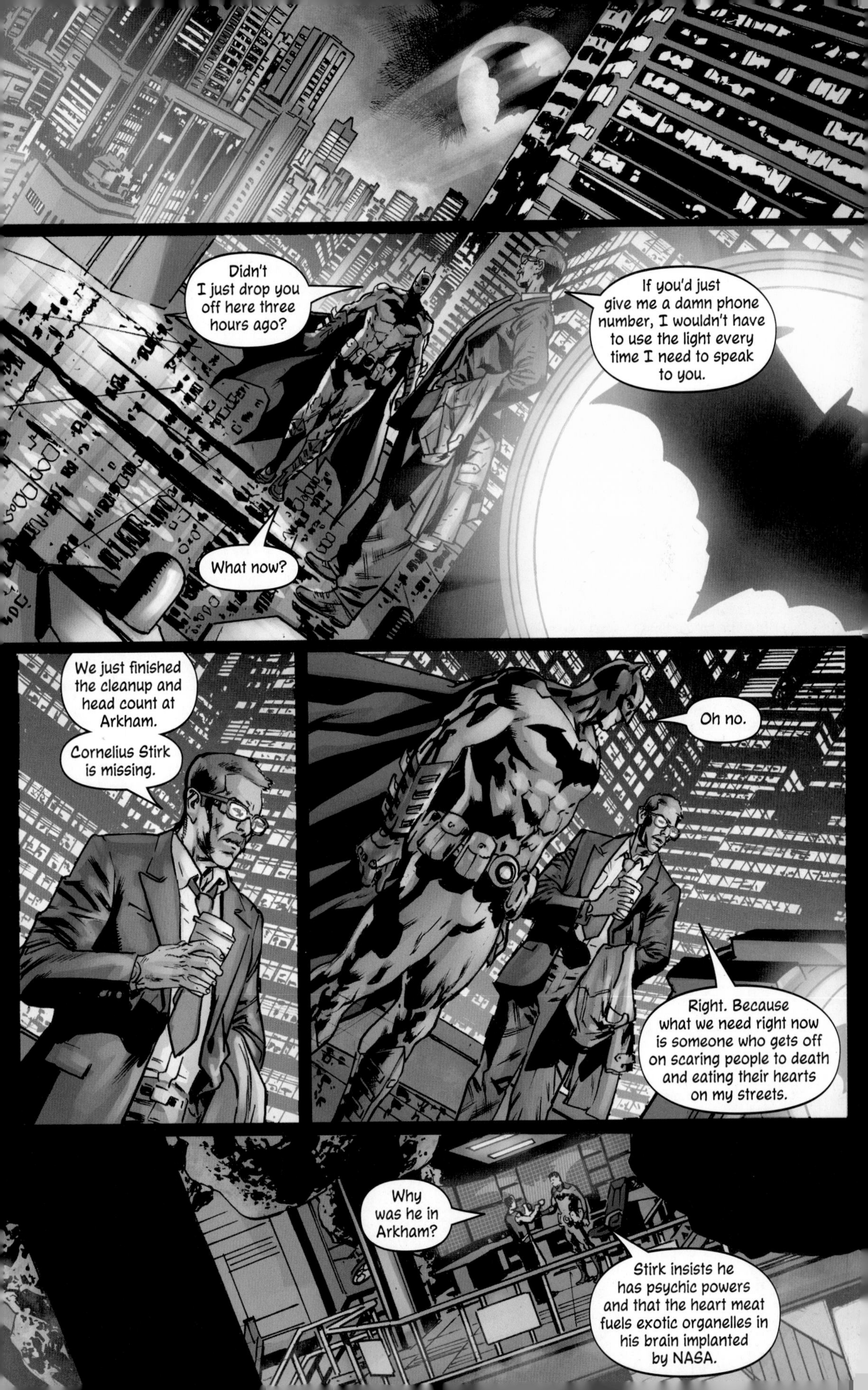
Didn't I just drop you off here three hours ago?
If you'd just give me a damn phone number, I wouldn't have to use the light every time I need to speak to you.
What now?
We just finished the cleanup and head count at Arkham.
Cornelius Stirk is missing.
Oh no.
Right. Because what we need right now is someone who gets off on scaring people to death and eating their hearts on my streets.
Why was he in Arkham?
Stirk insists he has psychic powers and that the heart meat fuels exotic organelles in his brain implanted by NASA.

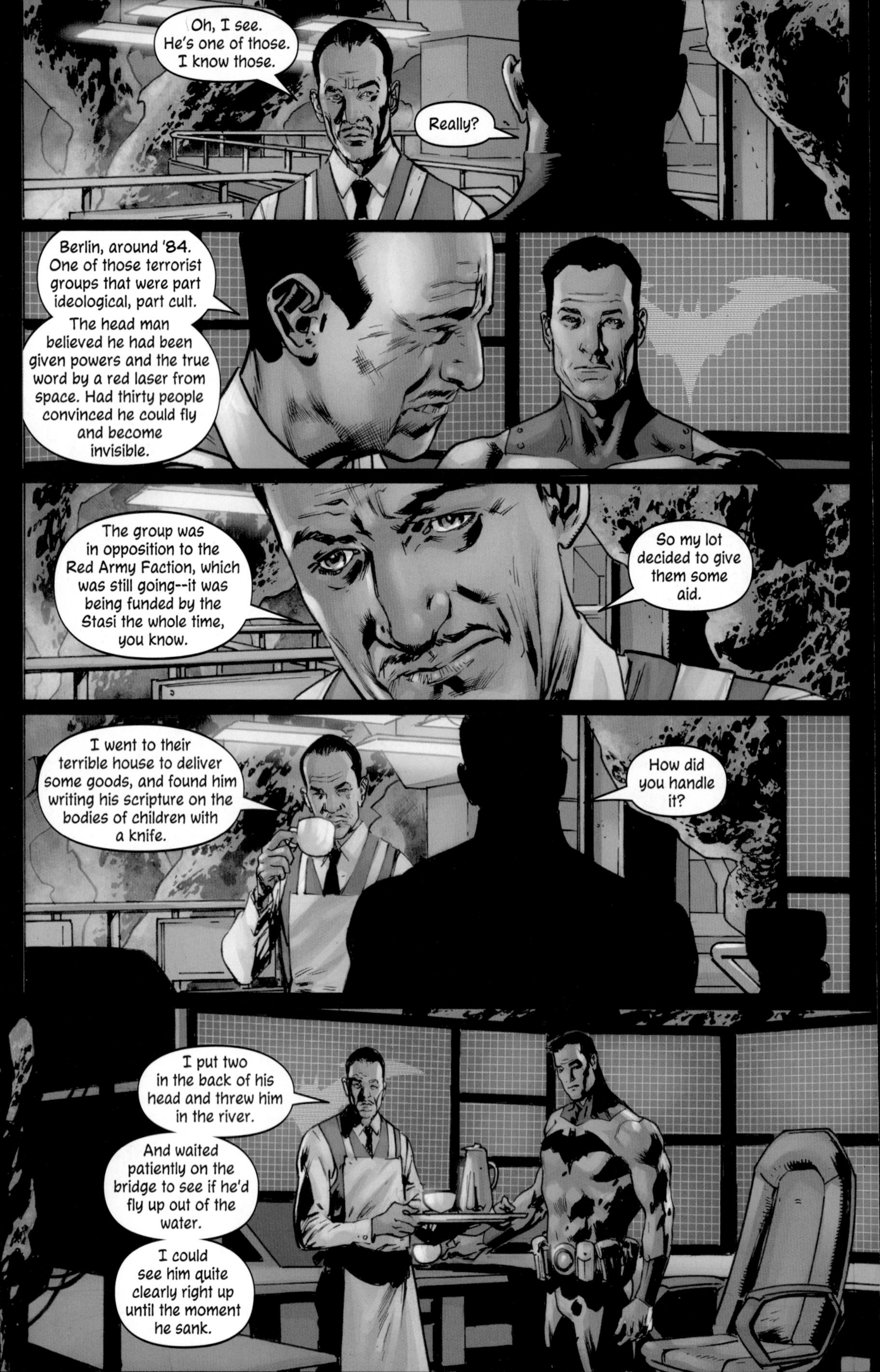

Oh, I see. He's one of those. I know those.
Really?
Berlin, around '84. One of those terrorist groups that were part ideological, part cult.
The head man believed he had been given powers and the true word by a red laser from space. Had thirty people convinced he could fly and become invisible.
The group was in opposition to the Red Army Faction, which was still going--it was being funded by the Stasi the whole time, you know.
So my lot decided to give them some aid.
I went to their terrible house to deliver some goods, and found him writing his scripture on the bodies of children with a knife.
How did you handle it?
I put two in the back of his head and threw him in the river.
And waited patiently on the bridge to see if he'd fly up out of the water.
I could see him quite clearly right up until the moment he sank.

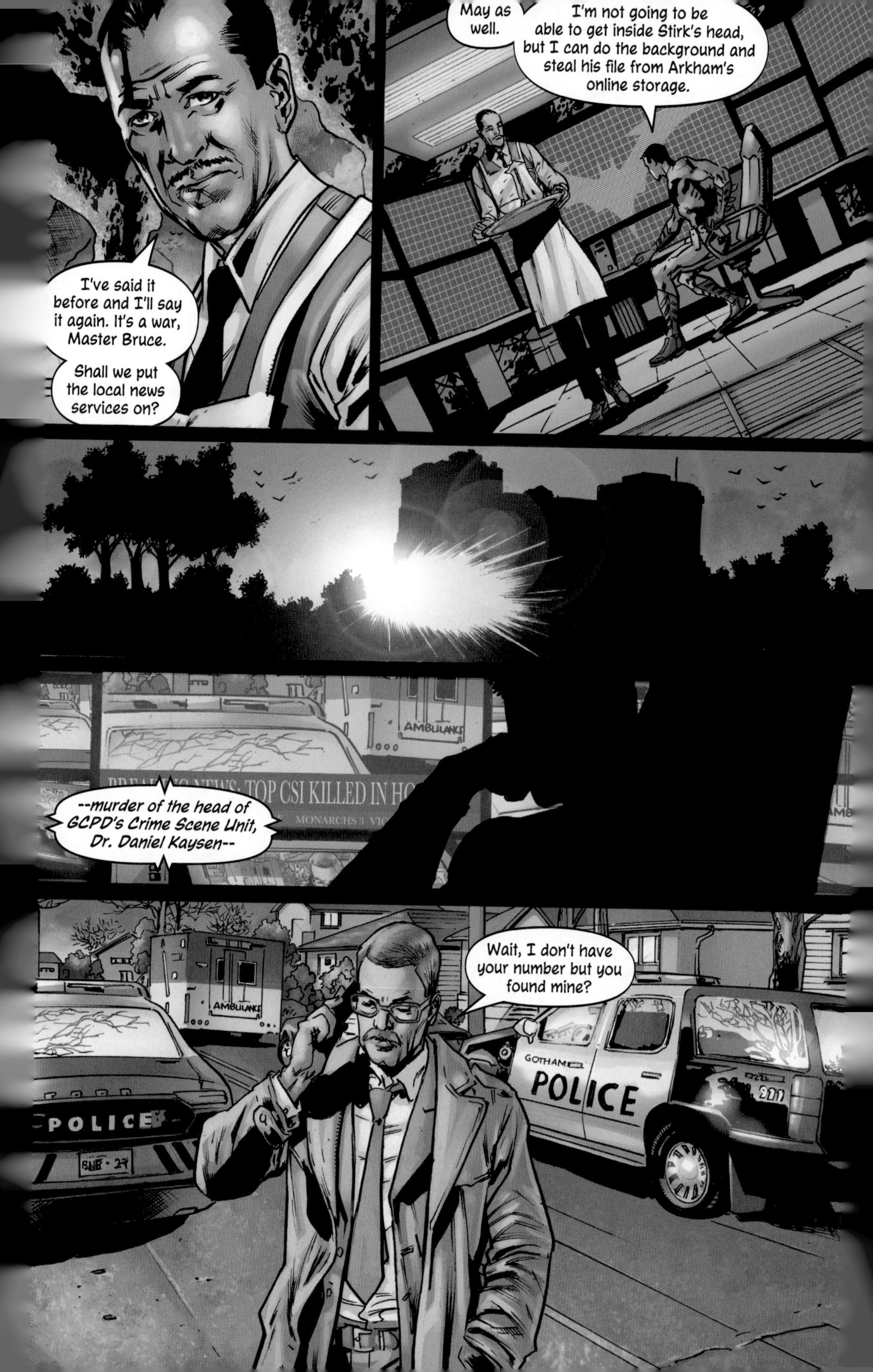
I've said it before and I'll say it again. It's a war, Master Bruce.
Shall we put the local news services on?
May as well.
I'm not going to be able to get inside Stirk's head, but I can do the background and steal his file from Arkham's online storage.
AMBULANCE
BREAKING NEWS: TOP CSI KILLED IN HO
MONARCHS 3
--murder of the head of GCPD's Crime Scene Unit, Dr. Daniel Kaysen--
AMBULANCE
Wait, I don't have your number but you found mine?
POLICE
GOTHAM
POLICE

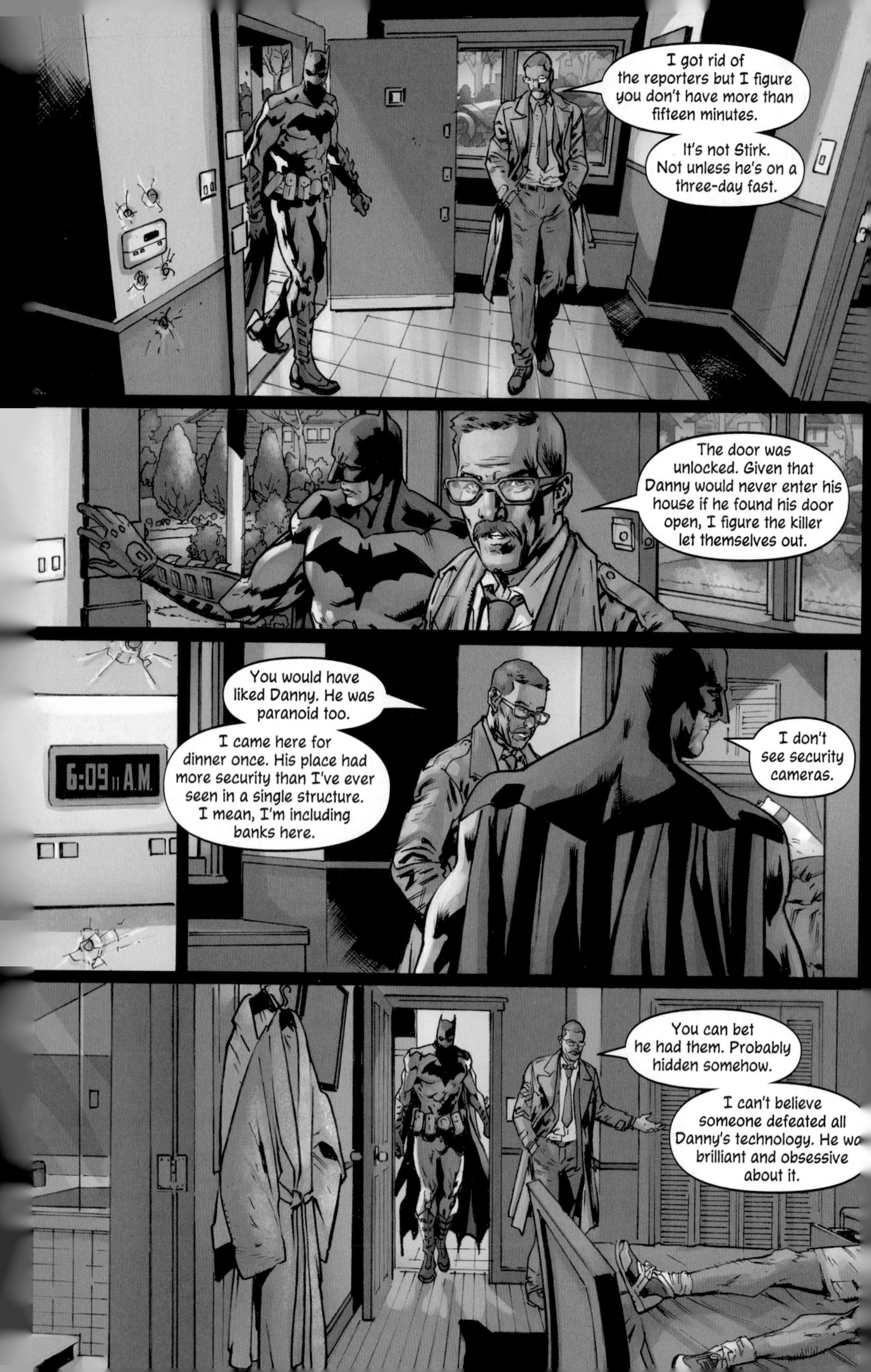

I got rid of the reporters but I figure you don't have more than fifteen minutes.
It's not Stirk. Not unless he's on a three-day fast.
The door was unlocked. Given that Danny would never enter his house if he found his door open, I figure the killer let themselves out.
You would have liked Danny. He was paranoid too.
I came here for dinner once. His place had more security than I've ever seen in a single structure. I mean, I'm including banks here.
6:09 11 A.M.
I don't see security cameras.
You can bet he had them. Probably hidden somehow.
I can't believe someone defeated all Danny's technology. He wa brilliant and obsessive about it.

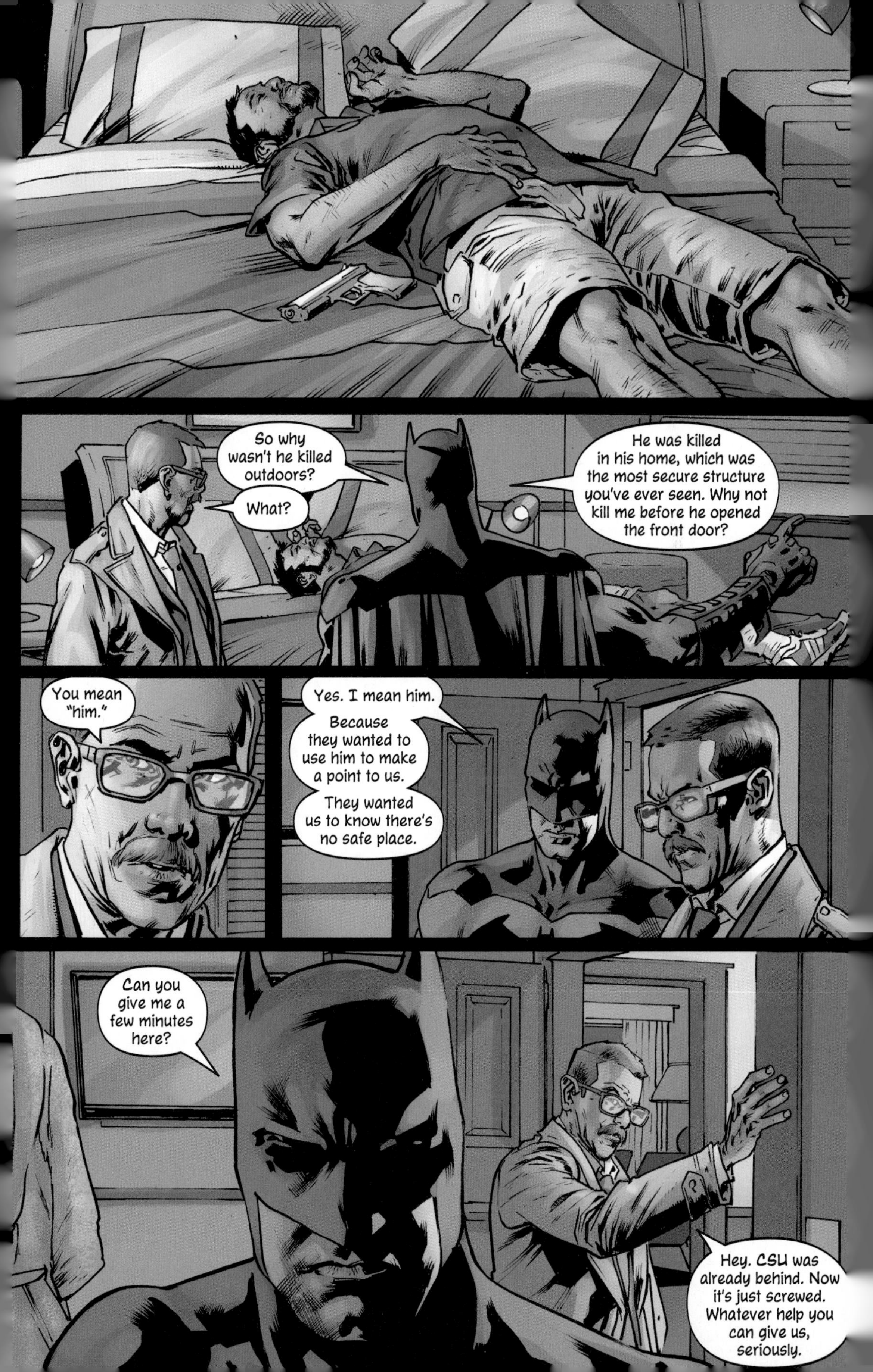
So why wasn't he killed outdoors?
What?
He was killed in his home, which was the most secure structure you've ever seen. Why not kill me before he opened the front door?
You mean "him."
Yes. I mean him.
Because they wanted to use him to make a point to us.
They wanted us to know there's no safe place.
Can you give me a few minutes here?
Hey. CSU was already behind. Now it's just screwed. Whatever help you can give us, seriously.

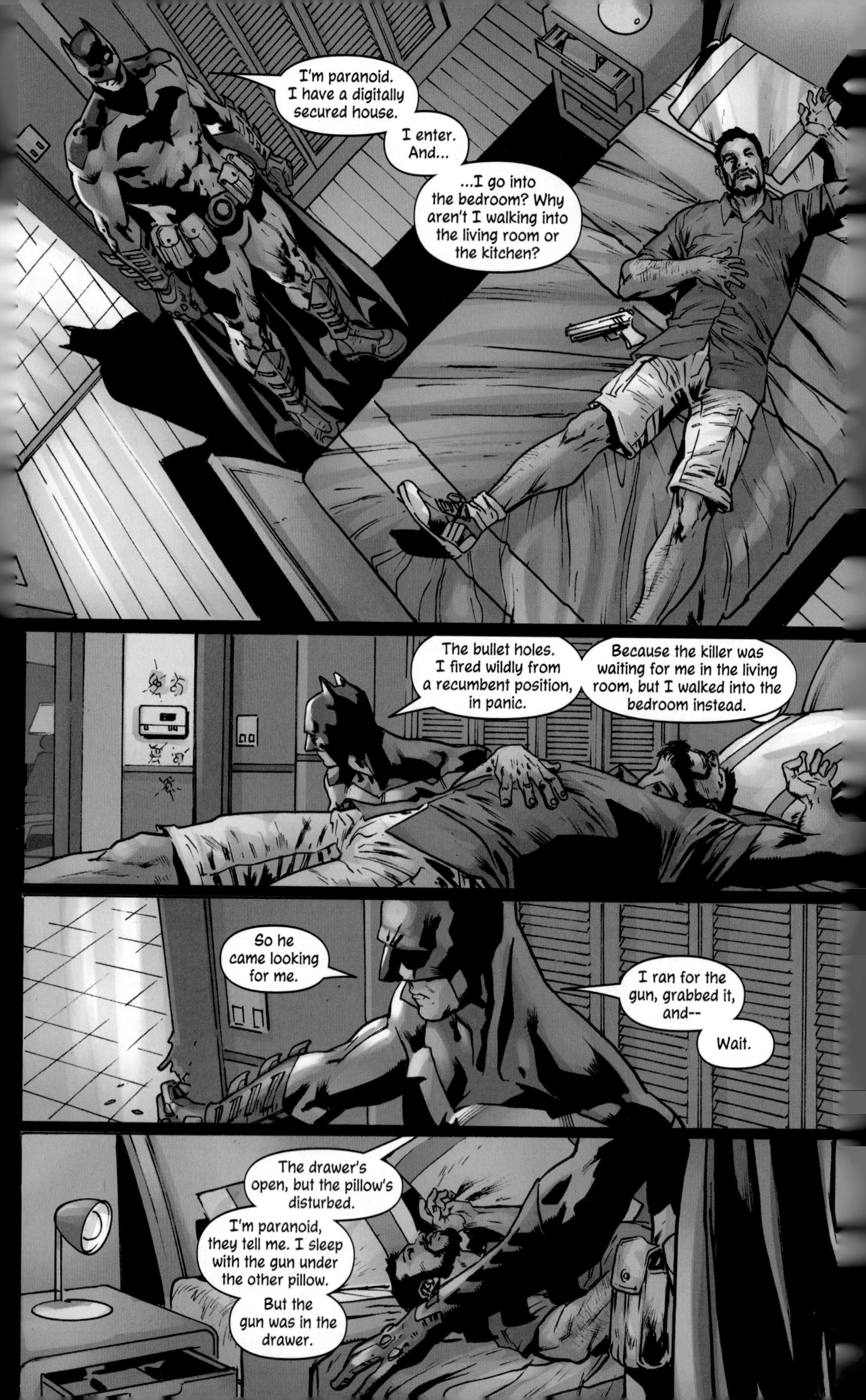
I'm paranoid. I have a digitally secured house.
I enter. And...
...I go into the bedroom? Why aren't I walking into the living room or the kitchen?
The bullet holes. I fired wildly from a recumbent position, in panic.
Because the killer was waiting for me in the living room, but I walked into the bedroom instead.
So he came looking for me.
I ran for the gun, grabbed it, and--
Wait.
The drawer's open, but the pillow's disturbed.
I'm paranoid, they tell me. I sleep with the gun under the other pillow.
But the gun was in the drawer.

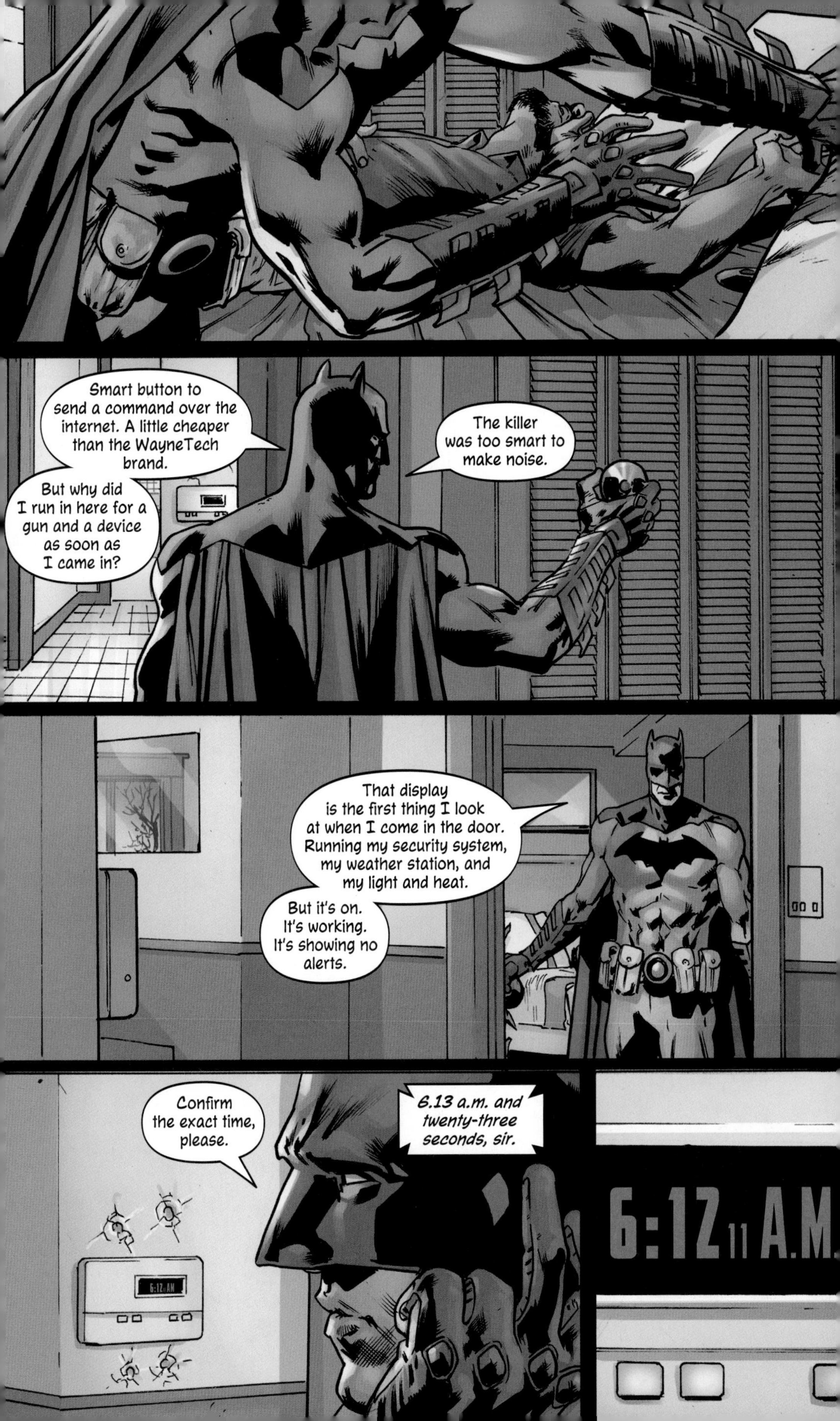
Smart button to send a command over the internet. A little cheaper than the WayneTech brand.
But why did I run in here for a gun and a device as soon as I came in?
The killer was too smart to make noise.
That display is the first thing I look at when I come in the door. Running my security system, my weather station, and my light and heat.
But it's on. It's working. It's showing no alerts.
Confirm the exact time, please.
6.13 a.m. and twenty-three seconds, sir.
6:12 11 A.M

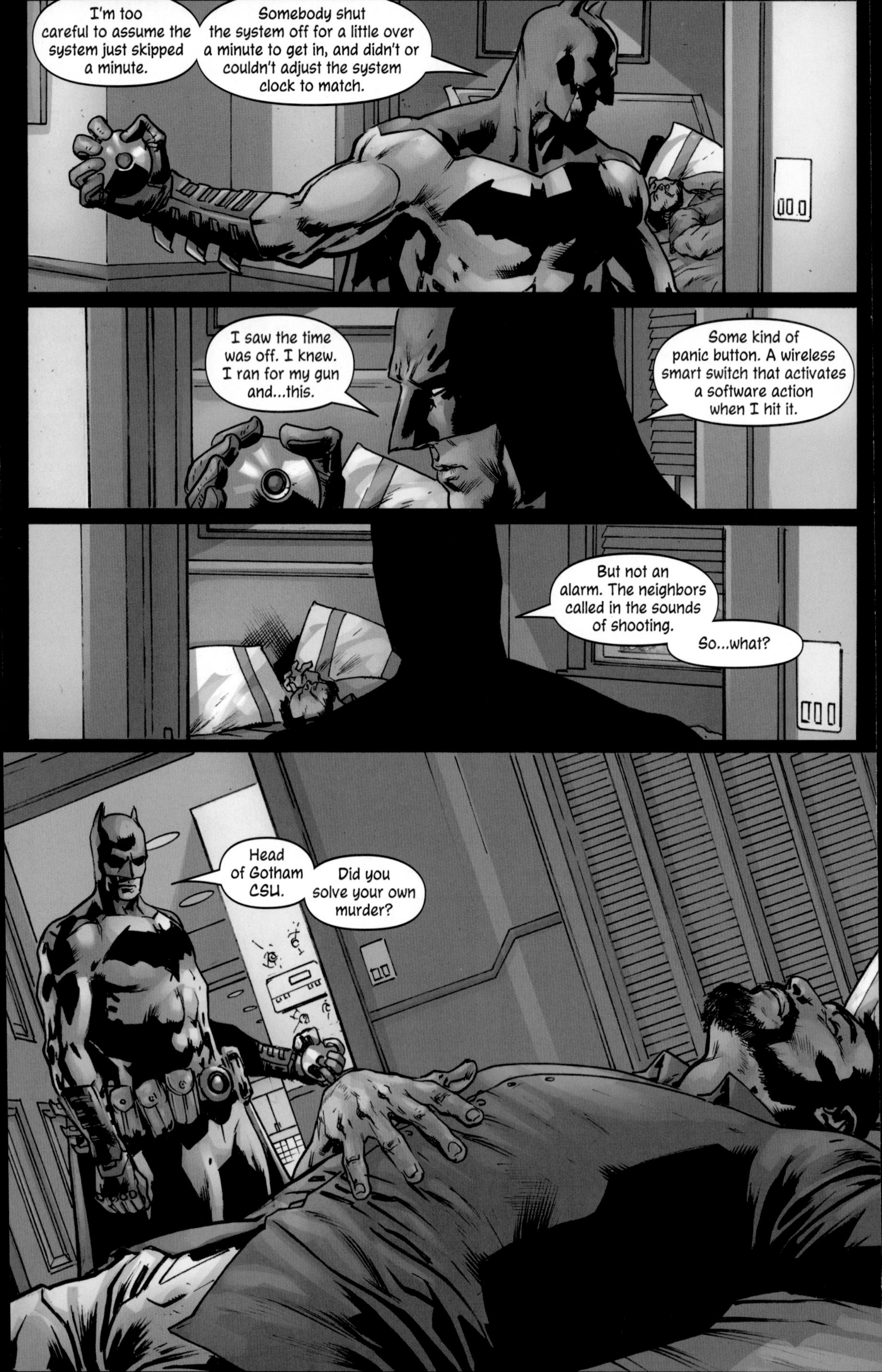
I'm too careful to assume the system just skipped a minute.
Somebody shut the system off for a little over a minute to get in, and didn't or couldn't adjust the system clock to match.
I saw the time was off. I knew. I ran for my gun and...this.
Some kind of panic button. A wireless smart switch that activates a software action when I hit it.
But not an alarm. The neighbors called in the sounds of shooting.
So...what?
Head of Gotham CSU.
Did you solve your own murder?

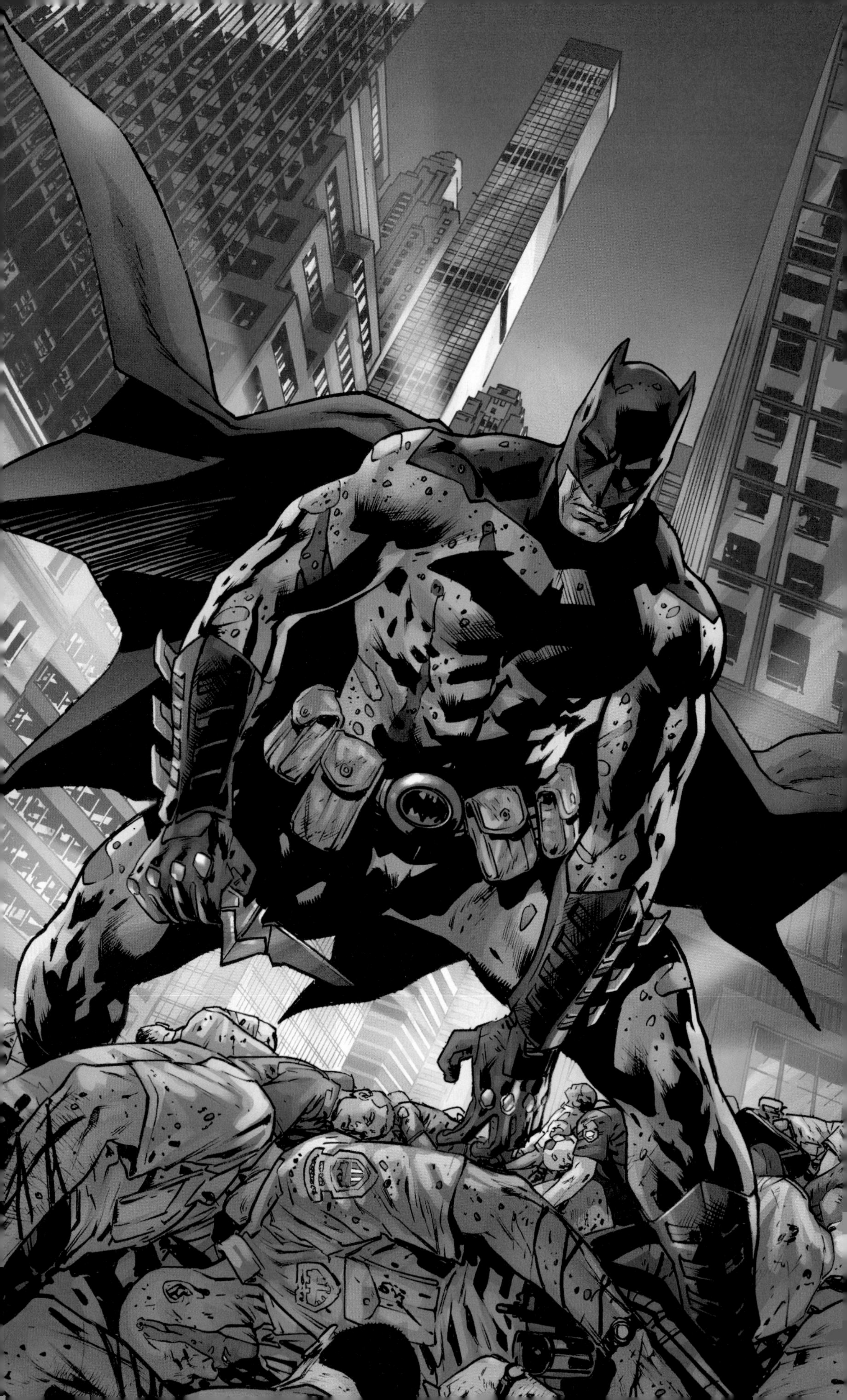

THE BATMAN'S GRAVE #7 variant cover
by FRANK QUITELY

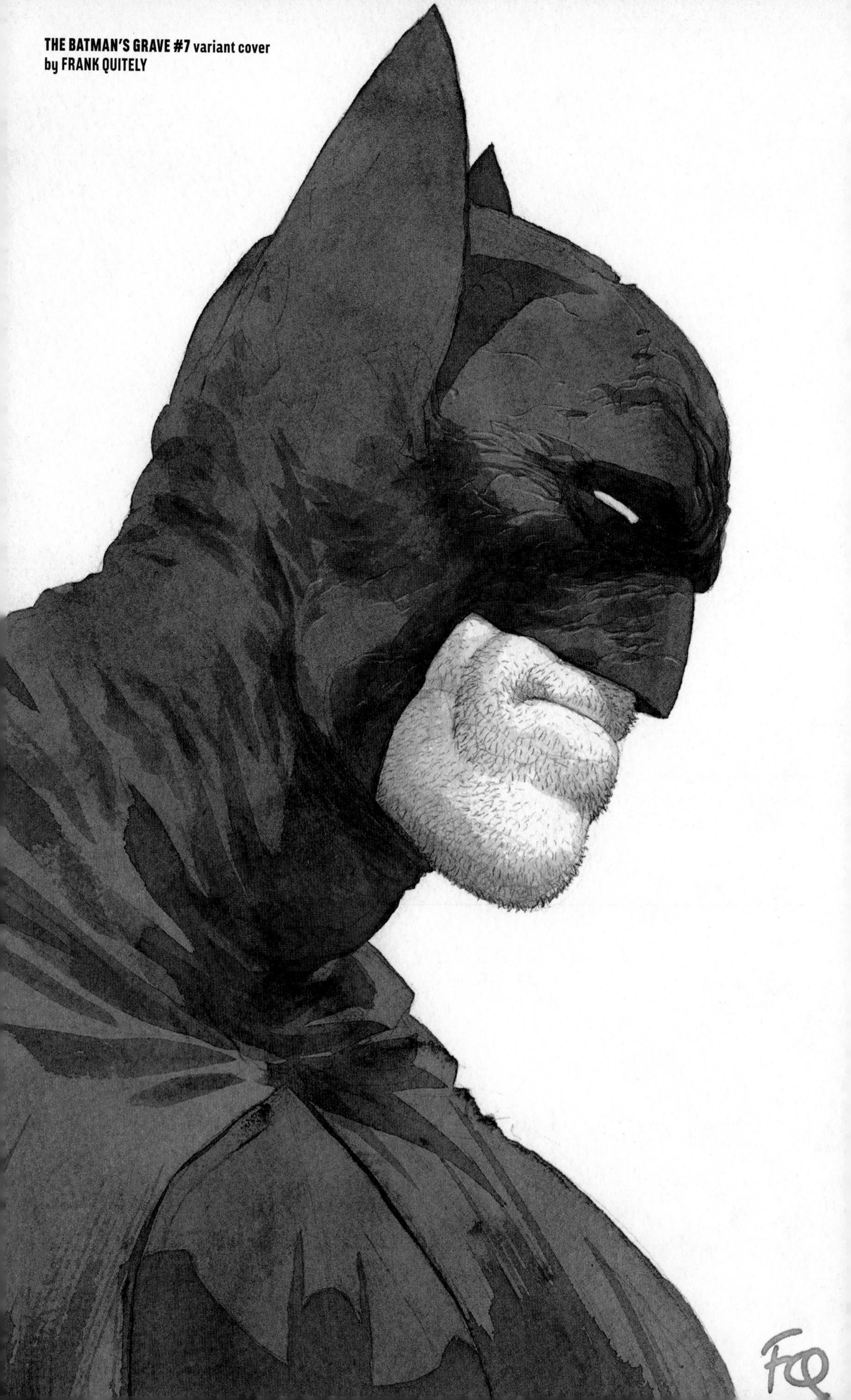
FQ

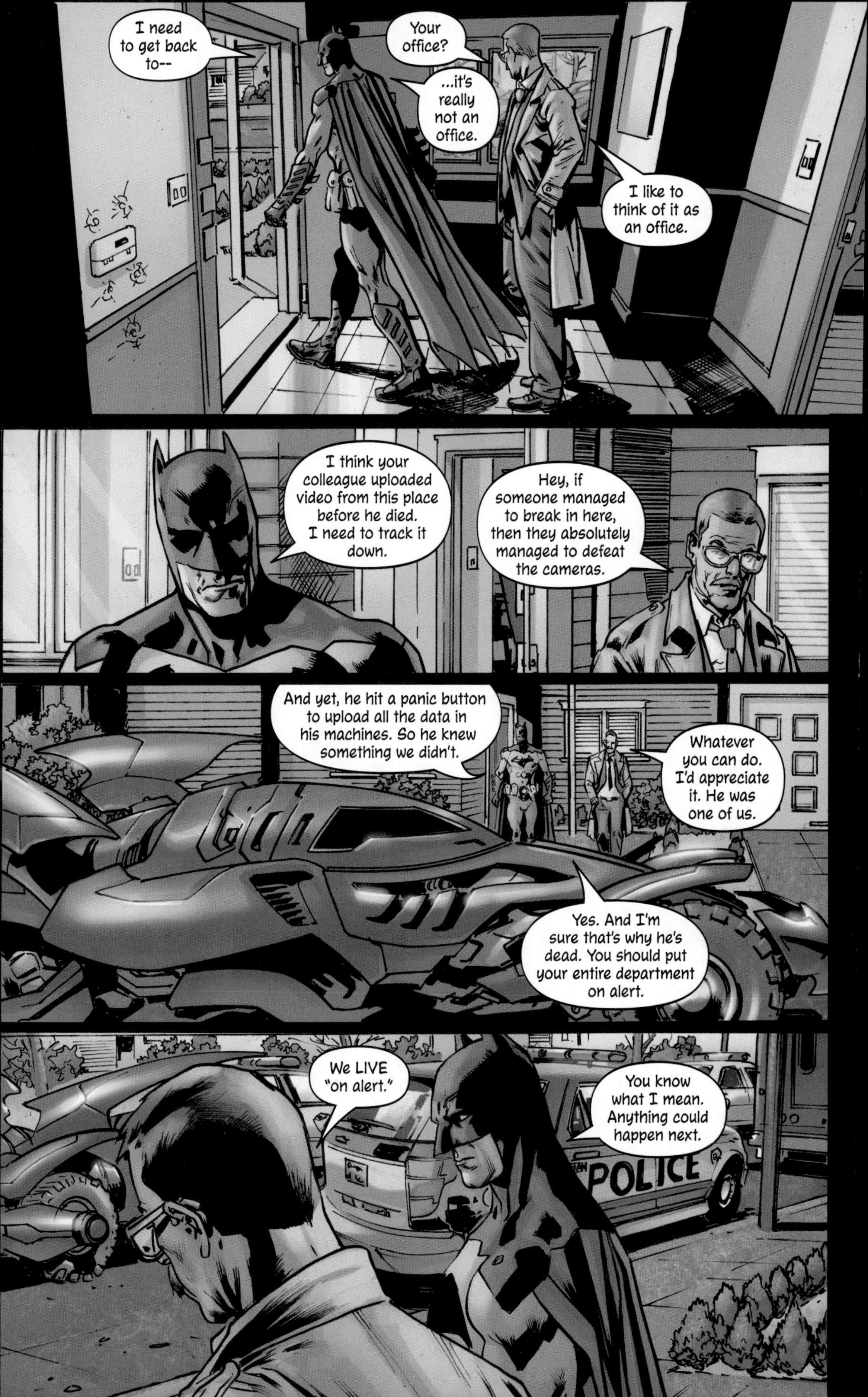
I need to get back to--
Your office?
...it's really not an office.
I like to think of it as an office.
I think your colleague uploaded video from this place before he died. I need to track it down.
Hey, if someone managed to break in here, then they absolutely managed to defeat the cameras.
And yet, he hit a panic button to upload all the data in his machines. So he knew something we didn't.
Whatever you can do. I'd appreciate it. He was one of us.
Yes. And I'm sure that's why he's dead. You should put your entire department on alert.
We LIVE "on alert."
You know what I mean. Anything could happen next.
POLICE

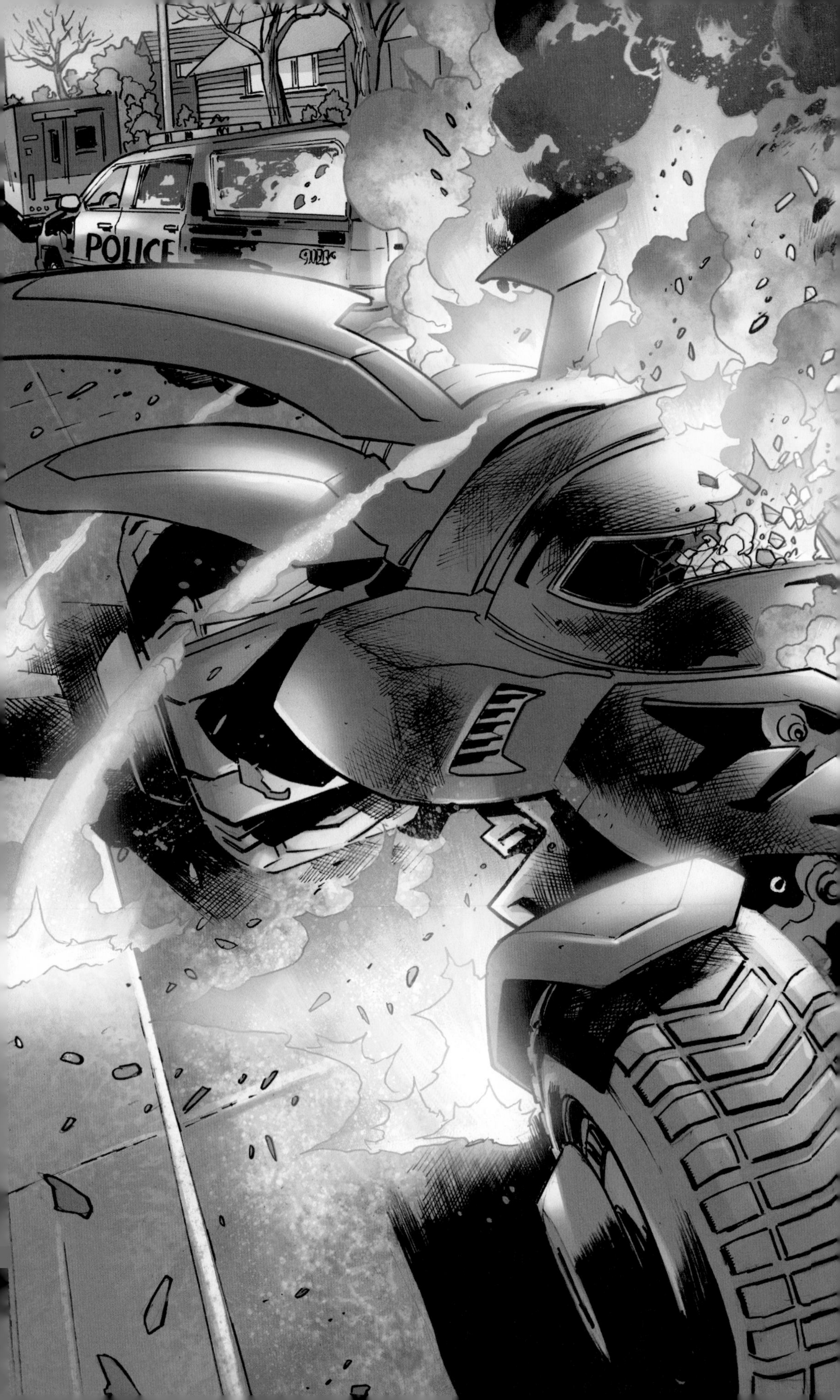
POLICE

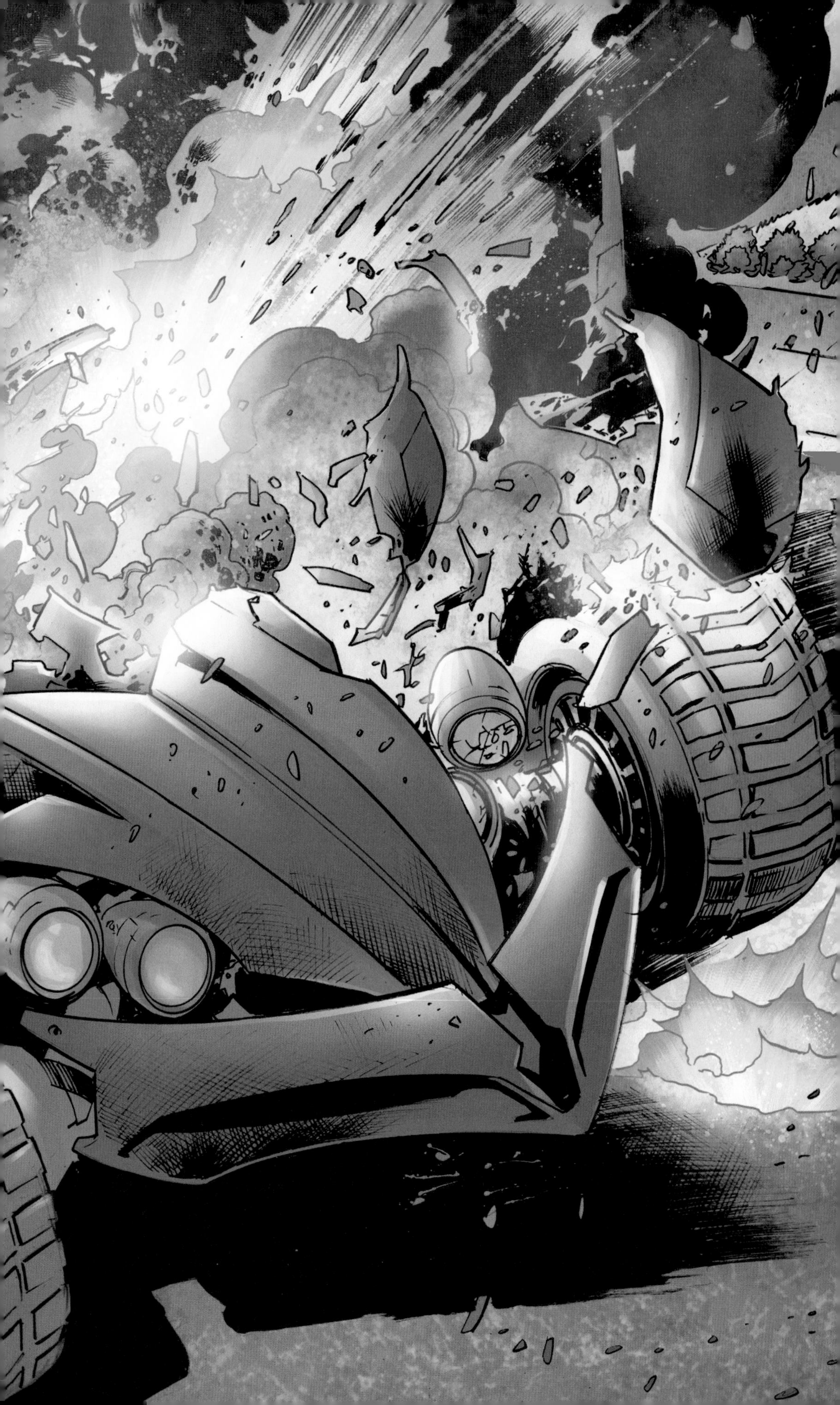

Yeah.

Chapter 7

Writer	Art
WARREN ELLIS	**BRYAN HITCH**

Colors	Letters
ALEX SINCLAIR	**RICHARD STARKINGS**

Cover	Variant Cover
BRYAN HITCH &	**FRANK**
ALEX SINCLAIR	**QUITELY**

Associate Editor	Editor
ANDREW MARINO	**MARIE JAVINS**

BATMAN created by BOB KANE with BILL FINGER

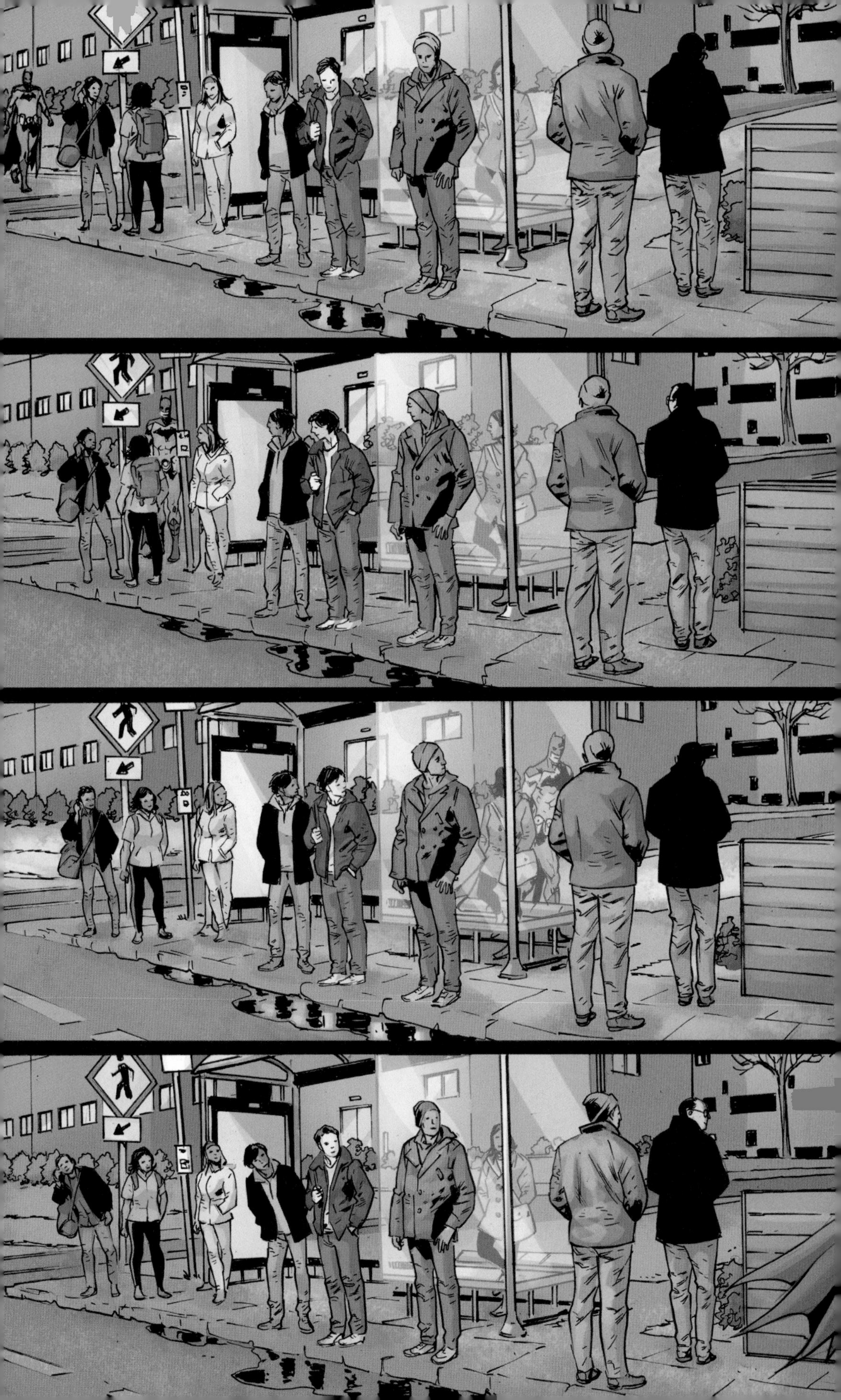

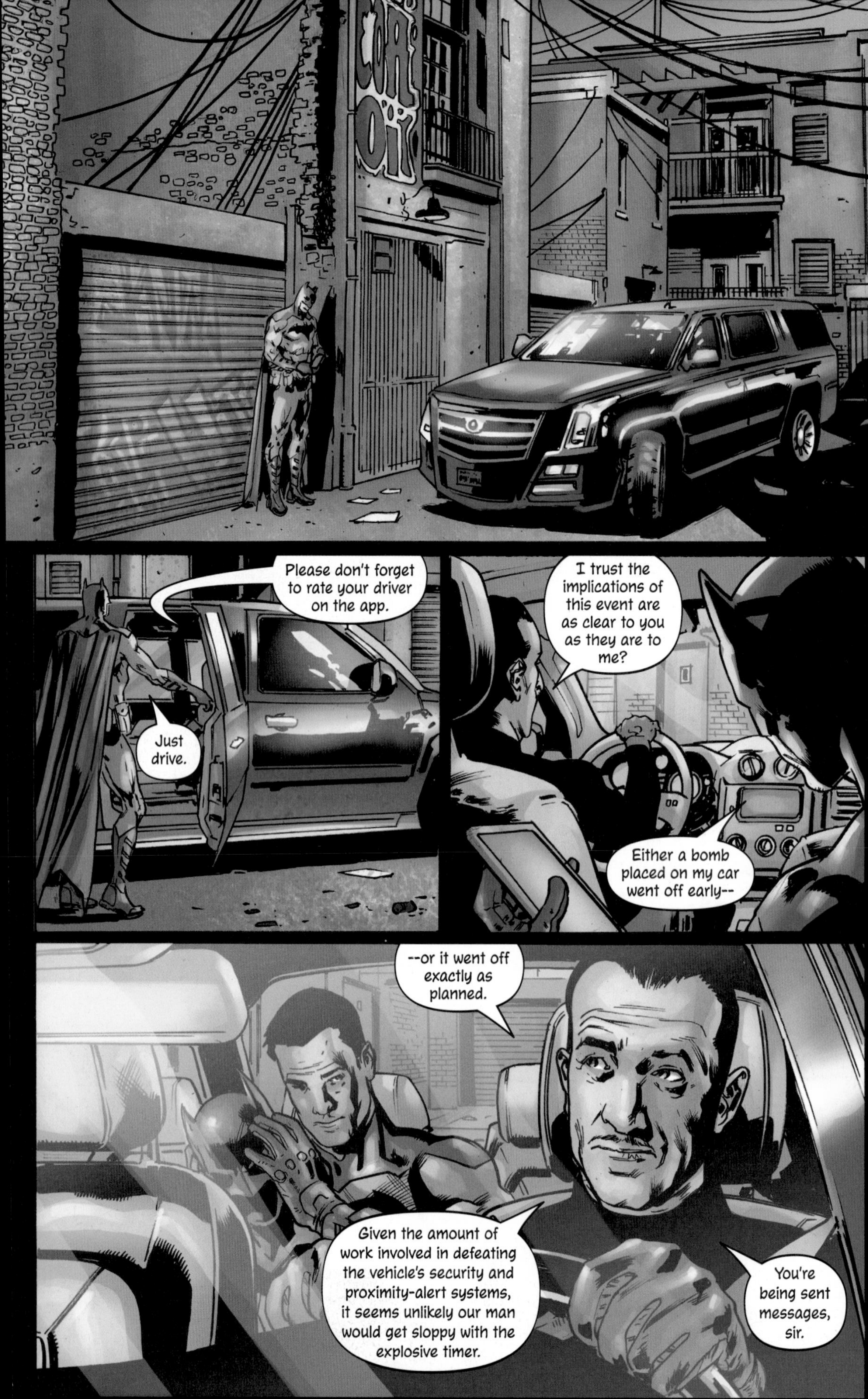
Please don't forget to rate your driver on the app.
Just drive.
I trust the implications of this event are as clear to you as they are to me?
Either a bomb placed on my car went off early--
--or it went off exactly as planned.
Given the amount of work involved in defeating the vehicle's security and proximity-alert systems, it seems unlikely our man would get sloppy with the explosive timer.
You're being sent messages, sir.

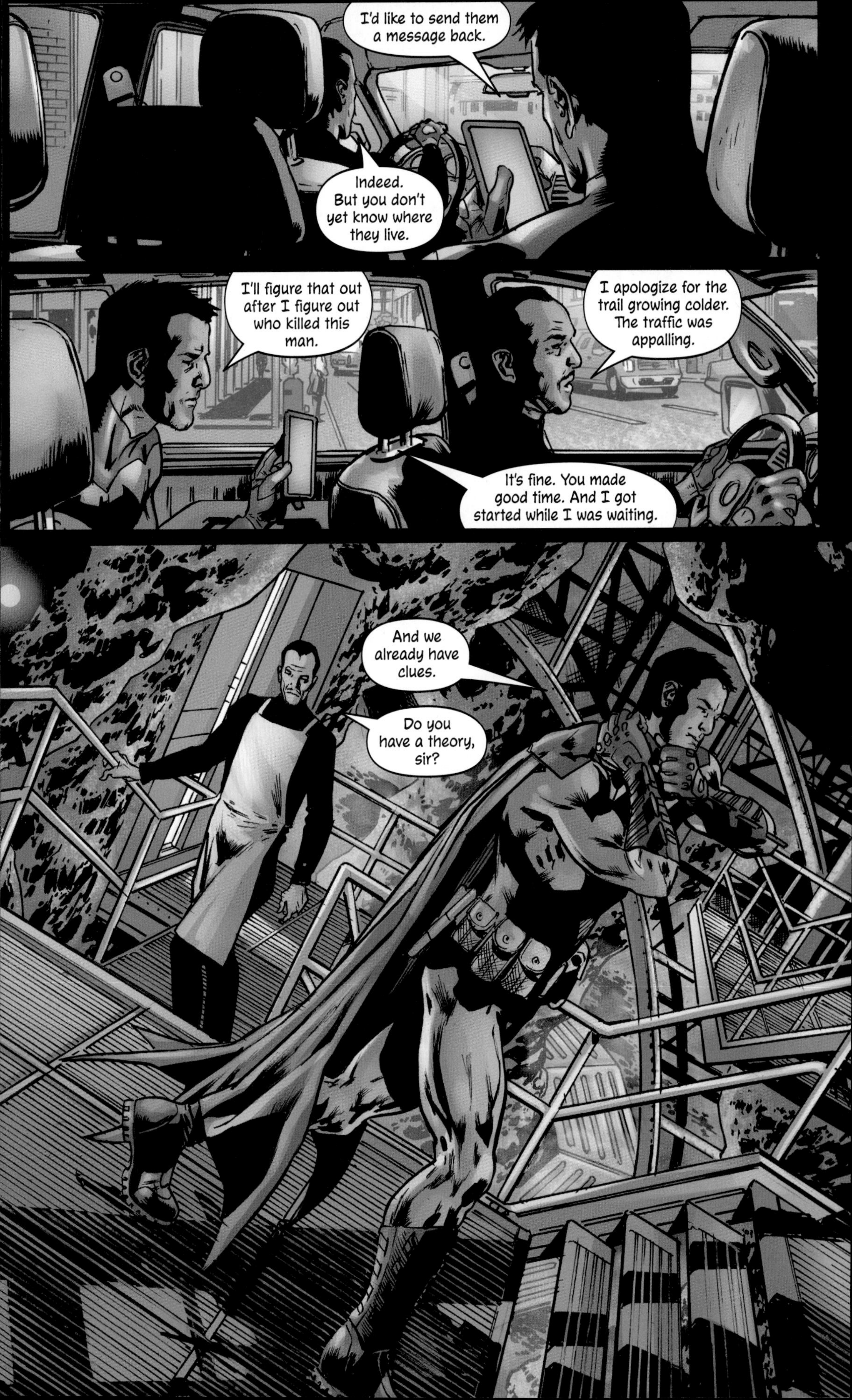
I'd like to send them a message back.
Indeed. But you don't yet know where they live.
I'll figure that out after I figure out who killed this man.
I apologize for the trail growing colder. The traffic was appalling.
It's fine. You made good time. And I got started while I was waiting.
And we already have clues.
Do you have a theory, sir?

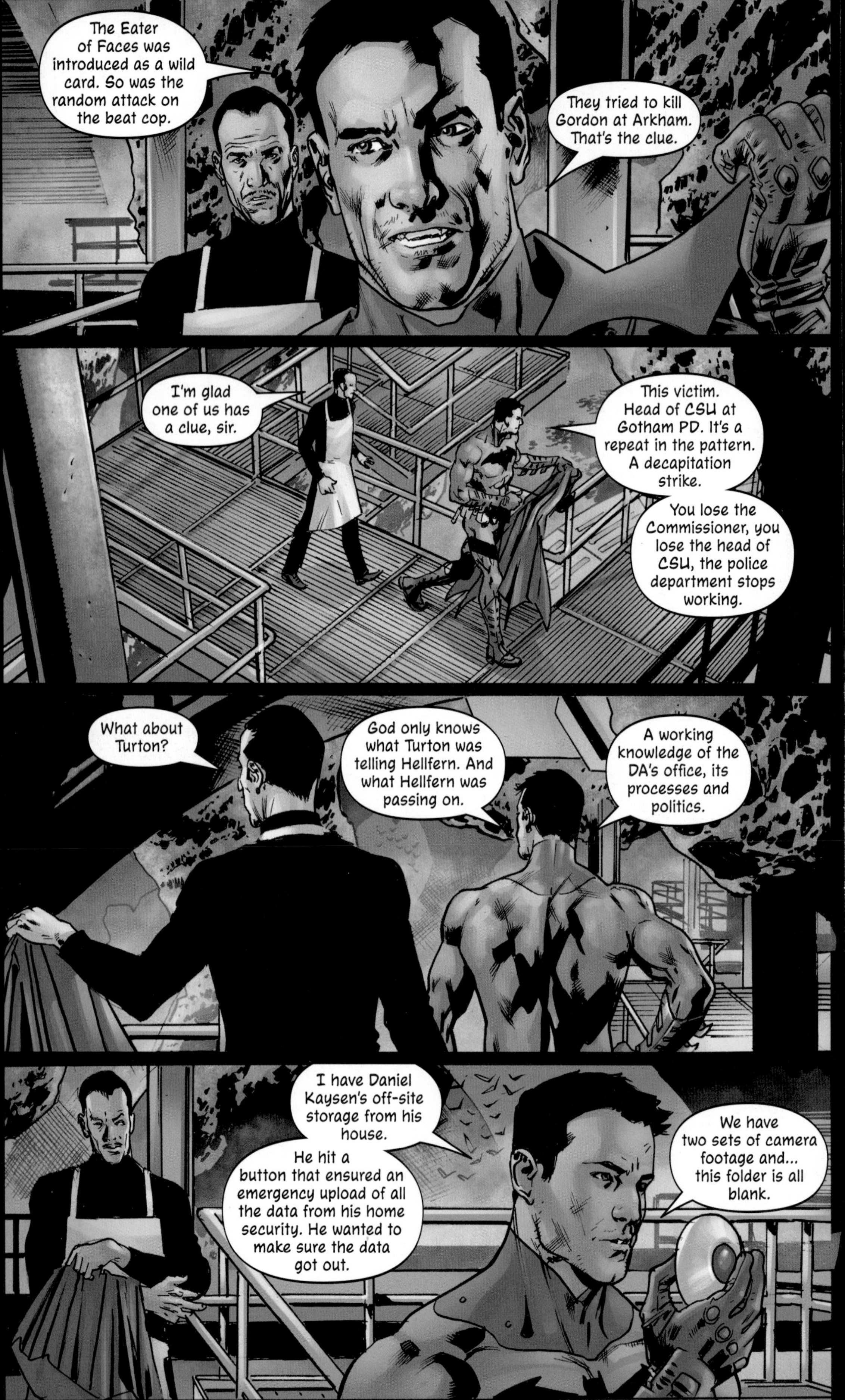
The Eater of Faces was introduced as a wild card. So was the random attack on the beat cop.
They tried to kill Gordon at Arkham. That's the clue.
I'm glad one of us has a clue, sir.
This victim. Head of CSU at Gotham PD. It's a repeat in the pattern. A decapitation strike.
You lose the Commissioner, you lose the head of CSU, the police department stops working.
What about Turton?
God only knows what Turton was telling Hellfern. And what Hellfern was passing on.
A working knowledge of the DA's office, its processes and politics.
I have Daniel Kaysen's off-site storage from his house.
He hit a button that ensured an emergency upload of all the data from his home security. He wanted to make sure the data got out.
We have two sets of camera footage and... this folder is all blank.

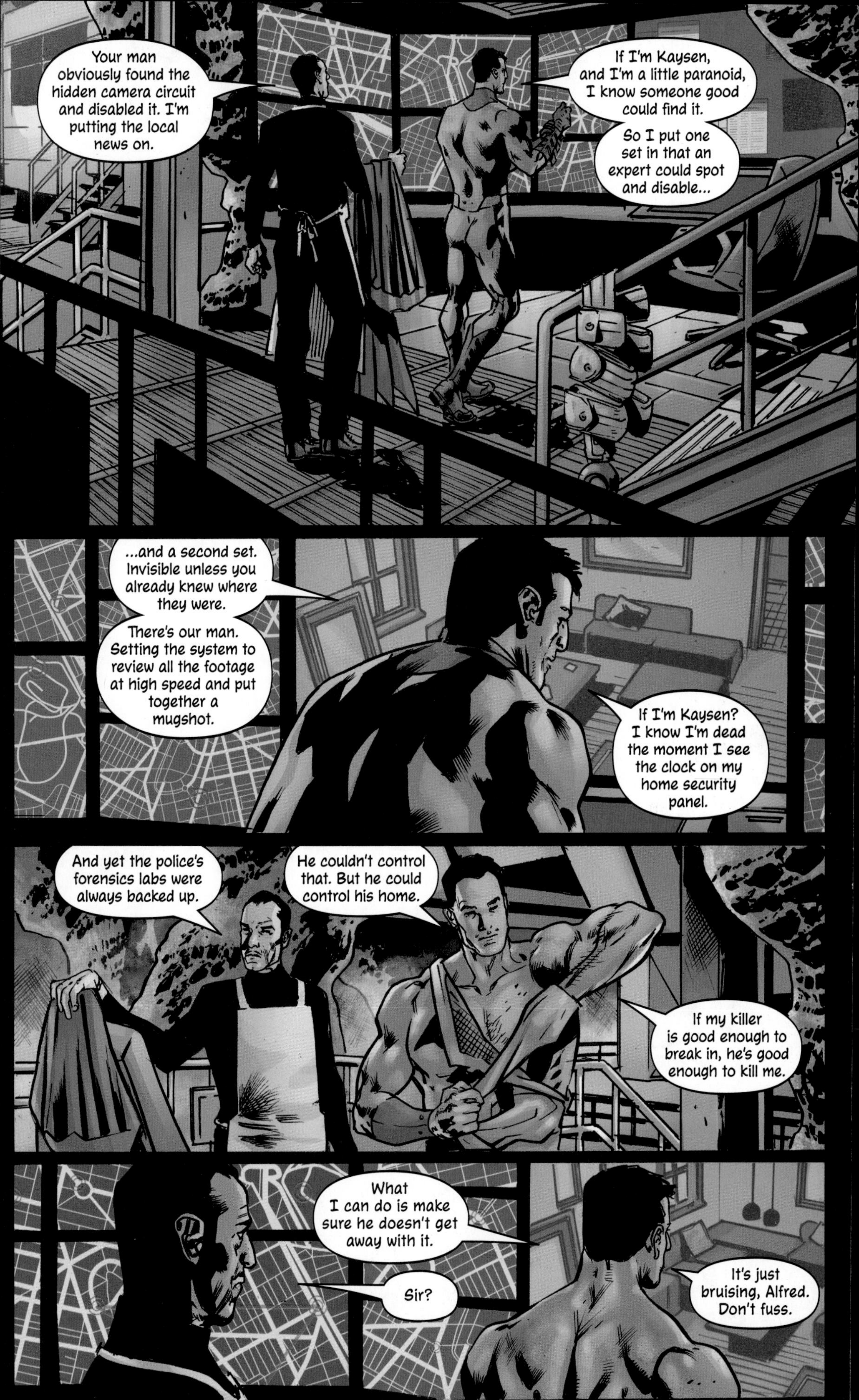
Your man obviously found the hidden camera circuit and disabled it. I'm putting the local news on.
If I'm Kaysen, and I'm a little paranoid, I know someone good could find it.
So I put one set in that an expert could spot and disable...
...and a second set. Invisible unless you already knew where they were.
There's our man. Setting the system to review all the footage at high speed and put together a mugshot.
If I'm Kaysen? I know I'm dead the moment I see the clock on my home security panel.
And yet the police's forensics labs were always backed up.
He couldn't control that. But he could control his home.
If my killer is good enough to break in, he's good enough to kill me.
What I can do is make sure he doesn't get away with it.
Sir?
It's just bruising, Alfred. Don't fuss.

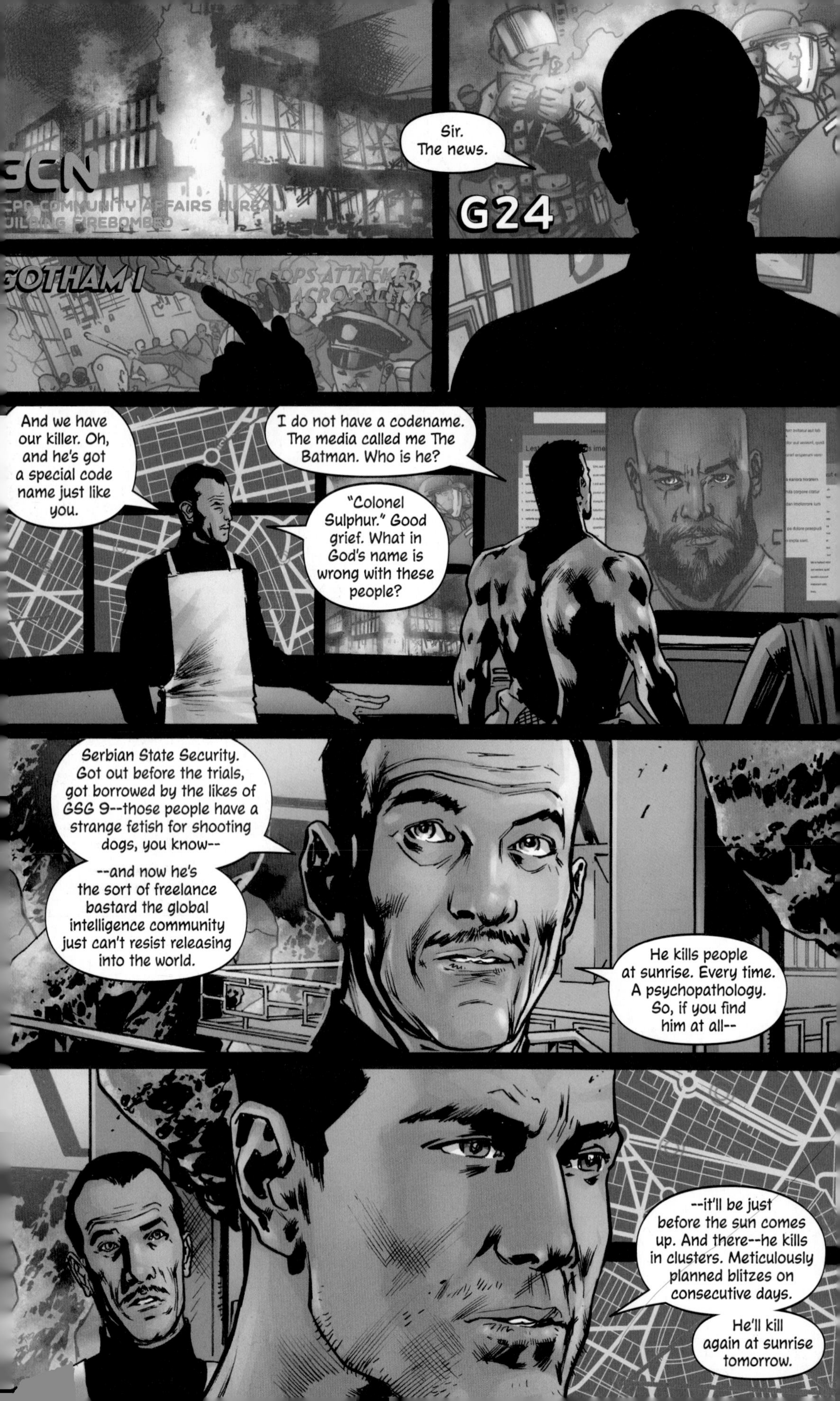
Sir.
The news.
G24
And we have our killer. Oh, and he's got a special code name just like you.
I do not have a codename. The media called me The Batman. Who is he?
"Colonel Sulphur." Good grief. What in God's name is wrong with these people?
Serbian State Security. Got out before the trials, got borrowed by the likes of GSG 9--those people have a strange fetish for shooting dogs, you know--
--and now he's the sort of freelance bastard the global intelligence community just can't resist releasing into the world.
He kills people at sunrise. Every time. A psychopathology. So, if you find him at all--
--it'll be just before the sun comes up. And there--he kills in clusters. Meticulously planned blitzes on consecutive days.
He'll kill again at sunrise tomorrow.

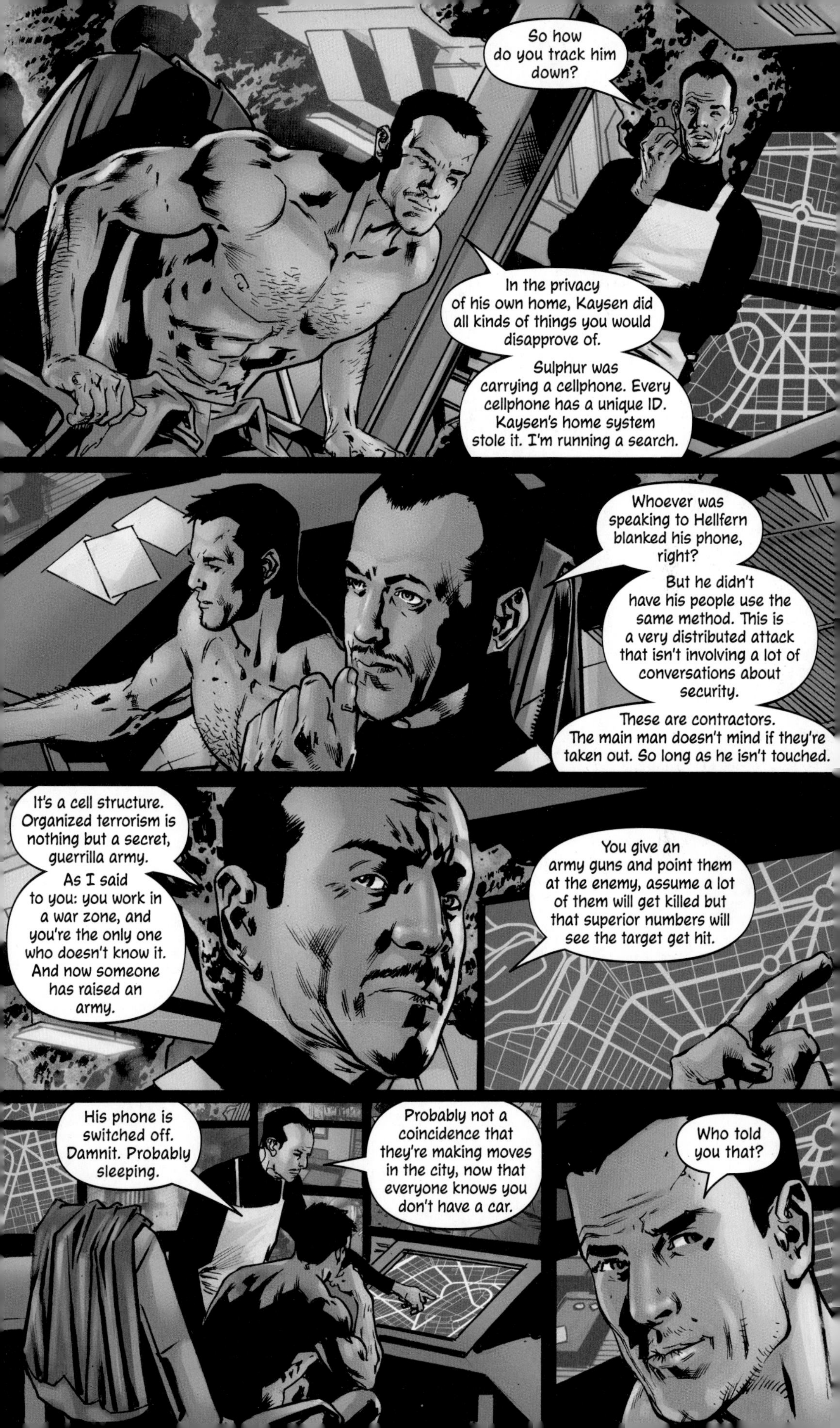

So how do you track him down?
In the privacy of his own home, Kaysen did all kinds of things you would disapprove of.
Sulphur was carrying a cellphone. Every cellphone has a unique ID. Kaysen's home system stole it. I'm running a search.
Whoever was speaking to Hellfern blanked his phone, right?
But he didn't have his people use the same method. This is a very distributed attack that isn't involving a lot of conversations about security.
These are contractors. The main man doesn't mind if they're taken out. So long as he isn't touched.
It's a cell structure. Organized terrorism is nothing but a secret, guerrilla army.
As I said to you: you work in a war zone, and you're the only one who doesn't know it. And now someone has raised an army.
You give an army guns and point them at the enemy, assume a lot of them will get killed but that superior numbers will see the target get hit.
His phone is switched off. Damnit. Probably sleeping.
Probably not a coincidence that they're making moves in the city, now that everyone knows you don't have a car.
Who told you that?

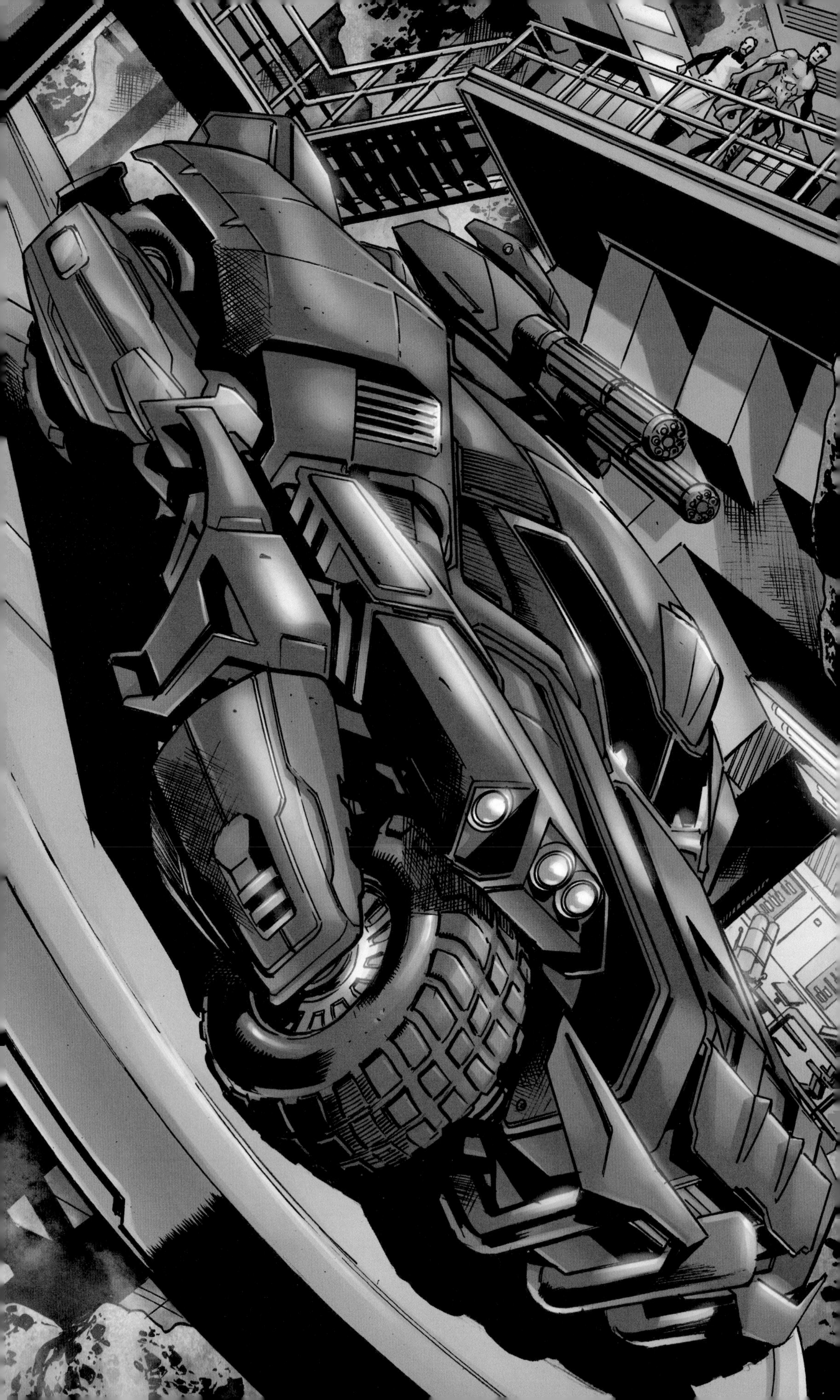

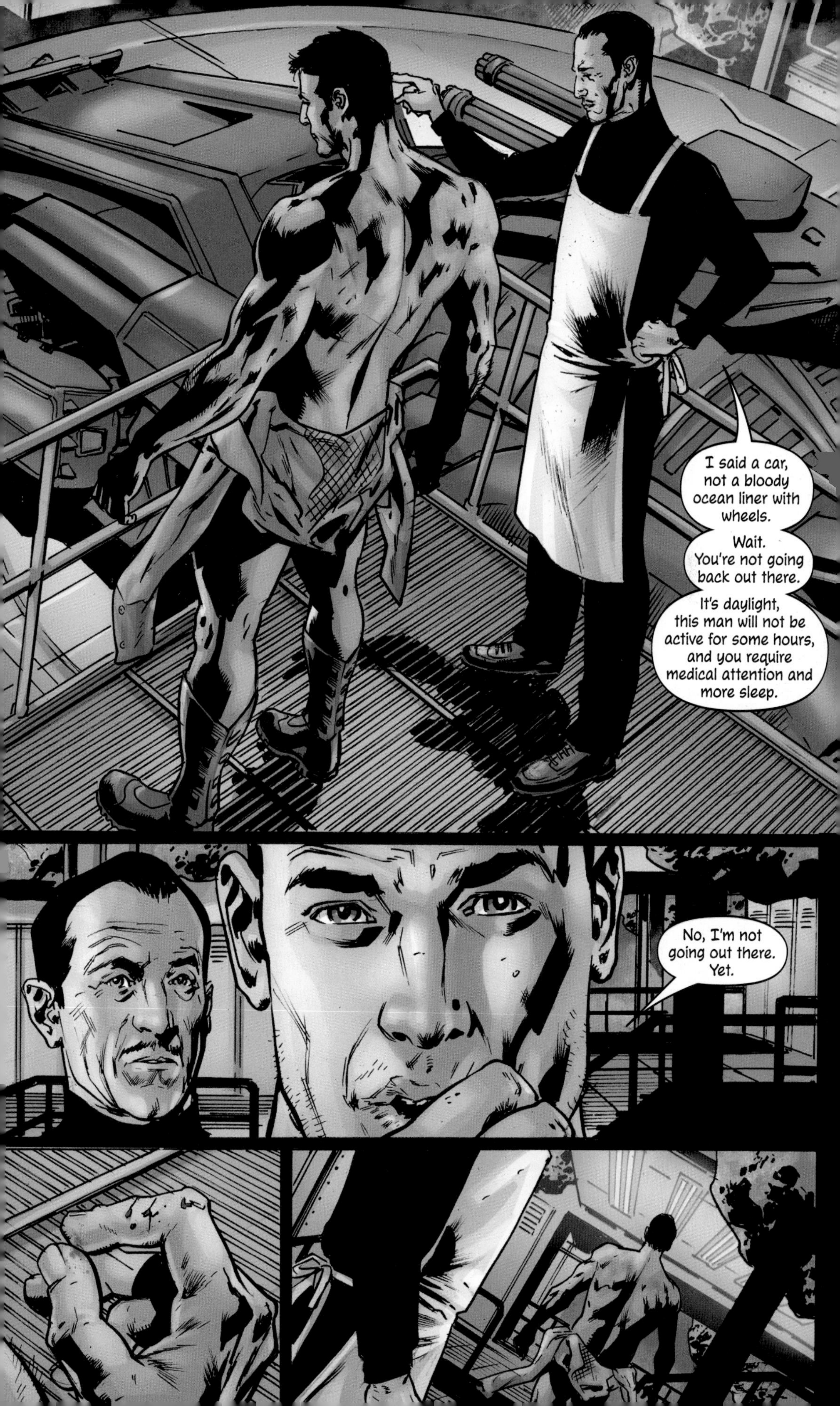
I said a car, not a bloody ocean liner with wheels.
Wait. You're not going back out there.
It's daylight, this man will not be active for some hours, and you require medical attention and more sleep.
No, I'm not going out there. Yet.

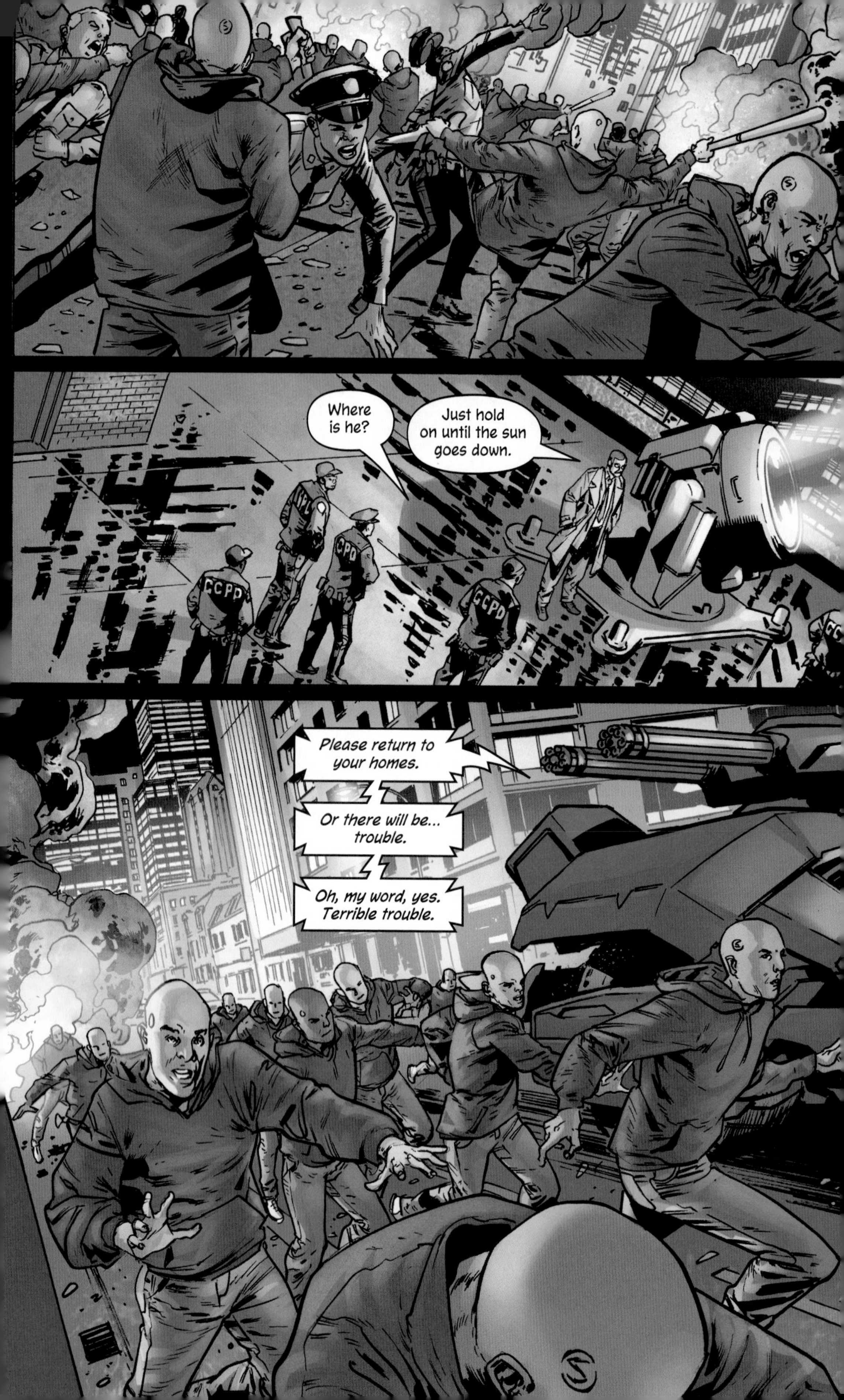
Where is he?
Just hold on until the sun goes down.
Please return to your homes.
Or there will be... trouble.
Oh, my word, yes. Terrible trouble.

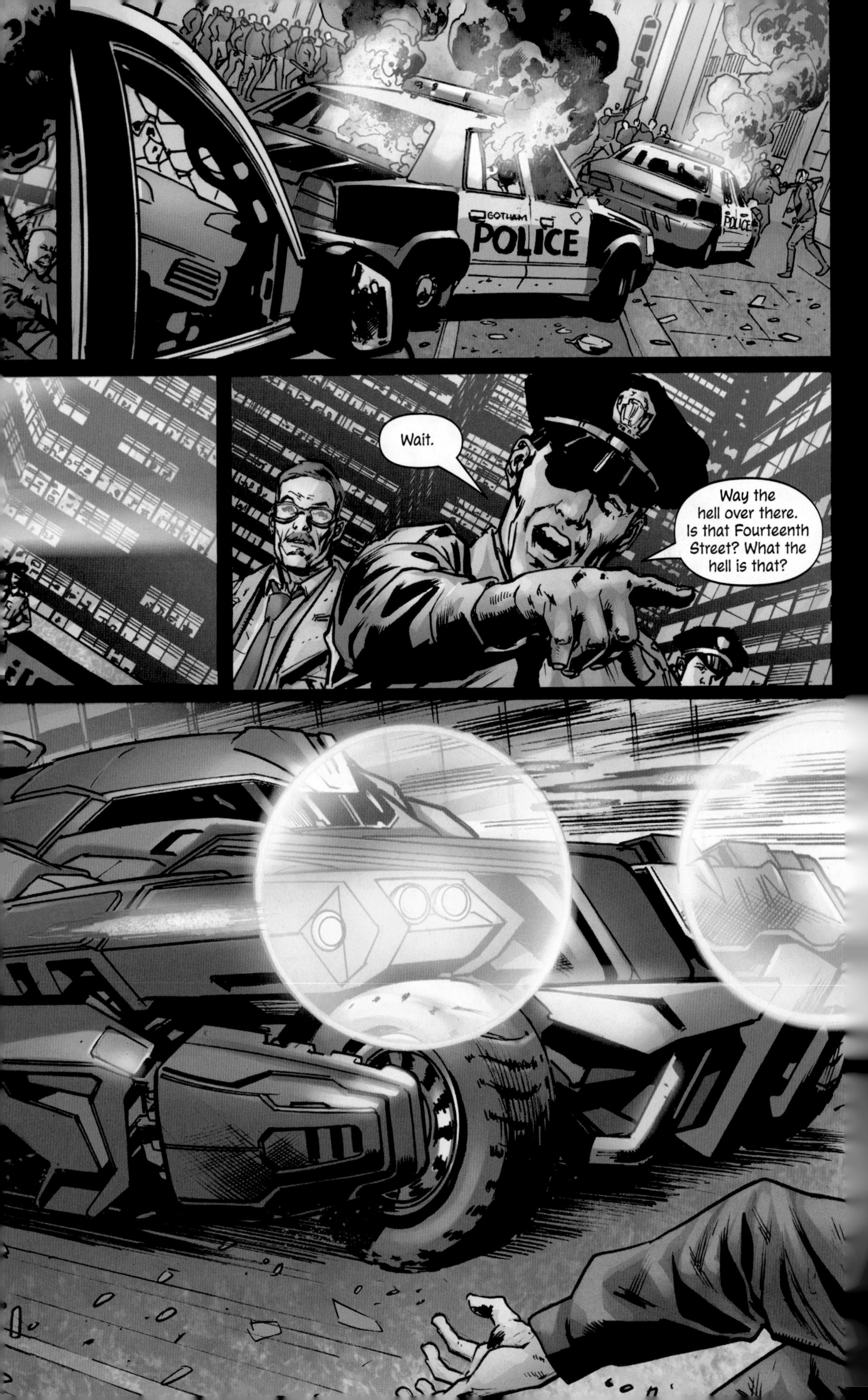
GOTHAM POLICE
POLICE
Wait.
Way the hell over there. Is that Fourteenth Street? What the hell is that?

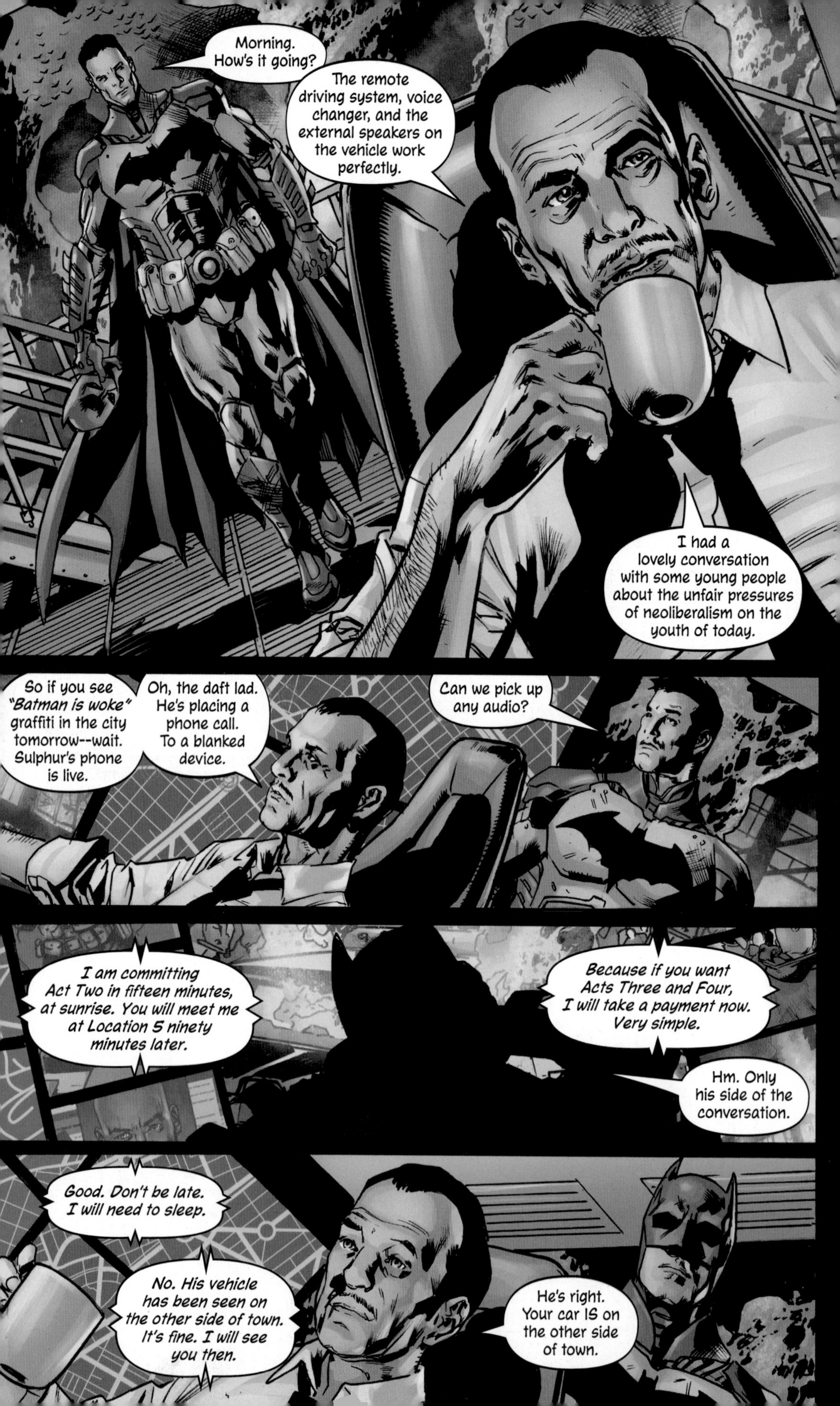
Morning. How's it going?
The remote driving system, voice changer, and the external speakers on the vehicle work perfectly.
I had a lovely conversation with some young people about the unfair pressures of neoliberalism on the youth of today.
So if you see "Batman is woke" graffiti in the city tomorrow--wait. Sulphur's phone is live.
Oh, the daft lad. He's placing a phone call. To a blanked device.
Can we pick up any audio?
I am committing Act Two in fifteen minutes, at sunrise. You will meet me at Location 5 ninety minutes later.
Because if you want Acts Three and Four, I will take a payment now. Very simple.
Hm. Only his side of the conversation.
Good. Don't be late. I will need to sleep.
No. His vehicle has been seen on the other side of town. It's fine. I will see you then.
He's right. Your car IS on the other side of town.

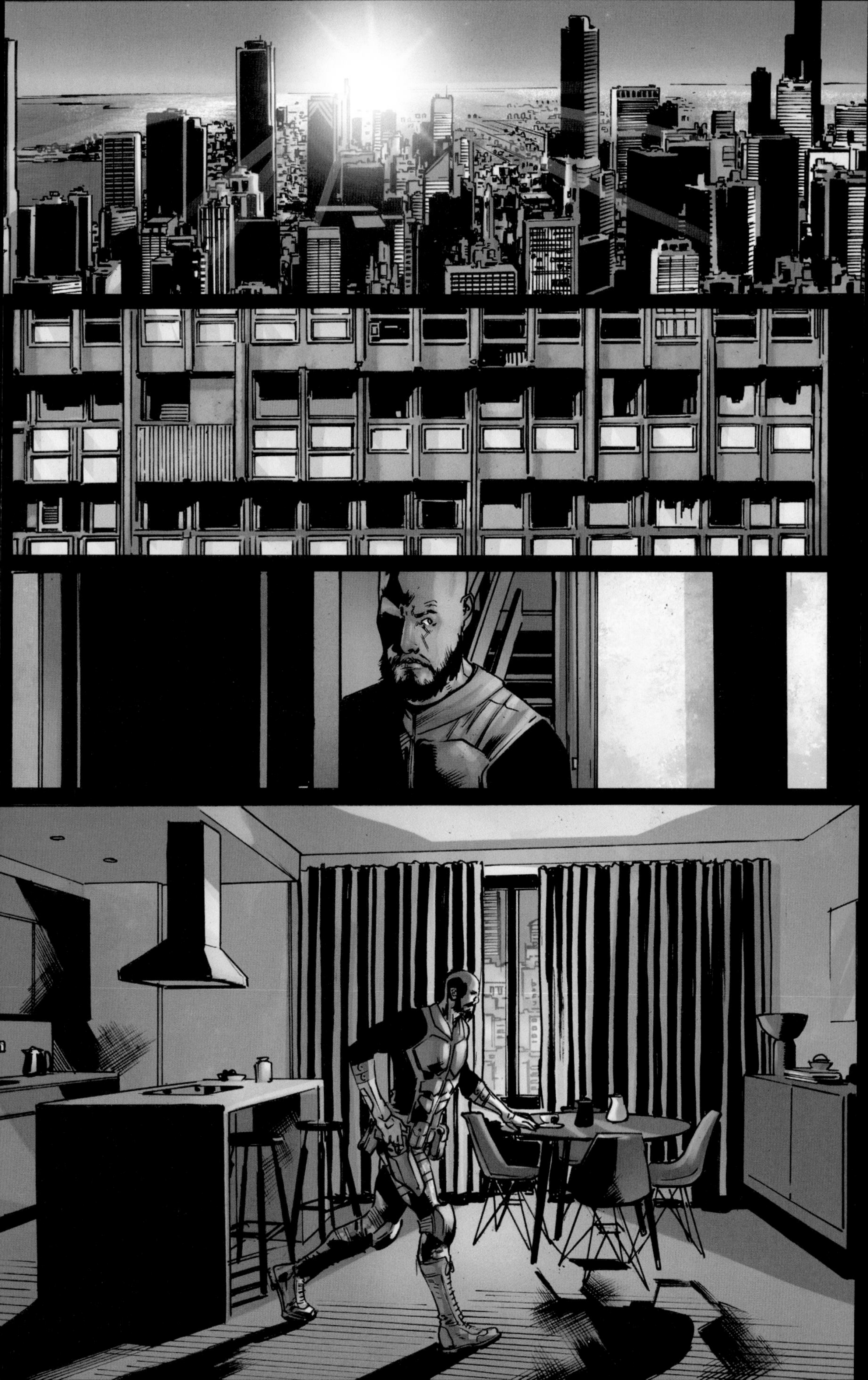

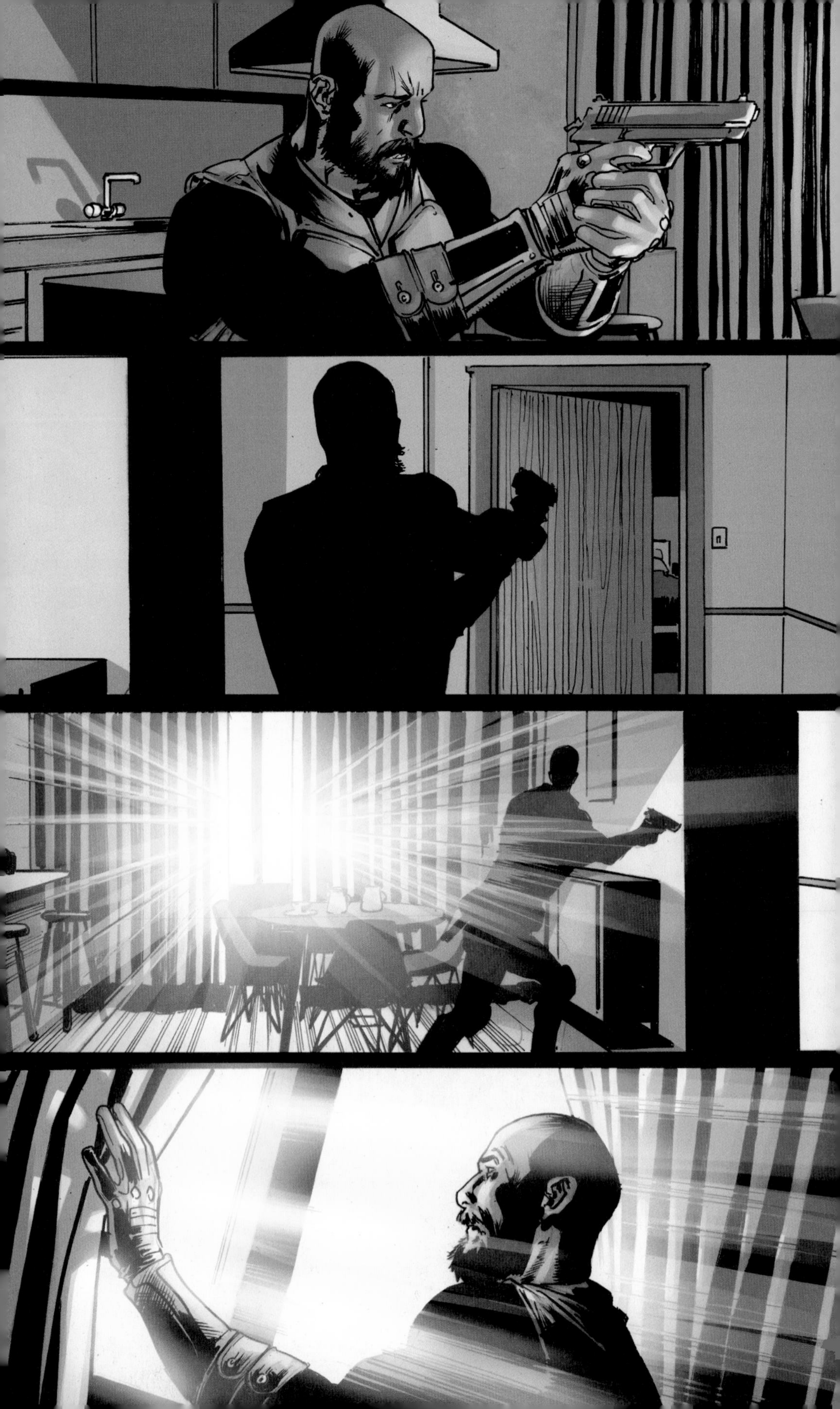

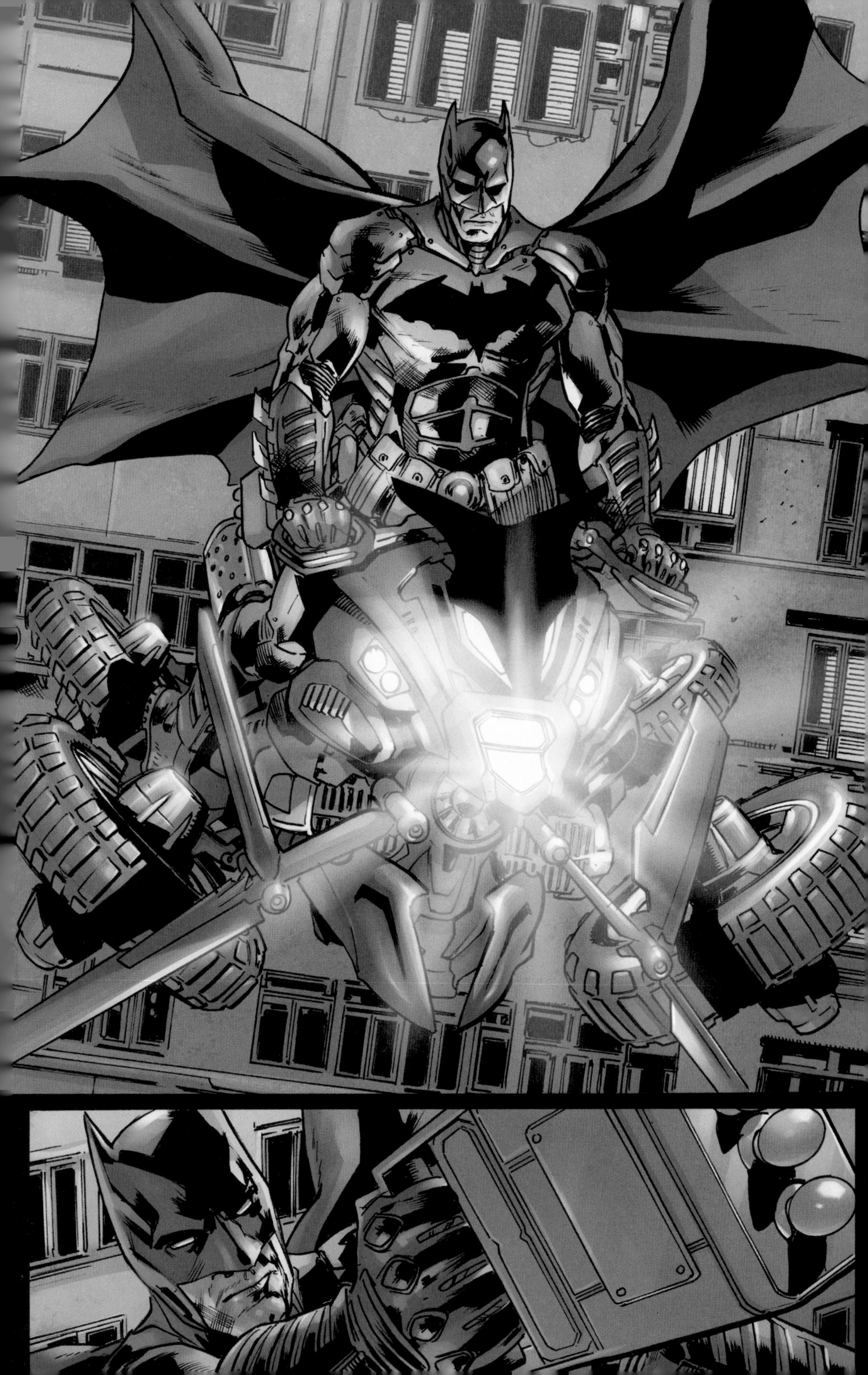

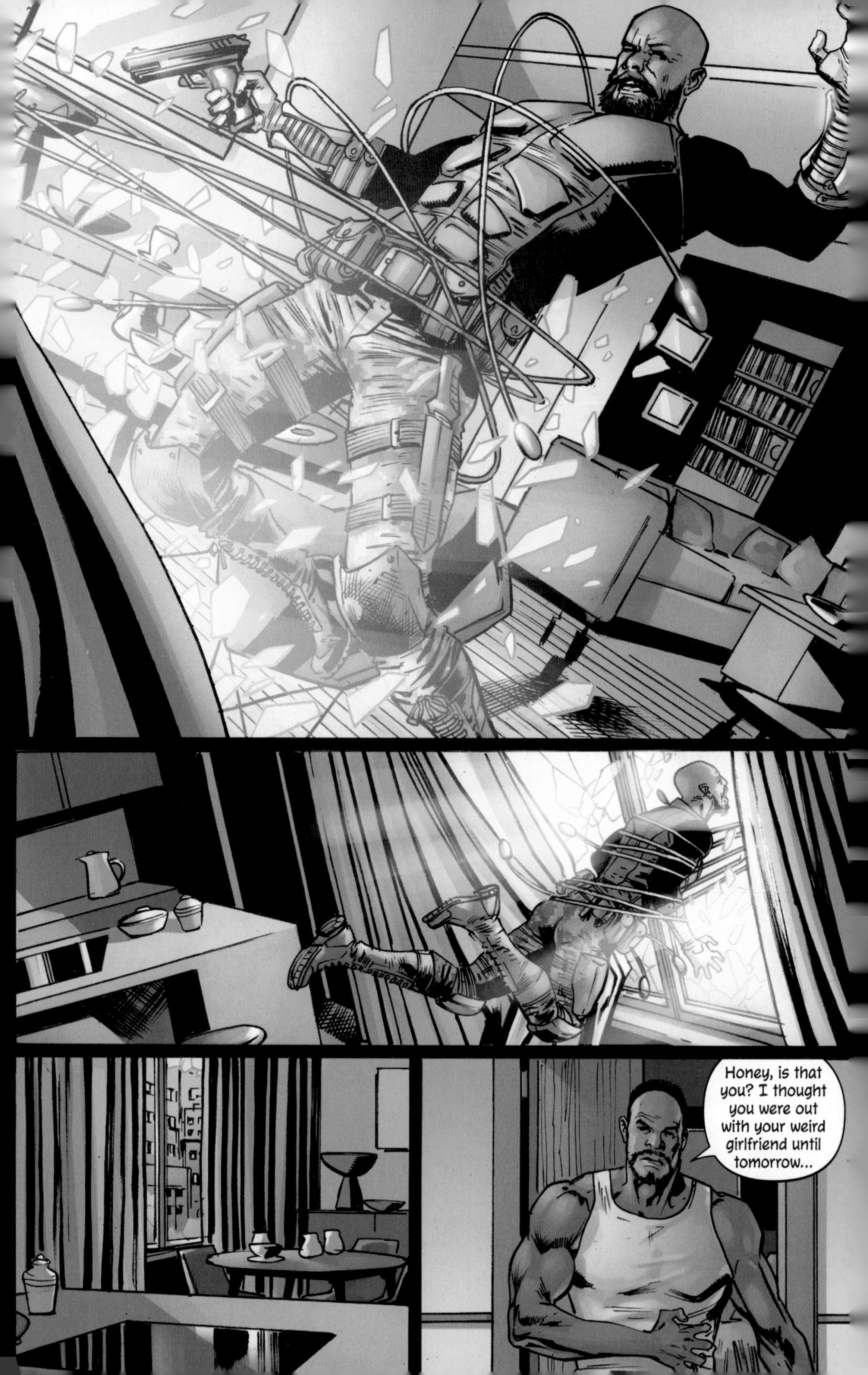
Honey, is that you? I thought you were out with your weird girlfriend until tomorrow...

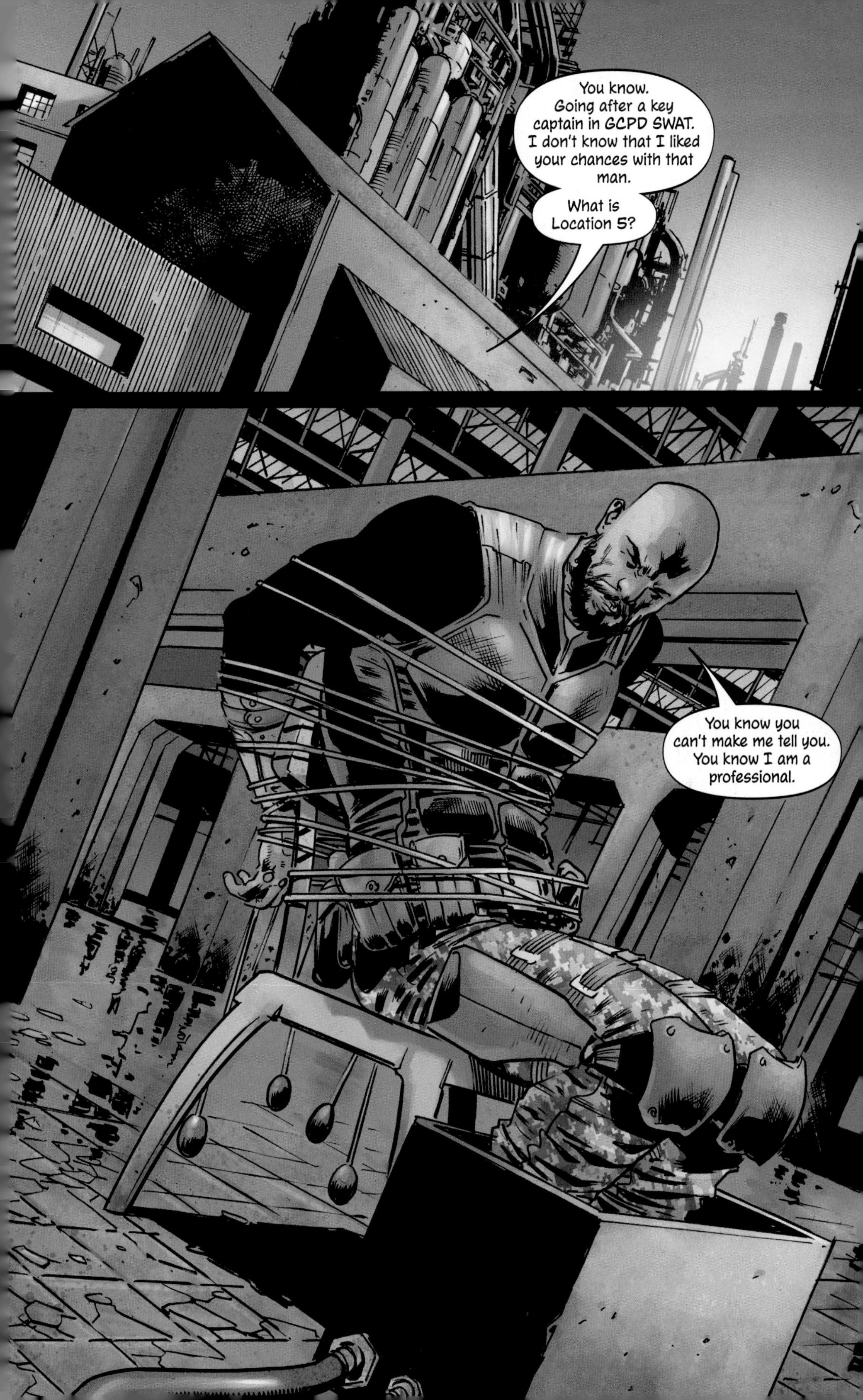
You know. Going after a key captain in GCPD SWAT. I don't know that I liked your chances with that man.
What is Location 5?
You know you can't make me tell you. You know I am a professional.

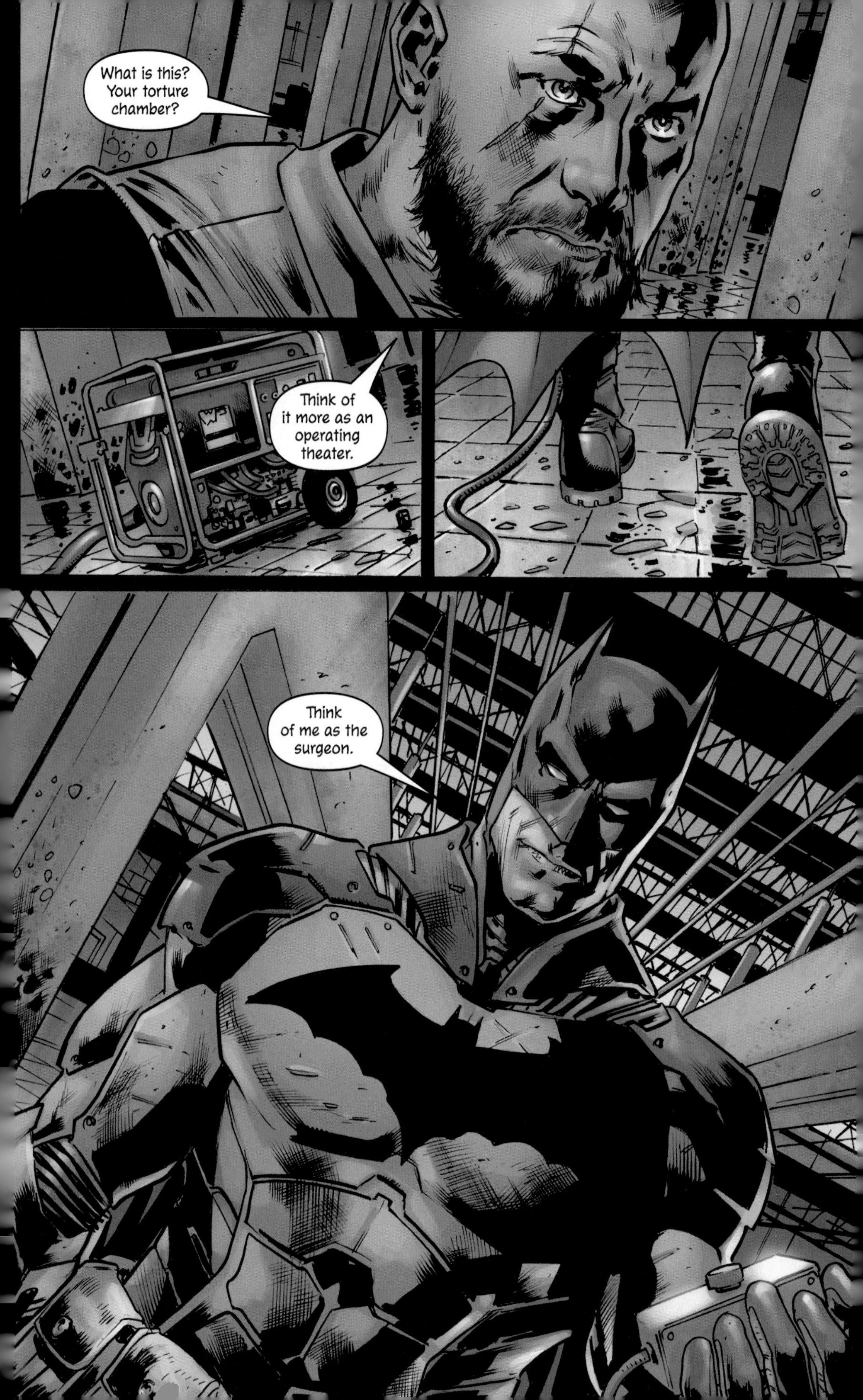
What is this? Your torture chamber?
Think of it more as an operating theater.
Think of me as the surgeon.

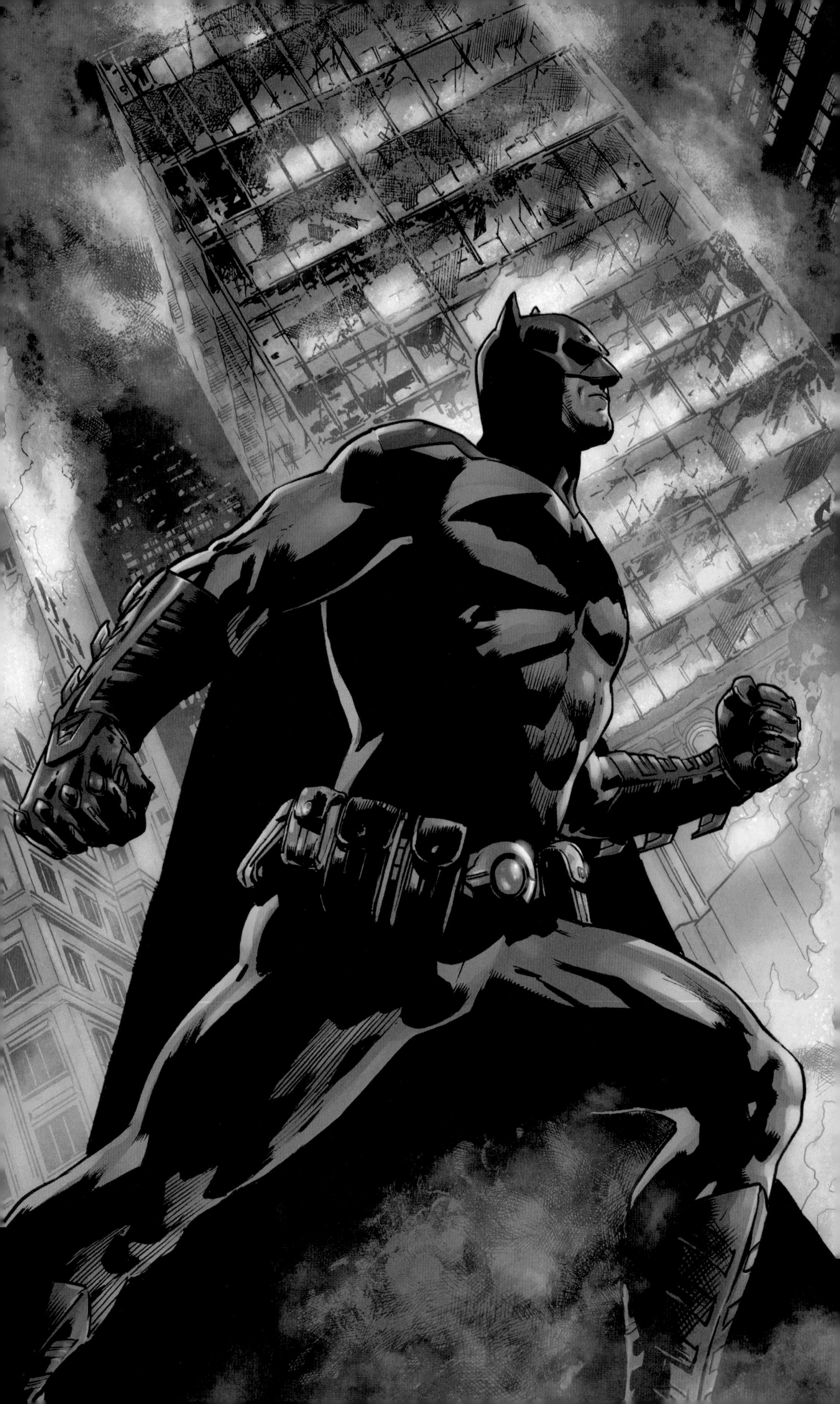

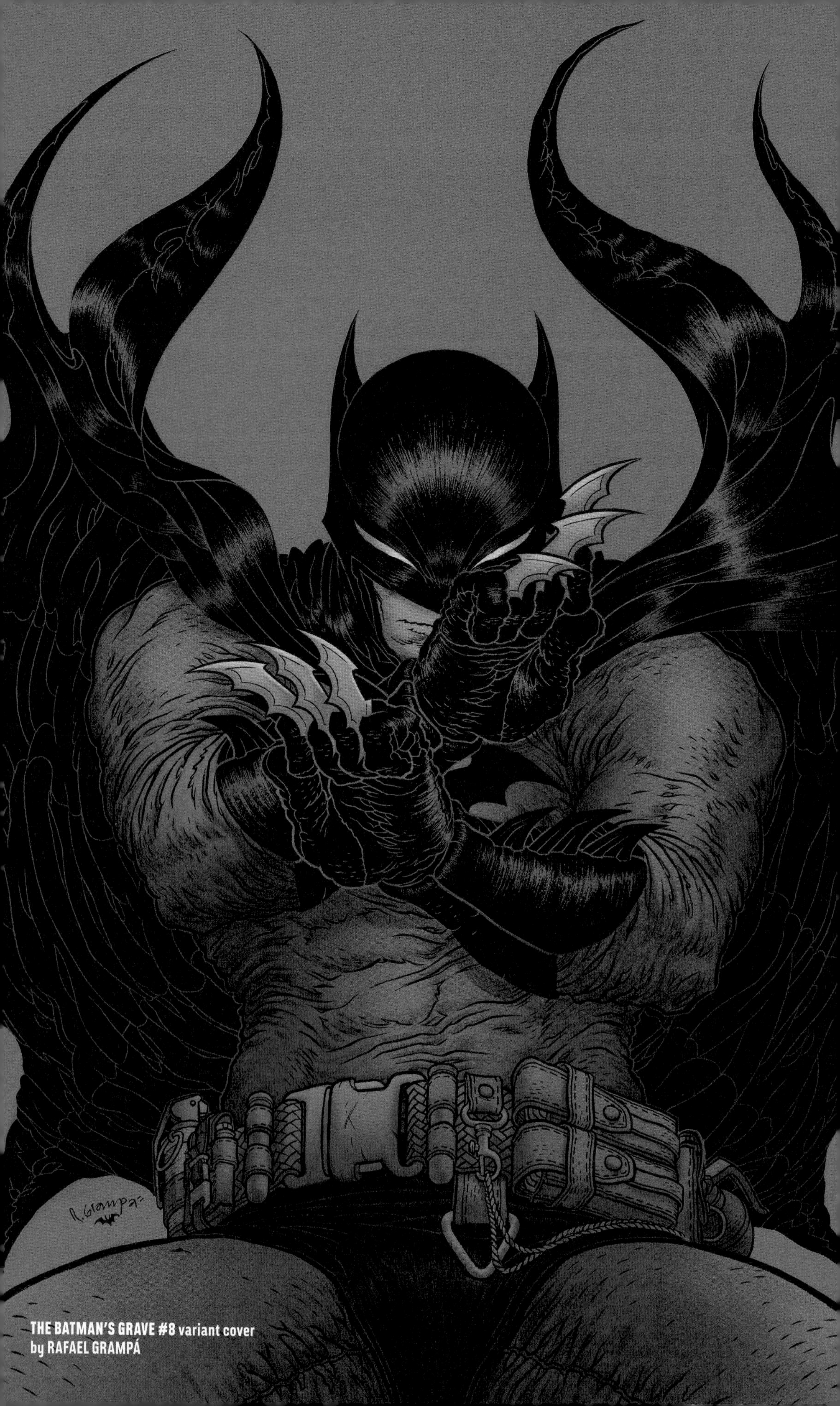
R. Grampá

THE BATMAN'S GRAVE #8 variant cover
by **RAFAEL GRAMPÁ**

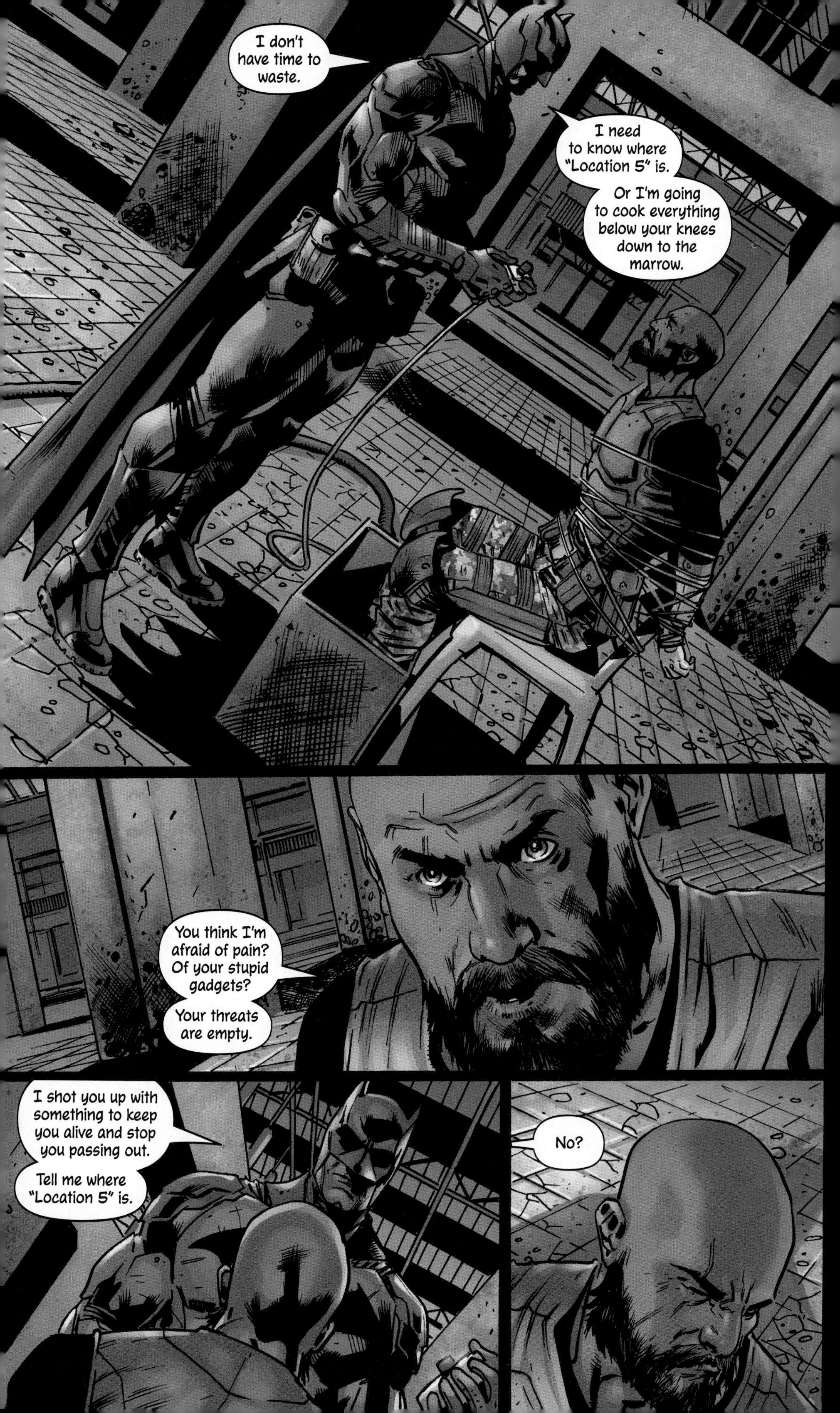
I don't have time to waste.
I need to know where "Location 5" is.
Or I'm going to cook everything below your knees down to the marrow.
You think I'm afraid of pain? Of your stupid gadgets?
Your threats are empty.
I shot you up with something to keep you alive and stop you passing out.
Tell me where "Location 5" is.
No?

AAAAAA

Chapter 8

Writer	Art
WARREN ELLIS	**BRYAN HITCH**

Colors	Letters
ALEX SINCLAIR	**RICHARD STARKINGS**

Cover	Varitant Cover
BRYAN HITCH &	**RAFAEL**
ALEX SINCLAIR	**GRAMPÁ**

Associate Editor	Editor
ANDREW MARINO	**MARIE JAVINS**

BATMAN created by BOB KANE with BILL FINGER

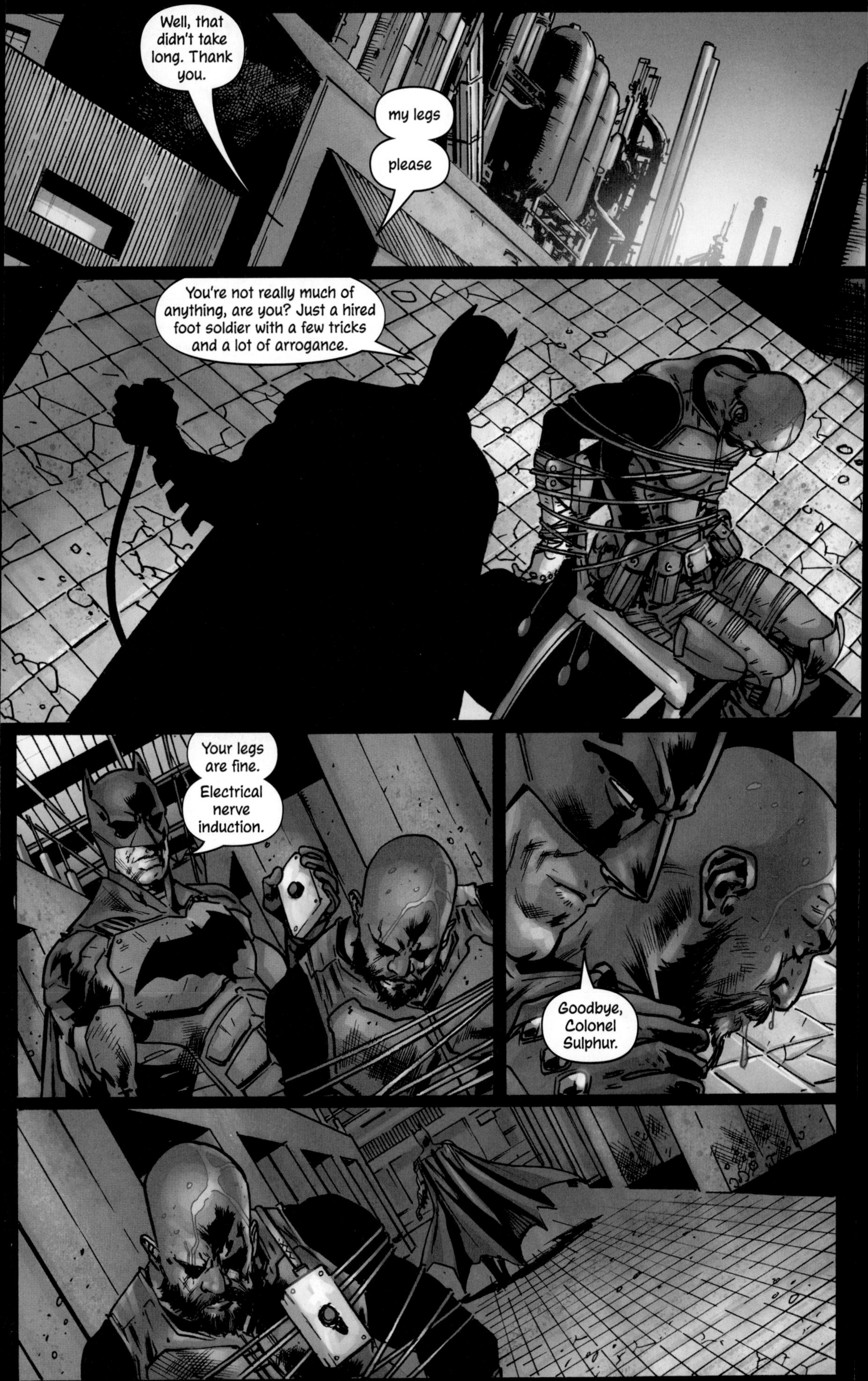
Well, that didn't take long. Thank you.
my legs
please
You're not really much of anything, are you? Just a hired foot soldier with a few tricks and a lot of arrogance.
Your legs are fine.
Electrical nerve induction.
Goodbye, Colonel Sulphur.

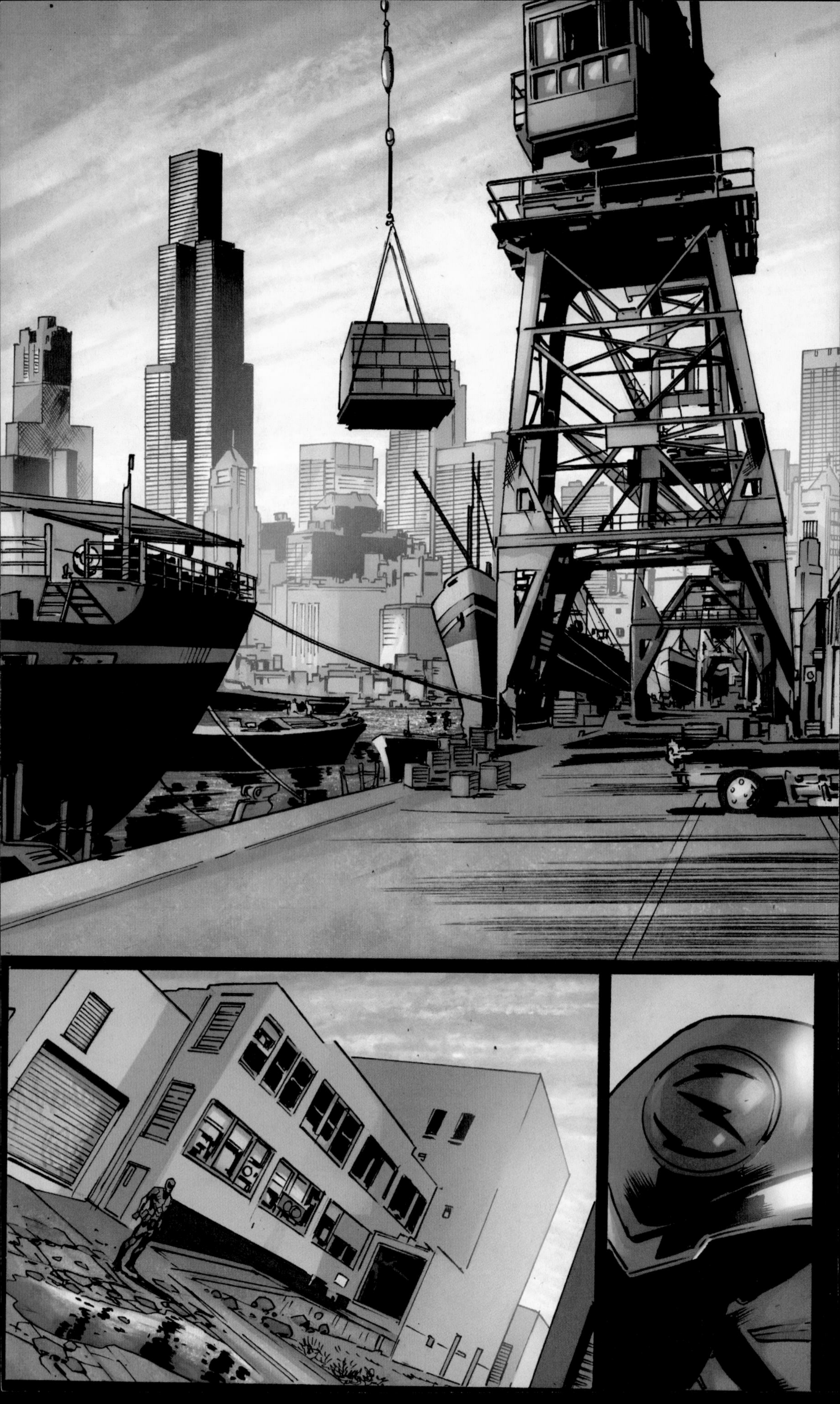

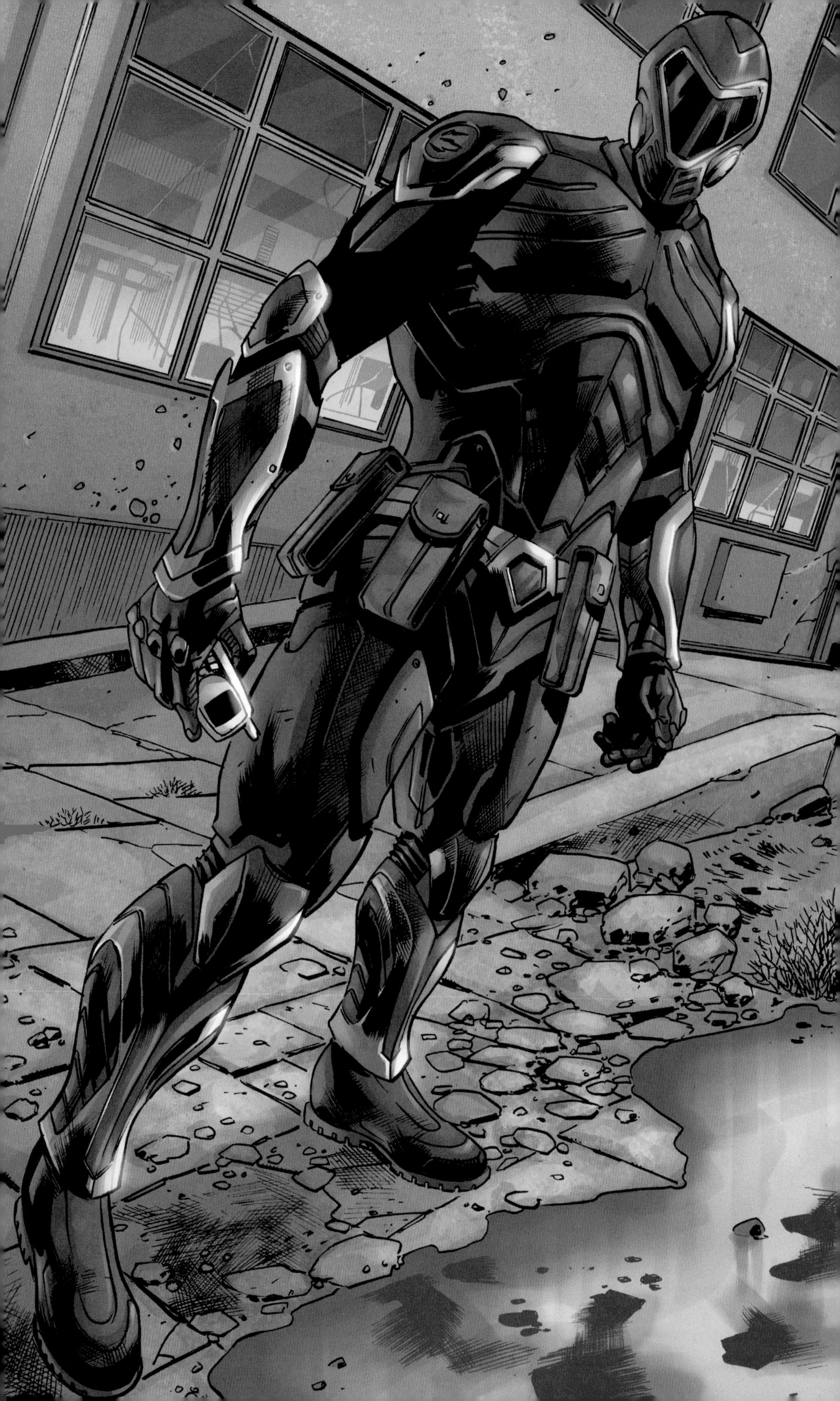

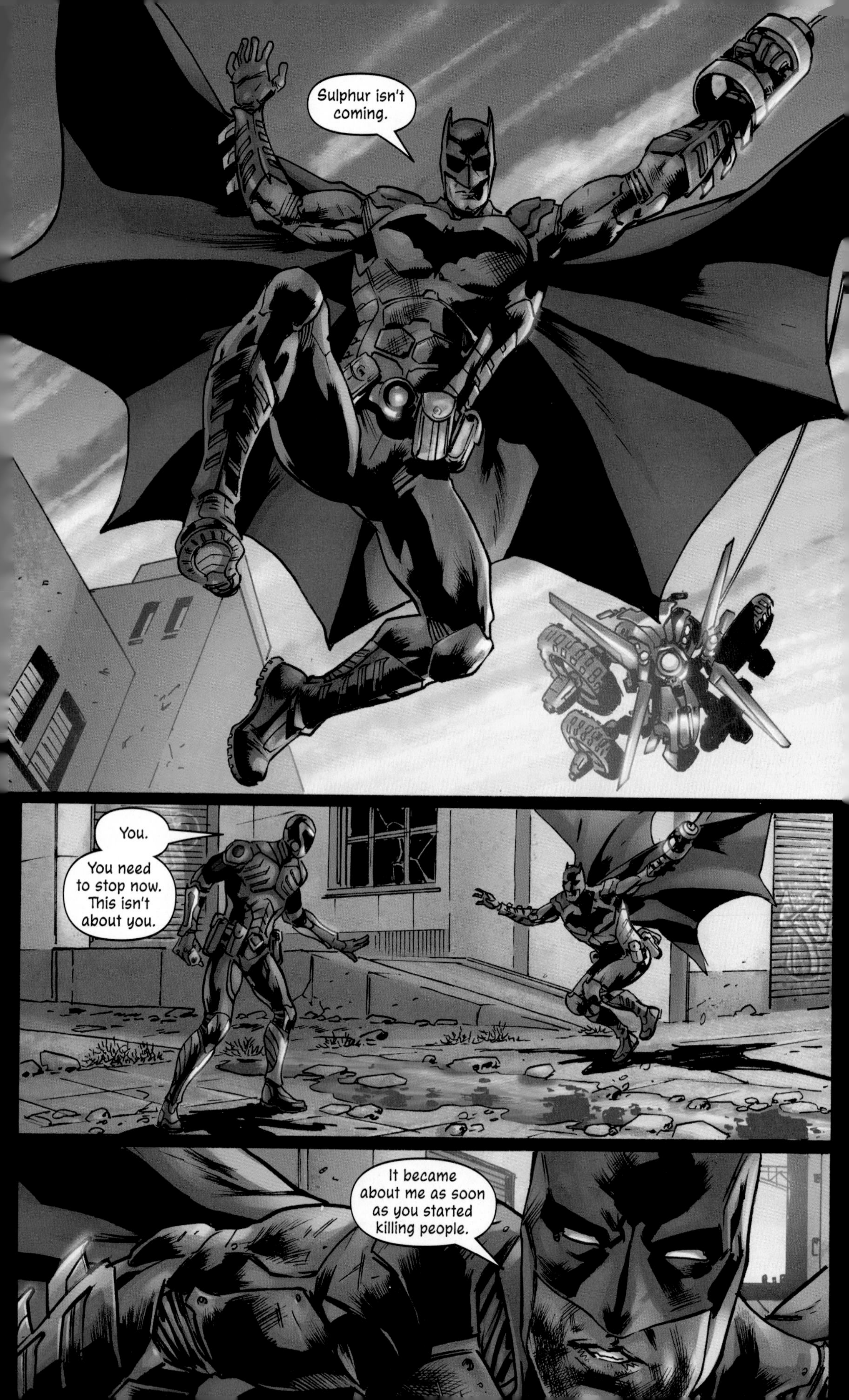
Sulphur isn't coming.
You.
You need to stop now. This isn't about you.
It became about me as soon as you started killing people.

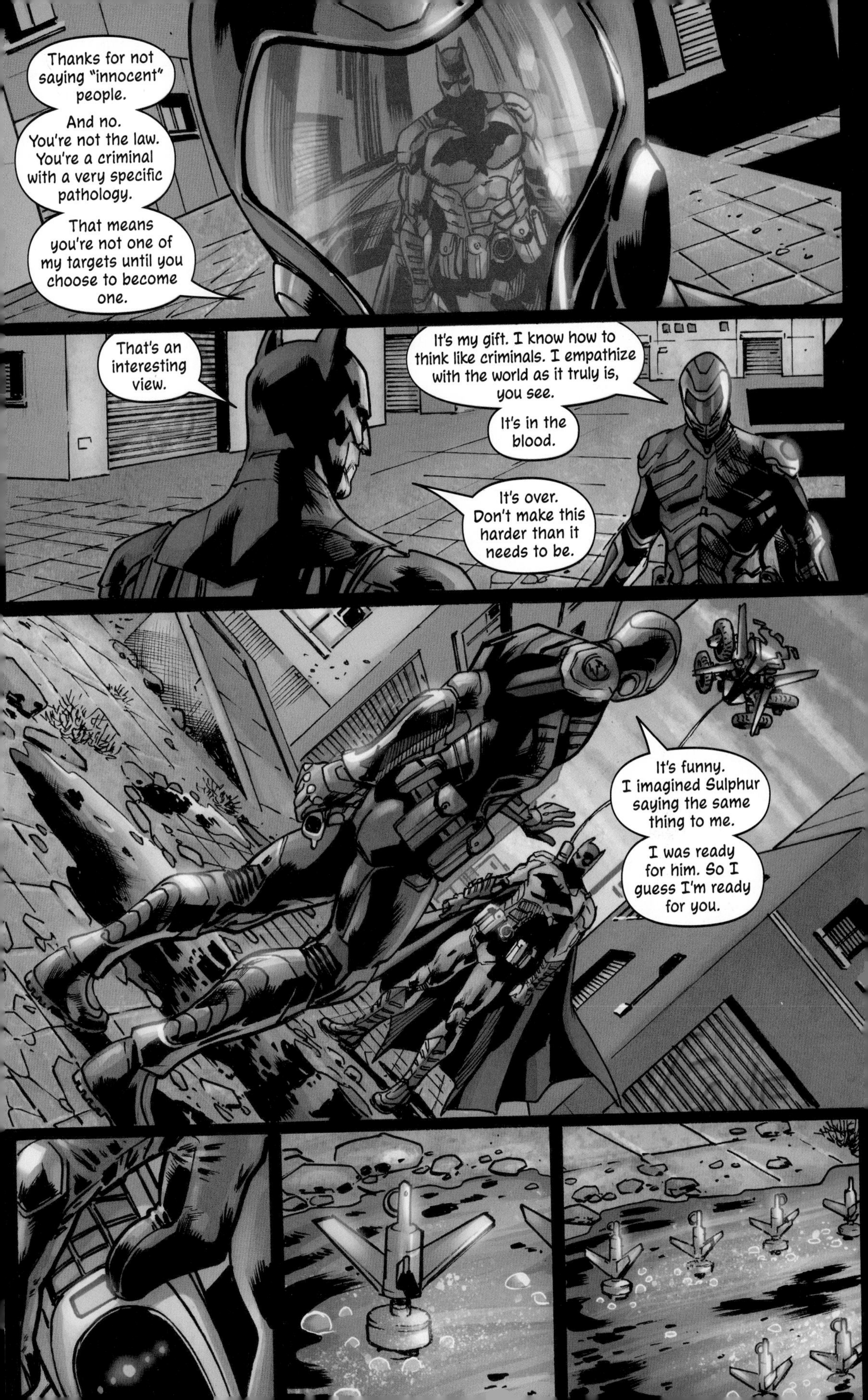
Thanks for not saying "innocent" people.
And no. You're not the law. You're a criminal with a very specific pathology.
That means you're not one of my targets until you choose to become one.
That's an interesting view.
It's my gift. I know how to think like criminals. I empathize with the world as it truly is, you see.
It's in the blood.
It's over. Don't make this harder than it needs to be.
It's funny. I imagined Sulphur saying the same thing to me.
I was ready for him. So I guess I'm ready for you.

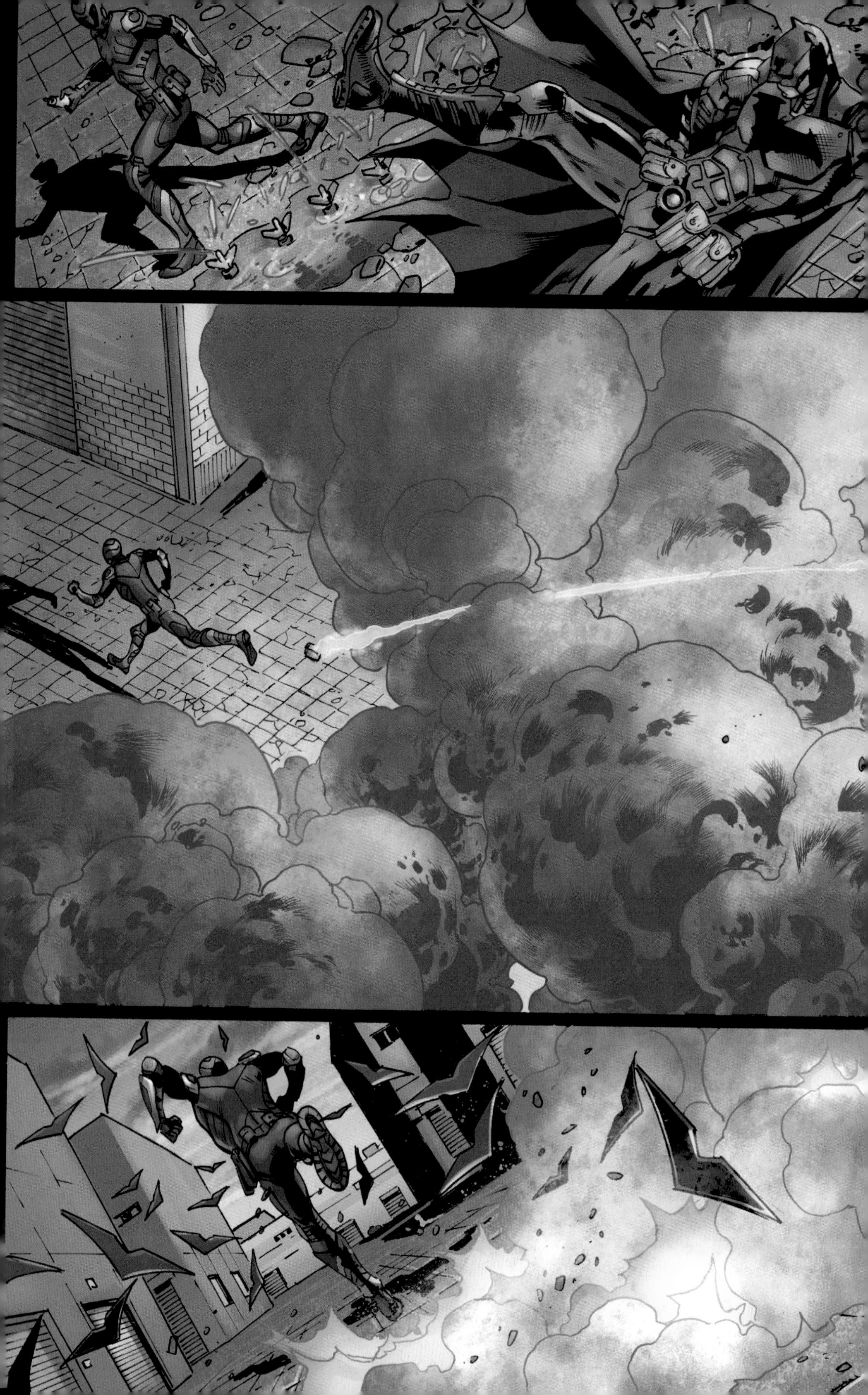

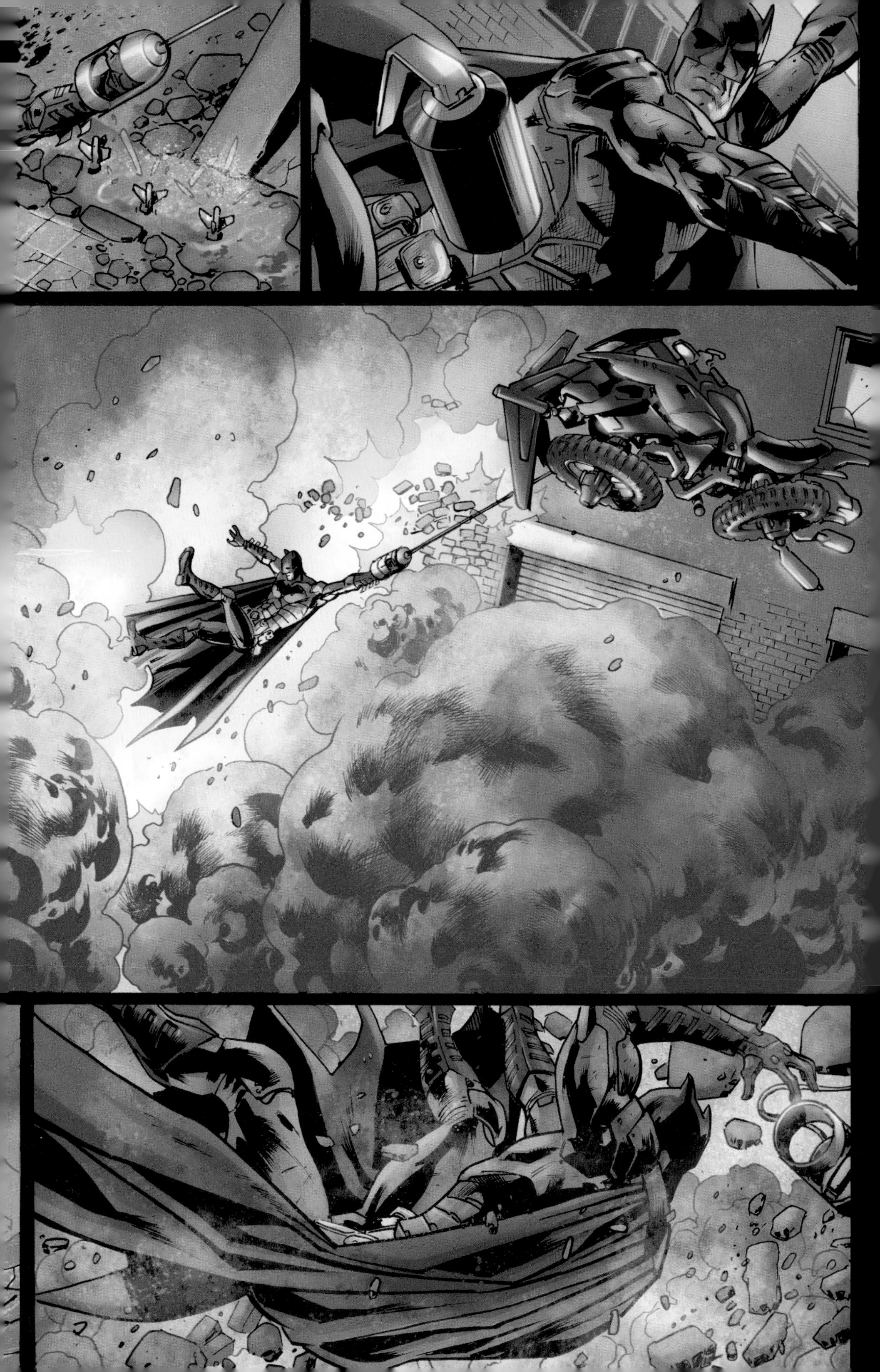

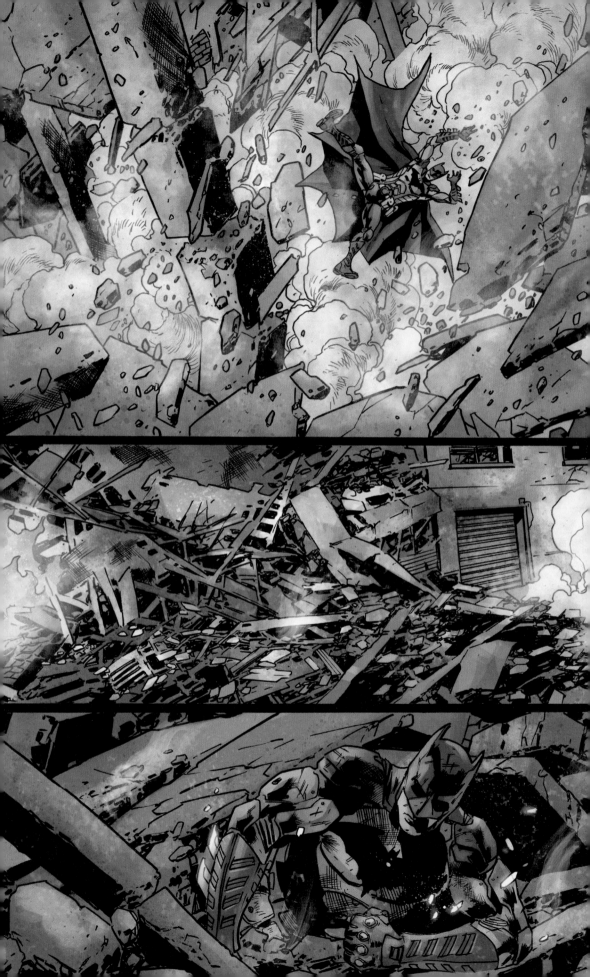

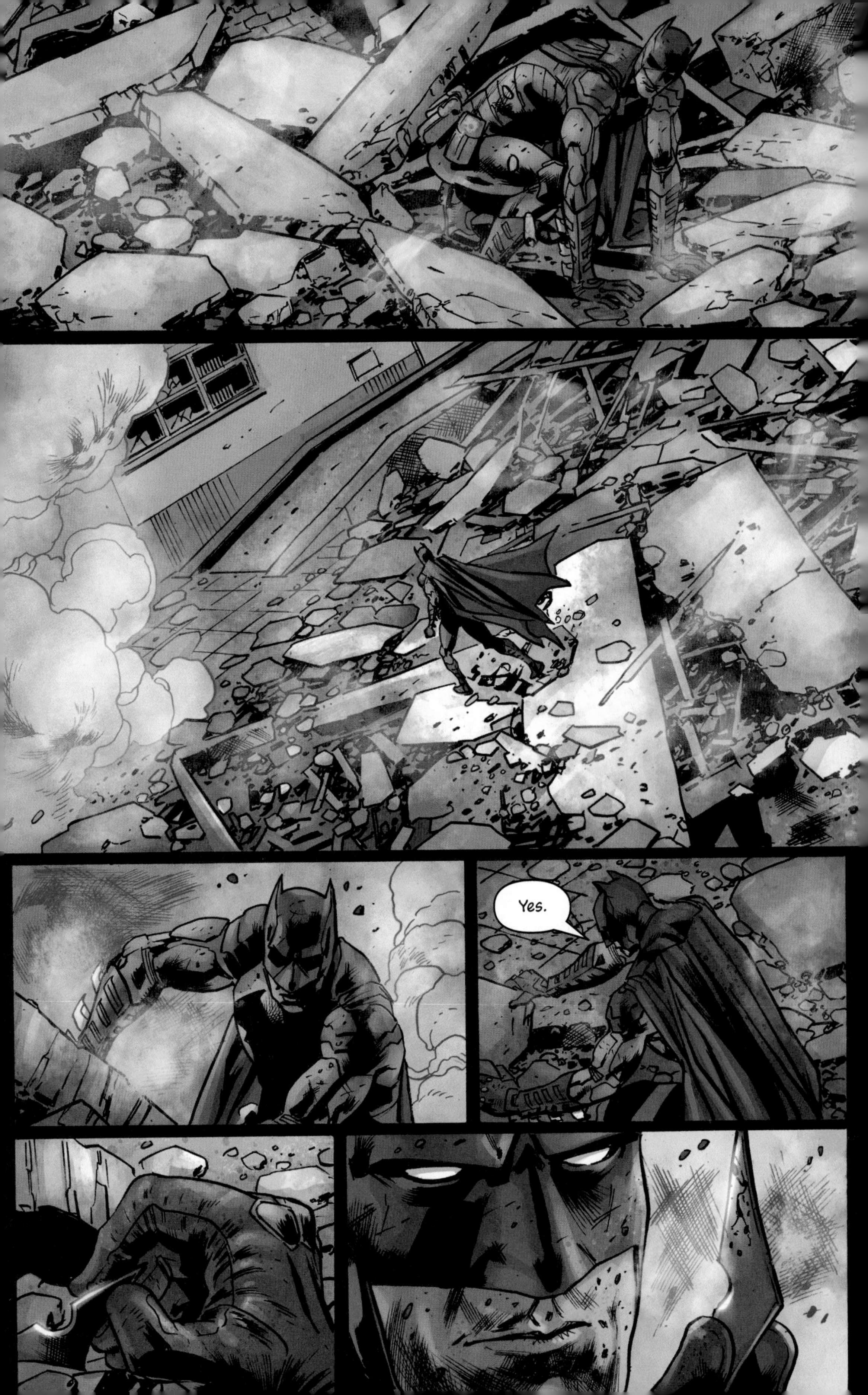
Yes.

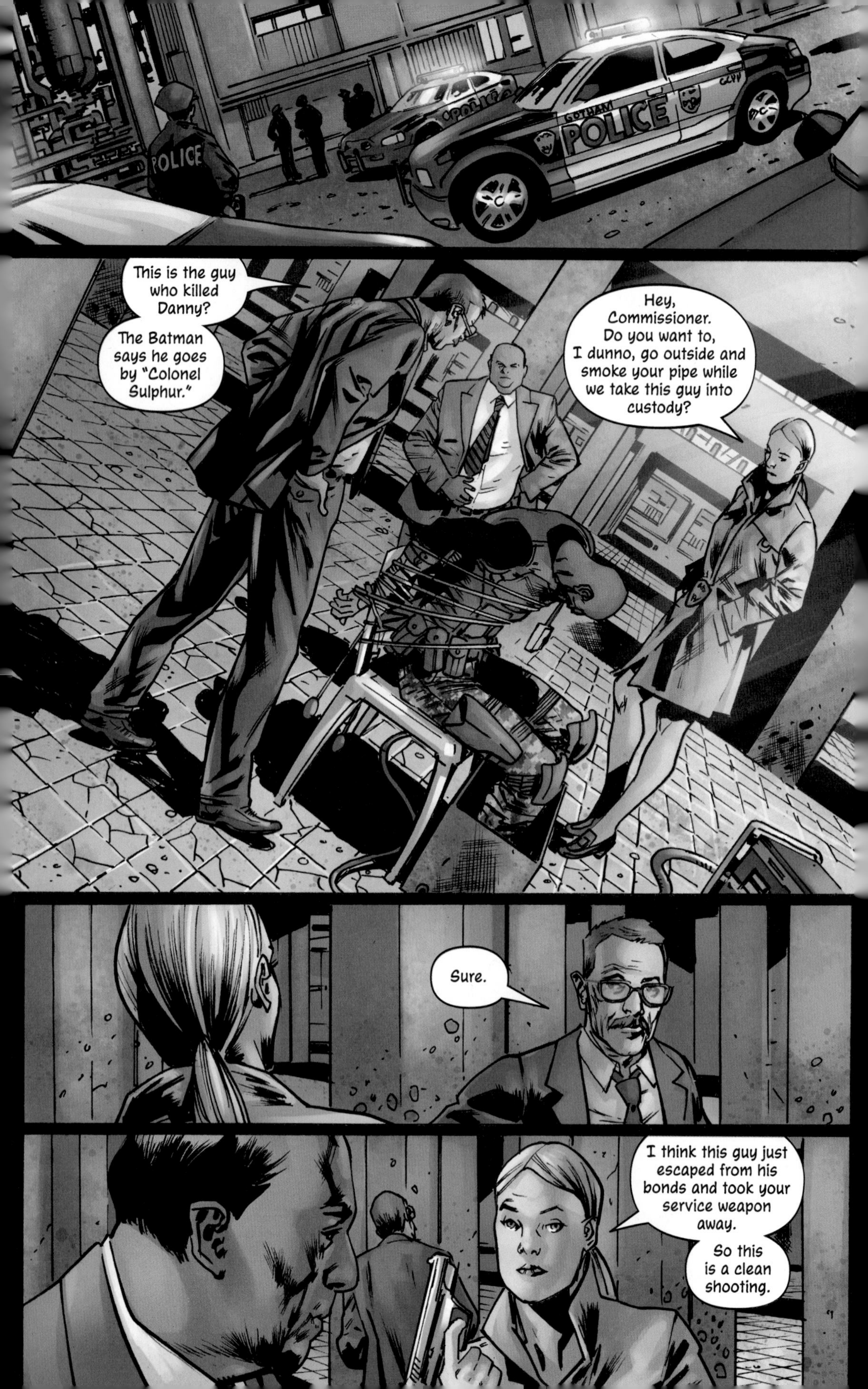

POLICE
GOTHAM POLICE
This is the guy who killed Danny?
The Batman says he goes by "Colonel Sulphur."
Hey, Commissioner. Do you want to, I dunno, go outside and smoke your pipe while we take this guy into custody?
Sure.
I think this guy just escaped from his bonds and took your service weapon away.
So this is a clean shooting.

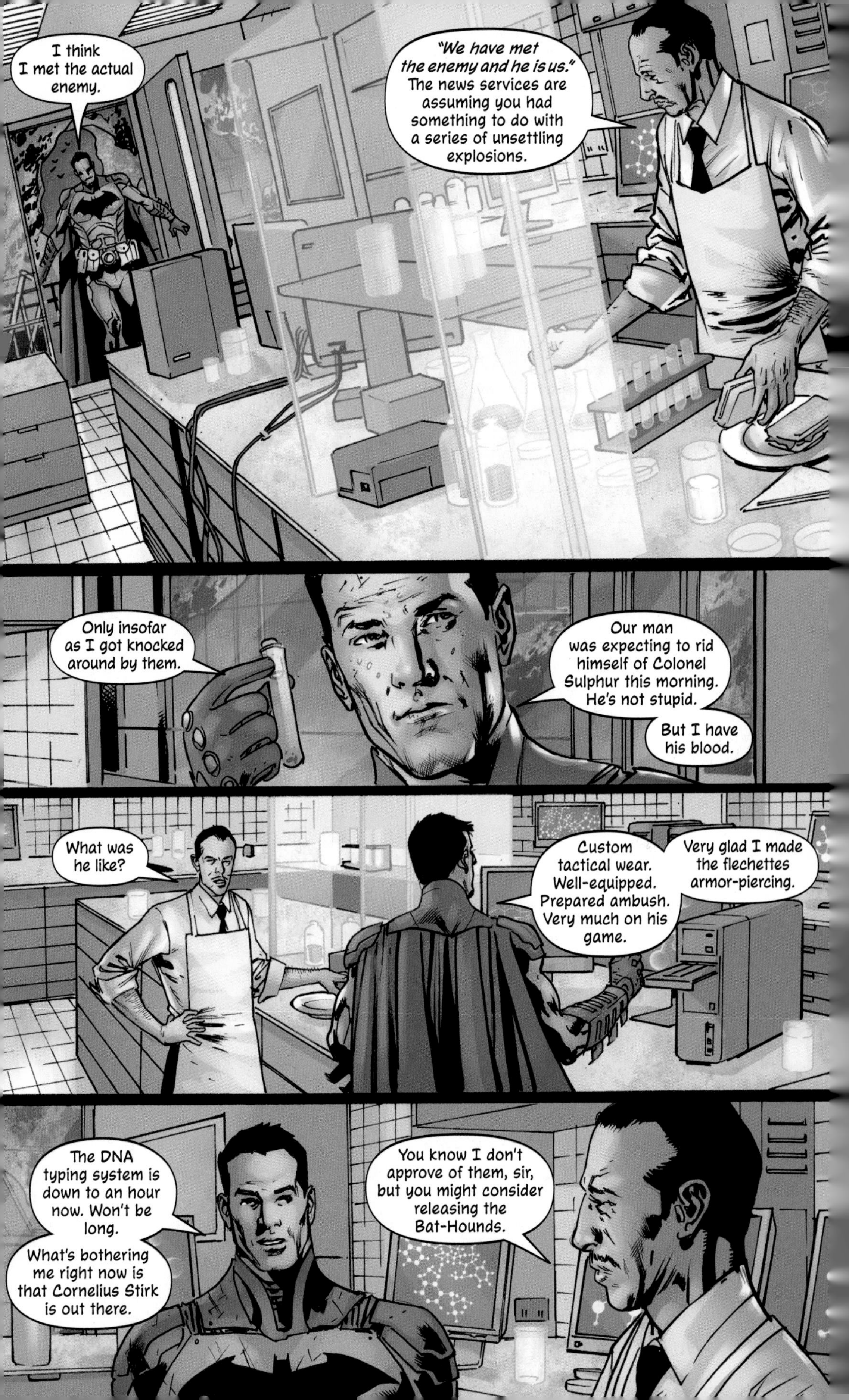
I think I met the actual enemy.
"We have met the enemy and he is us." The news services are assuming you had something to do with a series of unsettling explosions.
Only insofar as I got knocked around by them.
Our man was expecting to rid himself of Colonel Sulphur this morning. He's not stupid.
But I have his blood.
What was he like?
Custom tactical wear. Well-equipped. Prepared ambush. Very much on his game.
Very glad I made the flechettes armor-piercing.
The DNA typing system is down to an hour now. Won't be long.
What's bothering me right now is that Cornelius Stirk is out there.
You know I don't approve of them, sir, but you might consider releasing the Bat-Hounds.

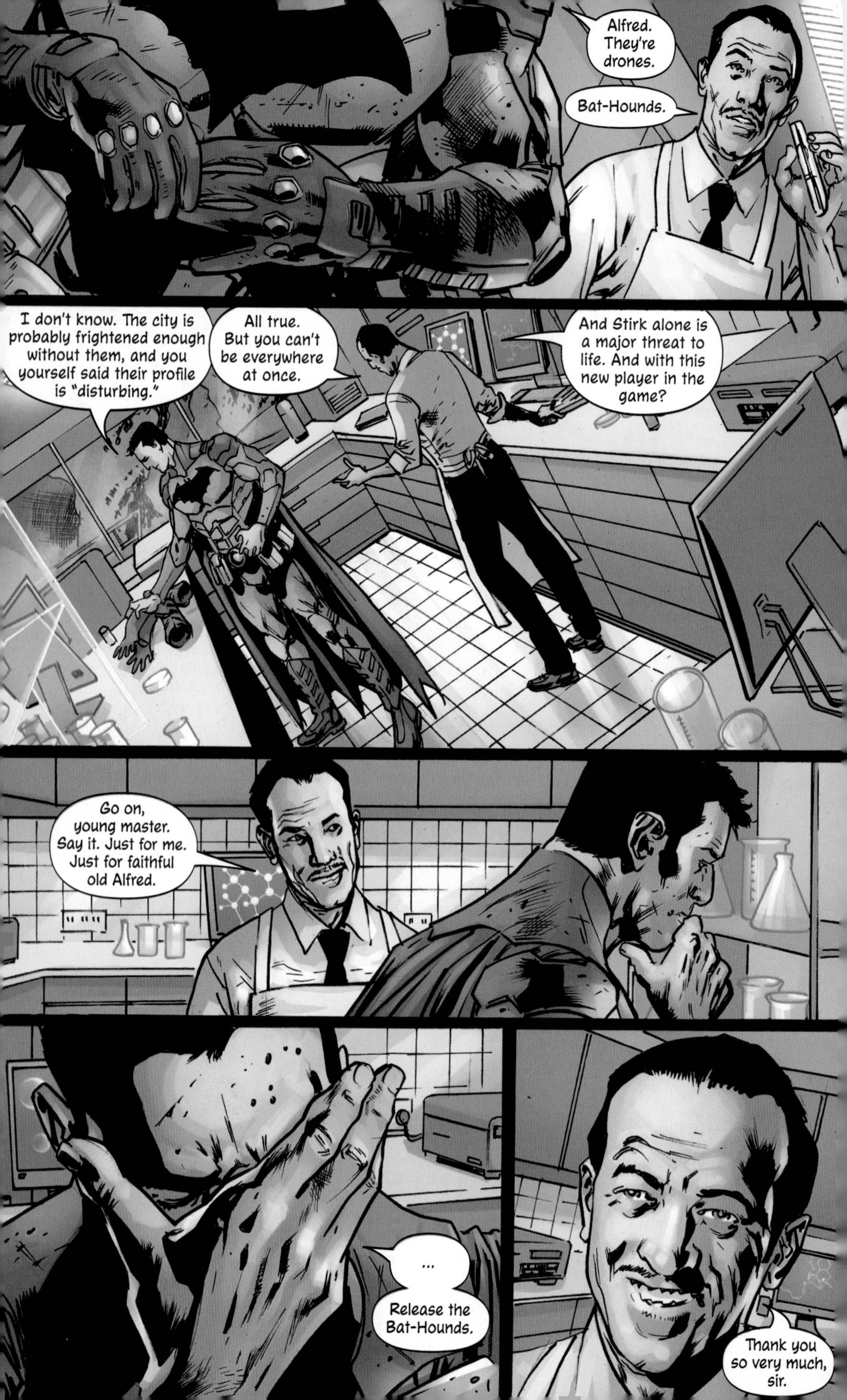
Alfred. They're drones.
Bat-Hounds.
I don't know. The city is probably frightened enough without them, and you yourself said their profile is "disturbing."
All true. But you can't be everywhere at once.
And Stirk alone is a major threat to life. And with this new player in the game?
Go on, young master. Say it. Just for me. Just for faithful old Alfred.
...
Release the Bat-Hounds.
Thank you so very much, sir.

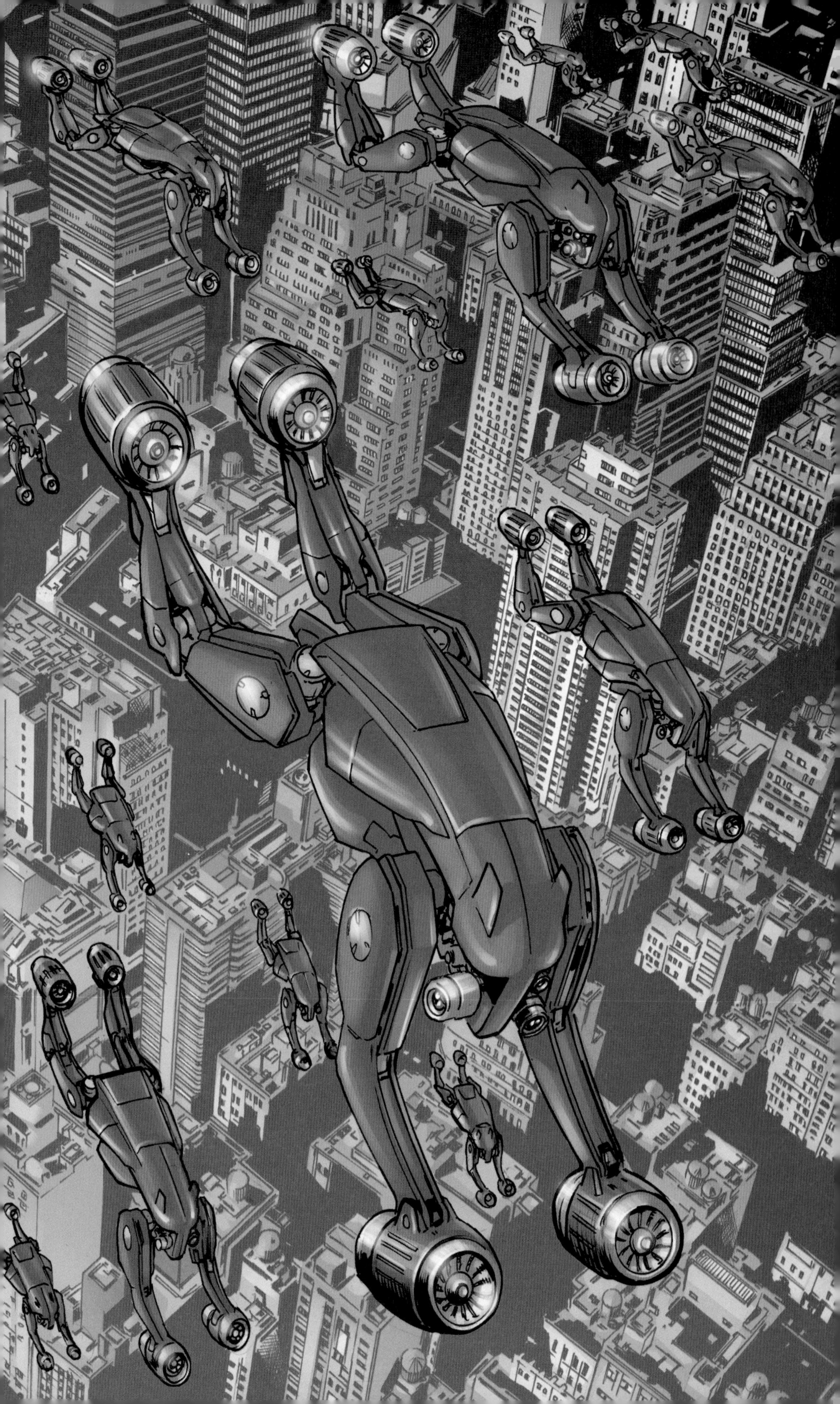

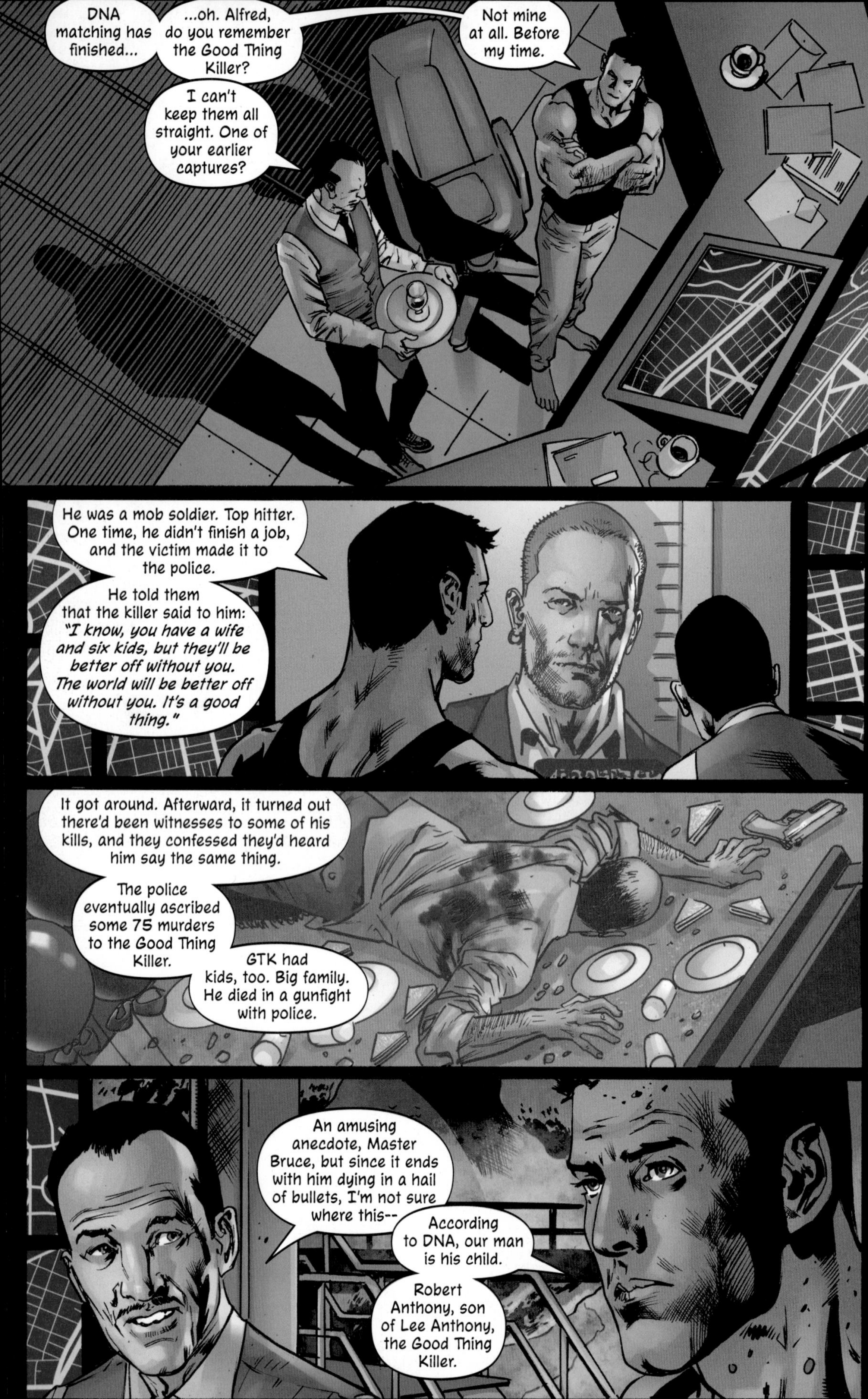
DNA matching has finished...
...oh. Alfred, do you remember the Good Thing Killer?
Not mine at all. Before my time.
I can't keep them all straight. One of your earlier captures?
He was a mob soldier. Top hitter. One time, he didn't finish a job, and the victim made it to the police.
He told them that the killer said to him: *"I know, you have a wife and six kids, but they'll be better off without you. The world will be better off without you. It's a good thing."*
It got around. Afterward, it turned out there'd been witnesses to some of his kills, and they confessed they'd heard him say the same thing.
The police eventually ascribed some 75 murders to the Good Thing Killer.
GTK had kids, too. Big family. He died in a gunfight with police.
An amusing anecdote, Master Bruce, but since it ends with him dying in a hail of bullets, I'm not sure where this--
According to DNA, our man is his child.
Robert Anthony, son of Lee Anthony, the Good Thing Killer.

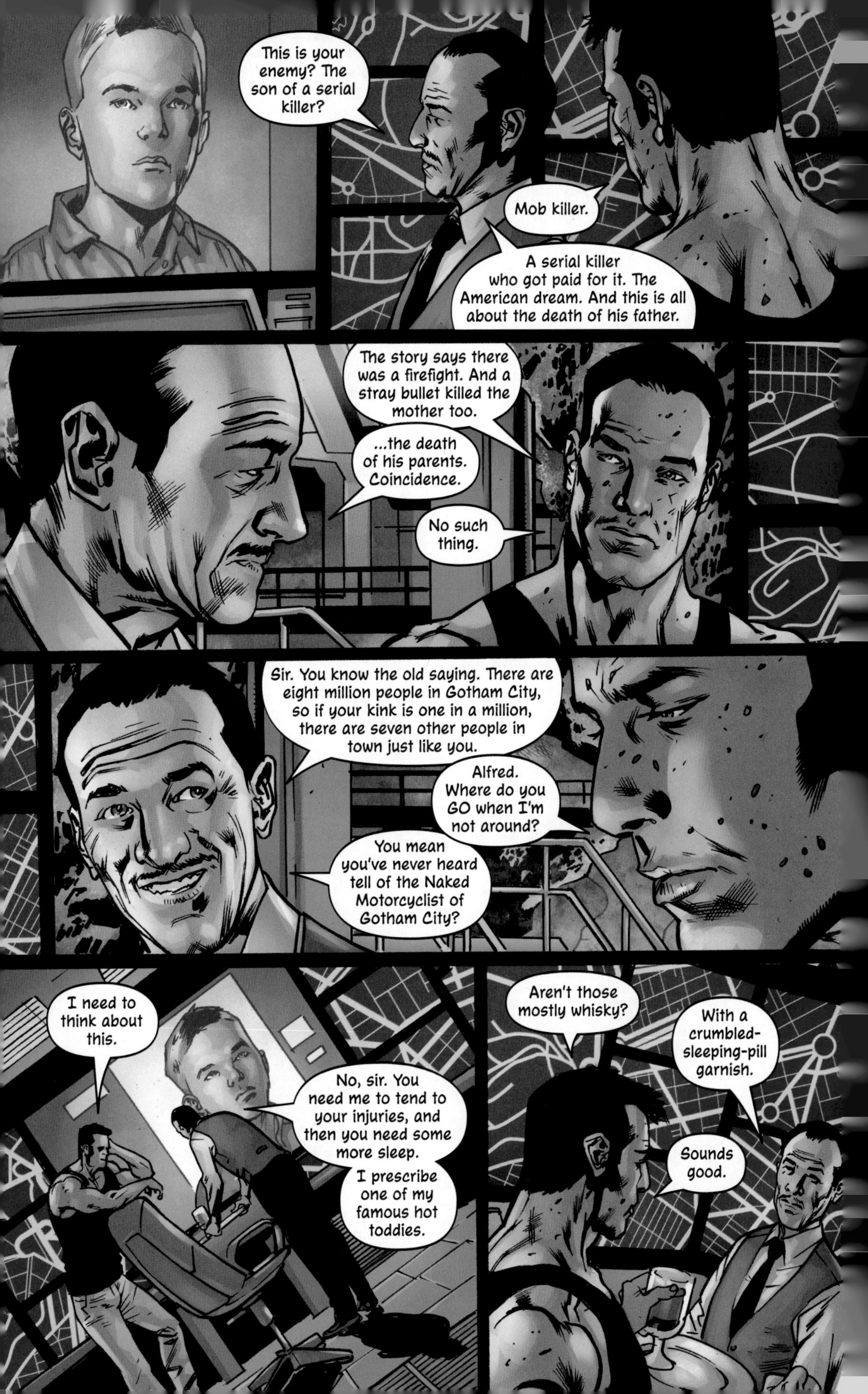
This is your enemy? The son of a serial killer?
Mob killer.
A serial killer who got paid for it. The American dream. And this is all about the death of his father.
The story says there was a firefight. And a stray bullet killed the mother too.
...the death of his parents. Coincidence.
No such thing.
Sir. You know the old saying. There are eight million people in Gotham City, so if your kink is one in a million, there are seven other people in town just like you.
Alfred. Where do you GO when I'm not around?
You mean you've never heard tell of the Naked Motorcyclist of Gotham City?
I need to think about this.
No, sir. You need me to tend to your injuries, and then you need some more sleep.
I prescribe one of my famous hot toddies.
Aren't those mostly whisky?
With a crumbled-sleeping-pill garnish.
Sounds good.

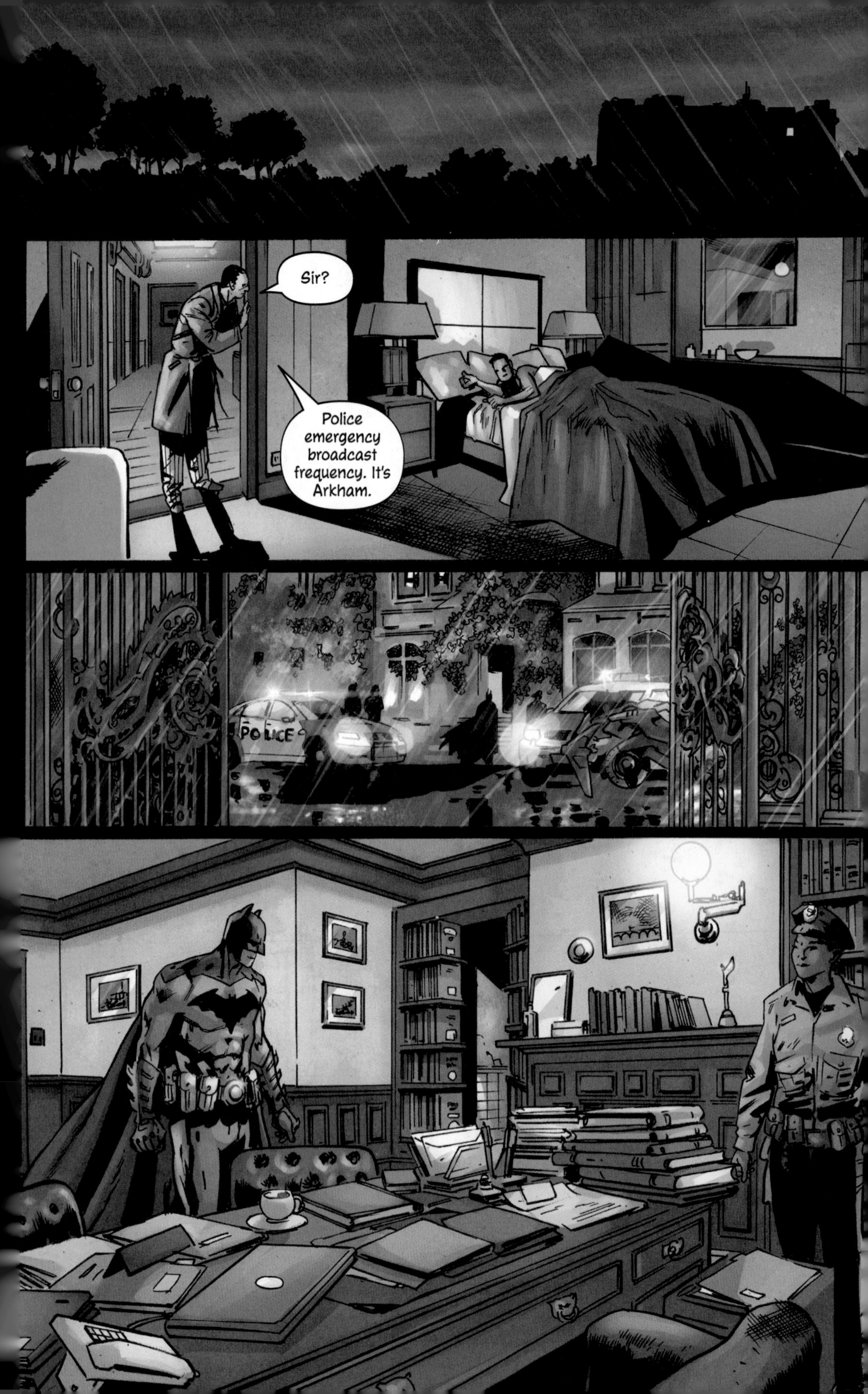
Sir?
Police emergency broadcast frequency. It's Arkham.
POLICE

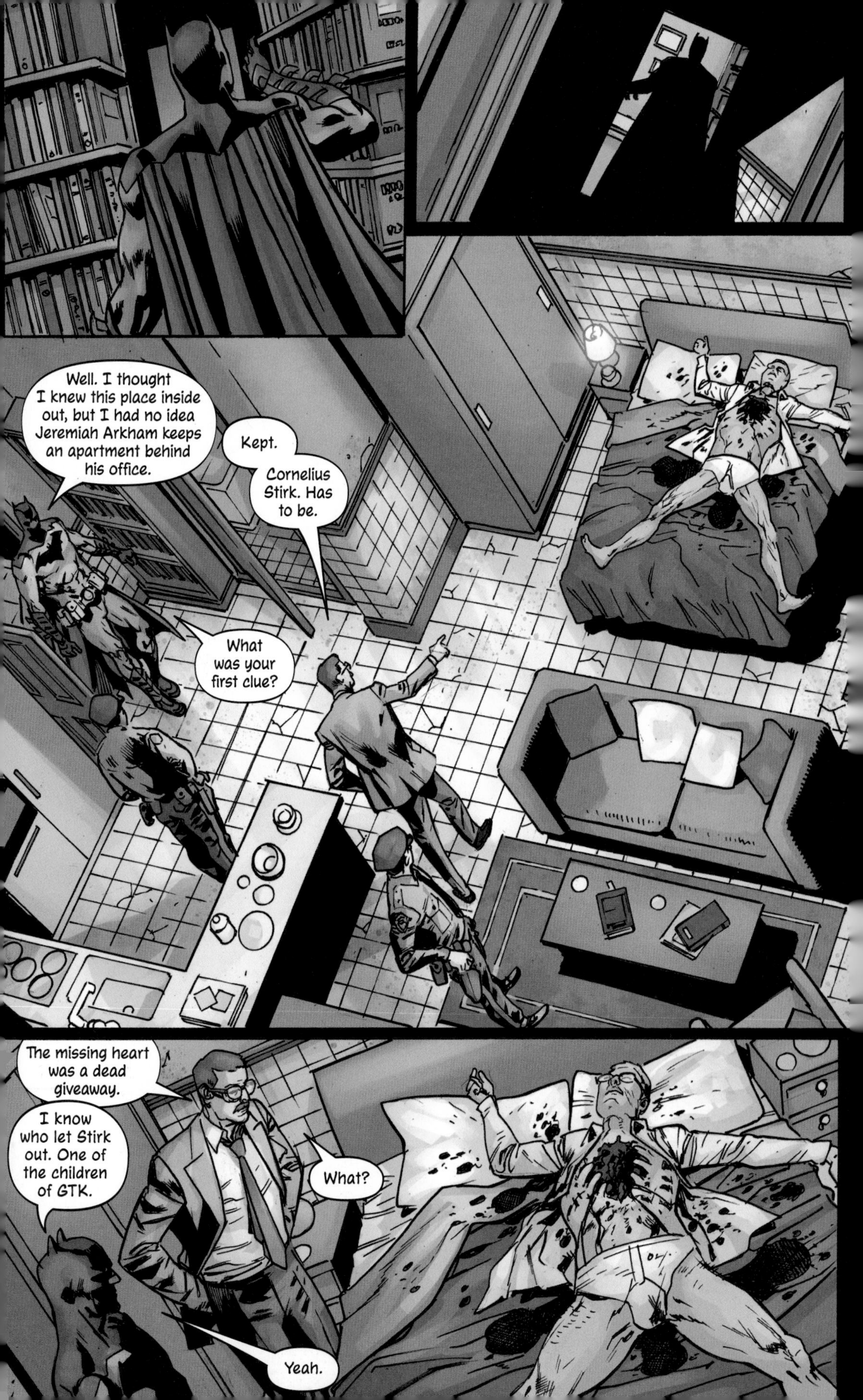
Well. I thought I knew this place inside out, but I had no idea Jeremiah Arkham keeps an apartment behind his office.
Kept.
Cornelius Stirk. Has to be.
What was your first clue?
The missing heart was a dead giveaway.
I know who let Stirk out. One of the children of GTK.
What?
Yeah.

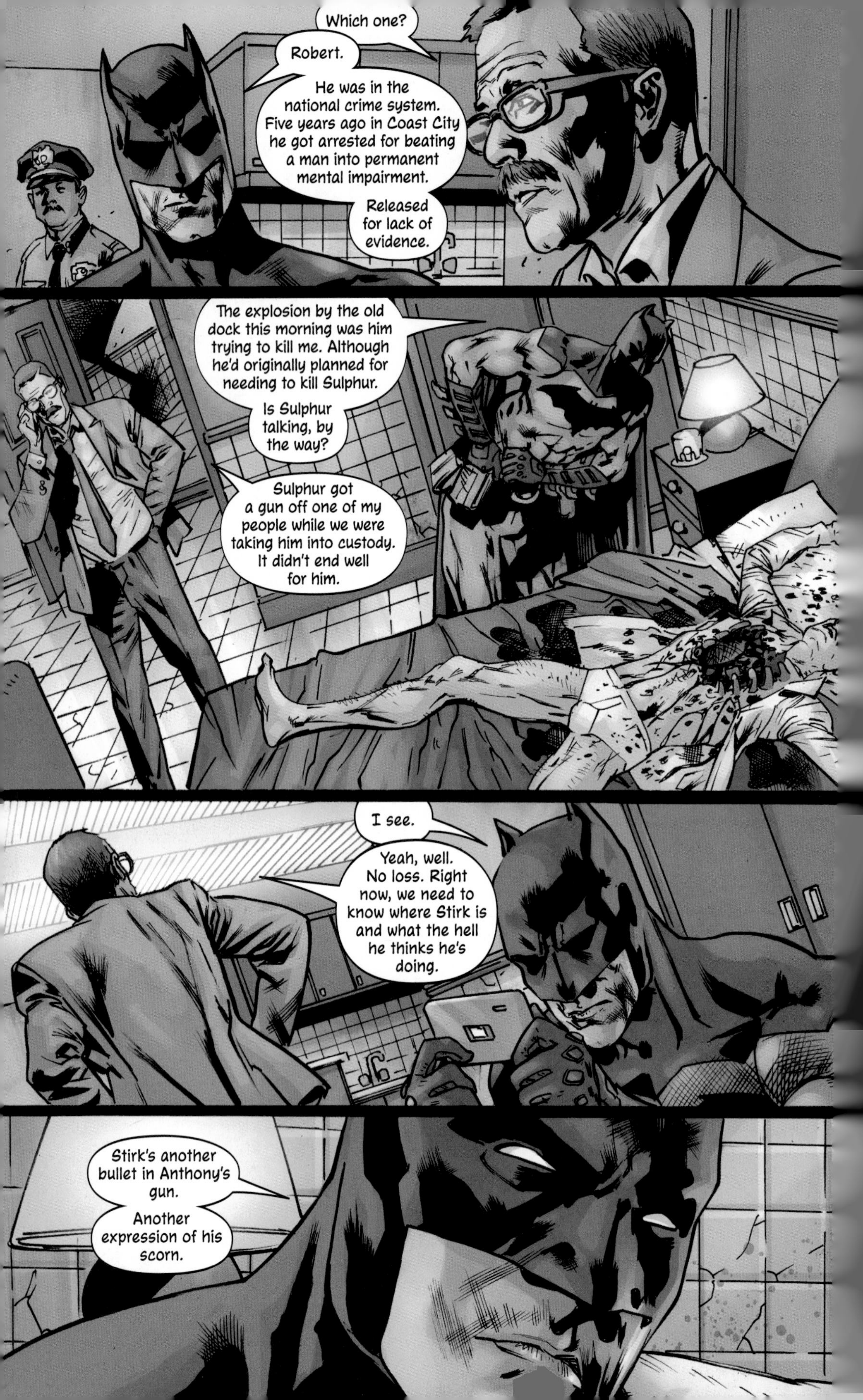
Which one?
Robert.
He was in the national crime system. Five years ago in Coast City he got arrested for beating a man into permanent mental impairment.
Released for lack of evidence.
The explosion by the old dock this morning was him trying to kill me. Although he'd originally planned for needing to kill Sulphur.
Is Sulphur talking, by the way?
Sulphur got a gun off one of my people while we were taking him into custody. It didn't end well for him.
I see.
Yeah, well. No loss. Right now, we need to know where Stirk is and what the hell he thinks he's doing.
Stirk's another bullet in Anthony's gun.
Another expression of his scorn.

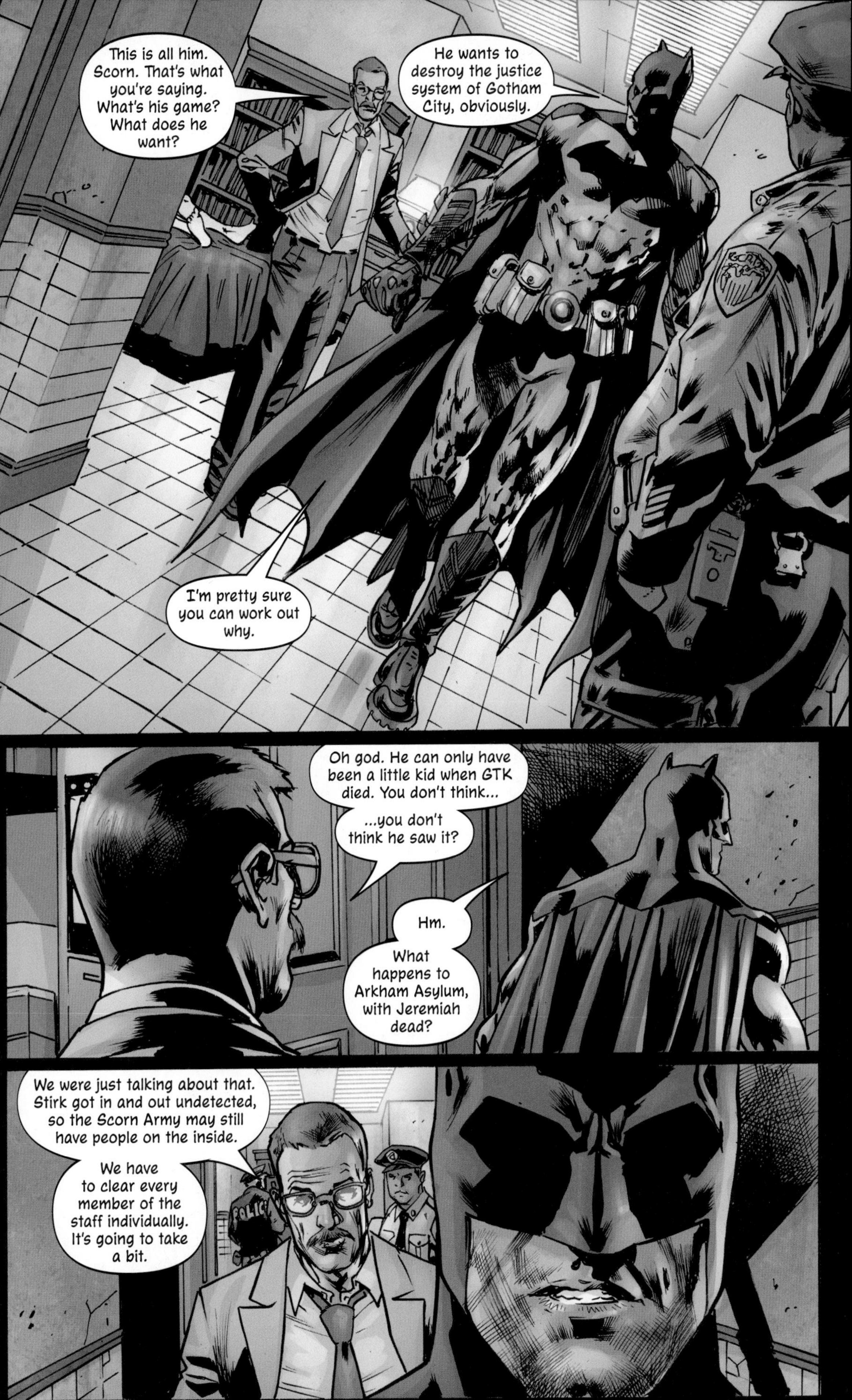
This is all him. Scorn. That's what you're saying. What's his game? What does he want?
He wants to destroy the justice system of Gotham City, obviously.
I'm pretty sure you can work out why.
Oh god. He can only have been a little kid when GTK died. You don't think...
...you don't think he saw it?
Hm.
What happens to Arkham Asylum, with Jeremiah dead?
We were just talking about that. Stirk got in and out undetected, so the Scorn Army may still have people on the inside.
We have to clear every member of the staff individually. It's going to take a bit.
POLICE

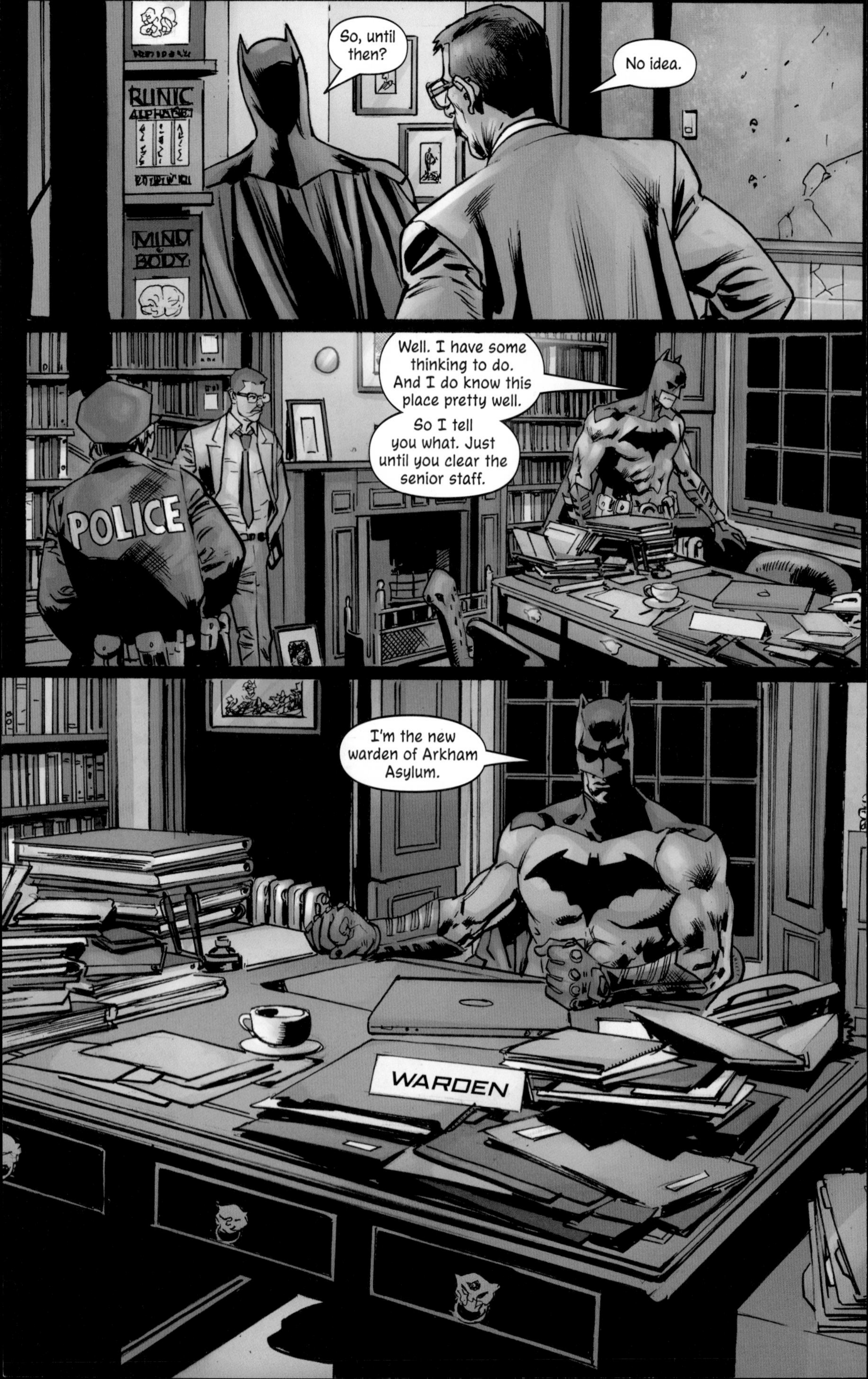
RUNIC ALPHABET
MIND BODY
So, until then?
No idea.
Well. I have some thinking to do. And I do know this place pretty well.
So I tell you what. Just until you clear the senior staff.
POLICE
I'm the new warden of Arkham Asylum.
WARDEN

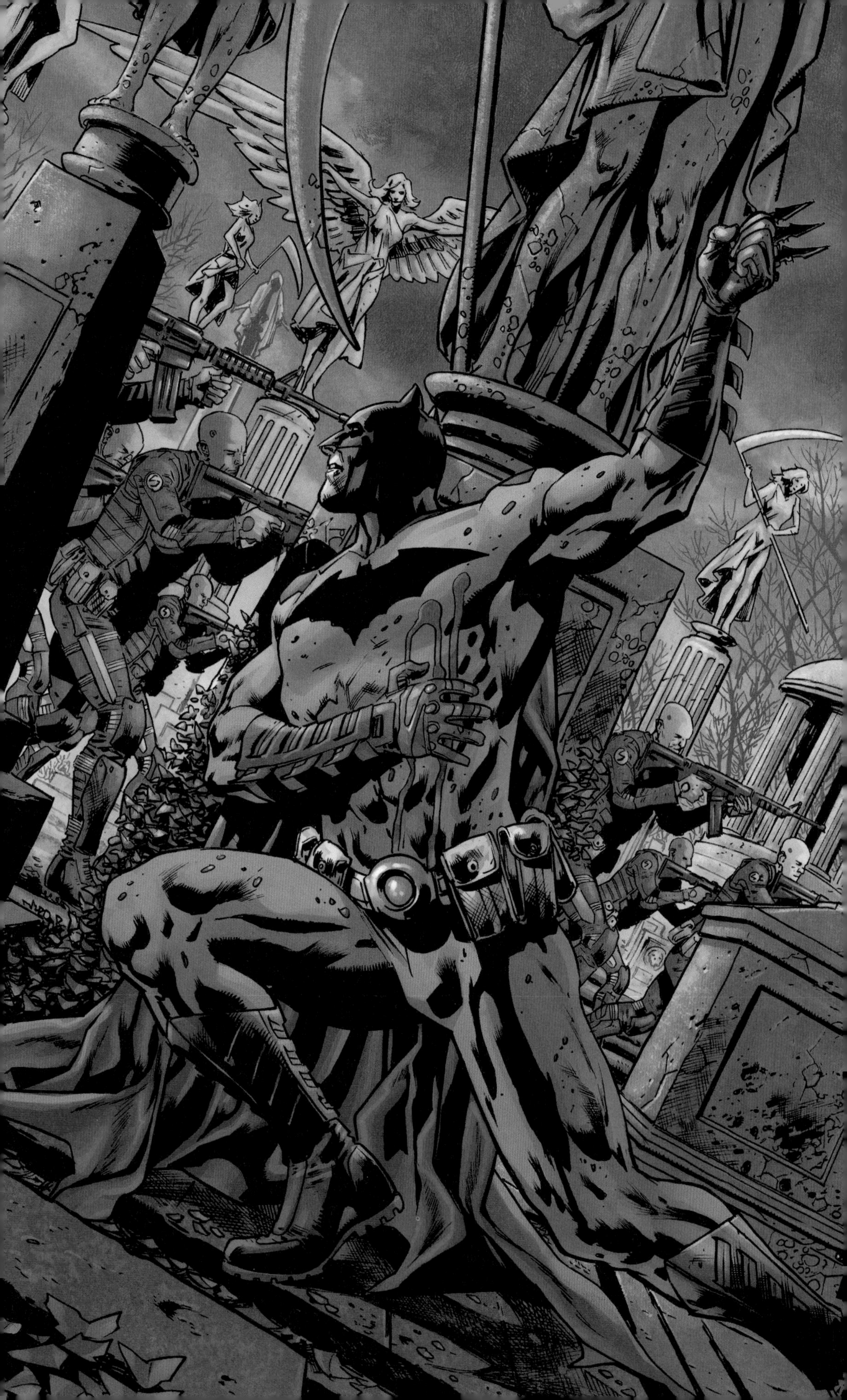

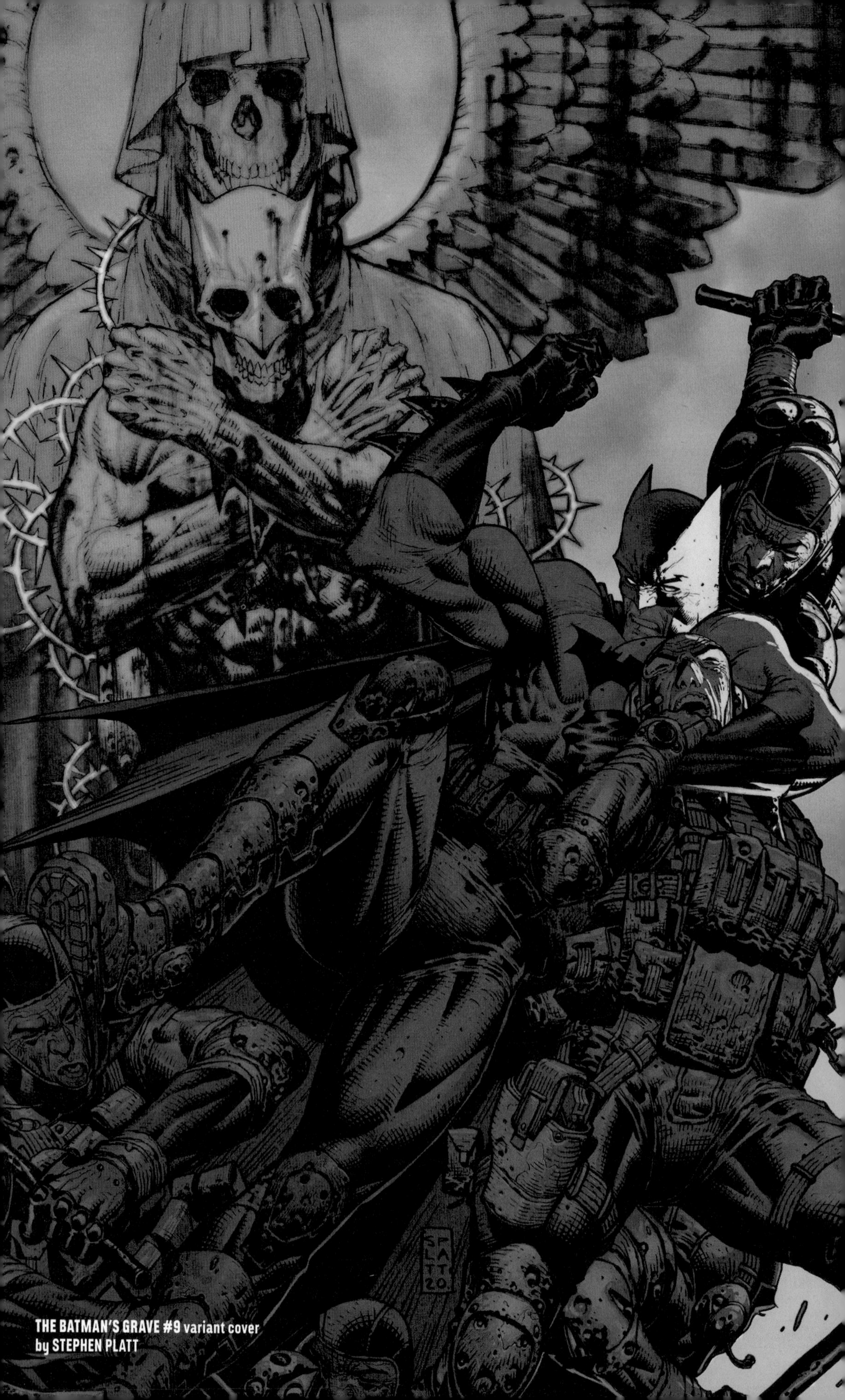

THE BATMAN'S GRAVE #9 variant cover
by **STEPHEN PLATT**

SCORN

MOB - D
MONEY

Chapter 9

Writer **WARREN ELLIS**	Art **BRYAN HITCH**
Colors **ALEX SINCLAIR**	Letters **RICHARD STARKINGS**
Cover **BRYAN HITCH &** **ALEX SINCLAIR**	Variant Cover **STEPHEN** **PLATT**
Associate Editor **ANDREW MARINO**	Editor **MARIE JAVINS**

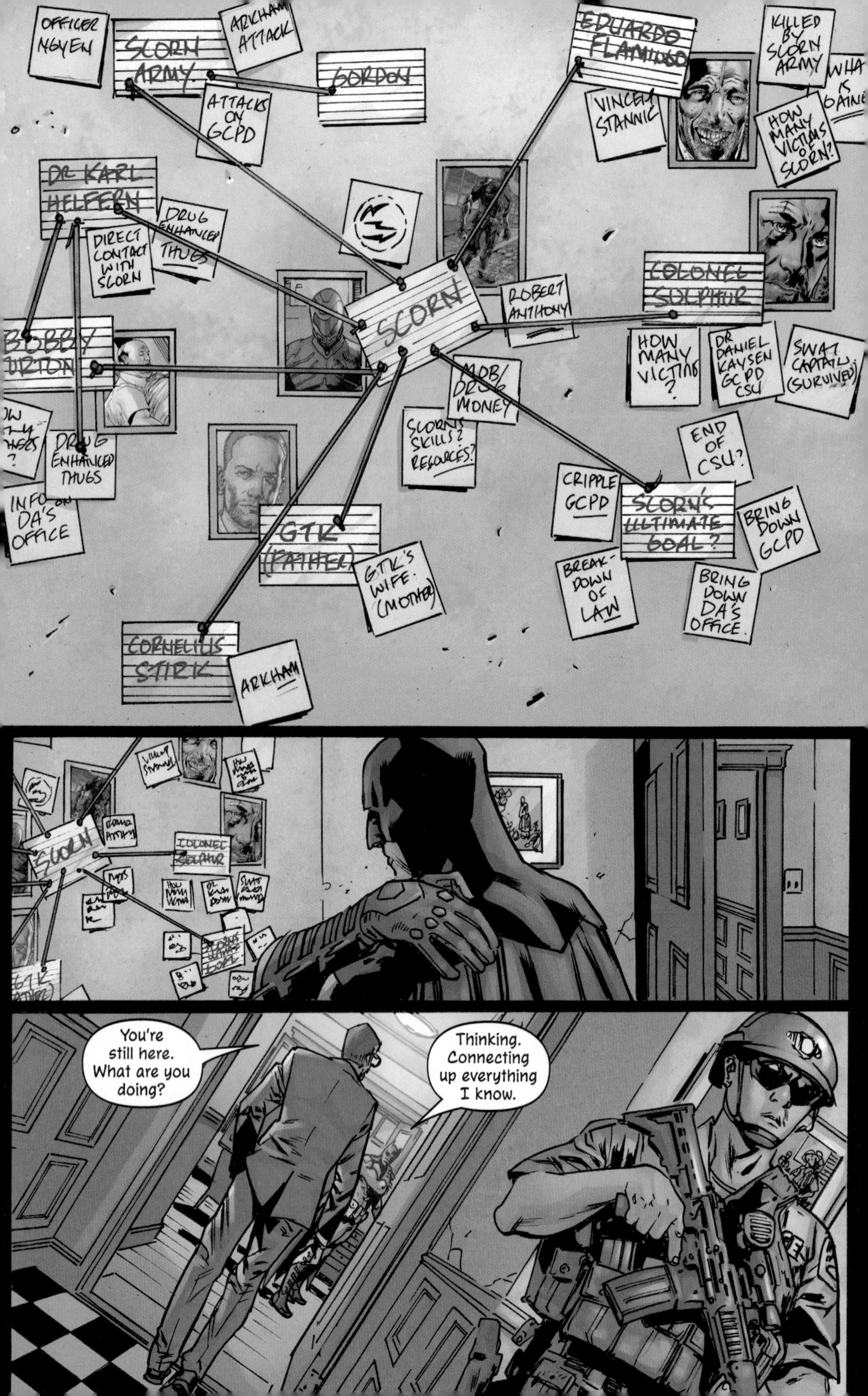
OFFICER NGYEN
SCORN ARMY
ARKHAM ATTACK
GORDON
ATTACKS ON GCPD
EDUARDO FLAMINGO
KILLED BY SCORN ARMY
HOW MANY VICTIMS OF SCORN?
DR KARL HELFERN
DRUG ENHANCED THUGS
DIRECT CONTACT WITH SCORN
SCORN
ROBERT ANTHONY
COLONEL SULPHUR
HOW MANY VICTIMS?
DR DANIEL KAYSEN GCPD CSU
SWAT CAPTAIN (SURVIVED)
MOB/DRUG MONEY
SCORN'S SKILLS? RESOURCES?
DRUG ENHANCED THUGS
INFO ON DA'S OFFICE
END OF CSU?
CRIPPLE GCPD
SCORN'S ULTIMATE GOAL?
BRING DOWN GCPD
GTK (FATHER)
GTK'S WIFE (MOTHER)
BREAK-DOWN OF LAW
BRING DOWN DA'S OFFICE
CORNELIUS STIRK
ARKHAM
You're still here. What are you doing?
Thinking. Connecting up everything I know.

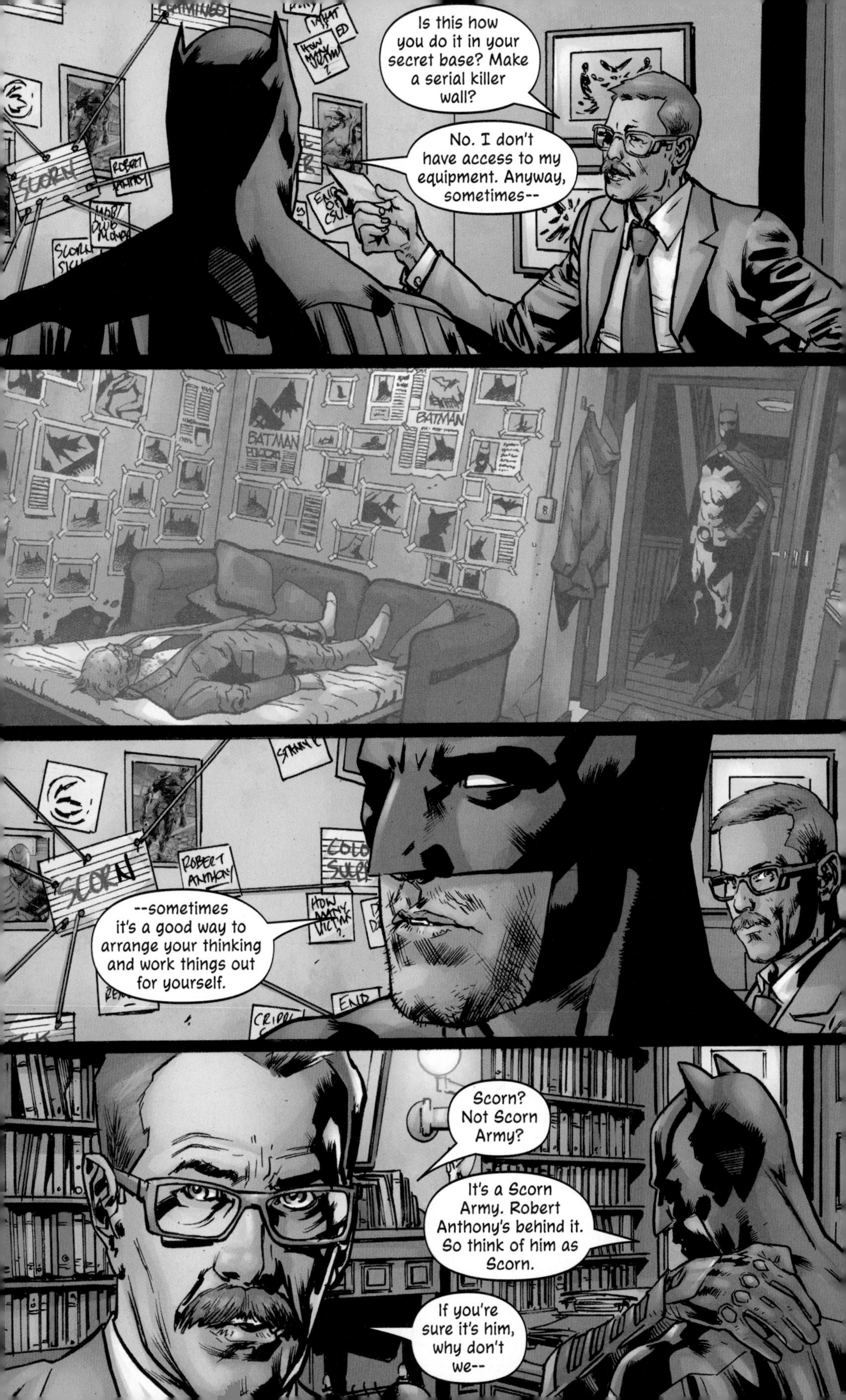
Is this how you do it in your secret base? Make a serial killer wall?
No. I don't have access to my equipment. Anyway, sometimes--
BATMAN
BATMAN
SCORN
ROBERT ANTHONY
--sometimes it's a good way to arrange your thinking and work things out for yourself.
Scorn? Not Scorn Army?
It's a Scorn Army. Robert Anthony's behind it. So think of him as Scorn.
If you're sure it's him, why don't we--

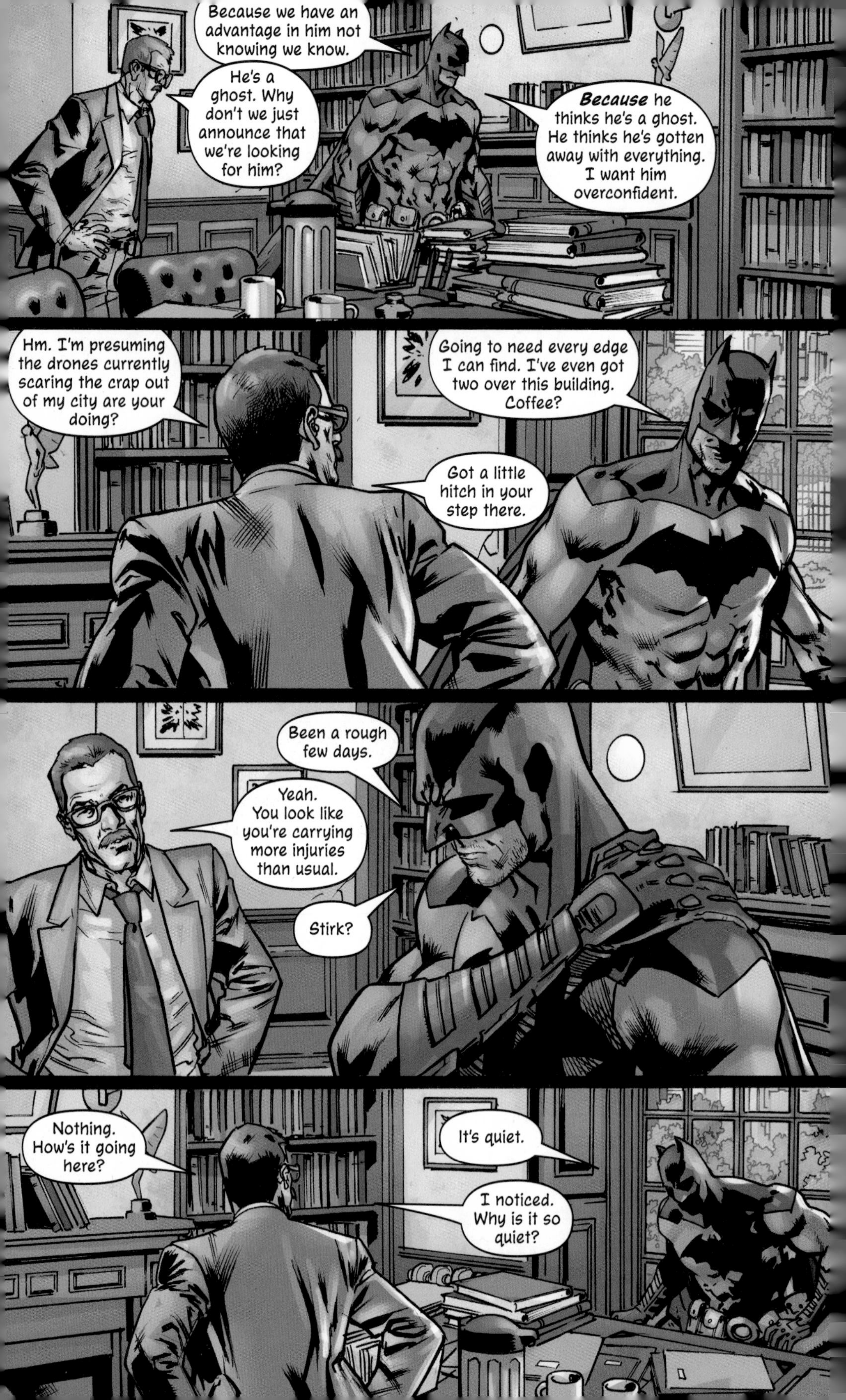
Because we have an advantage in him not knowing we know.
He's a ghost. Why don't we just announce that we're looking for him?
Because he thinks he's a ghost. He thinks he's gotten away with everything. I want him overconfident.
Hm. I'm presuming the drones currently scaring the crap out of my city are your doing?
Going to need every edge I can find. I've even got two over this building. Coffee?
Got a little hitch in your step there.
Been a rough few days.
Yeah. You look like you're carrying more injuries than usual.
Stirk?
Nothing. How's it going here?
It's quiet.
I noticed. Why is it so quiet?

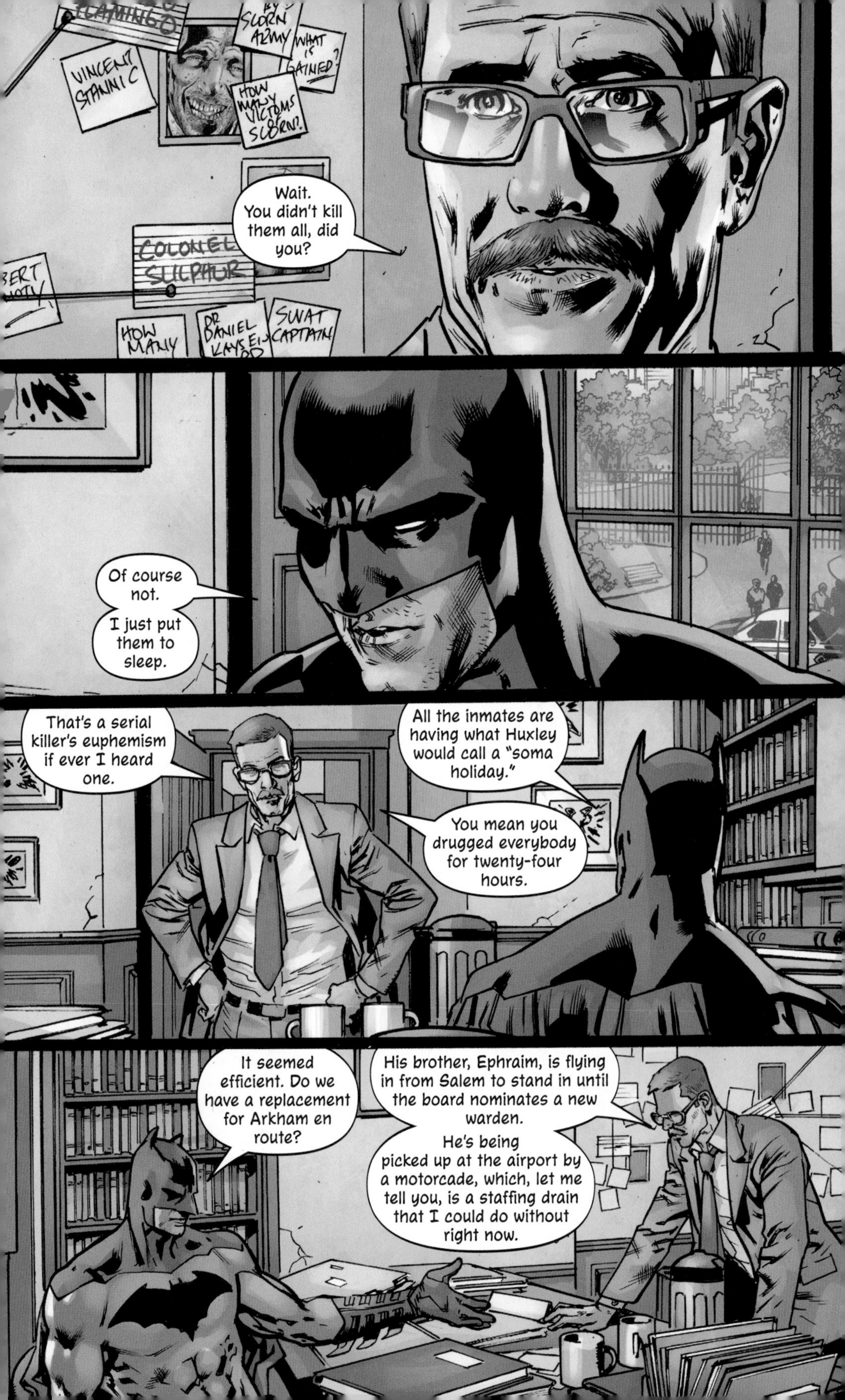

COLONEL SULPHUR
SWAT CAPTAIN
Wait. You didn't kill them all, did you?
Of course not.
I just put them to sleep.
That's a serial killer's euphemism if ever I heard one.
All the inmates are having what Huxley would call a "soma holiday."
You mean you drugged everybody for twenty-four hours.
It seemed efficient. Do we have a replacement for Arkham en route?
His brother, Ephraim, is flying in from Salem to stand in until the board nominates a new warden.
He's being picked up at the airport by a motorcade, which, let me tell you, is a staffing drain that I could do without right now.

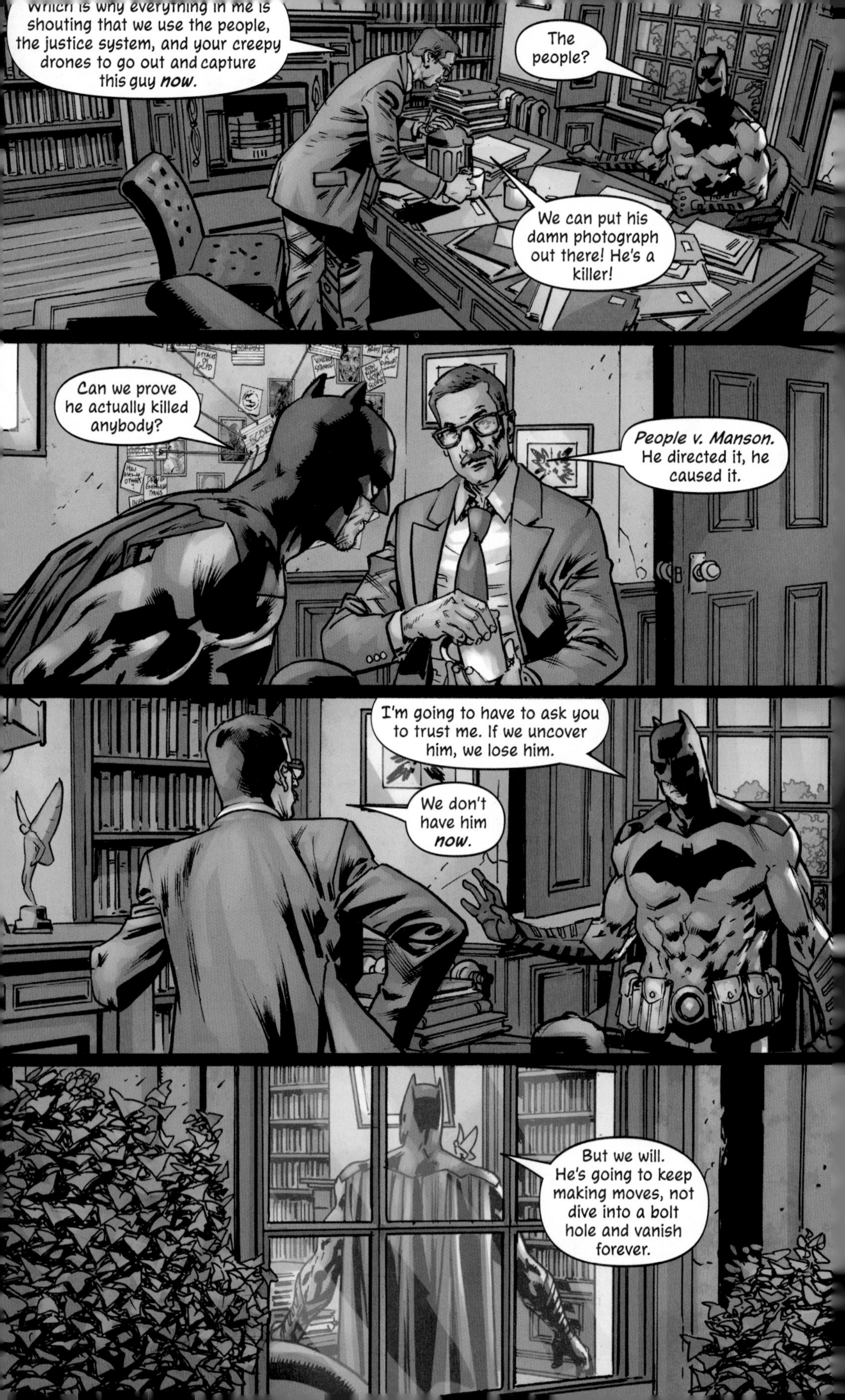
Which is why everything in me is shouting that we use the people, the justice system, and your creepy drones to go out and capture this guy **now**.
The people?
We can put his damn photograph out there! He's a killer!
Can we prove he actually killed anybody?
People v. Manson. He directed it, he caused it.
I'm going to have to ask you to trust me. If we uncover him, we lose him.
We don't have him **now**.
But we will. He's going to keep making moves, not dive into a bolt hole and vanish forever.

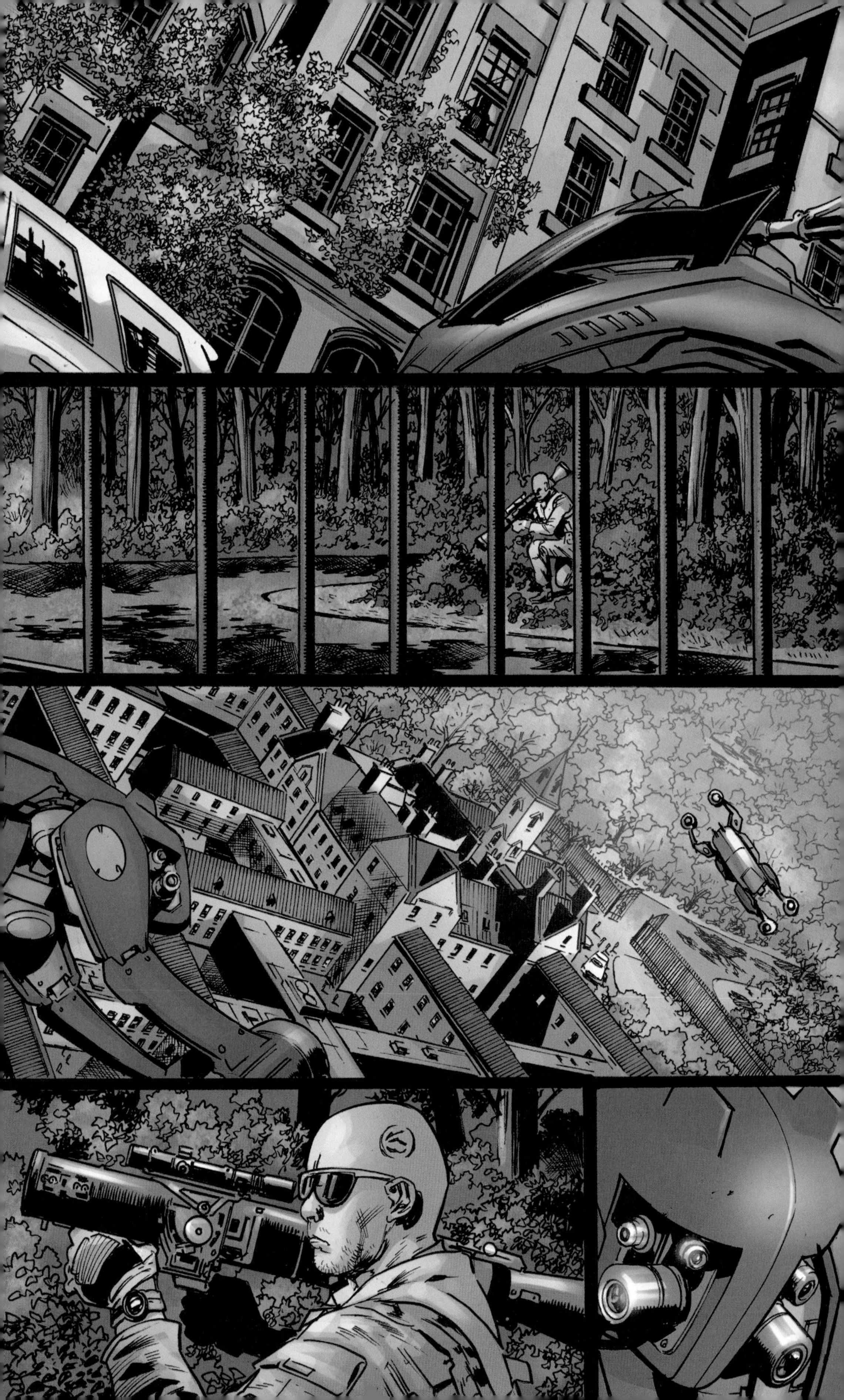

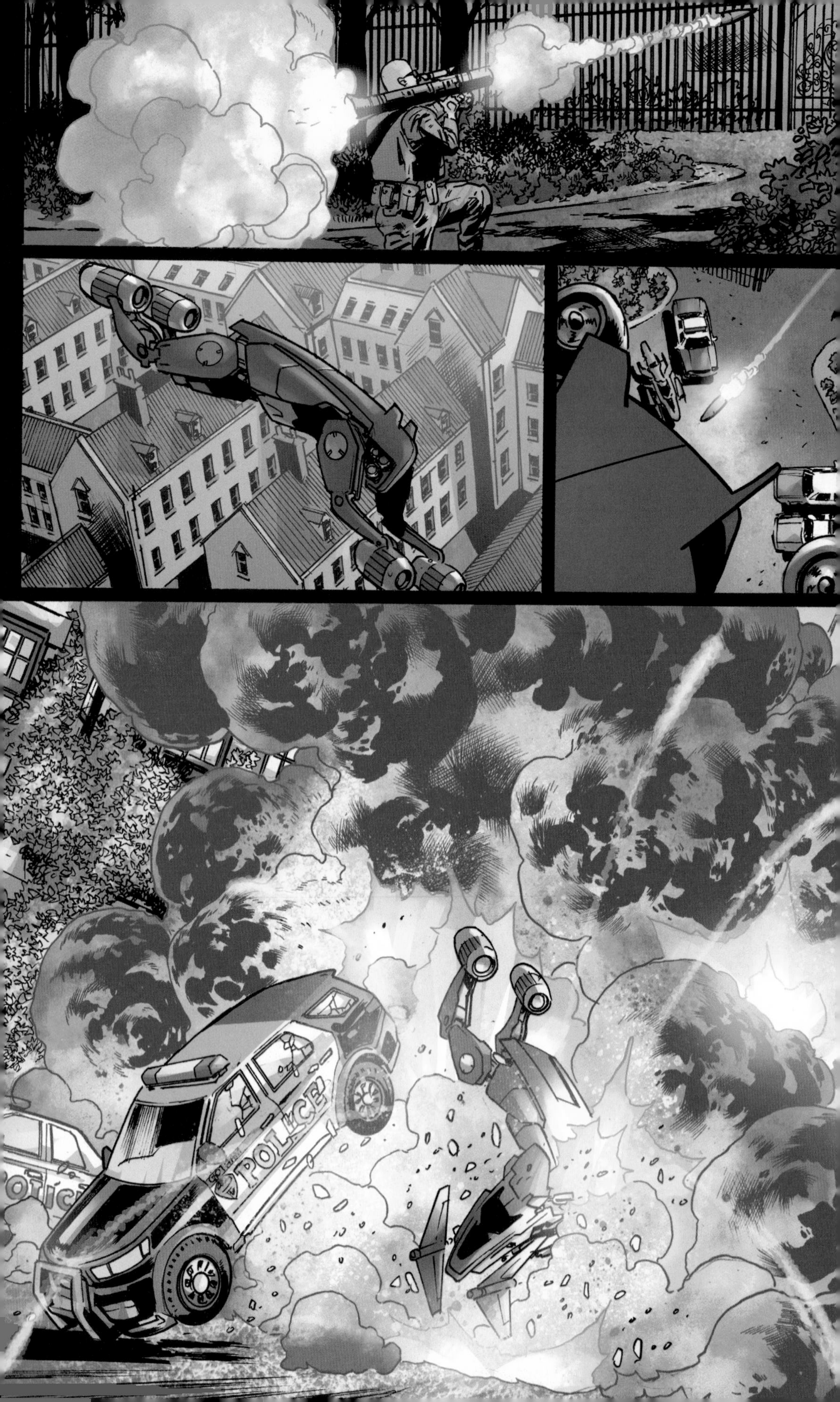
POLICE

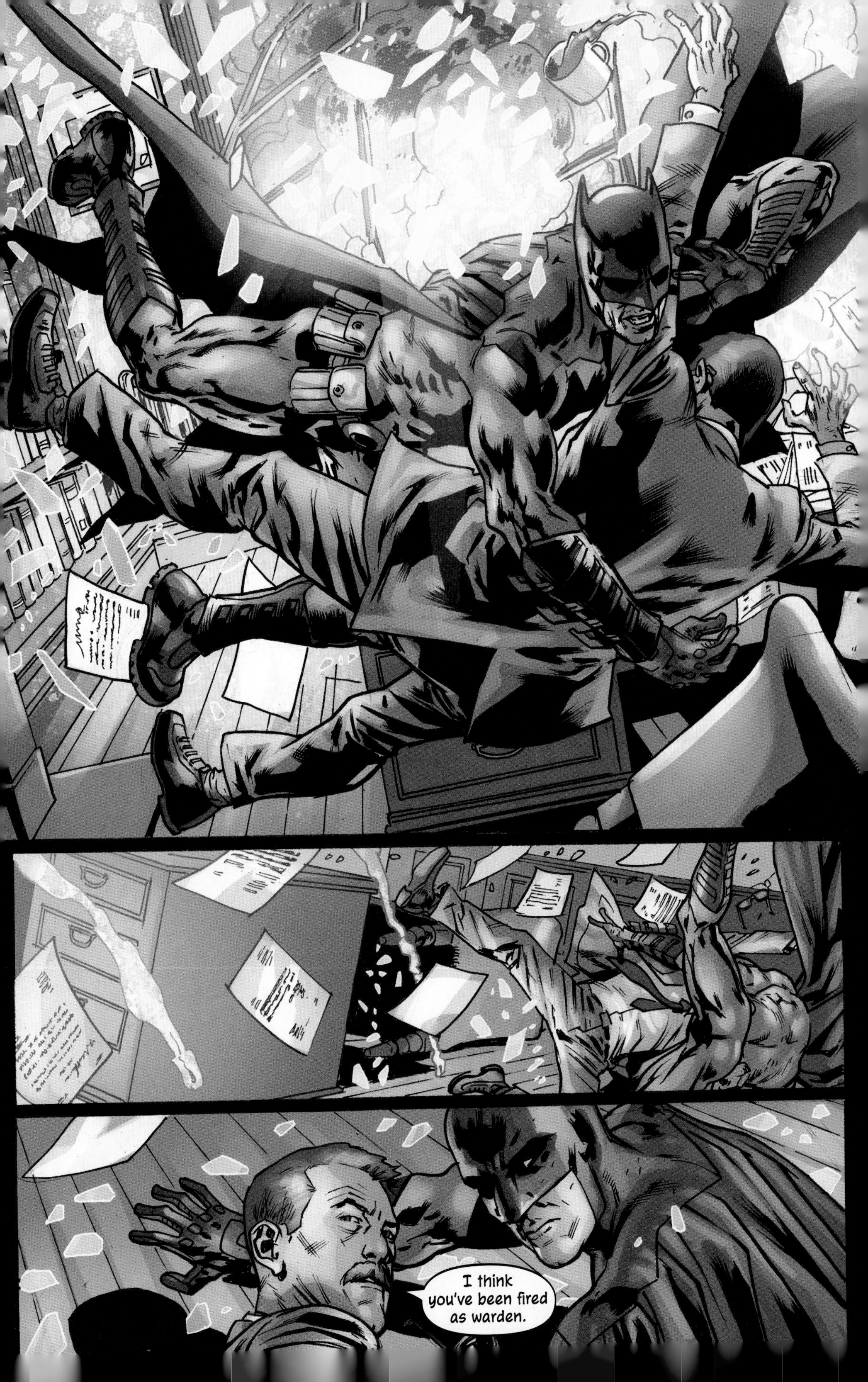
I think you've been fired as warden.

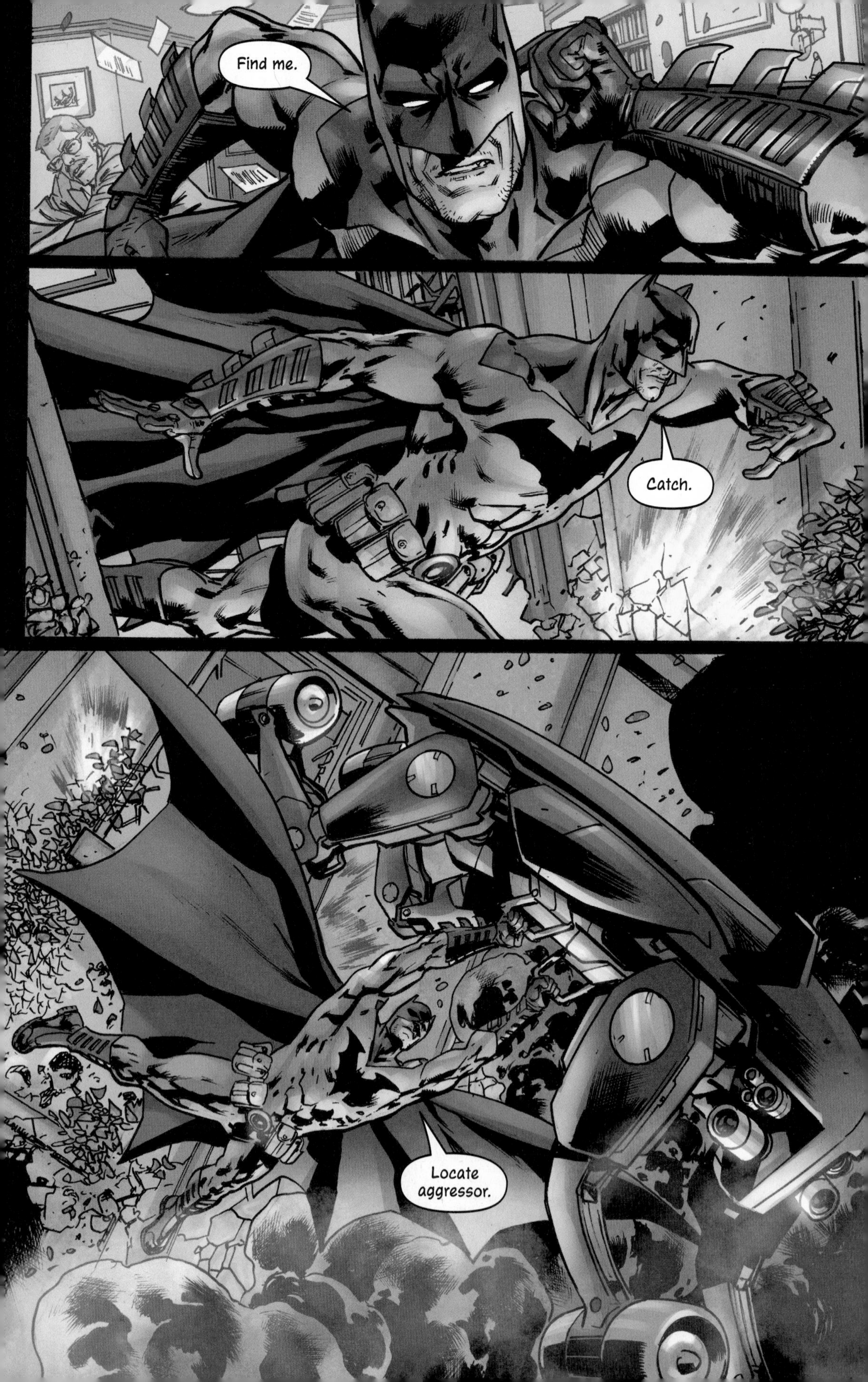
Find me.
Catch.
Locate aggressor.

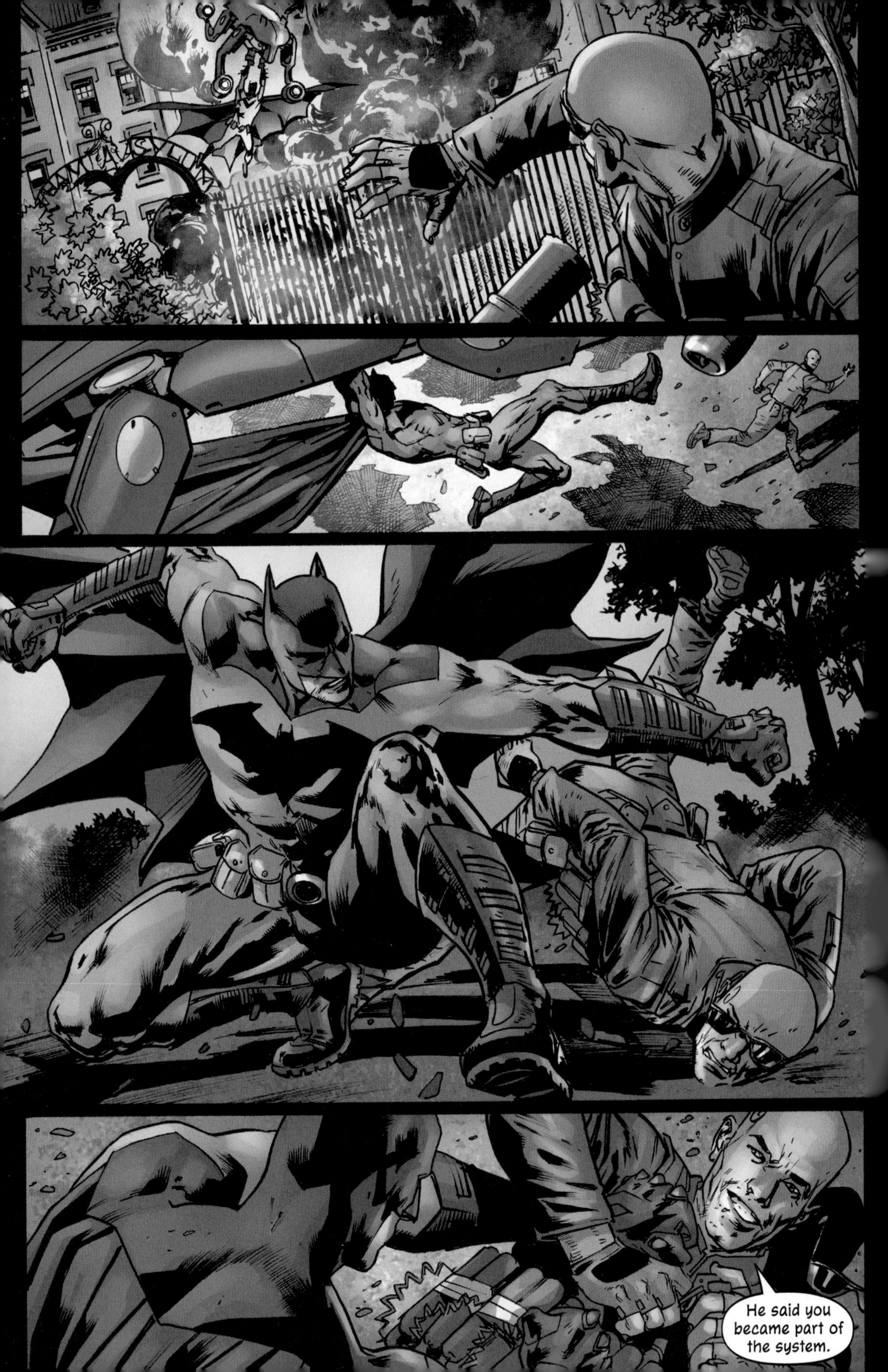
He said you became part of the system.

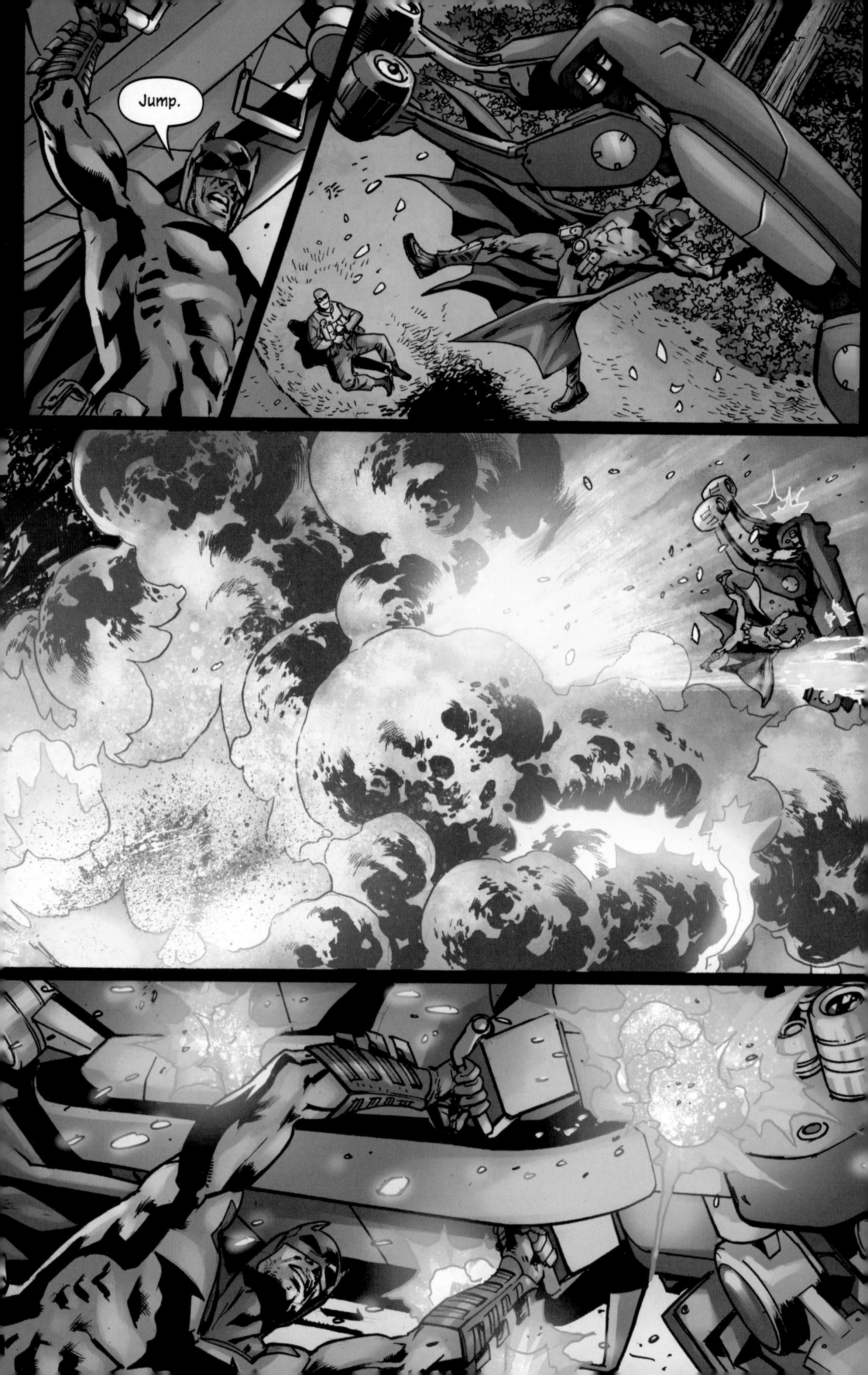
Jump.

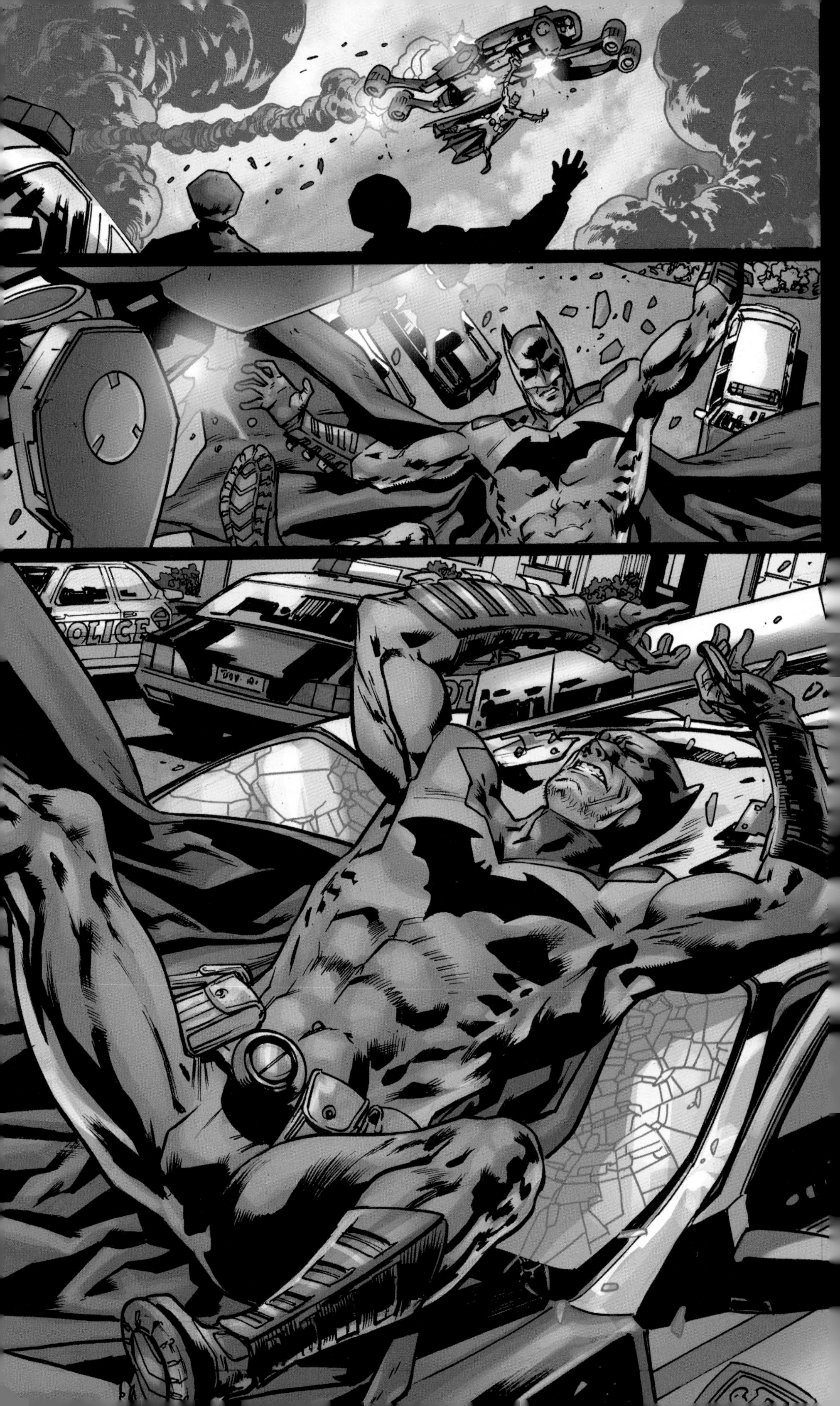

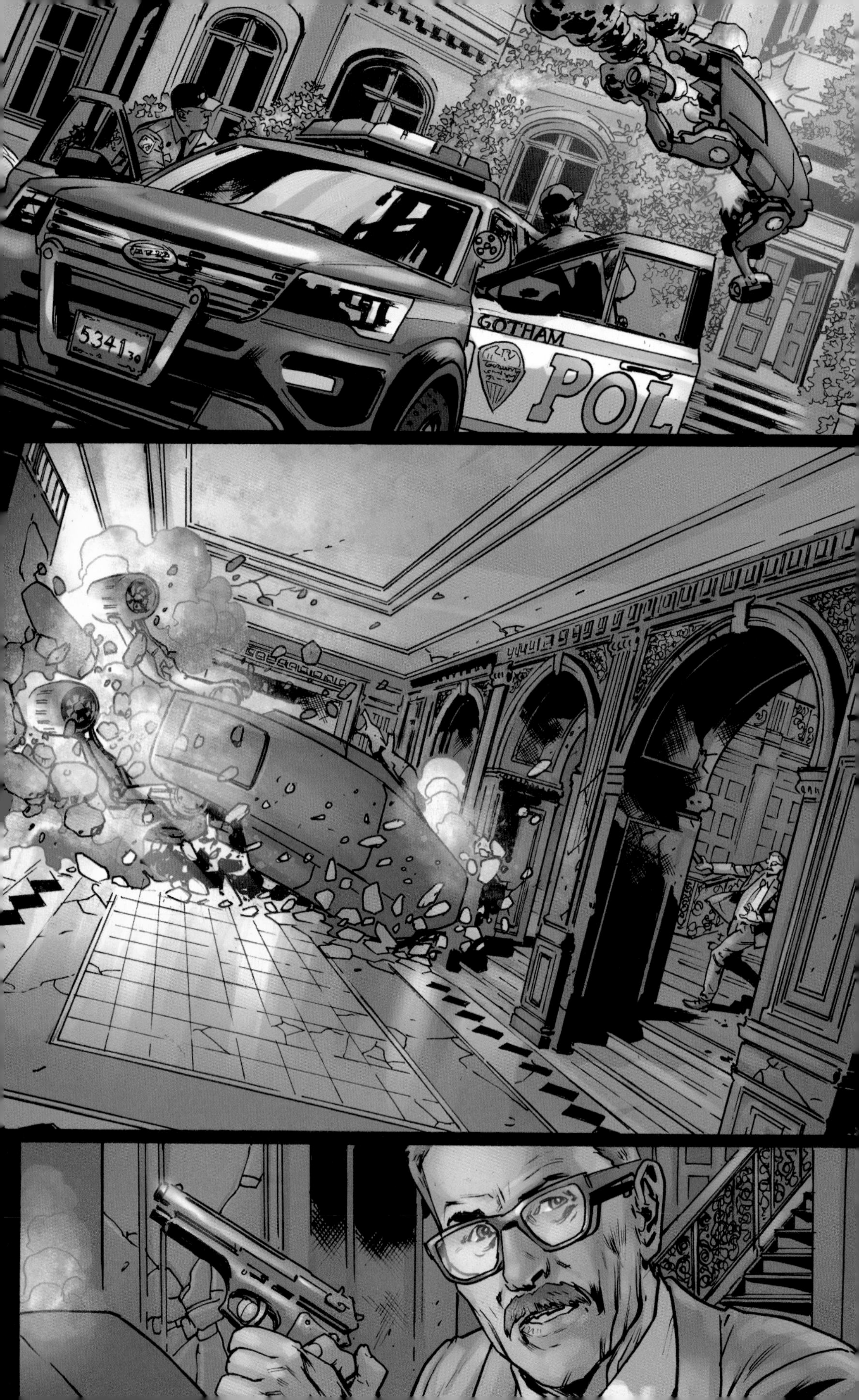
5341
GOTHAM
POL

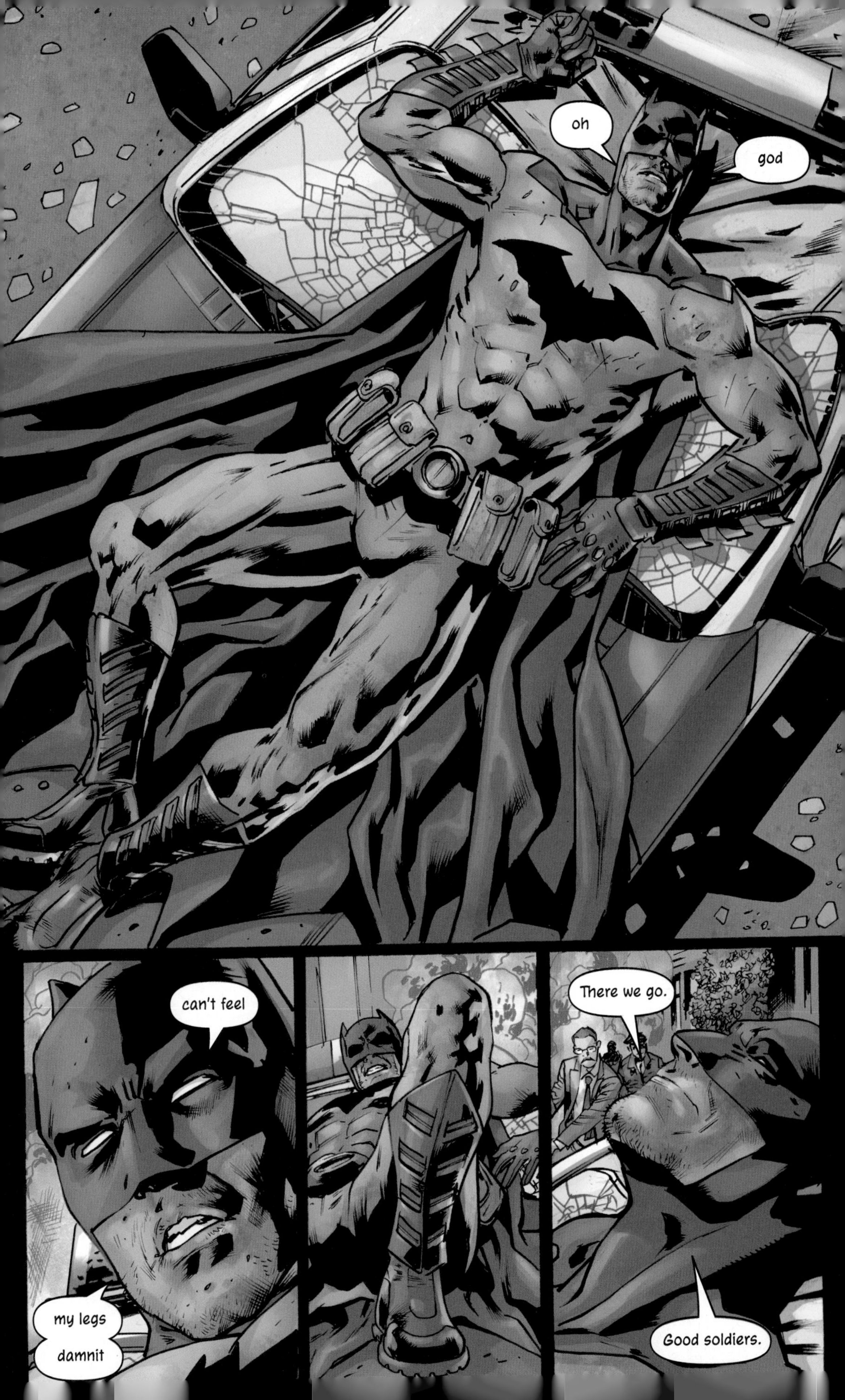
oh
god
can't feel
my legs
damnit
There we go.
Good soldiers.

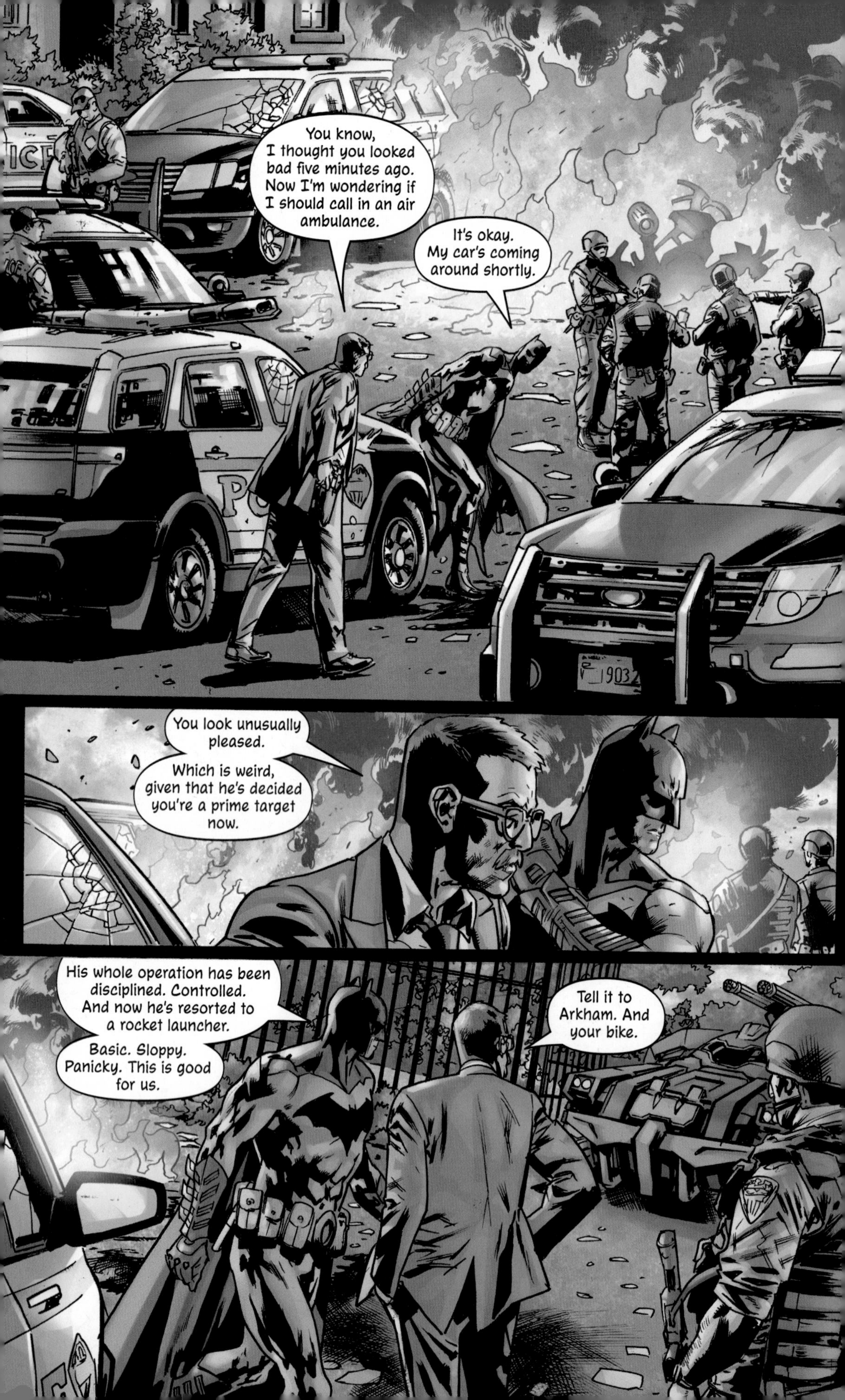
You know, I thought you looked bad five minutes ago. Now I'm wondering if I should call in an air ambulance.
It's okay. My car's coming around shortly.
You look unusually pleased.
Which is weird, given that he's decided you're a prime target now.
His whole operation has been disciplined. Controlled. And now he's resorted to a rocket launcher.
Basic. Sloppy. Panicky. This is good for us.
Tell it to Arkham. And your bike.

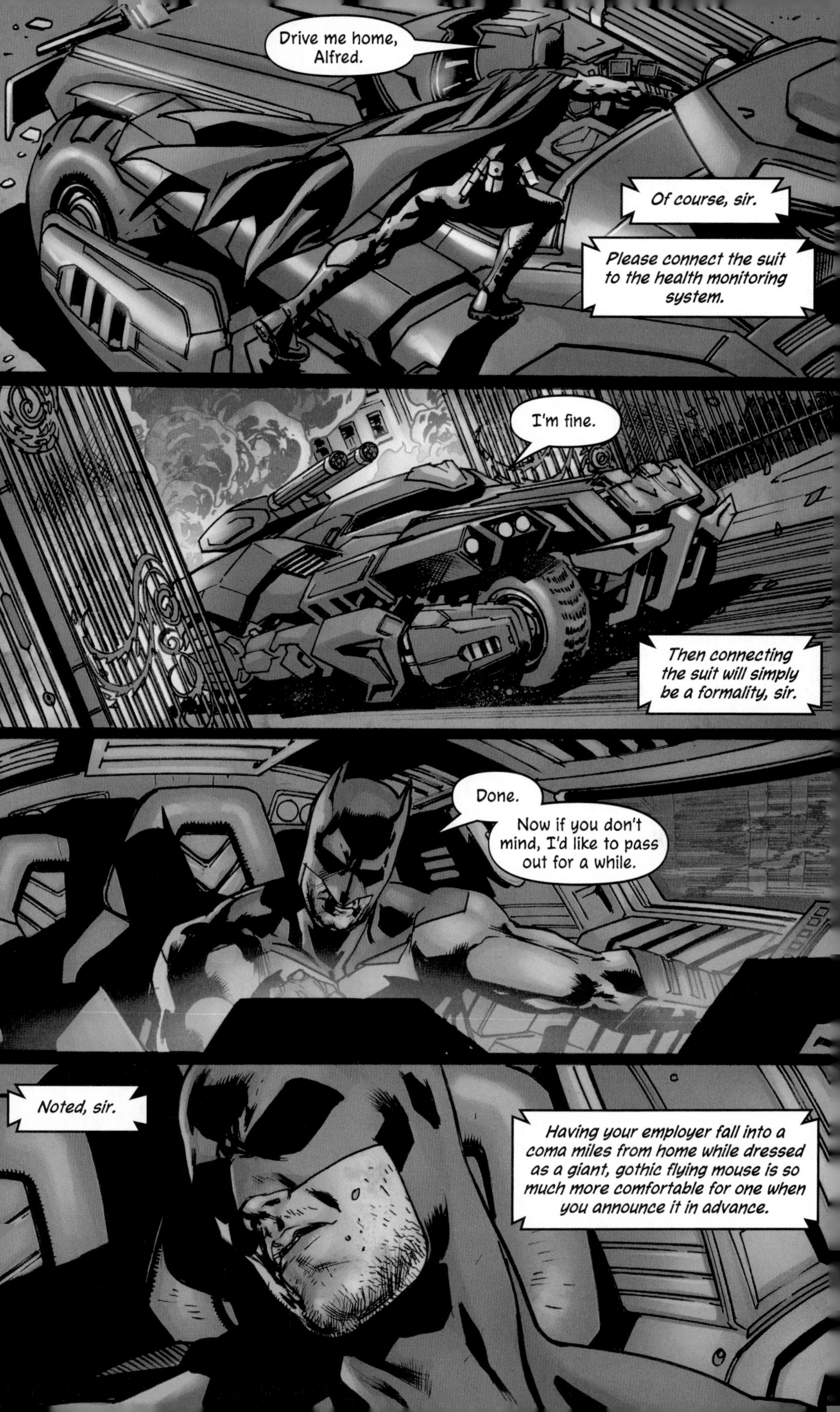
Drive me home, Alfred.
Of course, sir.
Please connect the suit to the health monitoring system.
I'm fine.
Then connecting the suit will simply be a formality, sir.
Done.
Now if you don't mind, I'd like to pass out for a while.
Noted, sir.
Having your employer fall into a coma miles from home while dressed as a giant, gothic flying mouse is so much more comfortable for one when you announce it in advance.

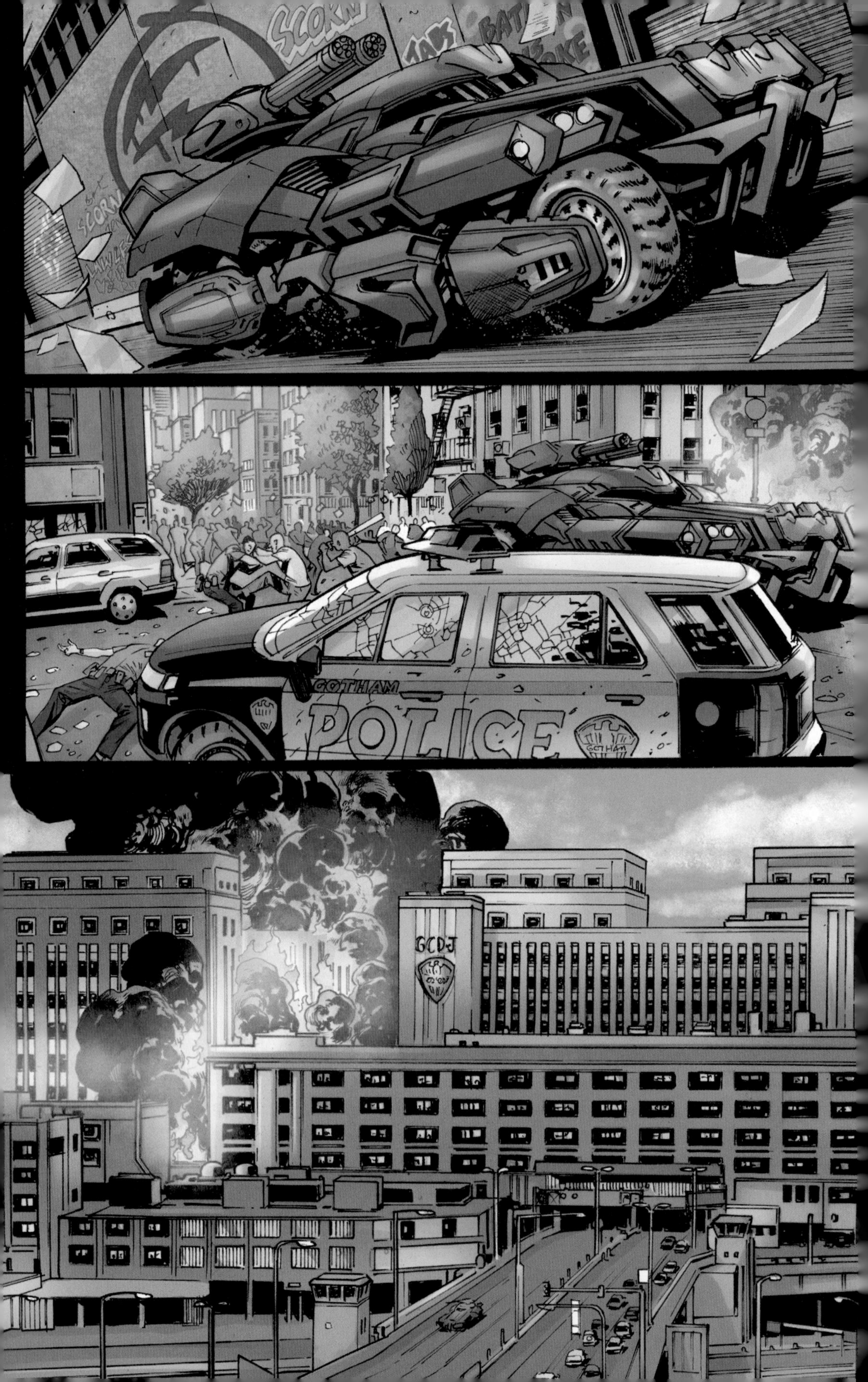
SCORN
GOTHAM
POLICE
GCDJ

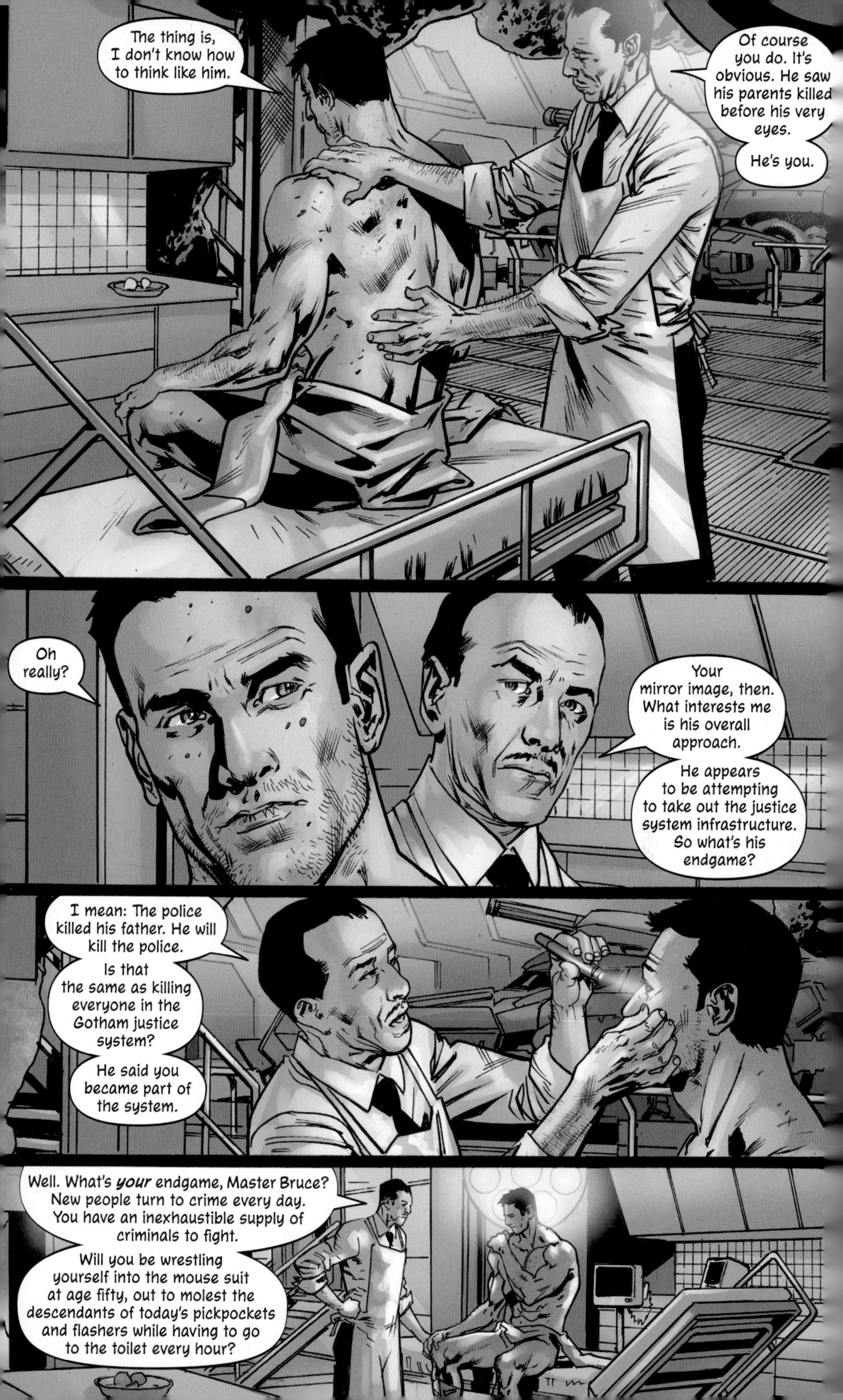
The thing is, I don't know how to think like him.
Of course you do. It's obvious. He saw his parents killed before his very eyes.
He's you.
Oh really?
Your mirror image, then. What interests me is his overall approach.
He appears to be attempting to take out the justice system infrastructure. So what's his endgame?
I mean: The police killed his father. He will kill the police.
Is that the same as killing everyone in the Gotham justice system?
He said you became part of the system.
Well. What's *your* endgame, Master Bruce? New people turn to crime every day. You have an inexhaustible supply of criminals to fight.
Will you be wrestling yourself into the mouse suit at age fifty, out to molest the descendants of today's pickpockets and flashers while having to go to the toilet every hour?

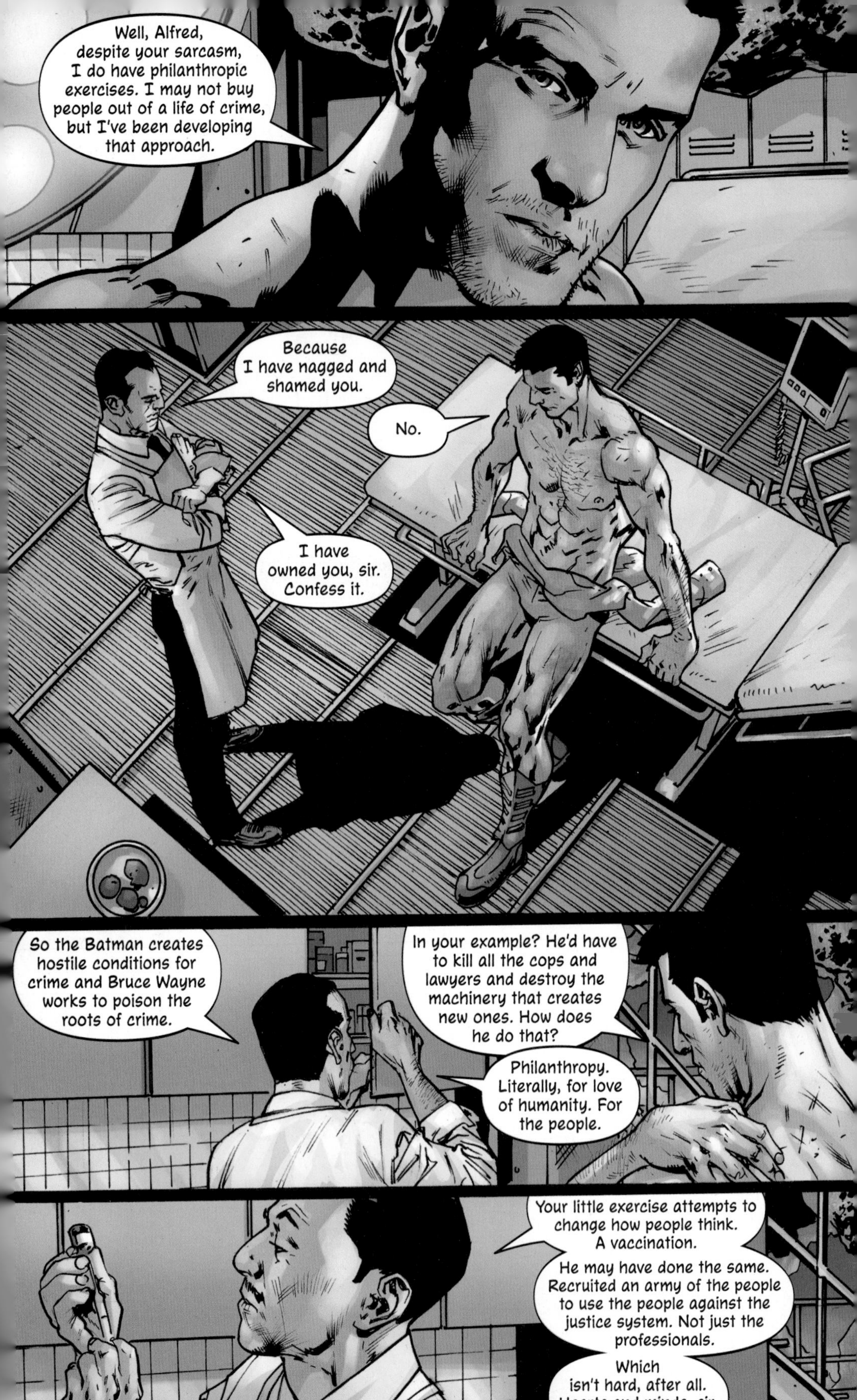
Well, Alfred, despite your sarcasm, I do have philanthropic exercises. I may not buy people out of a life of crime, but I've been developing that approach.
Because I have nagged and shamed you.
No.
I have owned you, sir. Confess it.
So the Batman creates hostile conditions for crime and Bruce Wayne works to poison the roots of crime.
In your example? He'd have to kill all the cops and lawyers and destroy the machinery that creates new ones. How does he do that?
Philanthropy. Literally, for love of humanity. For the people.
Your little exercise attempts to change how people think. A vaccination.
He may have done the same. Recruited an army of the people to use the people against the justice system. Not just the professionals.
Which isn't hard, after all. Hearts and minds, sir.

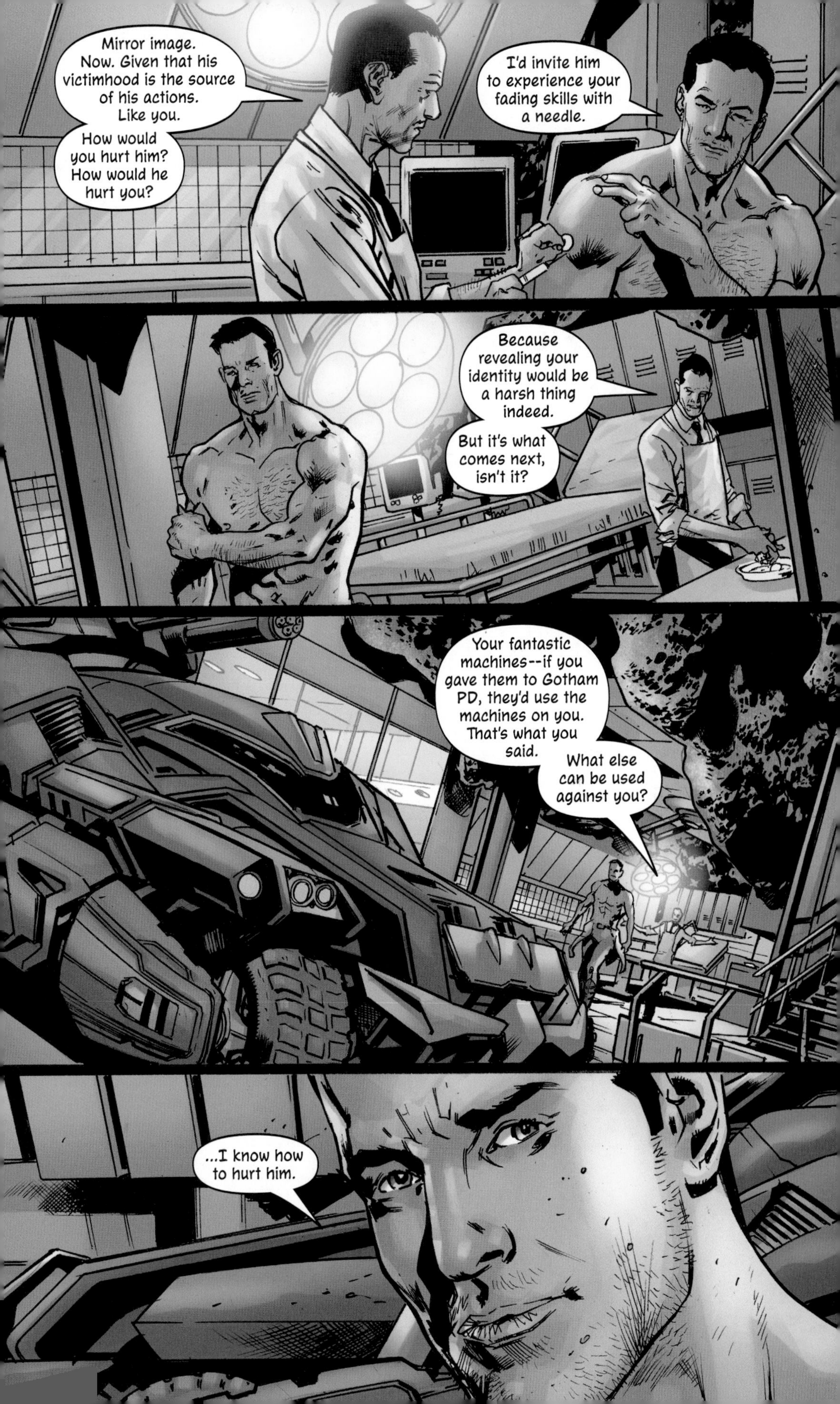
Mirror image. Now. Given that his victimhood is the source of his actions. Like you.
How would you hurt him? How would he hurt you?
I'd invite him to experience your fading skills with a needle.
Because revealing your identity would be a harsh thing indeed.
But it's what comes next, isn't it?
Your fantastic machines--if you gave them to Gotham PD, they'd use the machines on you. That's what you said.
What else can be used against you?
...I know how to hurt him.

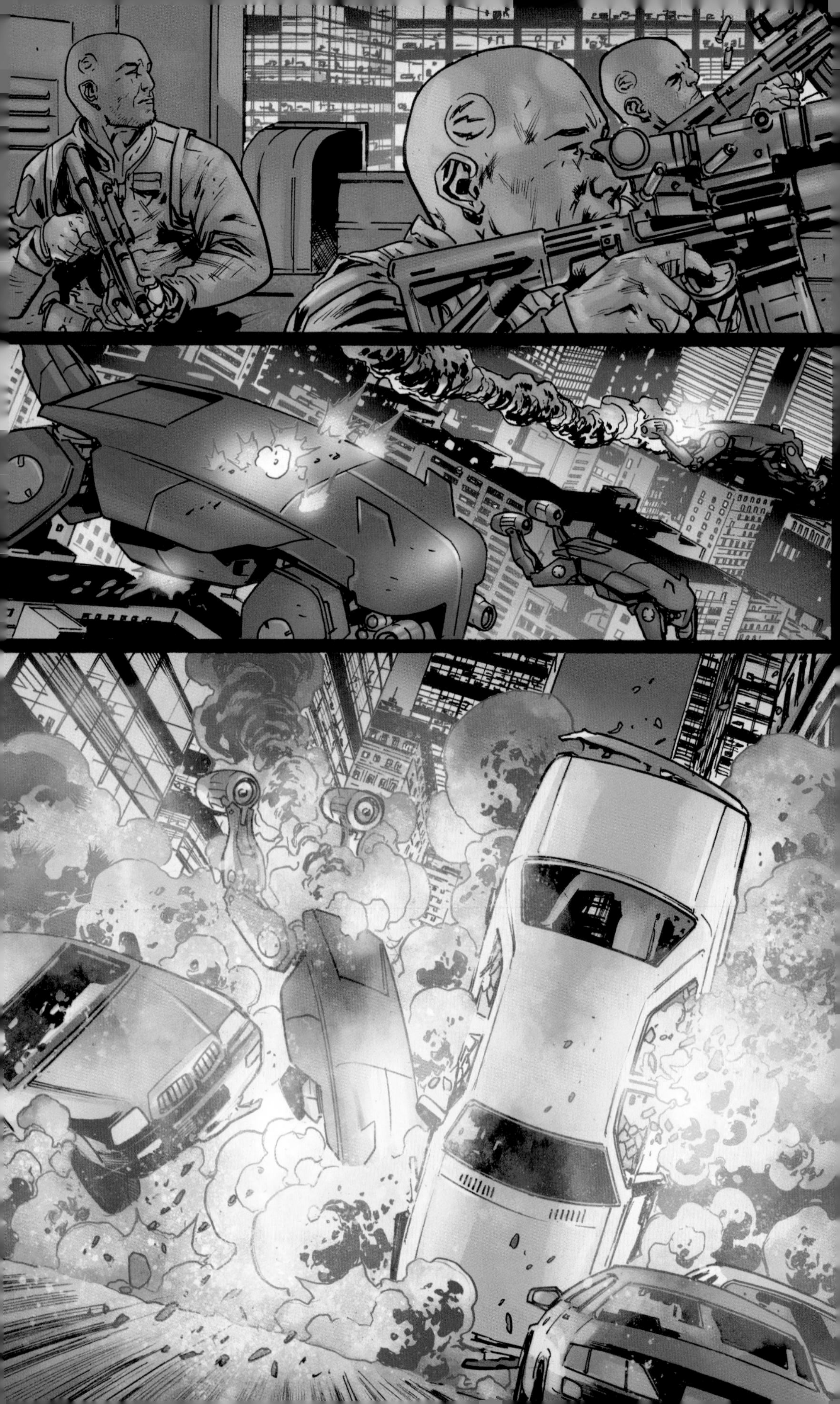

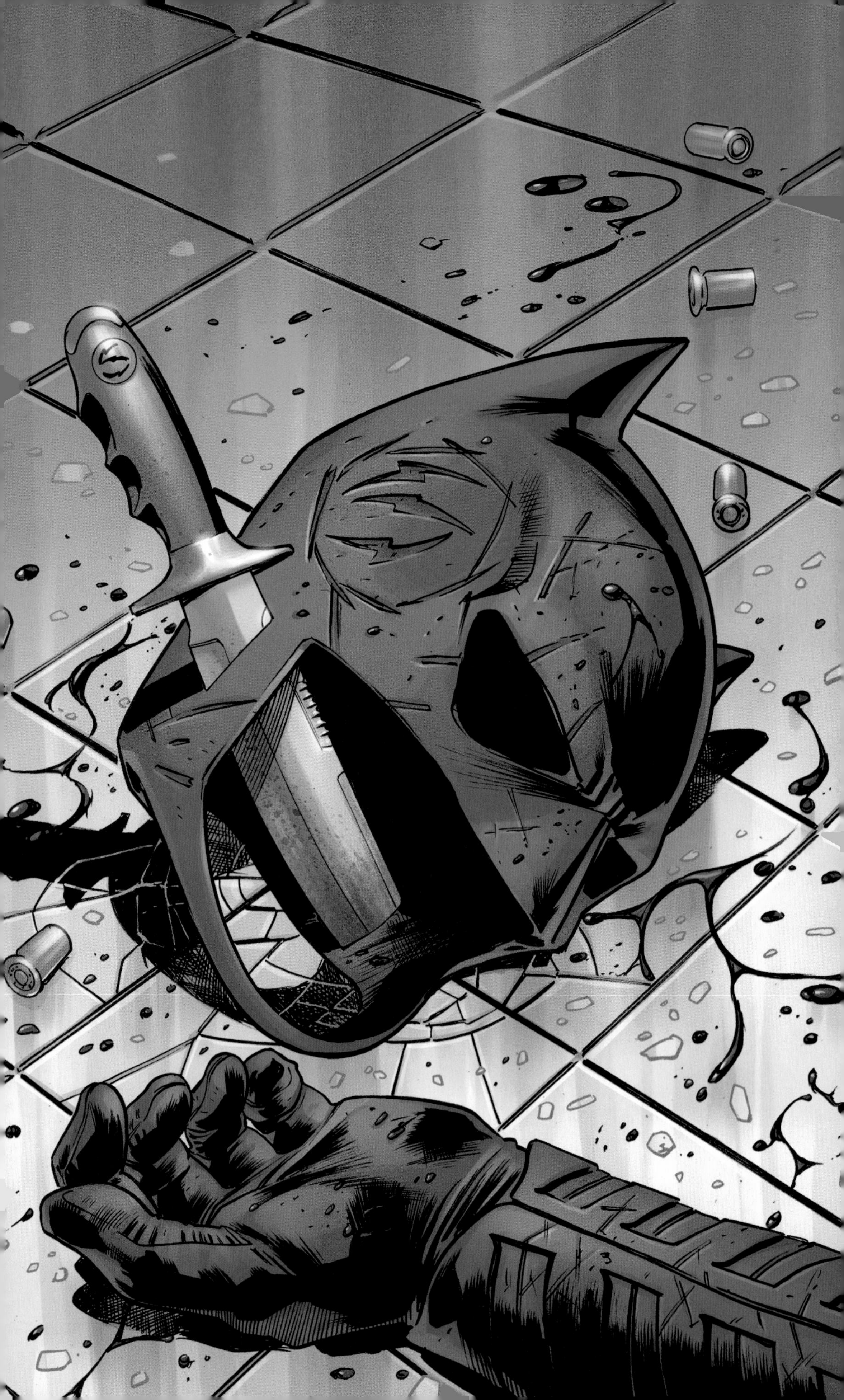

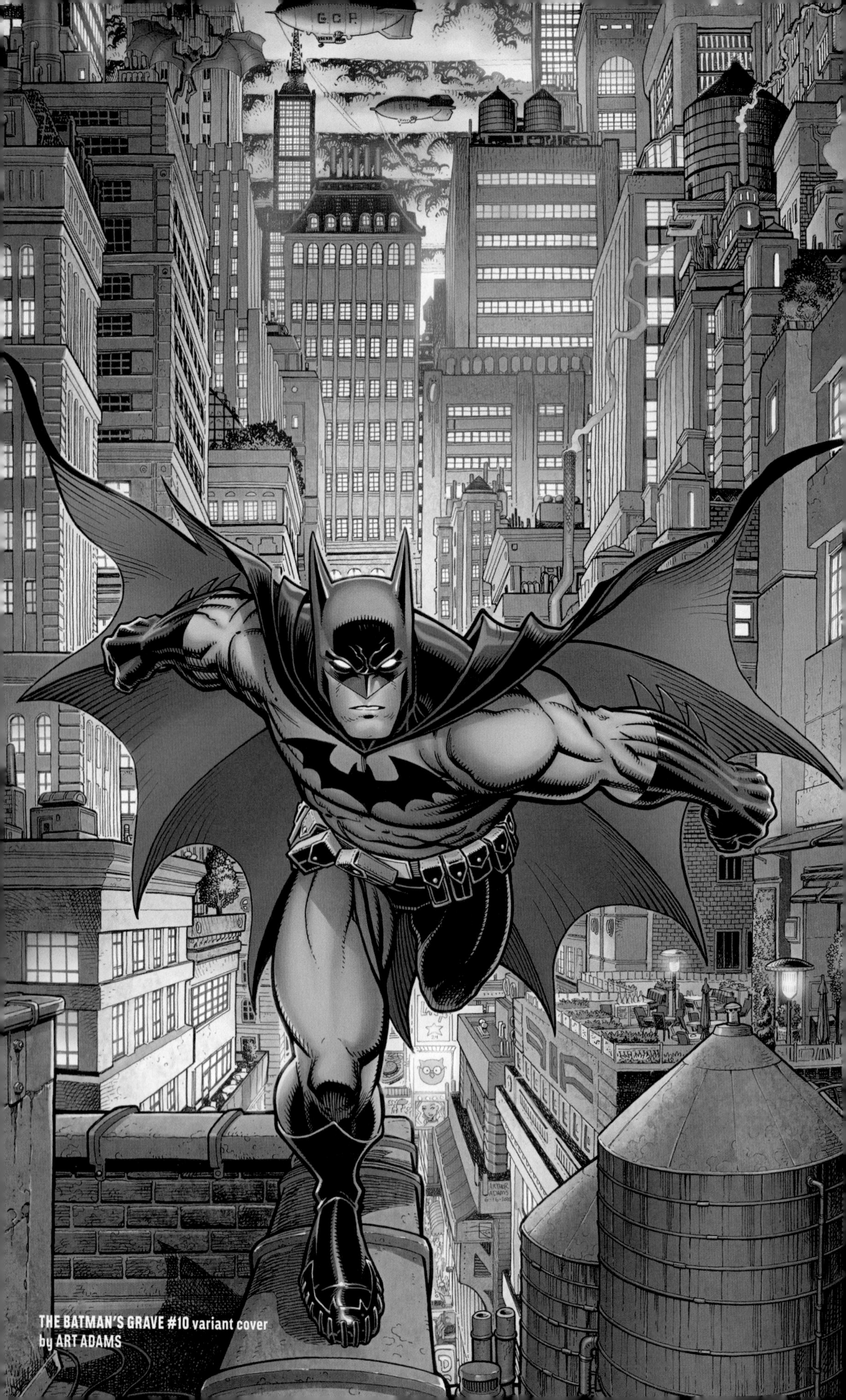
G.C.P.

THE BATMAN'S GRAVE #10 variant cover
by ART ADAMS

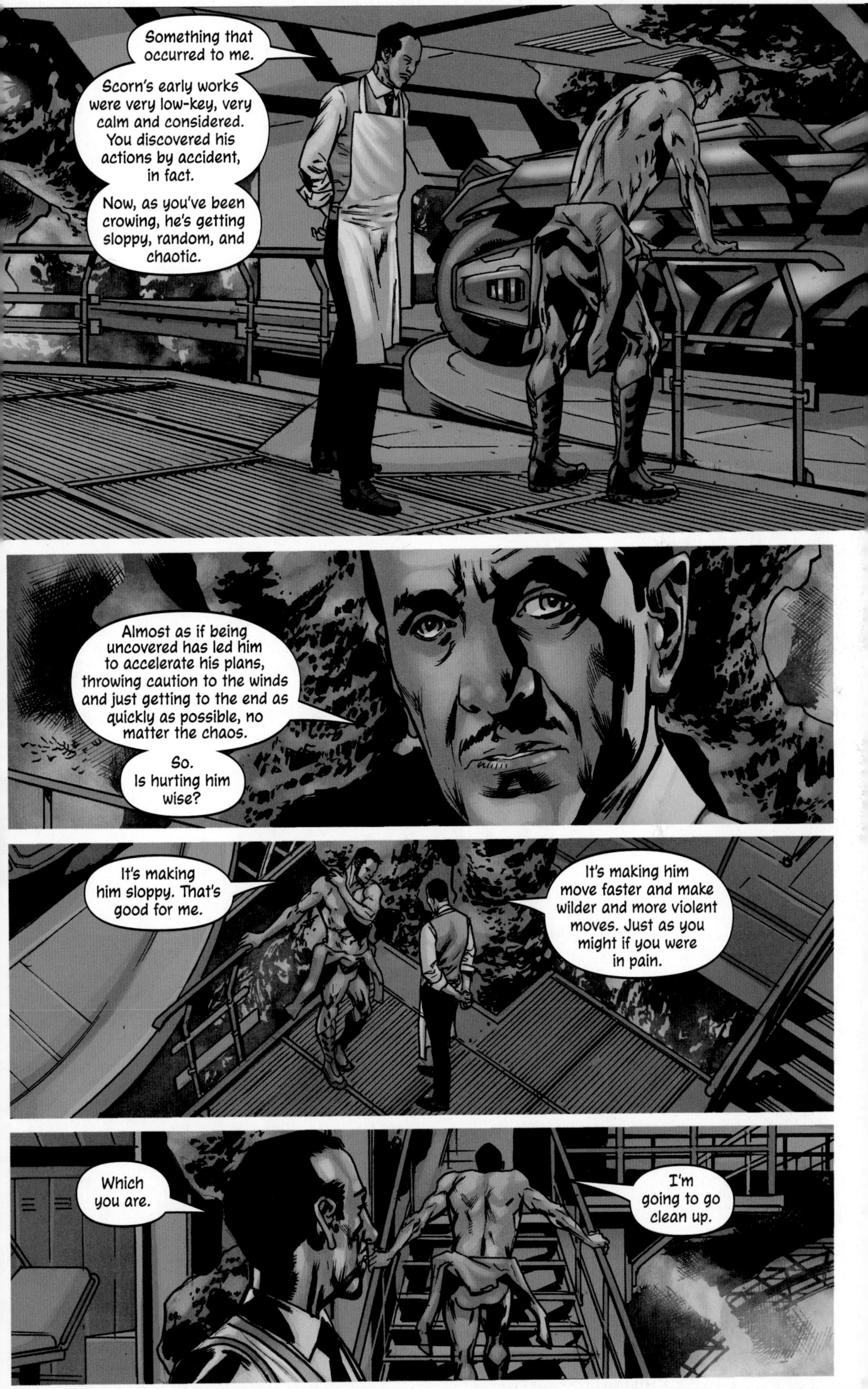
Something that occurred to me.
Scorn's early works were very low-key, very calm and considered. You discovered his actions by accident, in fact.
Now, as you've been crowing, he's getting sloppy, random, and chaotic.
Almost as if being uncovered has led him to accelerate his plans, throwing caution to the winds and just getting to the end as quickly as possible, no matter the chaos.
So. Is hurting him wise?
It's making him sloppy. That's good for me.
It's making him move faster and make wilder and more violent moves. Just as you might if you were in pain.
Which you are.
I'm going to go clean up.

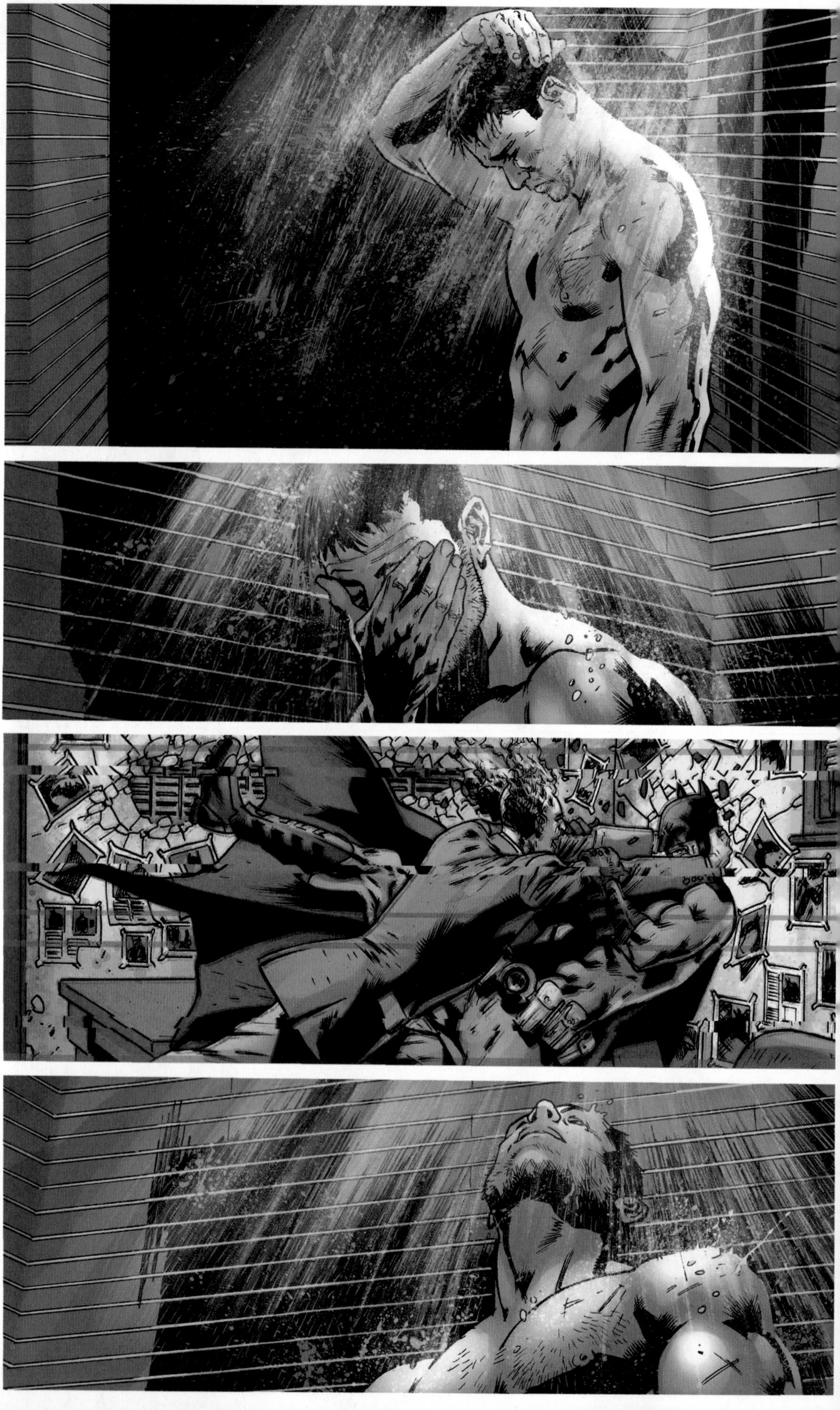

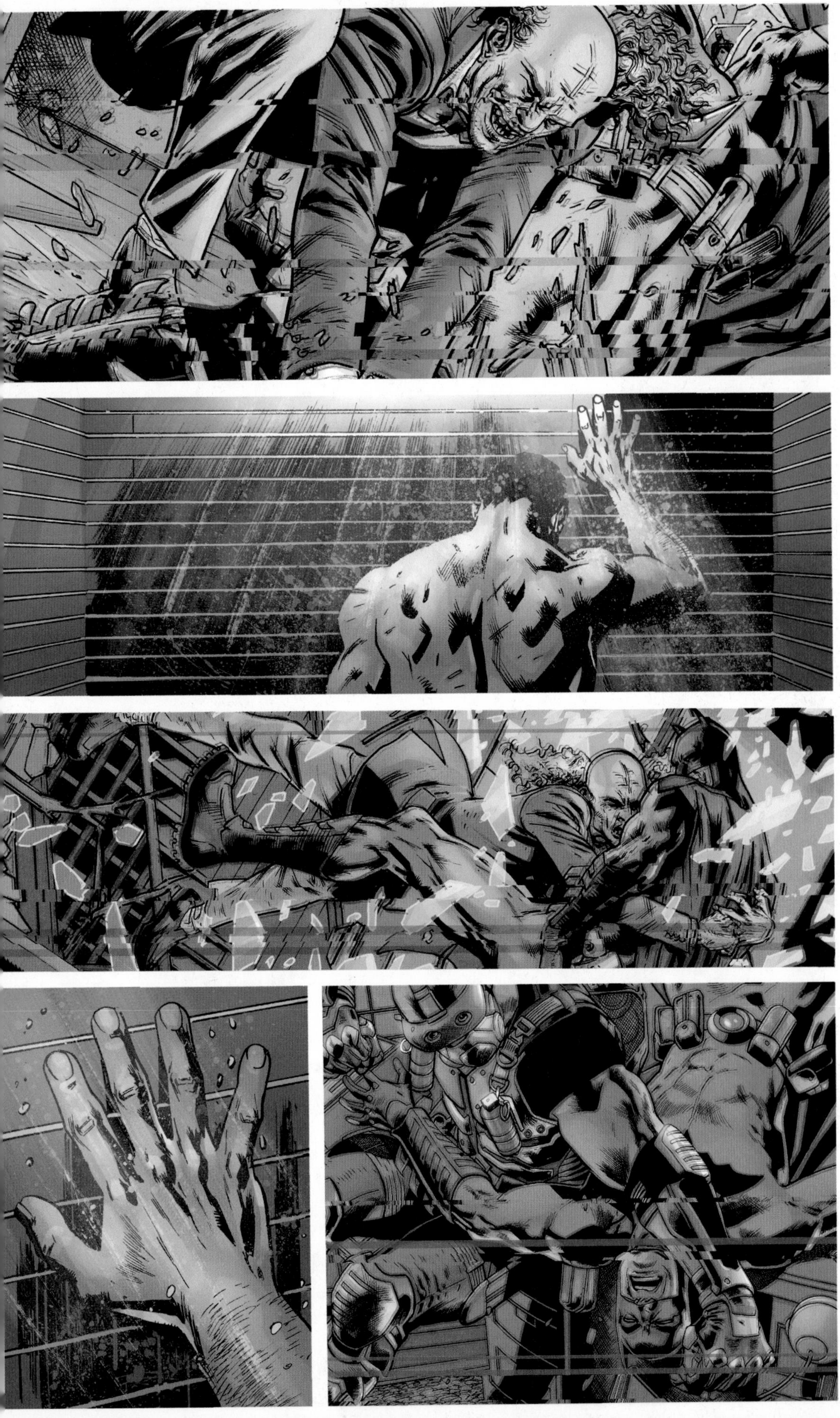

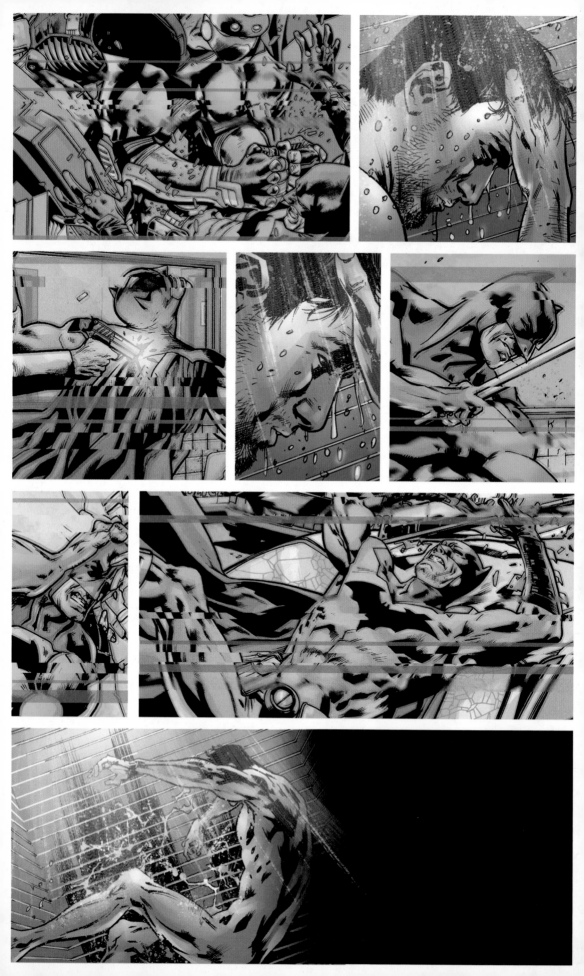

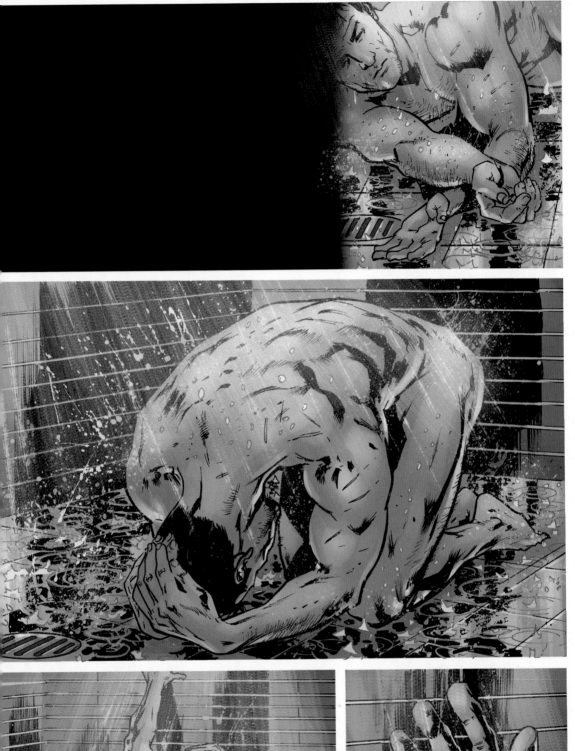

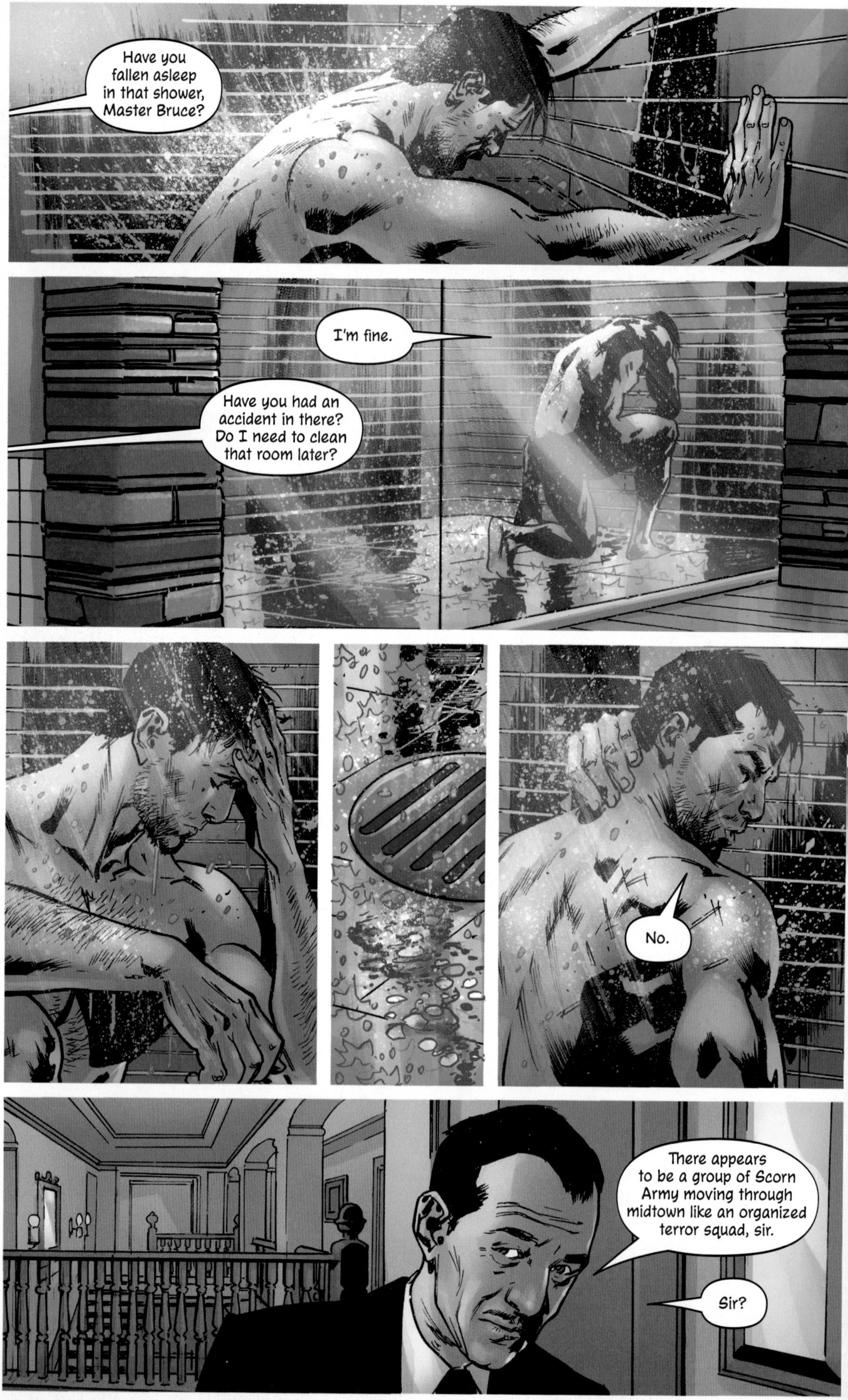
Have you fallen asleep in that shower, Master Bruce?
I'm fine.
Have you had an accident in there? Do I need to clean that room later?
No.
There appears to be a group of Scorn Army moving through midtown like an organized terror squad, sir.
Sir?

Chapter 10

Writer	Art
WARREN ELLIS	**BRYAN HITCH**

Colors	Letters
ALEX SINCLAIR	**RICHARD STARKINGS**

Cover	Variant Cover
BRYAN HITCH & **ALEX SINCLAIR**	**ART** **ADAMS**

Associate Editor	Editor
ANDREW MARINO	**MARIE JAVINS**

BATMAN created by **BOB KANE** with **BILL FINGER**

This isn't terrorism, Alfred. This is just organization.

They're locking down the district.

Scorn has a plan.

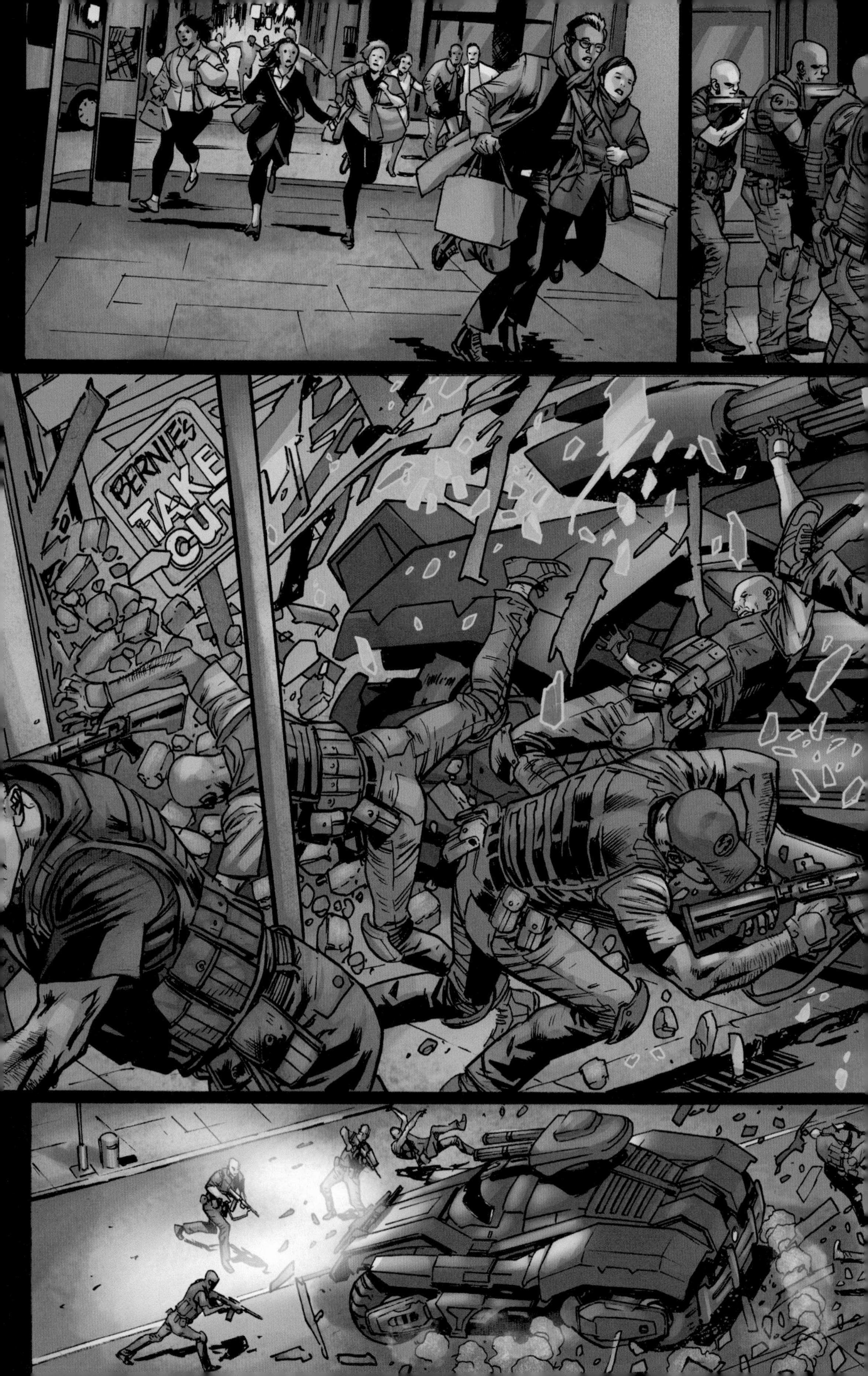
BERNIE'S
TAKE
OUT

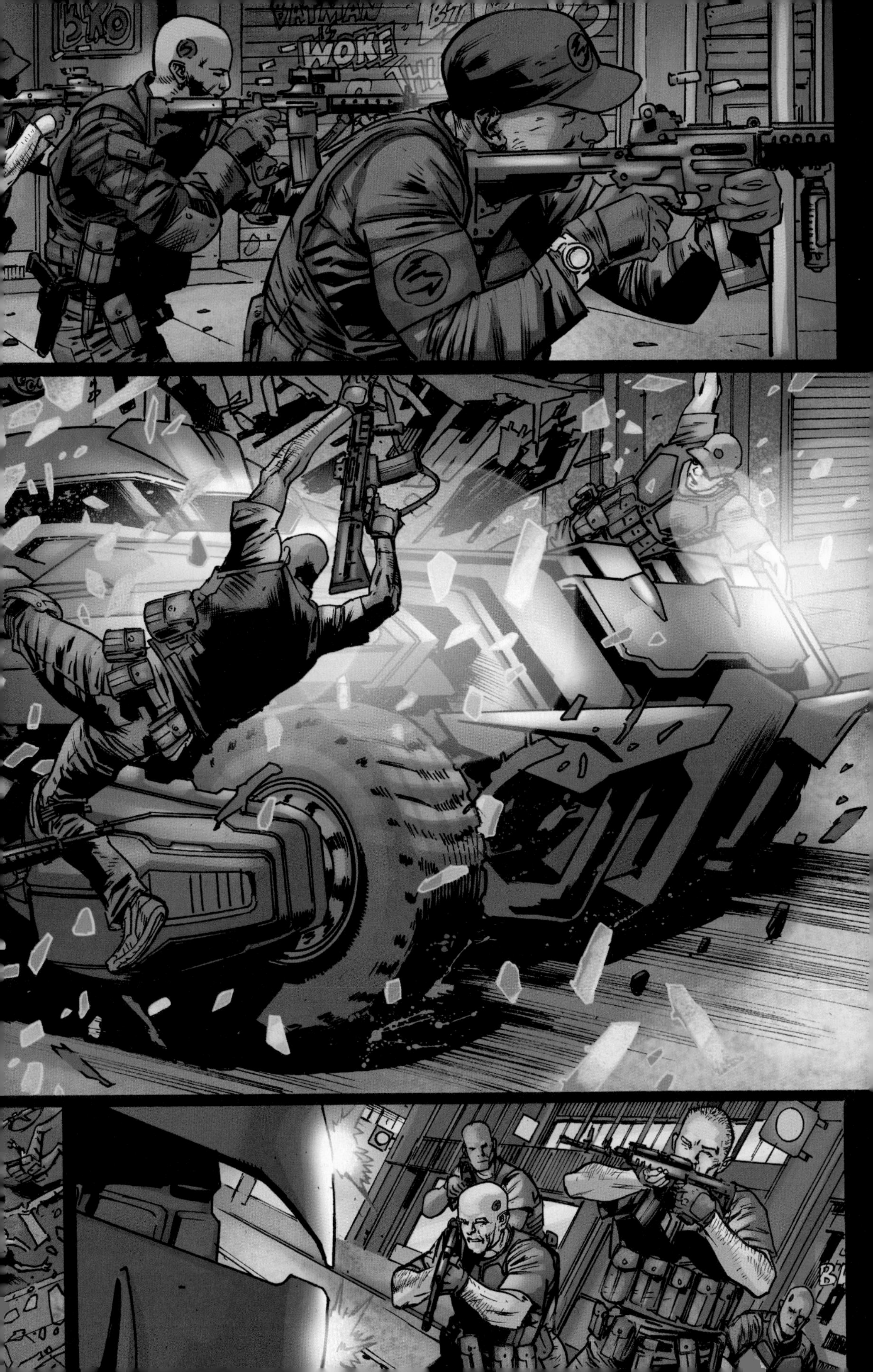
BATMAN
is
WOKE

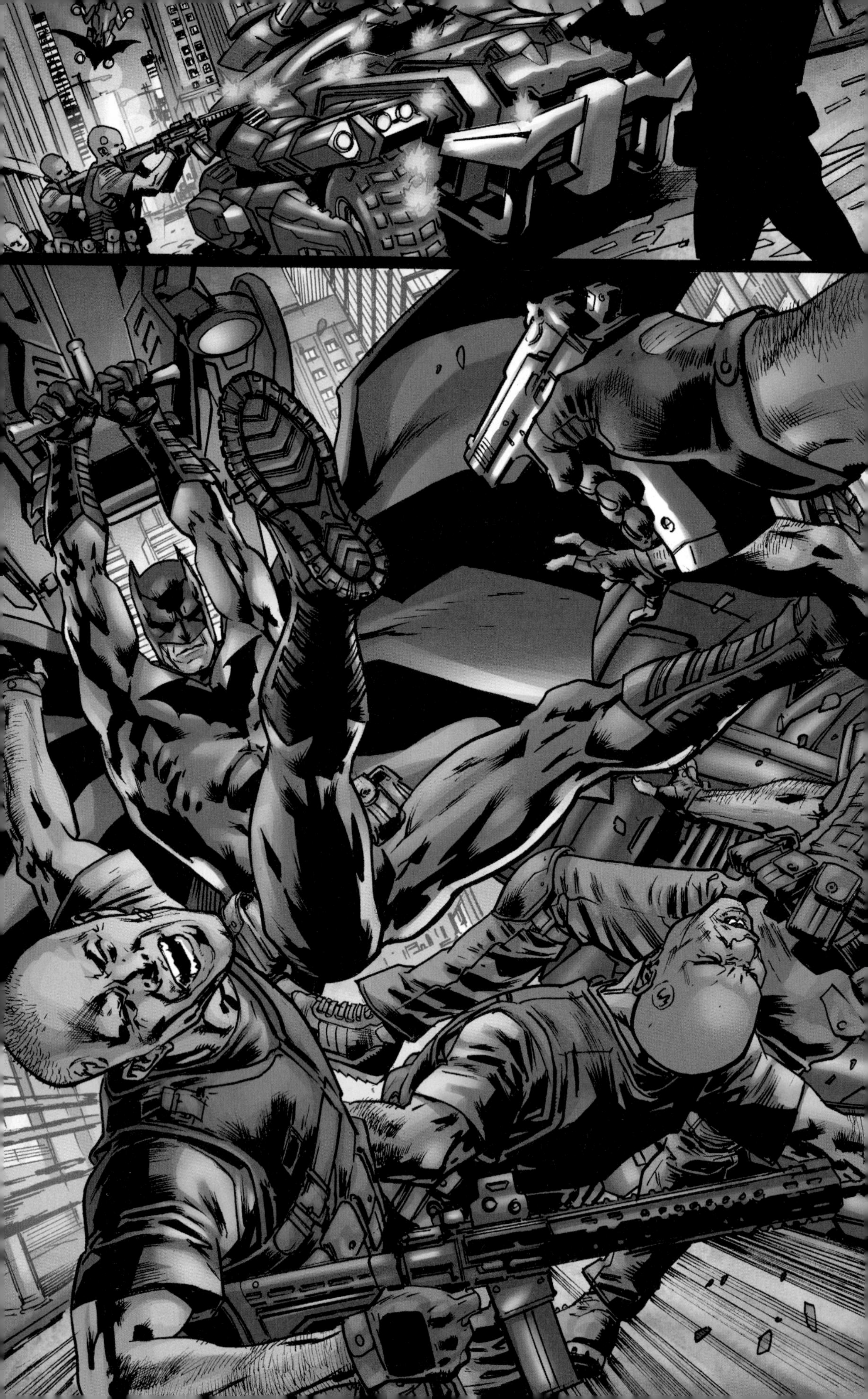

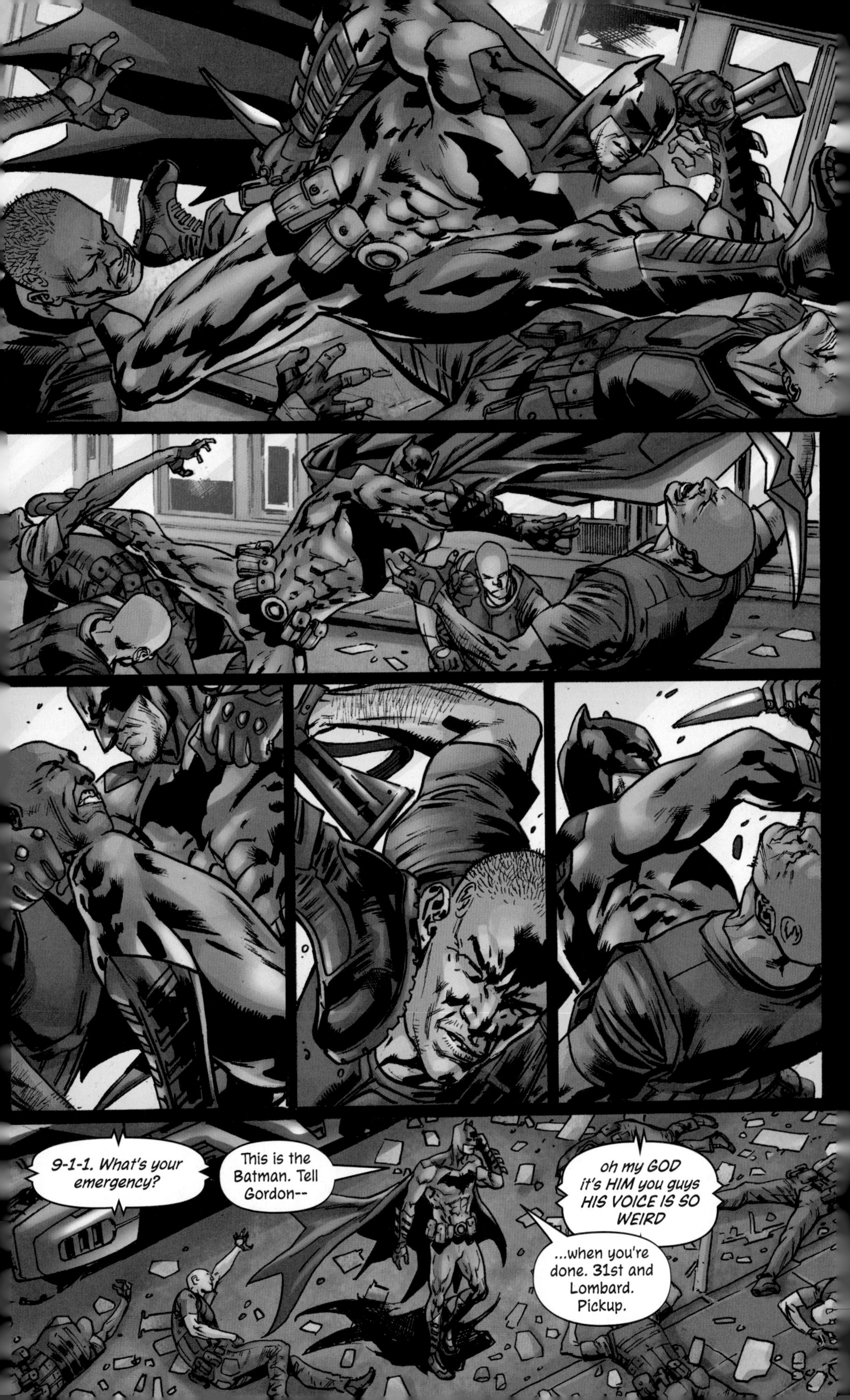

9-1-1. What's your emergency?
This is the Batman. Tell Gordon--
oh my GOD it's HIM you guys HIS VOICE IS SO WEIRD
...when you're done. 31st and Lombard. Pickup.

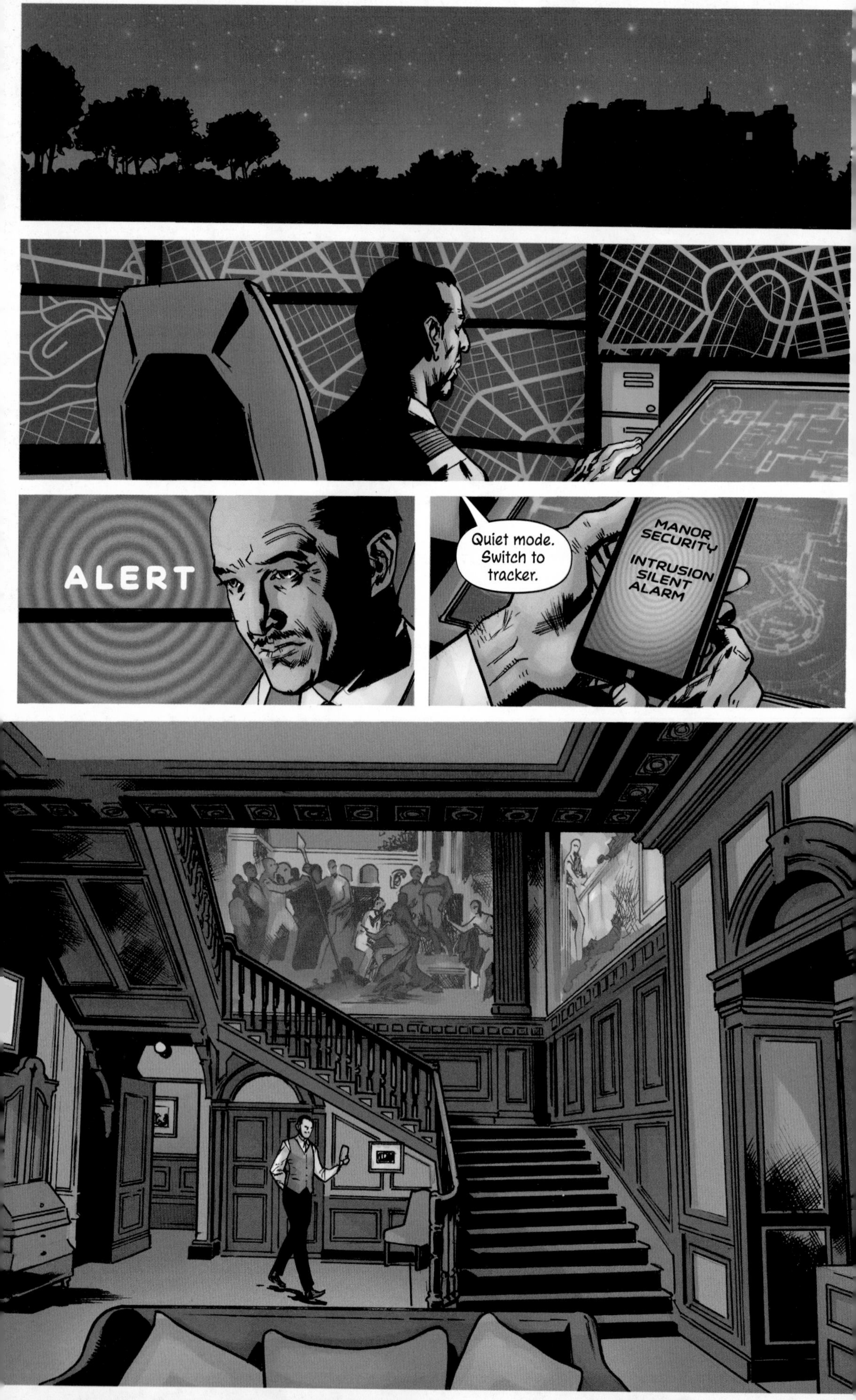
ALERT
Quiet mode. Switch to tracker.
MANOR SECURITY
INTRUSION SILENT ALARM

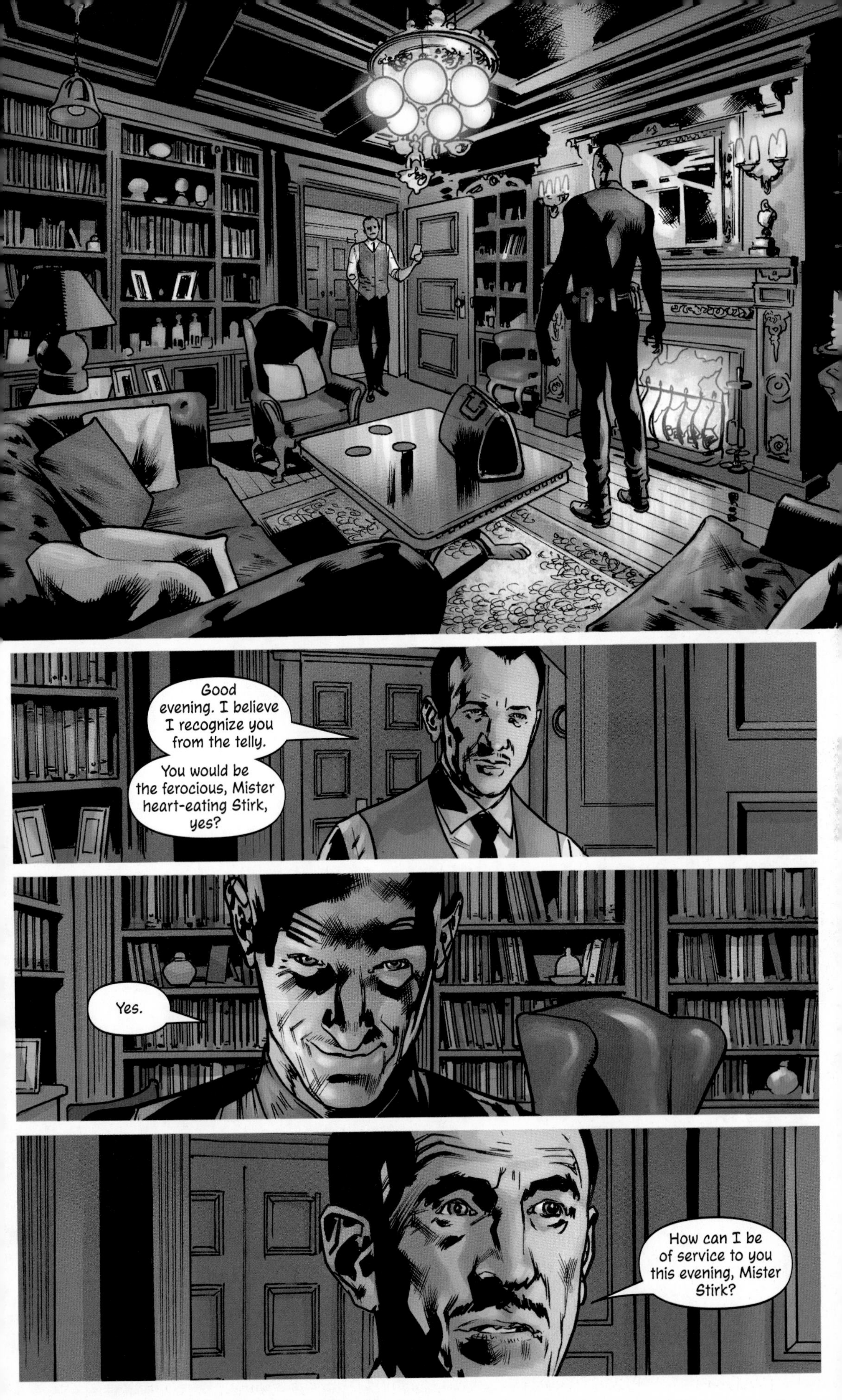

Good evening. I believe I recognize you from the telly.
You would be the ferocious, Mister heart-eating Stirk, yes?
Yes.
How can I be of service to you this evening, Mister Stirk?

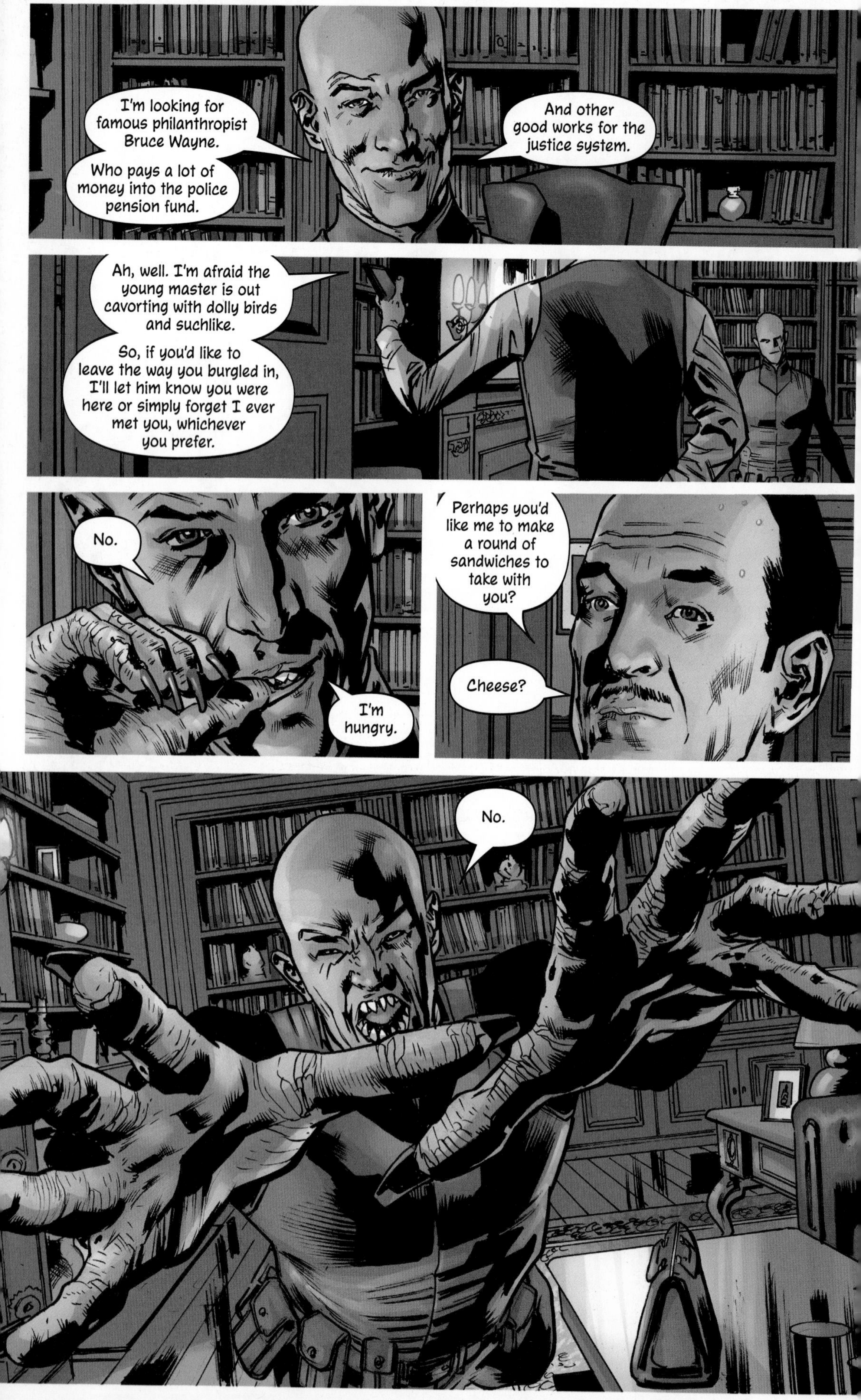
I'm looking for famous philanthropist Bruce Wayne.
Who pays a lot of money into the police pension fund.
And other good works for the justice system.
Ah, well. I'm afraid the young master is out cavorting with dolly birds and suchlike.
So, if you'd like to leave the way you burgled in, I'll let him know you were here or simply forget I ever met you, whichever you prefer.
No.
I'm hungry.
Perhaps you'd like me to make a round of sandwiches to take with you?
Cheese?
No.

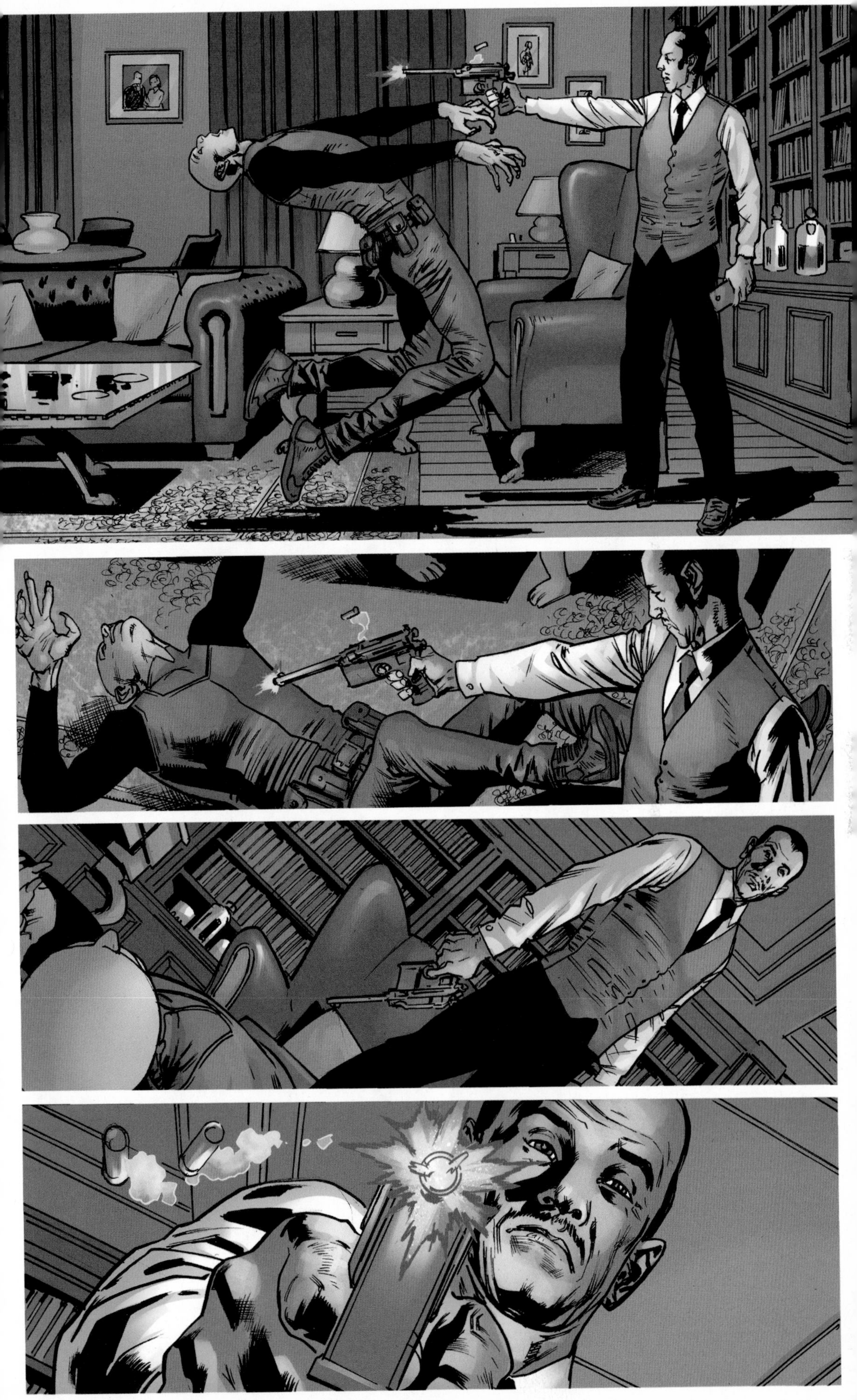

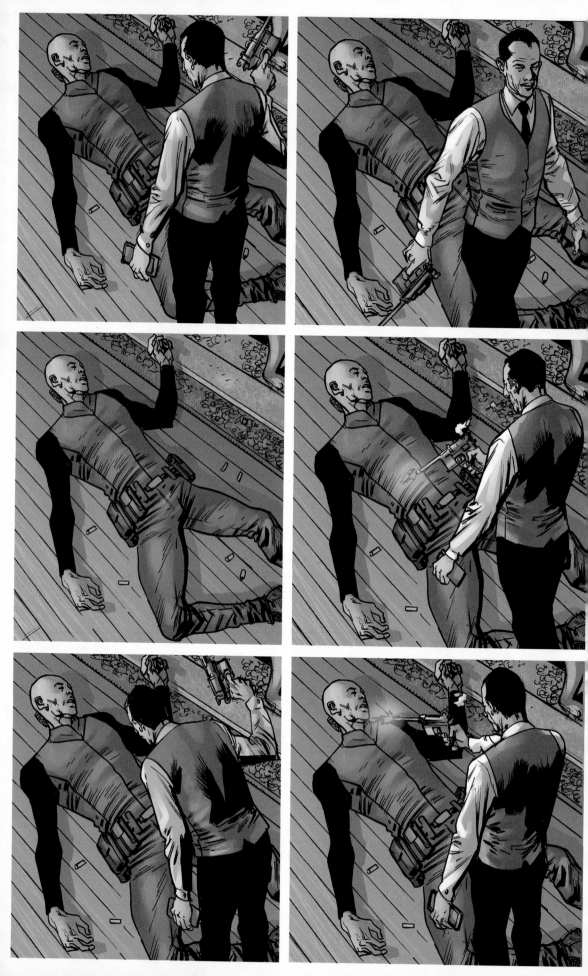

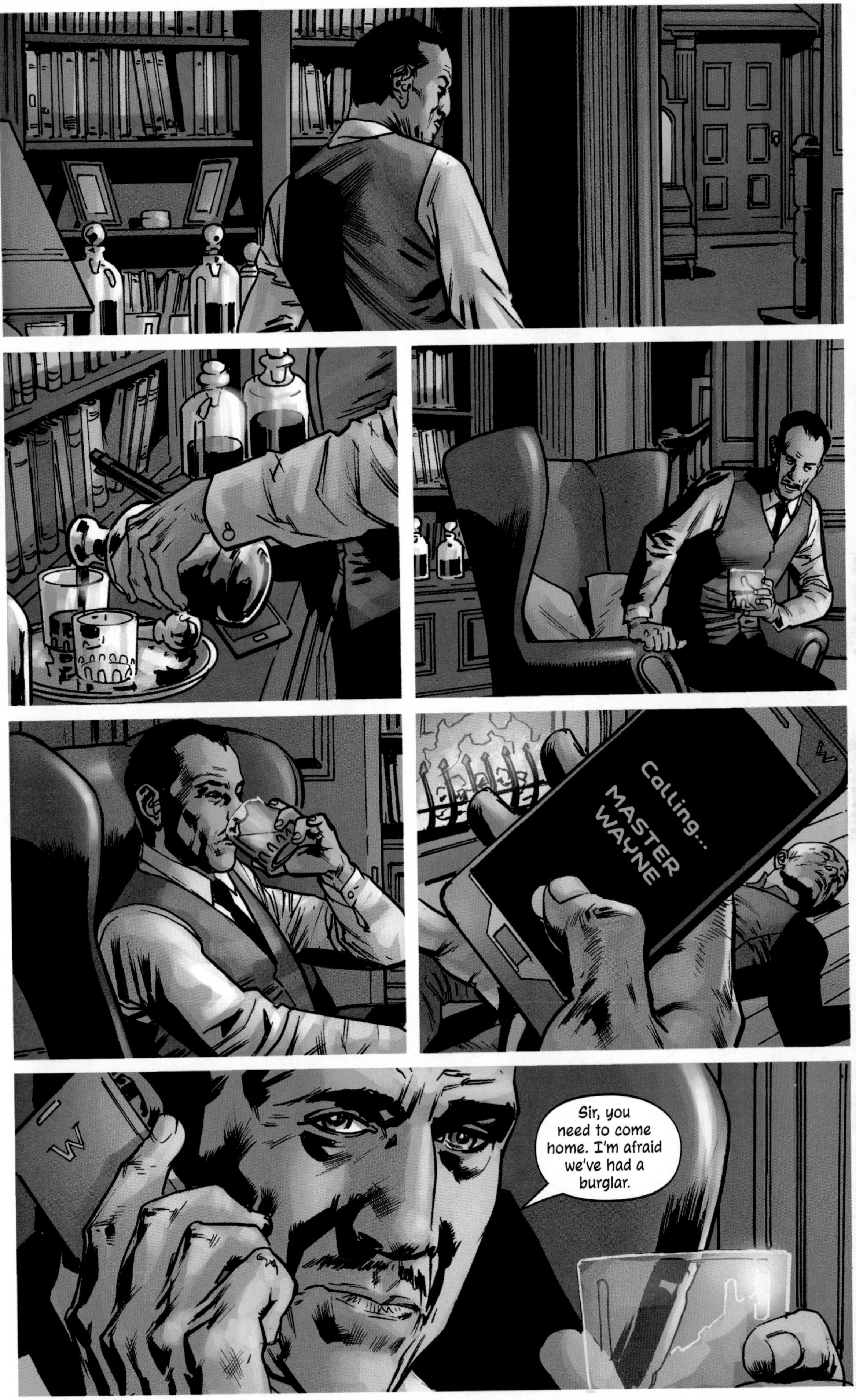
Calling...
MASTER WAYNE
Sir, you need to come home. I'm afraid we've had a burglar.

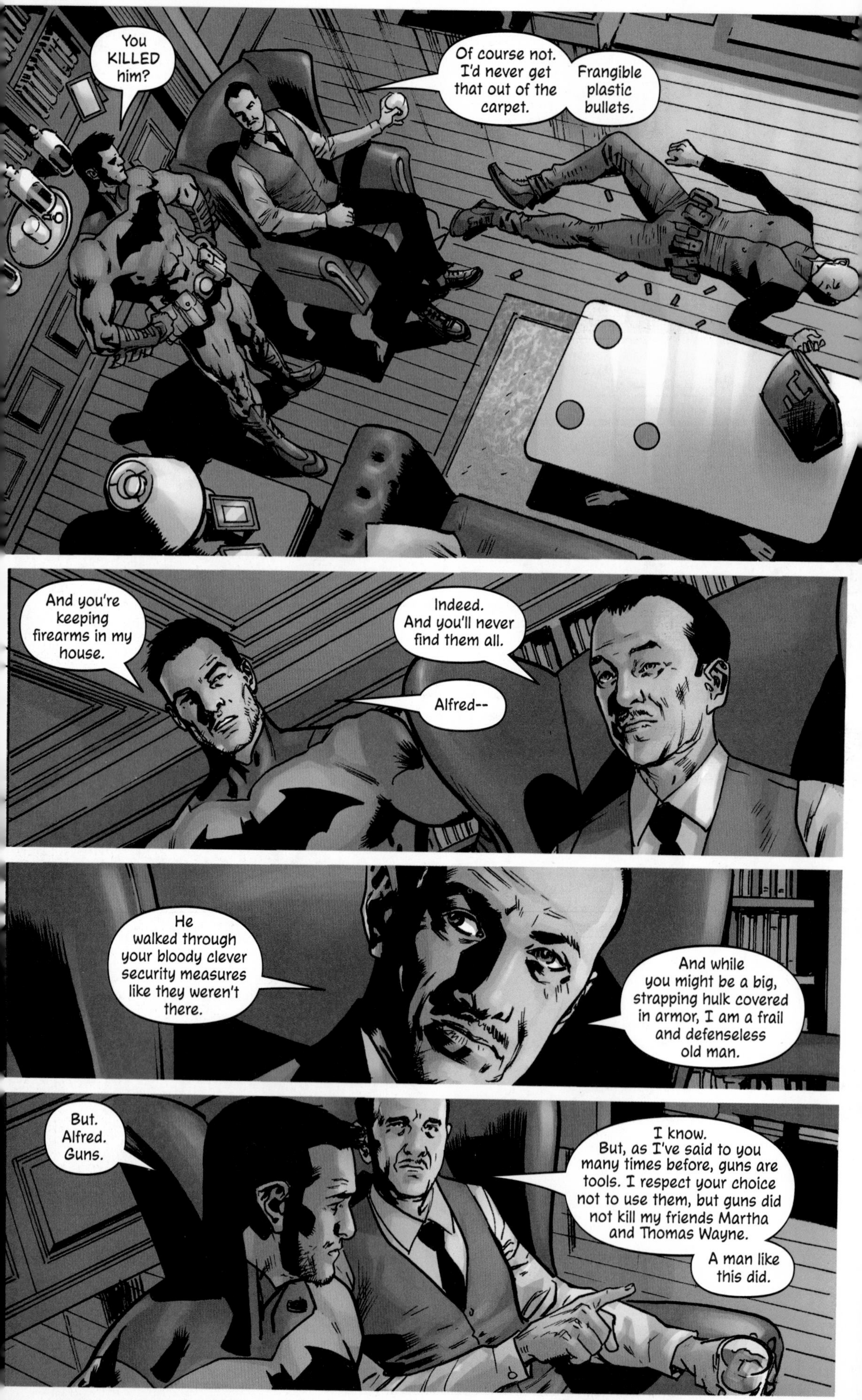
You KILLED him?
Of course not. I'd never get that out of the carpet.
Frangible plastic bullets.
And you're keeping firearms in my house.
Indeed. And you'll never find them all.
Alfred--
He walked through your bloody clever security measures like they weren't there.
And while you might be a big, strapping hulk covered in armor, I am a frail and defenseless old man.
But. Alfred. Guns.
I know. But, as I've said to you many times before, guns are tools. I respect your choice not to use them, but guns did not kill my friends Martha and Thomas Wayne.
A man like this did.

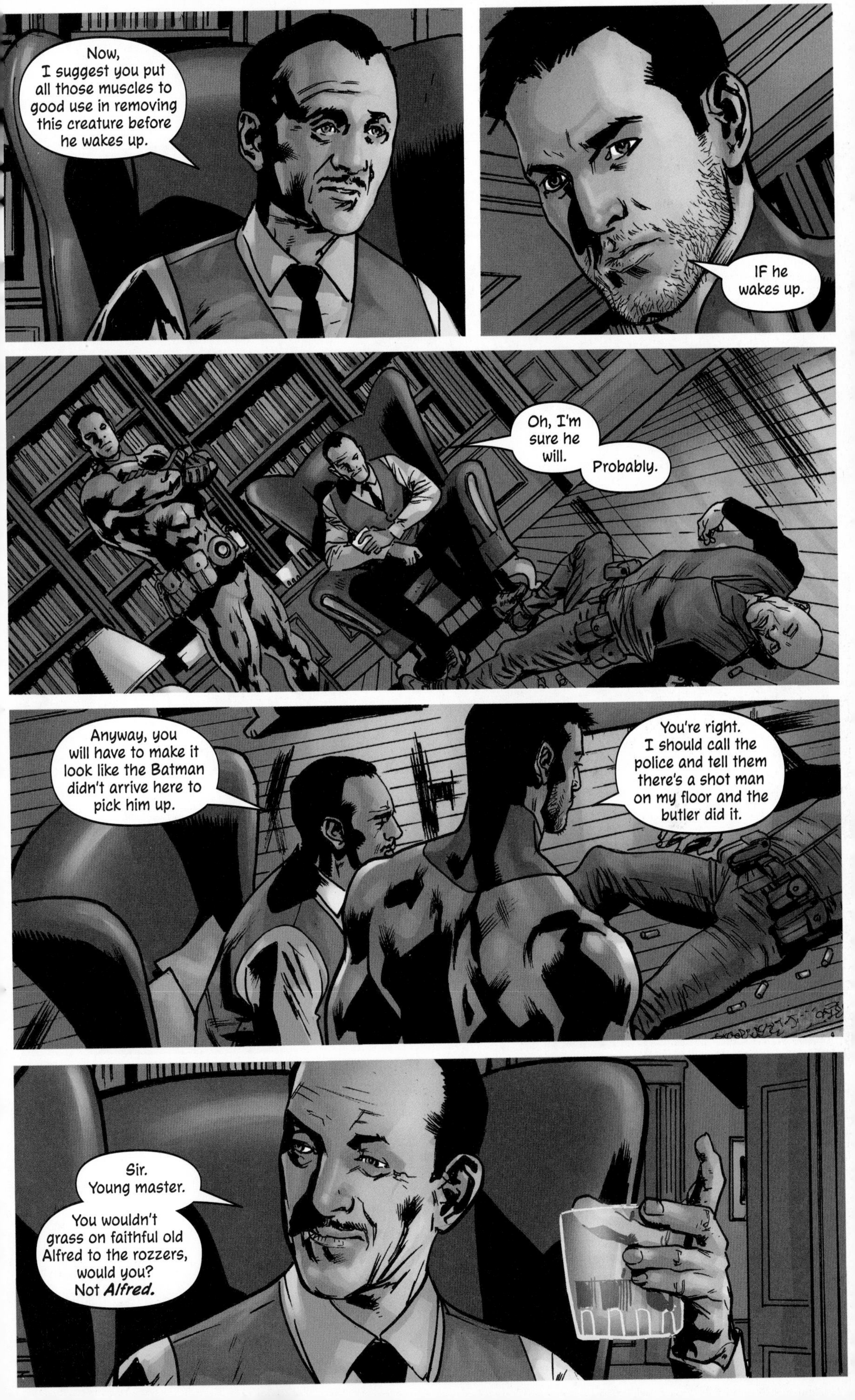
Now, I suggest you put all those muscles to good use in removing this creature before he wakes up.
IF he wakes up.
Oh, I'm sure he will.
Probably.
Anyway, you will have to make it look like the Batman didn't arrive here to pick him up.
You're right. I should call the police and tell them there's a shot man on my floor and the butler did it.
Sir. Young master.
You wouldn't grass on faithful old Alfred to the rozzers, would you? Not *Alfred.*

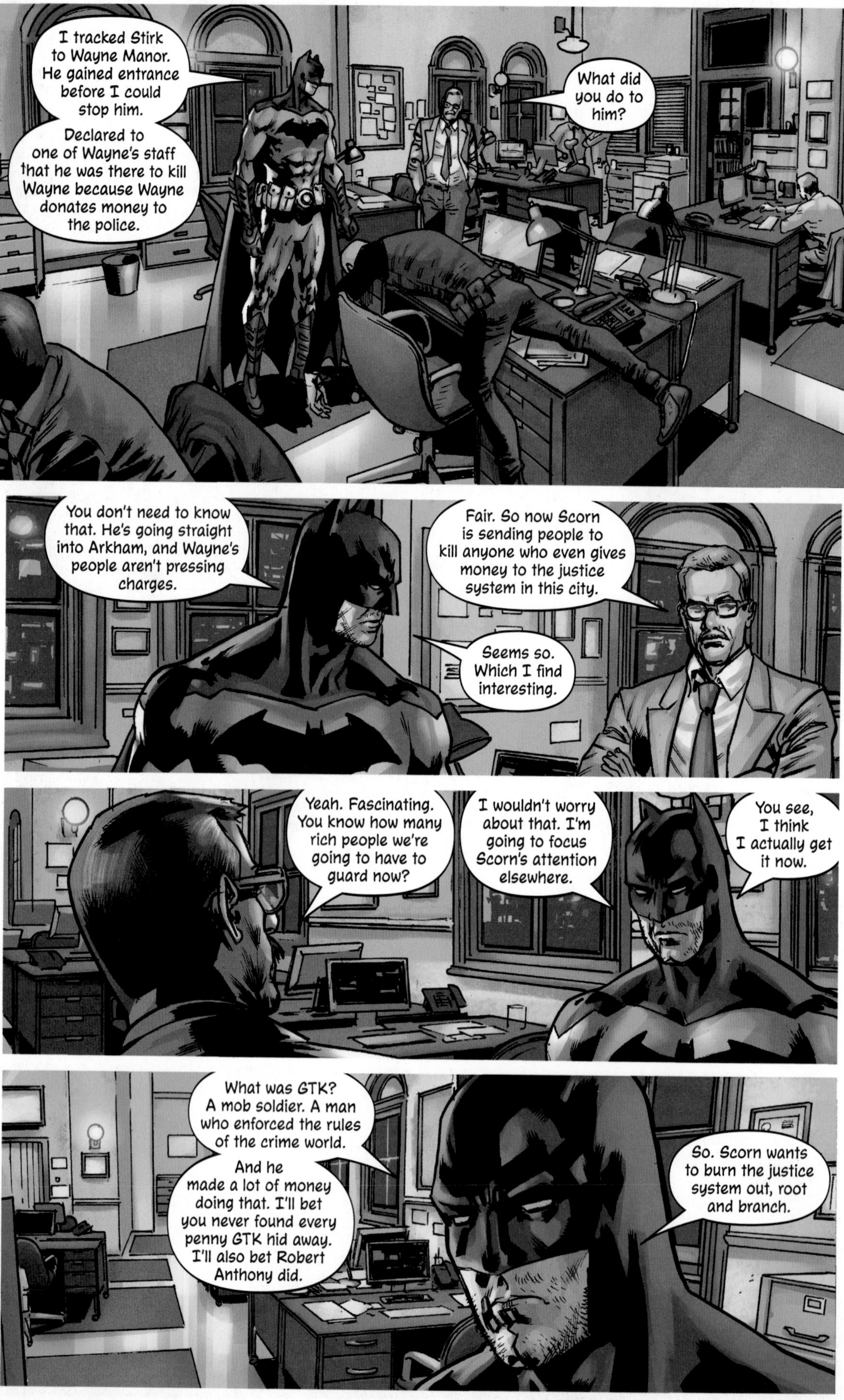
I tracked Stirk to Wayne Manor. He gained entrance before I could stop him.
Declared to one of Wayne's staff that he was there to kill Wayne because Wayne donates money to the police.
What did you do to him?
You don't need to know that. He's going straight into Arkham, and Wayne's people aren't pressing charges.
Fair. So now Scorn is sending people to kill anyone who even gives money to the justice system in this city.
Seems so. Which I find interesting.
Yeah. Fascinating. You know how many rich people we're going to have to guard now?
I wouldn't worry about that. I'm going to focus Scorn's attention elsewhere.
You see, I think I actually get it now.
What was GTK? A mob soldier. A man who enforced the rules of the crime world.
And he made a lot of money doing that. I'll bet you never found every penny GTK hid away. I'll also bet Robert Anthony did.
So. Scorn wants to burn the justice system out, root and branch.

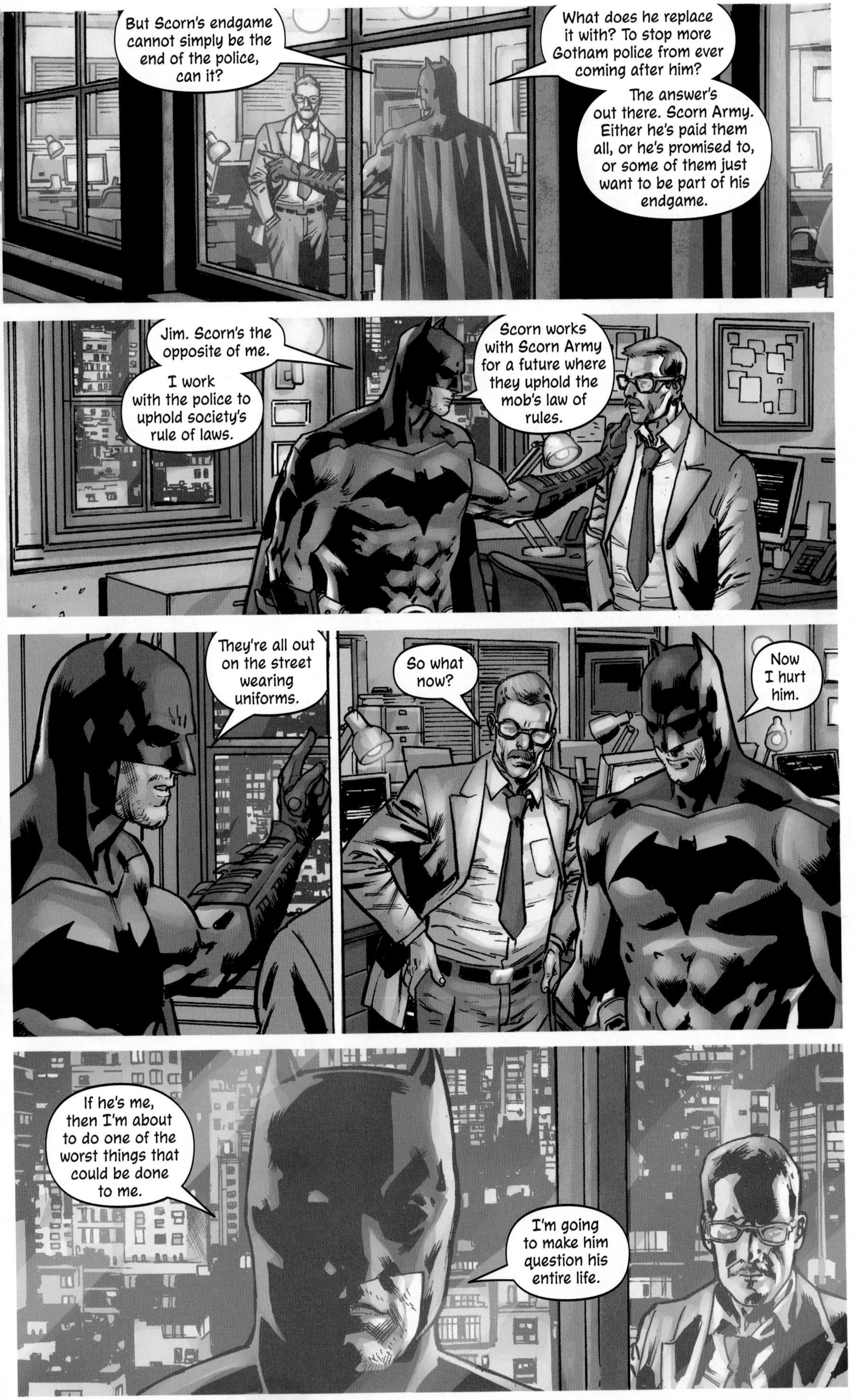
But Scorn's endgame cannot simply be the end of the police, can it?
What does he replace it with? To stop more Gotham police from ever coming after him?
The answer's out there. Scorn Army. Either he's paid them all, or he's promised to, or some of them just want to be part of his endgame.
Jim. Scorn's the opposite of me.
I work with the police to uphold society's rule of laws.
Scorn works with Scorn Army for a future where they uphold the mob's law of rules.
They're all out on the street wearing uniforms.
So what now?
Now I hurt him.
If he's me, then I'm about to do one of the worst things that could be done to me.
I'm going to make him question his entire life.

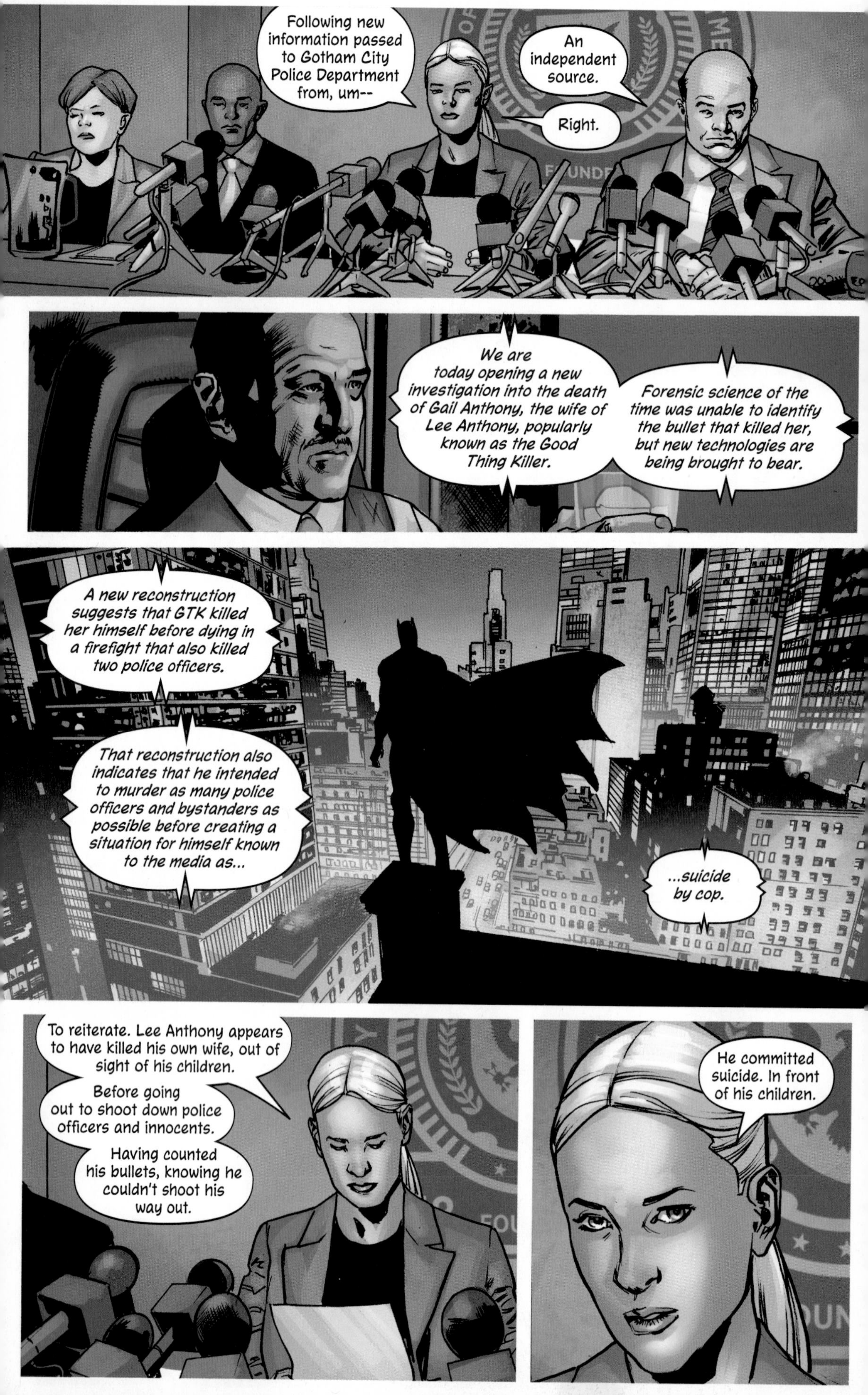
Following new information passed to Gotham City Police Department from, um--
An independent source.
Right.
We are today opening a new investigation into the death of Gail Anthony, the wife of Lee Anthony, popularly known as the Good Thing Killer.
Forensic science of the time was unable to identify the bullet that killed her, but new technologies are being brought to bear.
A new reconstruction suggests that GTK killed her himself before dying in a firefight that also killed two police officers.
That reconstruction also indicates that he intended to murder as many police officers and bystanders as possible before creating a situation for himself known to the media as...
...suicide by cop.
To reiterate. Lee Anthony appears to have killed his own wife, out of sight of his children.
Before going out to shoot down police officers and innocents.
Having counted his bullets, knowing he couldn't shoot his way out.
He committed suicide. In front of his children.

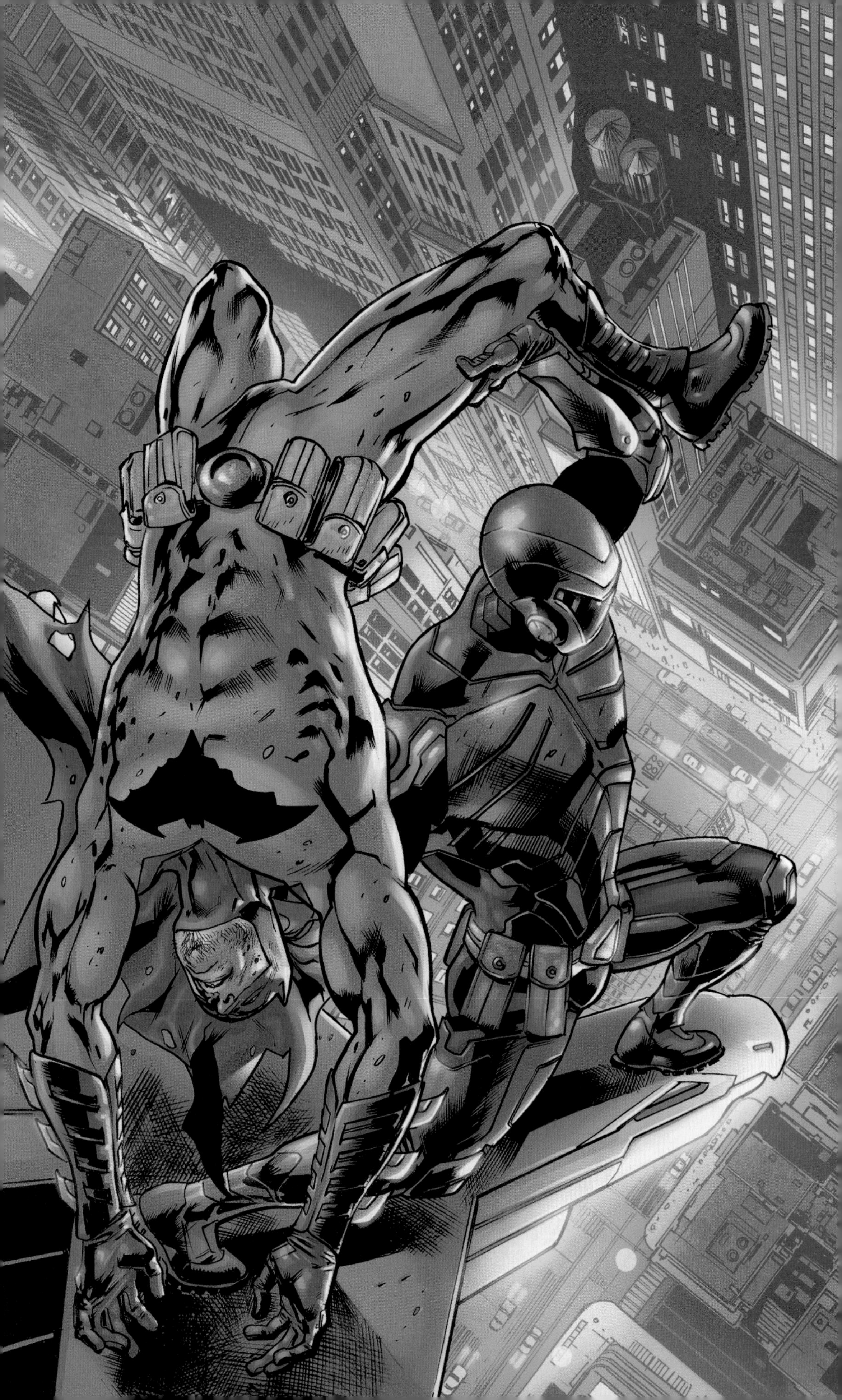

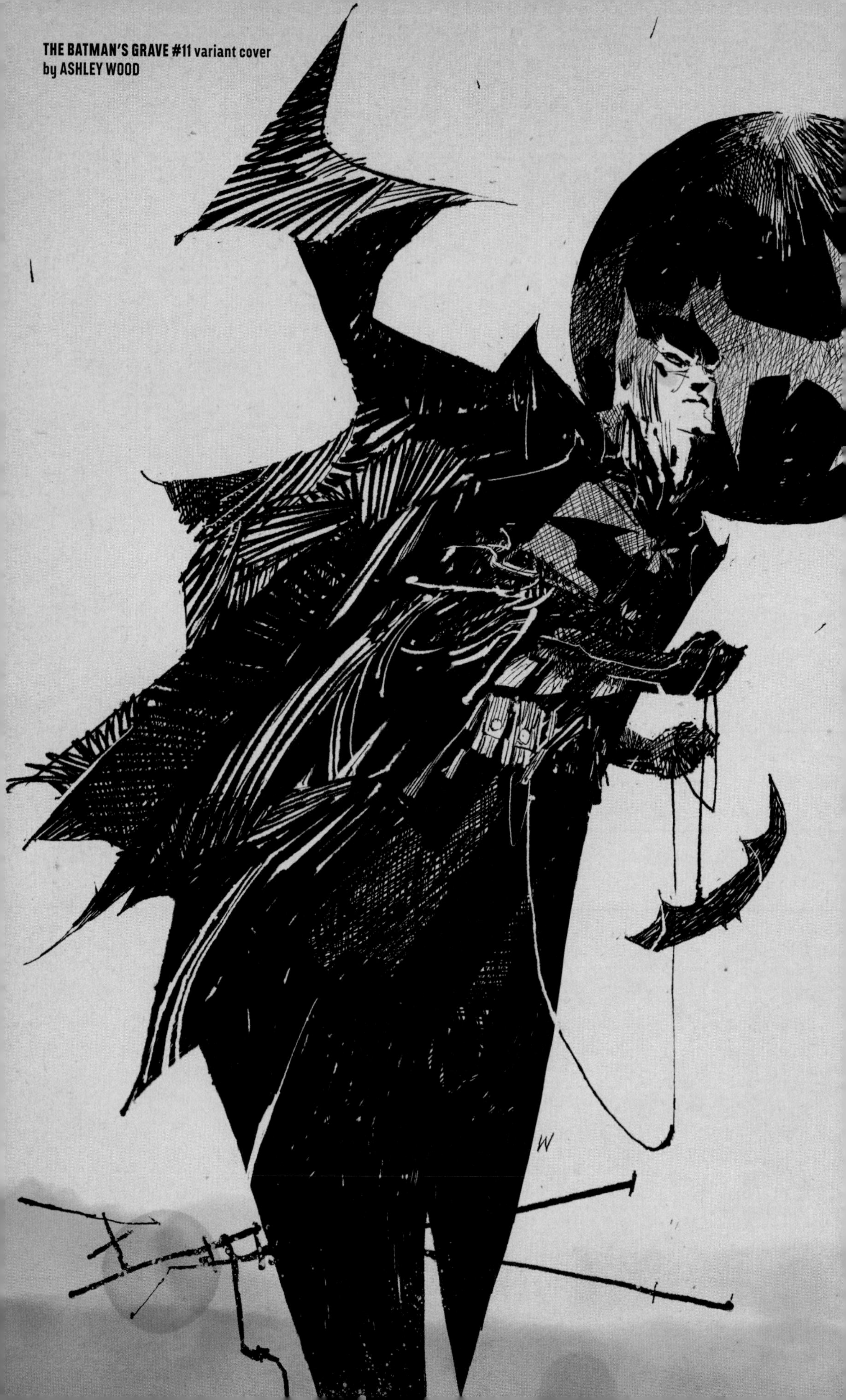

THE BATMAN'S GRAVE #11 variant cover
by ASHLEY WOOD

Chapter 11

Writer	Art
WARREN ELLIS	BRYAN HITCH

Colors	Letters
ALEX SINCLAIR	RICHARD STARKINGS

Cover	Variant Cover
BRYAN HITCH & ALEX SINCLAIR	ASHLEY WOOD

Associate Editor	Editor
ANDREW MARINO	MARIE JAVINS

BATMAN created by BOB KANE with BILL FINGER

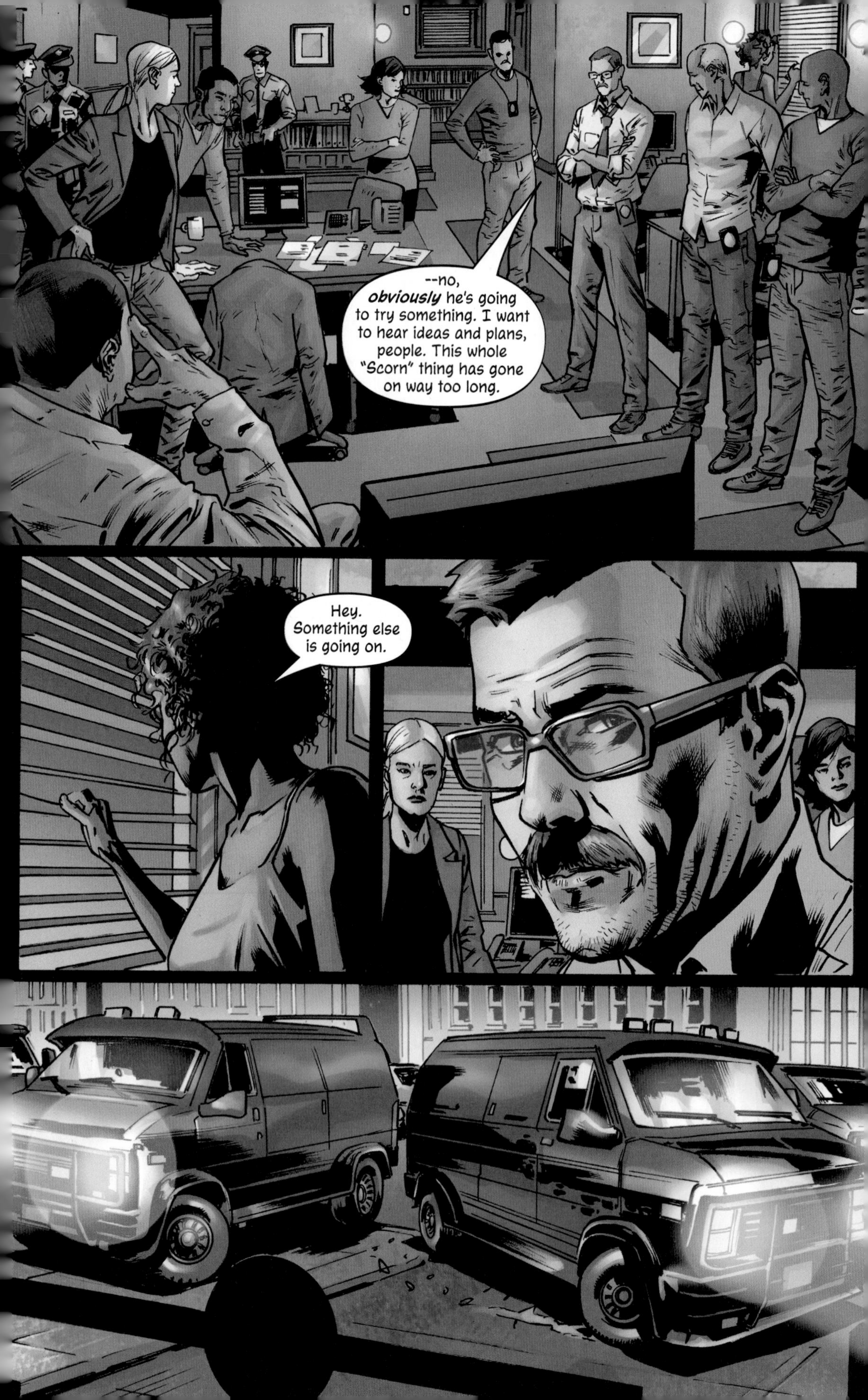
--no, *obviously* he's going to try something. I want to hear ideas and plans, people. This whole "Scorn" thing has gone on way too long.
Hey. Something else is going on.

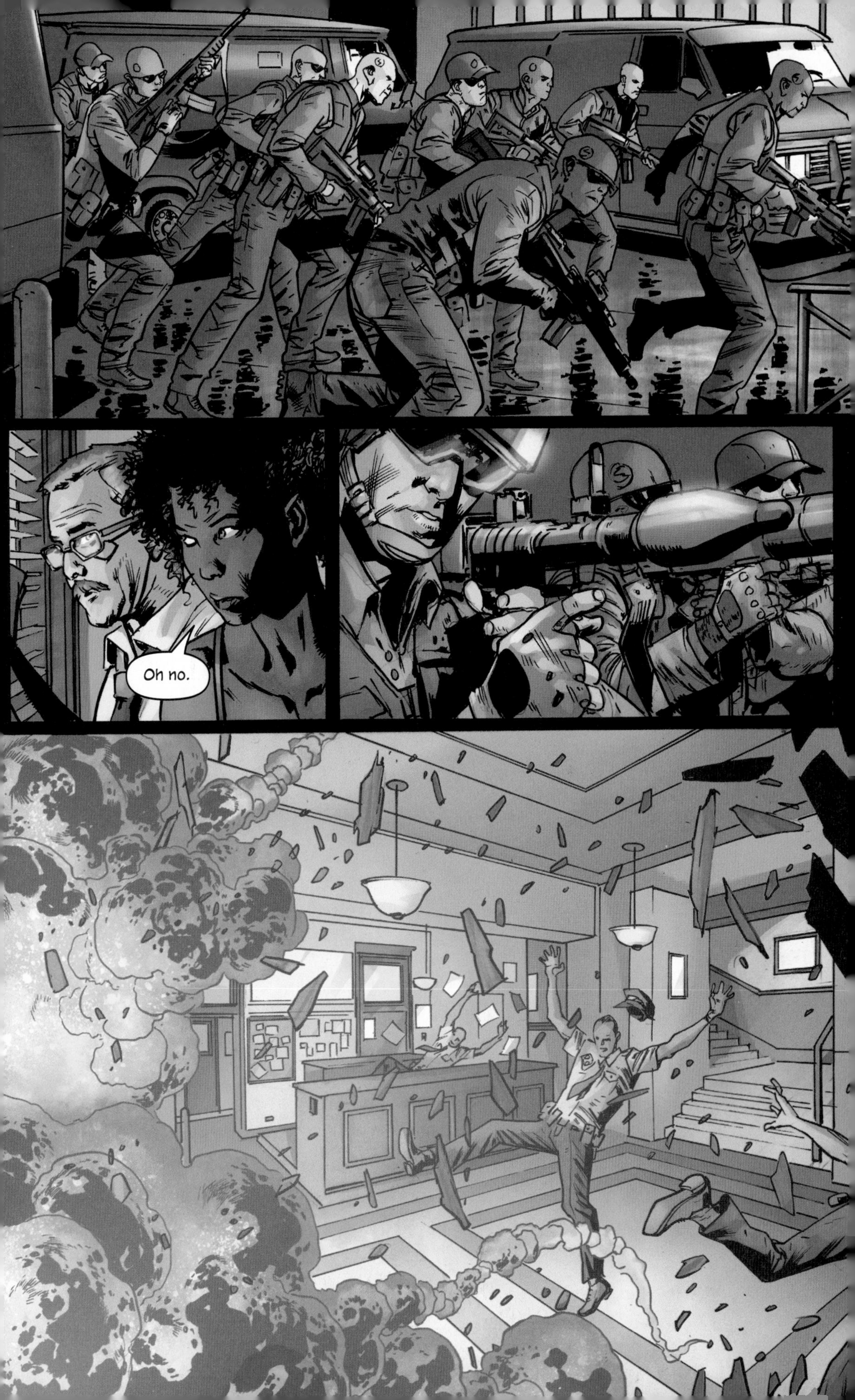
Oh no.

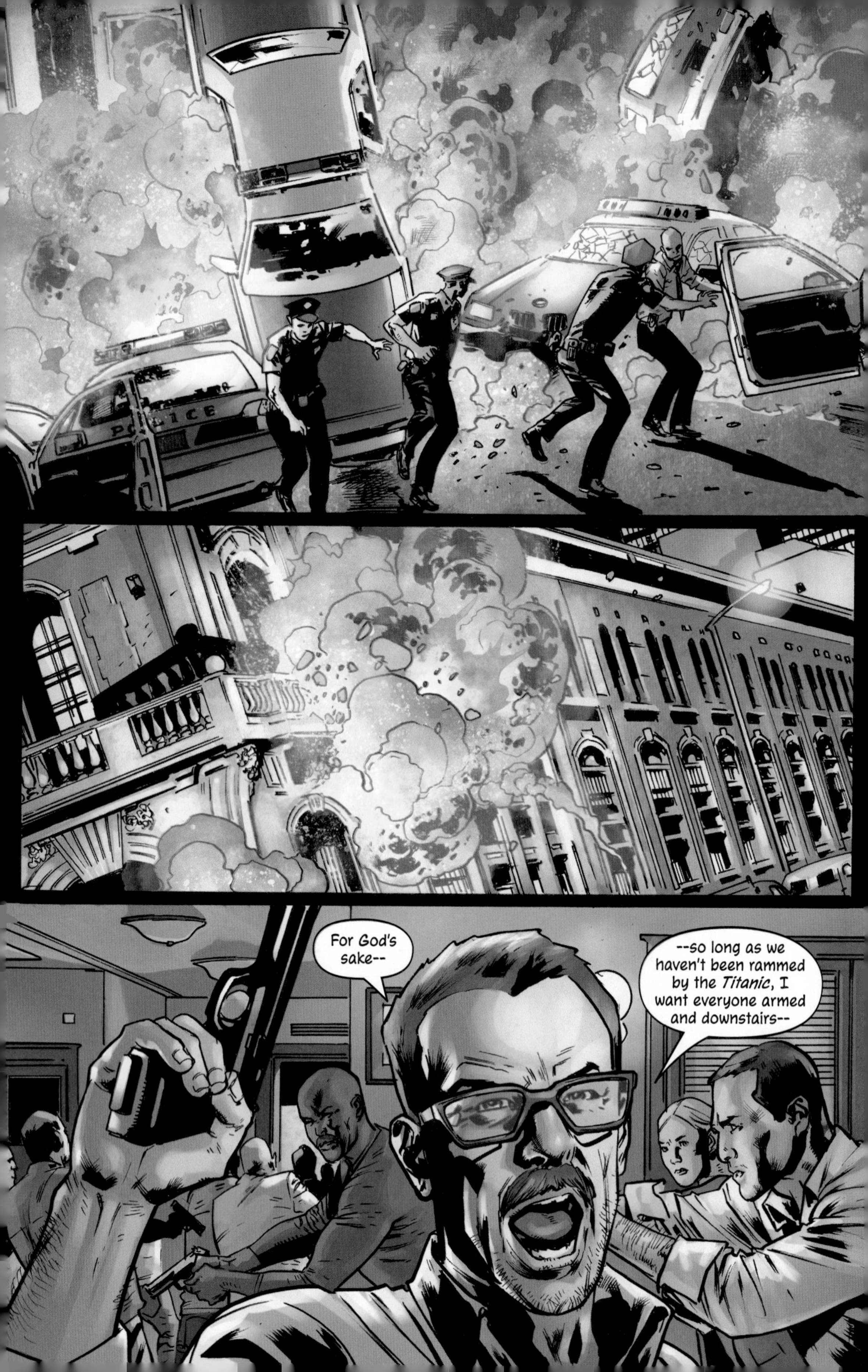
For God's sake--
--so long as we haven't been rammed by the *Titanic*, I want everyone armed and downstairs--

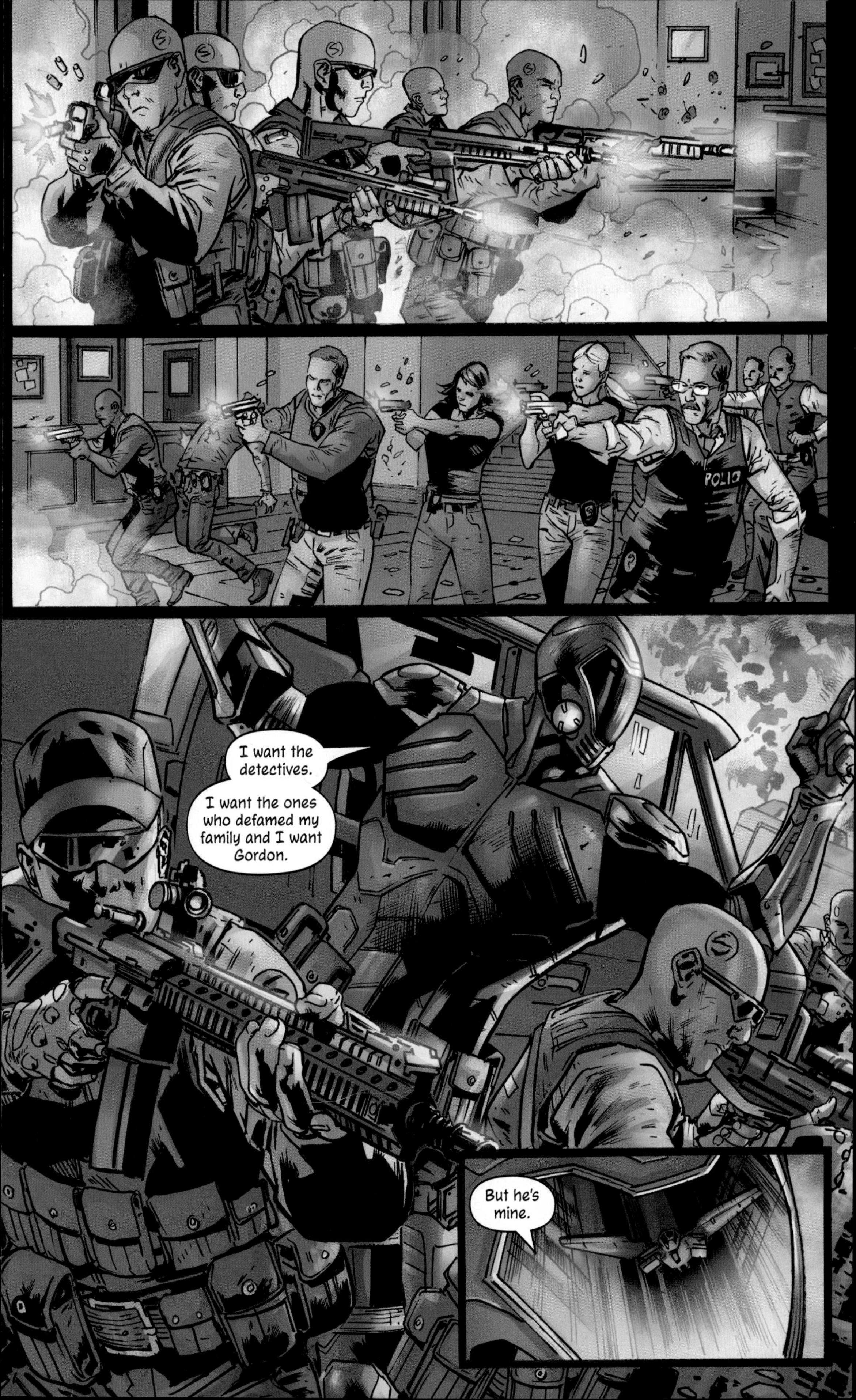
POLIC
I want the detectives.
I want the ones who defamed my family and I want Gordon.
But he's mine.

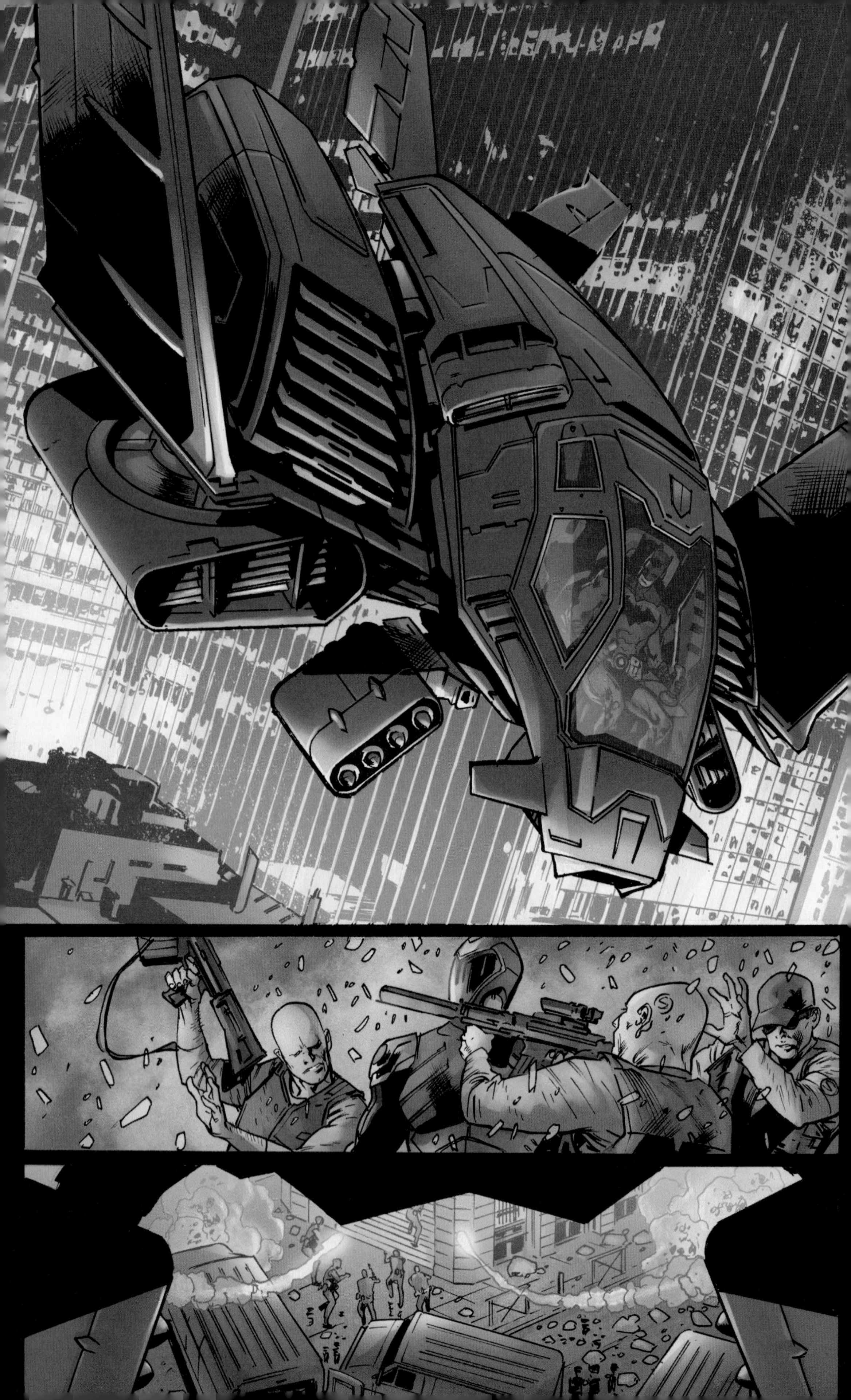

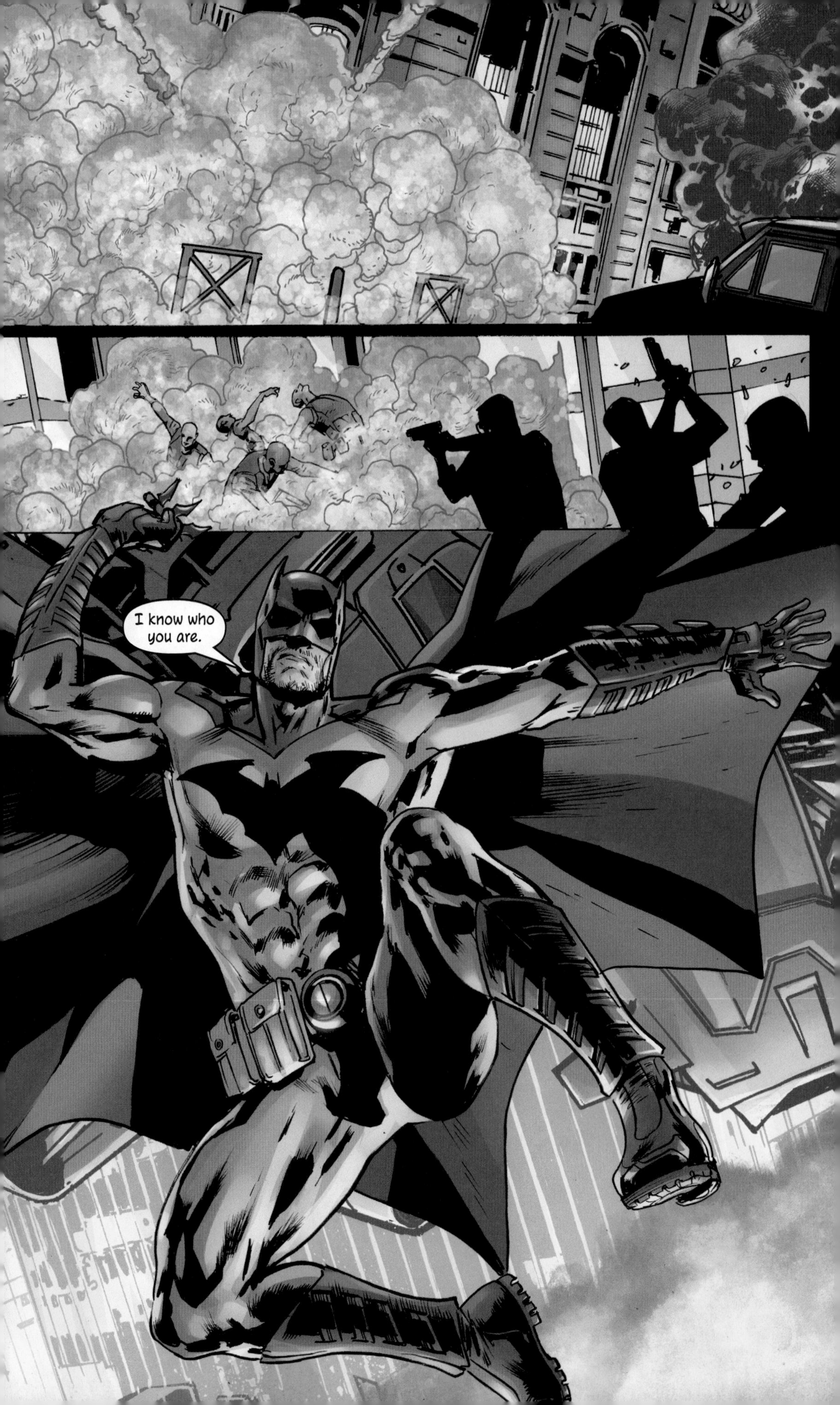
I know who you are.

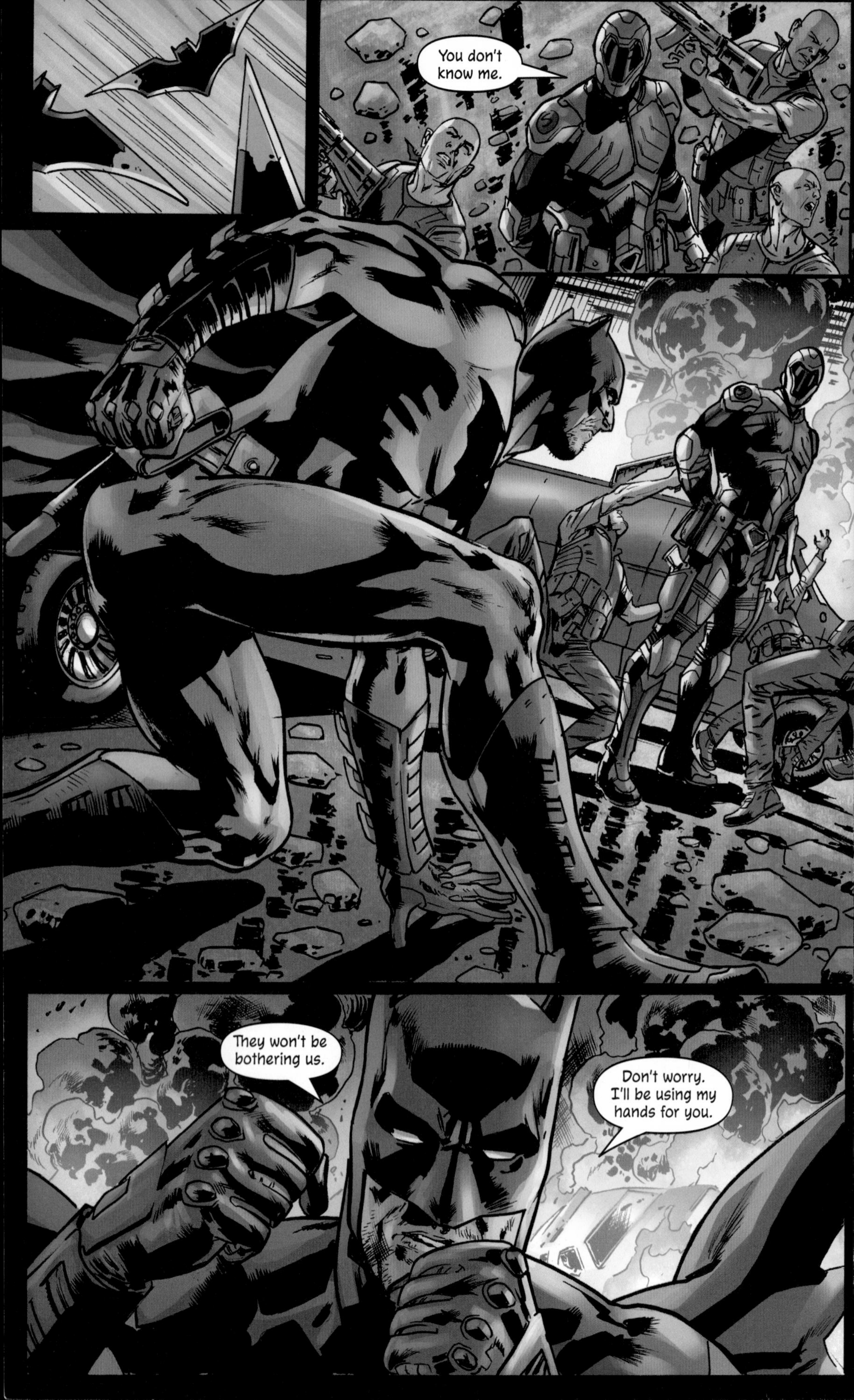
You don't know me.
They won't be bothering us.
Don't worry. I'll be using my hands for you.

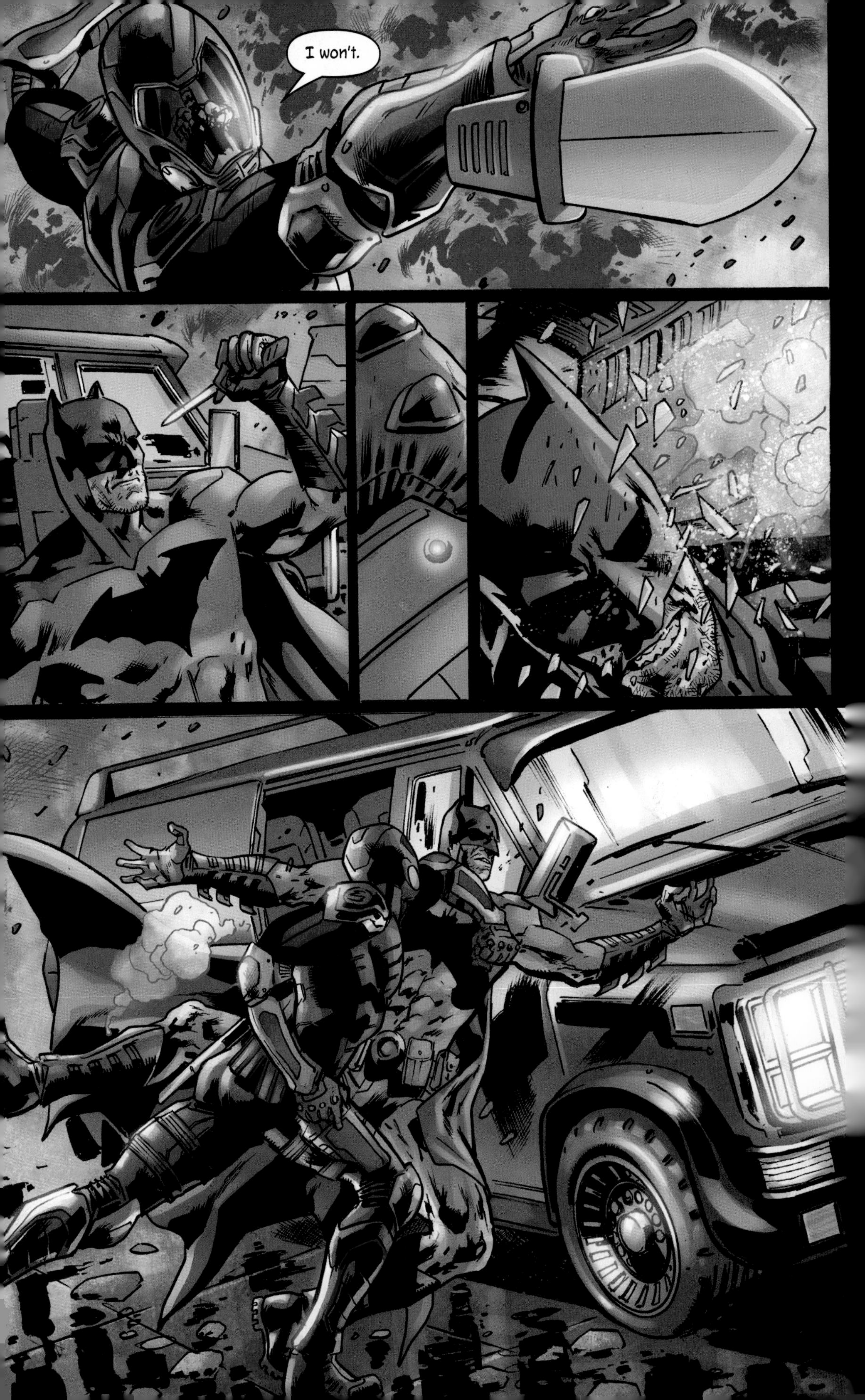
I won't.

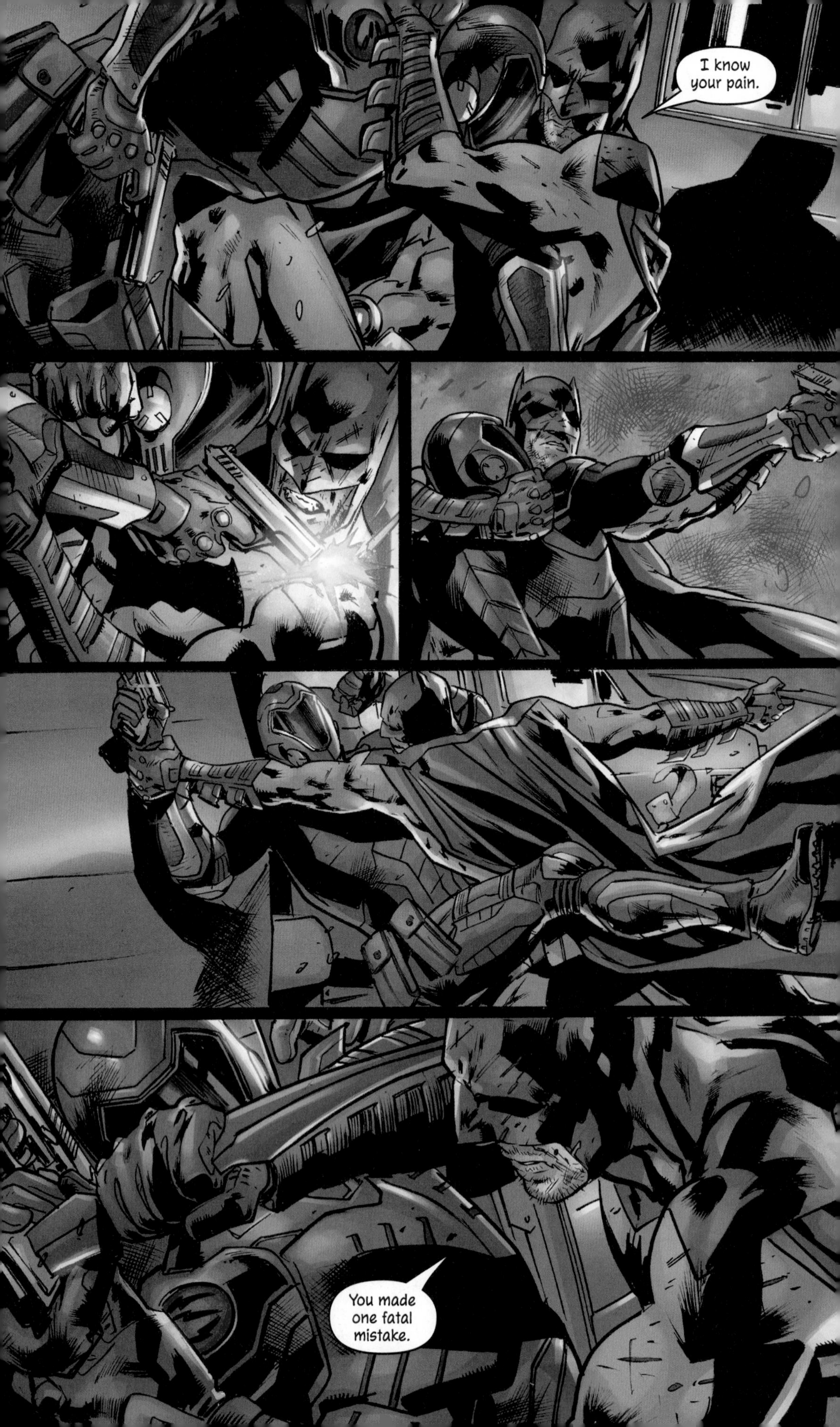
I know your pain.
You made one fatal mistake.

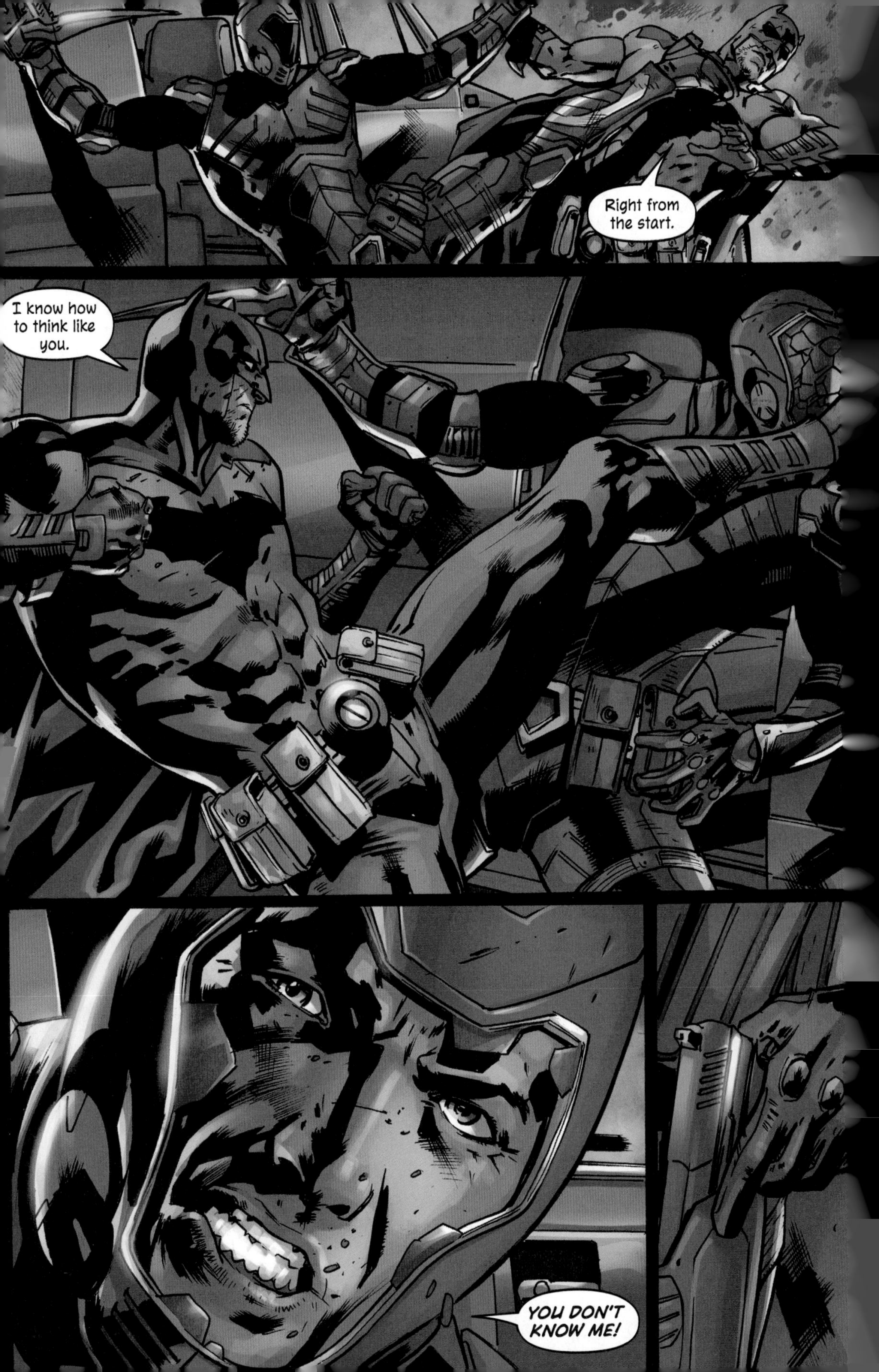
Right from the start.
I know how to think like you.
YOU DON'T KNOW ME!

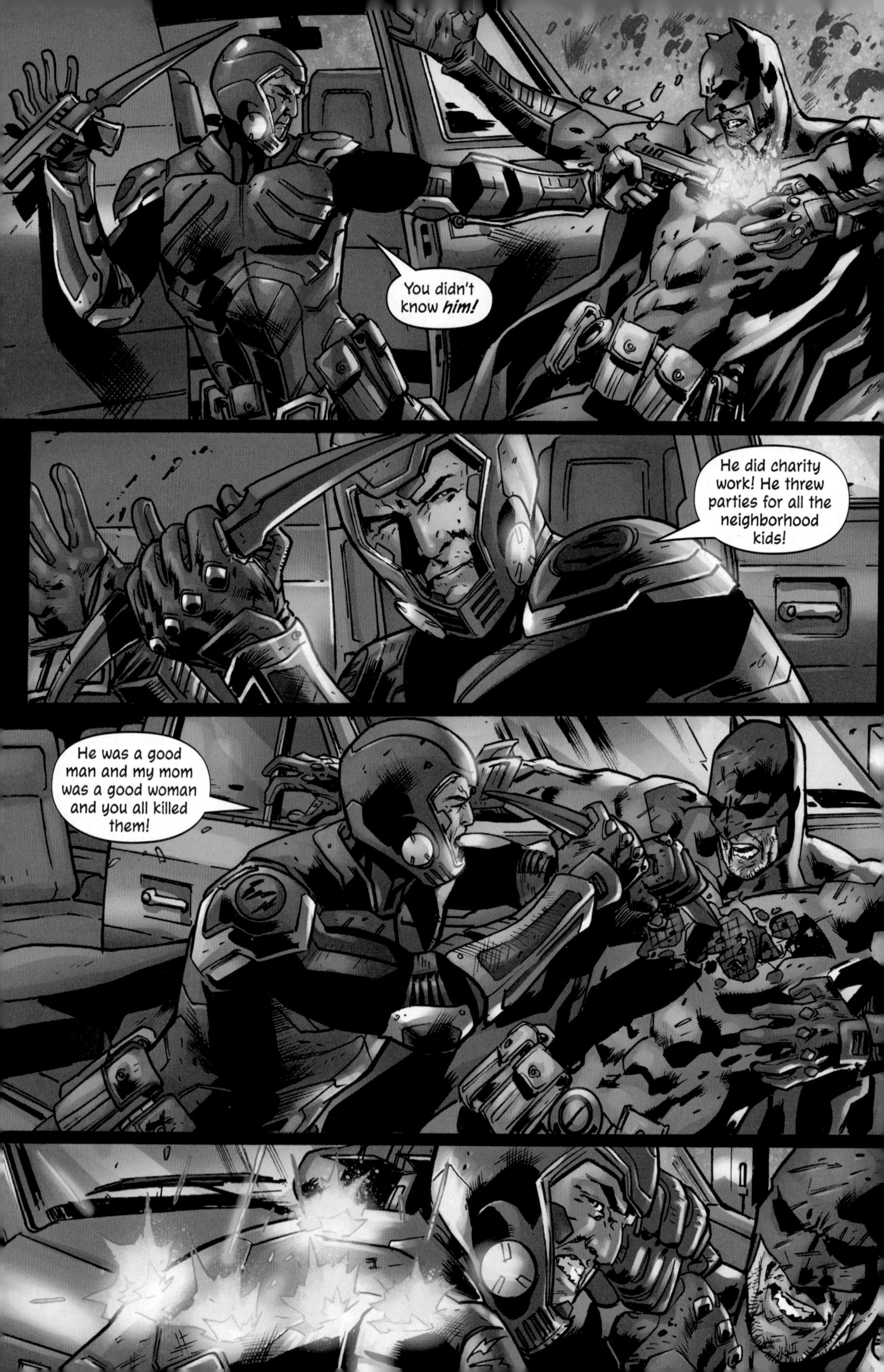
You didn't know *him!*
He did charity work! He threw parties for all the neighborhood kids!
He was a good man and my mom was a good woman and you all killed them!

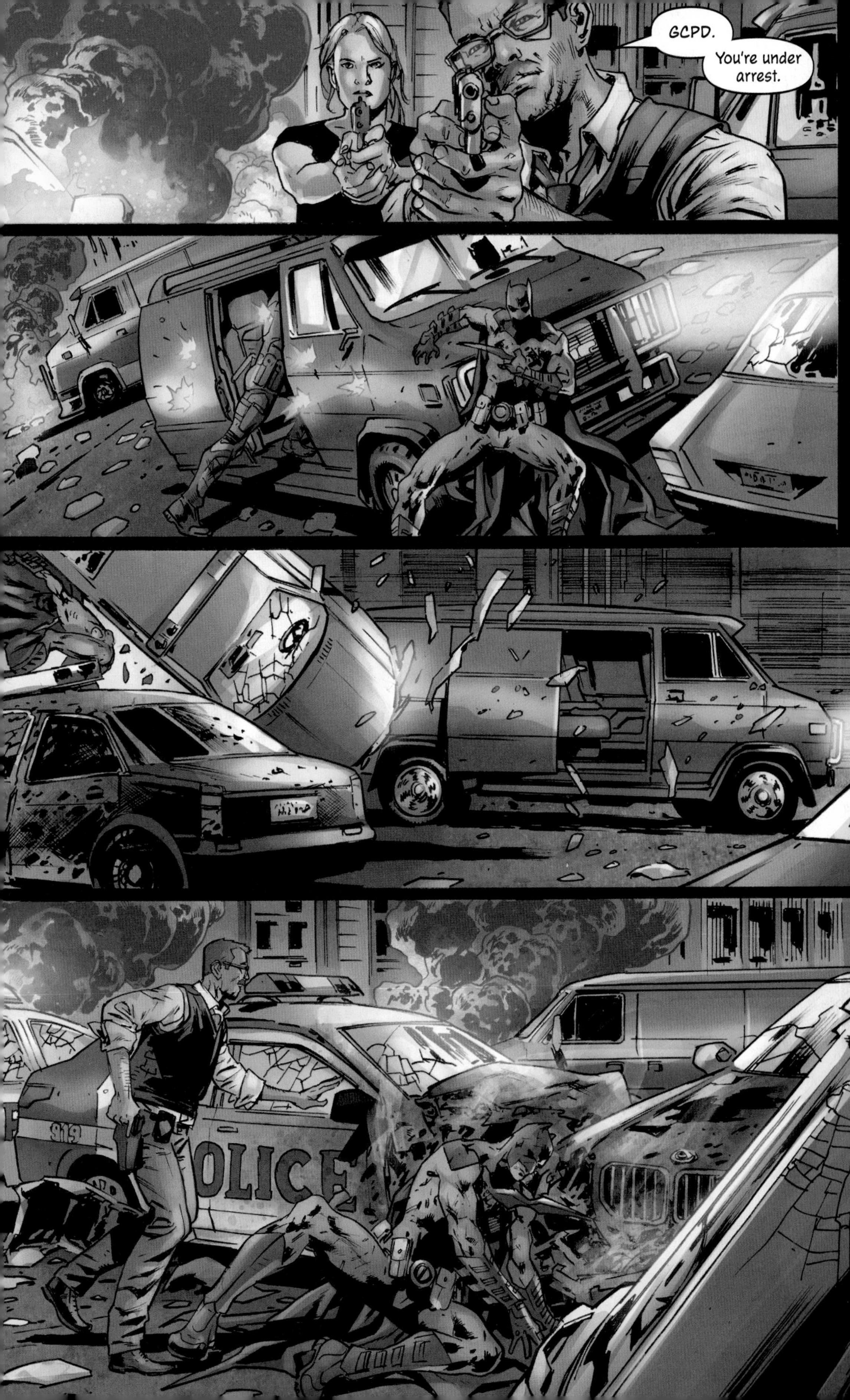
GCPD.
You're under arrest.
POLICE
9119

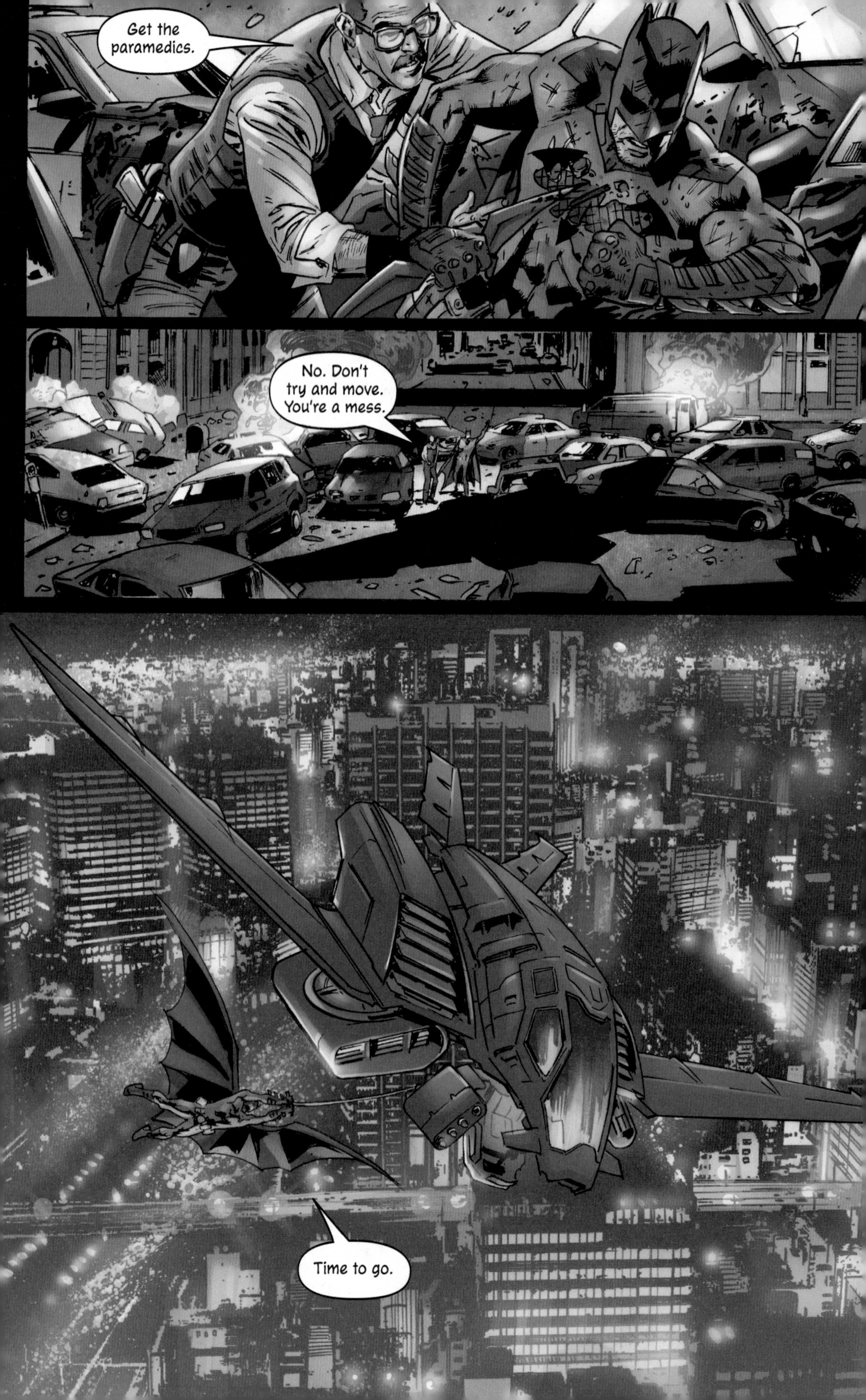
Get the paramedics.
No. Don't try and move. You're a mess.
Time to go.

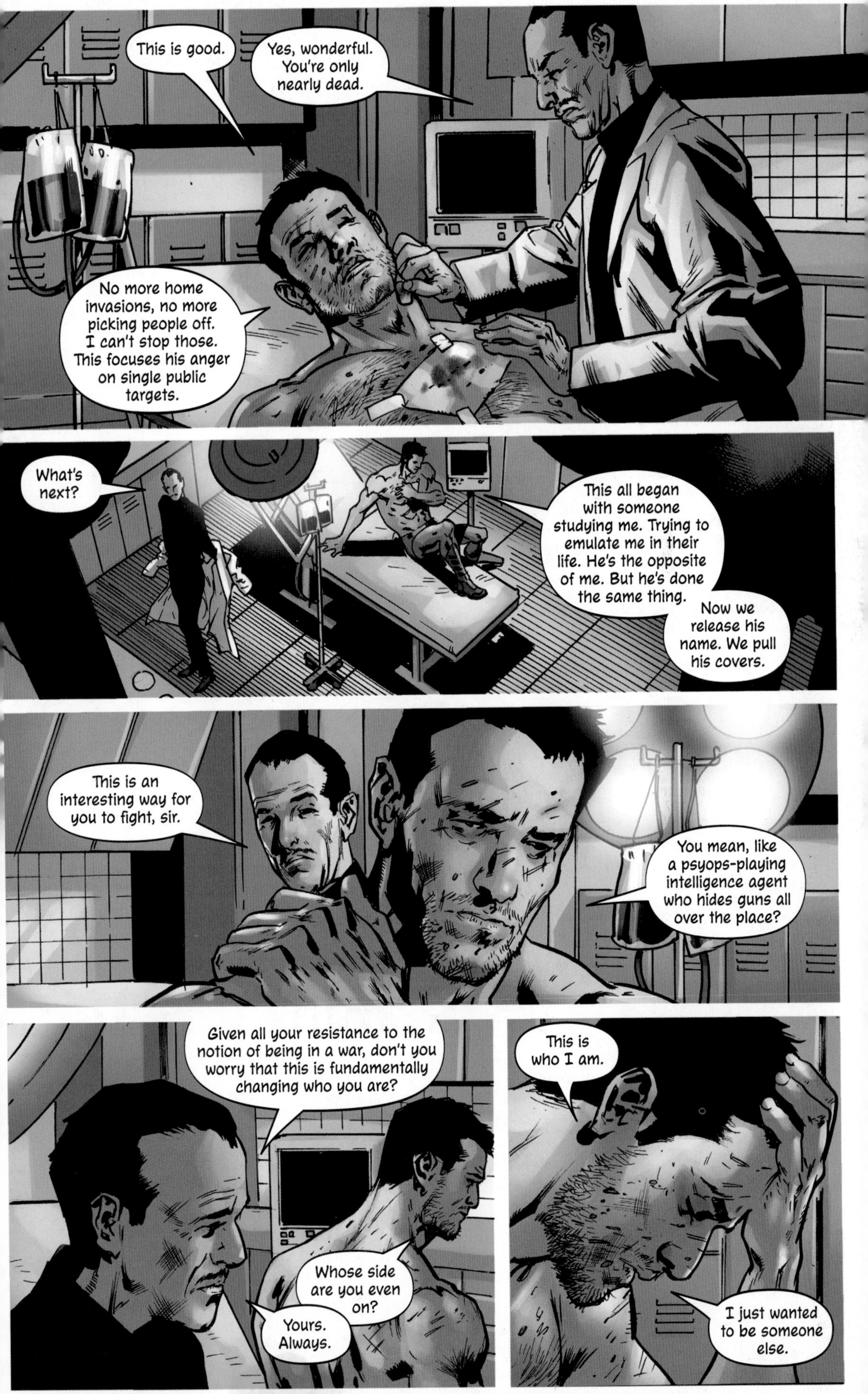

This is good.
Yes, wonderful. You're only nearly dead.
No more home invasions, no more picking people off. I can't stop those. This focuses his anger on single public targets.
What's next?
This all began with someone studying me. Trying to emulate me in their life. He's the opposite of me. But he's done the same thing.
Now we release his name. We pull his covers.
This is an interesting way for you to fight, sir.
You mean, like a psyops-playing intelligence agent who hides guns all over the place?
Given all your resistance to the notion of being in a war, don't you worry that this is fundamentally changing who you are?
Whose side are you even on?
Yours. Always.
This is who I am.
I just wanted to be someone else.

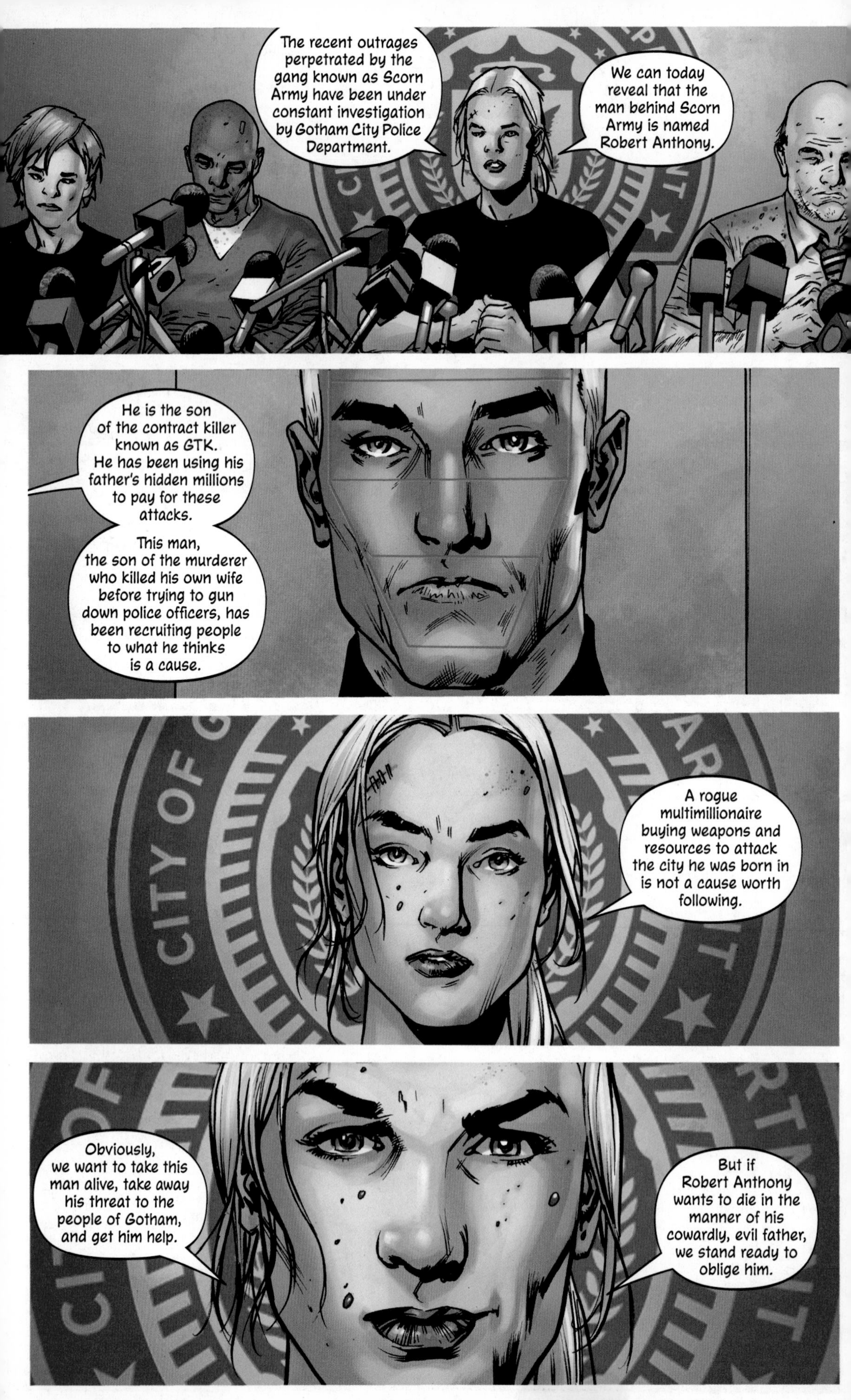
The recent outrages perpetrated by the gang known as Scorn Army have been under constant investigation by Gotham City Police Department.
We can today reveal that the man behind Scorn Army is named Robert Anthony.
He is the son of the contract killer known as GTK. He has been using his father's hidden millions to pay for these attacks.
This man, the son of the murderer who killed his own wife before trying to gun down police officers, has been recruiting people to what he thinks is a cause.
A rogue multimillionaire buying weapons and resources to attack the city he was born in is not a cause worth following.
Obviously, we want to take this man alive, take away his threat to the people of Gotham, and get him help.
But if Robert Anthony wants to die in the manner of his cowardly, evil father, we stand ready to oblige him.

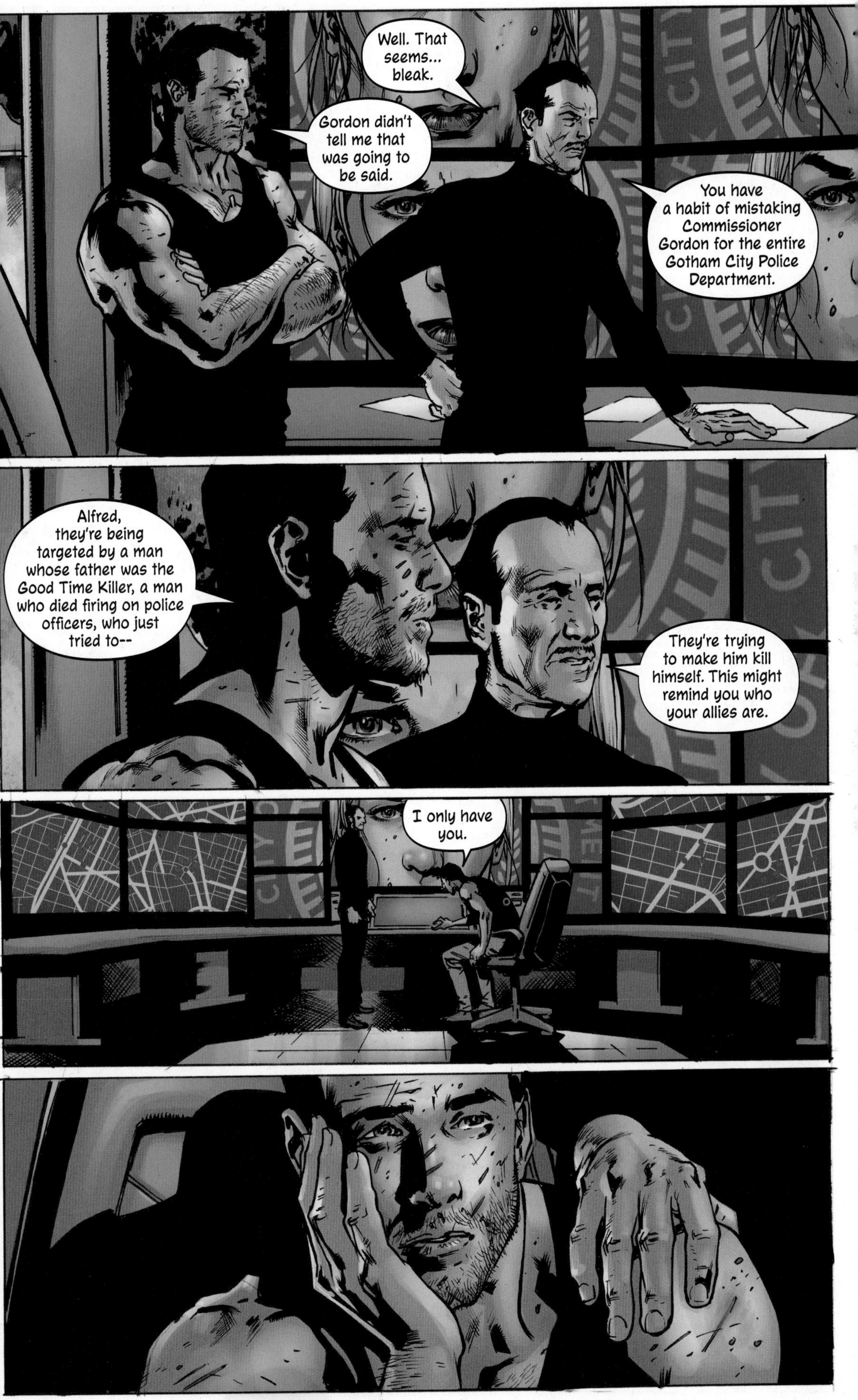
Well. That seems... bleak.
Gordon didn't tell me that was going to be said.
You have a habit of mistaking Commissioner Gordon for the entire Gotham City Police Department.
Alfred, they're being targeted by a man whose father was the Good Time Killer, a man who died firing on police officers, who just tried to--
They're trying to make him kill himself. This might remind you who your allies are.
I only have you.

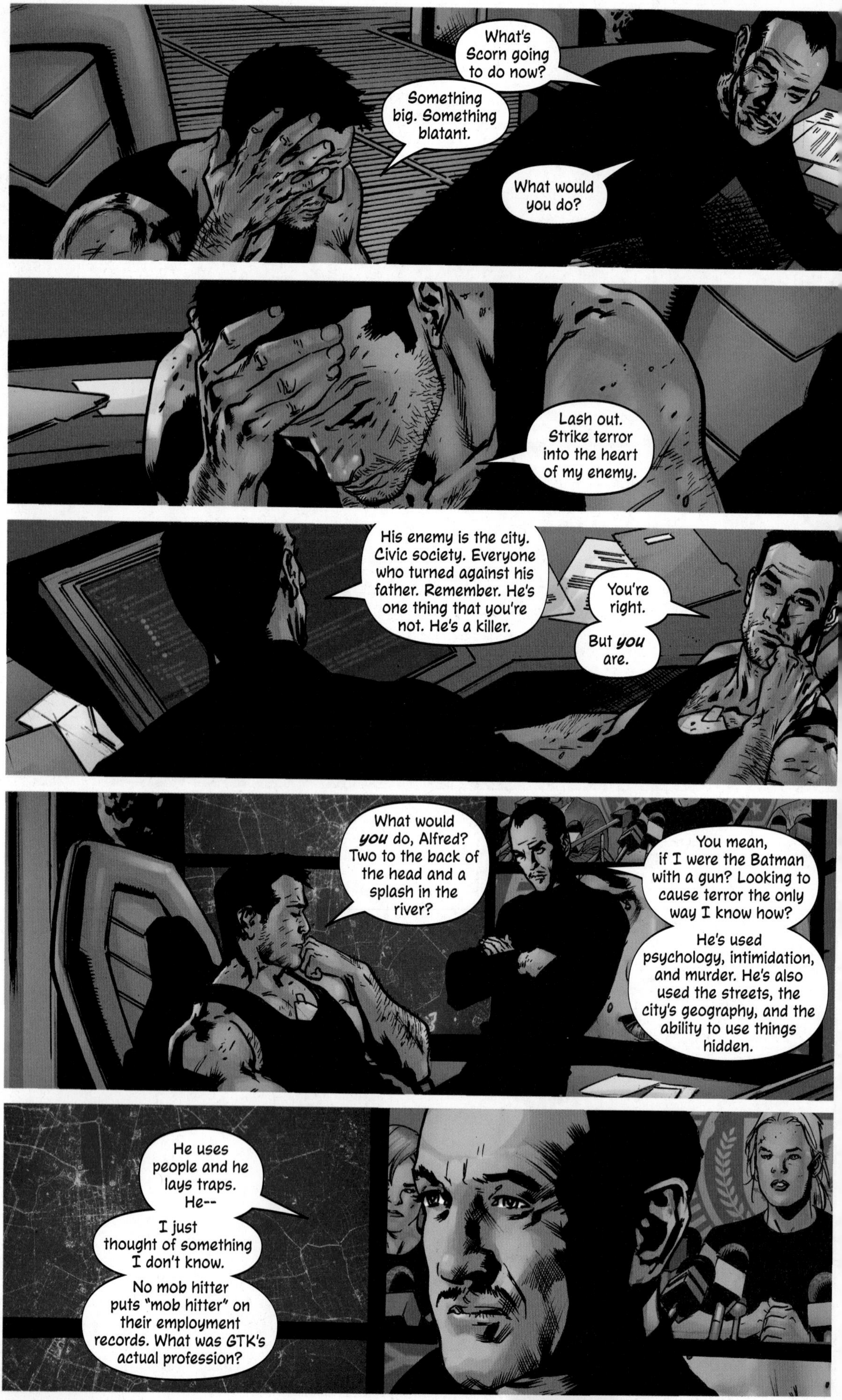
What's Scorn going to do now?
Something big. Something blatant.
What would you do?
Lash out. Strike terror into the heart of my enemy.
His enemy is the city. Civic society. Everyone who turned against his father. Remember. He's one thing that you're not. He's a killer.
You're right.
But *you* are.
What would *you* do, Alfred? Two to the back of the head and a splash in the river?
You mean, if I were the Batman with a gun? Looking to cause terror the only way I know how?
He's used psychology, intimidation, and murder. He's also used the streets, the city's geography, and the ability to use things hidden.
He uses people and he lays traps. He--
I just thought of something I don't know.
No mob hitter puts "mob hitter" on their employment records. What was GTK's actual profession?

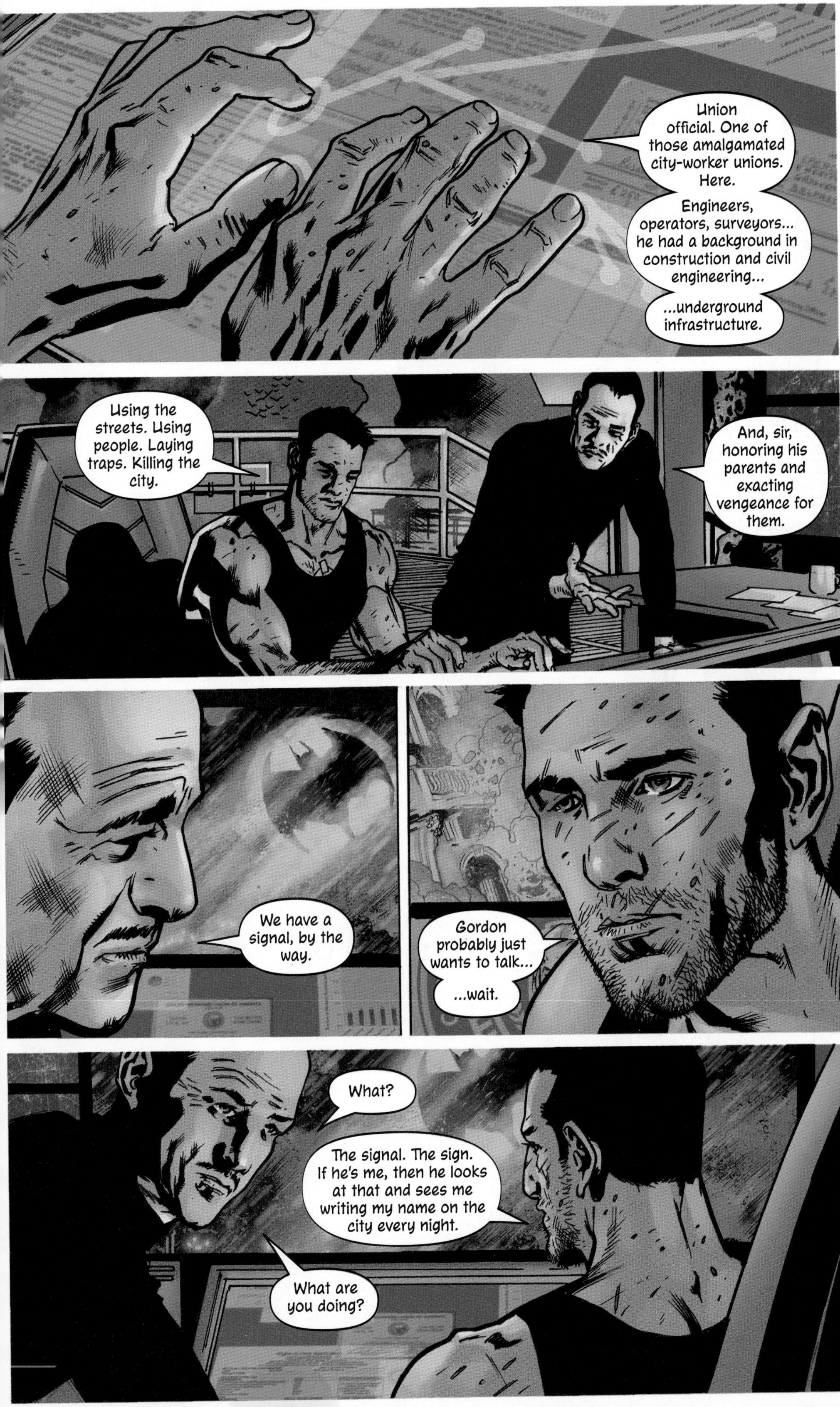
Union official. One of those amalgamated city-worker unions. Here.
Engineers, operators, surveyors... he had a background in construction and civil engineering...
...underground infrastructure.
Using the streets. Using people. Laying traps. Killing the city.
And, sir, honoring his parents and exacting vengeance for them.
We have a signal, by the way.
Gordon probably just wants to talk...
...wait.
What?
The signal. The sign. If he's me, then he looks at that and sees me writing my name on the city every night.
What are you doing?

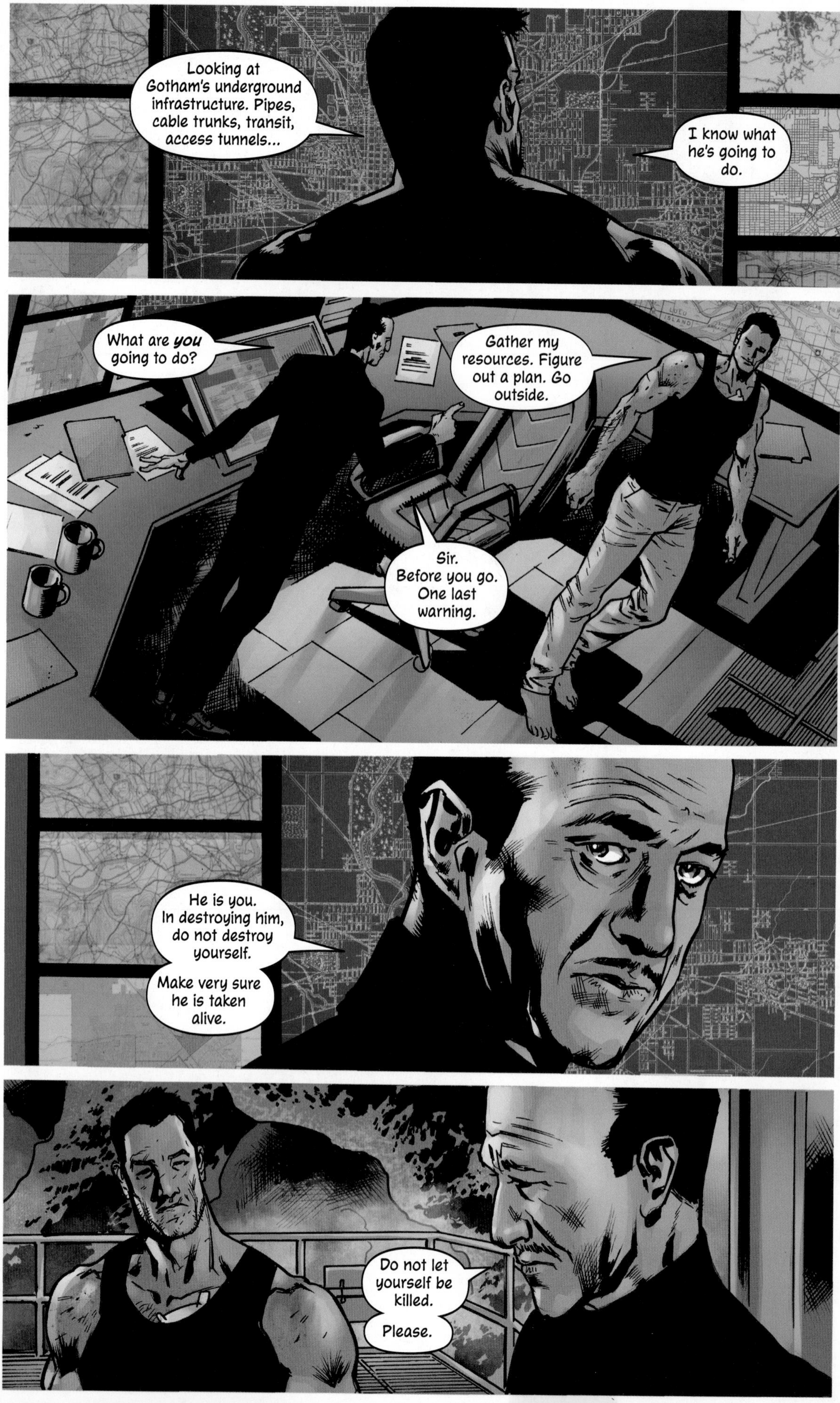
Looking at Gotham's underground infrastructure. Pipes, cable trunks, transit, access tunnels...
I know what he's going to do.
What are *you* going to do?
Gather my resources. Figure out a plan. Go outside.
Sir. Before you go. One last warning.
He is you. In destroying him, do not destroy yourself.
Make very sure he is taken alive.
Do not let yourself be killed.
Please.

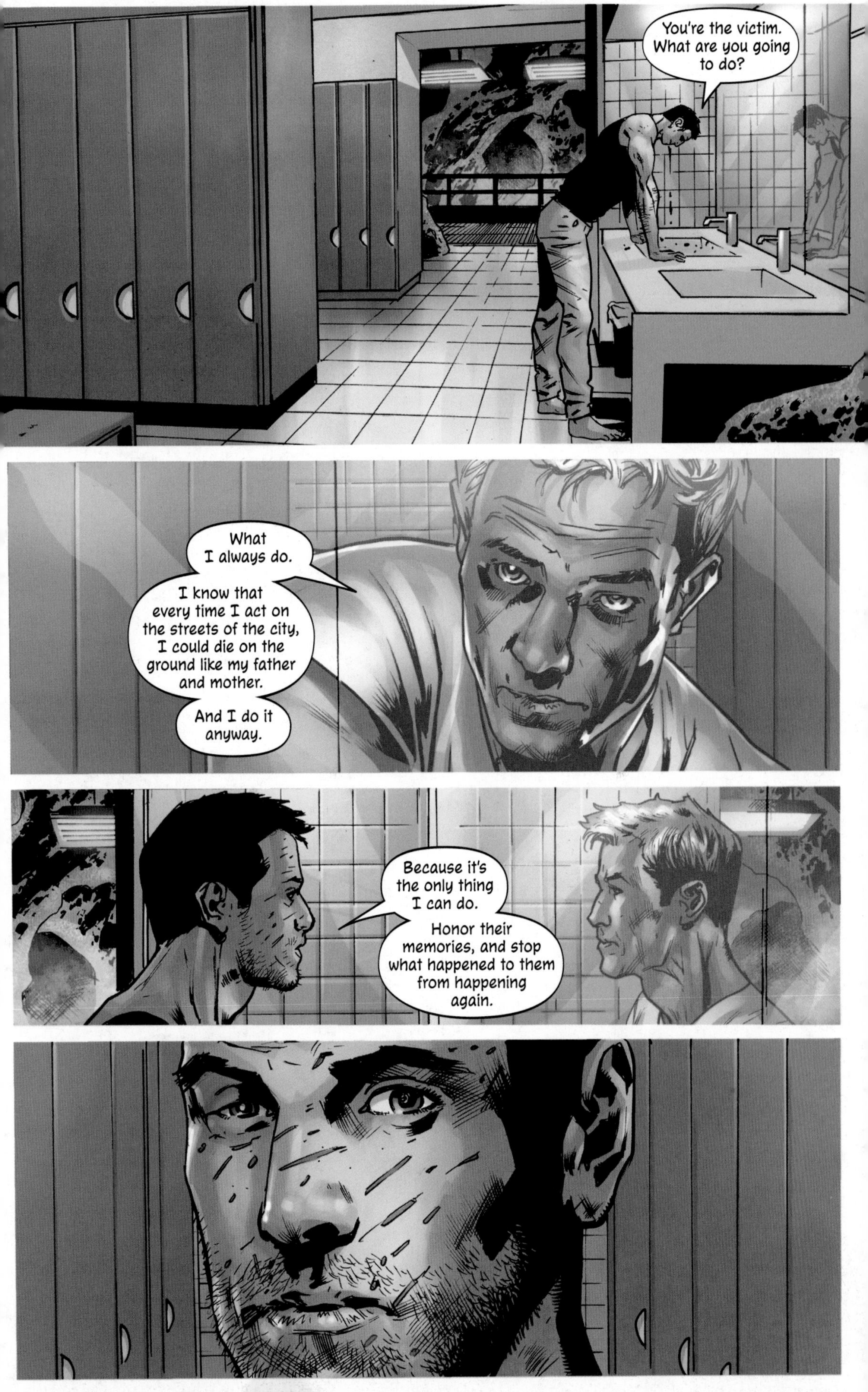

You're the victim. What are you going to do?
What I always do.
I know that every time I act on the streets of the city, I could die on the ground like my father and mother.
And I do it anyway.
Because it's the only thing I can do.
Honor their memories, and stop what happened to them from happening again.

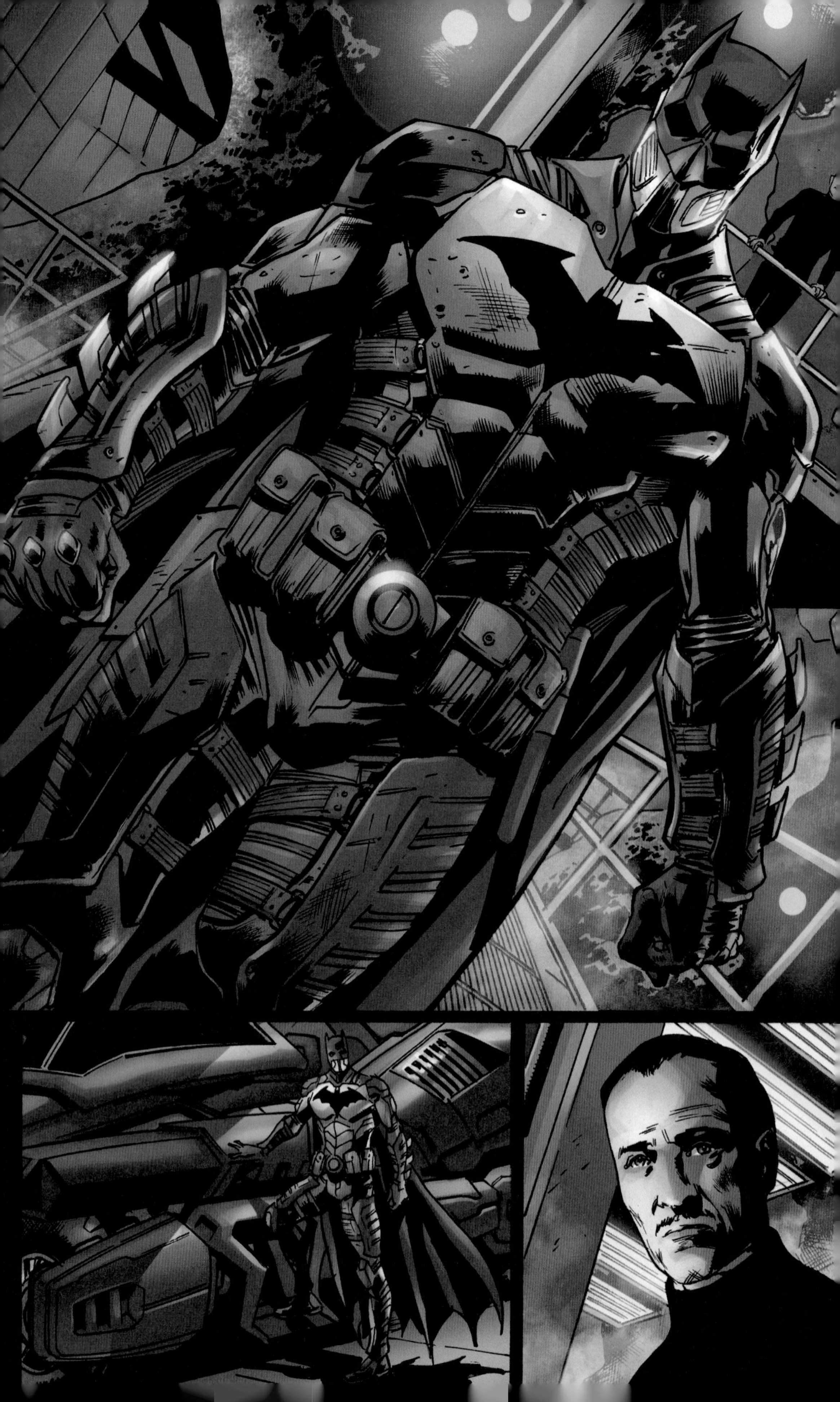

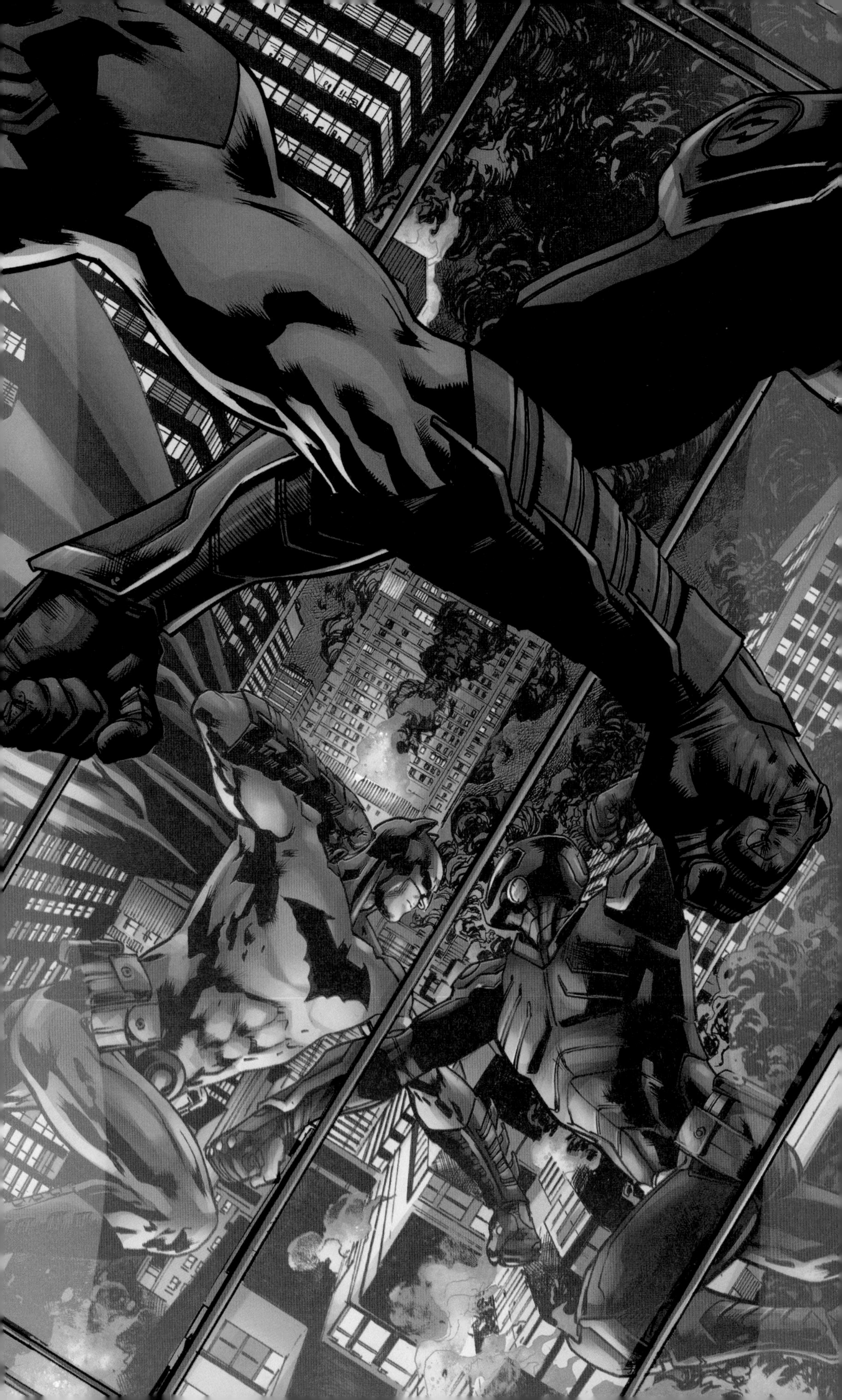

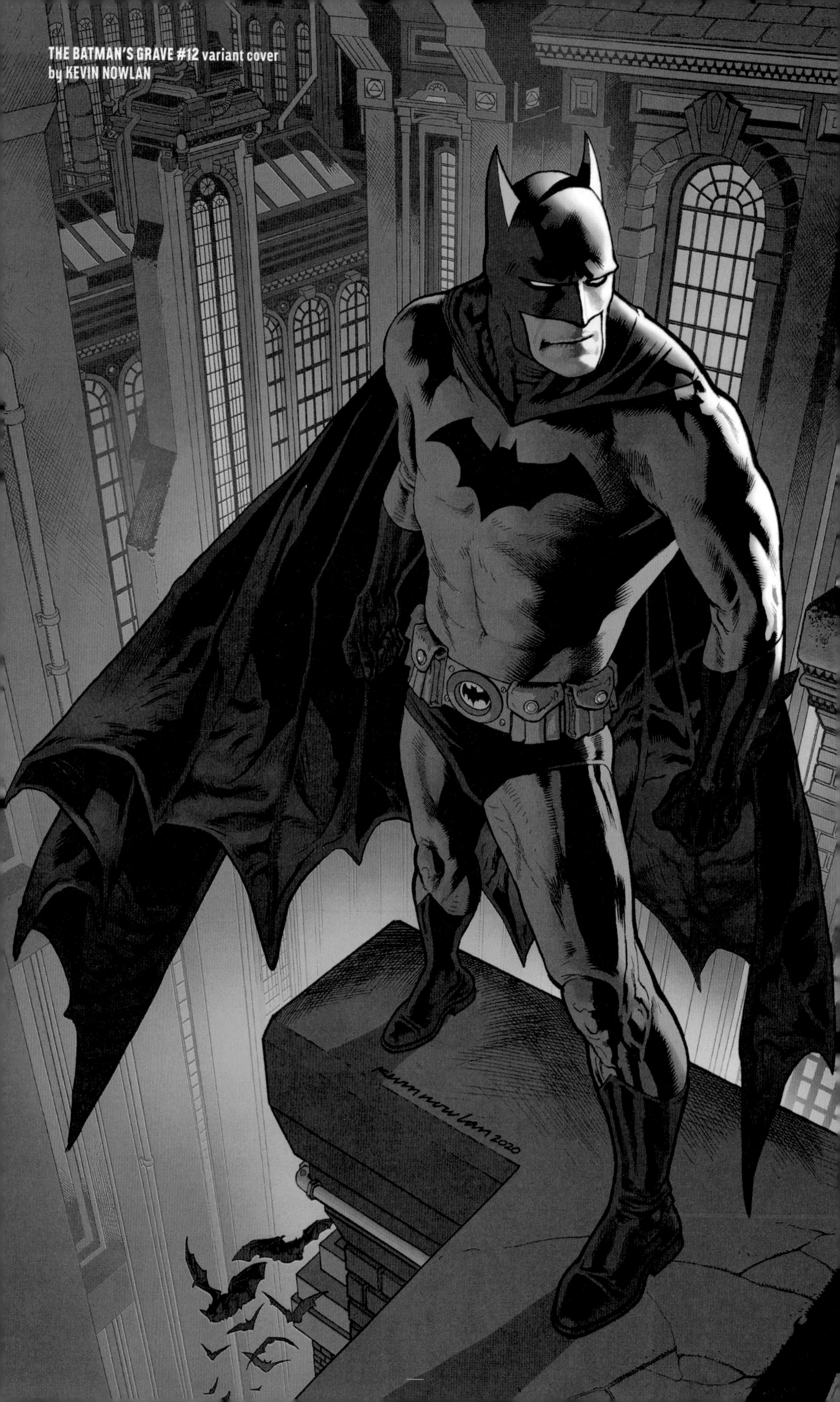

THE BATMAN'S GRAVE #12 variant cover
by KEVIN NOWLAN

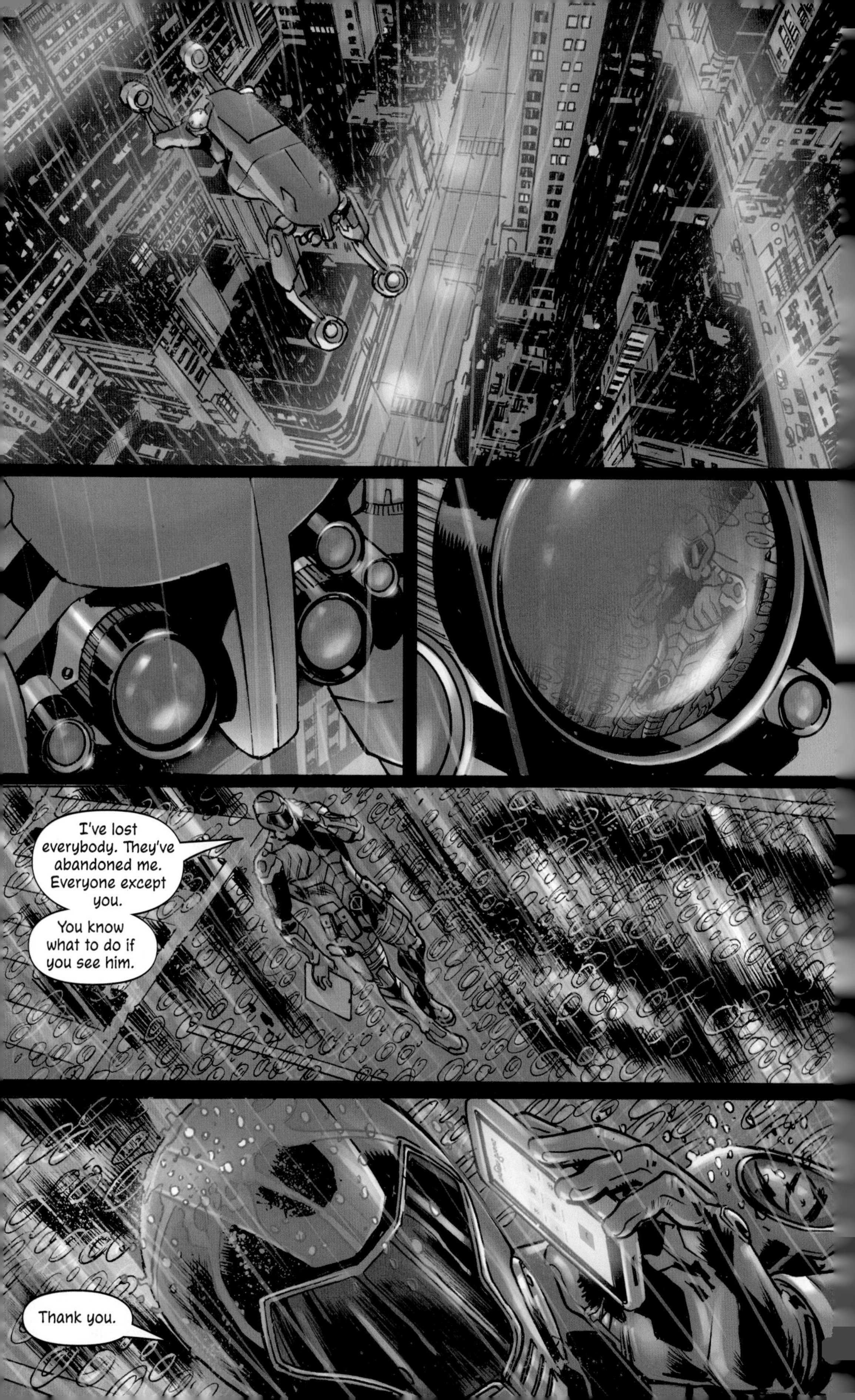
I've lost everybody. They've abandoned me. Everyone except you.
You know what to do if you see him.
Thank you.

Chapter 12

Writer	Art
WARREN ELLIS	**BRYAN HITCH**

Colors	Letters
ALEX SINCLAIR	**RICHARD STARKINGS**

Cover	Variant Cover
BRYAN HITCH & **ALEX SINCLAIR**	**KEVIN** **NOWLAN**

Associate Editor	Editor
ANDREW MARINO	**MARIE JAVINS**

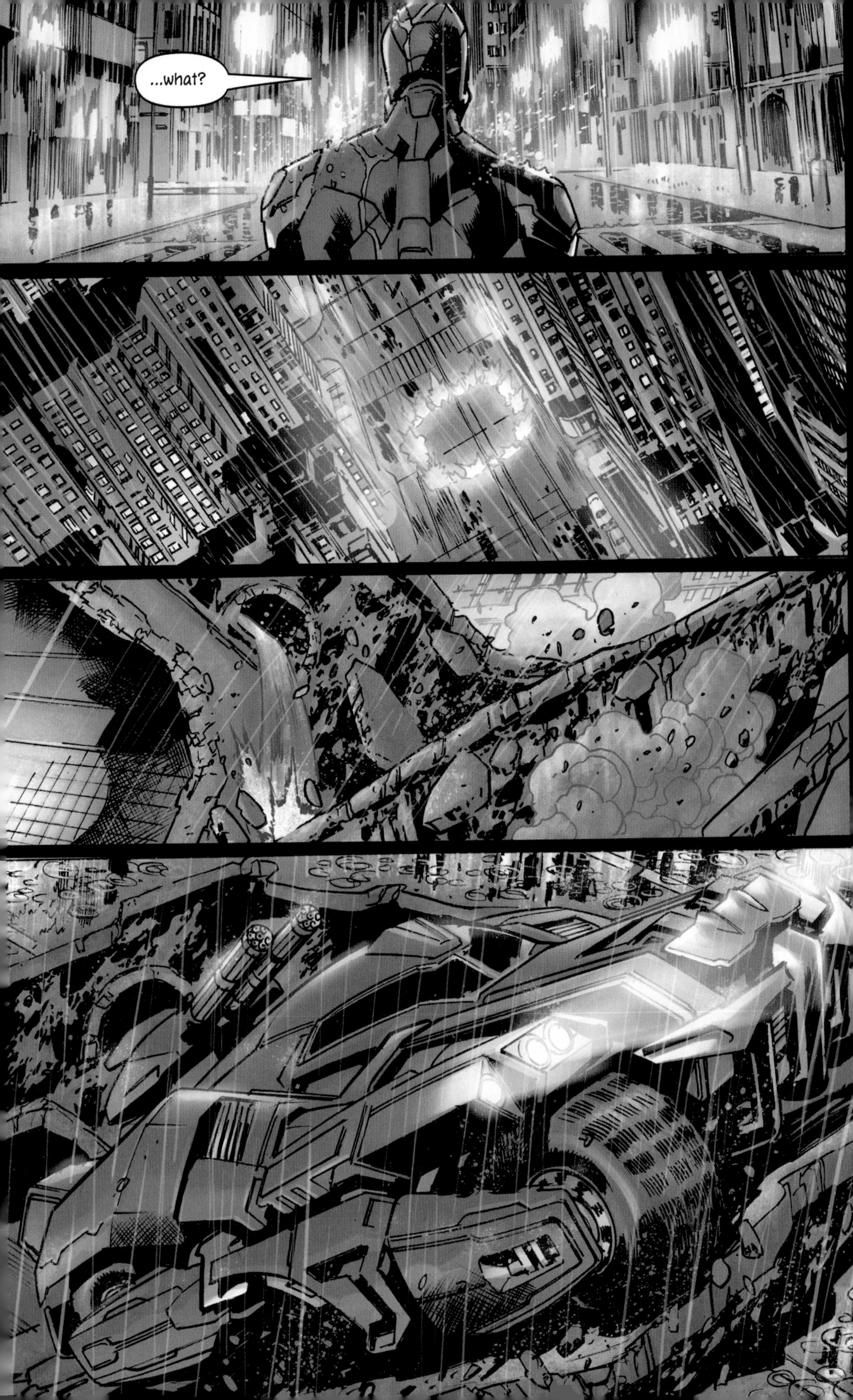
...what?

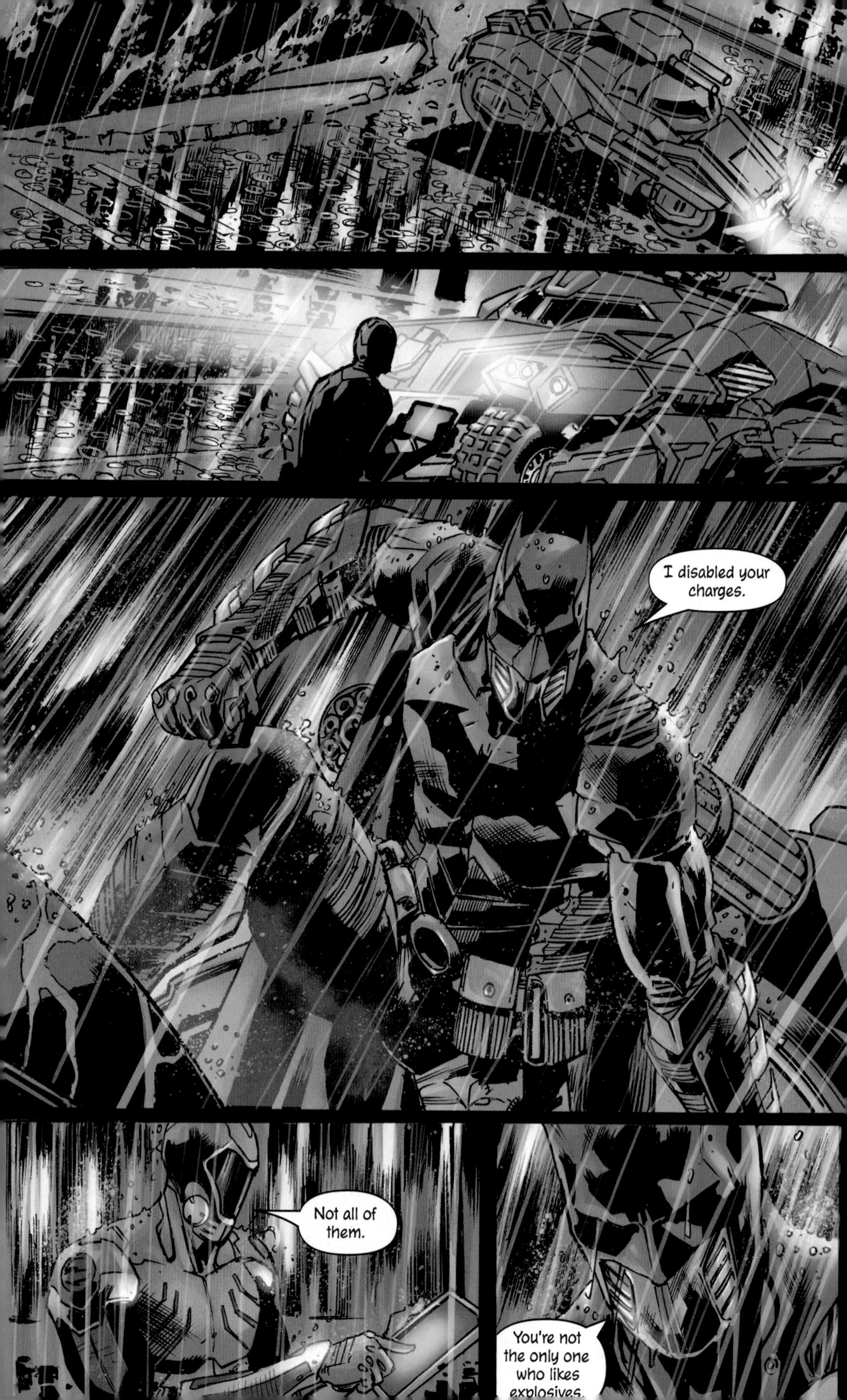
I disabled your charges.
Not all of them.
You're not the only one who likes explosives.

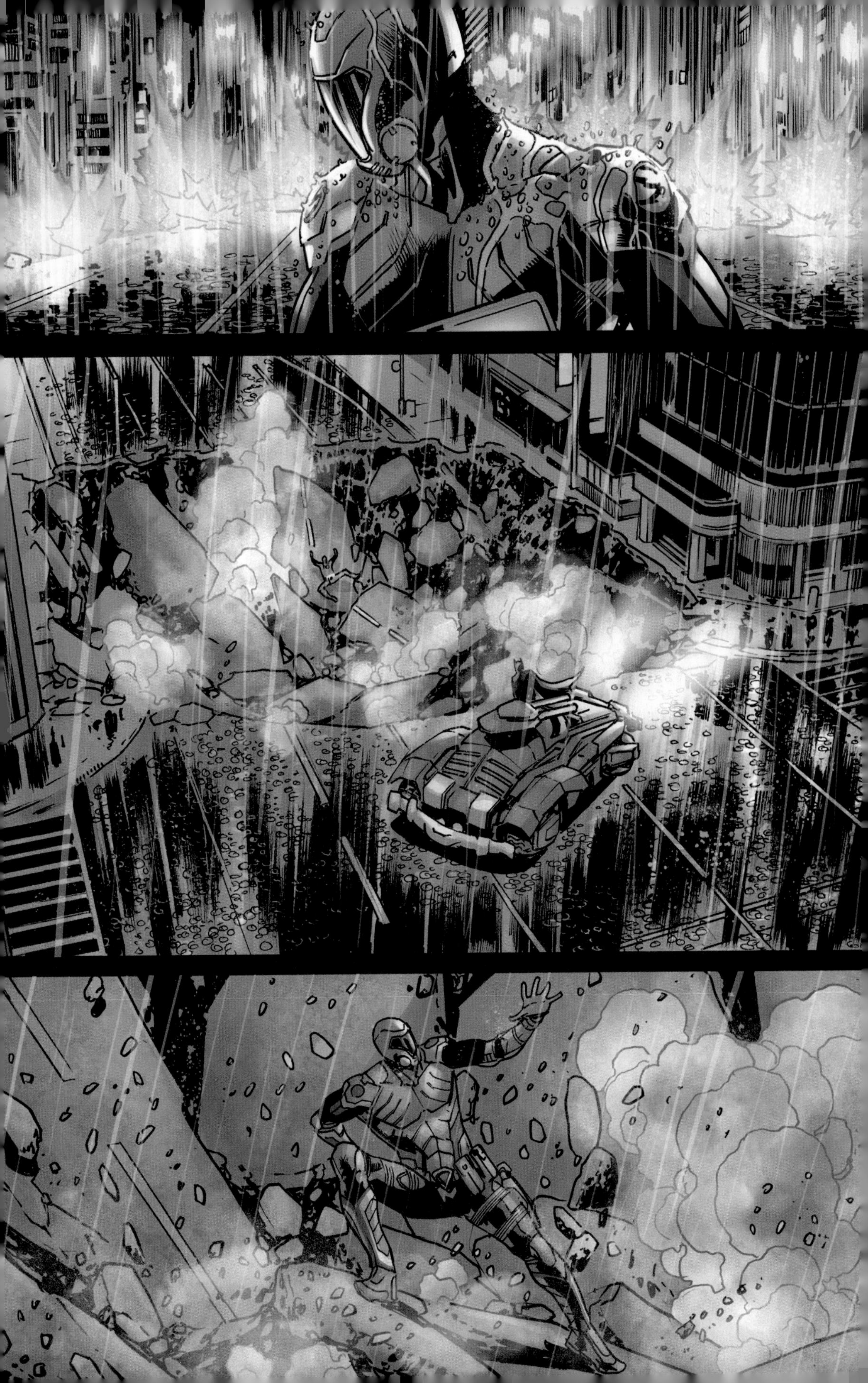

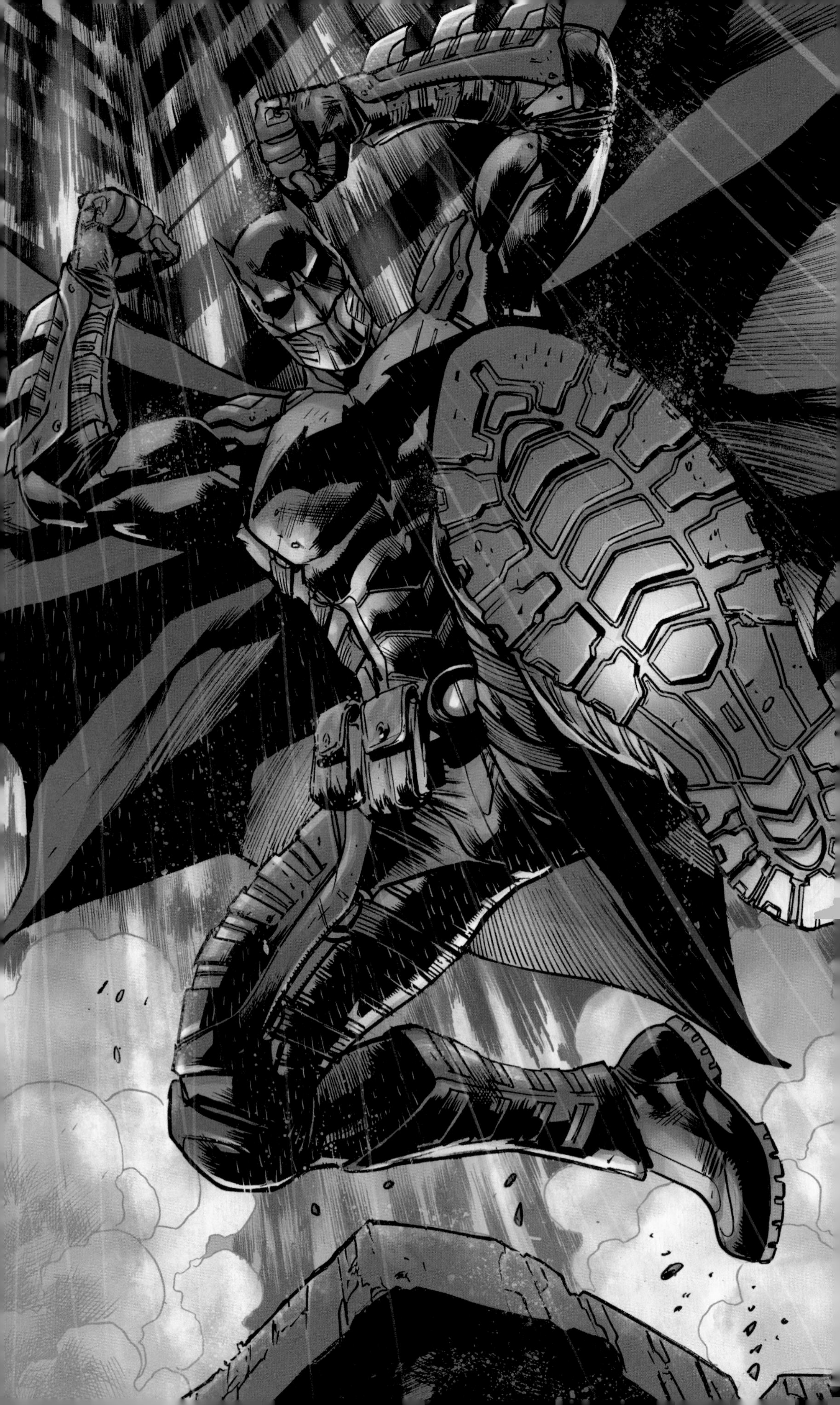

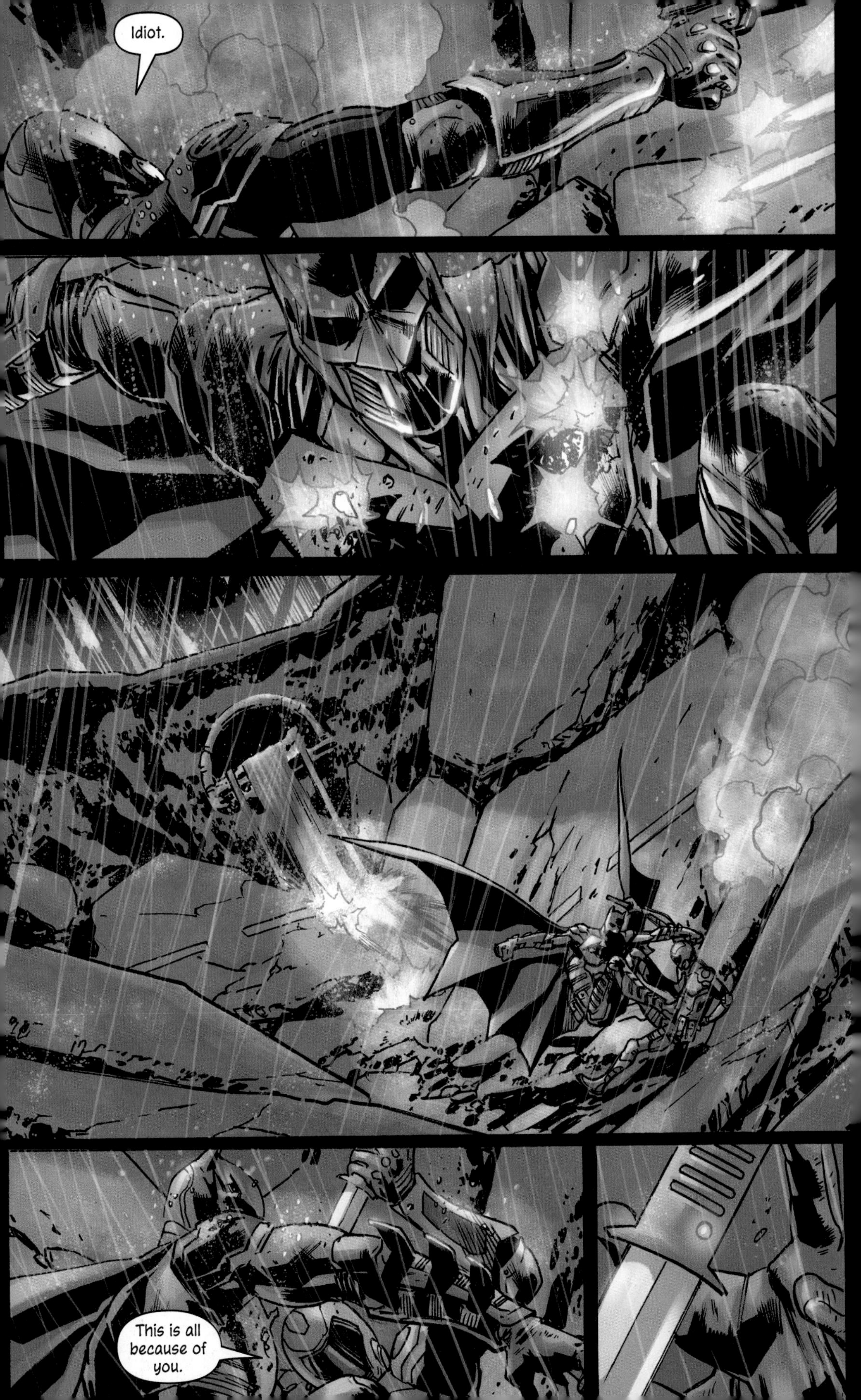
Idiot.
This is all because of you.

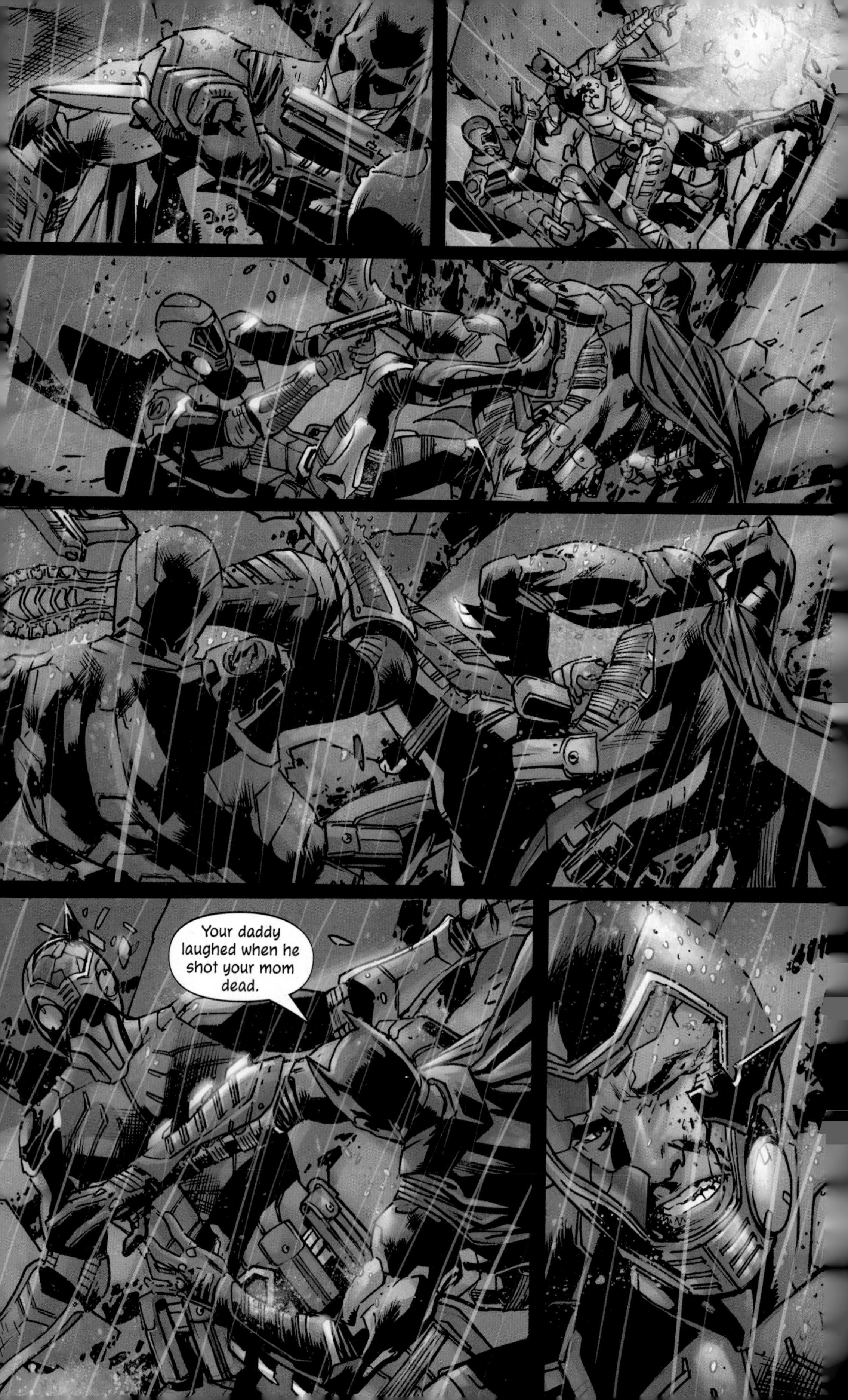
Your daddy laughed when he shot your mom dead.

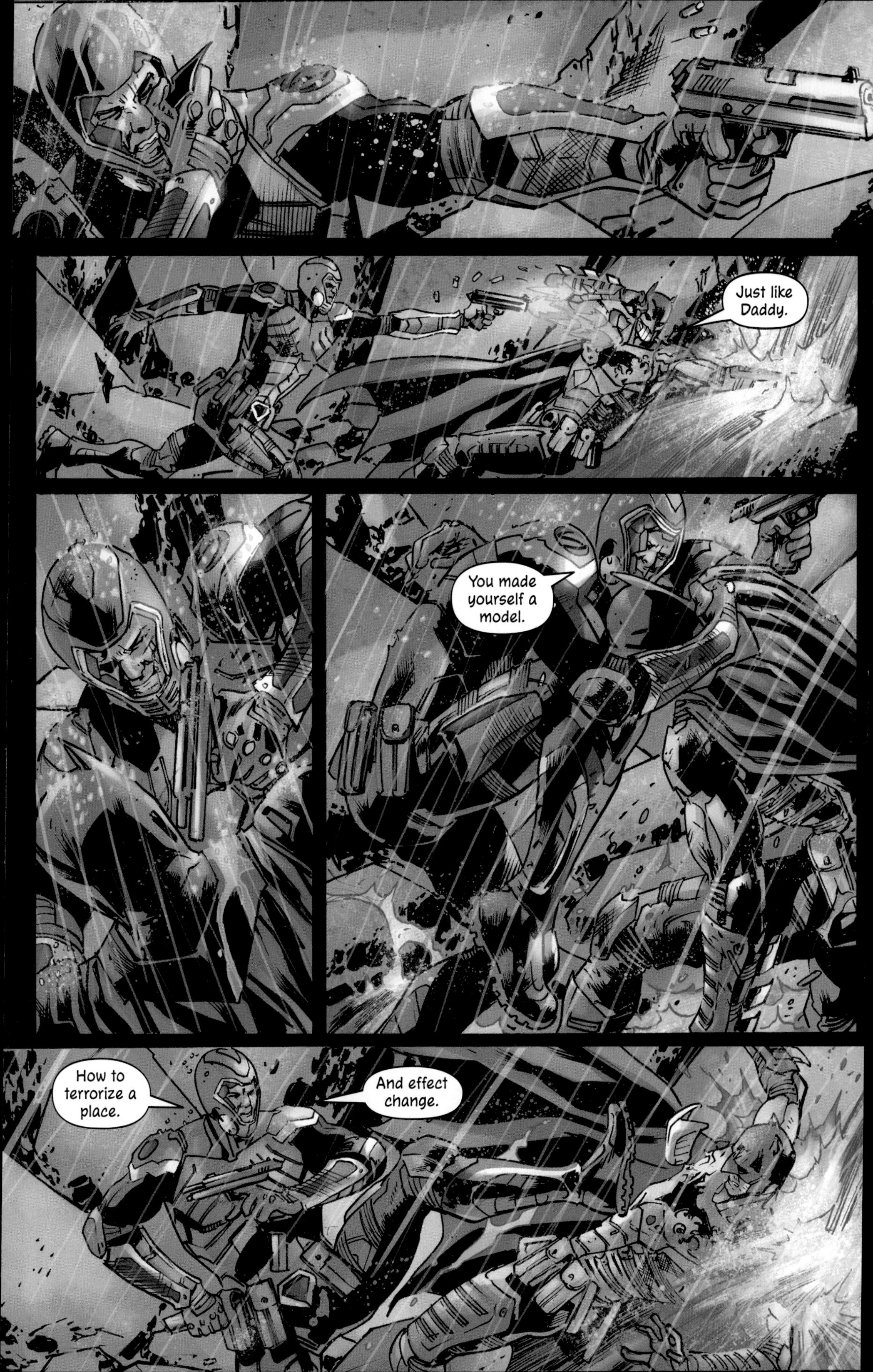
Just like
Daddy.
You made
yourself a
model.
How to
terrorize a
place.
And effect
change.

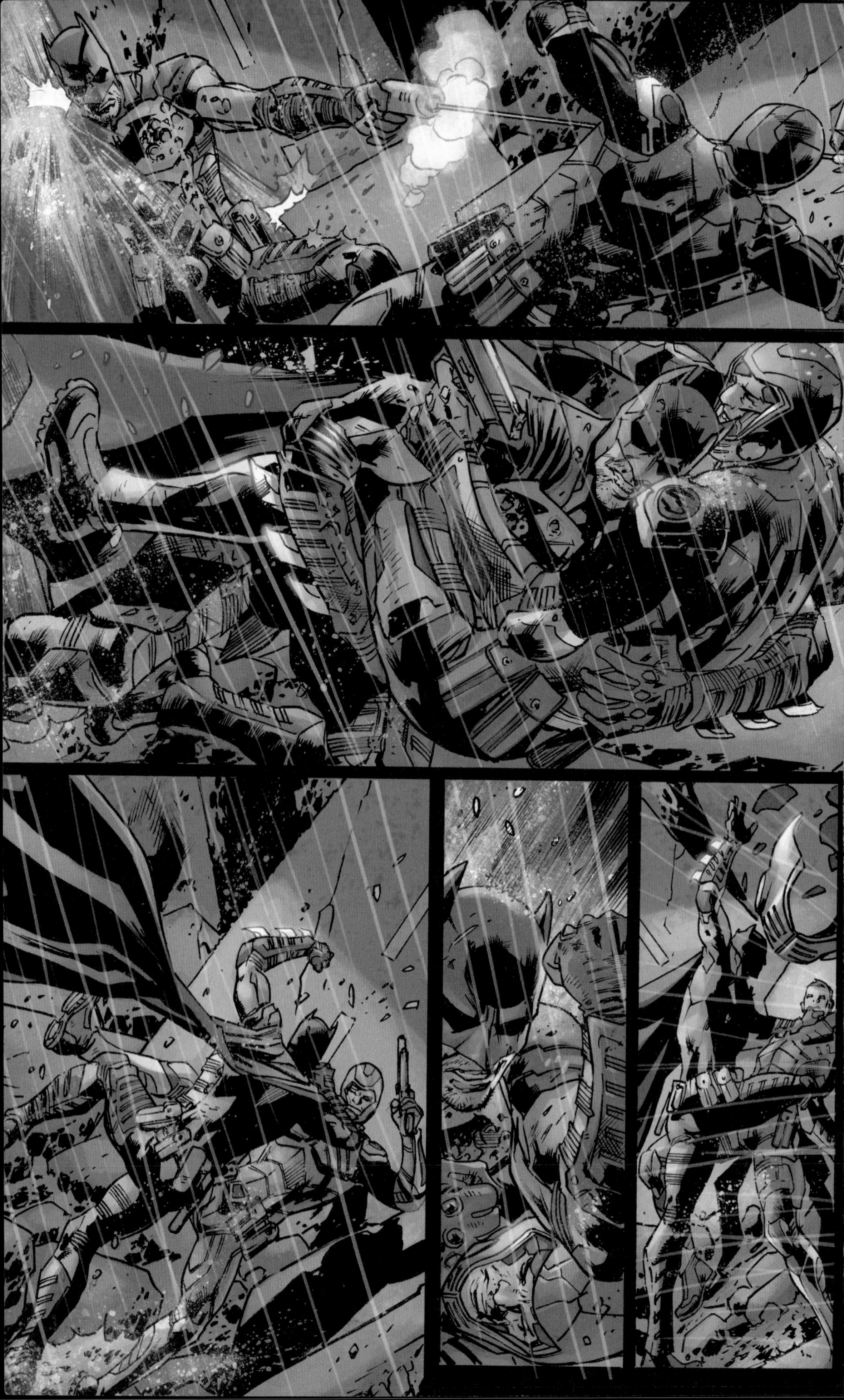

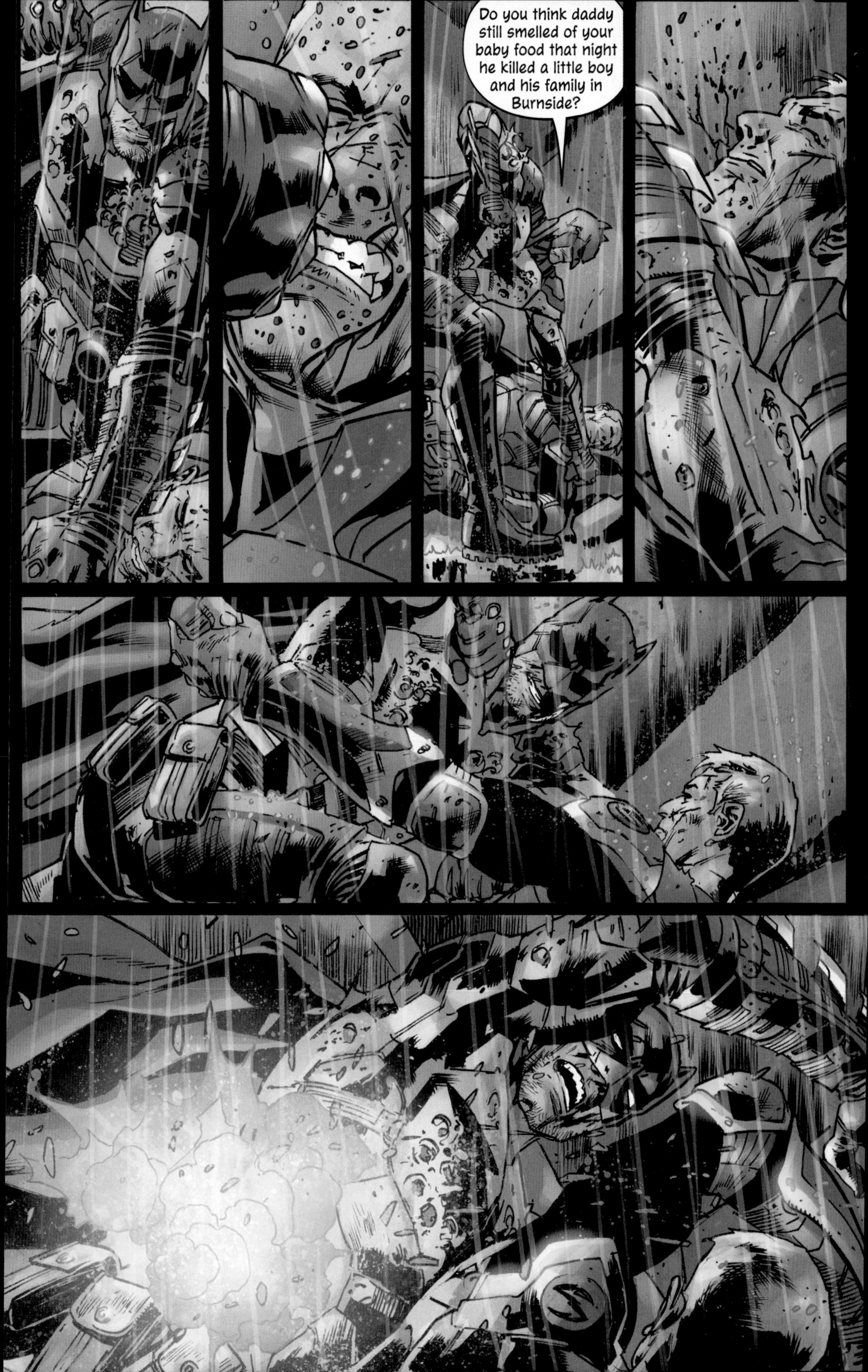
Do you think daddy still smelled of your baby food that night he killed a little boy and his family in Burnside?

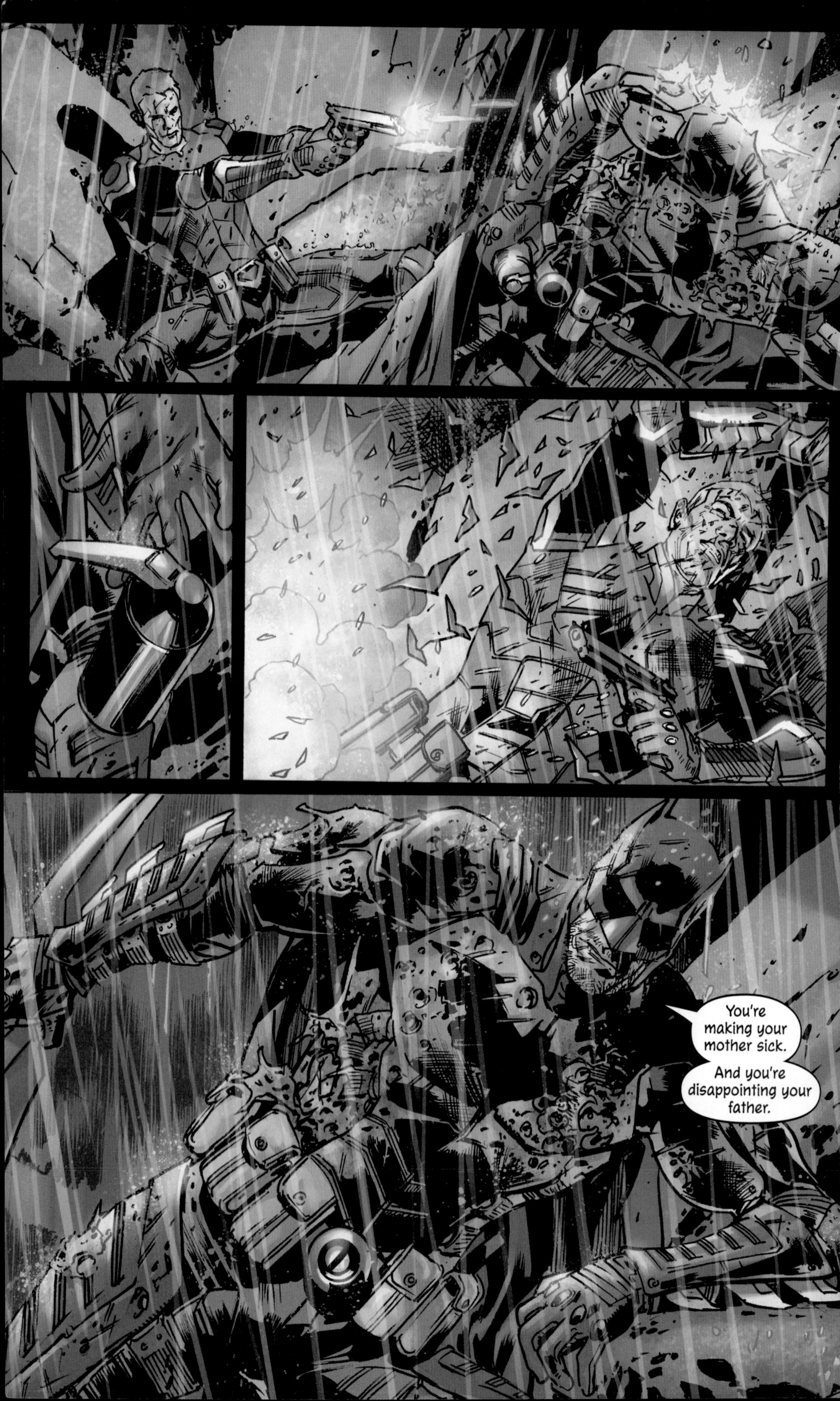
You're making your mother sick.
And you're disappointing your father.

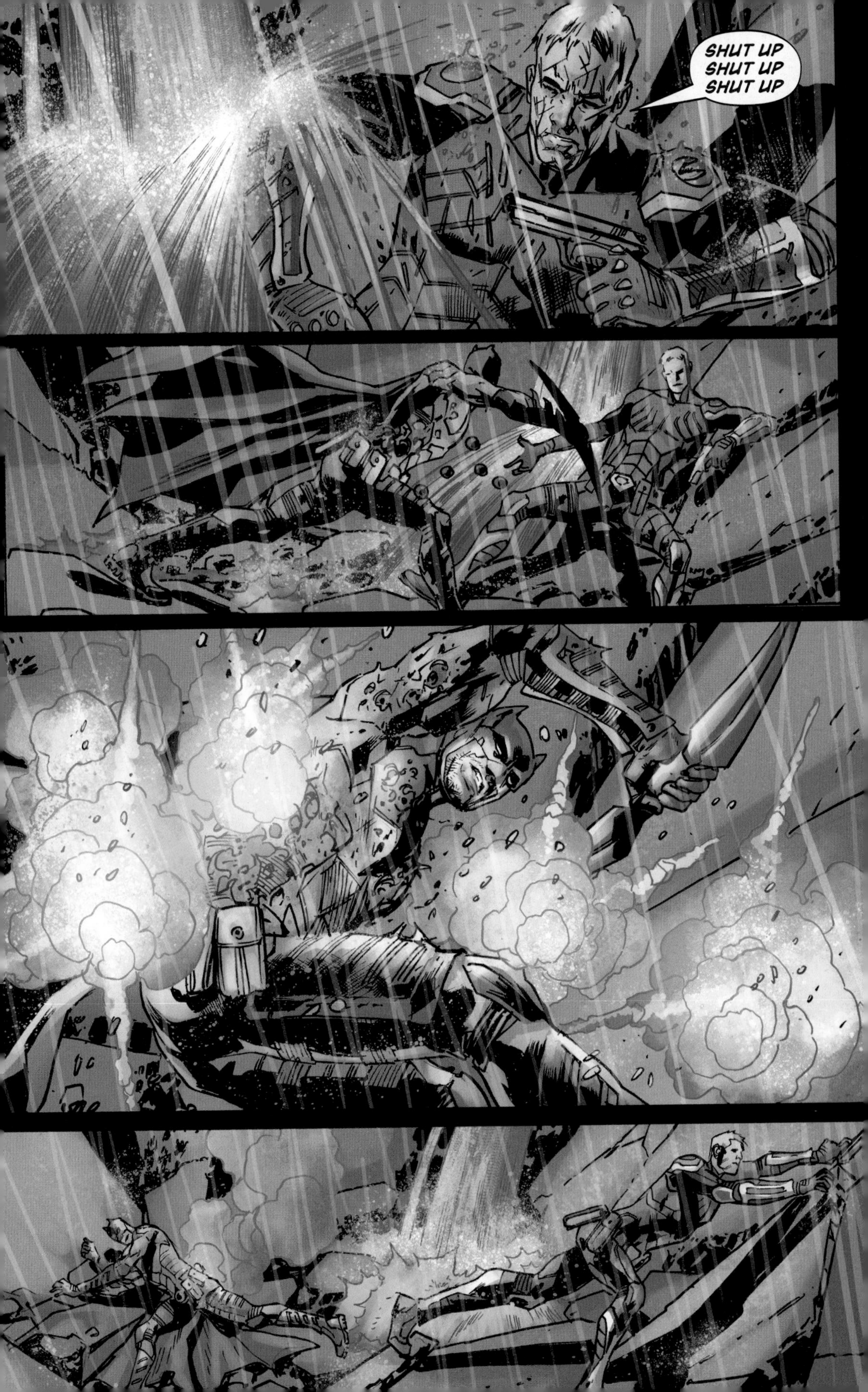
SHUT UP
SHUT UP
SHUT UP

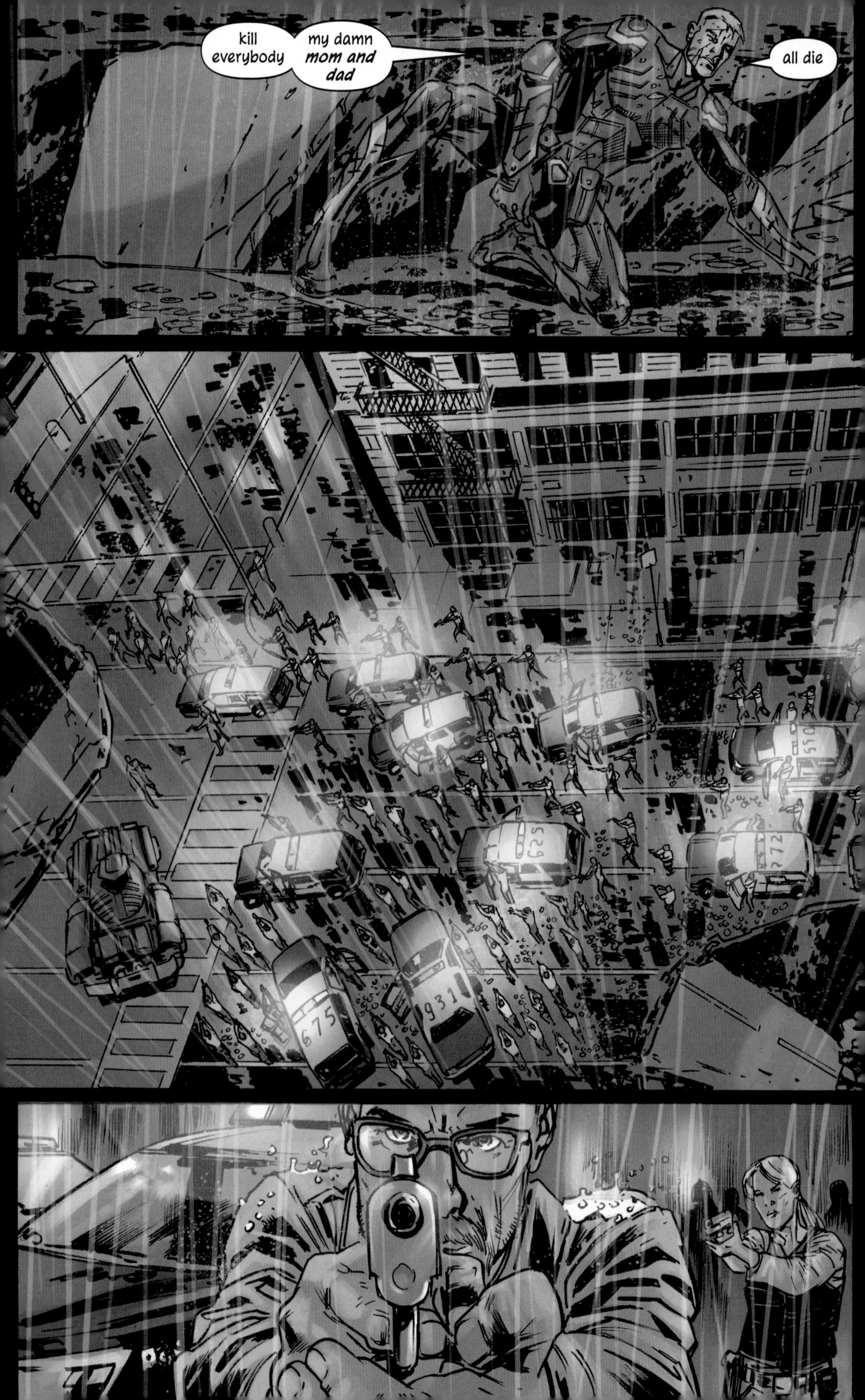
kill everybody
my damn *mom and dad*
all die

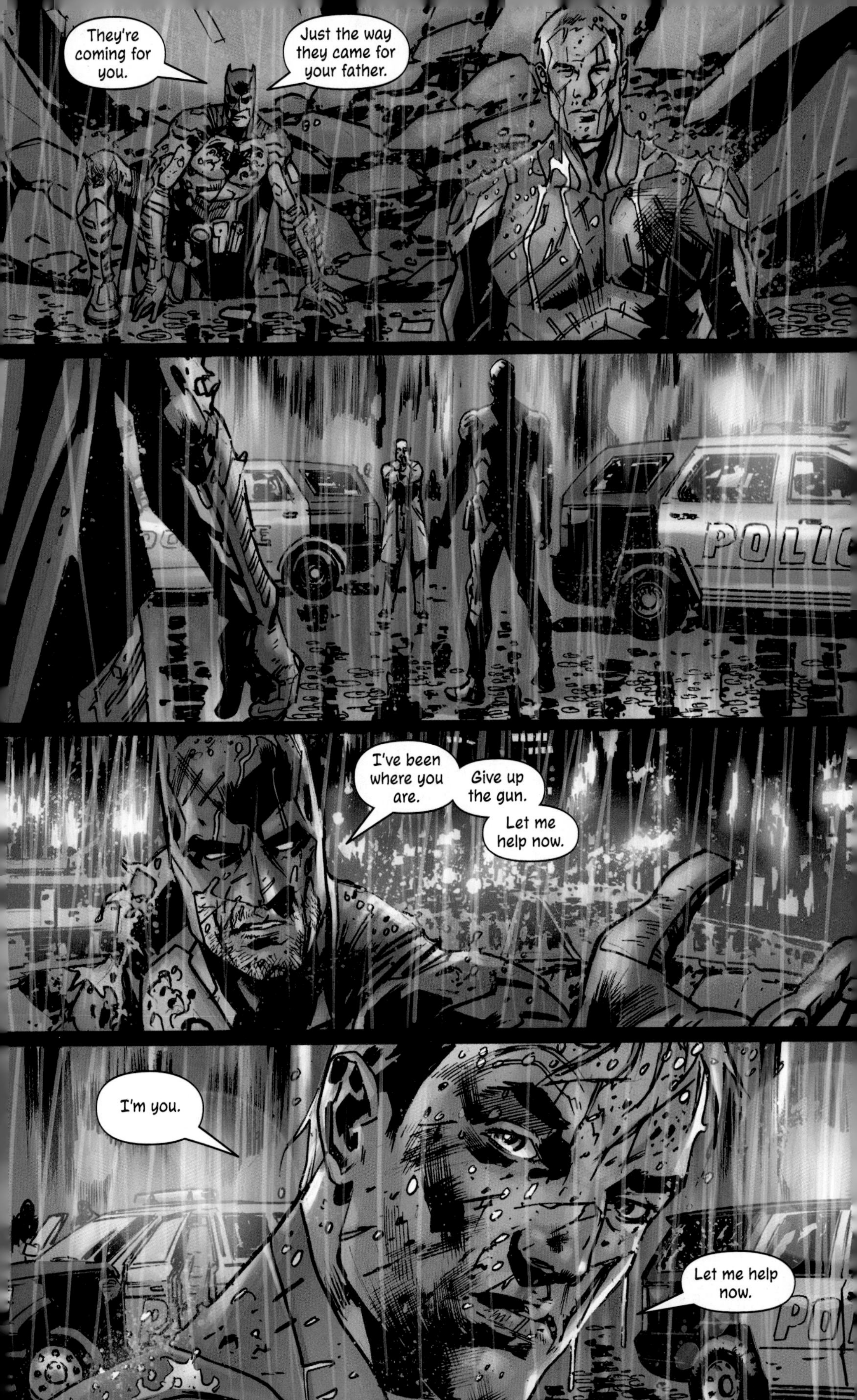
They're coming for you.
Just the way they came for your father.
I've been where you are.
Give up the gun.
Let me help now.
I'm you.
Let me help now.

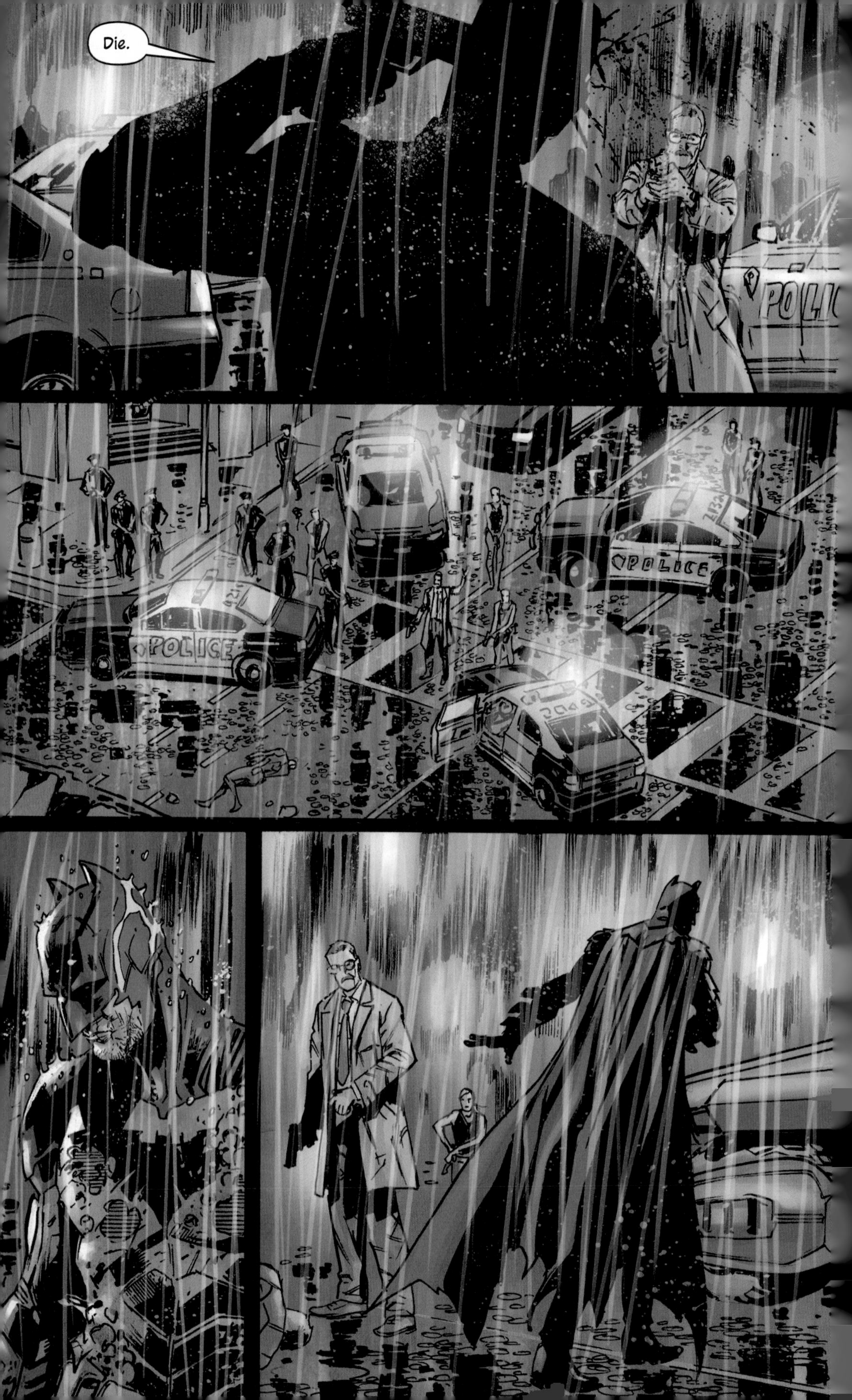
Die.
POLICE
POLICE
POLICE

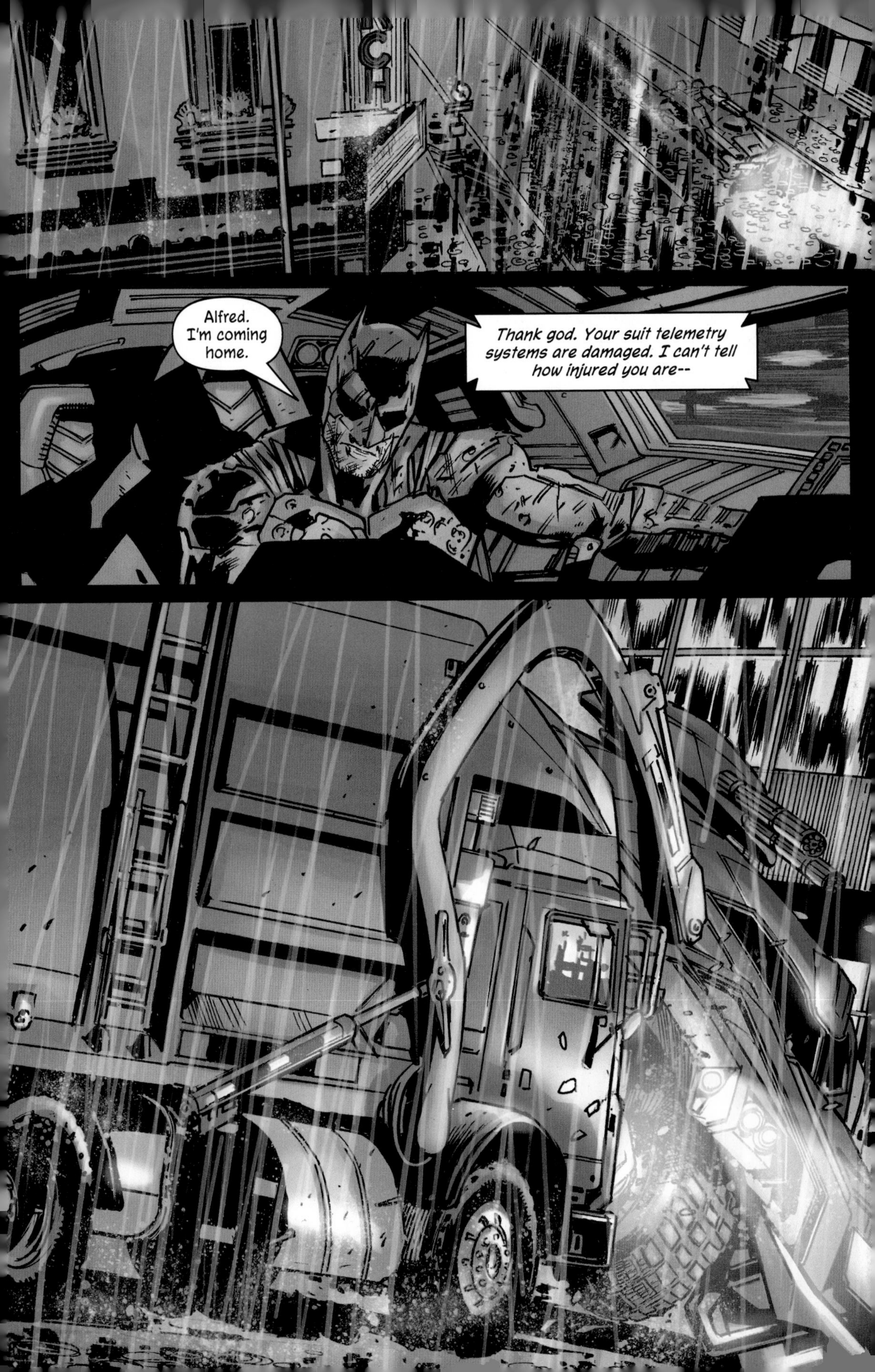
Alfred. I'm coming home.
Thank god. Your suit telemetry systems are damaged. I can't tell how injured you are--

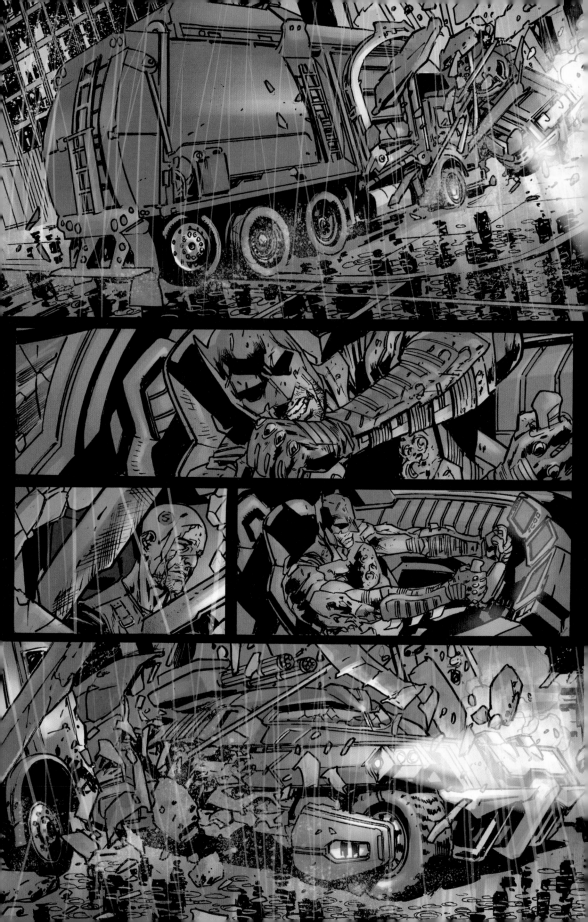

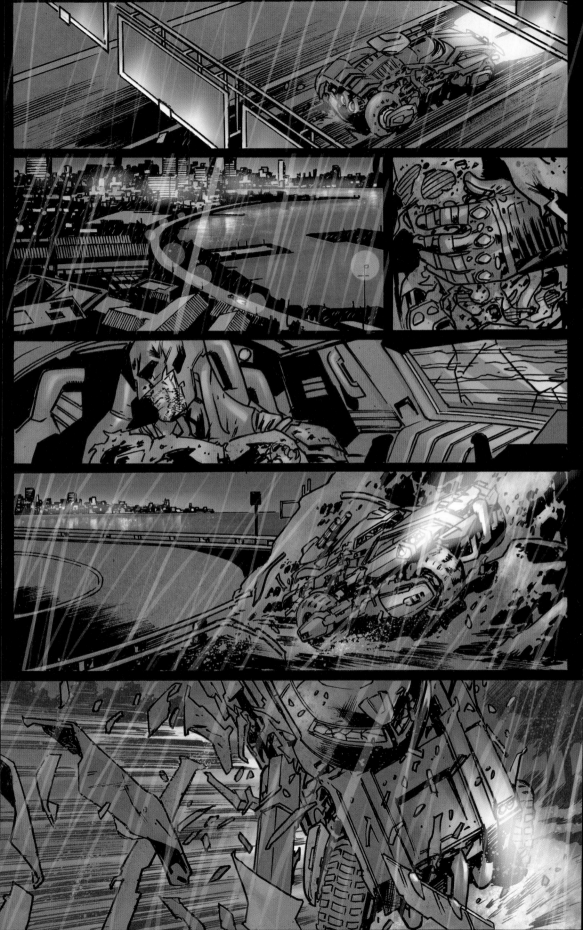

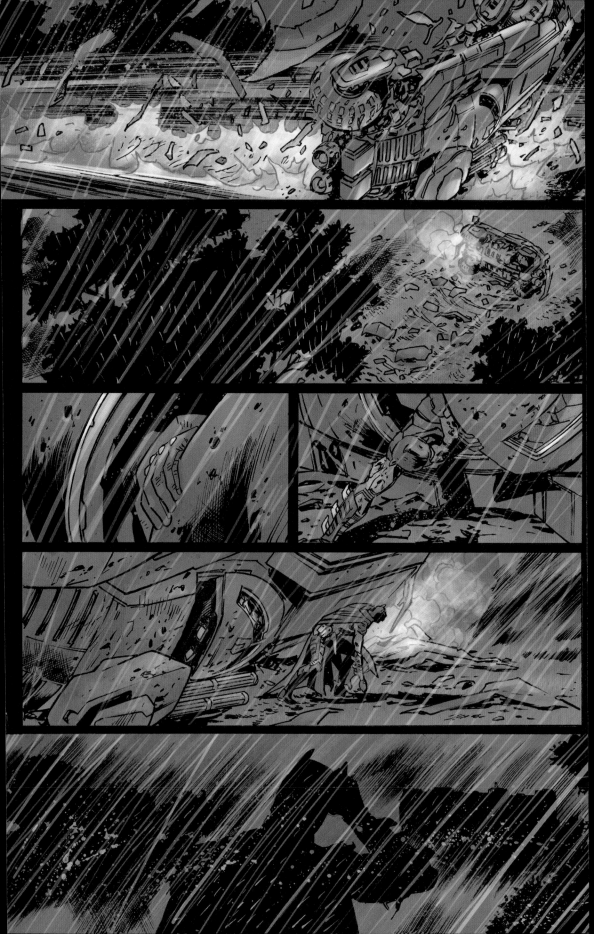

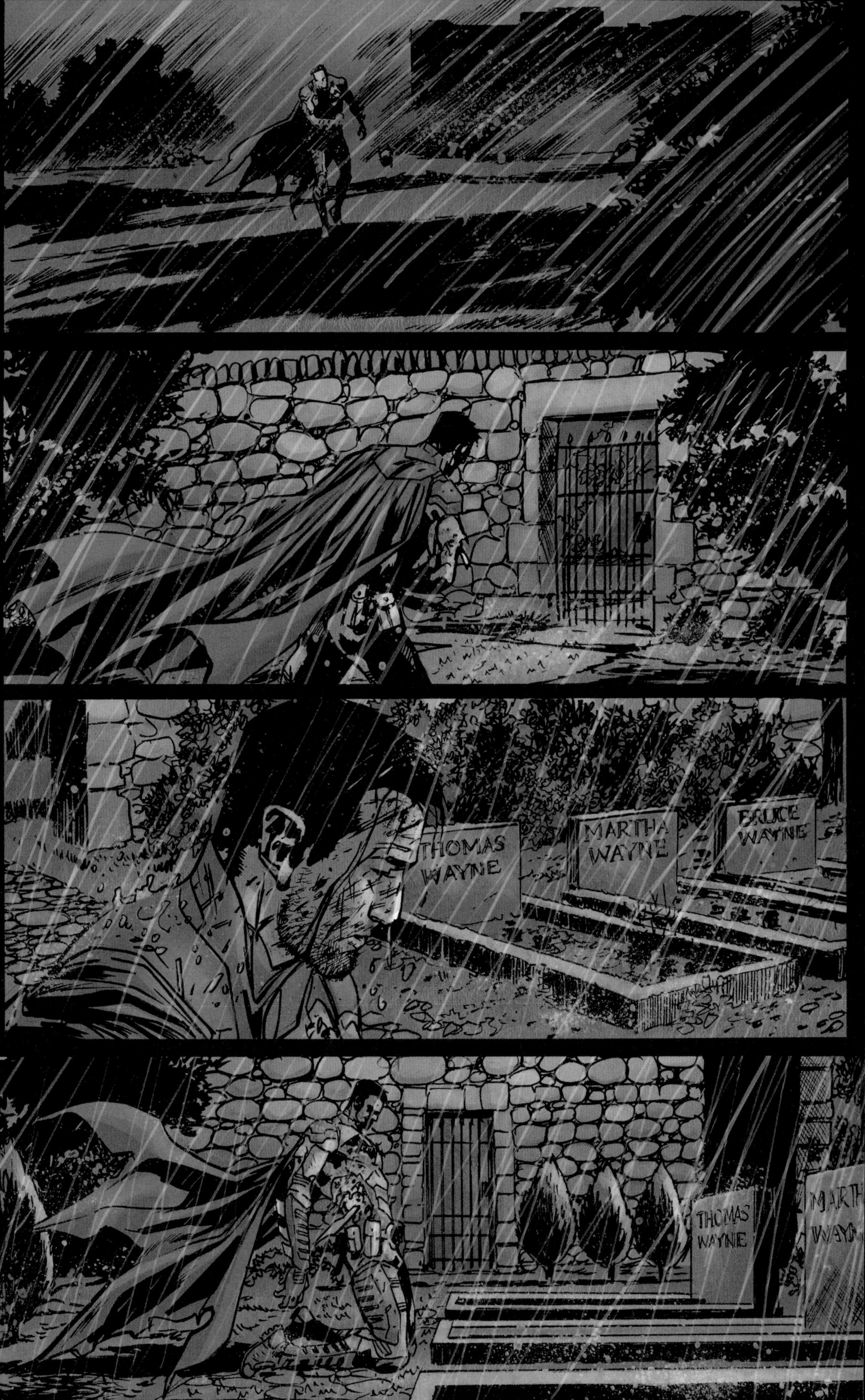

THOMAS WAYNE
MARTHA WAYNE
BRUCE WAYNE
THOMAS WAYNE

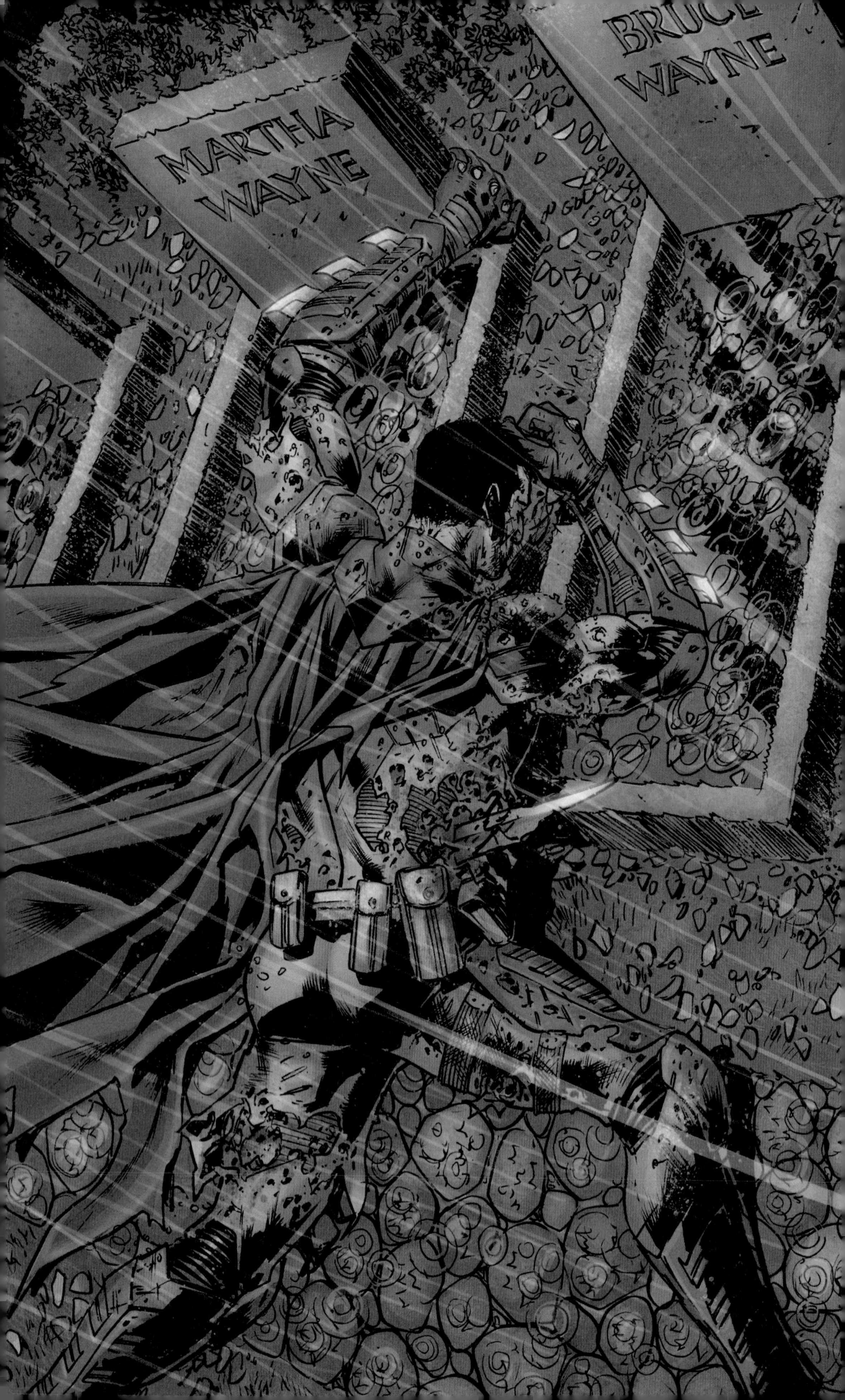
MARTHA WAYNE
BRUCE WAYNE

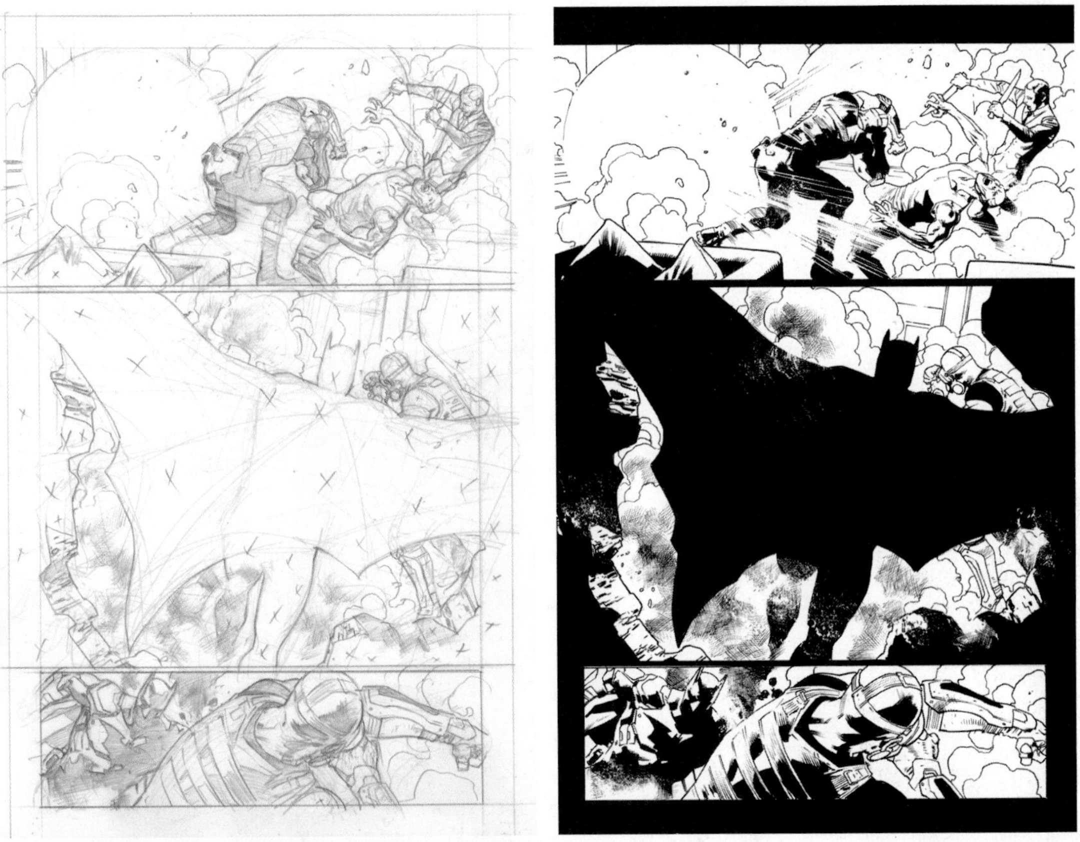

THE BATMAN'S GRAVE #4 Page 8 - Pencils and Inks by BRYAN HITCH

INTERIOR PROCESS

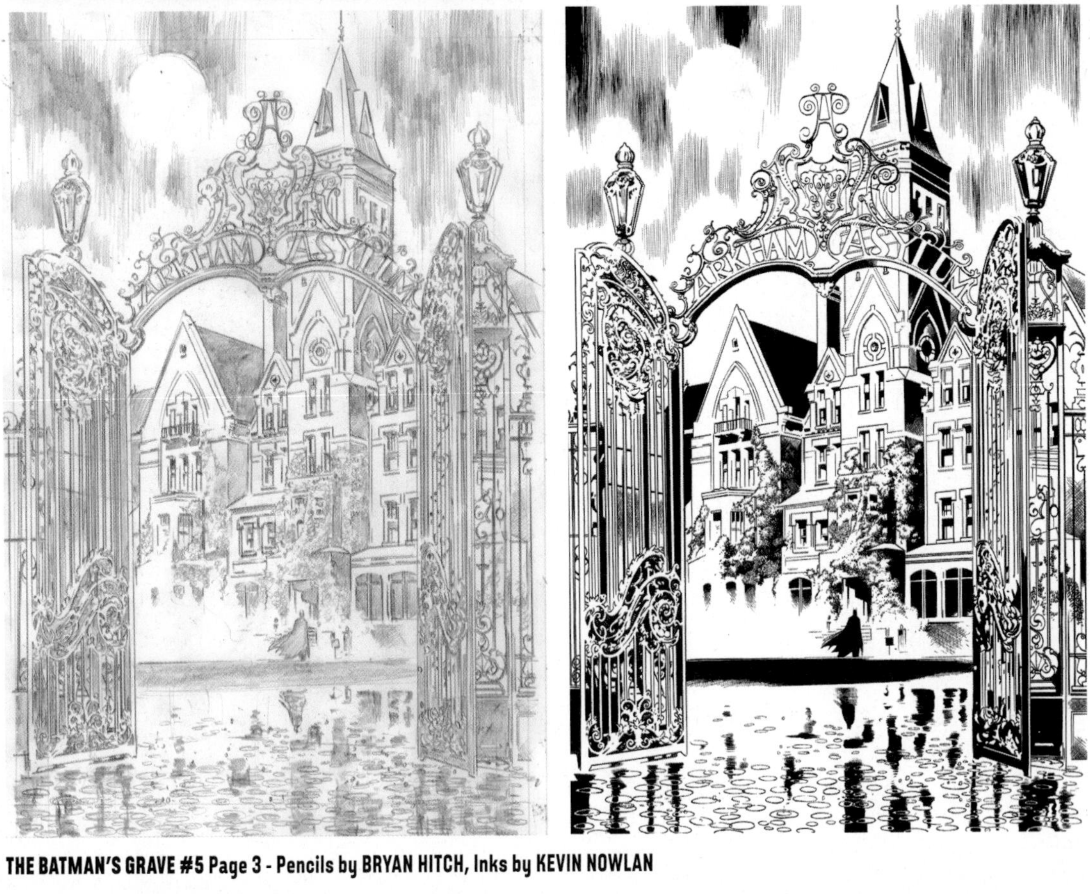
ARKHAM ASYLUM

THE BATMAN'S GRAVE #5 Page 3 - Pencils by BRYAN HITCH, Inks by KEVIN NOWLAN

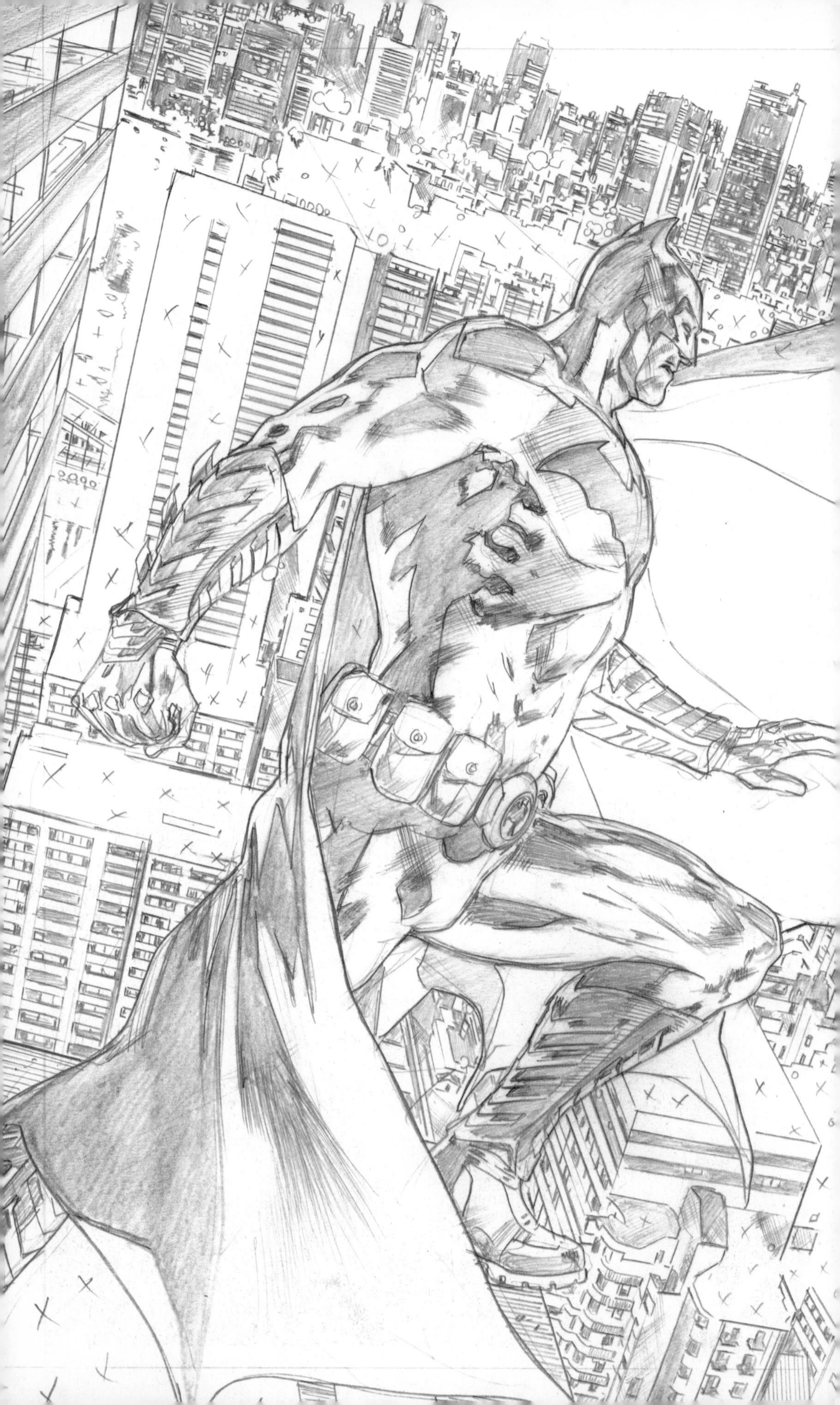

THE BATMAN'S GRAVE #1 Pages 4-5
Pencils by BRYAN HITCH
Inks by KEVIN NOWLAN

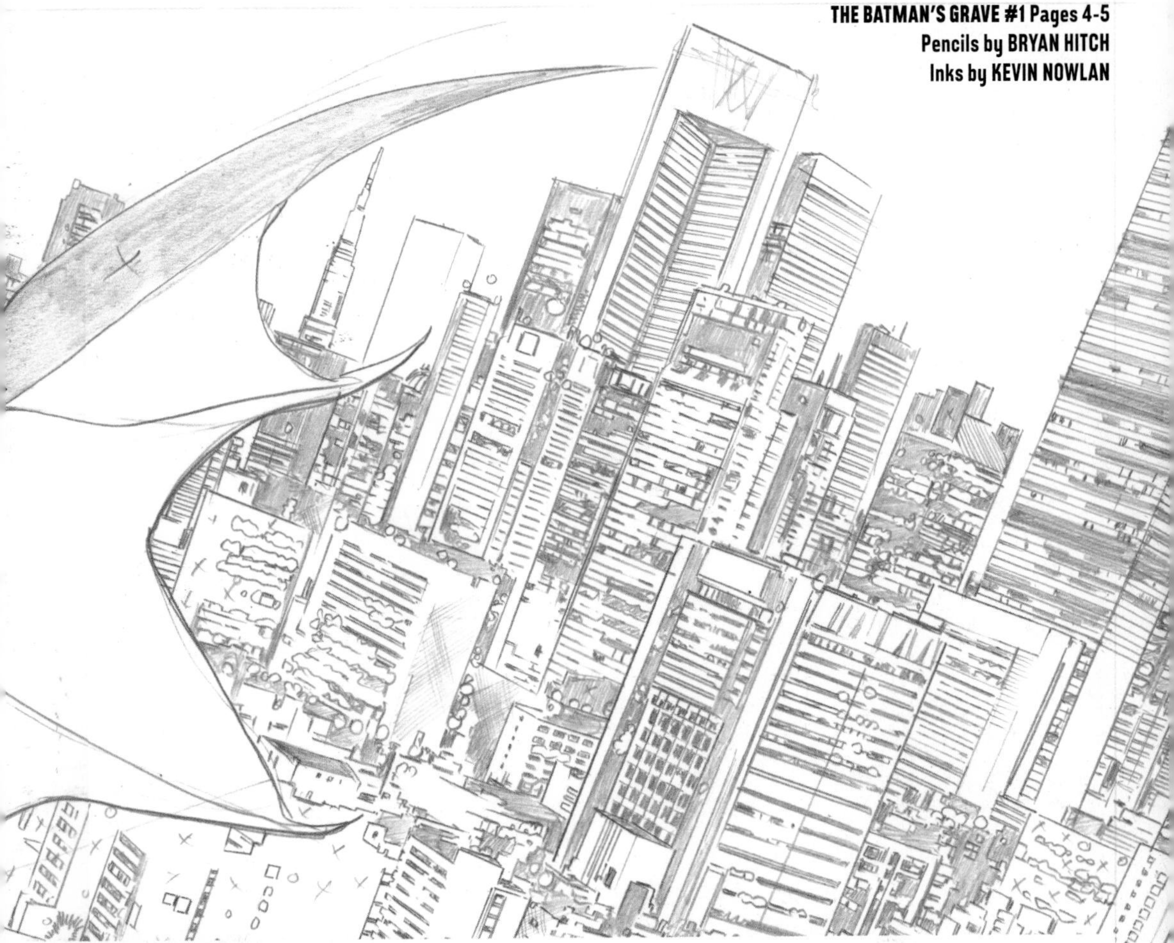

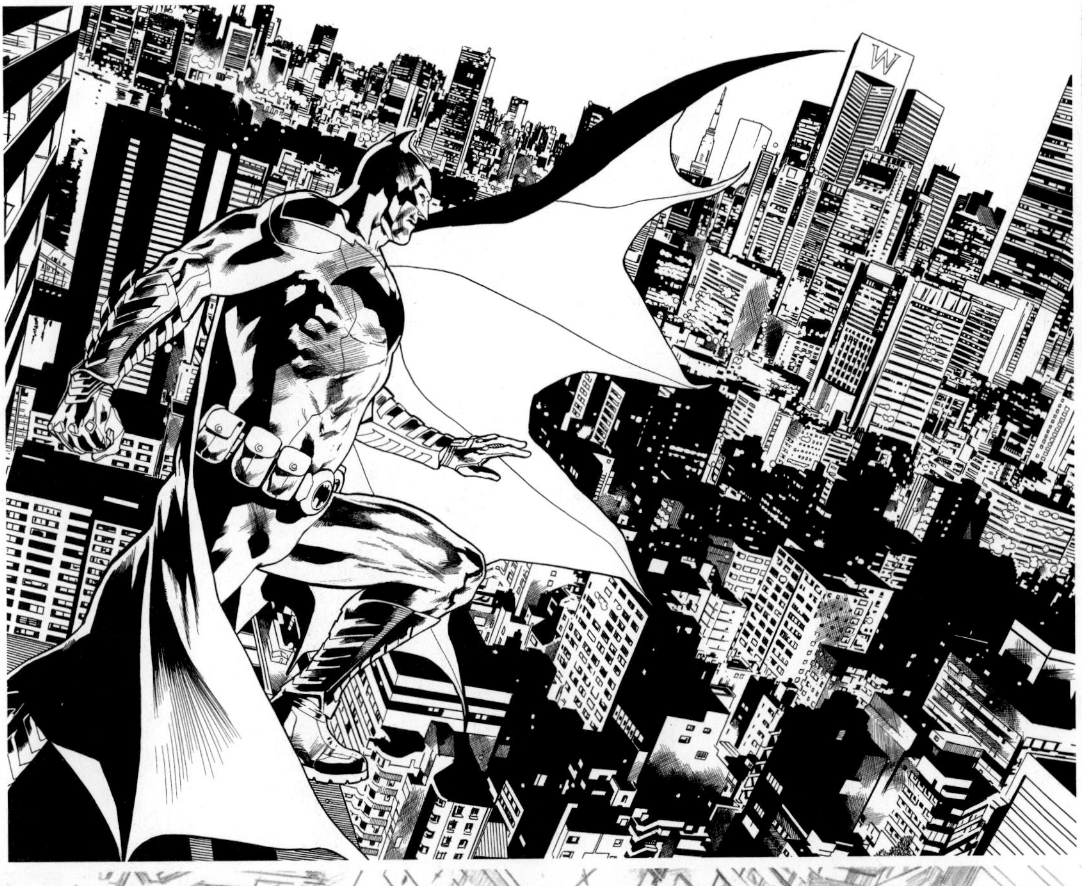

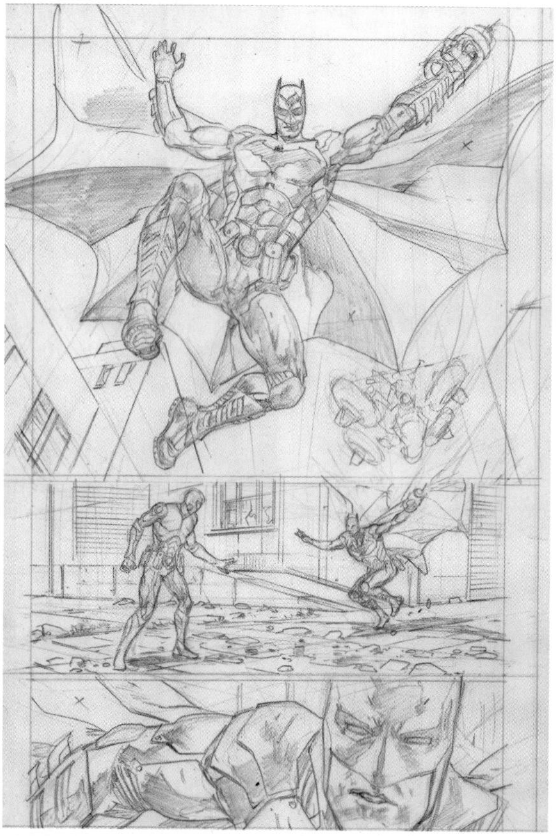
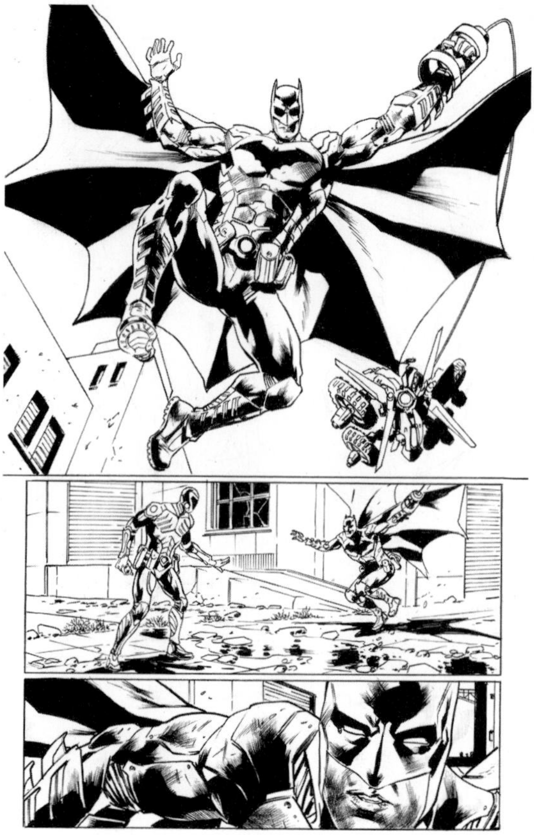

THE BATMAN'S GRAVE #8 Page 6 - Pencils and Inks by BRYAN HITCH

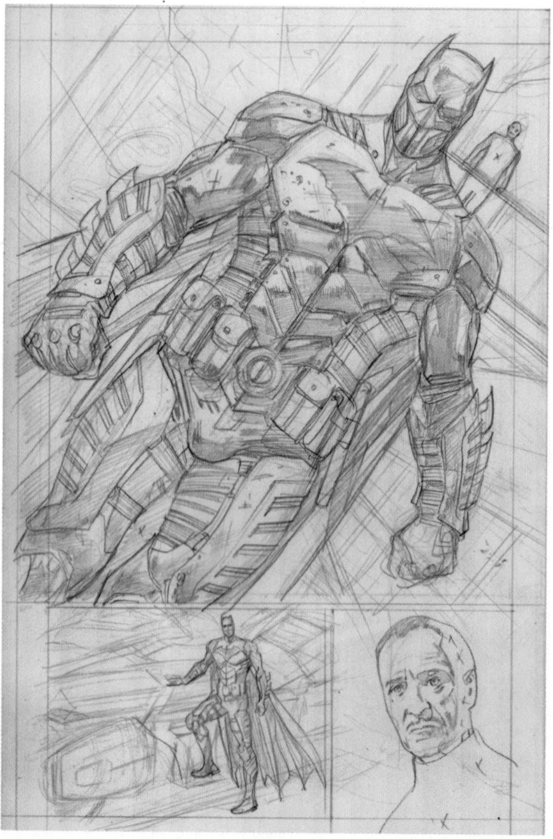
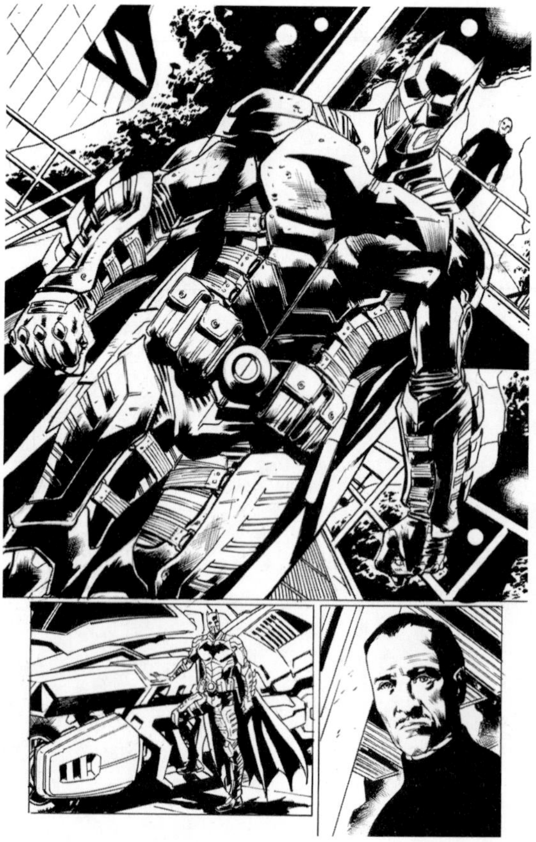

THE BATMAN'S GRAVE #11 Page 22 - Pencils and Inks by BRYAN HITCH